CAVALIERS AND PIONEERS

CAVALIERS AND PIONEERS

Abstracts of
Virginia Land Patents and Grants

Edited by
Dennis Ray Hudgins

VOLUME EIGHT: 1779–1782

Virginia Genealogical Society

Richmond • 2005

© Virginia Genealogical Society 2005
All rights reserved.

For ordering information contact the

Virginia Genealogical Society
5001 West Broad Street, Suite 115
Richmond, VA 23230-3023

CONTENTS

Preface i

Abbreviations v

Introduction vii

Abstracts:

    Grant Book A 1

    Grant Book B 67

    Grant Book C 107

    Grant Book D 139

    Grant Book E 205

    Grant Book F 281

Index

    A Note to the User 319

    Index 321

Preface

Commonwealth Grants of Virginia
from Williamsburg & Richmond

The fees for the early grants were paid into the Treasury of the Commonwealth at the rate (Ancient Composition Money) of one shilling sterling per 10 acres of land. Additionally, some early grants were issued for old pre-Revolutionary War surveys which were already paid for and those grants are in bold if the money was paid into **the late Receiver Generals Office** or **into the late Secretary's Office**.

The term "inclusive survey" is found in some of the grants which include old land. In the colonial patents, the terms "old land new land" or "old land" would have been used. In the early inclusive grants, there was an obvious attempt made to only charge for the new land. However, consistency and continuity were not the order for the new land office and we see various rates being charged which today do not make sense as well as a lack of chronological order in the dates of the early grants.

The date of the survey is usually included in the grant. This provides an important clue to when the land may have been taken-up by the original grantee or the subsequent assignees. As many as 55 years have been noted between the date of the original survey and the date of the Commonwealth grant.

The cost of land in the patents during the Royal/Regal Government was 10 acres per shilling (referred to as the "Ancient Composition" in the Grant Books) with the charges rounded-off to the next 5 shillings, i.e.: 100 acres for 10 Shillings; 200 acres for 20 Shillings or £1; and 400 acres for 40 Shillings or £2.

The cost of land in the Commonwealth grants (as a result of State Land Office Treasury Warrants and/or Preemption Treasury Warrants) was 8 shillings per acre with costs not rounded-off; therefore £'s, Shillings & pence were charged.

The first 400 acres allotted "by Certificate in Right of Settlement" was normally free or at the ancient composition. Land allotted for military service (State Land Office Military Warrants for military service in accordance with various Acts of the General Assembly passed in 1763, 1779 etc.) was also free or at the ancient composition.

Some of the costs for land at 8 shillings per acre follow:

10 acs. = £4	560 acs. = £224
50 acs. = £20	600 acs. = £240
100 acs. = £40	666⅔ acs. = £266.S13.d4
150 acs. = £60	700 acs. = £280
200 acs. = £80	760 acs. = £304
240 acs. = £96	900 acs. = £360
250 acs. = £100	907 acs. = £362.S16
300 acs. = £120	1000 acs. = £400
344 acs. = £137.S12	1200 acs. = £480
350 acs. = £140	1400 acs. = £560
400 acs. = £160	1500 acs. = £600
450 acs. = £180	1600 acs. = £640
500 acs. = £200	2000 acs. = £800
535 acs. = £214	2964 acs. = £1185.S12

This volume (Volume VIII) continues the series of Virginia patent abstracts begin by Nell Marion Nugent who abstracted the first fourteen patent books in three volumes. Volumes 4 through 7 completed the colonial patent series.

Volume I
PB 1	pp. 1-951	26 Jan 1621/22 to 10 Apr 1644
PB 2	pp. 1-369	24 Feb 1643/44 to 29 Jan 1651/52
PB 3	pp. 1-394	13 Dec 1653 to 6 Oct 1656
PB 4	pp. 1-643	2 Oct 1655 to 3 Oct 1664
PB 5	pp. 1-545 [669]	28 Jan 1662/63 to 7 Sep 1667

Volume II
PB 6	pp. 1-691	22 Oct 1666 to 30 May 1679
PB 7	pp. 1-718	25 Sep 1679 to 25 Apr 1689
PB 8	pp. 1-443	20 Oct 1689 to 21 Apr 1695

Volume III
PB 9	pp. 1-740	25 Oct 1695 to 10 Jun 1706
PB 10	pp. 1-462	12 Dec 1710 to 20 Feb 1719/20
PB 11	pp. 1-346	20 Feb 1719/20 to 8 Jul 1724
PB 12	pp. 1-538	9 Jul 1724 to 7 Jul 1726
PB 13	pp. 1-540	24 Mar 1725/26 to 28 Sep 1730
PB 14	pp. 1-537	28 Sep 1728 to 17 Jan 1732/33

Volume IV
PB 15		pp. 1-537	9 Oct 1732 to 19 Jun 1735
PB 16		pp. 1-531	1 Jul 1735 to 10 Jan 1735/36
PB 17		pp. 1-532	10 Jan 1735/36 to 16 Jun 1738
PB 18	(Volume 1 of 2)	pp. 1-566	16 Jun 1738 to 12 Mar 1739/40
PB 19	(Volume 2 of 2)	pp. 567-1140	12 Mar 1739/40 to 12 Oct 1741

Volume V
PB 20	(Volume 1 of 2)	pp.1-566	15 Oct 1741 to 30 Aug 1743
PB 21		pp.1-674	30 Jul 1742 to 25 Nov 1743
PB 22		pp.1-631	1 Mar 1743/44 to 20 Mar 1745/6
PB 23	(Volume 2 of 2)	pp.567-1147	30 Aug 1743 to 20 Aug 1745
PB 24		pp.1-631	20 Sep 1745 to 12 Jan 1746/7
PB 25		pp.1-635	20 Mar 1745/46 to 25 Jun 1747
PB 26		pp.1-723	25 Jun 1747 to 20 Aug 1748
PB 27		pp.1-533	1 Dec 1748 to 15 Dec 1749
PB 28	pp.1-730		12 Jan 1746/47 to 5 Sep 1749 [12 Mar 1749/50]

Volume VI
PB 29	pp.1-532	15 Dec 1749 to 5 Aug 1751
PB 30	pp.1-531	1 Jun 1750 to 16 Nov 1752
PB 31	pp.1-750	20 Sep 1751 to 10 Sep 1755

PB 32	pp.1-716	16 Nov 1752 to 10 Mar 1756
PB 33	pp.1-1095	8 Jun 1756 to 7 Aug 1761
PB 34	pp.1-1088	10 Mar 1756 to 24 Feb 1763 (25 Sep 1762)

Volume VII
PB 35 (Volume 1 of 2)	pp.1-556 25 Sep 1762 to 27 Jun 1764
PB 36 (Volume 2 of 2)	pp.557-1083 27 Jun 1764 to 12 Aug 1767
PB 37 (Volume 1 of 2)	pp.1-452 10 Jul 1767 to 20 Sep 1768
PB 38 (Volume 2 of 2)	pp.453-904 20 Sep 1768 to 12 May 1770
PB 39 (Volume 1 of 2)	pp.1-454 12 May 1770 to 16 Mar 1771
PB 40 (Volume 2 of 2)	pp.455-901 16 Mar 1771 to 1 Aug 1772
PB 41 (Volume 1 of 2)	pp.1-456 1 Aug 1772 to 15 Jun 1773
PB 42 (Volume 2 of 2)	pp.457-899 15 Jun 1773 to 7 Dec 1774

Volume VIII (this volume)
GB A pp. 1-685	23 Oct 1779 to 17 Jul 1780
GB B pp. 1-459	26 Oct 1779 to 20 Jul 1780
GB C pp. 1-555	1 Sep 1780 to 1 Mar 1781
GB D pp. 1-930	20 Jul 1780 to 10 Apr 1781
GB E pp. 1-38	1 May 1775 to 15 Mar 1776 [See the end of PB 42]
GB E pp. 38-929	14 Jul 1780 to 1 Feb 1781
GB F pp. 1-519	10 Apr 1781 to 1 Jun 1782

Volumes IX, X & XI will include
GB G pp. 1-320	1 Jun 1782 to 8 Apr 1783
GB H pp. 1-669	1 Jun 1782 to 7 Nov 1783
GB I pp. 1-559	20 May 1783 to 7 Apr 1784
GB K pp. 1-652	7 Nov 1783 to 1 May 1784
GB L pp. 1-738	1 Apr 1783 to 1 Jun 1784
GB M pp. 1-721	20 Apr 1784 to 27 Jan 1785
GB N pp. 1-719	20 Jun 1784 to 8 Mar 1785

GB O pp. 1-740	8 Mar 1785 to 23 May 1785
GB P pp. 1-735	1 Jun 1784 to 25 Jun 1785
GB Q pp. 1-733	1 Jun 1785 to [20] Jun 1785
GB R pp. 1-740	5 Jul 1785 to 9 Nov 1785
GB S pp. 1-722	20 Jun 1785 to 4 Jan 1786
GB T pp. 1p728	15 Dec 1785 to __ Jan 1786

GB U pp. 1-772	23 Nov 1785 to 20 Mar 1786
GB V pp. 1-7__	24 Dec 1785 to 10 Apr 1785
GB W pp. 1-735	21 Feb 1786 to 17 May 1786
GB X pp. 1-731	2 Dec 1785 to 2 Dec 1785
GB Y pp. 1-736	12 Dec 1785 to 3 Aug 1786
GB Z pp. 1-739	2 Dec 1785 to 26 Jun 1786

ABBREVIATIONS

A.C. = Ancient Composition (Money)
acs. - acres
adj. - adjoining, adjacent, joining, joyning
ass'ee = assignee
bef. - before
bet. - between, betwixt
Br., Brs. - Branch, Branches
c. - corner
ca. - circa
Chas. City - Charles City [Co.]
ch., chs. - chain, chaines/chains
Cl., Clk. - Clerk
Co. - County
Col. - Collo., Colo., Colonel
Cr. - Creek
Cultiv. - Cultivation
dec'd - deced, deceased
E, Ewd., Ely. - East, Eastward, Easterly
Esq. - Esqr., Esquire
g., gtd. - grant, granted
Genl. - Generll, General
Gent. - Gentleman
Govr. - Governor
Imp. - Importation
Improv. - Improvement
Is. of Wight - Isle/I'le of Wight
K. & Q. - King & Queen [Co.]
King Wm. - King William [Co.]
L. - Land
lb.,lbs. - pound, pounds [of tobacco]
LOTW # - Land Office Treasury Warrant number

Maj. - Majr., Major
Mr - Mister
Mrs - Mistress [not always a married woman]
MW # = Military Warrant number
N, Nwd., Nly. - North, Northward, Northerly
NL - New Land
Norf. - Norfolk [Co.]
OL - Old Land
p. - page
Par. - Parish
pat., ptd. - patent, patented
PB - Patent Book
Pers. - Person, Persons
Pr. Ann or Anne - Princess Ann/Anne
Pr. Geo. - Prince George [Co.]
PW # = Preemption Warrant number
PTW # = Preemption Treasury Warrant number
relinq. - relinquished
Riv. - River
S, Swd., Sly. - South, Southward, Southerly
sd - said, aforesaid
Shill. - Shillings
Spotsyl. - Spotsylvania [Co.]
St. - Saint
Sterl. = Sterling
Sw. - Swamp
TW # = Treasury Warrant number
W, Wwd., Wly. - West, Westward, Westerly

ff   transcribed as a capital F.
~   a tilde overscoring any letter is transcribed as a doubled letter, i.e.: Comander = Commander, Comon = Common.
( )   indicates a variant spelling, normally found in the index.
/   a virgule separates variant spellings within the text.
[ ]   brackets set off abstractor's comments.
?   indicates uncertainty.
—   indicates the absence of a word or letters.
...   replaces extraneous data

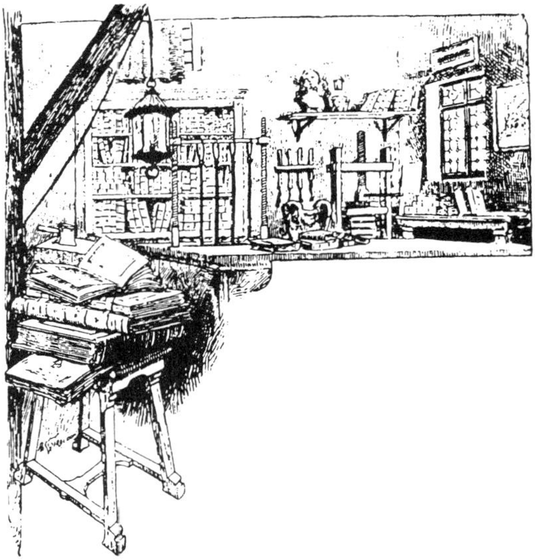

Introduction

On 7 December 1774 the last patent issued by the royal government was recorded. Almost five years later, on 23 October 1779 the first grant issued by the Commonwealth's Land Office was recorded, the act establishing the new land office having been passed by the General Assembly in May 1779. Settlement of new land had not halted during this period and as a result, the new government was faced with numerous conflicting land claims. In order to encourage continued settlement and discourage litigation the General Assembly at the same time it created the Land Office, established a special commission which it charged with the task of speedily settling the conflicting claims. The records generated by the commission as well as the patents resulting from its decisions provide the researcher with a wealth of information on the settlement of individuals on the western waters during and following the French and Indian War through 1779. The full text[1] of both acts follows:

May 1779—3rd of Commonwealth
CHAP. XII[2]

An Act for adjusting and settling the titles of claimers to unpatented lands under the present and former government, previous to the Establishment of the commonwealth's land office.[3]

1. **WHEREAS** the various and vague claims to unpatented lands under the former and present government, previous to the establishment of the

---

[1] William Waller Hening, *The Statutes at Large; Being a Collection of all the Laws of Virginia* . . ., vol. 10 (1822; reprint, Charlottesville, Va.: University Press of Virginia, 1969), 35–65.

[2] See 2 Rev. Code of 1819, p. 324 to 482 for this, and the subsequent acts.

[3] This act is published in Chan. Rev. p. 90, in which it is separated by *sections*, as here; which was not the case in the original.

commonwealth's land office, may produce tedious and infinite litigation and disputes, and in the mean time purchasers would be discouraged from taking up lands upon the terms lately prescribed by law, whereby the funds to be raised in aid of the taxes for discharging the publick debt, would be in a great measure frustrated; and it is just and necessary, as well for the peace of individuals as for the publick weal, that some certain rules should be established for settling and determining the rights to such lands, and fixing the principles upon which legal and just claimers shall be entitled to sue out grants; to the end that subsequent purchasers and adventurers may be enabled to proceed with greater certainty and safety: *Be it enacted by the General Assembly*, That all surveys of waste and unappropriated land made upon any of the western waters before the first day of January, in the year 1778, and upon any of the eastern waters at any time before the end of this present session of assembly, by any county surveyor commissioned by the masters of William and Mary college, acting in conformity to the laws and rules of government then in force, and founded either upon charter, importation rights duly proved and certified according to ancient usage, as far as relates to indented servants, and other persons not being convicts, upon treasury rights for money paid the receiver general duly authenticated upon entries on the western waters, regularly made before the 26th day of October, in the year 1763, or on the eastern waters at any time before the end of this present session of assembly, with the surveyor of the county for tracts of land not exceeding four hundred acres, according to act of assembly upon any order of council, or entry in the council books, and made during the time in which it shall appear either from the original or any subsequent order, entry, or proceedings in the council books, that such order or entry remained in force the terms of which have been complied with, or the time for performing the same unexpired, or upon any warrant from the governour for the time being for military service, in virtue of any proclamation either from the king of Great Britain[4] or any former governour of Virginia, shall be, and are hereby declared good and valid, but that all surveys of waste and unpatented lands made by any other person, or upon any other pretence whatsoever, shall be, and are hereby declared null and void, provided that all officers or soldiers, their heirs or assigns, claiming under the late governour Dinwiddie's proclamation[5] of a bounty in lands to the first Virginia regiment, and having returned to the secretary's office, surveys made by virtue of a special commission from the president and masters of William and Mary college, shall be entitled to grants thereupon on payment of the

---

[4] See Vol 7, p 663, for the king's proclamation of 1763.
[5] See Vol. 7, p. 661, for governour Dinwiddie's proclamation of 1754.

common office fees; that all officers and soldiers, their heirs or assigns under proclamation warrants for military service, having located lands by actual surveys made under any such special commission, shall have the benefit of their said locations, by taking out warrants upon such rights, resurveying such lands according to law, and thereafter proceeding according to the rules and regulations of the land office. All and every person or persons, his, her, or their heirs or assigns, claiming lands upon any of the before recited rights, and under surveys made as herein before mentioned against which no caveat shall have been legally entered, shall upon the plats and certificates of such surveys being returned into the land office, together with the rights, entry, order, warrant or authentick copy thereof upon which they were respectively founded, be entitled to a grant or grants for the same In manner and form herein after directed.

II. *Provided*, That such surveys and rights be returned to the said office within twelve months next after the end of this present session of assembly, otherwise they shall be, and are hereby declared forfeited and void. All persons, their heirs or assigns, claiming lands under the charter and ancient custom of Virginia, upon importation rights as before limited, duly proved, and certified in any court of record before the passing of this act; those claiming under treasury rights for money paid the receiver general duly authenticated, or under proclamation warrants for military service, and not having located and fixed such lands by actual surveys as herein before mentioned, shall be admitted to warrants, entries, and grants for the same, in manner directed by the act of assembly entitled "An act for establishing a land office, and ascertaining the terms and manner of granting waste and unappropriated lands,"[6] upon producing to the register of the land office the proper certificates, proofs, or warrants, as the case may be, for their respective rights within the like space of twelve months after the end of this present session of assembly, and not afterwards. All certificates of importation rights proved before any court of record according to the ancient custom, and before the end of this present session of assembly, are hereby declared good and valid: And all other claims for importation rights not so proved, shall be null and void; and where any person before the end of this present session of assembly, hath made a regular entry according to act of assembly, with the county surveyor for any tract of land not exceeding four hundred acres upon any of the eastern waters, which hath not been surveyed or forfeited, according to the laws and rules of government in force at the time of making such entry, the surveyor

---

[6] See the next chapter.

of the county where such land lies, shall after advertising legal notice thereof, proceed to survey the same accordingly, and shall deliver to the proprietor a plat and certificate of survey thereof within three months; and if such person shall fail to attend at the time and place so appointed for making such survey, with chain carriers and a person to mark the lines, or shall fail to deliver such plat and certificate into the land office, according to the rules and regulations of the same, together with the auditors certificate of the treasurers receipt for the composition money herein after mentioned, and pay the office fees, he or she shall forfeit his or her right and title; but upon performance of these requisitions, shall be entitled to a grant for such tract of land as in other cases.

III. *And be it enacted*, That all orders of council or entries for land in the council books, except so far as such orders or entries respectively have been carried into execution by actual surveys in manner herein before mentioned, shall be, and they are hereby declared void and of no effect; and except also a certain order of council for a tract of sunken grounds, commonly called the Dismal Swamp, in the south eastern part of this commonwealth, contiguous to the North Carolina line, which said order of council with the proceedings thereon and the claim derived from it, shall hereafter be laid before the general assembly for their further order therein. No claim to land within this commonwealth for military service founded upon the king of Great Britain's proclamation, shall hereafter be allowed, except a warrant for the same shall have been obtained from the governour of Virginia, during the former government as before mentioned; or where such service was performed by an inhabitant of Virginia, or in some regiment or corps actually raised in the same; in either of which cases the claimant making due proof in any court of record, and producing a certificate thereof to the register of the land office within the said time of twelve months, shall be admitted to a warrant, entry, and grant for the same, in the manner herein before mentioned; but nothing herein contained shall be construed or extend to give any person a title to land for service performed in any company or detachment of militia.

IV. And whereas great numbers of people have settled in the country upon the western waters, upon waste and unappropriated lands, for which they have been hitherto prevented from suing out patents or obtaining legal titles by the king of Great Britain's proclamations or instructions to his governours, or by the late change of government, and present war having delayed until now, the opening of a land office, and the establishment of any certain terms for granting lands, and it is just that those settling under such circumstances should have some reasonable allowance for the charge and risk they have incurred, and that the property so acquired should be secured to them: *Be it therefore enacted*,[7] That all persons who, at any time before the first day of January, in the year one thousand seven hundred and seventy eight, have really and bona fide settled themselves or their families, or at his, her, or their charge, have settled others upon any waste or unappropriated lands on the said western waters, to which no other person hath any legal right or claim, shall be allowed for every family so settled, four hundred acres of land, or such smaller quantity as the party chooses, to include such settlement. And where any such settler hath had any survey made for him or her, under any order of the former government, since the twenty sixth day of October, in the year one thousand seven hundred and sixty three, in consideration of such settlement for less than four hundred acres of land, such settler, his or her heirs, may claim and be allowed as much adjoining waste and unappropriated land, as together with the land so surveyed will make up the quantity of four hundred acres.

V. And whereas several families for their greater safety have settled themselves in villages or townships, under some agreement between the inhabitants of laying off the same into town lots, to be divided among them, and have, from present necessity, cultivated a piece of ground adjoining thereto in common: *Be it enacted*, That six hundred and forty acres of land whereon such villages and towns are situate, and to which no other person hath a previous legal claim, shall not be entered for or surveyed, but shall be reserved for the use and benefit of the said inhabitants until a true representation of their case can be made to the general assembly, that right and justice may be done therein; and in the mean time there shall be allowed to every such family, in consideration of their settlement, the like quantity of land as is herein allowed to other settlers adjacent, or convenient to their respective village or town, and to which no other person hath, by this act, the right of preemption, for which said quantities to be adjusted, ascertained, and certified by the commissioners to be appointed by virtue of this act, in manner herein after directed. The proper claimants shall be respectively entitled to entries with the surveyor of the county wherein the land lies, upon producing to him certificates of their rights from the said commissioners of the county, duly attested, within twelve months next after the end of this present Session of assembly, and not afterwards; which certificate the said surveyor shall record in his books, and then return them to the parties, and shall proceed to survey the lands so entered, according to law. And upon due return to the land office of the plats and

---

[7] See Journal of Convention of June 24, 1776—& 2 Rev Code of 1819, p. 350—See also vol. 9, p. 355, 356.

certificates of survey, together with the certificates from the said commissioners of the rights, by settlement upon winch the entries were founded, grants may and shall issue to them and their heirs or assigns, in manner before directed. And if any such settlers shall desire to take up a greater quantity of land than is herein allowed them, they shall on payment to the treasurer of the consideration money, required from other purchasers, be entitled to the preemption of any greater quantity of land adjoining to that allowed them in consideration of settlement, not exceeding one thousand acres, and to which no other person hath any legal right or claim. And to prevent doubts concerning settlements, *It is hereby declared*, That no family shall be entitled to the allowance granted to settlers by this act, unless they have made a crop of corn in that country, or resided there at least one year since the time of their settlement. All persons who, since the said first day of January, in the year one thousand seven hundred and seventy eight, have actually settled on any waste or unappropriated lands on the said western waters, to which no other person hath a just or legal right or claim, shall be entitled to the preemption of any quantity of land, not exceeding four hundred acres, to include such settlement at the state price to other purchasers. And all those who, before the said first day of January, in the year one thousand seven hundred and seventy eight, had marked out or chosen for themselves, any waste or unappropriated lands, and built any house or hut, or made other improvements thereon, shall also be entitled to the preemption upon the like terms, of any quantity of land, to include such improvements, not exceeding one thousand acres, and to which no other person hath any legal right or claim; but no person shall have the right of preemption for more than one such improvement; provided they respectively demand and prove their right to such preemption, before the commissioners for the county, to be appointed by virtue of this act within eight months, pay the consideration money, produce the auditor's certificate for the treasurer's receipt for the same, take out their warrants from the register of the land office within ten months, and enter the same with the surveyor of the county, within twelve months next after the end of this present session of assembly; and there after duly comply with the rules and regulations of the land office. All locations made by officers and soldiers upon the lands of actual settlers, shall be void but the said officers, soldiers, or their assignees, may obtain warrants on producing the commissioners certificate of their several rights, and locate their claims on other waste and unappropriated lands. To prevent the locations of those claiming under warrants for preemption, from interfering with such as claim under certificates for settlements, and to give due preference to the latter, so far as respects their rights to tracts of land not exceeding four hundred acres; the register of the land office shall particularly distinguish all preemption warrants by him issued, and no county surveyor shall admit any such warrant to be entered or located in his books, before the expiration of ten months as aforesaid. And where any such warrant shall not be entered and located with the county surveyor, within the before mentioned space of twelve months, the right of preemption shall be forfeited, and the lands therein mentioned may be entered for by any other person holding another land warrant; but such preemption warrant may, nevertheless, be located upon any other waste or unappropriated lands, or upon the same lands where they have not in the mean time been entered for by some other.

VI. *And be it farther enacted*, That all persons claiming lands, and suing out grants upon any such surveys heretofore made; either under entries with the surveyor of any county, or under any order of council, or entry in the council books, for which rights have not formerly been lodged in the secretary's office, and also those suing out grants for tracts of lands upon the western waters, not exceeding four hundred acres herein allowed them in consideration of their settlements, or under former entries with the county surveyor, for lands upon · the eastern waters, shall be subject to the payment of the usual composition money under the former government, at the rate of ten shillings stirling for every hundred acres, to be discharged in current money, at the rate of thirty three and one third per centum exchange, before the grant issues, and to no other charge or imposition whatsoever, save the common office fees. And to all such persons, their heirs or assigns, who having title to land under the former government, had not only surveyed the same, but had lodged their certificates of survey, together with their rights, in the secretary's office; and although no caveat hath been entered, have not obtained patents, grants shall issue in consideration thereof, upon the payment of the office fees only.

VII. And whereas it hath been represented to the general assembly, that upon lands surveyed for sundry companies by virtue of orders of council, many people have settled without specifick agreement, but yet under the faith of the terms of sale publickly offered by the said companies or their agents at the time of such settlements, who have made valuable improvements thereon: *Be it enacted and declared*, That all persons so settled upon any unpatented lands, surveyed as before mentioned, except only such lands as before the settlement of the same, were notoriously reserved by the respective companies for their own use, shall have their titles confirmed to them by the members of such companies, or their agents, upon payment of the price at which such lands were offered for sale when they were settled, together with interest thereon from the time of the respective settlements, provided they compromise their claims with the said companies, or lay them before the commissioners for their respective counties, to be appointed by virtue of this act, and have the same tried and determined by them, in manner herein after directed: And provided also, that where any such survey contains more than four hundred acres, no one settler shall be entitled to a greater quantity than three hundred acres, unless he takes the whole survey, to include his settlement, and leave the remainder in one entire and convenient piece where the same is practicable.

VIII. And whereas the claims of various persons to the lands herein allowed to the inhabitants, in consideration of their settlements, and of those who, by this act, are entitled to preemption at the state price; as well as of the settlers on the lands surveyed for sundry companies by orders of council as aforesaid, may occasion numerous disputes, the determination of which depending upon evidence, which cannot, without great charge and trouble, be collected, but the neighbourhood of such lands will be most speedily and properly made by commissioners in the respective counties: *Be it enacted*, That the counties on the western waters shall be allotted into districts, to wit: The counties of Monongalia; Yohogania, and Ohio, into one district; the counties of Augusta, Botetourt, and Greenbrier, into one district; the counties of Washington and Montgomery, into one other district; and the county of Kentucky, shall be another district; for each of which districts, the governour, with the advice of the council, shall appoint four commissioners under the seal of the commonwealth, not being inhabitants of such district (any three of whom may act) to continue in office eight months from the end of this present session of assembly, for the purpose of collecting, adjusting, and determining such claims, and four months thereafter for : the purpose of adjusting the claims of settlers on lands surveyed for the aforesaid companies. Every such commissioner, before he enters on the duties of his office, shall take the following oath of office: "I A.B. do swear that I will well and truly serve this commonwealth in the office of a commissioner for the district of _____ for collecting, adjusting, and settling the claims, and determining the titles of such persons as claim lands in the said district, in consideration of their settlements; of such as claim preemption to any lands therein, and also of such settlers as claim any lands surveyed by order of council, for sundry companies, according to an act of general assembly, entitled An act for adjusting and settling the titles of claimers to unpatented lands, under the former and present government, previous to the establishment of the commonwealth's land office; and that I will do equal right to all manner of people, without respect of persons; I will not take by myself, nor by any other person, any gift, fee, or reward for any matter done, or to be done by virtue of my office, except such fees or salary as the law shall allow me; and finally in all things belonging to my said office, I will faithfully, justly, and truly, according to the best of my skill and judgment, do equal and impartial justice, without fraud, favour, affection, or partiality. So help me God." Which oath shall be administered by any of the said commissioners to the first of them in nomination, who shall be present, and then by him to the others. The said commissioners shall have power to hear and determine all titles claimed in consideration of settlements to lands, to which no person hath any other legal title, and the rights of all persons claiming preemption to any lands within their respective districts, as also the rights of all persons claiming any unpatented lands, surveyed by order of council for sundry companies, by having settled thereon under the faith of the terms of sale publickly offered by such companies or their agents, and shall immediately upon receipt of their commissions, give at least twenty days previous notice by advertisements at the forts, churches, meeting houses, and other publick places in their district, of the time and place at which they intend to meet, for the purpose of collecting, hearing, and determining the said claims and titles, requiring all persons interested therein, to attend and put in their claims, and may adjourn from place to place, and time to time, as their business may require; but if they should fail to meet at any time to which they shall have adjourned, neither their commission nor any matter depending before them shall be thereby discontinued, but they shall proceed to business when they do meet, as if no such failure had happened. They shall appoint and administer an oath of office to their clerk; be attended by the sheriff, or one of the under sheriffs of the county; be empowered to administer oaths to witnesses or others, necessary for the discharge of their office; to punish contempts, enforce good behavior in their presence, and award costs, in the same manner with the county courts; they shall have free access to the county surveyor's books, and may order the same to be laid before them, at any time or place of their sitting, and shall pay to such surveyor, out of the fees received by them for certificates, the sum of three pounds for every day he shall attend, and to the sheriff for the like attendance, two pounds for each day's attendance. In all cases of disputes upon claims for settlement, the person who made the first actual settlement his or her heirs or assigns, shall have the preference, in all disputes for the right of preemptions for improvements made on the land, the persons, their heirs or assigns respectively, who made the first improvement, and the persons to whom any right of preemption on account of settlement or improvements shall be adjudged, shall fix the quantity at their own option at the time of the judgment, so as not to exceed the number of acres respectively allowed by this act, or to interfere with the just rights of others. The clerk shall keep exact minutes of all the proceedings of the commissioners, and enter the names of all the persons to whom either lands for settlement or right of preemption as the case is, shall be adjudged with their respective quantities and locations, and also the names of all such persons to whom titles shall be adjudged for lands within the surveys made by order of council for any company with the quantity of acres adjudged, and in what survey; and if the same is only part of such survey, in what manner it shall be located therein, the name or style of the company, and the price to be paid them, with the time from which the same is to bear interest. Upon application of any person claiming a right to any lands by virtue of this act, and complaining that another pretends a right in opposition thereto, the said clerk shall issue a summons, stating the nature of the plaintiffs claim and calling on the party opposing the same, to appear at a time and place certain therein to be named, and shew cause why a grant of the said lands may not issue, or a title be made to the said by plaintiff: The said summons shall be served on the party by the sheriff of the county where he resides, or wherein he may be found, and such service being returned thereon, and the party appearing or failing to reappear, the commissioners may proceed to trial, or for good cause shewn, may refer such trial to a farther day. The clerk shall also have power at the request of either party, to issue subpoenas for witnesses to appear at the time and place of trial, which shall be had in a summary way without pleadings in writing, and the court in conducting the said trial, in all matters of evidence relative thereto, and in giving judgment, shall govern themselves by such rules and principles of law or equity, as are applicable to the case, or would be the rule of evidence or of dicision, (sic) were the same before the ordinary courts of law or equity; save only as far as this act shall otherwise have specially directed. Judgment when rendered shall be final, except as herein after excepted, and shall give to the party in whose favour it is, a title against all others who were parties to the trial; and if after such judgment rendered, the party against whom it is, shall enter the said lands forcibly, or forcibly detain the same, it shall be lawful for the said commissioners or any one of them, or any justice of peace for the county, to remove such force, in like manner as it were committed on lands holden by grant actually issued. The said commissioners shall deliver to every person to whom they shall adjudge lands for settlement, a certificate thereof under their hands, and attested by the clerk, mentioning the number of acres, and the time of settlement, and describing as near as may be, the particular location, noting also therein the quantity of adjacent land to which such person shall have the right of preemption. And to every other person to whom they shall adjudge the right of preemption to any lands, they shall in like manner deliver a certificate, specifying the quantity and location of such land, with the cause for preemption, with a memorandum for the information of the party in each certificate of the last day on which the lands therein respectively mentioned can be entered with the county surveyor: For every hundred acres of land contained within the said certificates, the party receiving the same, shall pay down to the commissioners the sum of ten shillings, besides a fee of ten shillings to the clerk for each certificate so granted; and the said certificates produced within the times herein before respectively limited to the surveyor of the county, or to the register of the land office, with the auditors certificate of the treasurer's receipt for the payment due on the preemption, as the nature of the case may require, shall entitle the person respectively receiving them, to an entry and survey, or a warrant for the said lands, in such way, and on such terms as are herein before prescribed. And to prevent frauds or mistakes, the said commissioners immediately upon having completed the business in their district, shall transmit to the register of the land office, under their hands, and attested by their clerk, an exact list or schedule in alphabetical order, of all such certificates by them granted, and a duplicate so signed and attested to the county surveyor for their information. They shall in like manner, and upon payment of the same fees, deliver to every person to whom they shall adjudge, a title to any unpatented land, surveyed for any company by order of council, a certificate mentioning the number of acres to which they have adjudged the title, what particular survey the same is in, and for what company made, the price to be paid such company, and the date from which the same is to bear interest, and where there is a greater quantity of land contained in the survey, describe as near as may be, the manner the land to which they have adjudged title, shall be laid off and bounded; and shall also immediately upon having completed the business in their district, transmit to the clerk of the general court, under their hands, and attested by their clerk, a list or schedule in alphabetical order, containing exact copies of all such certificates by them granted, to remain in the said clerk's office for the information of the said companies, and as evidence and proof of the respective titles.

IX. *Provided nevertheless,* That if the parties, their heirs or assigns, to whom such titles shall have been adjudged, shall not within six months at farthest, from the time of their respective judgments in their favour, pay or tender to the company to whom the same is due, or their agent, the price and interest so fixed by the said commissioners, the title of every person so failing, shall be forfeited, and shall be from thence forward, to all intents and purposes, null and void; anything herein to the contrary thereof notwithstanding. The said commissioners for every day they shall be actually employed in the execution of their office, shall be allowed the sum of eight pounds each; they shall be accountable for all the money they shall have received upon issuing certificates as aforesaid, except the fee to the clerk, and shall settle a fair account upon oath, with the auditors, and receive from the treasurer whatever balance may appear due to them thereon, or pay to him any balance which shall be by them due to the commonwealth. The clerk and sheriff shall receive for their services, the fees heretofore allowed by law for the like services in the county court, and the witnesses the same allowance for their attendance, to be paid by the party, and collected in like manner as is directed in the ordinary cases of the same nature, and the clerk shall have the same power of issuing executions as the clerks of the county courts; provided that the clerk shall not be allowed any farther or other fee for entering and issuing a certificate than is herein before mentioned. But as by this summary mode of proceeding, some persons at a great distance may not have timely notice, and may be unable to appear in support of their claims, for remedy whereof, *Be it enacted,* That no grant shall issue upon any of the claims determined by the said commissioners until the first day of December, 1780, and in the mean time, any such person injured by their determination, his or her heirs or assigns, may enter a caveat against a grant thereupon, until the matter shall be heard before the general court, and may petition the said general court to have his or her claim considered; and upon its being proved to the court that he or she laboured under such a disability at the time of the meeting of the commissioners thereupon, the court shall grant him or her a hearing in a summary way, and if it shall appear upon trial, that the petitioners claim is just, such court may reverse the former determination, and order a grant to issue for such land or any part thereof, on the terms herein before mentioned, to the person to whom they shall adjudge the same.

X. *And be it farther enacted,* That all claims for lands upon surveys under any order of council or entry in the council books, shall by the respective claimers be laid before the court of appeals; which shall meet for that purpose on the sixteenth day of December next, and shall adjourn from day to day until the business be finished; or if it be proved to the court that any such claimer is unable to attend and prosecute his claim, or for other just cause to them shewn, they may order such claim to be tried before them on some future day. All such claims shall be heard and determined in a summary way, without pleadings in writing, upon such evidence as in the opinion of the court, the nature of the case may require; and no such claim shall be valid, but such only as shall be so heard and established by the said court of appeals, and on their certificate that any such claim hath been by them established, the register is hereby required to issue a warrant or grant thereupon, according to the nature of the case, and the rules and regulations of the land office; and the attorney general is hereby required to attend the said court on behalf of the commonwealth.

XI. *Provided always*, That nothing herein contained shall extend to officers, soldiers, or their assignees, claiming lands for military service. The register of the land office shall regularly record all land warrants issued by virtue of this act; they may be executed in one or more surveys, and may be exchanged or divided so as best to suit the purposes of the party, and shall remain in force until lands shall have been actually obtained for them, in the same manner with the warrants to be issued by virtue of the before recited act for establishing a land office. And when the said register shall make out a grant to any person or persons for lands due to him, her, or them, by virtue of this act, he shall recite therein as the consideration, the rights and cause for which the same became due, according to an act of general assembly, passed in the year of our Lord one thousand seven hundred and seventy nine, entitled "An act for adjusting and settling the titles of claimers to unpatented lands under the former and present government, previous to the establishment of the commonwealth's land office;" and if any part thereof is due in consideration of the ancient composition money, or the new purchase money paid to the commonwealth, the same shall be properly distinguished, and in every other respect the grant shall be drawn and pass in the form and manner prescribed by law for future grants of lands from the commonwealth.

XII. And whereas at the time of the late change of government, many caveats against patents for lands which had been entered in the council office, were depending and undetermined, Be it enacted, That all such caveats, with the papers relating thereto, shall be removed into the clerk's office of the general court, there to be proceeded on and tried in the manner directed by law for future caveats; but the same shall be determined according to the laws in force at the time they were entered; and upon the determination of any such caveat, a grant shall issue in the name of the person to whom such land shall be adjudged, his or her heirs or assigns, upon producing to the register of the land office, within three months at farthest from the time of such judgment, an authentick copy thereof, together with the auditor's certificate of the treasurer's receipt for the antient composition money due thereon, at the rate of exchange herein before mentioned; but where the person recovering had before paid rights into the secretary's office, a grant shall issue in consideration thereof upon payment of the office fees only.

CHAP. XIII

An act for establishing a Land office, and ascertaining the terms and manner of granting waste and unappropriated lands[8]

I. WHEREAS there are large quantities of waste and unappropriated lands within the territory of this commonwealth, the granting of which will encourage the migration of foreigners hither, promote population, increase the annual revenue, and create a fund for discharging the publick debt: *Be it enacted by the General Assembly*, That an office shall be, and is hereby constituted for the purpose of granting lands within this commonwealth, into which all the records now in the secretary's office, of patents or grants for lands heretofore issued, with all papers and documents relating thereto, and all certificates of surveys of lands now in the said office and not patented, shall be removed and lodged for their safe keeping; and, all future grants of lands shall issue from the said office in manner and form herein after mentioned. A register of the said land office shall be appointed, from time to time, by joint ballot of both houses of assembly, who shall give bond with sufficient security to the governour or first magistrate of this commonwealth, in the penalty of fifty thousand pounds current money; shall hold his office during good behaviour; be entitled to receive such fees as shall hereafter be allowed by law, and shall have power to appoint a deputy and clerks to assist in executing the business of the said office, but shall nevertheless reside there himself. If any vacancy shall happen by the death, resignation, or removal of a register during the recess of the general assembly, the governour or first magistrate of the commonwealth, by and with the advice of the council, may appoint some other person, giving bond and security in like manner, to act as register of the said office until the end of the next session of assembly. All copies of the records and other papers of the said office, or of the records and papers hereby directed to be removed from the secretary's office and lodged therein, duly attested by such register, shall be as good evidence as the originals would be.

II. And whereas a certain bounty in lands hath been engaged to the troops on continental establishment raised by the ordinances of convention or the laws this commonwealth, and to the troops upon Virginia establishment: Be it enacted, That the officers and soldiers of the said troops, as well as the officers and soldiers to whom a bounty in lands may, or shall be hereafter allowed by any law of this commonwealth, shall be entitled to the quantity of waste or

---

[8] Chan. Rev. p. 94.

unappropriated lands respectively engaged to them by such laws, a commissioned officer or his heirs, upon certificate from any general officer of the Virginia line, or the commanding officer of the troops on the Virginia establishment as the case may be, and a non-commissioned officer or soldier, or his heirs, upon certificate from the colonel or commanding officer of the regiment, or corps to which they respectively belonged, that such officer or soldier hath served the time required by law or hath been slain or died in the service, distinguishing particularly the time such officer or soldier hath served, and in what regiment or corps such service hath been performed, or death happened; and upon making proof before any court of record within the commonwealth by the persons own oath, or other satisfactory evidence of the truth and authenticity of the said certificate, and that the party had never before proved or claimed his right to land for the service therein mentioned, which proof the clerk of the court before whom it shall be made, is hereby empowered and required to endorse and certify upon the original certificate, making an entry or minute thereof in his order book and recording the same; and every county court shall annually, in the month of October, send to the register's office, a list of all certificates granted by their respective county courts upon any of the before mentioned rights, there to be recorded. And for creating a sinking fund in aid of the annual taxes to discharge the publick debt: *Be it enacted,* That any person may acquire title to so much waste and unappropriated land as he or she shall desire to purchase, on paying the consideration of forty pounds for every hundred acres, and so in proportion for a greater or smaller quantity, and obtaining certificate from the publick auditors in the following manner: The consideration money shall be paid into the hands of the treasurer, who shall thereupon give to the purchaser a receipt for the payment specifying the purpose it was made for, which being delivered to the auditors, they shall give to such person a certificate thereof, with the quantity of land he or she is thereby entitled to.

III. *And be it enacted,* That upon application of any person or persons, their heirs or assigns, having title to waste or unappropriated lands, either by military rights or treasury rights, and lodging in the land office a certificate thereof; the register of the said office shall grant to such person or persons a printed warrant under his hand and the seal of his office, specifying the quantity of land and the rights upon which it is due, authorizing any surveyor duly qualified according to law, to lay off and survey the same, and shall regularly enter and record in the books of his office, all such certificates and the warrants issued thereupon, which warrants shall be always good and valid until executed by actual survey, or exchanged in the manner hereinafter directed; provided that warrant on treasury rights, other than preemption warrants, to be obtained by virtue of this act, shall be granted or issued before the fifteenth day of October next nor shall the surveyor of any county admit the entry or location of any warrant on treasury rights except preemption warrants, in his books, before the first day of May next. Any person holding a land warrant upon any of the before mentioned rights, may have the same executed in one or more surveys, and in such case, or where the lands on which any warrant is located shall be insufficient to satisfy such warrant, the party may have the said warrant exchanged by the register of the land office for others of the same amount in the whole, but divided as best may answer the purposes of the party, or entitle him to so much land elsewhere as will make good the deficiency. A surveyor shall be appointed in every county to be nominated, examined, and certified able by the president and professors of William and Mary college, and if of good character, commissioned by the governour, with a reservation in such commission to, the said professors, for the use of the college, of one sixth part of the legal fees which shall be received by such surveyor, for the yearly payment of which, he shall give bond with sufficient security to the president and masters of the said college. He shall hold his office during good behaviour; shall reside within his county; and before he shall be capable of entering upon the execution of his office, shall before the court of the same county, take an oath and give bond with two sufficient sureties, to the governour and his successours, in such sum as he, with advice of his council, shall have directed for the faithful execution of his office. All deputy surveyors shall be nominated by their principals, who shall be answerable for them, examined and certifiedable by the president and masters of the said college, and if of good character, commissioned by the governour, and shall thereupon be entitled to one half of all fees received for services performed by them respectively, after deducting the proportion thereof due to the college. If any principal surveyor shall fail to nominate a sufficient number of deputies to perform the services of his office in due time, the court of the county shall direct what number he shall nominate, and in case of failure, shall nominate for him. And if any deputy surveyor, or any other on his behalf, and with his privity, shall pay or agree to pay any greater part of the profits of his office, sum of money in gross, or other valuable consideration to his principal for his recommendation or interest in procuring the deputation, such deputy and principal shall be thereby rendered for ever incapable of serving in such office; it shall not be necessary for the present chief or deputy surveyors of the several counties duly examined, commissioned, and qualified according to the laws heretofore in force, to be again commissioned and qualified under the directions of this act, nor in cases now depending before any court within this commonwealth. Every person having a land warrant founded on any of the before mentioned rights, and being desirous of locating the same on any particular waste and unappropriated lands, shall lodge such warrant with the chief surveyor of the county wherein the said lands or the greater part of them lie, who shall give a receipt for the same if required. The party shall direct the location thereof so specially and precisely, as that others may be enabled with certainty, to locate other warrants on the adjacent residuum; which location shall bear date the day on which it shall be made, and shall be entered by the surveyor in a book to be kept for that purpose, in which there shall be left no blank leaves or spaces between the different entries. And if several persons shall apply with their warrants at the office of any surveyor at the same time to make entries, they shall be preferred according to the priority of the dates of their warrants, but if such warrants be dated on the same day, the surveyor shall settle the right of priority between such persons by lot. And every surveyor shall, at the time of making entries for persons not being inhabitants of his county appoint a time for surveying their land, and give notice thereof in writing to the persons making the same. And if on such application at his office, the surveyor shall refuse to enter such location, under pretence of a prior entry for the same lands made by some other persons, he shall have a right to demand of the said surveyor a view of the original of such prior entry in his book, and also an attested copy of it. But it shall not be lawful for any surveyor to admit an entry for any land without a warrant from the register of the land office, except in the particular case of certificates from the commissioners of the county for tracts of land, not exceeding four hundred acres allowed in consideration of settlements, according to an act of assembly, entitled "An act for adjusting and settling the titles of claimants to unpatented lands, under the present and former government, previous to the establishment of the commonwealth's land office." No entry or location of land shall be admitted within the county and limits of the Cherokee Indians, or on the north west side of the Ohio river, or on the lands reserved by act of assembly for any particular nation or tribe of Indians, or on the lands granted by law to Richard Henderson and company,[9] or in that tract of country reserved by resolution of the general assembly[10] for the benefit of the troops serving in the present war, and

---

[9] See vol. 9, p. 571.

[10] The resolution above alluded to, is in the following words:
Saturday the 19th of December, 1778

Mr. Lyne from the committee to whom the memorial of the general and field officers was referred, reported that the committee had, according to order, had the same under their consideration, and had agreed Upon a report and come to several resolutions thereupon, which he read, in his place, and afterwards delivered in at the

[*footnote 10, continued*]
clerks table where the same were again read, and are as followeth, viz.

Resolved, That it is the opinion of this committee, that a certain tract of country to be bounded by the Green river and a south east course from the head thereof to the Cumberland mountains, with the said mountains to the Carolina line, with the Carolina line to the Cherokee or Tennessee River, with the said river to the Ohio river, and with the Ohio river to the said Green river, ought to be reserved for supplying the officers and soldiers in the Virginia line with the respective proportions of land which have been or may be assigned to them by the general assembly, saying and reserving the land granted to Richard Henderson and Company, and their legal rights to such persons as have heretofore actually located lands and settled thereon within the bounds aforesaid.

Resolved, That it is the opinion or this committee that the said officers and soldiers, or any of them, may be at liberty to locate their proportions of land on any other vacant and ungranted lands within this commonwealth.

Resolved, That it is the opinion of this committee, that the allowance of two hundred acres of land over and above the continental bounty, be given to all the soldiers in the Virginia line who have heretofore enlisted or shall hereafter enlist for the term of three years or during the war.

Resolved, That it is the opinion of this committee, that the several commissioned and noncommissioned officers in the Virginia line ought to have their allowance of lands increased in the same proportion as that of the soldiers are by the preceeding resolution. And whereas no provision hath been hitherto made for the general officers;

Resolved, That such general officers who were inhabitants of this state, be allowed the following proportions of land. upon the same terms and under the same restrictions with the lands engaged to the officers and soldiers raised in this commonwealth, that is to say, to the commander in chief _____ acres, to every major general _____ acres, and to every brigadier general _____ acres.

The first resolution being read a second time, was, upon the question put thereupon, agreed to by the house. Ordered, that Mr. G. Mason do carry the same to the senate and desire their concurrence. The second, third, fourth and fifth of the said resolutions, being read a second time, were ordered to lie on the table. [MS. Journal of the House of Delegates of October 1778, six pages from the end—the volume not being paged.]

A Message from the Senate by Mr. Ellzey

Mr. Speaker,

The senate have agreed to the resolution of this house for reserving certain lands on the waters of the Ohio and Green rivers for the use of the officers and soldiers, with an amendment to which they desire the concurrence of this house; and then he withdrew.

The house proceeded to consider the amendments proposed by the senate, to the resolution for reserving certain lands on the waters of the Ohio and Green rivers for the use of the officers and .soldiers, and the said amendment was read and agreed to by the house.

[MS Journal of House of Delegates of October 1778, 3rd and 4th pages from the end.]

bounded by the Green river and a south east course from the head thereof to the Cumberland mountains, with the said mountains to the Carolina line, with the Carolina line to the Cherokee or Tenesee(*sic*) river, with the said river to the Ohio river, and with the Ohio to the said Green river, until the farther order of the general assembly. Any chief surveyor having warrant for lands, and desirous to locate the same on lands within his own county, shall enter such location before the clerk of the county, who shall return the same to his next court, there to be recorded, and the said surveyor shall proceed to have the survey made as soon as may be, and within six months at farthest, by some one of his deputies, or if he hath no deputy, then by any surveyor or deputy surveyor of an adjacent county, or his entry shall be void, and the land liable to the entry of any other person. Every chief surveyor shall proceed with all practicable despatch, to survey all lands entered for in his office, and shall, if the party live within his county, either give him personal notice of the time at which he will attend to make such survey, or shall publish such notice by fixing an advertisement thereof on the door of the courthouse of the county, on two several court days, which time so appointed shall be at least one month after personal notice given, or after the second advertisement so published; and if the surveyor shall accordingly attend, and the party, or some one for him, shall fail to appear at the time with proper chain carriers, and a person to mark the lines, if necessary, his entry shall become void, the land thereafter subject to the entry of any other person, and the surveyor shall return him the warrant, which may, notwithstanding, be located anew upon any other waste or unappropriated lands, or again upon the same lands where it hath not, in the mean time, been entered for by another person. Where the chief surveyor doth not mean to survey himself, be shall immediately after the entry made, direct a deputy surveyor to perform the duty, who shall proceed as is before directed in the case of the chief surveyor. The persons employed to carry the chain on any survey, shall be sworn by the surveyor, whether principal or deputy, to measure justly and exactly to the best of their abilities, and to deliver a true account thereof to such surveyor, and shall be paid for their trouble by the party for whom the survey is made. The surveyor at the time of making the survey, shall see the same bounded plainly by marked trees, except where a water course or ancient marked line shall be the boundary, and shall make the breadth of each survey at least one third of its length in every part, unless where such breadth shall be restrained on both sides by mountains unfit for cultivation, by water courses, or bounds or lands before appropriated. He shall as soon, as it can conveniently be done, and within three months at farthest after making the survey, deliver to his employer, or his order, a fair and true plat and certificate of such survey, the quantity contained, the hundred (where hundreds are established in the county wherein it lies) the courses and discriptions of the several boundaries, natural and artificial, ancient and new, expressing the proper names of such natural boundaries, where they have any, and the name of every person whose former line is made a boundary; and also the nature of the warrant and rights on which such survey was made, and shall at the same time redeliver the said warrant to the party. The said surveyor may, nevertheless, detain the said certificates and warrants until the payment of his fees. The said plats and certificates shall be examined and tried by the said principal surveyor, whether truly made and legally proportioned as to length and breadth, and shall be entered within three months at farthest after the survey is made, in a book well bound, to be provided by the court of his county, at the county charge. And he shall in the month of July every year, return to the president and professors of William and Mary college, and also to the clerk's office of his county court, a true list of all surveys made by him, or his deputies, in the preceding twelve months with the names of the persons for whom they were respectively made, and the quantities contained in each, there to be recorded by such clerk; and no person after the first day of May next, shall hold the offices of clerk of a county court and surveyor of a county, nor shall a deputy in either office act as deputy or chief in the other. Any surveyor, whether principal or deputy, failing in any of the duties aforesaid, shall be liable to be indicted in the general court and punished by amercement or deprivation of his office and incapacity to take it again, at the discretion of a jury, and shall moreover be liable to any party injured, for all damages he may sustain by such failure. Every county court shall once in every year, and oftener if they see cause, appoint two or more capable persons to examine the books of entries and surveys in possession of their chief surveyor, and to report in what condition and order the same are kept; and on his death or removal, shall have power to take the same into their possession, and deliver them to the succeeding chief surveyor. Every person for whom any waste or unappropriated lands shall be so located and laid off shall within twelve mouths at farthest after the survey made, return the plat and certificate of the said survey into the land office, together with the warrant on which the lands were surveyed, and may demand of the register a receipt for the same, and on failing to make such return within twelve months as aforesaid, or if the breadth of his plat be not one-third of its length as before directed, it shall be lawful for any other person to enter a caveat in the said land office against the issuing of any grant to him, expressing therein for what cause the grant should not issue; or if any person shall obtain a survey of lands to which another hath by law a better right, the person having such better right, may in like manner enter a caveat to prevent his obtaining a grant until the title can be determined; such caveat also expressing the nature of the right on which the plaintiff therein claims the said land. The person entering any caveat, shall take from the register a certified copy thereof, which, within three days thereafter, he shall deliver to the clerk of the general court, or such caveat shall become void; the said clerk on receiving the same, shall enter it in a book, and thereupon issue a summons, reciting the cause for which such caveat is entered, and requiring the defendant to appear on the seventh day of the succeeding court and defend his right; and on such process being returned executed, the court shall proceed to determine the right of the cause in a summary way, without pleadings in writing, empanneling and swearing a jury for the finding of such facts as are material to the cause, and are not agreed by the parties; and shall thereupon give judgment, on which no appeal or writ of errour shall be allowed; a copy of such judgment, if in favour of the defendant, being delivered into the land office, shall vacate the said caveat; and if not delivered within three months, a new caveat may for that cause be entered against the grant; and if the said judgment be in favour of the plaintiff, upon delivering the same into the land office, together with a plat and certificate of the survey, and also producing a legal certificate of new rights on his own account, he shall be entitled to a grant thereof but on failing to make such return and produce such certificates within six months after judgment so rendered, it shall be lawful for any other person to enter a caveat for that cause against issuing the grant; upon which subsequent caveats, such proceedings shall be had as are before directed in the case of an original caveat; and in any caveat where judgment shall be given for the defendant, the court. shall award him his costs, and may compel the plaintiff in any caveat, if they think fit, to give security for costs, or on failure thereof, may dismiss his suit; and in case the plaintiff in any such caveat shall recover, the court may, if they think it reasonable, award costs against the defendant; provided that where any lands surveyed upon a land warrant as aforesaid, shall, in consequence of any judgment upon a caveat, be granted to any other person than the party claiming under such warrant, such party shall be entitled to a new warrant from the register for the quantity of land so granted to another, reciting the original warrant and rights, and the particular cause of granting the new warrant. And to prevent confusion and mistakes in the application, exchange, or renewal of warrants, the register of the land office is hereby directed and required to leave a sufficient of his margin in the record books of his office, and whenever any warrant shall be exchanged, renewed, or finally carried into execution by a grant, to note the same in the margin opposite to such warrant, with folio references to the grant, or other mode of application; and also to note in the margin opposite to each grant, the warrant or warrants and survey on which such grant is founded, with proper folio references to the books in which the same are recorded. All persons, as well foreigners, as others, shall have right to assign or transfer warrants or certificates of survey for lands, and any foreigner purchasing warrants for lands, may locate and have the same surveyed, and after returning a certificate of survey to the land office shall be allowed the term of eighteen months either to become a citizen, or to transfer his right in such certificate of survey to some citizen of this, or any other of the United States of America. When any grant shall have been finally completed, the register shall cause the plat and certificate of survey on which such grant is founded, to be exactly entered and recorded in well bound books, to be provided for that purpose at the publick charge. Due returns of the several articles herein before required being made into the land office, the register, within not less than six, nor more than nine months, shall make out a grant by way of deed poll to the party having right, in the following form: "A. B. esquire, governour of the commonwealth of Virginia, to all to whom these presents shall come greeting: Know ye that in consideration of military service performed by C. D. to this commonwealth, &c. (or in consideration of military service performed by C. D. to the United American States, or in consideration of the sum _____ of current money, paid by C. D. into the treasury of this commonwealth, &c.) there is granted by the said commonwealth unto the said C. D. a certain tract or parcel of land containing _____ acres lying in the county of _____, and hundred of _____, &c. (describing the particular bounds of the land and the date of the survey upon which the grant issues) with its appurtenances, to have and to hold the said tract or parcel of land with its appurtenances to the said C. D. and his heirs for ever. In witness whereof the said A. B. governour of the commonwealth of Virginia, hath hereunto set his hand, and caused the seal of the said commonwealth to be affixed at _____ on the _____ day of _____ in the year of our Lord and of the commonwealth. A.B.

Upon which grant the said register shall endorse that the party hath title to the same; whereupon it shall be signed by the governor, sealed with the seal of the commonwealth, and then entered of record at full length in good well bound books to be provided for that purpose at the publick expense and kept by the register, and being so entered, shall be certified to have been registered and then be delivered, together with the original certificate of survey to the party or his order. Where a grant shall be made to the heir or assignee of a person claiming under any of the before mentioned rights, the material circumstances of the title shall be recited in such grant: And for preventing hasty and surreptitious grants and avoiding controversies and expensive law suits, *Be it enacted*, That no surveyor shall at any time within twelve months after the survey made, issue or deliver any certificate, copy or plat of land by him surveyed, except only to the person or persons for whom the same was surveyed; or to his, her, or their order, unless a caveat shall have been entered against a grant to the person claiming under such survey, to be proved by an authentick certificate of such caveat from the clerk of the general court produced to the surveyor; and if any surveyor shall presume to. issue any certificate, copy, or plat as aforesaid, to any other than the person or persons entitled thereto, every surveyor so offending shall forfeit and pay to the party injured, his or her legal representatives or assigns, fifty pounds current money for every hundred acres of land contained in the survey whereof a certificate, copy, or plat shall be so issued, or shall be liable to the action of the party injured at the common law for his or her damages at the election of the party. Any person possessing high lands, to which any swamp, marshes, or sunken grounds are contiguous, shall have the preemption of such swamps, marshes, or sunken grounds for one year, from and after the passing of this act, and if such person shall not obtain a grant for such swamps; marshes, or sunken grounds within the said year, then any other person may enter on and obtain, a grant for the same in the like manner as is directed in the case of other unappropriated lands. But nothing herein contained shall be construed or extend to give liberty to any person to survey, take up, or obtain a grant for any swamps, marshes, or sunken grounds lying contiguous to the high lands of any feme covert, infant under the age of twenty one years, person not being compos mentis, or person out of the commonwealth, according to the regulations of an act entitled "An act declaring who shall be deemed citizens of this commonwealth," but all such persons shall be allowed one year after the removal of their several disabilities for the preemption of such lands.

IV. And whereas, through the ignorance, negligence, or fraud of surveyors, it may happen that divers persons now do or may hereafter hold within the bounds expressed in their patents or grants, greater quantities of land than are therein mentioned; for quieting such possessions, preventing controversies, and doing equal justice to the commonwealth and its citizens, *Be it enacted*, That it shall not be lawful for any person to enter for, survey, or take up; any parcel of land held as surplus in any patent or grant, except during the life time of the patentee or grantee, and before any transference, conveyance, or other alienation shall have been made of the lands contained in such patent or grant, and until the party intending to enter and take up the same, shall have given one full years notice to such patentee or grantee of such his intentions, and in case such patentee or grantee shall not within the year, obtain rights and sue forth a patent for the surplus land by him held, it shall be lawful for the person who gave notice as aforesaid, upon producing a certificate from the clerk of due proof of such notice before the court of the county wherein such patentee or grantee resides, to demand from the register of the land office, a warrant to the surveyor of the county wherein such lands lie, to resurvey at the proper charge of the person obtaining such warrant, the whole tract within the bounds of the patent or grant, and upon such persons returning into the land office a plat and certificate of such resurvey, together with the warrant on which it is founded, and obtaining and producing new rights for all the surplus land found within the said bounds, he may sue forth and obtain a new grant for such surplus, which shall be granted to him in the same manner as waste or unappropriated lands; but the former patentee or grantee may assign such surplus land in any part of his tract as he shall think fit in one entire piece, the breadth of which shall be at least one third of the length and in such new grant there shall be a recital of the original patent or grant, the resurvey of which the surplus was ascertained and of other material circumstances.

V. *Provided always*, That if upon notice given as aforesaid, the original patentee or grantee shall within the year resurvey his tract, and it be thereupon found that he hath no more than the quantity of land expressed in his patent or grant, with the allowance hereinafter mentioned, the party giving such notice shall be liable to pay all charges of such resurvey, for which he shall give sufficient security to the said patentee or grantee at the time of the notice, otherwise such notice shall be void and of no effect; and moreover for his unjust vexation, shall also be liable to an action upon the case at the suit of the party grieved, and that in all such new surveys, the patentee or grantee shall have an allowance at the rate of five acres in every hundred, for the variation of instruments.

VI. *And be it enacted,* That where any person shall find any mistake or uncertainty in the courses or description of the bounds of his land, and desires to rectify the same, or shall hold two or more tracts of land adjoining to each other, and is desirous to include them in one grant, he may in either case, having previously advertised his intentions and the time of application, at the door of the courthouse on two several court days, and also having given notice to the owners of the adjoining lands; present a petition to the court of the county wherein such lands lie, reciting the nature and truth of the case, and such court may, and is hereby empowered to order the surveyor of their county to resurvey such lands at the charge of the party, according to his directions and the original or authentick title papers, taking care not to intrude upon the possessions of any other person, and to return a fair plat and certificate of such resurvey into the said court, to be examined and compared with the title papers;

and if such court shall certify that in their opinion such resurvey is just and reasonable, the party may return the same, together with his material title papers in the land office, and demand the register's receipt for them; and in case any caveat shall be entered against his obtaining a new grant upon such resurvey, the same proceedings shall be had therein as is directed in the case of other caveats, and the general court upon hearing the same, may either prohibit such new grant, or vacate the caveat as to them shall seem just; but if no caveat shall be entered within six months after such return, or if a caveat shall be entered and vacated as aforesaid, the party upon producing new rights for whatever surplus land appears to be within the bounds, more than the before mentioned allowance of five acres for every hundred, may sue out and obtain a new grant for such lands thereupon, in which shall be recited the dates and other material circumstances of the former title, and the title papers shall be delivered by the register to the new owner. The judges of the general court shall once in every year and oftener if they see cause, appoint-two or more capable persons to examine the record books and papers in the land office, and report in what condition and order they are kept, who shall compare all warrants of survey returned to the said office executed, with the list of those issued therefrom, and cancel all such as shall appear to have been properly executed or exchanged, an account of which shall be kept by the register, charging therein those issued, and giving credit for those cancelled aforesaid. The treasurer for the time being shall annually enter into bond with sufficient security to the governour in the sum of one hundred thousand pounds for the just and faithful accounting for according to law, all money which shall come to his hands by virtue of this act. And that the proprietors of lands within this commonwealth may no longer be subject to any servile, feudal, or precarious tenure, and to prevent the danger to a free state from perpetual revenue; *Be it enacted,* That the reservation of royal mines of quitrents, and all other reservations and conditions in the patents or grants of land from the crown of England or of Great Britain, under the former government, shall be, and are hereby declared null and void and that all lands thereby respectively granted, shall be held in absolute and unconditional property to all intents and purposes whatsoever, in the same manner with the lands hereafter to be granted by the commonwealth by virtue of this act; and no petition for lapsed land shall be admitted or received for or on account of any failure or forfeiture whatsoever, alledged to have been made or incurred after the twenty ninth day of September, in the year of our Lord one thousand seven hundred and seventy five. *And be it farther enacted,* That he or she be adjudged a felon and not have the benefit of clergy, who shall steal, or by other means take from the possession or custody of another, any warrant from the register of the land office of this commonwealth, to authorize a survey of waste and unappropriated lands; or who shall alter, erase, or aid or assist in the alteration or erasement of any such warrant; or forge or counterfeit, or aid, abet, or assist in forging or counterfeiting any written or printed paper, purporting to be such warrant: or who shall transfer to the use of another, or for his or her own use, present or cause to be presented to the register for the exchange thereof, or to a surveyor for the execution thereof, any such warrant or paper purporting to be such warrant, knowing the same so transferred or presented for the exchange or the execution thereof to be stolen, or by other means taken from the possession or custody of another, or altered or erased, or forged or counterfeited; and he or she shall be adjudged a felon and not have the benefit of clergy, who shall falsely make or counterfeit, or aid, abet, or assist, in safely keeping or counterfeiting any instrument stamping an impression in the figure and likeness of the seal officially used by the register of the land office, or who shall have in his or her possession or custody such instrument, and shall wilfully conceal the same, knowing it to be falsely made or counterfeited. So much of all former acts of assembly as concern or relate to the entering, taking up, or seating lands, or direct the mode of proceeding in any case provided for by this act, shall be, and are hereby repealed.

Grant Book A

23 Oct 1779 to 12 January 1780

EVAN SHELBY, 2,000 acs. Kentucky Co. on the Waters of Elkhorn Cr. a br. of the Kentucky, adj. William Prestones Land called *the Cave Spring tract*; 23 Oct 1779 in the *4th year of the Commonwealth* In Witness whereof the sd Thomas Jefferson Esqr. Governor of the Commonwealth of Virginia hath hereunto Set his Hand and Caused the seal of the sd Commonwealth to be affixed at **Williamsburg**, p.1. *by Virtue and in consideration of Military Service performed by Evan Shelby according to the King of Great Britains Proclamation of 1763.*

JAMES TAYLOR Heir at Law to GEORGE TAYLOR, 1,000 acs. Kentucky Co. on the Waters of the Ohio, Beginning on the bank of a Cr. being a fork of Harrods Cr.; 23 Oct 1779, p.2. *in consideration of Military Service performed by George Taylor according to the term of the King of Great Britains Proclamation of 1763* there is Gtd. to James Taylor his Heir at Law the said George Taylor being Decd.

EDMUND TAYLOR ass'ee of ANDREW WAGGONER Heir at Law of the said THOMAS WAGGONER Decd., 3,000 acs. Kentucky Co. on the South fork of Elkhorn Cr. a br. of Ohio, adj. the L. Surveyed for Slaugter & Jones; 23 Oct 1779, p.3. *in consideration of Military Service performed by Thomas Wagner a Capt. in the late War between Great Britain and France according to the terms of the King of Great Britains Proclamation of 1763.*

EDMUND TAYLOR Ass'ee of ANDREW WAGGONER Heir at Law of sd EDMUND WAGGONER Decd., 1,000 acs. Kentucky Co. on the Head brs. of Bargrass Cr. the Waters of the Ohio, adj. the L. of John Ashby; 23 Oct 1779, p.4. *in consideration of Military Service performed by Edmund Waggoner as a Subaltern Officer in the Virginia Service according to the terms of the King of Great Britains Proclamation of 1763.*

WILLIAM ATKINS, 135 acs. [Brunswick Co.] on the S side of the three Creeks, adj. Parham & Adams; 26

Oct 1779, p.5. in consideration of 15 shill. sterl. paid by William Atkins into the Treasury of the Commonwealth it being the Ancient Composition Money. [This land separates John Shearing's PB 15 p.412 from his PB 19 p.763 & is North of Isaac Adams's PB 34, p.326]

RICHARD HARTWELL, 17 acs. Brunswick Co. on the S side Meherrin Riv., adj. James Hinton & William Sims; 23 Oct 1779, p.6. A.C. of 5 shill. sterl.

THOMAS BRANSCOMB, 200 acs. [Brunswick Co.] on the Rocky run, along the fourt Road; adj. Douglass, Branscomb & Chapman; 26 Oct 1779, p.7. A.C. of 20 Shill. Sterl. this Tract is the Same that was formerly Surveyed for *Jacob Jones* and Transfered by *his son Isaac (Jones)* to this Thomas Bransco[m]b.

HARMON HARRISON Ass'ee of WILLIAM NIAX who was ass'ee of JOSEPH PRINCE who was ass'ee of JAMES WALL, 316 acs. Brunswick Co. on the N side of the fort road, adj. John Eves; 26 Oct 1779, p.8. A.C. of 35 Shill. sterl.

SAMUEL CRAWFORD, 170 acs. Botetourt Co. on the N Brs. of Back Cr. being the Waters of James Riv., on a high hill, adj. Stewarts Survey & Clerks line; 26 Oct 1779, p.9. A.C. of 20 Shill. Sterl.

JOSEPH RAGSDALE, 430 acs. Lunenburg Co. on both sides Chesnut Cr., adj. Caldwell; 23 Oct 1779, p.10. A.C. of 45 Shill. sterl.

WILLIAM FURGUSON, 427 acs. Henry Co. on Nicholas's Cr., crossing the North fork of sd Cr., crossing a Bold br., adj. Alley; 20 Oct 1779, p.11. A.C. of 45 Shill. sterl.

JAMES MARTIN, 538 acs. Pittsylvania Co. on the brs. of Chesnut Cr., crossing a bold br., adj. sd James Martin; 20 Oct 1779, p.12. A.C. of 55 Shill. sterl.

JOHN DOUGHTON, 198 acs. Henry Co. on the brs. of Chesnut Cr.; adj. James Calloway, his own line & Smith; 20 Oct 1779, p.13. A.C. of 20 Shill. sterl.

SAMUEL EMMERSON, 400 acs. Pittsylvania Co. on the East fork of Bearskin Cr., along John Piggs road, adj. Edward Hodges; 20 Oct 1779, p.13. A.C. of 40 Shill. sterl.

THOMAS PRENTY, 354 acs. Henry Co. on the Waters of Snow Cr., on Keytons Br., crossing the South fork of Guttery Run, crossing the fork of Gullery Runs; adj. Jeremiah Morrow, Lewis & Choise; 20 Oct 1779, p.14. A.C. of 35 Shill. Sterl.

JOHN HARPER (ass'ee of THOMAS MOODY), 9 acs. Lunenburg Co. on the E side of Stony Cr.; adj. Thomas Moore & Henry Collises's line; 20 Oct 1779, p.15. A.C. of 5 Shill. sterl. [The margin note has Jno. Harper ass'ee of Jno. Moody] [For Thomas Moore's, see PB 32 p.656 to William Newsum]

PETER GRUHEART, 343 acs. Henry Co. on the head of hacket run and Rounding Mill br. [Pounding Mill Br.] waters of Pigg Riv.; adj. James Turpin, Springlan, James Calloway, Henry Jones & James Rentfrow; 20 Oct 1779, p.16. A.C. of 35 Shill. sterl.

WATERS DUNN, 247 acs. Halifax Co. on both sides of Leatherwood Cr.; 20 Oct 1779, p.17. A.C. of 25 Shill. Sterl.

JAMES STANDEFER SENR., 493 acs. Henry Co. on Stony Cr., adj. William Davis; 20 Oct 1779, p.18. A.C. of 50 Shill. Sterl.

THOMAS BABER SENR., 400 acs. Fluvanna Co. on the N side of the Rivanna Riv. and on the Brs. of Ballengers Cr.; adj. Thomas Baber Junr., Winston, & John Strange; 20 Oct 1779, p.20. A.C. of 40 Shill. Sterl.

JOHN WOODS, 424 acs. Pittsylvania Co. on the Brs. of Greasy fork of Chesnut Cr.; adj. Hugh Woods, Hanking, & James Martin; 20 Oct 1779, p.21. A.C. of 45 Shill. Sterl.

WILLIAM DUNNING, 244 acs. Pittsylvania Co. on the brs. of Stinking Riv.; adj. Thomas Farr or Farris, Earbyes Line, Hughin [Hughes?], Barret & the Wests line; 20 Oct 1779, p.23. A.C. of 25 Shill. Sterl.

NATHAN THURMAN, 669 acs. Pittsylvania Co. on both Sides the old Womans Cr. of Stanton Riv., adj. John Whealer; 20 Oct 1779, p.24. A.C. of £3.S10 sterl.

HENRY JONES, 288 acs. Henry Co. on hatchett run and brs. of Pigg Riv., near the Whistling hill, near the Road, adj. his own line & Hill; 20 Oct 1779, p.25. A.C. of 30 shill. Sterl.

WILLIAM VASON, 601 acs. Pittsylvania Co. on the Waters of Allens Cr., adj. John Ballenger; 12 Oct 1779, p.26. A.C. of £3 Sterl.

HENRY HARDEN, 364 acs. Pittsylvania Co. on the Draughts of Sweetnings fork and Sandy Cr., Crossing Sweetens fork, adj. Thomas Hardy & Certain; 26 Oct 1779, p.27. A.C. of 40 Shill. Sterl. Thomas Jefferson Governor of the Commonwealth of Virginia hath hereunto Set his hand and Caused the ~~Lesser~~ seal of the said Commonwealth to be affixed at **Williamsburg**.

ROBERT SPENCER ass'ee of the sd JOSEPH CARTER, 75 acs. Brunswick Co. on the three Creeks, up Kettlestick run, down the Dividing br.; adj. Smith, & Frederick Maclin; 26 Oct 1779, p.28. 10 Shill. sterl. **paid into the late Receiver Generals Office** by Joseph Carter. [Included in sd Robert Spencer's GB 3 p.213 dated 23 Jun 1786 which also included 31 acs. of William Gower's 554 acs. in PB 19 p.975 and Richard Carter's 273 acs. in PB 13 p.440, regranted to James Gee in PB 28 p.226]

WILLIAM HAMBLETT, 65 acs. Halifax Co. on Draughts of Mirery Cr., near the sd Hambletts Mills; adj. the sd Hambletts line, Charles Witt & the old Line; 26 Oct 1779, p.29. A.C. of 10 Shill. Sterl.

MARK HARDEN, 378 acs. Pittsylvania Co. on the brs. of Shoco Cr., crossing a br. of John run [Johns Run], Beginning on the top of Banisters Mountain, adj. Claybrook; 26 Oct 1779, p.30. A.C. of 40 Shill. sterl.

THEODORICK CARTER, 2,472 acs. Pittsylvania Co. on the Brs. of Sweatons fork of Sandy Cr., Crossing Sweatings fork; adj. King, Kerby, Henry Hardin, Shepherd, Hardy, Campbell, Waller, & Fennys order line; 26 Oct 1779, p.31. A.C. of £12.S10 Sterl.

JOHN ROBINSON, 78 acs. Pittsylvania Co. now Henry Co. on the waters of Pigg

Riv., adj. Calloway; 26 Oct 1779, p.33. A.C. of 10 Shil. sterl.

THOMAS HALL, 163 acs. Pittsylvania Co. on both sides of Pigg Riv., down the Gundstone Br. [Grindstone Br.], adj. sd Hills line; 26 Oct 1779, p.34. A.C. of 20 Shill. sterl.

HENRY JONES, 340 acs. Pittsylvania Co. on the Draughts of Pigg Riv., adj. John Jones, Johns, Robert Jones, Isaac Jones & Abraham Jones; 26 Oct 1779, p.35. A.C. of 35 Shill. Sterl.

PETER GILLUM, 112 acs. Henry Co. on black water Riv., at a Meadow, to a Gray Rock, adj. Chirtwood; 26 Oct 1779, p.36. A.C. of 15 Shill. Sterl.

JOHN FREDERICK MILLER, 305 acs. Pittsylvania Co. on both Sides of Stones Cr.; 26 Oct 1779, p.37. A.C. of £1.S15 Sterl.

FREDERICK FARMER, 349 acs. Halifax Co. on the Brs. of Berches Cr., down a bold br.; adj. Champness Terry, John Nobb, Edwards, & Thos. Wilson; 26 Oct 1779, p.38. A.C. of £1.S15. Sterl.

WILLIAM SUMMERS, 357 acs. Pittsylvania Co. on the Brs. of Sandy Cr.; adj. James Walker, Donalson & Lawless; 26 Oct 1779, p.39. A.C. of 40 Shill. Sterl.

THOMAS DODSON, 210 acs. Halifax Co. on the brs. of Birches Cr.; adj. Philip Going, Thomas Wilson & Jacob Midriff; 26 Oct 1779, p.40. A C. of 25 Shill. Sterl.

WILLIAM COTTRILL, 369 acs. Pittsylvania Co. on Fall Cr., adj. Fowless; 26 Oct 1779, p.41. A.C of £2 sterl.

AMBROSE NELSON, 136 acs. Pittsylvania Co. on both sides the main fall Cr., on a naked ridge; adj. John Donalson, Freeman, & John Kirby; 26 Oct 1779, p.42. A.C. of 15 Shill. Sterl.

NICHOLAS FORMBY, 290 acs. Halifax Co. on the Brs. of Birches Cr., near the little Cr., up the Ivry Br.; adj. John Ecoles, Hickey, Champness Terry & Philip Gowing; 26 Oct 1779, p.43. A.C. of £1.S10 sterl.

HENRY HARDEN, 363 acs. Pittsylvania Co. on the brs. of Sandy Cr., crossing the head brs. of Peters br.; adj. Mack Harden, Sweeting, Mark Harden, Shepherd, & John Cerby; 26 Oct 1779, p.44. A.C. of 40 Shill sterl.

WILLIAM TAYLOR Ass'ee of NEAL ONEAL, 323 acs. Pittsylvania Co. on bull Run of Horn Pasture Cr., adj. Randolph; 20 Oct 1779, p.45. A.C. of 35 shill.

ROBERT MAVILY, 110 acs. Henry Co. on little Otter Cr., on a Ridge; adj. Christopher Choat & Ragland; 20 Oct 1779, p.46. A.C. of 15 Shill. Sterl.

ABRAHAM HITE Ass'ee of PETER STEINBERGEN, 2,000 acs. Kentucky Co. on Hickmans Cr. a br. of Kentucky riv., adj. a Survey Made for James Douglass; 28 Oct 1779, p.47. *in consideration of Military Service Performed by Peter Steinbergen [Slunbergen?] a Lieut. in the late War between Great Britain and France according to the King of Great Britains Proclamation of 1763.*

THOMAS READ (Ass'ee of MARY GORDON) 63 acs. Charlotte Co., adj.

Leddesdale, Watson, Samuel Cobb & Matthew Cunningham; 26 Oct 1779, p.48. A.C. of 10 Shill. Sterl. [This is the 1st grant (or patent) to contain reference letters denoting the survey corners: "Beginning at Leddesdales corner Small red oak at A. thence from A. to B. on Watsons line N51E 46 poles to Pointers on Samuel Cobbs line to C. on his line N46W 278 poles to Matthew Cunninghams Corner Hickory C. to D. on his line S8W 29 poles to a Small hickory D. to E. N60W 52 poles to Leddesdale Corner 2 Small red oaks E. to F. on his line S25W 53 poles to a Small white oak F. to G. S73E 180 poles to a white oak G. to A. S34E 120 poles to the Beginning"] [For Leddesdale's line, see Brunswick Co. PB 23, p.796 to Alexander Spalding & John Lidderdale; for Watson's line, see Amelia Co. PB 37, p.347 to William Watson; & for Samuel Cobb's line, see Amelia Co. PB 34, p.515 to Edith Cobbs]

THOMAS HANCOCK, 90 acs. Pittsylvania Co. on Beard Cr.; 20 Oct 1779, p.49. A.C. of 10 Shill. sterl.

THOMAS JONES, 507 acs. Pittsylvania Co. on the Draughts of Nicholas's Cr., crossing Stony Cr., adj. Choat; 20 Oct 1779, p.50. A.C. of 55 Shill. Sterl.

THOMAS HAIL, 50 acs. Pittsylvania Co. on Pigg Riv., adj. Verdiman & Jones; 10 Nov 1779, p.51. A.C. of 5 Shill. sterl.

ROBERT JONES, 59 acs. Pittsylvania Co. on the waters of Nicholas's Cr., adj. Jones; 20 Oct 1779, p.52. A.C. of 10 shill.

SHADRACH TURNER, 330 acs. Pittsylvania now Henry Co. on the S side Town Cr., Beginning at his Corner; 20 Oct 1779, p.53. A.C. of 35 Shill. sterl.

WILLIAM HURD, 335 acs. Henry Co. on Indian br. of Snow Cr., adj. Randolph & Morrow; 2 Nov 1779, p.54. A.C. of 35 Shill. sterl.

MOSES SWINNY, 200 acs. Pittsylvania Co. on both sides the North br. of Great Cherry Stone Cr.; 2 Nov 1779, p.54. A.C. of 10 Shill. sterl. [Should be 20 Shill. or £1]

THOMAS & SWINKFIELD HILL Executors and Legatees of ROB. HILL Decd., 468 acs. Henry Co. on Hatchetts Run, on the top of the Whistling hill, crossing a Road; adj. William Coocks New Survey, Caloway, Early & Cook; 20 Oct 1779, p.55. A.C. of 50 shill. sterl.

WILLIAM YOUNG, 232 acs. Pittsylvania Co. on the waters of Pigg Riv.; 20 Oct 1779, p.56. A.C. of 25 Shill. sterl.

ALEXANDER SPOTSWOOD DANDRIDGE Ass'ee of the sd ALEXANDER SPOTSWOOD, 2,000 acs. Kentucky Co. on the Waters of Elk-horn Cr. a North br. of the Kentucky Riv. being the Waters of the Ohio Riv. about 90 Miles from the Same and on the South side thereof, adj. William Nashes Land; 20 Nov 1779, p.57. *in consideration of the late Governor Dunmores Warrant to Alexander Spotswood for Military Service performed during the Late War between Great Britain and France according to the terms of the King of Great Britains Proclamation of 1763.*

ALEXANDER SPOTSWOOD DANDRIDGE Ass'ee of sd ALEXANDER

SPOTSWOOD, 1,000 acs. Kentucky Co. on the waters of Bear grass Cr. a South br. of the Ohio Riv., Beginning on the N side of the South fork of the Cr. 650 poles from the falls of the Ohio, to the upper End of a Tract of L. Surveyed for Colo. Preston in a line of Hancock Taylor Ass'ee of Waugh, adj. a Tract of L. Surveyed for Capt. Ware; 2 Nov 1779, p.58. *in consideration of the late Governor Dunmores Warrant to Alexander Spotswood for Military Service performed During the Late War Between Great Britain & France according to the Terms of the King of Great Britains Proclamation of 1763.*

JEREMIAH SHROUSBURY, 171 acs. Pittsylvania Co. on the waters of Black Water Riv., adj. James Sandefur, the sd Standefers old line; 20 Oct 1779, p.59. A.C. of 20 Shill. Sterl.

JOHN DILLARD, 320 acs. Halifax Co. on the birch br. of Straitstone Cr., adj. Thomas Dillard & Hunt; 20 Oct 1779, p.60. A.C. of 35 Shill. sterl.

OWEN RUBLE, 100 acs. Henry Co. on Pinners of Pigg Riv.; 20 Oct 1779, p.61. A.C. of 10 Shill. Sterl.

JOHN BUCKLEY, 528 acs. Pittsylvania Co. on the waters of Allens Cr.; adj. Langford, Bullerton, Ballenger, Pemberton, Faris, Morgan & Harness; 20 Oct 1779, p.62. A.C. of 55 Shill. Sterl.

DAVID HUMPHREY, 361 acs. Fluvanna Co. & Louisa Co. on the S side of the Rivanna Riv. [sic - Southanna Riv.] and on Each side of the Byrd Cr. and its Brs.; 359¼ acs. part in Fluvanna Co. and 1¾ acs. the Residue in Louisa Co., to the Horse pen br. & the white oak br.; adj. R. Watson, E. Humphrey, J. Holland, W. Lovell, H. Taylor & John Holland; 20 Oct 1779, p.63. A.C. of 40 Shill. sterl.

ISRAEL STANDEFER, 600 acs. Henry Co. on Standefers Br. adj. the Land sd Standefer sold to Edmundson; 20 Oct 1779, p.65. A.C. of £3 sterl.

DANIEL SPANGLEG, 197 acs. Henry Co. on the S side of Pigg Riv., Beginning near a Great fowls [falls], adj. William Cook; 20 Oct 1779, p.65. A.C. of 20 Shill. Sterl.

JOHN GIVENS, 50 acs. Augusta Co. on the N side of the Middle Riv. of Shanadow; adj. his old line, Samuel Henderson & Patrick Crawford; 26 Oct 1779, p.67. A.C. of 5 Shill. sterl.

SAMUEL EMMERSON, 390 acs. Pittsylvania Co. on the Brs. of Bearskin Cr., along John Piggs Road, on Robins Br.; adj. his, Duen & Twedwell; 26 Oct 1779, p.68. A.C. of 40 Shill. sterl.

DERBEY RYAN/RION, 120 acs. Halifax Co. on both sides of Nicholas's Cr.; 20 Oct 1779, p.69. A.C. of 15 Shill. sterl.

ROBERT SHAW, 400 acs. Rockbridge Co. up the Merry Cr., adj. James McClung & Shaws old line; 26 Oct 1779, p.69. A.C. of 40 Shill. sterl.

LUKE WILLIAMS, 987 acs. Pittsylvania Co. adj. McDaniel, Currie, Benjamin Davis, Channey & Glascock; 26 Oct 1779, p.71. A.C. of £5 Sterl. *the 987 acs. Including 3 Several Tracts, one for 454 acs. Surveyed 20 May 1767, one other for 142 acs., a third for 391 acs.*

Surveyed for Edmund Cornwell and Trasfered to the sd Williams.

JOSEPH ROGERS, 696 acs. Inclusive, Pittsylvania Co. on the brs. of the Dry Fork of White oak Cr.; adj. Isaac Carter & the said S. Carter; 26 Oct 1779, p.72. A.C. of £3.S10 sterl.

HENRY KERBY, 323 acs. Pittsylvania Co. on the Brs. of Sandy Cr., crossing Ivi Br.; adj. Mack Harden, Henry Harden, Donalson & the sd Richard Kerby; 2 Nov 1779, p.73. A.C. of 35 Shill. sterl.

WILLIAM LYNCH, 930 acs. Pittsylvania Co. on the Brs. of fall Cr.; adj. the sd William Lynch, William Freeman, Benj: Porter, Donalson, Thomas Burgess & Benj: Lawless; 2 Nov 1779, p.75. A.C. of £4.S15. sterl.

JOHN WILSON, 564 acs. Pittsylvania Co. on the S side Dan Riv., adj. His back line; 20 Oct 1779, p.76. A.C. of £3 Sterl.

WILLIAM WILSON, 768 acs. Pittsylvania Co. on the N brs. of Dan riv., down White Walnut Cr.; adj. sd Wilsons lines, William Shelton & Chaldwell; 20 Oct 1779, p.77. A.C. of £4 Sterl.

JOHN WILSON, 75 acs. Pittsylvania Co. on both sides of Sandy Riv., adj. Peter Wilson & Smith; 20 Oct 1779, p.78. A.C. 10 Shill. sterl.

JOHN WILSON, 400 acs. Pittsylvania Co. on a br. of Sandy Cr., adj. Jasper Billings; 20 Oct 1779, p.79. A. C. £2. Sterl.

JOHN SMITH, 400 acs. Pittsylvania Co. on both sides the South fork of Sandy Riv., crossing two forks of sd Riv., adj. Cloud & Waller; 20 Oct 1779, p.79. A.C. £2.

BARTHOLOMEW DANDRIDGE Ass'ee of the said TURNER SOUTHALL, 2,000 acs. in Kentucky Co. on Elkhorn Cr. a North br. of the Kentucky Riv. and About 70 Miles from the Ohio and on the S Side thereof, Beginning at 3 Double Sugar trees on the South Bank by a large Buffaloe foard 360 poles above Cave Run, by a Draft and Meadow at the foot of a Hill, on the side of a flat Ridge, Crossing the Ridge, on the Bank of the Cr. by a small Gully at the lower End of an Island Opposite to a High Hill; 5 Nov 1779, p.80. *in Consideration of Military Service Performed by Turner Southall in the late War between Great Britain and France according to the term of the King of Great Britains Proclamation of 1763.*

BARTHOLOMEW DANDRIDGE ass'ee of EDWARD DEAN Heir at Law to the said THOMAS DEAN, 200 acs. Kentucky Co. on the S Side of the Ohio Riv. in the first Large Bottom above the big Miami Riv. about 9 Miles above sd Riv., on the Point of a Ridge, adj. Hugh Mersers Survey; 5 Nov 1779, p.82. *in Consideration of Military Service Performed by Thomas Dean in the late War between Great Britain and france according to the terms of the King of Great Britains Proclamation of 1763.*

THOMAS SMITH, 382 acs. Pittsylvania Co. on the Brs. of Sandy Riv.; adj. Evan Stokes, Billings his Mill Survey & Edward Smith; 20 Oct 1779, p.83. A.C. of £2 Sterl.

THOMAS MASHALL, 248 acs. Halifax Co. on the Brs. of Terrible Cr.; adj. Nathaniel Hunt, Powel, Fenny, &

Alexander Anderson; 2 Nov 1779, p.84. A.C. of 25 Shill. Sterl.

THOMAS WEIR, 186 acs. Pittsylvania Co. on the Brs. of fall Cr., adj. Wadey & the sd Cargels former line; 20 Oct 1779, p.85. A.C. of £1 Sterl.

HEZEKIAH SMITH, 164 acs. Pittsylvania Co. on the Brs. of Sandy Riv., adj. Givens; 20 Oct 1779, p.86. A.C. of 20 Shill. sterl.

CHARLES BURTON, 112 acs. Pittsylvania Co. on the waters of Sandy Riv., adj. Billings; 20 Oct 1779, p.86. A.C. of 15 Shill. Sterl.

JOHN SOUTHERLIN/SUTHERLIN, 420 acs. Pittsylvania Co. on both sides of Bold Br. of Sandy Cr. and on the N side white oak Mountain; adj. John Asworth, Hall & the sd Aswoerth; 20 Oct 1779, p.87. A.C. of £2.S5 Sterl.

ISAAC CLEMMENT/CLEMENTS, 400 acs. Pittsylvania Co. on the forks of Pudding Cr., Crossing the South & Middle forks of the sd Cr., at a point of Rocks on the sd Cr.; 20 Oct 1779, p.88. A.C. of £2 Sterl.

RICHARD EDMONSON, 126 acs. Pittsylvania Co. on the Drafts of Black Water Run, adj. his own line; 20 Oct 1779, p.89. A.C. of 15 Shill. Sterl.

JAMES FULTON, 220 acs. Pittsylvania Co. on the Main Sandy Cr., adj. Dodson; 20 Oct 1779, p.90. A.C. of £1.S5.

JOHN KEMP, 345 acs. Henry Co., Crossing Camp br. of black water & up Black Water Riv., adj. Edmonson & Kemp; 20 Oct 1779, p.91. A. C. of 35 Shill. sterl.

JOHN HEARD/HEAD, 362 acs Henry Co. on the head of Maple Br. and head of Robersons Br., crossing Robinsons Br., adj. Roberson; 20 Oct 1779, p.92. A.C. of 40 Shill. sterl.

ELIJAH CRAIG Ass'ee of JOHN CARTER who was ass'ee of the sd MATTHEW ANDERSON, 200 acs. Kentucky Co. on the Ohio Riv. about 19 Miles above the falls, Beginning at the Mouth of a Cr. just above the Third Island above the falls; 7 Nov 1779, p.93. *in Consideration of Military Service performed by Matthew Anderson in the Late War Between Great Britain and france according to the Term of the King of Great Britains Proclamation of 1763.*

ELIJAH CRAIG Ass'ee of JOHN CARTER Representative of the sd THOMAS CARTER dec'd, 2,000 acs. Kentucky Co. on the Brs. of Elkhorn Cr. a North Br. of the Kentucky Riv. & the Brs. running into the sd Riv. above Elkhorn being the Waters of the Ohio and on the South side of the same, adj. William Phillips; 7 Nov 1779, p.94. *in Consideration of Military Service performed by Thomas Carter Dec'd During the Late war between Great Britain & france according to the King of Great Britains Proclamation of 1763.*

RICHARD CAVE Ass'ee of the sd JOHN WARE, 100 acs. Kentucky Co. on the Brs. of Elkhorn Cr. a north Br. of the Kentucky Riv. about 90 Miles from the Ohio Riv. and on the S Side the Same, adj. a Survey of Colo. Christian; 10 Nov 1779, p.95. *in Consideration of Military Service performed by John Ware in the late War between Great Britain & france according to the Terms of the King of Great Britains Proclamation of 1763.*

SHADRACH VAUGHAN, 2,000 acs. Kentucky Co. on the Waters of Elkhorn Cr. a North Br. of the Kentucky Riv. and about 25 Miles from the Same and about 95 Miles from the Ohio Riv. on the S side thereof, adj. William Russels Land; 17 Oct 1779, p.96. *in Consideration of Military Service Performed During the late War between Great Britain & France by Shadrach Vaughan according to the Terms of the King of Great Britains Proclamation of 1763.*

JOHN SMITH, 104 acs. Pittsylvania Co. on the Brs. of Sandy Riv., to Hicky's Road; adj. Yarrington, & John Morton; 20 Oct 1779, p.97. A.C. of 10 Shill. sterl.

THOMAS JONES, 310 acs. Pittsylvania Co. on the Brs. of Pigg Riv., adj. Robert Jones; 20 Oct 1779, p.98. A.C. of 35 Shill. Sterl.

THOMAS COOPER, 159 acs. Pittsylvania Co. on Beaver Cr., adj. Shelton; 20 Oct 1779, p.99. A.C. of 20 Shill. sterl.

ROBERT JONES, 204 acs. Halifax Co. on the South fork of Pigg Riv., adj. Rentfrow; 20 Oct 1779, p.100. A.C. of 15 Shill. Sterl.

THOMAS HILL, 278 acs. Henry Co. on the S side of Pigg Riv.; adj. his own, Daughton & Roads [Rhodes?] lines; 20 Oct 1779, p.101. A.C. of 30 Shill. Sterl.

SAMUEL EMMERSON, 198 acs. Pittsylvania Co. on the Brs. of Bearskin Cr., on Robbins Br.; adj. Tweedwell, & John Pigg; 26 Oct 1779, p.102. A.C. of 20 Shill. sterl.

JOHN HARRESS [jor.?], 39½ acs. Albemarle Co. on both Sides the North fork of Hardware Riv., Beginning on the East Bank of the River where Colo. E. Carters line Crosses it; adj. Colo. Carter, William Hamner & the Land formerly Thomas Bookers; 20 Oct 1779, p.103. A.C. of 10 Shill. Sterl.

WILLIAM LAUDERDALE, 46 acs. Botetourt Co. on a Br. of Miligans Run the Waters of James Riv. joining the Land he lives on, on the Ridge, in the Gap of the Ridge near a Sink hole; 30 Oct 1779, p.104. A.C. of 5 Shill. Sterl.

JOHN REAVES, 83 acs. Bedford Co. on the Brs. of Hurricane Cr., adj. his own Line; 20 Oct 1779, p.105. A.C. of 10 Shill. sterl.

JOHN FULTON 311 acs. Pittsylvania Co. on the N side of Sandy Riv., adj. Billings; 20 Oct 1779, p.106. A.C. of £1.S15 Sterl.

THOMAS SMITH, 281 acs. Pittsylvania Co. on the Waters of Sandy Riv.; 20 Oct 1779, p.107. A.C. of £1.S10 sterl.

WILLIAM WATKINS, 405 acs. Pittsylvania Co. on the Brs. of Birches Cr.; adj. Moore, & Mach or Mack Shelton; 20 Oct 1779, p.108. A.C. of £2.S5 Sterl.

JOHN FULTON, 299 acs. Pittsylvania Co. on the Waters of Stewarts Cr.; adj. John Smith, Bethony Hayes [his lines] & the sd Fultons Lines; 20 Oct 1779, p.109. A.C. of £1.S10 Sterl.

THOMAS SMITH, 324 acs. Pittsylvania Co. on the Brs. of Sandy Riv., adj. James Fulton; 20 Oct 1779, p.110. A.C. of £1.S15 Sterl.

NATHANIEL HUGHS, 402 acs. Pittsylvania Co. on Birches Cr., near Burches Cr.; adj. Moore, Joseph Terry, William Walter & Weatherford; 20 Oct 1779, p.111. A.C. of £2 Sterl.

JONATHAN ROSSER, 230 acs. Bedford Co. on the E side of Mortons fork of Falling Riv.; adj. Harry Terrel, M. Randolph, John Wood, his own line & David Rosser; 20 Oct 1779, p.112. A.C. of 25 Shill. Sterl.

HEZEKIAH PIGG, 800 acs. Pittsylvania Co. on the S side Banister Riv. & on both Sides Pudding Cr., in the Bent of sd Cr., adj. John Pigg & Christopher Hutchings; 20 Oct 1779, p.113. £4 sterl.

JAMES DIVEN, 129 acs. Pittsylvania Co. on the Brs. of Banister, Crossing little Cr.; adj. White, & William Diven; 20 Oct 1779, p.115. A.C. of 15 Shill. Sterl.

JOHN WILLIS, 174 acs. Henry Co. on Hatchett Run, near the Road; adj. Henry Jones, Hill, James Turpin & Willis; 20 Oct 1779, p.115. A.C. of 20 shill. sterl.

JOHN SMITH, 272 acs. Pittsylvania Co. on Both Sides of the long Br. and Pole Bridge Br.; adj. Francis Mabray, Fulton, Moses Vincent & James Robert; 20 Oct 1779, p.116. A.C. £1.S10 Sterl.

WILLIAM LEFTWITCH Ass'ee of JNO. CROUCH, 150 acs. Bedford Co. on Buffaloe fork of Back Cr., Beginning near his house on the S Side of sd fork, down Prize Run; adj. Leftwick, Hall & his old line; 8 Oct 1779, p.117. A.C. of 15 Shill. Sterl.

ROBERT MASON, 236 acs. Pittsylvania Co. on Both Sides the Muddy fork of Chesnut Cr., on the top of Chesnut Mountain, adj. Robert Frazer & Hodges; 20 Oct 1779, p.118. A.C. of 25 Shill. Sterl.

JAMES JONES, 213 acs. Maclenburg Co. on the S Side of Arons Cr., near Aarons Cr.; adj. John Jones, Joseph Gell, Hutchings, Coak & Gill; 20 Oct 1779, p.119. A.C. of 25 Shill. sterl.

WILLIAM JOHNSON, 326 acs. Charlotte Co. on both sides Bantrees fork of Chesnut Cr., crossing Main fork, on a Ridge, Crossing Bantree fork to the Beginning, adj. his own line; 20 Oct 1779, p.120. A.C. of 35 Shill. sterl.

JOHN MARTIN, 209 acs. Fluvanna Co. on the N Side of Rivanna Riv. on both Sides Arbor Road and on some of the Brs. of Ballengers Cr., to Arbox Road, on Lick Br.; adj. Thomas Baber Junr., Jones Hacketts line, sd Hatchett, Samuel Davis & sd Martin; 20 Oct 1779, p.121. A.C. of 25 Shill. Sterl.

ROBERT BAKER, 270 acs. Botetourt Co. on the Waters of Tinker Cr. a Br. of Roan oak joining the Land of James Robinson, in a Draft, in a Gully, to Thomas Prentys Corner; 20 Oct 1779, p.123. A.C. of 30 Shill. Sterl.

JOSIAH CARTER, 200 acs. Halifax Co. now Henry on both Sides Black Water Riv.; 20 Oct 1779, p.124. A.C. of 20 Shill. sterl.

GEORGE HARDEN, 300 acs. Louisa Co. on some of the small Brs. of Machunk Cr.; adj. Nathaniel Waid [Ward?], Doctor Walker, Howett, & Morris Roberts; 20 Nov 1779, p.125. A.C. of 30 Shill. sterl.

JOHN HOPKINS Ass'ee of SAMUEL HOPKINS, 350 acs. Fluvanna Co. on the S Side of the Rivanna Riv. on the Brs. of the white oak, Burks's and Adreans Creeks; Crossing the white oak Br.; adj. Grey Smith, Dolton Hopkins, Robert Eliot/Elliot & Isaac Dirkam; 12 Nov 1779, p.126. A.C. of 35 Shill. Sterl.

JOHN BAYS, 146 acs. in Pittsylvania Co. on Reed Cr.; adj. Kersey, Terrys order line & John Terrell; 20 Oct 1779, p.127. 15 Shill. A.C. of 15 Shill. sterl.

JOSHUA CANTRILL, 337 acs. Pittsylvania Co. on Nals [Nats] fork of Strawberry Cr., adj. Chamberlain; 20 Oct 1779, p.128. A.C. of 35 Shill. sterl.

RICHARD PHILLIPS, 107 acs. in Trinity Par. Louisa Co. on the Waters of Pamonky Riv.; adj. Richard Phillips Senr., Richard Anderson & Harley [Hailey]; 20 Oct 1779, p.129. A.C. of 15 Shill. sterl.

JAMES McCLUNG, 43 acs. Augusta Co. on the Waters of Mary Cr. a br. of James Riv., Crossing three Drafts to the End of a Spur near a br., up the side of the Spur & Crossing a Draft, adj. sd James McClung; 20 Oct 1779, p.130. A.C. of 5 Shill. sterl.

JOHN RAMSEY, 346 acs. Henry Co. on the Brs. of Chesnut Cr., adj. Standefer; 20 Oct 1779, p.131. A.C. of 35 Shill. sterl.

FRANCIS WRIGHT, 426 acs. Pittsylvania Co. on the Brs. of Birches Cr.; adj. Harris, Givens, Shelton, Joseph Terry & Robert Walters Lines; 20 Oct 1779, p.132. A.C. of 45 Shill. Sterl.

JAMES DIVEN, 240 acs. Pittsylvania Co. on both Sides the Head brs. of Bannister Riv., On the Court house Road, crossing Banister Riv.; adj. sd Diven, Emmerson, William Diven & William Coock; 20 Oct 1779, p.133. A.C. of 25 Shill. sterl.

JOHN SHEPHERD Ass'ee of GABRIEL PENN, 370 acs. Amherst Co. on the Brs. of Juniper, to the Middle fork & North fork of Juniper; 20 Oct 1779, p.134. A.C. of 40 Shill. sterl.

JOHN WILLIS, 384 acs. Henry Co. on the Waters of Hatchett Run; adj. Turpin, Melton, Hill, his own line & Hilton; 20 Oct 1779, p.135. A.C. of 40 Shill. sterl.

JAMES COOLEY, 154 acs. Henry Co. on the N Brs. of the North fork of Chesnut Cr., adj. Warren & Richards; 20 Oct 1779, p.136. A.C. of 15 shill. Sterl.

WILLIAM BASKET, 109 acs. Fluvanna Co. on the N Side of the Rivanna Riv., to Phills Cr.; adj. sd Barkets Line formerly Gray Smiths, Benjamin Johnston, sd Johnson & Thomas Thurmand; 20 Oct 1779, p.136. A.C. of 15 Shill. Sterl. [The scribe used page 136 twice and skipped page 137]

WILLIAM BASKET, 334 acs. Fluvanna Co. on Long Island Cr. the N Brs. of the Rivanna, crossing the Road; adj. sd Basket, Appleberry, Bethell, Quarles & Lentecom; 20 Oct 1779, p.138. A.C. of 30 Shill. Sterl.

JAMES WILSON, 321 acs. Pittsylvania Co. on the waters of Dan Riv.; adj. Richard Guin, Southerlin & Bostick; 20 Oct 1779, p.139. A.C. of £1.S15. sterl.

SAMUEL MATHEWS, 399 acs. Halifax Co. on the Brs. of Lower Double Creeks; adj. Robert Wilkins, Bird, & Charles Weatherford; 20 Oct 1779, p.140. A.C. of 40 shill. Sterl.

DAVID PREWIT, 264 acs. Henry Co. on Camp Br. of Snow Cr., Crossing a road, on his old line near a Spring; 20 Oct 1779, p.141. A.C. of 30 Shill. sterl.

SAMUEL WALKER, 185 acs. Augusta Co. on the fork of James Riv. adj. his own Land his old Survey, crossing Cedar Cr.; 20 Oct 1779, p.142. A.C. of 20 Shill.

JOHN COX, 400 acs. Pittsylvania Co. on the Brs. of Horse Shoe and Mill Cr., Crossing Pigg River Road, Crossing the Horse Shoe Br.; adj. Edward Gray, Philemon Payne, Mrs Purnell [her Line] & Edmond Gray; 20 Oct 1779, p.143. A.C. of 40 Shill. Sterl.

JOHN FORBIS, 400 acs. Bedford Co. on the East br. of Beaver Cr.; adj. Andrew Hainston [Hairston], Fleming, Parrow & Hauston; 20 Oct 1779, p.144. A.C. of 40 shill. sterl.

JOHN REAVES, 104 acs. Bedford Co. on the head Brs. of Hurricane Cr., on a Spur of Hurricane Mountain; adj. Thomas Milum, Richards & Milam; 20 Oct 1779, p.145. A.C. of 10 Shill. sterl.

ARCHIBALD WOODS, 50 acs. Botetourt Co. on the Waters of Cataber Cr. a Br. of James Riv., Beginning on the Side of a Stony hill; 20 Oct 1779, p.145. A.C. of 5 Shill. Sterl.

NICHOLAS MEREWETHER, 212 acs. Louisa Co. in Trinity Par. on the S Side Pamonkey Riv. on Knuckold Br.; adj. Richard Phillips, Richard Anderson, Hailey, & John Richmond; 20 Oct 1779, p.146. A.C. of 25 Shill. sterl.

HENRY WILLIS, 62 acs. Henry Co. on a Br. of Black Water; adj. Hilton, Lewis Deiver/Dewer, Spangler, & John Willis; 20 Oct 1779, p.147. A.C. of 10 Shill. sterl.

SAMPSON & GEORGE MATHEWS /MATTHEWS & PATRICK LOCKHART Ass'ees of MICHAEL WOODS, 216 acs. by Survey Dated 27 Nov 1771 in Botetourt Co. on Burdens Run a Br. of James Riv., adj. Michael Woods & Hawkins; 10 Nov 1779, p.148. A.C. of 25 Shill. Sterl. **paid into the Late Receiver Generals Office**.

PETER PALSEL Ass'ee. of JOHN SEHORN who was Ass'ee of NICHOLAS SEHORN, 216 acs. by Survey 3 Dec 1754 in Augusta Co. on Lime Stone Ridge, on the Boundry Line [N46°W] Between Lord Fairfax & the Commonwealth of Virginia at the Side of a Small meadow; 10 Nov 1779, p.149. A.C. of 25 Shill. sterl.

JAMES ROBERTSON, 184 acs. by Survey 28 Jan 1767 in Augusta Co. on the South fork of Roan oak Riv.; 10 Nov 1779, p.150. A.C. of 20 Shill. Sterl. [Repeated in GB B, p.43]

HUGH DONOGHO, 80 acs. Augusta Co. on the N Side the North Riv. of Shandore, adj. Donogho; 10 Nov 1779, p.151. A.C. of 10 Shill. sterl. **paid into the Late Receiver Generals Office.**

HUGH DONOGHO, 50 acs. Augusta Co. on the S side of the North Riv. of Shandow, Beginning by a Road, on a Ridge; adj. David Loard, Joseph Dickinson, William Moira, Hugh Donogho & Beard; 10 Nov 1779, p.151. A.C. of 5 Shill. sterl. **paid into the late Receiver Generals Office.**

JAMES BARNETT Ass'ee of WALTER CROCKET who was ass'ee of DAVID ROBERTSON, 47 acs. by Survey 10 Nov 1772 in Botetourt Co. on the S side of the South fork of Roan oak; adj. James Barnetts new Survey and the Land of Crockett & Barnet on the River Bank; 20 Oct 1779, p.152. A.C. of 5 Shill. **paid into the Late Receiver Generals Office.**

PETER DYERLY, 43 acs. (by Survey 25 May 1768) in Botetourt Co. on Roan oak Riv., on the Bank by a heap of Rocks, adj. Alexander Love; 20 Oct 1779, p.153. A.C. of 5 Shill. sterl.

PETER DYERLY, 19 acs. by Survey 25 May 1768 in Botetourt Co. on Roan Oak Riv., by a Ri[d]ge on the S side the Riv.; 20 Oct 1779, p.154. A.C. of 5 Shill. sterl.

THOMAS FITZPATRICK, 32 acs. Botetourt Co. on the South fork of Cedar Cr. a Br. of Jacksons Riv., Beginning in a flat ground on the N side the Cr., by the foot of a hill near a Sw.; 20 Oct 1779, p.155. 5 Shill. sterl. **paid into the late Receiver Generals Office.**

ROBERT HILL, 379 acs. Halifax Co. on the S Side of black Water Riv., crossing the Pounding Mill br., adj. Randolph; 20 Oct 1779, p.155. A.C. of 40 Shill. Sterl.

PETER DYERLY, 243 acs. by Survey 4 Nov 1772 in Botetourt Co., on the N Side of Road oak Riv. [Roan oak Riv.], adj. his other Survey; 20 Oct 1779, p.156. A.C. of 25 Shill. Sterl.

CUTHBERT BULLET Devisee of the sd THOMAS BULLET, 1,240 acs. by Survey 24 May 1775 in Botetourt Co. on the forks of Elk Riv. and the Great Kenhawa and on the lower Side of of Elk Riv., down the Elk Riv. to the point Below Elk, down the Great Kenhawa; 20 Oct 1779, p.157. *in Consideration of Military Service performed by Thomas Bullet in the late War between Great Britain & France according to the Terms of the King of Great Britains Proclamation of 1763.*

CUTHBERT BULLET Devisee of THOS. BULLET Dec'd, 400 acs. by Survey 3 Dec 1766 in Augusta Co. near *the hot Spring*, Beginning on the Side of a Mountain, in A line of the Hot Spring Survey, adj. Andrew Lewis & Gabriel Jones; 20 Oct 1779, p.158. A.C. of 40 Shill. Sterl.

JOSHUA STONE, 184 acs. Pittsylvania Co. On the waters of Allens Cr.; adj. Luke Smith, Inness, & James Degarnet; 13 Nov 1779, p.159. A.C. of 20 Shill. Sterl.

PETER PERKINS/PURKINS ass'ee of THOMAS SCOTT JUNR., 800 acs. Halifax Co. on Sandy Cr.; adj. Follin, Givens & Fallen; 22 Nov 1779, p.160. in Consideration of the A.C. of £4 Sterl. paid by Peter Perkins ass'ee of the sd Thomas Scott Junr. **paid into the late**

Receiver Generals Office. *Whereas by pat. under the Seal of the Colony and Dominion of Virginia bearing date 25 Mar 1762 Granted unto George Walton and whereas the sd George Walton hath failed to pay the Quitrents that Were Due thereon and Thomas Scott Junr. had before the late Revolution petition'd the then president of the King of Great Britains Counsil of the said Colony and had obtained a Grant for the Same.*

[Margin note: "**This Grant is not to Issue**"]
CHARLES WINDHAM, 140 acs. Surry Co. on the S side of the Main Black water Sw., down the Black Sw., adj. Richard Tomlinson; 18 Oct 1779. p.162. A.C. of 15 Shill. Sterl. [This Sussex Co. land may have been allotted to Francis Reading or was part of John Goodwin's PB 27, p.81 dated 1 Dec 1748. For Richard Tomlinson's land see PB 11, p.264 to Thomas Weekes dated 5 Sep 1723]

THOMAS HEARD, 290 acs. Pittsylvania Co. on both Sides of Jacks Cr.; 20 Oct 1779, p.162. A.C. of 30 Shill. Sterl.

WILLIAM CHRISTIAN, 1,000 acs. Kentucky Co. on Salt Riv. a br. of the Ohio about 20 Miles from the Great falls which Tracts Includes a Salt Spring and Buffaloe lick, Beginning on the River bank at the Mouth of a Small Gut, near a Small Cr.; 24 Nov 1779, p.163. *in Consideration of the Military Service performed by William Christian in the late War between Great Britain and France According to the Terms of the King of Great Britains Proclamation of 1763.*

WILLIAM MAVITY, 366 acs. Henry Co. on the N Brs. of Pigg Riv., on the top of the Whilting hill; adj. Jones's old line, D. Rion, & Hills new lines; 20 Oct 1779, p.164. A.C. of 40 Shill. Sterl.

ROBERT GOOD ass'ee of SAMUEL GOOD who was Assee. of ABSALOM FEARS, 340 acs. Pr. Edward Co. on both Sides the North fork of Sawneys Cr., adj. Hill; 20 Nov 1779, p.165. A.C. of 35 Shill. Sterl.

SAMUEL MORTON, 44 acs. Pr. Edward Co. on the Brs. of Sandy Riv.; adj. Pineaes, Morton, Mortons fence, Hamlin, & Pennixes line; 25 Nov 1779, p.166. A.C. of 5 Shill. Sterl.

SAMUEL HUGHES/HUGES, 370 acs. Pittsylvania Co. on Both Sides of Bear Skin Cr., on a Ridge, adj. Owen Atkins & Pigg; 16 Nov 1779, p.167. A.C. of 40 Shill. sterl.

JOHN DAUGHTON/DOUGHTON, 400 acs. Pittsylvania Co. on the Waters of Pigg Riv., up Buck Br., adj. Swinfield Hill; 20 Oct 1779, p.168. A.C. of 40 Shill. sterl.

DANIEL MORGAN, 249 acs. Pittsylvania Co. on the Waters of Allens Cr., adj. Harness & Baker; 20 Nov 1779, p.169. A.C. of 25 Shill. sterl.

EDMUND FITZGARRELL, 215 acs. Pittsylvania Co. on the Brs. of Sandy Cr., crossing Johns Br., Beginning in the old line, along the Dividing Line; 16 Nov 1779, p.170. A.C. of 25 Shill. sterl.

ZEBULON BRINSON, 244 acs. Pittsylvania Co. on both Sides of a bold

Br. of Mill Cr., adj. Gray & Bynam; 16 Nov 1779, p.171. A.C. of 25 Shill. sterl.

EDWARD BURGESS, 270 acs. Pittsylvania Co. on the Brs. of Sandy Cr., Crossing a Br. of the Little fork, up Bays Br.; adj. John Owen, Roger Atkisson, Thomas Payne & William Payne; 15 Oct 1779, p.172. A.C. of 30 Shill. sterl.

ABRAHAM SHELTON, 296 acs. Pittsylvania Co. on both Sides the Glady fork of white thorn Cr., adj. his former line; 11 Nov 1779, p.173. A.C. of 30 Shill. sterl.

JAMES MOORE, 212 acs. Pittsylvania Co. on the Camp Br. of Allens Cr.; adj. John Donalson, Pemberton, Joseph Slater, Vaughan, John Chrisam & Mathew Vaner; 30 Nov 1779, p.174. A.C. of 30 Shill. sterl.

BENJAMIN LANGFORD, 380 acs. by Survey 18 Apl. 1774 in Pittsylvania Co. on a Steep Br. of Alens Cr. [Allens Cr.]; adj. Heart, Hampton & Langford; 22 Nov 1779, p.175. A.C. of 40 Shill. sterl.

JOHN COLYER, 217 acs. Pittsylvania Co. on Both Sides of the Old Womans Cr., adj. Wheler/Whealer; 11 Nov 1779, p.176. A.C. of 25 Shill. Sterl.

NIMROD NEWMAN, 354 acs. by Survey 23 Mar 1776 in Bedford Co. on Glady Br., adj. Hale & Mead; 1 Dec 1779, p.176. A.C. of 35 Shill. Sterl.

JOHN GARLAND, 321 acs. by Survey 2 Feb 1779 in Lunenburg Co. adj. Singleton, Barrott & Upshar; 1 Dec 1779, p.178. A.C. of 35 Shill. sterl. [This is the same land ptd. by William Saffold in PB 31 p.342 but as 293 acs. on the Miry Br.; for Singletons line see James Daws' PB 34 p.114; for Upshaw's see PB 42 p.775 to John Blanks on the Watry Br. of Crooked Cr.; and for Barrott's see John Edloe's PB 30 p.445 included in William Barrett's GB W p.27]

JOHN TALBOT, 400 acs. Bedford Co. on both Sides of the North fork of Enocks Cr. a South Cr. of Goose Cr.; adj. Stith, Orrick, Yates & Holland; 1 Dec 1779, p.179. A.C. of 40 Shill. sterl.

NOVELL BLANKENSHIP ass'ee of JOHN MILLER who was ass'ee of JOHN JOHNSON who was ass'ee of CHARLES MOORMAN who was Ass'ee of ZACHERIAH MOORMAN who was ass'ee of JOHN CAUDLER who was ass'ee of GEORGE STONE, 200 acs. by Survey 25 Mar 1776 in Bedford Co. on the head Brs. of Fishing Cr., adj. Edward Clark; 1 Dec 1779, p.180. A.C. of 20 Shill. sterl.

DANIEL CANDLER ass'ee of ARCHELAUS GILLIAM, 370 acs. (by Survey 19 Jan 1770) in Bedford Co. on both Sides of flat Cr. & Possum Cr. Including their Heads, on Glady Br. of flat Cr., on the Brow of a Hill of Possum Cr., adj. [Stemmon]; 1 Dec 1779, p.181. A.C. of 40 Shill. sterl.

GEORGE STOVALL, 240 acs. by Survey 19 Feb 1768 in Amherst Co. on the South Brs. of Stovalls Cr.; adj. George Jefferson, Micajah Clark & Henry Fry; 1 Dec 1779, p.182. A.C. of 20 Shill. Sterl.

THOMAS RUTHERFORD of Berkley Co., 1,000 acs. by Survey 2 Apl. 1775 in Ohio Co. on the River Ohio at the Mouth of Hardens run, Crossing sd run,

Crossing a Drain, up the River Crossing 2 Drains and the Mouth of 2 other Drains; 23 Dec 1779, p.182. *in Consideration of Military Service by Thomas Rutherford in the Late War between Great Britain & France according to the Terms of the King of Great [Britains] Proclamation of 1763.*

ROBERT RUTHERFORD Esq. of Berkley Co. Ass'ee of sd JOHN WEST, JUNIOR, 1,300 acs. by Survey 5 Apl. 1775 in Yohogania Co. on Mill Cr. a br. of the Ohio, Beginning on a Level about 160 poles on the East of the falls of the aforesaid Cr., crossing 3 Brs. to a ridge, crossing [various] Drains, on the W side of Mill Cr. opposite a parcel of Rocks; 23 Dec 1779, p.184. *in Consideration of Military Service performed by John West Junr. in the late War between Great Britain & France according to the Terms of the King of Great Britains Proclamation of 1763.*

JOSEPH CALDWELL, 35 acs. by Survey 20 Apr 1779 in Rockbridge Co.; 5 Jan 1780, p.185. A.C. of 5 Shill. Sterl.

ROBERT KINCAID/KINGCAID ass'ee of HENRY McCURDY, 70 acs. by Survey 8 Dec 1770 in Rockbridge Co. joining the Lines of [The said] McCurdy on Burtons run a br. of Buffaloe Cr. the Waters of James Riv., by a path; 5 Jan 1780, p.186. A.C. of 10 Shill. Sterl.

JOHN TEDFORD ass'ee of DAVID LOGAN who was ass'ee of JOHN McKEE, 60 acs. by Survey 20 Nov 1772 in Rockbridge Co. on the Waters of Buffaloe Cr. a br. of James Riv. and joining the Lines of sd McKees L., by a Sink hole, on the Top of & down a ridge; 5 Jan 1780, p.187. A.C. of 10 Shill. sterl.

WALTER STEWART, 200 acs. by Survey 10 Jul 1776 in Kentucky Co. on a Br. of Licking Cr. a br. of the Ohio; 5 Jan 1780, p.188. *in consideration of Military Service performed by Walter Stewart in the late War between Great Britain & France according to the Terms of the King of Great Britains Proclamation of 1763.*

SAMUEL MILLER ass'ee of JOSEPH BLAINE, 80 acs. by Survey 23 Oct 1767 in Rockbridge Co. on both sides Cedar Cr. and in the fork of James Riv., adj. his old Line; 5 Jan 1780, p.189. 10 Shill. sterl.

JOHN STANDUFF ass'ee of JOHN NEELY, 60 acs. by Survey 12 Mar 1766 in Rockbridge Co. on a Draft Between two Spurs of the house Mountain in the fork of James Riv.; 5 Jan 1780, p.190. A.C. of 10 Shill. sterl.

THOMAS CUNNINGHAM ass'ee of JOHN BOLES, 50 acs. by Survey 6 Jun 1771 in Botetourt Co. on the Waters of Collins Cr. a br. of James Riv., on a Grassy hill, in a bottom, in a Draft; adj. Moses Collins L. & a Survey belonging to sd Roles; 5 Jan 1780, p.191. A.C. of 5 Shill. **paid into the late Receiver Generals Office**.

THOMAS CUNNINGHAM Ass'ee of JOHN BOLES, 50 acs. by Survey 2 Oct 1770 in Botetourt Co. on a Br. of Collins Cr. joining the sd Boles L. and in the fork of James Riv., adj. his Patent Land, by a Sorry run, by the head of a Spring; 5 Jan 1780, p.192. A.C. of 5 Shill. Sterl. **paid into the late Receiver Generals Office**.

PATRICK McCOLAN, 98 acs. by Survey 6 Apr 1767 in Rockbridge Co. in the forks of James Riv., up a Steep hill,; adj. his own Land, McCorkle & sd McClans line; 5 Jan 1780, p.193. A.C. of 10 Shill. Sterl.

WILLIAM McFEETERS, 45 acs. by Survey 14 Mar 1753 in Augusta Co. on the W side of Catheyes Riv., on the top of a ridge; adj. a line of Beverly McCanner [Mannor] & the Land sd McFeeters Lives on; near a line of sd Manner; 5 Jan 1780, p.194. A.C. of 5 Shill. Sterl.

CHARLES WINGFIELD ass'ee of JOSEPH WHITTLE, 92 acs. by Survey 11 May 1756 in Albemarle Co. on the N Side the Buffaloe Ridge and in the Coves; adj. Cheswell, Matt Whittle & James Xlian [Christian]; 5 Jan 1780, p.195. A.C. of 10 Shill. sterl. [Regranted to Robert Clopton ass'ee of William Ford ass'ee of David Staples heir at Law to John Staples decd in GB 4 p.629, dated 9 Oct 1786, Amherst formerly Albemarle Co., by survey dated 11 May 1756]

EDWARD CARTER & PETER F. TRENT Ass'ees of JOHN CAMPBELL, 54 acs. by Survey 13 Apr 1768 in Amherst Co. on the S Brs. of Stony run of Rockfish Riv., adj. Samuel Doaks & Thomas West/Uest; 12 Jan 1780, p.196. A.C. of 5 Shill. sterl.

PETER FIELD, 145 acs. by Survey 15 Dec 1760 in Albemarle Co. on the head of the Brs. of South Hardware Riv., adj. Jacob Cleveland; 12 Jan 1780, p.197. A.C. of 25 Shill. sterl.

JOHN WILSON/WILLSON, 60 acs. by Survey 6 May 1773 in Augusta Co. joining to the W Side of his own Land on Jacksons Riv., Crossing a Br. and Steep Bank to a Draft; 12 Jan 1780, p.198. A.C. of 10 Shill. sterl.

JOHN POAGE ass'ee of JOHN WIER, 76 acs. by Survey 1 Nov 1773 in Augusta Co. on the White Walnut Bottom a br. of South Mill Cr.; 12 Jan 1780, p.198. A.C. of 10 Shill. sterl.

WILLIAM KENNON ass'ee of RICHARD JOHNSON, 68 acs. by Survey 14 Jul 1779 in Louisa Co. on Head of Roundabout Cr., on the Goochland Co. Line, adj. William Kennon; 27 Jan 1780, p.199. A.C. of 10 Shill. sterl.

WILLIAM PRICE, 110 acs. by Survey 1775 in Louisa Co. on the Brs. of fork Cr.; adj. Clarks Old line & Diggs line formerly F. Clarkes; 27 Jan 1780, p.200. A.C. of 15 Shill. sterl.

NICHOLAS MEREWETHER, 1,204 acs. Louisa Co. on Beaver Dam Cr. and the head of Camp Cr., up the road, to the Three Notched Road near the head of the south fork of Beaverdam, near Browns line, East along a path, adj. Charles Fan & William Pettet; 12 Jan 1780, p.201. A.C. of £6 sterl.

ROBERT BIBB, 180 acs. by survey 27 Jan 1778 in Louisa Co. on the N Side of Pamonkey and on some of the small brs. thereof; adj. Moses White, William White, Gentry Thomason, Major Thomas Johnson, Harris & Wood; 12 Jan 1780, p.202. A.C. of 20 Shill. sterl.

ZACHERIAH GILLAM ass'ee of EDWARD DONOHOE, 562 acs. by Survey 2 Dec 1773 in Bedford Co. on both Sides of Difficult Cr. a north br. of Goose Cr.; adj. Overstreet, Dabney &

Hailes; 12 Jan 1780, p.203. A.C. of £3 Sterl. [For Overstreet's land, see PB 39, p.267 to Charles Irby. For Hailes land, see GB E, p.373 to William Mead]

WILLIAM LEAR ass'ee of CHARLES CAMPBELL, 50 acs. by Survey 20 Dec 1770 in Bedford Co. on the E Brs. of Hurricane; adj. his old line, Holt, Mead & the patent Line; 12 Jan 1780, p.204. A.C. of 5 Shill. sterl.

ROBERT CARTER NICHOLAS, a certain 9½ acs. Island in the Fluvanna Riv. in Albemarle Co. opposite the Mouth of Rock Island Cr. between the Lands of Harden Purkens on the S [side of the River] & sd Nicholas on the N side the River; 12 Jan 1780, p.205. A.C. of 5 Shill. sterl.

SAMUEL PHELPS ass'ee of HENRY BARTMAN, 619 acs. by Survey 18 Nov 1751 or 1754 in Lunenburg Co. on the fork of Allens Cr., crossing a Great br.; adj. James Tucker, George Walton, Thomas Farrow, Clark & Ruffin; 12 Jan 1780, p.205. A.C. of £3.S5. sterl. **paid into the late Receiver Generals Office**. [For James Tucker's, see his PB 42 p.469; for Thomas Farrow's, see PB 34 p.389 to Thomas Farrer; for Clark's, see PB 28 p.132 & p.136 to Francis Ealidge/Elledge which both adj. James Clark's PB 33 p.927; for George Walton's, see PB 32 p.559 to Col. John Ruffin & Col. James Baker]

JOHN GILES, 170 acs. by Survey 6 Mar 1778 in Bedford Co. on Prathers run a South br. of Stanton Riv., adj. Calloway & Watts; 12 Jan 1780, p.206. A.C. of 20 Shill. sterl.

GEORGE RUSHER, 99 acs. by survey 15 Mar 1775 in Bedford Co. on the Brs. of Falling Cr. of Stanton Riv., Beginning near a Lick; 12 Jan 1780, p.207. A.C. of 10 Shill. sterl.

JOHN CHRISTOPHER LAINHART, 347 acs. by Survey 16 Dec 1771 in Bedford Co. on both Sides of Otter Riv., Crossing the North fork & the South fork of the Riv., adj. Casper Read; 12 Jan 1780, p.208. A.C. of 35 Shill. sterl.

WILLIAM BUFORD, 224 acs. by Survey 15 Oct 1777 in Bedford Co. on Enochs Cr., along a Waggon Road, to top of a Mountain; adj. Holland, & Joseph Baynes; 12 Jan 1780, p.209. A.C. of 25 Shill. sterl.

GEORGE RUSHER, 240 acs. by Survey 15 Mar 1775 in Bedford Co. on falling Cr., adj. Weaver; 12 Jan 1780, p.210. A.C. of 25 Shill. sterl.

WALTER ONEAL, 249 acs. by Survey 4 Apr 1774 in Bedford Co. on Sycamore Cr., down Roaring run; adj. Tracy, Goodman & Lainhart; 12 Jan 1780, p.211. A.C. of 25 Shill. sterl.

SIMON MILLER, 330 acs. by Survey 25 Feb 1779 in Bedford Co. on the Waters of Otter Riv.; adj. Rushes line, his own line, Crews line, Rusher & Bramble; 12 Jan 1780, p.212. A.C. of 35 Shill. sterl.

JOHN KENNADY Ass'ee of PETER FORGUSON who was ass'ee of JAMES & WILLIAM BRYANT, 400 acs. by Survey 12 Nov 1774 in Bedford Co. on the Brs. of Hurricane Cr.; adj. Milloner, Logwood, Alley & Milam; 12 Jan 1780, p.213. A.C. of 40 Shill. sterl.

STEPHEN ENGLISH/INGLISH, 186 acs. by Survey 30 Mar 1778 in Bedford Co. on the both Sides of Stanton Riv., adj. his old line; 12 Jan 1780, p.214. A.C. of 20 Shill. Sterl.

JOHN HAYNES ass'ee of AQUELLA GREAR, 860 acs. by Survey 14 Mar 1772 in Bedford Co. on the S Side of Stanton Riv., by the road; adj. his line, James Grear, Joseph Greer & Brown; 12 Jan 1780, p.215. A.C. of £3.S15 sterl. Including 110 acs. Gtd. to sd Grear by Pat. 20 Aug 1760 [Lunenburg Co. PB 34, p.664 to Acquilla Grier]

THOMAS BUFORD, 99 acs. by Survey 2 Apr 1774 in Bedford Co. on Beaverdam Cr., by the road side; adj. John Wright/Write, Walton, Tolbert & Finley; 12 Jan 1780, p.216. A.C. of 10 Shill. sterl.

THOMAS DOOLEY, 93 acs. by Survey 18 Dec 1771 in Bedford Co. on the S Side of the South fork of Otter Riv., adj. Beard & Ewing; 12 Jan 1780, p.216. A.C. of 10 Shill. sterl.

THOMAS COCKRAN, 400 acs. by Survey 5 Apr 1775 in Augusta Co. bet. Jannings & Folfits Brs.; adj. Michael Hogshead, James Campbell, Edmiston, & John Hogshead; 12 Jan 1780, p.217. A.C. of 40 Shill. sterl.

NICHOLAS SHEVER ass'ee of CORNELIUS RIDDELL, 192 acs. by Survey 5 Sep 1774 in Augusta Co. on the W side of Linvells Cr., Beginning on the S side the North Br. of Shanandoe, by a Meadow; adj. David Roberson, another Tract of sd Riddles Land, John Bumks Corner & one Hunters line; 12 Jan 1780, p.218. C.C. of 20 Shill. sterl.

JOHN BIFE ass'ee of CORNELIUS RIDDLE, 335 acs. by Survey 5 May 1774 in Augusta Co. on the Western br. of long Meadow a br. of the North fork of Shanadow, Beginning on a ridge, adj. Matthias Laces lines & sd Riddles L.; 12 Jan 1780, p.219. A.C. of 35 Shill. Sterl.

ABRAHAM HITE & PETER HOGG assignees of sd WILLIAM PRESTONE, 1,000 acs. by Survey 9 Aug 1775 in Kentucky Co. on the SE side of Kentucky Riv. about 25 Miles from the Mouth, Beginning on the Brow of a Ridge, to the Mouth of Salt Spring Cr., on a large Buffaloe Road, on the point of a ridge; 1 Feb 1780, p.220. *in consideration of Military Service performed by William Prestone in the late War between Great Britain & France according to the Terms of the King of Great Britains Proclamation of 1763.*

CHARLES SMITH, 162 acs. by Survey 4 Jul 1773 in Augusta Co. on the South fork of Patowmack, by the Riv. above the Mouth of a Small Br. thence down sd Riv. to a Bent thence Cross the Same, at the foot of the Mountain, on a Ridge; 12 Jan 1780, p.221. A.C. of 20 Shill. Sterl. Including a Tract of 76 acs. Gtd. to sd Charles Smith by Pat. 6 Apr 1769 [PB 38, p.603] the Remaining 86 Never before ptd.

JOHN POAGE ass'ee of JOHN DAVIS, 153 acs. by Survey 10 Oct 1772 in Augusta Co. on the E Side of Back Cr. against William Cunninghams L., Beginning on the Side of a Ridge below Lewis's L., by the Branch in a Gap; 12 Jan 1780, p.222. A.C. of 15 Shill. Sterl.

ROBERT GOODWYN, 311 acs. by Survey 21 Apr 1779 in Louisa Co. on the little Riv., adj. John Bullock & James Terry; 12 Jan 1780, p.223. A.C. of 35 Shill. sterl. 250 acs. of which is Patent Land and 49 the Residue never before Gtd.

THOMAS ADAMS, 545 acs. by Survey 5 Jul 1771 in Augusta Co. on the W Side of the Calf Pasture Riv.; adj. Robert Gay, the L. formerly William Campbells, & William Logherd; 12 Jan 1780, p.224. A.C. of 55 Shill. Sterl. Including a Tract of L. of 110 acs. first Gtd. to Robert McKittrick [PB 34, p.298 to Robert McCetrick] by Pat. 12 May 1759 & by Sundry Conveyances the Property is now Vested in sd Adams the Remaining 435 acs. Never Ptd.

JOSEPH LIVELY ass'ee of JNO. MOORE SENR., 231 acs. by Survey 21 Sep 1774 in Louisa Co. on a br. of Camp Cr. Commonly Called and Known by the Name of Sycamore fork, in the head of a Glade, adj. Joseph Carver & Harlow; 12 Jan 1780, p.226. A.C. of 15 Shill. sterl.

SAMUEL OWINGS ass'ee of sd WILLIAM CROMWELL, 1,700 acs. Augusta Co., Beginning at a white oak Standing on the SE Side of the West fork of Shirtee Cr. Letter'd **W.C.** at the point of an Island, on the bank of the South fork of Shirtee, to the point of the forks of sd Cr. thence Extending up the West Br.; 22 Mar 1780, p.227. *in consideration of Military Service performed by William Cromwell as a* **Subaltern** *in the Late War between Great Britain & France according to the Terms of the King of Great Britains Proclamation of 1763.*

ELEXANDER WELLS ass'ee of SARAH GIBBS, Legal Representative of the sd THOMAS GIBBS, 200 acs. by Survey 18 Jan 1775 in Augusta Co. on a Small Br. of Hard Bargain Cr. a Br. of Ohio joining to Harman Great House in the Cove, Beginning on the Side of a hill about 30 poles from the End of a Small pond; 27 Mar 1780, p.228. *in Consideration of Military Service by Thomas Gibbs in the late War between Great Britain and France according to the Terms of the King of Great Britains Proclamation of 1763.*

DAVID PATTERSON ass'ee of JOHN WARD Gent., 41,477 acs. by Survey 24 Oct 1770 in Pittsylvania Co. on the Head Brs. of Dan Riv. and on both Sides of Reed Island Cr. of New Riv., Crossing 3 Brs. of Smiths Riv., Crossing a Br. of Rock Castle and 4 Brs., Crossing a Br. of Burks fork, to a Synamon Tree & to a Waughoo Tree, Down a Br. of Reed Island to the Cr. thence up the Same, Crossing a fork of Read Island, up a fork of Reed Island, Crossing Robertsons Cr., Crossing 2 forks of Dan to the Beg.; adj. Twitty, Ward, Willis & Cos. Line, & Twilley; 1 May 1780, p.229. A.C. of £275.S9.d4 Sterl. *In Witness whereof the sd Thomas Jefferson Esq. Governor of the Commonwealth of Virginia hath hereunto Set his hand and Caused the Seal of the said Commonwealth to be affixed at* **Williamsburg**.

LODOWICK TUGGLE, 174 acs. By Survey 7 Oct 1776 in Pittsylvania Co. on the Brs. of Pigg Riv., along the old line; **1 May** 1780, p.233. A.C. of 20 Shill. Sterl. *In Witness whereof the sd Thomas Jefferson Esq. Governor of the Commonwealth of Virginia hath hereunto Set his hand and Caused the Seal of the sd Commonwealth to be affixed at* **Richmond**.

JOHN TERRELL ass'ee of JOHN CONARY, 336 acs. by Survey 7 Nov 1769 in Henry Co. on Great Sycamore Cr., adj. White; 1 May 1780, p.234. A.C. of 35 Shill. Sterl.

JOHN WATKINS, 273 acs. (by Survey 16 Nov 1774) in Pittsylvania Co. on the South fork of Stinking Riv.; adj. Thomas Farriss, Jonathan Jones & David Mitchell; 1 May 1780, p.235. A.C. of 30 Shill. sterl.

BENJAMIN SHELTON, 456 acs. by Survey 23 Dec 1778 in Pittsylvania Co. on the Brs. of Panther Cr.; adj. Joseph Johnson, Wade, & Abraham Shelton; 1 May 1780, p.236. A.C. of 50 Shill. Sterl.

WILLIAM HAYMES, 354 acs. by Survey 26 Sep 1778 in Pittsylvania Co. on the horse Shoe Brs. of White thorn Cr., Crossing Pigg River Road, on Mill Cr.; adj. sd William Hames/Haymes, Edmund Payne, Richard Perriman, John Medirff & John Cox; 1 May 1780, p.237. A.C. of 35 Shill. sterl.

JAMES BOAZ, 371 acs. by Survey 12 Dec 1777 in Pittsylvania Co. on both Sides of Little Leewatts Cr. of Sandy Riv., adj. Barnett McColough; 1 May 1780, p.238. A.C. of 40 Shill. sterl.

RICHARD BROWN, 204 acs. by Survey 12 Jun 1779 in Pittsylvania Co. on the Br. of Shocks Cr., on Shoco Cr.; adj. William Williams, Markham, Claybrook & the sd Brown; 1 May 1780, p.239. A.C. of 20 Shill. sterl.

JOHN BALLENGER, 152 or 150 acs. by Survey 4 Feb 1780 in Pittsylvania Co. on the Draughts of Straight Stone Cr.; adj. Shadrach Tribble, Gilbert Hunt, David Hunt, Dillard, & John Vaughan; 1 May 1780, p.239. A.C. of 15 shill. sterl.

ROBERT DOLTON/DALTON ass'ee of JAMES PARBARY, 109 acs. by Survey 20 Oct 1755 in Halifax Co. on Turkey Cock Cr. a South Br. of Irven Riv., adj. Webb; 1 May 1780, p.240. A.C. of 15 Shill. Sterl.

ABRAHAM SHELTON, 394 acs. by Survey 11 Jan 1766 in Halifax Co. on the Glady fork of white thorn Cr.; 1 May 1780, p.241. A.C. of 40 Shill. Sterl.

ABRAM SHELTON, 400 acs. by Survey 21 Feb 1780 in Pittsylvania Co. on the Glady fork of White thorn Cr., adj. sd Sheltons former Line; 1 May 1780, p.242. A.C. of 40 Shill. sterl.

ARMSTED/ARMSTRONG/ARMSTEAD SHELTON, 295 acs. by Survey 28 Nov 1775 in Pittsylvania Co. on both Sides of Georges Cr., adj. James Farriss; 1 May 1780, p.243. A.C. of 30 Shill. sterl.

ARTHER KERSEE, 432 acs. by Survey 15 Apr 1774 in Pittsylvania Co. on both Sides Bird Cr.; adj. Samuel Matthews, & Terry's Order; 1 May 1780, p.243. A.C. of 45 Shill. sterl.

JOHN HAMMOND SENR., 245 acs. by Survey 2 Feb 1774 in Pittsylvania Co. on the Waters of Shocks Cr., adj. his former Line & Terry's order; 1 May 1780, p.244. A.C. of 20 Shill. sterl.

THOMAS JONES, 400 acs. by Survey 28 Feb 1771 in Pittsylvania Co. on Mill Cr., adj. Gray & Polly; 1 May 1780, p.245. A.C. of 40 Shill. sterl.

DANIEL JINKINGS, 296 acs. by Survey 12 Aug 1772 in Pittsylvania Co. on the Brs. of fly Blow and Allens Creeks, up the West fork of Allens Cr.; adj. John Short, [Jacob] Farriss & Thomas Vaughan; 1 May 1780, p.246. A.C. of 30 Shill. sterl.

JAMES BOAZ, 363 acs. by survey 24 Mar 1779 in Pittsylvania Co. on both Sides of the Grassy fork of Stewarts Cr.; adj. Maxwell, the sd James Boaz, & Thomas Boaz old line; 1 May 1780, p.247. A.C. of 40 Shill. sterl.

JOSEPH MAYS, 400 acs. by survey 25 Mar 1754 in Halifax Co. on the Brs. of Childrys Cr.; adj. Prewit, Booker & Cunningham; 1 May 1780, p.248. A.C. of 40 Shill. sterl.

JOHN VAUGHAN, 182 acs. by Survey 2 Feb 1770 in Pittsylvania Co. on the Brs. of Straight Stone Cr.; adj. John Vaughan, Tribble, Moses Dillard & Hubboard; 1 May 1780, p.248. A.C. of 20 Shill. sterl.

WILLIAM WILLIAMS, 50 acs. by Survey 21 Oct 1774 in Pittsylvania Co. on the Draughts of Shoco Cr., adj. his old line & Hugh Henry; 1 May 1780, p.249. A.C. of 5 Shill. Sterl.

JOSEPH MAYS, 420 acs. by Survey 16 Apr 1774, 300 acs. Together with 120 acs. of new Land, surveyed 12 Jun 1779 in Pittsylvania Co. on the River & along the Mountain; adj. Henry Banks, Claybrook, Markam, & Stephen Terry; 1 May 1780, p.250. A.C. of 45 Shill. sterl.

WILLIAM WILLIAMS, 306 acs. by Survey 21 Oct 1774 in Pittsylvania Co. on the Brs. of Shoco Cr.; adj. his own Line, Terrys Order line & Hutchings Line; 1 May 1780, p.251. A.C. of 35 Shill. sterl.

CALEP/CALEB HUNDLEY, 400 acs. by Survey 9 Feb 1774 in Pittsylvania Co. on the Brs. of Coartks Cr., crossing Jefferson Road; adj. Daniel Witoker, the sd Withers line; 1 May 1780, p.252. A.C. of 40 Shill. sterl.

[*The next 15 grants were issued at Richmond even though they were dated prior to 1 May 1780*]

JAMES BECKHAM, 282 acs. by survey 9 Feb 1764 in Buckingham Co. on both Sides of Witch Island Cr., adj. John Coleman & Jeremiah Whitney; 1 Feb 1780, p.253. A.C. of 30 Shill. sterl. [This Appomattox Co. land is on Wreck Island Cr. near Colemans Road. For Jeremiah Whitney's land see Thomas Oglesby's GB A p.486 and for John Coleman's land see John McKenny's PB 35 p.44]

DAVID BELL, 113 acs. by Survey 7 Jul 1773 in Augusta Co. on the Br. of the West fork of Black Thorn above Trimbles Survey, to a Bunch of Maples by a Spring; 12 Jan 1780, p.254. A.C. of 10 Shill. sterl. [This land is also granted on p.684]

CHRISTIAN WAGGONER, 89 acs. by Survey 7 Apr 1772 in Augusta Co. on the Middle Br. of Crab apple the Head Waters of the South Br. of Potomack, on the N Side of a Ridge; adj. Barnet Lancer & Armouist?; 12 Jan 1780, p.254. A.C. of 10 Shill. sterl.

ELIAS TOMASON/THOMASON, 521 acs. in Louisa Co. on the Waters of North East Cr. and near the head thereof; adj.

Whitlock, Waddy Thompson, John Rice, Samuel Tomason & Freeman; 12 Jan 1780, p.255. A.C. of 55 Shill. sterl.

JOHN HEMPHILL ass'ee of JOHN CAUCHEY, 213 acs. by Survey 16 Jul 1775 in Augusta Co. on Some Brs. of Walkers Run brs. of the Middle Riv. of Shanadore; adj. John Bumsider, Thomas Francis, John Campbell, John McMahan & Samuel McKee; near Walkers corner; 12 Jan 1780, p.256. A.C. of 25 Shill. Sterl.

NICHOLAS MEREWETHER, 183 acs. Louisa Co. adj. Wady Thompson, Elias Thomerson & Garret; 12 Jan 1780, p.257. A.C. of 20 shill. sterl.

WILLIAM AKERS, 400 acs. Henry Co. by Survey 12 Oct 1773 on Lazy run of Black Water Riv., Crossing Lick Cr.; adj. Thomas Miller, Calloway & Rentfrow; 1 Feb 1780, p.258. A.C. of 40 Shill. sterl.

JOHN POAGE & JOHN SKIDMORE, 400 acs. by Survey 15 Apr 1775 in Augusta Co. on the head Waters of the South Br. of Potomack on the SE side of Pater Neals Land above the Colt Spring, Beginning at the foot of the Mountain; 12 Jan 1780, p.259. A.C. of 40 Shill. sterl.

SIMON MILLER ass'ee of WILLIAM MEAD, 137 acs. by Survey 4 Apr 1774 in Bedford Co. on the S Side of Roaring Run; adj. Strol/Stort, his own line & Goodman; 12 Jan 1780, p.260. A.C. of 15 Shill. Sterl.

JOHN TURDALE/TIRDLE, 450 acs. by Survey 16 Mar 1771 in Louisa Co. on the Brs. of Reedy Cr., on the S Side of the old Mountain Road, in a Slash; adj. John Ross, John Ragland, Miller, Mills, old Mills line, Andrew Hunter & sd Tirdle; 12 Jan 1780, p.261. A.C. of 45 Shill. sterl.

JAMES HOGG, 170 acs. by Survey 5 Jul 1773 in Augusta Co. on the E side of Black Thorn, adj. March Sevadleys Survey & Bastion Hooe; 12 Jan 1780, p.262. A.C. of 10 Shill. Sterl.

HENRY MORRIS ass'ee of JNO. WHITE who was ass'ee of THOMAS MATTHEWS, 128 acs. by Survey 19 Mar 1771 in Buckingham Co. on the head of dry Beaver Pond Cr., adj. Richard Taylor; 1 Feb 1780, p.262. A.C. of 15 Shill. Sterl.

CHARLES PATTERSON ass'ee of EDWARD FURGASON, 329 acs. by Survey 25 Mar 1773 in Buckingham Co. on both sides the West fork of Wolf Cr.; adj. Ezekiel Carson, William Furguson, Bartholemy Zachery & Nicholas Hay; 1 Feb 1780, p.263. A.C. of 35 Shill. sterl. [For Carson's land, see John Carson's PB 34, p.413. For Zachery's land see Alexander Hunter's 334 acs. in PB 34, p.380. For Nicholas Hays land see Alexander Hunter's 200 acs. in PB 34, p.381]

THOMAS WOOLDRIDGE ass'ee of HICKERSON BARKSDALE, 275 acs. by Survey 23 Feb 1762 in Buckingham Co. on the Br. called the long Br. and Cattail brs. of the South fork of Willis's Cr.; adj. Alexander Stinson, John Sanders & his own line formerly John Woodnetts; 1 Feb 1780, p.264. A.C. of 30 Shill. Sterl.

ALEXANDER SMITH ass'ee of WILLIAM GILLIAM, 187 acs. by Survey 13 Feb 1764 in Buckingham Co.

on the Brs. of the S side Wreck Island Cr.; adj. Nimrod Riches Corner, the Sd Gilliams own Line, John Cox & John Clemon; 1 Feb 1780, p.265. A.C. of 20 Shill. Sterl.

CHARLES GALLOWAY & Co., 574 acs. by Survey 27 Mar 1770 in Pittsylvania Co. Inclusively, Crossing Sugar tree Cr., up Sandy Riv.; adj. Burnett, Cunningham, Shud & Burnet; 4 May 1780, p.266. A.C. of £3 Sterl.

CONSTANT PERKINS/PURKINS, 639 acs. by Survey 21 Mar 1770 in Pittsylvania Co. on the Open ground fork of Beans Cr., Crossing the South fork, to *the Pilate Pine*, adj. Duncan & Chadwell; 4 May 1780, p.267. A.C. of £3.S5 Sterl.

CONSTANT PERKINS/PURKINS, 12 acs. by Survey 18 Mar 1778 in Pittsylvania Co. on the S Side of Dan Riv., along the County Line [East - the Country Line], adj. his own line; 4 May 1780, p.268. A.C. of 5 Shill. Sterl.

CONSTANT PERKINS, 392 acs. by Survey 19 Mar 1770 in Pittsylvania Co. on the Waters of Dan Riv., Beginning at *the Pilate Pine*, adj. Duncan; 1 May 1780, p.269. A.C. of 40 Shill. Sterl.

CONSTANT PERKINS, 296 acs. by Survey 8 Mar 1779 in Pittsylvania Co. on both Sides of the Pond Br. of Dan Riv.; adj. William Wadlow, Stone, Charles Duncan & McGuff; 1 May 1780, p.270. A.C. of 30 Shill. Sterl.

NICHOLAS PERKINS, 340 acs. by Survey 18 Oct 1762 in Pittsylvania Co. on Moberlys Cr. and the Brs. of Mountain Cr., adj. Harris & Co. [Company]; 4 May 1780, p.271. A.C. of 35 Shill. sterl.

PETER PERKINS, 440 acs. by Survey 14 Oct 1762 in Pittsylvania Co. on the East fork of Cascade Cr., adj. Walton & Watson; 4 May 1780, p.272. A.C. of 45 Shill. sterl.

JOHN MARR, 16,336 acs. by Survey 21 Mar 1752 in Henry Co. on Dan Riv. and the Arrarat Riv.; Crossing Elk Cr., a Bent of Peters Cr. & a Bent of Bells Riv.; along the Country Line [N88½°W, S88½°E]; on Rocky Cr.; Crossing a Br. of Clerks Cr. 8 times; up Bells Mountain; on the head of [Arrarat] Riv. on a Gap of the sd Mountain; Crossing Boings Cr.; on Jones's Cr.; Crossing Beaver Cr. to the W side of the Arrarat Riv.; crossing the Arrarat Riv., flat Cr., Rocky Cr. 5 times, Dan Riv. 6 times, Bells [Riv.] Elk Cr. 3 times to Peters Cr., adj. Gray, to a Corner that was made for Dawson & Co. [Company] thence Including the sd Land; 4 May 1780, p.273. A.C. of £81.S15 sterl. [This survey includes the 2,816 acs. Lunenburg Co. in PB 33, p.559 to John Dawson (& Co.) dated 26 Apr 1759]

RICHARD RIPLEY, 182 acs. by Survey 18 Mar 1757 in Albermarle Co. [Buckingham Co.] amongst the Brs. of Waltons fork and Arthers Cr. [of Slate Riv.]; adj. William Nowland, William Chambers, Thomas Patterson, Isaiah Burton & Richd. Ripley; 1 Feb 1780, p.276. A.C. of 20 Shill. Sterl.

JOHN FURGASON/FURGUSON, 398 acs. by Survey 16 Mar 1750/51 in Albermarle Co. [Buckingham Co.] among the Brs. of Wolf Cr. and on both Sides of Bairds Road, adj. Phillip

Matthews/Mathews & Philip Major [Philip Mayo]; 1 Feb 1780, p.277. A.C. of 40 Shill. sterl. [This land is between Samuel Staples' PB 39 p.8 and John Carson's PB 34, p.413]

MASON BISHOP, 319 acs. by Survey 5 Mar 1774 in Lunenburg Co. on the Head Brs. of Stony Cr.; adj. Edward Ragsdale, Henry Gee, Thomas Green & William Brintle; 1 Feb 1780, p.278. A.C. of 35 Shill. Sterl. [This land is surrounded by William Clopton's PB 33, p.428, David Garland's PB 36, p.733, Henry Gee's PB 33, p.54, David Mason's PB 35, p.235 & John Williams etc. GB E, p.67]

JOHN LAND ass'ee of HICKERSON BARKDALE, 275 acs. by Survey 23 Feb 1762 in Buckingham Co. adj. Alexander Stinson, William Curd & John Sanders; 1 Feb 1780, p.279. A.C. of 30 Shill. sterl.

ISAAC STAPLES, 222 acs. by Survey 4 Feb 1756 in Albermarle Co. on the S Brs. of Stone Wall Cr. on the S side Fluvanna Riv., crossing a Br. of Wreck Island, adj. James Christian; 1 Feb 1780, p.280. A.C. of 30 Shill. Sterl.

BENJAMIN WITT, 700 acs. by Survey 3 Dec 1773 in Bedford Co. on the head of Island and falling Creeks; adj. Solomon Smith, Austin, Butler & Michell; 1 Feb 1780, p.281. A.C. of £3.S10. Sterl.

WILLIAM TONEY, 525 acs. by Survey 2 Mar 1774 in Bedford Co. on the N Brs. of Black Water Riv., Beginning in the old line; 1 Feb 1780, p.282. A.C. of 55 Shill. Sterl.

DAVID ROSS, Merchant in Petersburg, 5,709 acs. by Inclusive Survey made 3 Mar 1780 in Fluvanna Co., Beginning at the Point of fork that makes the Fluvanna and Rivanna Rivers, up the Fluvanna River 2,306 poles, to a Stake in an old field, Crossing the North fork of Crooks Cr.; down the Rivanna River 473 poles; 11 May 1780, p.283. *A.C. of £198,795 Current Money of Virginia Paid to Thomas Napier Gent. Escheator for Fluvanna Co. being the Escheated Land of Walter King a Subject of Great Britain which was laid off in lotts and then Sold by the sd Thomas Napier unto the sd David Ross by Virtue of And agreeable to two acts of Assembly Passed in 1779 the one Intitled an act concerning Escheats and forfeitures from British Subjects and the other Intitled an act Concerning Escheators.* [Most of this land was ptd. by Dudley Digges, 5,000 acs. in Henrico Co. in PB 12, p.329 dated 26 Oct 1725, which went up the Fluvanna River 1,760 poles]

JOHN SHORT, 354 acs. by Survey 29 Oct 1774 in Pittsylvania Co. on the Brs. of Banister Riv. & on the S Side thereof, along Rocky Br., adj. Finnys order & Claybrook; 4 May 1780, p.285. A.C. of 35 Shill. Sterl.

HAYNES MORGAN, 318 acs. by Survey 14 Jan 1765 in Pittsylvania Co. on the N Brs. of Banister Riv.; adj. Turner, John Steen, Doss, Morton, & Joseph Ray; 1 May 1780, p.286. A.C. of 5 Shill. Sterl.

JOSEPH COLLINGS, 87 acs. by Survey 17 Dec 1765 in Halifax Co. on the S side of Childry's Cr., along his own line; 4 May 1780, p.287. A.C. of 10 Shill. Sterl.

BRYANT WARD NOWLING ass'ee of RICHARD HANCOCK, 244 acs. by Survey 18 Dec 1764 in Halifax Co. on both Sides of Potters Cr., adj. Roberson;

4 May 1780, p.288. A.C. of 25 Shill. Sterl. **paid into the late Receiver Generals Office.**

SARAH VAUGHAN, 149 acs. by Survey 7 Jun 1774 in Pittsylvania Co. on the Brs. of Fly blow Cr.; adj. Vaughan, Farris & Anderson; 1 May 1780, p.289. A.C. of 15 Shill. Sterl.

DANIEL BATES, 152 acs. by Survey 15 Apr 1774 in Pittsylvania Co. on the S side of Banister Riv., adj. Samuel Mathews & Turner; 4 May 1780, p.290. A.C. of 15 Shill. Sterl.

DRURY OLIVER, 268 acs. by Survey 27 Mar 1779 in Pittsylvania Co. on both sides of the little Cr. of Banister Riv., Crossing 2 forks of the sd Cr., adj. John Wimbush & Green; 4 May 1780, p.290. A.C. of 20 Shill. Sterl.

[The next grants to David Ross are for Escheated land now in Goochland Co. & Fluvanna Co. This land was ptd. by Capt. John Martin in PB 13, p.164, 6,186 acs. Henrico Co. dated 13 Oct 1727, which included most of John Thornton's 3,600 acs. Henrico Co. dated 6 Nov 1721 in PB 11, p.64]

DAVID ROSS, Merchant, ass'ee of WILLIAM ANDERSON & THOMAS PLEASANTS JUNR., 400 acs. by Survey 24 Nov 1779 in Goochland Co. which was laid off in Lotts and the said Lott sold by the sd William Harrison unto the sd William and Thomas Pleasants Junior and by them Sold and ass'd to the sd David Ross; Beginning on the North Bank of James Riv., on the Mouth of a Gut, down the Bird & a Drain to sd Riv., adj. Charles Lewis; 11 May 1780, p.292. *£20,510 paid to William Harrison Gent.*

Escheator for Goochland Co. being part of the Esche[a]ted Land of Lewis Burwell Martin a Subject of Great Britain ... Agreeable to two Acts of Assembly Passed in 1779 the one Intitled an Act Concerning Escheats & Forfeitures from British Subjects the other Intitled an Act Concerning Escheators.

DAVID ROSS, Merchant in Petersburg, ass'ee of WILLIAM ANDERSON & THOMAS PLEASANTS JUNR., 400 acs. by Survey 24 Nov 1779 being part of the Escheated land and layed of in one Lot and Sold by William Harrison the Sd Escheator to sd William Anderson & Thomas Pleasants Junr. and by them Ass'd. to the sd David Ross; Beginning at the Mouth of Island Gut, at the Edge of the low grounds, to **Rocks Called Golgotha Rocks of James River**; 11 May 1780, p.293. *£23,500 Current Money of Virginia paid by David Ross, Merchant in Petersburg to William Harrison Gent. Escheator for Goochland Co. ... a Greeable to two Acts of Assembly Pass'd in 1779 the one Intituled an "act concerning Escheats and forfeitures from British Subjects and the other Intituld "an act Concerning Escheators.* [This is a duplicate of his grant on p.308]

DAVID ROSS, Merchant, ass'ee of THOMAS PLEASANTS, 339 acs. by Survey 24 Nov 1779 being part of the Escheated Land of Samuel Martin a Subject of Great Britain, in Fluvanna Co. which sd Lott was layed off and then sold by sd Thomas Napier Escheator unto sd Thomas Pleasants Junior and by him sold and ass'd to the sd David Ross; adj. J. Bryan; 11 May 1780, p.294. *£1,120 Current Money of Virginia paid by David Ross Merchant to Thomas Napier Gent.*

Escheator of Fluvanna Co. .... agreeable to two Acts of Assembly Passed in 1779 the one Intituled an act Concerning Escheats & forfeitures from British Subjects the other Intituld an act Concerning Escheators.

DAVID ROSS, Merchant, ass'ee of THOMAS PLEASANTS JUNR., 400 acs. by Survey made 24 Nov 1779 being part of a Larger Tract of Escheat Land of Samuel Martin a Subject of Great Britain, in Fluvanna Co. which was laid off and Sold by sd Thomas Napier Escheator unto sd Thomas Pleasants Junior and by him Sold And Assigned to sd David Ross; on the N Side of Bryants Road; 11 May 1780, p.295. *£3,004 Current Money of Virginia Paid by David Ross Merchant to Thomas Napier Escheator for Fluvanna Co. ... A Greeable to two Acts of Assembly Passed in 1779 the one Intituled an act Concerning Escheats and Forfeitures from British Subjects the other Intituled an act Concerning Escheaters.*

DAVID ROSS, Merchant, ass'ee of THOMAS PLEASANTS JUNR., 400 acs. by Survey made 24 Nov 1779 being Part of the Escheated Land of Samuel Martin a Subject of Great Britain in Fluvanna Co. and Goochland Go. which sd Lott Was lay'd off and Then Sold by the sd Thomas Napier Escheator, 284 acs. of the sd Lott in Fluvanna Co. to the sd Thomas Pleasants Junior and by him Sold and Ass'd to David Ross; to **Golgotha** on James River thence up James River and Rivanna Riv., near Gum Cr., adj. Cockes line; 11 May 1780, p.296. *in Consideration of the A. C. of the Sum of £16,000 Current Money of Virginia by David Ross Merchant to Thomas Napier Escheator for sd Co. ... A Greeable to two Acts of Assembly Passed in 1779 the one Intituled an Act Concerning Escheats and forfeitures from British Subjects the Other Intitul'd an act Concerning Escheators.*

DAVID ROSS, Merchant as ass'ee of WILLIAM ANDERSON & THOMAS PLEASANTS JUNIOR, 307 acs. by Survey made 24 Nov 1779 being part of the Escheated Land of Samuel Martin a Subject of Great Britain, in Goochland Co. which sd Lott was lay'd off and Sold by the sd William Harrison Escheator unto the sd William Anderson and Thomas Pleasants Junior and by them Assigned to the sd David Ross; down & crossing the Bird to the Mouth of a Gut, down & crossing the Cr. to the old Mill thence down the Bird, up the Main Road, to a Weavers Shop, to a Smiths Shop, adj. John Ward; 11 May 1780, p.297. *in consideration of £6,526 Current Money of Virginia paid by David Ross, Merchant to William Harrison Escheator for Goochland Co. ... a Greeable to two Acts of Assembly Passed in 1779 the one Intitul'd an act Concerning Escheats and forfeitures from British Subjects the other Intituled an Act Concerning Escheators.*

DAVID ROSS ass'ee of WILLIAM ANDERSON & THOMAS PLEASANTS JUNIOR, 400 acs. by Survey made 24 Nov 1779 being part of the Escheated Land of Lewis Burwell Martin a Subject of Great Britain, in Goochland Co. & Fluvanna Co. which sd Lott was lay'd off and then Sold by sd William Harrison Esq. Escheter to sd William Anderson & Thopmas Pleasants Junior and by them Sold & Ass'd to the sd said Ross; up the Road, to a Weavers Shop, to a Black Smiths Shop; 11 May 1780, p.298. *£3,000 Current Money of Virginia paid* by David Ross Merchant to William Harrison Escheator for Goochland Co. ... by Virtue and a Greeable to two Acts of Assembly Passed in 1779 the one Intituled An Act Concerning Escheats and forfeitures from British Subjects and the other Intituled an act concerning Escheators.

DAVID ROSS ass'ee of THOMAS PLEASANTS, JUNIOR, 475 acs. by Survey 24 Nov 1779 being part of Escheated Land of Samuel Martin a Subject of Great Britain in Fluvanna Co. which sd Lott was lay'd off and Sold by sd Thomas Napier Escheator unto sd Thomas Pleasants Junior and by him Sold and Assd. unto sd David Ross; on the N side the Bird Cr., to the Mouth of Elk Br.; 11 May 1780, p.300. £4,000 Current Money of Virginia paid by David Ross Merchant to Thomas Napier Gent. Escheator for Fluvanna Co. ... A Greeable to two Acts of Assembly Passed in 1779 the one Intituld an Act Concerning Escheats and forfeitures from British Subjects the other Concerning Escheators.

DAVID ROSS ass'ee of WILLIAM ANDERSON & THOMAS PLEASANTS, JUNIOR, 400 acs. by Survey 24 Nov 1779 being part of the Escheated Land of Samuel Martin a Subject of Great Britain in Goochland Co. which sd Lott was layed off and Sold by sd William Harison Escheator unto William Anderson and Thomas Pleasants Junior and by them Sold and Assigned to sd David Ross; Down the Main River Road, up the Bird to the Mouth of a Canel [Channel or Canal]; 11 May 1780, p.300. £5,090 Current Money of Virginia Paid by David Ross Merchant to William Harrison Gent. Escheator of Goochland Co. ... A Greeable to two Acts of Assembly passed in 1779 the one Intituled an act Concerning Escheats and Forfeitures form British Subjects the other and the other Concerning Escheators.

DAVID ROSS ass'ee of THOMAS PLEASANTS, JUNIOR, 400 acs. by Survey 24 Nov 1779 being part of the Escheated Land of Samuel Martin a Subject of Great Britain in Goochland Co. which sd Lott was layed off and then sold by sd Thomas Napier Escheater unto sd Thomas Pleasants Junior & by him Sold and Assigned to sd David Ross; on the N side the Rivanna Riv., to a Spanish oak at the Mouth of Gum Cr. but not found, on Cockes line; 11 May 1780, p.302. £10,000 Current Money of Virginia paid by David Ross Merchant to Thomas Napier Escheater for Fluvanna Co. ... a Greeable to two Acts of Assembly passed in 1779 the one Intituld an Act Concerning Escheats and forfeitures from British Subjects the other Intituld an act Concerning Escheators.

DAVID ROSS ass'ee of THOMAS PLEASANTS, JUNIOR, 400 acs. by Survey 24 Nov 1779 in Goochland Co. being part of the Escheated Land of Lewis Burwell Martin a Subject of Great Britain which sd Lott was laid off and then sold by the sd William Harrison unto Thomas Pleasants Junr. and by him Sold and Assd. to David Ross; up the River Road ; 11 May 1780, p.303. £4,110 Current Money of Virginia paid by David Ross Merchant to William Harrison Escheator for Goochland Co. ... a Greeable to two Acts of Assembly Passed in 1779 the one Intituled an Act Concerning Escheats and forfeitures *from British Subjects and the other Intituled an act Concerning Escheators.*

DAVID ROSS ass'ee of WILLIAM ANDERSON & THOMAS PLEASANTS JUNIOR, 299 acs. by Survey made 24 Nov 1779 being part of the Escheated Land of Lewis Burwell Martin a Subject of Great Britain, in Goochland Co. which sd Lott was laid off and then Sold by sd William Harrison Escheator unto sd William Anderson and Thomas Pleasants Junr. and by them Sold and Assignd unto the sd David Ross; on the Edge of a Cr., on a Ridge, up the Bird Cr.; 11 May 1780, p.304. *£2,520 Current Money of Virginia Paid by David Ross Merchant to William Harrison Gent. Escheator for Goochland Co. ... Agreeable to two Acts of Assembly Passed in 1779 and the one Intituld an act Concerning Escheat and forfeitures from British Subjects the other Intituld an act Concerning Escheators.*

DAVID ROSS Ass'ee of WILLIAM ANDERSON & THOMAS PLEASANTS JUNR., 400 acs. by Survey made 24 Nov 1779 being Part of the Escheated Land of Samuel Martin a Subject of Great Britain in Fluvanna Co. & Goochland Co. which sd Lot was layd off and Sold by the sd Thomas Napier Escheator unto sd William Anderson & Thomas Pleasants Junr. and by them Sold and Assigned to sd David Ross; on Cockes line near Gum Cr.; 11 May 1780, p.305. *£2,610 Current Money of Virginia paid by David Ross Merchant to Thomas Napier Gent. Escheator for Fluvanna Co. ... a Greeable to two Acts of Assembly Passed in 1779 the one Intituld an Act Concerning Escheats and forfeitures from British Subjects the other Intituld an Act Concerning Escheators.*

DAVID ROSS ass'ee of THOMAS PLEASANTS, JUNIOR, 400 acs. by Survey made 24 Nov 1779 being part of the Escheated Land of Samuel Martin a Subject of Great Britain in Fluvanna Co. which sd Lot was laid off and then sold by sd Thomas Napier Escheator unto sd Thomas Pleasants Junior and by him Sold and Assigned to the sd David Ross; on the N side of the Bird, adj. Henry and Thomas Crenks [Crank's] line on Elk Br., down Lillys Br.; 11 May 1780, p.306. *£1,013 Current Money of Virginia Paid by David Ross, Merchant to Thomas Napier Esq. Escheator for Fluvanna Co. ... A Greeable to two Acts of Assembly Passed in the year 1779 the one Intituld an Act Concerning Escheats and forfeitures from British Subjects the other Intitud an Act Concerning Escheaters.*

DAVID ROSS ass'ee of THOMAS PLEASANTS JUNIOR, 409 acs. by Survey made 24 Nov 1779 being part of the Escheated Land of Samuel Martin A Subject of Great Britain in Fluvanna Co. which sd Lott was laid off by sd Thomas Napier Escheator unto sd Thomas Pleasants Junior and by him Sold and Assignd to sd David Ross; on the N side of the Bird, up Elk br., adj. Thomas and Henry Crank; 11 May 1780, p.306. *£3,003 Current Money of Virginia paid by David Ross Merchant in Petersburg to Thomas Napier Escheator for Fluvanna Co. ... a Greeable to two Acts of Assembly Passed in 1779 the one Intitueled an act Concerning Escheats and forfeitures from British Subjects the other Intituld an act Concerning Escheators.*

DAVID ROSS ass'ee of WILLIAM ANDERSON & THOMAS PLEASANTS, JUNIOR, 400 acs. by

Survey made 24 Nov 1779 being part of the Escheated Land of Lewis Burwell Martin a Subject of Great Britain in Goochland Co. which sd Lott was laid off and sold by sd William Harrison Escheator to the sd William Anderson & Thomas Pleasants Junr. and by them Sold and Assignd to sd David Ross; Beginning on the Bank of James Riv., at the foot of the River Hill, at the Mouth of Island Gut on the Riv.; 11 May 1780, p.307. *£20,000 Current Money of Virginia paid by David Ross Merchant at Petersburg to William Harrison Gent. Escheator for Goochland Co. ... a Greeable to two Acts of Assembly Passed in 1779 the one Intituld an act concerning Escheats and forfeitures from British Subjects the other Intituld an act Concerning Escheators.*

DAVID ROSS ass'ee of WILLIAM HARRISON & THOMAS PLEASANTS JUNR., 400 acs. by Survey made 24 Nov 1779 being Part of the Escheated Land of Samuel Martin a Subject of Great Britain in Goochland Co. and layed off in one lott and Sold by William Harrison the sd Escheator to sd William Anderson & Thomas Pleasants Junior and by them Assigned and Disposed of to the sd David Ross; Beginning at the Mouth of Island Gut, at the Edge of the Low grounds, to **Rocks Call'd Golgotha Rocks on James River**; 11 May 1780, p.308. *£23,500 Current money of Virginia paid by David Ross Merchant to William Harrison Gent. Escheator for Goochland Co. ... a Greeable to two Acts of Assembly Passed in 1779 the one Intitul'd an act Concerning Escheats and forfeitures from British Subjects the other Intituld an act Concerning Escheators.* [This is a duplicate of his grant on p.293]

JOHN DAVIS ass'ee of DAVID McCAINES, 150 acs. by Survey 7 Nov 1751 in Augusta Co. on the Waters of Thimade between Mossey Cr. and the North Riv., adj. his Land & Hugh Dives Survey; 4 May 1780, p.310. A.C. of 15 Shill. sterl.

SIMON JUSTICE ass'ee of JAS. JUSTICE who was ass'ee of JAMES WILLIAM, 210 acs. by Survey 11 Mar 1762 in Halifax Co. on Harping Cr., down the Rocky fork of sd Cr.; adj. Walton, Stone & Shockley; 4 May 1780, p.310. A.C. of 25 Shill. Sterl.

JOHN BALLENGER, 210 acs. by Survey 2 Feb 1770 in Pittsylvania Co. on Camp Br. of Straight Stone Cr., adj. John Ballenger & William Collen/Collin/Colling; 4 May 1780, p.311. A.C. of 20 Shill. Sterl.

THOMAS BENNET Ass'ee of ALEXANDER MOORE, 100 acs. by Survey 30 Jan 1769 in Pittsylvania Co. on the Brs. of Potters Cr., near a Meadow, adj. Bryant Ward Nowling & Daniel McKinsey; 4 May 1780, p.312. A.C. of 10 Shill. Sterl. **paid into the late Receiver Generals Office**.

JAMES MITCHELL, 294 acs. by Survey 28 Feb 1774 in Pittsylvania Co. on the Brs. of Harpin Cr., along Pigg River Road; adj. Harmon Cook, Shockley, Williams & Walton; 4 May 1780, p.313. [Entered incorrectly by the scribe as p.213] A.C. of 30 Shill. Sterl.

JOSEPH STANDLEY, 260 acs. by Survey 16 Feb 1774 in [Pittsylvania] Co. on the Brs. of Bearskin Cr., adj. Owen Adkerson & John Wimbut; 11 May 1780, p.314. A.C. of 30 Shill. Sterl.

SHERWOOD WALTON, 400 acs. by Survey 3 Apr 1754 in Halifax Co. on Both Sides of Dry Cr., crossing a Br. of Chesnut Cr., adj. William Powell & Terry; 4 May 1780, p.315. A.C. of 40 Shill. sterl.

JACOB EARLEY, 87 acs. by Survey 7 Mar 1780 in Bedford Co. on the West br. of Elk Cr., adj. Calloway & his own line; 4 May 1780, p.315. A.C. of 10 Shill. Sterl.

MICHAEL GILBERT, 231 acs. by Survey 18 Feb 1777 in Pittsylvania Co. on both Sides of Johnakin Cr., adj. Henry Conway; 4 May 1780, p.316. A.C. of 25 Shill.

THOMAS RUTLIDGE Ass'ee of DAVID ROBERSON, 114 acs. by Survey 23 Dec 1771 in Botetourt Co. on the S side Paris Mountain and on the E Side the Path that leads from William Robinsons, along the Top of and down sd Mountain; 4 May 1780, p.317. A.C. of 15 Shill. Sterl.

MOSES WALDEN, 259 acs. by Survey 24 Jun 1773 in Halifax Co. on the Brs. of Childreys Cr.; adj. Handcock, William Mulling, the old line, John Maulding & William Braze; 11 May 1780, p.318. A.C. of 30 Shill. sterl.

WILLIAM THOMAS, Gent., 320 acs. by Survey 22 Mar 1775 in Pittsylvania Co. on the Brs. of Dan; adj. James Glasbey, the sd Thomas's line, Cargett [Cargill], & John Owen; 11 May 1780, p.319. A.C. 40 Shill. Sterl.

MATTOX MAYS, 440 acs. by Survey 12 Jun 1779 in Pittsylvania Co. on the Brs. of Banister Riv. and Bird Cr., on the Mountain; adj. Joseph Mays Corner, Henry Blanks Corner, Samuel Matthews's line, Joshua Mathews Corner, John Terril line, Richard Brown & Claybrook; 10 Jun 1780, p.320. A.C. of 45 Shill.

MOZO HURT, 542 acs. by Survey 6 Oct 1779; 20 acs. which with two Surveys, 193 acs. & 225 acs. amounts to 438 acs.; which with 104 acs. Gtd. by Pat. 1 Mar 1743/44 to Roger Neal and Properly Conveyed; amounts to 542 acs. in Bedford Co. on the N Side of Stanton Riv., near a large Br.; adj. Murray, Marshall, his own & Littlebury Epperson; 4 May 1780, p.321. A.C. of £2.S15. Sterl.

THOMAS RUTLEDGE/RUTLIDGE Ass'ee of DAVID ROBERSON, 99 acs. by Survey 16 Jan 1772 in Botetourt Co. on the Dividing Ridge and on the Brs. of the North br. of Roanoak, Beginning near a Spring; 11 May 1780, p.323. A.C. of 10 Shill. Sterl.

ROBERT HUCHENSON, 180 acs. by Survey 6 Apr 1773 in Botetourt Co. on John Cr. a Br. of James Riv., adj. William Eaken; 11 May 1780, p.324. A.C. of 20 Shill. sterl.

THOMAS RUTLEDGE Ass'ee of DAVID ROBERTSON, 191 acs. by Survey 16 Jan 1772 in Botetourt Co. on the Dividing Ridge Including Some Brs. of the North fork of Roan [Roanoak Riv.], Beginning near a Spring, on a Ridge, near the Great Road; 11 May 1780, p.324. A.C. of 20 Shill. Sterl.

THOMAS AKIN, 204 acs. by Survey 13 Dec 1771 in Botetourt Co. on Johns Cr., Crossing the Cr. above the falls, by a Cabbin, adj. the Tract he lives on; 11 May 1780, p.325. A.C. of 10 Shill. Sterl.

JOSHUA HARDY Ass'ee of JOHN HALL who was ass'ee of THOMAS HARDY, 300 acs. by Survey 3 Nov 1762 in Halifax Co. on the Brs. of the Double Creeks, by the School House Spring, adj. John Wadden & Watkins line; 18 May 1780, p.326. A.C. of 30 Shill. Sterl.

MILES SELDON JUNR. on His own Right & as ass'ee of RICHARD HOLLAND, 2 acs. by Survey Made 3 Oct 1775 in the Town of Richmond, Escheated from Thomas Atcheson; Bounded by the Main Street, River Street & Cross Street; 20 May 1780, p.327. 6 Shill. and 8 Pence Sterl. paid in the late Receiver Generals Office.

PETER POYTHRESS, Nearly 13 acs. by Survey 24 Nov 1779 in Bath Par. Dinwiddie Co. on the S Side of Butterwood Cr.; adj. Peter Wynnes line now Polly Pothress, & his Own line; 29 May 1780, p.328. A.C. of 5 Shill. Sterl.

CALEB WALLACE Ass'ee of ISRAEL CHRISTIAN who was ass'ee of ROBERT NEILLY, 152 acs. by Survey 7 Aug 1767 in Botetourt Co. on the Waters of Roan-oak; adj. the Land formerly Archibald Grahams, Grahams old place, & William Christian; 29 May 1780, p.329. A.C. of 15 Shill. Sterl.

THOMAS MADISON Ass'ee of PATRICK HENRY who was Ass'ee of JAMES ROBINSON, 1,000 acs. by Survey 15 Jul 1774 in Kentucky Co. on the N Brs. of Kentucky Riv. about 5 Miles East of the head of E[l]khorn Cr. about 30 Miles from the Kentucky being the Waters of the Ohio Riv. on the S Side thereof and about 110 Miles from the Same; adj. his land & Thomas Hind; 29 May 1780, p.330. *in Consideration of Military Service performed by James Robinson in the late War Between Great Britain & Fra[n]ce According to the Terms of the King of Great Britains Proclamation of 1763.*

THOMAS MADISON Ass'ee of PATRICK HENRY who was Ass'ee of sd JOHN WARE, 1,000 acs. by Survey 15 Jul 1774 in Kentucky Co. on the N Brs. of Kentucky River above 5 Miles East of the head of Elkhorn Cr. being on the S Side of the Ohio Riv. and about 110 Miles from the Same, adj. Samuel Meredith & his own Land; 29 May 1780, p.331. *in Consideration of Military Service performed by John Ware as Capt. in the late War Between Great Britain & France according to the terms of the King of Great Britains Proclamation of 1763.*

ROSANNA CHRISTIAN, 150 acs. by Survey 5 Aug 1767 in Augusta Co. on Buffaloe Cr. a Br. of Roanoak, in a Valley, adj. Israel Christian; 29 May 1780, p.331. in Consideration of the A. C. of 15 Shill. sterl.

THOMAS MADISON Ass'ee of PATRICK HENRY who was ass'ee of the sd THOMAS FLEMING, 3,000 acs. by Survey 7 Jul 1774 in Kentucky Co. on a North Br. of Kentucky River Called the Elkhorn Cr. about 80 Miles from the Ohio River and on the S Side thereof, Beginning by the Side of a Small Draft which runs into the South fork of sd Cr., Crossing the North fork of the Cr. to a Bend in the Same, Near where a Small Cr. Joins the large one; 29 May 1780, p.332. *in Consideration of Military Service performed by Thomas Fleming as a Capt. in the late War Between Great Britain & France According to the Terms of the King of Great Britains Proclamation of 1763.*

WILLIAM JONES ass'ee of CHARLES JONES & JOSHUA COOK, 915 acs. by Survey 17 Mar 1773 in Brunswick Co. on Peahill, up the Great Br.; adj. William Huskey, Wm. Jones, Jones & Harmon, Harman, Ledbetter, John Ledbetter & Thomas Bausher; 30 May 1780, p.333. A.C. of £4.S15 sterl. [The survey in this grant is corrected on p.370]

Messrs. CARTER & TRENT [EDWARD CARTER & PETER F. TRENT] Ass'ees of WILLIAM BAILEY who was ass'ee of JEDIAS WEBB, 133 acs. by Survey 21 Feb 1767 in Amherst Co. on the N Brs. of Tye Riv., adj. Col. Henry; 30 May 1780, p.334. A.C. of 15 Shill. sterl.

MANN SOWELL Ass'ee of JOHN FORD who was ass'ee of HENRY MARTIN who was ass'ee of GRAY SMITH, 400 acs. by Survey 13 Jun 1755 in Albemarle Co. on the S Side the Rivanna Riv. on the Brs. of Adrians Cr. and Johnsons Br., Crossing a Bent of Adrian's Cr., adj. his own line & Henry Martin; 31 May 1780, p.335. A.C. of 40 Shill. Sterl.

HENRY MARTIN, 116 acs. by Survey 18 Mar 1752 in Albemarle Co. on the S Brs. of Rivanna Riv.; adj. John Payne, Julius Saunders/Sanders & Chamberlain; 1 Jun 1780, p.336. A.C. of 15 Shill. Sterl.

JOSEPH PEEBLES, 65 acs. by Survey 9 Dec 1774 in Brunswick Co. down Speeds br.; adj. his old Corner, Colo. John Macklin & Lightfoot; 1 Jun 1780, p.337. A.C. of 10 Shill. sterl.

LEWIS CRAIG ass'ee of MARY FRAZIER who is the only Daughter and heir at Law of GEORGE FRAZIER dec'd, 2,000 acs. in Kentucky Co. on E[l]khorn Cr. the Waters of the Ohio Riv.; 1 Jun 1780, p.338. in Consideration of Military Service Performed by George Frazier a Lieut. in the late War between Great Britain & France According to the Terms of the King of Great Britains Proclamation of 1763.

JOHN COX, 200 acs. by Survey 22 Jan 1763 in Pittsylvania Co. on the Brs. of mill Cr. of Panther Cr., Crossing Pigg River Road; adj. his former line, David Haley & Muston; 1 Jun 1780, p.339. A.C. of 20 Shill. Sterl.

JOHN COLLY, 256 acs. by Survey 1 Mar 1772 in Pittsylvania Co. on the Waters of Sandy Riv., adj. Burnet & Oak; 1 Jun 1780, p.339. A.C. of 30 Shill. Sterl.

ANDREW LEWIS, 1,170 acs. by Survey 29 Apr. 1750 in Greenbrier Co. on a br. of Greenbrier Riv. on the W side of a hill Known by the Name of a high Knob, in a Glead, on a little Sinking Cr.; 2 Jun 1780, p.340. A.C. of £6 Sterl. **paid into the late Receiver Generals Office**.

WILLIAM CHRISTIAN ass'ee of sd JOHN BLAGG & WILLIAM BRADLEY, 2,000 acs. by Survey 7 Jun 1774, 1,000 acs. thereof by in Part of the Sd Blaggs Warrent and the other 1,000 acs. in Part of the sd Bradleys Warrant Granted them by Lord Dunmore & Assigne[r] of the sd William Christian, in Kentucky Co. on Bargrass Cr., Beginning at Hugh Allens Survey about 2 Miles from the Riv., Crossing a Cr. twice which Empties into the Ohio below Harrods Cr. Crossing Beargrass Cr., adj. John Floyd;

2 Jun 1780, p.341. *in Consideration of Military Service Performed by John Blagg & William Bradly as Capts. in the late War between Great Britain & France according to the Terms of the King of Great Britains Proclamation of 1763.*

ANDREW LEWIS, 480 acs. by Survey 11 Oct 1751 in Greenbrier Co. on both sides Greenbrier Riv. at the Mouth of Ewin Cr., Beginning near the E Side Ewins Cr., on the Low Grounds; 2 Jun 1780, p.342. A.C. of £2.S10 Sterl.

ANDREW LEWIS, 400 acs. by Survey 28 Apr 1780 in Botetourt Co. at a Place Called the Cove on the Head Waters of Back Cr. a Br. of James Riv. near the Sweet Springs, along the Mountain; 2 Jun 1780, p.343. A.C. of 40 Shill. sterl.

PETER FIELD TRENT ass'ee of PETER GARLAND, 765 acs. by Survey 8 Feb 1774 in Lunenburg Co. on the head Brs. of flat Rock & Hounds Cr., near Ready Cr.; adj. John Hardy, Thomas Hardy, James Buford, Aron Drummon, Lazs. Williams & Samuel Wynn; 13 May 1780, p.344. A.C. of £4 Sterl.

WILLIAM CHRISTIAN ass'ee of sd SAMUEL OVERTON, 3,000 acs. by Survey 11 Jul 1774 in Kentucky Co. on the Waters of Elkhorn Cr a North Br. of the Kentucky Riv. about 87 Miles from the Ohio & on the S side thereof, Crossing by the Head of a Spring and 2 Brs. to an Elm Hoopwood and large Ash in a Cane Break, adj. John Ware; 2 Jun 1780, p.345. *in Consideration of Military Service Performed by Samuel Overton as Captain during the late War Between Great Britain & France According to the Terms of the King of Great Britains Proclamation of 1763.*

WILLIAM CHRISTIAN ass'ee of sd WILLIAM HENRY, 1,000 acs. by Survey 16 May 1774 in Kentucky Co. on the S Side of the Ohio Riv. 3 Miles above the Mouth of Kentucky Riv., Beginning on the River bank Corner to Peachys Land; 2 Jun 1780, p.346. *in Consideration of Military Service Performed by William Henry in the late War between Great Britain & France according to the Terms of the King of Great Britains Proclamation of 1763.*

JOHN COX Gent., 229 acs. by Survey 25 Jun 1773 in Pittsylvania Co. on the Brs. of Bearskin Cr., Crossing the Road; 2 Jun 1780, p.347. A.C. of 25 Shill.

BARTLEY FOLEY, 171 acs. by Survey 22 Nov 1768 in Henry Co. on Sycamore Cr.; adj. his own line, Harbour, & Adams Order; 5 Jun 1780, p.347. 20 Shill. Sterl.

WALTER COLES, 298 acs. by Survey 11 Feb 1763 in Halifax Co. on the Brs. of Bulskin [Buckskin] & Hunting Creeks; adj. Thomas Clark & the sd Coles Hunting Creek Land & his River Land; 5 Jun 1780, p.348. A.C. of 30 Shill. Sterl.

ALEXANDER WELLS & NATHAN CROMWELL Ass'ees of HENRY GAINS Heir at Law to the sd ROBERT GAINS Dec'd, 1,500 acs. by Survey 15 Jan 1775 in Ohio Co. on the forks of Cross Cr. a Br. of the Ohio, Beginning by Estimation 150 Poles below the forks of the Cr. and 25 Poles on the S Side of sd Cr., on a Ridge; 3 Jun 1780, p.349. *in Consideration of Military Service performed by Robert Gains Dec'd in the late War between Great Britain &*

ALEXANDER WELLS Ass'ee of SARAH GIBBS Representative of the sd JOHN McNELLY Dec'd, 200 acs. by Survey 6 Jun 1775 in Ohio Co. on the Eastern Brs. of Ohio Riv. Including the lower end of a larg[e] Rich Bottom Generally Called the Mingo Bottom Opposite the Old Mingo Town on the sd Riv., Beginning on the sd Riv. near and on the Lowest Side of a Drain or Small Br.; 3 Jun 1780, p.350. *in Consideration of Military Service Performed by John McNelly Dec'd in the late War Between [Great Britain] & France According to the Terms of the King of Great Britains Proclamation of 1763.*

ALEXANDER WELLS & NATHAN CROMWELL Ass'ees of HENRY GAINS who was Heir at Law to sd ROBERT GAINS Dec'd, 500 acs. by Survey 17 Jan 1775 in Yohogania Co. on the North fork of Cross Cr. a Br. of the Ohio, Beginning at 2 white oaks Marked A.W. Standing in the Fork of a Run; 6 Jun 1780, p.352. *in Consideration of Military Service Performed by Robert Gains Dec'd in the late War between Great Britain & Fra[n]ce according to the Terms of the King of Great Britains Proclamation of 1763.*

ANTHONY LAWSON, by Estimation 400 acs. being Part of an Undivided Tract of Marsh Land in Pr. Anne Co. lately the property of John Saunders a British Subject and Sold under two Acts of Assembly the one Intituled an act Concerning Escheats and Forfeitures from British Subjects the other Intitul'd an act Concerning Escheators; 6 Jun 1780, p.352. A.C. of £705 Current Money of Virginia paid by Anthony Lawson to Thomas P. Walker Escheator for Pr. Anne Co.

THOMAS SMITH, one Unimproved Lott in Hanover Town in Hanover Co. being lately the Property of James Eslin a British Subject & Sold a Greeable to two acts of Assembly passed in 1779 the one Intituled an Act Concerning Escheats & forfeitures from British Subjects the other Intitul'd an Act Concerning Escheators which sd Lott is Marked in the Number of the Town one hundred & fifty [Lott #150] with its Appurtenances; 6 Jun 1780, p.353. £200 current Money of Virginia paid to Bartlett Anderson Esq. Escheator for Hanover Co. [Margin note: *one Improved Lott. Examd.*]

LAZARUS DE FRANCEY, a certain Lott or parcel of L. in the Town of Hanover in Hanover Co. containing one Lott with the Houses and Improvements thereon belonging which Lott is Marked in the Plan of the sd Town Number forty three [Lott #43] and was lately the property of Archibald Govern a British Subject And Sold by the sd Bartlett Anderson to the sd Lazarus de Francey a greeable to two Acts of Assembly the one Intituled an act concerning Escheats & Forfeitures; 6 Jun 1780, p.354. £2,000 current Money of Virginia paid to Bartlett Anderson Gent. Escheator for Hanover Co.

LAZARUS DE FRANCEY, 2 Lotts with the houses & Improvements thereunto Belonging in the Town of Hanover & Hanover Co. which Lotts are Marked in the Plann of the sd Town No. 31 and 32 & Were lately the Property of Donalds, Scott & Company British Subjects and

Sold by Bartlett Anderson Escheator for the sd Co. to sd Lazarus de Francey a Greeable to two Acts of Assembly the one Intitul'd an act Concerning Escheats and forfeitures from British Subjects the other Intitul'd an Act Concerning Escheators; 6 Jun 1780, p.354. £10,000 Current Money of Virginia paid to Bartlett Anderson Esq. Escheator for Hanover Co.

PETER STEPHEY, 123 acs. by Survey 21 Jan 1772 in Botetourt Co. on a Br. of Ingle Mill Cr. being the Waters of Roan oak, adj. John Robinsons land; 7 Jun 1780, p.355. A.C. of 15 Shill. sterl. [As Peter Stephens in adj. GB 54 p.464, 160 acs. Montgomery Co. to Charles Taylor dated 16 Apr 1806 which also adj. John Robinson's 200 acs., 160 acs. & 115 acs. surveys]

JEREMIAH WHITE, 400 acs. by Survey 14 Mar 1755 in Lunenburg Co. [now Charlotte Co.] on both Sides of the Lick fork of the horsepen Cr., adj. Joshua Chaplin & Zacheriah Davis; 7 Jun 1780, p.356. A.C. of 40 Shill. Sterl. [This is the earliest survey in the grant or patent books to contain reference letters denoting the survey corners: Beginning at Joshua Chaplins [Joshua Chafin] corner white oak at it thence from a. to b. on his line N50°W 84P to a white oak B. to C. new lines N30°W 44P to 2 Dogwoods on a Branch C. to D. N50°E 420P to a Small Jack in Zacheriah Davises line D. to E. on his line S35½°E 58P to a Small Red oak on the same. E. to F. new lines S22°W 312P to a pine F. to A. N81½°W 178P to the Beginning]

JOHN FULTON, 184 acs. by Survey 27 Nov 1765 in Pittsylvania Co. on Morsons br. of Sandy Riv.; 7 Jun 1780, p.356. A.C. of 20 Shill. Sterl.

MOSES AYRES, 304 acs. by Survey 24 Mar 1775 in Pittsylvania Co. on the brs. of Sandy Cr.; adj. Roberts line, Thomas Hardy & John Payne; 7 Jun 1780, p.357. A.C. of 30 Shill. Sterl.

CHARLES CLAY, 336 acs. by Survey 24 Oct 1774 in Pittsylvania Co. on the Waters of White oak Cr.; adj. Mosby/Mosbey, Hall & Porter; 20 Aug 1783 In Witness whereof the sd Benjamin Harrison Esq. Governor in the *8th year of the Commonwealth*, p.358. in Consideration of the A.C. of 35 Shill. [Margin note: *This Grant was Obtained in the name of Governor Harrison Dated the 20th of Augt. because ye Grant was made out in the name of Governor Jefferson who Resign'd before it Could be Seal'd*]

JAMES McGEEHEE/McGEHEE /McGEEHE, 262 acs. by Survey 18 Apr 1770 in Pittsylvania Co. on the Waters of Banister; 7 Jun 1780 In Witness whereof the sd Thomas Jefferson Esq. Governor in the *4th year of the Commonwealth*, p.359. A.C. of 30 Shill. sterl.

JOHN MARTIN Ass'ee of EPHRODITUS WHITE, 121 acs. by Survey 27 Nov 1765 in Pittsylvania Co. on both Sides of Sandy Riv., on the Ruis/Rius Br.; 7 Jun 1780, p.360. A.C. of 15 shill. sterl.

WILLIAM COLLAICE/COLLICE Ass'ee of JAMES COLLICE, 304 acs. by Survey 25 Mar 1775 in Pittsylvania Co. on the Brs. of Sandy Cr.; adj. William Tredwell, Achold, Wynn, & William Owen; 7 Jun 1780, p.361. A.C. 30 Shill. Sterl.

THOMAS BOAZ, 408 acs. by Survey 24 Mar 1779 in Pittsylvania Co. on both Sides the Grassy fork of Stewarts Cr., adj. James Boaz & sd Thomas Boaz's old line; 7 Jun 1780, p.362. A.C. of 45 shill. Sterl.

JOHN WILSON, 139 acs. by Survey 23 Apr 1768 in Pittsylvania Co. on Milbery Cr.; 7 Jun 1780, p.363. A.C. of 15 Shill. Sterl.

THOMAS CHAMBERS, 400 acs. by Survey 27 Mar 1778 [Pittsylvania Co.] on the brs. of Sandy Cr. [of Banister Riv.]; adj. Burwell Bowder [Browder?], Donelson, Elijah King & Claybrook; 7 Jun 1760, p.363. A.C. of 40 Shill. Sterl.

THOMAS BOAZ, 262 acs. by Survey 2 Mar 1779 [Pittsylvania Co.] on both sides of Stewarts Cr.; adj. John Smith, Bernet McColloug, Maxwell, James Boaz & Barnet McColloug; 8 Jun 1760, p.364-p.366. A.C. of 25 Shill. Sterl. [p.365 skipped by the scribe]

HUGH HENRY, 223 acs. by Survey 21 Feb 1774 [Pittsylvania Co.] on the North Br. of Shocco Cr.; adj. William Wright, William Williams & Terrys Order Line; 8 Jun 1760, p.366a. A.C. of 25 Shill. Sterl.

WILLIAM CHRISTIAN, 1,000 acs. by Survey 17 Jul 1774 in Kentucky Co. on the Waters of Elkhorn Cr. a north Br. of Kentucky Riv. being about 100 Miles from the Ohio Riv. and on the S Side thereof, by a Draft, adj. Barnes; 2 Jun 1780, p.367. *in Consideration of Military Service performed by William Christian in the late War between Great Britain & France According to the Terms of the King of Great Britains Proclamation of 1763.*

MATOX MAYS, 66 acs. by Survey 19 Mar 1767 on the Drafts of Ellises Cr. and on Mays Cr.; adj. his former Corner, Vaughan, Coles Lewis, Bardel & Mays; 8 Jun 1780, p.367a. A.C. of 45 Shill. sterl. [The cost should have been only 10 Shill.] [Halifax Co. or Pittsylvania Co.]

BARNET McCOLOUGH, 304 acs. by Survey 11 Dec 1779 in Pittsylvania Co. on both Sides little Stewarts Cr., adj. John Fulton; 7 Jun 1780, p.368. A.C. of 30 Shill. sterl.

WALKER DANIEL [DANIEL WALKER?], 245 acs. by Survey 7 Oct 1771 in Halifax Co. on the Brs. of Hunting Cr.; adj. Morehead, Richard Womack & John Owen; 2 Jun 1780, p.368a. A. C. of 25 Shill. Sterl.

THOMAS HARDY, 413 acs. by Survey 8 Dec 1776 [Pittsylvania Co.] on the South Brs. of Banister Riv., adj. Finny; 8 Jun 1780, p.369. A.C. of 45 Shill. sterl.

WILLIAM JONES Ass'ee of CHARLES JONES & JOSHUA COOK, 915 acs. by Survey 17 Mar 1773 [in Brunswick Co. on Peahill Cr.], up the Great Br.; adj. William Huskey, William Jones, Richard Jones, Harmon/Harman, Ledbetter, John Ledbetter & Thomas Bousher; 8 Jun 1780, p.370. A.C. of £4.S15. sterl. [This grant contains an apparent corrected survey of that on p.333]

ISAAC ADAMS, 100 acs. by Survey 1 May 1758 in Brunswick Co. on the S side of Meherrin Br.; adj. Tatum, Jackson, Lanier & Gouer; 8 Jun 1780, p.371. A.C. of 15 Shill. Sterl. [The Meherrin Br. runs into the three Creeks near the Brunswick/Greensville Co. line. For Gower's land see PB 34, p.162 to John

Maclin; for Jackson's land see PB 29, p.490 to Thomas Jackson]

JOHN ANGLIN, 238 acs. by Survey 3 Nov 1774 [Pittsylvania Co.] on the Brs. of Sandy Cr., along John Piggs Road, On a Ridge, in a Bottom; adj. Dolson [Dotson or Donnelson?], & Jesse Barker; 8 Jun 1780, p.372. A.C. of 45 Shill. sterl.

WILLIAM VAUGHAN, 50 acs. by Survey 22 Nov 1771 in Brunswick Co. on the S Side of Meherin Riv.; adj. his own line, Charles Letbetter & Henry Munger; 8 Jun 1780, p.373. A.C. of 5 Shill. Sterl.

BENJAMIN WHITE, 200 acs. by Survey 13 Mar 1770 [Pittsylvania Co.] on the Waters of Sandy Riv., Beginning at Gammons Cr., down the great Br.; adj. sd Billings Line, Owen & Gammon; 8 Jun 1780, p.374. A.C. of 25 Shill. sterl.

MOSES JOHNSON, 200 acs. by Survey 25 Mar 1779 [Pittsylvania Co.] on the Brs. of Trawbury Cr. [Strawberry Cr.], on Johnson Br.; adj. Adkerson, Joshua Cantrill & Edward Atkins line; 8 Jun 1780, p.375. A.C. of 20 Shill. Sterl.

WILLIAM WYCH, 200 acs. by Survey 4 Feb 1746/47 in Brunswick Co. on the N side of Meherin riv.; adj. Henry Tatum, Colo. Lightfoot, John Moore, Clack, & Henry Jackson; 8 Jun 1780, p.376. A.C. of 20 Shill. sterl. [This land was already gtd. to William Wyche in PB 29, p.234 dated 12 Jul 1750]

STERLING CATO, 252 acs. by Survey 13 Dec 1777 [Pittsylvania Co.] on the brs. of Sandy Riv., adj. the old line & John Smith; 8 Jun 1780, p.377. A.C. of 25 Shill. Sterl.

THOMAS ROBERSON, 327 acs. by Survey 30 Mar 1773 [Pittsylvania Co.] on Stewarts Cr., Crossing the Grassy fork, adj. Lumpkins; 8 Jun 1780, p.378. A.C. of 35 Shill. Sterl.

THOMAS BOAZ, 810 acs. by Survey 7 Dec 1777 [Pittsylvania Co.] on the Brs. of Stewarts Cr.; adj. sd Thomas Boaz, Randolph & Spilson; 9 Jun 1780, p.379. A.C. of 85 Shill. sterl.

EDWARD ATKINS, 376 acs. by survey 25 Mar 1775 [Pittsylvania Co.] on the E side of Strawberry Cr.; adj. sd Atkins his former Survey, Cantrell & Joel Slow the sd Slows former Line; 9 Jun 1780, p.380. A.C. of 40 Shill. sterl.

JAMES GLASBY, 400 acs. by Survey 22 Mar 1775 in Pittsylvania Co. on the Brs. of Dan Riv.; adj. John Owen, Lewis, & William Thomas; 9 Jun 1780, p.382. A.C. of 40 Shill. sterl.

LAZARUS DODSON, 202 acs. by Survey 10 Dec 1778 [Pittsylvania Co.] on the Brs. of Sandy Cr.; adj. the Order line, John Curl & George Hardy; 9 Jun 1780, p.383. A.C. of 20 Shill. sterl.

THOMAS HARDY, 350 acs. by Survey 16 Feb 1774 [Pittsylvania Co.] on Green Rock Cr.; adj. Jeremiah Washam, Petty, Robertson, Christian Hutchings line, Pigg & Pattey; 9 Jun 1780, p.384. A.C. of 35 Shill. sterl.

THOMAS GRESHAM, 142 acs. by Survey 22 Nov 1765 [Pittsylvania Co.] on the Brs. of the south fork of Sandy Riv., Crossing a Br. of Sugar tree Cr.;

adj. Lumpkin, Shield, Thomas & the sd Gresham; 8 Jun 1780, p.385. A.C. of 15 Shill. Sterl.

JOHN LYNCH & PETER STEPNEY /STEPHEY, 257 acs. by Survey 1 Jan 1772 in Botetourt Co. on the Brs. of Ingles Mill Cr. being the Waters of Roanoak; 8 Jun 1780, p.386. A.C. of 30 Shill. Sterl.

JOHN JACKSON JUNR., 400 acs. by Survey 3 Mar 1778 in Halifax Co. on both sides of Terrible Cr.; 9 Jun 1780, p.387. A.C. of 40 Shill. sterl. **paid into the late Receiver Generals Office** ... it being part of 800 acs. Lapsed for the non-payment of his Majestys quitrents from Anthony Griffin to whom it was gtd. by Patent 16 Aug 1756 [Lunenburgh Co. PB 33, p.61] & Since Devised to the sd John Jackson Junr. by the Honble. General Court.

JOHN STILE, 404 acs. by Survey 15 Dec 1777 [Pittsylvania Co.] on the S side of Sandy Riv. & on both sides the long br.; adj. Patrick Still, John Smith, Gouern, & Smiths new line; 9 Jun 1780, p.388. 40 Shill. Sterl.

BARNET McCOLOUGH, 324 acs. by survey 11 Dec 1777 [Pittsylvania Co.] on the brs. of Sandy Riv., adj. James Fulton; 9 Jun 1780, p.389. A.C. of 35 Shill. Sterl.

JOHN COX Gent., 384 acs. by Survey 16 Mar 1774 [Pittsylvania Co.] on the head Brs. of Mill Cr. and brs. of Cherry Stone, on Pigg River Road, Crossing a Bold Br.; adj. Edmund Gray, Philemon Payne, Donelsons order line & Henry; 9 Jun 1780, p.390. A.C. of 40 Shill. sterl.

MARTIN KEY JUNR., 200 acs. by Survey 10 Apr 1780 in Bedford Co. on the S Brs. of Magotty Cr.; adj. Ray, Wright & Murphey; 9 Jun 1780, p.391. A.C. of 20 Shill. sterl.

ALEXANDER BAINE Ass'ee of JAMES BATES, 200 acs. by Survey 7 Dec 1767 in Augusta Co. on a Small br. of Roan oak below the Lick run; 9 Jun 1780, p.392. A.C. of 20 Shill. Sterl.

ALEXANDER BOYD, 248 acs. by Survey 10 Feb 1764 in Augusta Co. on the Roan oak joining the Land whereon he dwells, Beginning on the N Side of the River at the Mouth of a Run Corner to his Patent L. and to the L. of Joseph Love, by a Lick hole, on a Ridge; 9 Jun 1780, p.393. A.C. of 25 Shill. sterl.

ABRAHAM SMITH & JOHN SKIDMORE, 390 acs. by Survey 14 Apr 1765 in Augusta Co. on the head waters of the South Br. of Patomack; adj. Peter Hole, Peter Hoal; 10 Jun 1780, p.394. A.C. of 40 Shill. sterl.

JOHN KERBY, 429 acs. by Survey 15 Mar 1770 [Pittsylvania Co.] on the Brs. of Sandy Cr.; adj. William Lynch, Samuel Harris, Givens Line, Cannon & Kerby; 12 Jun 1780, p.395. A.C. of 45 Shill. sterl.

HENRY DOOLEY, 133 acs. by Survey 8 May 1772 in Botetourt Co. on a Br. of Gralde Cr. being the Waters of Roan oak, adj. Maxes [or Mayes] Survey; 10 Jun 1780, p.396. A.C. of 15 Shill. Sterl.

JOHN LAMONT, 404 acs. by Survey 19 May 1777 in Bedford Co. on the head Brs. of Goose Cr., Beginning at his own Corner on oars Nob, by a Path, on the

Mountain thence along the Top of the Main Ridge as it Meanders, adj. his own lines; 7 Jun 1780, p.396. A.C. of 40 Shill. sterl. [Included with his 730 acs. in GB 9 p.598 dated 18 Jul 1787 in his 2,090 acs. PB 28 p.348 dated 7 June 1793]

WILLIAM SPENCER, 365 acs. by Survey 7 Mar 1780 in Amherst Co. on both Sides the South fork of Rucker Run, Beginning at Pointers Corner to North eight on the North Bank of the South fork of Ruckers Run, to Pointers Corner to Thomas Griffin and with his lines, to Pointers Corner to North six and with its line, to Pointers Corner to North eight & with his line; 11 Jun 1780, p.397. *£2,315 paid by William Spencer to David Shepherd Gent. Escheator for Amherst Co. ... part of a larger Tract was lately the Property of Walter King a British Subject which was Escheated & Sold by Virtue of & a Greeable to two Acts of Assembly passed in 1779 the one Intituled "an act Concerning Escheat and forfeitures from British Subjects the other Intituld "an act Concerning Escheators.*

DANIEL LOVELL, 92 acs. by survey 30 Jan 1766 in Halifax Co. on the long Br. of Great Cherry Stone Cr.; adj. Snelson & Turner; ["to a hickory in the said Tawn & line"]; 12 Jun 1780, p.399. A.C. of 10 Shill. Sterl.

MARTIN KEY, 230 acs. by Survey 10 Apr 1774 in Bedford Co. on the Brs. of Griffiths Cr., adj. Griffith & Anderson; 7 Jun 1780, p.400. A.C. of 25 Shill. Sterl.

JOEL ADKINS Ass'ee of HENRY ATKINS, 294 acs. by Survey 16 Feb 1774 in Pittsylvania Co. on both Sides of bold br. of Cherry Stone Cr.; adj. William Right; 7 Jun 1780, p.401. A.C. of 30 Shill. sterl.

WILLIAM DIX ass'ee of JOHN CARGETTS, 391 acs. by Survey 29 Jan 1766 in Pittsylvania Co. on the Brs. of Dan Riv.; adj. James Hogan, his new Survey, Terry, & Cargetts line; 7 Jun 1780, p.402. A.C. of 40 Shill. Sterl.

JOSIAH COOK, 261 acs. by Survey 25 Mar 1779 in Pittsylvania Co. on the Brs. of Sandy Cr.; adj. Francis Mabary, Thomas Boaz & Dodson; 12 Jun 1780, p.403. A.C. of 30 Shill. sterl.

THOMAS BROWN, 180 acs. by Survey 12 Mar 1771 in Pittsylvania Co. on Lawless's fork of Fall Cr., adj. James Jones & Lawless; 12 Jun 1780, p.404. A.C. of 20 Shill. Sterl.

THOMAS SMITH Gent., 146 acs. by Survey 5 Nov 1774 in Pittsylvania Co. on the Brs. of Sandy Cr., in a bottom, adj. James Roberts line; 12 Jun 1780, p.405. A.C. of 15 Shill. Sterl.

GEORGE WOOLDRIGE/WOOLDRIDGE, [MOSES DUNLAP], 31 acs. by Survey 30 Oct 1771 in Botetourt Co. on the S Side of Roan oak joining and below the Land of Isaac Taylor, Beginning at the head of a Spring, adj. Taylor; 12 Jun 1780, p.406. 5 Shill. sterl. **The above Grant to George Wooldridge is void, having issued to him thro' mistake, a new one is issued to Moses Dunlap this 28th. Nov. 1794.**
[Margin note: *"There is a Transfur on the back of the Survey now lying in the Land Office Vesting this Grant of 31 acres of Land in Moses Dunlap in whom the right appears to be*
 Edmund Thomas C.L. Off.]

[*See GB 31 pp.91-92 containing the same survey, abstracted as follows:*

MOSES DUNLAP Ass^{ee}. of GEORGE WOOLDRIDGE, 31 acs. by Survey 30 October 1791, in Botetourt Co. on the S side of Roan Oke Riv. joining and below the Land of Isaac Taylor, Beginning at the head of a Spring thence N16°W 52 poles to a hickory in Taylors line; 28 Nov 1794 in the 19th year of the Commonwealth, James Wood esq. Lieutenant Governor of the Commonwealth of Virginia, in consideration of the A.C. of 5 shillings Sterling paid by Moses Dunlap]

JOHN DIX Ass'ee of JOHN OWENS, 357 acs. by Survey 25 Jan 1766 in Halifax Co. on both Sides Hanus Cr. [Hances Cr.], on the N Side Dan Riv., along the Country Line [West]; adj. Hance Hendrick, Hogan & Atkinson; 7 Jun 1780, p.407. A.C. of 40 Shill. Sterl.

HARRY TERRY, 400 acs. by Survey 10 Dec 1778 in Pittsylvania Co. on the Brs. of Sandy Cr.; adj. the Order Line, Parish, King, & Peter Terry; 7 Jun 1780, p.408. A.C. of 40 Shill. Sterl.

JOHN WILKINS, 90 acs. by Survey 10 May 1776 in Mecklenburg Co. on the S Side of Swepstone Mill Cr.; adj. Mallott, Egleston & Newell/Nowill; 7 Jun 1780, p.409. A.C. of 10 Shill. sterl.

JOHN COX, 578 acs. by Survey 10 Apr 1770 in Pittsylvania Co. on both Sides of Strawberry Cr., to Wetsleave Cr.; adj. Chamberlain, Adam Lackey, Watkins line & White; 7 Jun 1780, p.410. A.C. of £3. Sterl.

WILLIAM McDOWELL, 69 acs. by Survey 12 Jan 1773 in Augusta Co. on *the Lime Stone Ridge* Near Smiths Cr., on a Ridge, adj. his old Line & Scham/Scam; 20 Jun 1780, p.411. A.C. of 10 Shill. Sterl. **paid into the Late Receiver Generals Office.**

MICHAEL FORD, 88 acs. by Survey 18 Feb 1773 in Rockingham Co. on the W Side of Brock Cr., at the foot of the Mountain, adj. John Phip & Samuel Conner; 7 Jun 1780, p.412. A.C. of 10 Shill. Sterl.

ISABELLA EAKINS [and her Heirs for Ever], by Survey 7 Nov 1754, for CONROD HARCHY, 66 acs. Which was Transfered by William Prestone Surveyer of Botetourt Co. unto the sd Isabella Eakins in the sd Co., crossing the Cr. to a Sw., adj. sd Harcheys old Survey; 7 Jun 1780, p.413. A.C. of 10 Shill. Sterl.

FRANCIS SMITH [and his Heirs for Ever], 226 acs. by Survey 26 Nov 1772 in Botetourt Co. on Some of the Draughts of James Riv., on a Ridge, by a Sink hole on a Ridge, adj. the L. of John McRoberts & Rolston; 7 Jun 1780, p.413. A.C. of 36 Shill. Sterl.

ARON & ABRAHAM FOUNTAIN Legatees of PETER FOUNTAIN Dec'd, 2,000 acs. by Survey 13 Mar 1779 in Henry Co. on this County line and Crooked Cr. and the Mayo Riv., Beginning in the County Line at the Place where the Line Corners which Divided Survey from Gilford County, on the S Side of Mayos Riv.; adj. Walton & a Line of 800 acs. Land Survey'd for the sd Fountain; 7 Jun 1780, p.415. A.C. of £10 Sterl. [The County Line in the survey was apparently the Country Line, East 1,724 Poles]

JOHN HERDMAN Ass'ee of THOMAS CAMPBELL, 54 acs. by Survey 2 Dec 1767 in Rockingham Co. on the head Drafts of the West fork of Cooks Cr., Beginning by a Sinkhole on the S Side of his other L., also adj. Mr Millers Line; 7 Jun 1780, p.416. A.C. of 5 Shill. Sterl.

WILLIAM HEATH, 200 acs. by Survey 17 Apr 1775 in Augusta Co. on the North fork of the South Br. of Patomack, to a Spruce Pine by a Bank, adj. Joseph Bennet; 7 Jun 1780, p.416a. A.C. of 20 Shill. Sterl.

DANL. RAGSDALE Ass'ee of JOHN BAILEY who was Ass'ee of JOHN TALIAFERRO, 400 acs. by Survey 17 Feb 1774 in Pittsylvania Co. on the Waters of Banister Riv. & White oak Cr., adj. Leiches corner, Finney, Christopher Hutching & Talliaferro; 7 Jun 1780, p.417. A.C. of 30 Shill. Sterl.

JONATHAN HILL, 303 acs. by Survey 5 Nov 1762 in Halifax Co. on the Brs. of the Lower double Cr.; adj. Thomas Warter, Willson & Wetherford; 7 Jun 1780, p.418. A.C. of 30 Shill. Sterl.

NATHANIEL HUGHES Ass'ee of JOHN WATKINS, 369 acs. by Survey 13 Feb 1766 in Pittsylvania Co. on the Brs. of Burches Cr., near the Pulpits Spring; adj. Joseph Terry, John Madding & Thomas Hardy; 7 Jun 1780, p.419. A.C. of 40 Shill. Sterl.

JOSEPH JACKSON Ass'ee of BENJAMIN LAWLESS, 480 acs. by Survey 15 Mar 1771 in Pittsylvania Co. on the Brs. of Sandy Cr.; adj. Moses Terry, sd Lawless's old Line & the Order Line; 14 Jun 1780, p.420. A.C. of 50 Shill. Sterl.

JOHN KING, 650 acs. by Survey 10 Jan 1767 in Pittsylvania Co. on the S Brs. of Sandy Cr.; adj. Williams Kennon, sd John Kings Old Line, Joseph Terry, Thomas Terry, Joseph Ironmunger, James Terry & Benjamin Terry; 14 Jun 1780, p.422. A.C. of 65 Shill. Sterl.

HENRY EUING/EWING, 128 acs. by Survey 7 Jul 1773 in Augusta Co. on the head drafts of the West fork of Cooks Cr., on a ridge; adj. his and Harrisons Lands, & William Euing; Near John Hendersons line; 14 Jun 1780, p.423. A.C. of 15 Shill. Sterl.

JOHN WALTERS, 314 acs. by Survey 1 Apr 1774 in Pittsylvania Co. on the Brs. of Sandy Cr., Crossing the Road, in a Pond; adj. Weatherford, & Robert Walther; 14 Jun 1780, p.424. A.C. 35 Shill. sterl.

TIMOTHY STAMPS/STAMPTS, 576 acs. by Survey 3 Feb 1766 in Pittsylvania Co. on the Brs. of Sandy Cr. and the upper double Cr.; adj. William Payne, Parrither, Election Musick, William King, William Russell & Thomas Hardy; 14 Jun 1780, p.425. A.C. of 60 Shill. Sterl.

SARAH CANTRIL, 20 acs. by Survey 14 Mar 1775 in Bedford Co. on the Brs. of Gills Cr., on the Waggon Road, adj. Ellison & Mead; 11 Jun 1780, p.427. A.C. of 5 Shill. Sterl.

WILLIAM GRAVES Ass'ee of JOHN COX, 201 acs. by Survey 16 May 1770 in Henry Co. on the Waters of Smiths

Riv.; adj. Randolph, Chandler & Gray; 4 Jun 1780, p.428. A.C. of 20 Shill. sterl.

HENRY VESTLER Ass'ee of JOHN DUNBORE, 60 acs. by Survey 4 Mar 1773 in Augusta Co. on the E Side of Cooks Cr., on a Ridge, adj. His old Line & Samuel Nicholas; 14 Jun 1780, p.429. A.C. of 20 Shill. Sterl.

JAMES SHANKS, 50 acs. by Survey 4 Feb 1767 in Augusta Co. on the head of Carrs Cr., adj. Mapes Cunningham & Napper; 14 Jun 1780, p.430. A.C. of 5 Shill. Sterl.

GEORGE MOFFETT, 1,000 acs. by Survey 1 Jul 1775 in Kentucky Co. about 5 Miles from the Kentucky on the Waters of Turkey Cr., on a Rissing Ground, by a Small Draught, near a large Buffaloe Road; 14 Jun 1780, p.431. *in Consideration of Military Service performed by George Moffett in the late War between Great Britain & France according to the Terms of the King of Great Britains Proclamation of 1763.*

EDMUND WILSON, 106 acs. by Survey 6 Apr 1757 in Albermarle Co. [Amherst Co. now Nelson Co.] on the S Side of Indian Cr. and in the Coves of the Mountain, adj. John Harris Dec'd.; 7 Jun 1780, p.432. A.C. of 15 Shill. sterl.

THOMAS BURGESS, 92 acs. by Survey 18 Feb 1774 in Pittsylvania Co. on the North fork of Freeding, adj. his own Line; 12 Jun 1780, p.433. A.C. of 10 Shill. Sterl.

JONAS LAWSON, 324 acs. by Survey 26 Oct 1778 in Pittsylvania Co. on the Waters of White oak Cr., adj. Payne; 12 Jun 1780, p.434. A.C. of 35 Shill. sterl.

ROBERT WALTERS, 376 acs. by Survey 29 Mar 1774 in Pittsylvania Co. on both Sides of Burches Cr., adj. Joseph Terry & Dodson; 12 Jun 1780, p.435. A.C. of 40 Shill. sterl.

PATRICK NAPIER, 200 acs. by Survey 24 Jan 1780 in Fluvanna Co. which was lately the Property of William Ainge a Subject of Great Britain and Sold by the sd Thomas Napier Gent. Escheator for the Co. Aforesaid unto the sd Patrick Napier, on the Riv. adj. his Corner; 16 Jun 1780, p.436. *£1,005 Current Money of Virginia Paid by Patrick Napier unto Thomas Napier Gent. Escheator for Fluvanna Co. ... by Virtue and a Greeable to two Acts of Assembly Passed in 1779 the one Intituld "an act Concerning Escheats and forfeitures from British Subjects the other Intituld "an act Concerning Escheators.*

JOHN SMITH, 136 acs. by Survey 17 Mar 1779 in Pittsylvania Co. on the S Brs. of Sandy Riv.; adj. Henry Richardson, Mack Mattenly, Watson & Sparks Line; 12 Jun 1780, p.437. A.C. of 15 Shill. Sterl.

WILLIAM CARR Gent., a Certain Lott or parcel of Land Containing ½ acres in Pr. William Co. and in the Town of Dumfries Laid down in a Plott in the said Town Number 146 which said Lott or half acre was lately the Property of **Colin, Dunlop, Son, and Co:y** Merchants of Great Britain and was Sold by the sd Henry Peyton Gent. Escheator for said Co. unto sd William Carr Gent. with Store Houses and appurtenances belonging to said Lott late the Property of the said Dunlop & Co.; 16 Jun 1780, p.438. *£8,550 Current Money of Virginia paid by William Carr Gent. unto*

Henry Peyton Escheator for Pr. William Co. ... by Virtue of and a Greeable to two late acts of Assembly Passed in 1779 the one Intituld "an Act Concerning Escheats and forfeitures from British Subjects and the other Intuld "an Act Concerning Escheators.

HENRY LEE Esq., four Lotts in Pr. William Co. and in the Town of Dumfries laid down in the Plan of the sd Town and Number'd, Viz, 151, 152, 154, 155 the said Lotts being lately the Property of William Cunningham and Company Subjects of Great Britain and was Sold by the sd Henry Peyton Gent. Escheator for sd Co. unto the sd Henry Lee Esq. with Store Houses and Appurtenances Appurtaining; 16 Jun 1780, p.438a. *£13,320 Current Money of Virginia paid unto William Peyton Gent. Escheator for Pr. William Co. by Henry Lee Esq. the said Lotts late the Property of sd William Cunningham & Company ... by Virtue of and a Greeable to two Acts of Assembly Passed in 1779 the one Intituld "an Act Concerning Escheats and forfeitures from British Subjects the other concerning Escheators.*

ABIA CHEATHAM, 400 acs. by Survey 17 Nov 1779 in Pittsylvania Co. on the Brs. [of] Fall Cr., up Finns br., adj. Harris & Clay; 12 Jun 1780, p.438b. A.C. of 40 Shill. Sterl.

JOHN ASHWORTH, 121 acs. by Survey 2 Nov 1774 in Pittsylvania Co. on the Brs. of Sandy Cr. on the S Side of white oak Mountain, in the head of a br. on the N Side the Mountain, adj. Charles Clay & James Lawless; 12 Jun 1780, p.439. A.C. of 15 Shill. sterl.

ADAM STEPHENS Esqr., 1,000 acs. by Survey 23 May 1774 in Kentucky Co. on the S Side the Ohio Riv., Beginning at a Buckey Hoopash and Sycamore Trees 3,570 Poles above the Mouth of the Kentucky, thence up the Ohio; 16 Jun 1780, p.440. *in Consideration of Military Service Performed by Colo. Adam Stephens in the late War between Great Britain and France according to the Terms of the King of Great Britains Proclamation of 1763.*

ADAM STEPHENS, 1,000 acs. by Survey 19 Jul 1774 in Kentucky Co. on the N Side of the Kentucky Riv. a br. of the Ohio and Jessemine Cr.; Beginning at a Red oak and 2 Mulberrys in broken down timber at Buffaloe Road at A. Running N60W 420 Poles to 3 hickories a Red oak and ash at B. thence S20W 400 Poles to 2 Red oaks and 2 hickories at C. thence S60E 420 Poles to 3 Red oaks and a hickory at D. thence N20E 400 Poles to the Beg.; 16 Jun 1780, p.442. *in Consideration of Military Service Performed by Adam Stephens as Colo. in the late War between Great Britain and France According to the Terms of King of Great Britains Proclamation 1763.*

DAVID TYRCE ass'ee of JOHN ROOKER HOY [JOHN BOOKER HOY?], 72 acs. by Survey 30 Jan 1773 in Buckingham Co. on the head brs. of Appamatox Riv.; adj. John Patterson, James Loaes Line, David Tyrce & Phelps; 14 Jun 1780, p.443. A.C. of 10 Shill. sterl. [adj. Thomas Phelps's PB 37 p.392 & John Patterson's PB 24 p.324 & PB 35 p.192]

THOMAS BURGESS, 416 acs. by Survey 14 Mar 1771 in Pittsylvania Co. on the Brs. of Sandy Cr. and fall Cr.; adj. Ben. Lawless & Fowles; 13 Jun 1780, p.444. A.C. of 45 Shill. Sterl.

THOMAS TOWNS, 217 acs. by Survey 9 Nov 1771 in Halifax Co. on the Draughts of Buck horn, up Boyds Ferry Road, adj. Wall; 13 Jun 1780, p.445. A.C. of 25 Shill. Sterl.

JAMES McDOWELL Heir at Law to sd JAMES McDOWELL, 1,000 acs. by Survey 14 Jun 1775 in Kentucky Co. on the south fork of Licking Cr. a br. of Ohio, crossing three forks & two forks of the Cr. adj. the Land of _____; 20 Jun 1780, p.446. *in Consideration of Military Service performed by James McDowell in the late War between Great Britain and France according to the Terms of the King of Great Britains Proclamation of 1763.*

JAMES McDOWELL Heir at Law to sd JAMES McDOWELL, 1,000 acs. by Survey 14 Jun 1775 in Kentucky Co. on a South fork of Licking Cr., in a flatt, adj. Hugarts L.; 20 Jun 1780, p.447. *in Consideration of Military Service performed by James McDowell in the late War between Great Britain and France according to the Terms of the King of Great Britains Proclamation of 1763.*

ADAM STEPHEN, 2,000 acs. by Survey 29 Jun 1774 in Kentucky Co. on the N Side of the Kentucky Riv. a br. of the Ohio & on the NW side of Elk horn Cr. about 8 Miles from a Remarkable Buffaloe fording Place Crossing Kentucky Riv., Beginning in the fork of a br. of Elk horn Cr. near Colo. A. Lewis's Corner, to 3 Double Sugar trees at C. Near Buffaloe ford; 19 Jun 1780, p.448. *in Consideration of Military Service performed by Colo. Adam Stephen in the late War between Great Britain and France according to the Terms of the King of Great Britains Proclamation of 1763.*

SILVANUS STOCKS [STOKES], 200 acs. by Survey 26 Oct 1774 in Pittsylvania Co. on the Waters of White oak Cr.; adj. William Payne, Adams & Lawson; 13 Jun 1780, p.449. A.C. of 20 Shill. sterl.

ADAM STEPEN/STEPHEN Esq. Heir at Law to sd ALEXANDER STEPEN Dec'd, 2,000 acs. by Survey 11 Jul 1774 in Kentucky Co. on the N side of the Kentucky Riv. a Br. of the Ohio the South Br. of Elkhorn Cr. adj. a Tract of L. Surveyed for Edward Ward on the SW side, at C. being the SW Corner of the Honble. Colo. Byrds L.; 19 Jun 1780, p.450. *in Consideration of Military Service performed by Alexander Stepen in the late War between Great Britain and France according to the Terms of the King of Great Britains Proclamation of 1763.*

STEPHEN HEARD, 342 acs. by Survey 10 Dec 1778 in Henry Co. on black Water Riv., adj. John Heard & Dillan; 20 Jun 1780, p.451. 35 Shill. Sterl.

SAMUEL McDOWELL, 380 acs. by Survey 3 Mar 1780 in Rockbridge Co., Crossing the Great Road; adj. Roger Key, Samuel [McDowell], McDowell, Lysle, & John Paul; 19 Jun 1780, p.452. A.C. of 40 Shill. Sterl.

MARTHA HAWKINS, 3,553 acs. by Survey 21 Apr 1773 in Botetourt Co. on the W Side of the Blue Ridge of Mountains and on a Br. of James Riv. Call'd Catawba Cr., adj. Boulden's old Patent, to an old Corner in the Patent which the trees Cut down being in John Hewits Plantation; 20 Jun 1780, p.454. Know ye, that Benjamin Hawkins and Martha his Wife did by their Council Produce in General Court held at the Capitol in Williamsburg 12 Apr 1775 an Original Patent under the Seal of the then Colony Granted to Benjamin Borden 9 Mar 1740/41, For 3,553 acs. of L. lying in that Part of Orange Co. Call'd Augusta Now Botetourt Co. and Suggested that the last Course of the Bounds of the sd L., To Wit, N49W 340 Poles to the Beginning Omitted out of the sd Patent by a Mistake in the Surveyor in his Certificate Returned to the Secretarys Office on which the sd Patent Issued and Prayed they might be admitted to Surrender to the sd Patent to be Cancil'd = and that a new Patent might be granted them for the said L. and it appearing by the Original Plann and anew Survey lately made that Such Suggestion is true it is Decreed and Ordered that the sd former Patent and the Record thereof be Cancell'd and that another Patent for the said L. Including the Course aforesaid be Granted to the said Benjamin Hawkins and Martha his Wife and the Heirs of the said Martha now Know ye, that in Pursuance of the said Judgment there is Granted by the said Commonwealth unto Martha Hawkins (the said Benjamin being Decd.)

ROBERT WALTERS, 504 acs. by Survey 6 Apr 1779 [Pittsylvania Co.] on the Brs. of fall Cr.; adj. Orlander Smith Corner, Robert Walters line, Thomas Walters line & William Russells line; 30 Jun 1780, p.456. A.C. of 50 Shill. Sterl.

WILLIAM BOOKER, 241 acs. by Survey 10 Apr 1779 in Pittsylvania Co. on both Sides of Chain Cr., on the Road, adj. Adkerson & John Jones; 30 Jun 1780, p.457. A.C. of 15 Shill. sterl.

GAWIN HAMILTON, 125 acs. by survey 29 Apr 1774 in Augusta Co. bet. Muddy Cr. and Dry Riv. Brs. of Shanadore, by a Road, adj. Alexander Millers Survey, to an Apple tree on his old lines; 13 Jun 1780, p.458. A.C. of 15 Shill. sterl.

ABRAHAM SMITH, 198 acs. by Survey 11 Apr 1774 in Augusta Co. on the E Side of Crab Apple Waters, near the Mountain; 13 Jun 1780, p.459. A.C. of 20 Shill. Sterl.

THOMAS WALTERS, 110 acs. by survey 12 Feb 1766 in Halifax Co. on both sides Watkins's fork of the Lower Double Cr.; adj. Watkins, sd Thomas Walters old line & John Moddings Lines; 13 Jun 1780, p.460. A.C. of 15 Shill. sterl.

JOHN EUING, 19 acs. by Survey 8 Jul 1773; in Augusta Co. on the head Drafts of the West fork of Cooks Cr., adj. William Shannon Junior [on the West line] & his old line; 13 Jun 1780, p.462. A.C. of 5 Shill. Sterl.

JOSEPH GOODWIN, 39 acs. by Survey 16 Apr 1768 [Henry Co.] on Smiths Riv.; 10 Jun 1780, p.463. A.C. of 5 Shill. sterl.

LUKE STANDEFORD, 138 acs. [Henry Co.] by Survey 17 Oct 1772 on the south fork of Stony Cr. [Story Cr.]; 20 Jun 1780, p.464. A.C. of 15 Shill. Sterl.

BENJAMIN TERRY, 564 acs. by Survey 24 Nov 1779 in Pittsylvania Co. on the N Brs. of Sandy Cr. and Johns Run; adj. Joseph Motley, Fitzgarrett, Reuben White, the sd Terry, Farmer [or Tanner] & Elijah King; 19 Jun 1780, p.465. A.C. of £3 Sterl. 264 acs. of which was Surveyd 8 Dec 1778 by John Donelson Junr. for the sd Terry, 200 acs. Transfered from Henry McDonold & 80 acs. transferd from Archabald Robertson to gether with 12 acs. of new land.

ZACHERY TAYLOR Heir at Law to HANCOCK TAYLOR who was ass'ee of ALEXANDER VAUGH [WAUGH] who was ass'ee of the sd JOHN WALLER, 1,000 acs. by Survey 20 Jun 1774 in Kentucky Co. on the Waters of Elkhorn Cr. a N Br. of the Kentucky Riv.; 21 Jun 1780, p.466. *in Consideration of Military Service Performed by John Waller as a Lieutenant in the 2nd. Virga. Regt. rais'd during the late War between Great Britain and france according to the Terms of the Kings of Great Britains Proclamation of 1763.*

WILLIAM THURMON, 209 acs. by Survey 12 Nov 1771 in Pr. Edward Co. on Both Sides of Rockey Br. a fork of the South fork of Appamatox Riv., Crossing the South fork of Rough Cr., adj. his own old Line & James Ross; 21 Jun 1780, p.467. A.C. of 25 Shill. Sterl.

WILLIAM HAMILTON Ass'ee of EDMUNDS BARKER ass'ee of JNO. MOSELY, 191 acs. By Survey 16 Nov 1762 in Brunswick Co., adj. Barker & Jones; 23 Jun 1780, p.469. A.C. of 20 Shill. Sterl.

MALLORY TODD, One Lott and House in the Town of Smithfield Marked in the Plann of the sd Town Number 2 being lately the Property of John Williams of Bermuda a British Subject and Sold by Samuel Hardy Escheator as aforesaid unto the sd Mallory Todd; 22 Jun 1780, p.470. *£1,010 paid by Mallory Todd to Saml. Hardy Esq. Escheator for Isle of Wight Co. ... Agreeable to two Acts of Assembly Passed in 1779 the one Intituld "an act Concerning Escheats and forfeitures from British Subjects the other Intituld "an Act Concerning Escheators.*

JEREMIAH WHITNEY, 272 acs. by Survey 5 Mar 1755 in Albemarle Co. adj. David Rogers; 22 Jun 1780, p.471. A.C. of 30 Shill. sterl. [This land was referred to as Richard Taylor's in PB 33 p.749 to David Rogers & PB 36 p.842 to John Beard, both on Wreck Island Cr. S of the Fluvanna Riv. now in Appomattox Co.]

JOHN BROWN, 70 acs. by Survey 16 Nov 1772 in Buckingham Co. on the brs. of Davids Cr. on the W side of the Naked Mountain; adj. John Brown, William Patterson & his Own line; 24 Jun 1780, p.472. A.C. of 10 Shill. Sterl.

JOHN COUCH Ass'ee of THEO-DORICK WEBB who was Ass'ee of JACOB WEBB, 200 acs. by Survey 20 Apr 1775 in Buckingham Co. on the lower fork of Thomas's Cr. a br. of Fluvanna Riv., near John Bowcocks fence, in a thick Place of a Br.; adj. his own Line, George Damson, Howard & sd John Bowcock; 23 Jun 1780, p.473. A.C. of 20 Shill. sterl.

JAMES SOUTHERN, 225 acs. by Survey 9 Dec 1773 in Buckingham Co. on both sides Willis's Cr., adj. Dyche Gilliam & William Kensly [or Hensly]; 22 Jul 1780, p.474. A.C. 25 Shill. sterl.

THOMAS TURPIN, JUNIOR, 400 acs. by Survey 9 Dec 1779 in Fluvanna Co. being part of a larger Tract lately the Property of Samuel Martin and Sold by the sd Thomas Napier Escheator as Aforesd., at the Mouth of Dog Cr. [of the Rivanna Riv.], adj. Sylvanus Bryant; 2 Jun 1780, p.476. *£2,300 Current Money paid to Thomas Napier Esq. Escheator for Fluvanna Co. ... a Greeable to two Acts of Assembly passed in 1779 the one Intituld "an act Concerning Escheats and Forfeitures from British Subjects the other Intituld and act Concerning Escheators.* [Part of Capt. John Martin's 6,186 acs. Henrico Co. in PB 13 p.164]

PETER DAVID Ass'ee of PHILIP BEASLEY who was Ass'ee of RICHARD BALLARD SENR., 359 acs. by Survey 27 Sep 1773 in Pittsylvania Co. on both Sides of Bull Run of Black Water Riv.; adj. Haynes, Wilson & Henry Haynes; 26 Jun 1780, p.477. A.C. of 30 Shill. sterl.

FRANCIS AMOS, 218 acs. by Survey 12 Nov 1772 in Buckingham Co. on the S Brs. of the Middle fork of Slate Riv.; adj. his own Line & Nicholas Corners the sd Conners line; 24 Jun 1780, p.478. A.C. of 25 Shill. Sterl.

JAMES BURNETT, 157 acs. by Survey 19 Nov 1772 in Buckingham Co. on the W Brs. of Davids Cr., adj. his Own Lines & William Clerk; 26 Jun 1780, p.479. A.C. of 20 Shill. Sterl.

JOHN DICKINSON, 466 acs. by Survey 1 Dec 1778 in Henry Co. on the Cool Br. of black Water riv., down the Road that leads to Anthony Ford, adj. Cowans line; 26 Jun 1780, p.480. A.C. of £2.S10. Sterl.

FRANCIS AMOS, 300 acs. by Survey 12 Nov 1772 in Buckingham Co. on the Brs. of the Middle Fork of Slate Riv., adj. Nicholas Conner; 24 Jun 1780, p.481. A.C. of 30 Shill. sterl.

HUGH DIVER, 120 acs. by Survey 12 Mar 1749/50 in Rockingham Co. at the Lower end of a Great Meadow, Crossing Beaver Cr. to the Points of a hill & adj. the sd Divers L. & Silas Hart; 24 Jun 1780, p.482. A.C. of 15 Shill Sterl. **paid into the late Receiver Generals Office**.

WILLIAM GRAHAM ass'ee of CORNELIUS RUDDLE who was Ass'ee of JAMES CARR, 400 acs. by Survey 25 Nov 1771, in Augusta Co. adj. sd Kerrs old Survey, Thomas Stewart & Samuel Black; 25 Jun 1780, p.483. A.C. of 40 Shill. Sterl.

THOMAS WRIGHT Ass'ee of THOMAS HUGART Heir at Law of WILLIAM HUGART Dec'd, 1,000 acs. by Survey 14 Jun 1775 in Kentucky Co. on Licking Cr. a br. of the Ohio, adj. Land; 25 Jun 1780, p.484. *in Consideration of Military Service Performed by William Hugart as a Lieutenant in the late War between Great Britain and France according to the terms of the King of Great Britains Proclamation of 1763.*

JACOB RUBSAMAN Esquire, 400 acs. more or Less in the Town of Manchester and Chesterfield Co. bounded by the Lands of Richard James and the Lotts marked in the Plann of the sd Town Number 237, 225, 213, 201, 187, 188, 189, 202, 214, 226 and 239 and was lately the Property of William Cunningham & Co. and Sold by sd Jesse Cogbill unto sd Jacob Rubsamon; 25 Jun 1780, p.485. *£15,000 Current Money* *paid by Jacob Rubsaman Esq. to Jesse Cogbill Escheator for Chesterfield County ... a Greeable to two Acts of Assembly passed in 1779 the one Intutuld an act Concerning Escheats and forfeitures from British Subjects the other Intituld an Act Concerning Escheators.*

THOMAS OGLESBY ass'ee of sd WILLIAM PHELPS, 378 acs. by Survey 21 Aug 1771 in Buckingham Co. on the Small Brs. of the Fluvanna Riv. and Wreck Island Cr. and the Ridge between the Same in the Co. aforesd., Crossing Colemans Road; adj. Hancocks line where it Crosses a North Br. of sd Cr.; Christian & Mr Whitney; 25 Jun 1780, p.486. A.C. of 40 Shill. sterl.

JOHN WALLER, 335 acs. by Survey 1 Apr 1774 in Pittsylvania Co., Crossing a Br. of Sandy Cr.; adj. William Russell, Timothy Stamp, King, Robert Waller, Talley & sd Tallys New Survey; 26 Jun 1780, p.488. A.C. of 35 Shill. Sterl.

ARCHELUS HUGHES, 239 acs. by Survey 9 Dec 1773 in Henry Co. on the Brs. of the North fork of Mayo's Riv., adj. Gray; 6 Jun 1780, p.489. A.C. of 25 Shill. sterl.

JOHN JEFFERSON, 53 acs. by Survey 17 Nov 1772 in Cumberland Co. on the Brs. of Crooms Quarter Br.; adj. Alexander Trent, John Thomas, Job Thomas & sd John Jefferson; 5 Jun 1790, p.490. A.C. of 5 Shill. sterl.

EVAN LEE, 370 acs. by Survey 20 Feb 1756 in Albemarle Co. on both sides Fish Pond Cr.; adj. Thomas Sanders in a Flat near a Br., Valentine Allen, his own Line & Thomas Lee; 25 Jun 1780, p.491. A.C. of 40 Shill. sterl.

JOHN DUNCAN Ass'ee of BENJAMIN MEGGINSON who was Ass'ee of JOHN MERIMON who was Ass'ee of ROBERT WOODING (for whom the Survey was Originally made), 390 acs. by Survey 9 Oct 1747 in Buckingham Co. on both Sides of Horse Pen Cr. of Glover Cr.; 25 Jun 1780, p.492. A.C. of 40 Shill. sterl. [Adj. John Cox's PB 41 p.180]

WILLIAM INGLES, 1,000 acs. by Survey 18 Jul 1774 in Kentucky Co. on the Waters of Elkhorn Cr., Beginning on the S side of a North Br. of sd Cr., adj. John Drapur or Drapier; 25 Jun 1780, p.493. *in Consideration of the Military Service Performed by William Ingles as a Lieutenant in the late War Between Great Britain and France according to the Terms of the King of Great Britains Proclamation of 1763.*

SAMPSON & GEORGE MATHEWS and PATRICK LOCKHART, Ass'ee of WILLIAM PRESTON & WILLIAM THOMSON, Executors of the sd JAMES PATTON Dec'd, 64 acs. Botetourt Co. in a Bent of Craigs Cr., down the Cr. to the Mouth of a Gully; 27 Jun 1780, p.494. 10 Shill. Sterl. paid by Sampson and George Mathews and Patick Lockhart **paid unto the late Receiver Generals Office**. Whereas by Pat. under the Seal of the Colony and Dominion of Virginia 3 Nov 1750 Gtd. to James Patton Dec'd in Botetourt Co. (formerly Augusta) and Whereas George Tredley in Whom the Right and Title has Since become Vested has faild to pay the Quitrents that Were due thereon and William Preston and William Thomson Exrs. to the sd James Patton Decd. had before the late Revolution Petitioned the then President of the King of Great Britains Council of sd Colony and had Obtained a Grant for the sd 64 acs.

EPAPHRODITUS SYDNOR, 58 acs. by Survey 10 May 1769 in Halifax Co. on both Sides of Fall Cr.; adj. Bailey, Irby & McEndry; 27 Jun 1780, p.495. A.C. of 10 Shill. sterl.

WILLIAM OLIVER Ass'ee of WILLIAM DUNCAS, 100 acs. by Survey 13 Jan 1746/47 in Halifax Co. on the lower side of Childreys Cr.; 27 Jun 1780, p.496. A.C. of 10 Shill. sterl.

PETER FORD, 386 acs. by Survey 1 Mar 1749/50 in Buckingham Co. on the head of the Brs. of Hubboards Cr. a South Br. of Slate Riv., Crossing Glovers Road; adj. Peter Salley, Matthew Agus, Colo. Fry; 25 Jun 1780, p.497. A.C. of 4 Shill. sterl.

ISAAC DAVID Ass'ee of LUKE HUGGINGS, 192 acs. by Survey 2 Dec 1778 in Henry Co. on the Brs. of Bull Run; adj. Henry Hains, Richard Walden, Maxy & Haynes; 27 Jun 1780, p.498. A.C. of 20 Shill. sterl.

JOHN NEADHAM, 60 acs. by Survey 30 Oct 1770 in Augusta Co on the E Side of Smiths Cr.; 28 Jun 1780, p.499. A.C. of 10 Shill. sterl.

REUBEN HARRISON, 194 acs. by Survey 30 Oct 1770 in Augusta Co. on the W side of Smiths Cr.; 27 Jun 1780, p.501. A.C. of 20 Shill Sterl.

JAMES MONTGOMERY, 100 acs. by Survey 17 Jan 1762 in Botetourt Co. on the Lick run a Br. of the North fork of Roan Oak on the E Side of the Tract he lives on, his old Patent Line; 27 Jun 1780, p.502. A.C. of 10 Shill. sterl.

JAMES OAKS, 120 acs. by Survey 19 Oct 1763 in Pittsylvania Co. on both Sides Mountain Cr., adj. Kurkland; 27 Jun 1780, p.503. A.C. of 15 Shill.

PETER PERKINS, 67 acs. by Survey 14 Apr 1763 in Pittsylvania Co. on the County Line [West, the Country Line], adj. John Lankford & Perkins; 27 June 1780, p.504. A.C of 10 Shill. Sterl.

JOHN CHAPMAN, 59 acs. by Survey 1 Nov 1769 in Pittsylvania Co. on the head of the North fork of Buffaloe Cr., on the top of a Spur of the Main Mountain; 28 Jun 1780, p.504. A.C. 10 Shill. Sterl.

RICHARD FORREST, 400 acs. by Survey 15 Mar 1753 in Halifax Co. on the S Side Stanton Riv. and both sides Wenfords Cr.; adj. Booker, Talbott & sd John Guilintines former Line; 29 Jun 1780, p.505. A.C. of 40 Shill. Sterl.

WILLIAM GILL, SENIOR, 408 acs. by Survey 28 Apr 1772 in Mecklenburg Co. adj. his New Survey on the Waters of Arons Cr.; adj. his Line, Guin/Guinn, Shotwell & Taylor; 28 Jun 1780, p.507. A.C. of 45 Shill. sterl.

GILBERT HUNT, 347 acs. by <u>Inclusive Survey</u> made 23 Feb 1780 in Pittsylvania Co. on the Brs. of Stinking Riv.; adj. Benjamin Gudgens, Jones, Michael Farriss, Cheldress, Arthur Kesee & Benjamin Gradge; 28 Jun 1780, p.508. A.C. of 35 Shill. sterl.

ALEXANDER CHEZENHALL /CHITZENHALL, (by Survey) 200 acs. Halifax Co. on the N side of Bannister

Riv., adj. William Law & Smith; 25 Jun 1780, p.509. A.C. of 20 Shill. Sterl.

ROBERT CLOPTON Ass'ee of WILLIAM FORD who was Ass'ee of WILLIAM WATSON, 400 acs. by Survey 10 Mar 1750/51 in Pr. Edward Co. on the fork of Spring Cr., adj. Collins & Baldwin; 25 Jun 1780, p.510. A.C. of 40 Shill. sterl. paid by Robert Clopton **into the late Receiver Generals Office**.

THOMAS HUST, 400 acs. by Survey 30 Oct 1771 in Halifax Co. on the drafts of Aarons Cr. adj. the County Line/Country Line [West] & Tucker; 25 Jun 1780, p.511. A.C. of 40 Shill. Sterl.

WILLIAM GILL SENIOR, 400 acs. by Survey 28 Apr 1772 in Mecklenburg Co. on the Waters of Aarons Cr., in a Valley; adj. the County Line/Country Line [West], his own line & Guin; 29 Jun 1780, p.512. A.C. of 40 Shill. sterl.

WILLIAM GILL, 400 acs. by Survey 23 Oct 1771 in Halifax Co. on the Brs. of little Blue Wing, Crossing a Br. and Road; adj. Harbert Hawkins, John Childress & William Hawkins; 25 Jun 1780, p.513. A.C. of Shill. sterl.

JAMES TREDWAY, 400 acs. by Survey 30 Oct 1753 in Halifax Co. on both Sides of Brush Cr., Crossing two forks of sd Cr., adj. Thomas Dandy; 30 Jun 1780, p.514. A.C. of 40 Shill. sterl.

PRESBY HARRISON, 415 acs. by Survey 24 Oct 1770 in Halifax Co. on both sides and forks of Seths Br. of Hico, Crossing the North fork and South fork of sd Br., adj. Robert Hutchings; 30 Jun 1780, p.515. A.C. of 45 Shill. sterl.

ROBERT STEWART, 9½ acs. by Survey 17 Oct 1774 in Pr. Geo. Co. on the N side of Black Water Sw., to sd Stewarts Corner upon the Hill on the S side of the Great Road; adj. William Brown, Joseph Hardway & sd Stewart; 30 Jun 1780, p.516. A.C. of 5 Shill. sterl.

ROBERT JOHNSON Ass'ee of PATRICK HENRY who was Ass'ee of the sd JAMES CLARK, 2,000 acs. by Survey 8 Jul 1774 in Kentucky Co. on the North Br. of Kentucky Riv. Called Elkhorn Cr., on a rise, Crossing 3 Brs. and the Big Cr., Crossing the Small and large Cr. and a br.; adj. sd Henry Survey of 3,000 acs. & his own Land near a very large Buffaloe Road Crossing Place; 25 Jun 1780, p.517. *in Consideration of Military Service Performed by James Cla[r]k as a Lieutenant in the late War between Greets Britain and France according to the Terms of the King of Great Britains Proclamation of 1763.*

ANTHONY THOMPSON ass'ee of ROBERT JOHNSON ass'ee of PATRICK HENRY who was Ass'ee of the sd ~~JAMES~~ RICHARD OMOHUNDRO, 200 acs. by Survey 2 May 1774 in Kentucky Co. on the Ohio Riv. Opposite to the Mouth of Sciotto Riv., Beginning 200 Poles above sd Riv., Crossing a Draft, on the Point of a Ridge; 30 Jun 1780, p.518. *in Consideration of Military Service Performed by Richard Omohundro as Corporal in the late War between Great Britain & France According to the Terms of the King of Great Britains Proclamation of 1763.*

ANTHONY THOMPSON who was Ass'ee of PATRICK HENRY who was Ass'ee of sd FRANCIS DRAKE, 200 acs. by Survey 2 May 1774 in Kentucky Co.

on the Ohio Riv. joining and below the Survey made Opposite to the Mouth of Sioto Riv., Beginning on the River Bank Corner to the first Survey, on the Point of a Ridge, in a flat; 30 Jun 1780, p.519. *in Consideration of Military Service Performed by Francis Drake as a Corporal in the late War between Great Britain and France according to the Terms of the King of Great Britains Proclamation of 1763.*

PETER PERKINS, 240 acs. by Survey 16 Nov 1764 in Pittsylvania Co. on the Pond br. of Dan Riv.; adj. John Wilson, Charles Duncan, Henry Stone & Georg[e] Chadwell; 30 Jun 1780, p.520. A.C. of 25 Shill. sterl.

JAMES WILSON, 176 acs. by Survey 2 Feb 1769 in Pittsylvania Co. on Smiths Riv.; adj. his old line on sd Riv., Lomax & Webb; 30 Jun 1780, p.521. A.C. of 20 Shill. sterl.

RICHARD GWYN, 330 acs. by Survey 3 Aug 1773 in Pittsylvania Co. on the Brs. of Sandy Cr., adj. Kerby & Kennon; 25 Jun 1780, p.522. A.C. of 35 Shill. sterl.

WILLIAM WADLOW, 300 acs. by Survey 15 Nov 1764 in Pittsylvania Co. on Beens Cr., Crossing the Road; adj. Been, Chadwell & George Chadwell; 25 Jun 1780, p.523. A.C. of 30 Shill. sterl.

EDWARD GIVINS/GIVANS, 727 acs. by an Inclusive Survey 26 Mar 1770 in Pittsylvania Co. on the S side of Sandy Riv., on Rocky Br.; adj. Thomas Owen, Gammon & Watson; 25 Jun 1780, p.524. A.C. of £3.S15.

BERNARD RANDLE, 611¾ acs. by Survey 16 Mar 1773 in Brunswick Co., Beginning in the head of the saw Scaffold Br., on the N side of a Road; adj. John Randel, Carpenter, Woolster, James Hynton, John Adkins & Wheeler; 23 Jun 1780, p.525. A.C. of £3.S5. sterl. paid by Bernard Randle **into the late Receiver Generals Office**. being part [of] 700 acs. which was Gtd. by order of Councel to William Randle and Surveyed 20 Nov 1746.

JOSEPH DODSON, 195 acs. by Survey 5 Feb 1762 [Halifax Co.] on Jeremiah fork of Birches Cr., adj. John Davidson in the low grounds; 30 Jun 1780, p.526. A.C. of 20 Shill. sterl.

GEORGE SOUTHERLAND, 76 acs. by Survey 16 Mar 1770 in Pittsylvania Co. on the N side of Sandy Riv., adj. Walton & the sd Southe[r]land; 25 Jun 1780, p.527. A.C. of 10 Shill. sterl.

PETER PERKINS, 224 acs. by Survey 23 Mar 1770 in Pittsylvania Co. on Mountain Cr.; adj. sd Lankford, Payne & Harris; 25 Jun 1780, p.528. A.C. of 25 Shill.

WILLIAM GILL, SENIOR, 412 acs. by Survey 28 Apr 1772 in Mecklenburg Co. on the Waters of Arons Cr.; adj. his old lines, Stafford, Shotwell in a Meadow & sd Gills new Survey; 30 Jun 1780, p.529. A.C. of 45 Shill. sterl.

RICHARD GWINN, 3,800 acs. by Survey 11 Feb 1774 in Pittsylvania Co. on both sides of Cherry Stone Cr. and Harpin Cr., Crossing Jeffersons Road, up Pigg River Road; adj. Walton & George Peak; along the Order line; 1 Jul 1780, p.530. A.C. of £19 sterl.

PETER PERKINS ass'ee of THOMAS CARNALL who was Ass'ee of JOHN

MODSFIELD, 697 acs. by Survey 3 Nov 1774 in Pittsylvania Co. on the head Brs. of Sandy Cr.; adj. John Hall, Ashworth & Robert Adams; 1 Jul 1780, p.533. A.C. of £3.S10. sterl.

PETER WILSON, 131 acs. by Survey 26 Mar 1771 in Pittsylvania Co. on Rocky run; adj. Gammon, Owen & Givins or Gwins Lines; 3 Jun 1780, p.534. A.C. of 15 Shill. sterl.

WILLIAM HARRISON, 66 acs. by Survey 17 Mar 1779 in Pittsylvania Co. on the N Brs. of Dan Riv., crossing the double Cr., adj. William Wadlow & Harrison; 3 Jun 1780, p.535. A.C. of 10 Shill. sterl.

FRANCIS GILL Ass'ee of JOSEPH GILL, SENIOR, 395 acs. by Survey 2 Oct 1772 in Halifax Co. on the drafts of dry Cr. and Blue Wing; adj. Sizemore, sd Gills line & Clift; 3 Jun 1780, p.536. A.C. of 40 Shill.

CHARLES WOMACK Ass'ee of sd JOHN COX who was Ass'ee of RICHARD JONES who was Ass'ee of JOSEPH AUSTIN, 373 acs. by Survey 8 Dec 1752 in Halifax Co. on the Brs. of Sandy Cr.; 3 Jun 1780, p.537. for the A.C. of 40 Shill. Sterl. paid by Charles Womack into the Treasury of this Commonwealth. *Whereas by Pat. under the Seal of the Colony and Dominion of Virginia 15 Jul 1760 there was Gtd. to Richard Jones ass'ee of Joseph Austin 373 acs. in sd Co. which sd Tract or parcel of L. was Gtd. on Condition of the Payments of his Majestys Quitrents and of the making Cultivation and Improvements as in the sd Patent is Express'd and Whereas the sd Richard Jones in Whom the right and title of sd 373 acs. has since become Vested had fail'd to pay the Quitrents that were due thereon John Cox had before the late Revolution Petition'd the then President of the King of Great Britains Council and had obtained a G. for the sd 373 acs.*

PETE PERKINS, 110 acs. by Survey 23 Mar 1770 in Pittsylvania Co. on the drafts of Mountain Cr.; adj. sd Perkins Line near a Pond, John Lankford & the Country Line [East]; 31 Jun 1780, p.538. A.C. of 15 Shill. sterl.

DAVID BUCHELLOR, 400 acs. by Survey 13 Oct 1774 in Pittsylvania Co. on the Waters of Pigg Riv., Crossing Buck Br.; 3 Jul 1780, p.539. A.C. of 40 Shill. Sterl. [DAVID BUCHELLOR could be DAVID BACHELLOR. This scribe occasionally writes his letter a like a letter u]

JOSHUA HUDSON Ass'ee of RALPH SHELTON, 82 acs. by Survey 10 Nov 1776 in Henry Co. on the Brs. of the Mayo Riv. and Russells Cr., Beginning on the Ridge; 3 Jul 1780, p.540. A.C. of 10 Shill.

RICHARD GIVEN/GIVENS, 400 acs. by Survey 17 Jan 1763 in Halifax Co. on Panther Cr., Beginning at the lower end of a Meadow on sd Cr. side; Crossing the Timber fork, the Glady fork & a bold Br.; 3 Jul 1780, p.541. A.C. of 40 Shill. Sterl.

WILLIAM HARRISON, 344 acs. by Survey 14 Jun 1774 in Pittsylvania Co. on Mobberleys Cr.; adj. Hardeman, Perkins, Dunkin, York, Harrison, the same Harris [sic] & Hardyman; 21 Jun 1780, p.543. A.C. 35 Shill. sterl.

TULLY CHOICE, 153 acs. by Survey 14 Mar 1753 in Pittsylvania Co. on the draughts of Gutterys Run of Snow Cr., adj. his old line; 4 Jul 1780, p.544. A.C. of 15 Shill. sterl.

JOHN TUNLEY/TUNLY ass'ee of JAMES BEAVER, 145 acs. by Survey 3 Mar 1763 in Henry Co. on the Brs. of the Crab tree fork of Snow Cr., on the Spur of the Mountain, adj. Walker; 4 Jul 1780, p.545. A.C. of 15 Shill. sterl.

JOHN LENEAUE/LEENEVE & WILLIAM BOOKER, 338 acs. by Survey 25 Mar 1780 in Pr. Edward Co. on the W Brs. of Bryery Riv. and on the heads of the Brs. of Buffalow Riv.; adj. Brown, Andersons old lines & Halecombs old Corner in the read [road]; 4 Jul 1780, p.546. A.C. of 35 Shill. sterl.

WILLIAM YOUNG, 392 acs. by Survey 30 Mar 1775 in Pittsylvania Co. on the Brs. of Pigg Riv., Crossing Hungry Camp Br. & the Corner Br., adj. John Childs line; 4 Jul 1780, p.548. A.C. of 40 Shill. sterl.

WILLIAM YOUNG, 111 acs. by Survey 10 Apr 1765 in Halifax Co. on the drafts of Snow Cr., Crossing Harbour Br.; 4 Jul 1780, p.549. A.C. of 10 Shill. sterl.

JOHN SMITH, 185 acs. by Survey 12 Dec 1764 in Pittsylvania Co. on the long Br. of Bull run, Beginning near the head of sd fork; 4 Jul 1780, p.550. A.C. of 20 Shill. sterl.

WILLIAM YOUNG, 400 acs. by Survey 31 Mar 1775 in Pittsylvania Co. on the Brs. of Bigg Riv. [Pigg Riv.]; adj. his own, Richardson & Ephraim Witcher; 4 Jul 1780, p.551. A.C. of 40 Shill. sterl.

WILLIAM YOUNG, 279 acs. by Survey 20 Feb 1769 in Pittsylvania Co. on the first fork of Snow Cr., adj. sd Youngs line; 4 Jul 1780, p.552. A.C. of 30 Shill. sterl.

GARROT BIRCH, 412 acs. by Survey 3 Nov 1779 in Henry Co. on the dung Br. of Leatherwood Cr., adj. Lomax and Company; 4 Jul 1780 *in the 4th year of the Commonwealth*, p.553. A.C. of 45 Shill. Sterl.

ROBERT STOCKTON, 172 acs. by Survey 27 Mar 1769 in Henry Co. on the Waters of Smiths Riv., adj. his old line; 5 Jul 1780 *in the 5th year of the Commonwealth*, p.554. A.C. of 20 Shill. sterl.

DAVID CLARKSON, 146 acs. by Survey 28 Sep 1773 in Pittsylvania Co. on the Brs. of Bull Run; adj. William Haynes, Richard Ballard & Wilson; 4 Jul 1780, p.555. A.C. of 15 Shill. sterl.

DAVID ROGERS, 322 acs. by Survey 16 Mar 1768 in Pittsylvania Co. on Rossels Cr. [Russels Cr.], Crossing the North fork of sd Cr.; 5 Jul 1780, p.556. A.C. of 40 Shill. sterl.

JOHN PARR, 105 acs. by Survey 30 Mar 1768 in Pittsylvania Co. on the Meadowry Cr.; 3 Jul 1780, p.557. A.C. of 15 Shill. Sterl.

MARGARET BROWN Ass'ee of JAMES BROWN, 200 acs. by Survey 10 Mar 1775 in Bedford Co. on Camping run of Linvels Cr., *Part of a large Survey made for William Mead by Isham Talbot*; Beginning at a Poplar of sd Camp and run; 5 Jul 1780, p.559. A.C. of 20 Shill. sterl.

REUBEN NANCE, 182 acs. by Survey 20 Nov 1765 in Henry Co. on the draughts of Leathe[r]wood Cr., adj. Terry; 4 Jul 1780, p.560. A.C. of 20 Shill. sterl.

EDWARD WATTS Ass'ee of GEORGE SIMMONS, 309 acs. by Survey 14 Dec 1762 in Bedford Co. on the S side of Stanton Riv., Beginning on the Riv. at a Clift of Rocks; 5 Jul 1780, p.561. A.C. of 35 Shill. sterl.

THOMAS SOWELL ass'ee of GEORGE THOMPSON, 48 acs. by Survey 7 Feb 1778 in Fluvanna Co., near a ridge Path; adj. John Moore, the sd Thompsons Line, the sd Thompsons Barnet Line, the sd Thompson Barnet, John Thompson & Baine; 5 Jul 1780, p.562. A.C. of 5 Shill. sterl.

SUSANNA REYNOLDS Ass'ee of JACOB CODGAR, 38 acs. by Survey 24 Apr 1754 in Henry Co. on the N Side of the South Br. of the North Br. of Mayo Riv., Crossing a fork of the Same; 5 Jul 1780, p.563. A.C. of 5 Shill. sterl.

JOSEPH MOTLEY, 400 acs. by Survey 14 Mar 1747/48 in Pittsylvania Co. on the S side of Shocco Cr.; 5 Jul 1780, p.564. A.C. of 40 Shill. sterl.

THOMAS SOWELL ass'ee of GEO. THOMPSON, 70 acs. by Survey 4 Nov 1775 in Fluvanna Co. on the N side of the Rivanna Riv. and on the Waters thereof, to the Church Road, to Hardens road; adj. John Strange, John Moore, Leonard Thompson & Benjamin Maddox; 5 Jul 1780, p.565. A.C. of 10 Shill. sterl.

ABSALOM McCLANAHAN Ass'ee of WILLIAM BUFORD who was Ass'ee of HENRY SMITH, 91 acs. by Survey 7 May 1770 in Bedford Co. on the head Brs. of Otter Riv.; 5 Jul 1780, p.566. A.C. of 10 Shill. sterl.

MARK COLE, 245 acs. by Survey 11 Dec 1753 in Bedford Co. on the little Cr.; 4 Jul 1780, p.567. A.C. of 25 Shill. sterl.

JAMES LEWIS, 129 acs. by Survey 16 Mar 1772 in Bedford Co. on the Brs. of Magotty Cr., adj. George Johnson; 5 Jul 1780, p.568. A.C. of 15 Shill. sterl.

PETER HOLLAND, 121 acs. by Survey 11 Apr 1770 in Bedford Co. on the N Side of Black Water Riv.; 5 Jul 1780, p.569. A.C. of 15 Shill. sterl.

WILLIAM BABER, 224 acs. by Survey 9 Mar 1770 in Pittsylvania Co. on the Waters of Stanton Riv., Crossing the Great Br.; 5 Jul 1780, p.570. A.C. of 25 Shill. sterl.

STEPHEN HEARD, 254 acs. by Survey 8 Dec 1778 in Henry Co. on the Brs. of Black Water Riv., to a Post oak near a Ridd [Ridge?]; adj. Mead, Ward, & Witton and Company; 5 Jul 1780, p.571. A.C. of 25 Shill. sterl.

AGUILLA GREAR, 400 acs. by Survey 16 Apr 1754 in Pittsylvania Co. on both sides of Bull Cr. of Black Water Riv., adj. John Gilmore; 5 Jul 1780, p.572. A.C. of 40 Shill. sterl.

MARK COLE, 328 acs. by Survey 11 Dec 1753 in Bedford Co. on both Sides a Br. of little Cr.; 5 Jul 1780, p.573. A.C. of 30 Shill. sterl.

JOHN GILL Ass'ee of JOHN EWING, 53 acs. by Survey 9 May 1770 in Bedford Co. on McFalls Mountain, by a Path, up

Gap Br., adj. Clark; 6 Jul 1780, p.574. A.C. of 5 Shill. sterl.

THOMAS DUMOSS, 194 acs. by Survey 1 May 1771 in Bedford Co. on the Brs. of Gills Cr.; 6 Jul 1780, p.576. A.C. of 20 Shill. sterl.

JOSEPH SIMMONS, 380 acs. by Survey 12 Mar 1775 in Bedford Co. on the little linvel Cr., on a new Road, Crossing 2 forks of sd Linvell Cr., adj. Mead; 6 Jul 1780, p.577. A.C. of 40 Shill. sterl.

WILLIAM BOARD, 390 acs. by Survey 7 Mar 1775 in Bedford Co. on Prathers Run, on Linvell Mountain, adj. Calloway; 6 Jul 1780, p.578. A.C. of 40 Shill. sterl.

RICHARD HATCHER Ass'ee of HENRY HAYNES, 192 acs. by Survey 29 Oct 1771 in Bedford Co. on the Brs. of Craddocks Cr. a North Br. of Stanton Riv., adj. Stephen Hail; 6 Jul 1780, p.579. A.C. of 20 Shill. sterl.

RICHARD BROWN, 80 acs. by Survey 14 Mar 1774 in Bedford Co. on the Brs. of Magotty Cr.; adj. Wright, Ray & Randolph; 6 Jul 1780, p.580. A.C. of 10 Shill. sterl.

JOEL MEADOR, 140 acs. by Survey 5 Mar 1775 in Bedford Co., by the sd Road; adj. Mead, Talbot/Talbott, Bradshaw, Meador, Holland & Calloway; 6 Jul 1780, p.581. A.C. of 15 Shill. sterl.

JOHN WALTON, 160 acs. by Survey 8 Mar 1774 in Bedford Co. on Griffiths Cr., adj. George Griffith; 5 Jul 1780, p.582. A.C. of 20 Shill sterl.

RICHARD KELLO, 1,070 acs. by Survey 14 Dec 1764 in Nottoway Par. Southampton Co. on the N Side of Round Hill Sw., Beginning at the Mouth of Cabben Br. on sd Sw., in the Head of the Cabbin br., in the Reedy Br.; adj. Moses Phillips, Hartwell Phillips, Stephen Simmons, Henry Brown & Robert Exum; 7 Jul 1780, p.583. £6 Sterl. paid by Richard Kello. 125 acs. part thereof was part of a Pat. formerly Gtd. to William Exum 5 Sep 1723 [Is. of Wight Co. PB 11, p.248], 100 acs. other part thereof part of a Pat. Gtd. to one John Ingram 12 Feb 1742/43 [200 acs. Is. of Wight Co. PB 20, p.460], 100 acs. other part thereof is part of a Pat. of 200 acs. Gtd. to John Branch [Is. of Wight Co. PB 11, p.167 dated 18 Feb 1722/23], 390 acs. other Part thereof was Gtd. to Joseph Exum by Pat. 20 May 1734 [Is. of Wight Co. PB 15, p.233 dated 25 May 1734], which sd Tract or Parcel of Land by Divers Conveyances and Since become Vested in the sd Richard Kello and 355 acs. the Residue Never before Gtd.

RICHARD WALDEN, 530 acs. by Survey 14 Feb 1775 in Pittsylvania Co. on the Brs. of Stanton Riv., Crossing Jaspers Cr., adj. Ward; 5 Jul 1780, p.586. A.C. of 15 Shill. sterl.

THOMAS PATTON, 96 acs. by Survey 30 Jan 1773 in Bedford Co. on the Lick Run; adj. Austin, Adams, Thompson & his own line; 6 Jul 1780, p.587. A.C. of 10 Shill. sterl.

ALLEN CONNER, 50 acs. by Survey 17 Jan 1775 in Bedford Co. on the E Side of Falling Riv., adj. Thomas Rafferty; 6 Jul 1780, p.588. A.C. of 5 Shill. sterl.

ANN WILL/WITT, 230 acs. by Survey 10 Oct 1777 in Bedford Co. on the Mouth of Island Cr. on the S Side of

Otter Riv., adj. White & Walton; 8 Jul 1780, p.589. A.C. of 25 Shill. sterl. [Included with William Mead's 200 acs. in GB B p.397 as part of William Irvine's 430 acs. in GB 32 p.248 dated 26 May 1795]

JOHN McDANIEL, 176 acs. by Survey 15 Dec 1772 in Bedford Co. on both Sides of Back br. of flat Cr., along the Church road, adj. his own line; 5 Jul 1780, p.590. A.C. of 20 Shill. Sterl.

CHARLES WYNN, 614 acs. by Survey 6 Mar 1771 in Pittsylvania Co. on the Waters of Rutledges Cr., with the County Line/Country Line [East]; adj. Mr Million [McMillion?], Wynn, Stellwell & Mr Hoone; 8 Jul 1780, p.591. A.C. of £3.S5 sterl.

JOHN SMALL Ass'ee of DARBY RION Heir at Law to AARVIEL RION Dec'd, 340 acs. by Survey 6 Nov 1753 in Halifax Co. on both Sides of Gills Cr., down the Haw br.; 6 Jul 1780, p.593. 30 Shill. sterl.

SAMUEL HAIRSTON, 249 acs. by Survey 18 Dec 1754 in Bedford Co. on both Sides bever Cr., adj. his own Line at a heap of Stones; 6 Jul 1780, p.594. A.C. of 25 Shill. sterl.

ELIPHAZ SHELTON, 846 acs. Inclusive by Survey 30 Oct 1783 in Henry Co. on Bull Mountain fork of Mayo Riv.; 6 Jul 1780, p.595. A.C. of £4.S5 sterl.

WALTER POOLE Ass'ee of JOHN TAYLOR DUKE, 440 acs. by Survey 22 Apr. 1749 in Mecklenburg Co. on the brs. of flatt Cr.; adj. Larkes line, Beaver, Duke, Poole, Taply & Roberson; 10 Jul 1780, p.597. A.C. of 45 Shill. sterl. paid by Walter Pooles **unto the late Receiver Generals Office**.

JOHN WILLIAMSON, 172 acs. by Survey 15 Oct 1772 in Mecklenburg Co. on the head brs. of Bever Pond, on a Ridge; adj. his own lines, Plunkett, Newton, William Taylor & Archibald Clark; 10 Jul 1780, p.598. A.C. of 20 Shill. sterl. **into the late Receiver Generals Office**.

JOEL MEADOR, 400 acs. by Survey 10 Dec 17__ in Bedford Co. on Indian Run, adj. Talbot & Dun; 7 Jul 1780, p.599. A.C. of 40 Shill. Sterl.

MARK COLE, 300 acs. by Survey 12 Dec 1753 in Bedford Co. on both sides of little Back Cr. and both sides the Back run, Beginning where James Coles line Crosses little Cr.; 8 Jul 1780, p.600. A.C. of 30 Shill. Sterl.

ROBERT HAIRSTON, 428 acs. by Survey 8 Nov 1773 in Pittsylvania Co. on Runnett Bagg Cr. and Otter Cr., adj. Peters old line; 6 Jul 1780, p.601. A.C. of 50 Shill. sterl.

ABRAHAM WARWICK, 385 acs. by Survey 15 Mar 1780 in Amherst Co. on the North Ruckers run, with the Pat. lines, to a Stake in John Buches field; 6 Jul 1780, p.603. *£1,000 Current Money of Virginia paid unto David Shepherd Gent. Escheator for Amherst Co. by Abraham Warwick ... being part of a large tract lately the Property of John Harmer a British Subject and was Sold by the sd David Shepherd Escheator unto the sd Abraham Warwick a Greeable to two Acts of Assembly passed in 1779 the one Intituld "an Act Concerning Escheats and forfeitures from British*

Subjects the other Intituld "an Act Concerning Escheators.

JAMES PRENTY, 232 acs. by Survey 2 Sep 1779 in Henry Co. on the Brs. of Grassy fork of Snow Cr.; adj. Bradshaws now Rions Line, Randolph, Smith, Stegal, Lawrence, & Ryons new line; 7 Jul 1780, p.604. A.C. 25 Shill. sterl.

WILLIAM HIX, 225 acs. by Survey 15 Apr 1774 in Bedford Co. on lick run a North Br. of Stanton Riv., adj. Meador & Mead; 7 Jul 1780, p.605. A.C. of 25 Shill. sterl.

THOMAS FARLOW, 327 acs. by Survey 13 Apr 1778 in Bedford Co. on the S Side of black Water Riv., adj. Clay; 8 Jun 1780, p.606. A.C. of 35 Shill. sterl.

JAMES SEAL, 165 acs by Survey 14 May 1767 in Halifax Co. on the Brs. of the lower double Cr.; adj. Nash, Timothy Stamp, William Russell & William Payne; 18 May 1780, p.607. A.C. of 15 Shill.

LEWIS HANSFORD & ROBERT TAYLOR, 4 Certain Lotts or parcel of Land Containing half an acres Each in Is. of Wight Co. and in the town of Smithfield Laid down [in] a platt of the sd town Number 47, 48, 62 & 63; 12 Jul 1780, p.608. *£16,000 Current Money of Virginia paid unto Samuel Hardy Gent. Escheator for Is. of Wight Co. by Lewis Hansford and Robert Taylor ... which sd lotts or half Acres was lately the Property of Andrew Symm & Co. British Subjects and was Sold by sd Samuel Hardy Escheator aforesd Unto sd Lewis Hansford & Robert Taylor A Greeable to two acts of assembly passed in 1779, the one Intituld "an Act Concerning Escheats and Forfeitures from British Subjects the other Intituld "an act Concerning Escheators.*

JOHN TAYLOR, one unImproved Lott or parcel of L. Containing half an acre in Is. of Wight Co. and in the town of Smith field Laid down in the plann of the sd town No. 30; 12 Jul 1780, p.609. ~~Ancient Composition~~ *Sum of £204 Current Money of Virginia paid unto Samuel Hardy Gentleman Escheator for Is. of Wight Co. ... which sd Lott or half acre was lately the Property of Messrs. John Heyndman and Company British Subjects and was Sold by the sd Samuel [Hardy] Escheator for aforesd Co. unto the sd John Taylor A Greeable to two Acts of Assembly passed in 1779 the one Intituld an act Concerning Escheats and forfeitures from British Subjects the other Intituld an act Concerning Escheators.*

THOMAS KING, one Certain Uni[m]proved Lott or parcel of L. Containing half an acre in Is. of Wight Co. and in the town of Smithfield Laid down in the platt of the said Town No. __; 12 Jul 1780, p.610. *£150 Current Money of Virginia paid unto Samuel Hardy Gent. Escheator for Is. of Wight Co. by Thomas King of Is. of Wight Co. ... which sd Lott or half acres was lately the Property of Messrs. Hunter & Blair British Subjects and was Sold by the sd Samuel Hardy Escheator as aforesd unto the sd Thomas King agreeable to two acts of Assembly passed in 1779 the one Intituld "an act Concerning Escheats & Forfeitures from British Subjects the other Intituld "an act Concerning Escheators.*

JOSEPH CHAPMAN, one Lott Unimproved or parcel of L. Containing half an acre in Isle of Wight Co. and in the town of Smith field Laid down in the Platt of sd town Number 29; 12 Jul 1780, p.611. *£112 Current Money of Virginia paid unto Samuel Hardy Gent. Escheator for Is. of Wight Co. by Joseph Chapman ... which sd Lott or half acre was late the property of Messrs. Hyndman & Co. British Subjects and was Sold by sd Samuel Hardy Escheator as aforesd unto the sd Joseph Chapman a Greeable to two acts of Assemby passed in 1779 the one Intituld "an act Concerning Escheats and Forfeitures from British Subjects the other Intituld "an act Concerning Escheators.*

ANDREW MACKIE, 400 acs. Is. of Wight Co. bounded on one side of the Lands of George Purdie and on the other side by Lands of William Davis and James Day; 12 Jul 1780, p.612. *£36,000 Current Money of Virginia paid Unto Samuel Hardy Gent. Escheator for Is. of Wight Co. by Andrew Mackie ... which sd L. was Lately the Property of John Goodrich British Subject and was Sold by the sd Samuel Hardy Escheator as aforesd unto the sd Andrew Mackie a Greeable to two Acts of Assembly passed in 1779, the one Intituld an act Concerning Escheats and Forfeitures from British Subjects the other Intituld an act Concerning Escheators.*

GEORGE PURDIE, Two Certain Lotts or parcels of Lands Containing half an Acre Each in Is. of Wight Co. and in the town of Smith field Laid down in a Platt of the sd Town No. 12, and 65; 12 Jul 1780, p.613. *£2,257 Current Money of Virginia paid by George Purdie unto Samuel Hardy Gent. Escheator for Is. of Wight Co. ... which sd Lotts or half Acres of L. was the Property of John Hyndman British Subjects and was Sold by sd Samuel Hardy Escheator as aforesd unto the sd George Purdie agreeable to two acts of Assembly passed in 1779, the one Intituld "an Act Concerning Escheats and forfeitures from British Subjects the other Intituld an act Concerning Escheators.* also 400 aces. in sd Co. [bounded as followeth, to Wit, Beginning at a Marked Pine the E side of the Miry Branch near the dwellings house thence by a Line of Marked trees SExE 76 Poles to a Gum Stand[ing] in a Branch of Gualtney Swamp thence down the sd Branch NNE 132 Poles to Gua[l]tney Swamp thence down the sd Swamp to the Mouth of Wicks Branch SExE 40 Poles thence up Wicks Branch SSW 166 Poles to a hickory thence up the sd Branch WSW 34 Poles a white oak thence NW 16 Poles to a Small Branch thence down the sd Branch North 46 Poles to a red oak a Corner tree thence West half North 40 Poles to a red oak Corner tree on the Cart Path on Char[l]es Chapmans line thence SW 80 Poles along the Cart Path by Marked trees on Chapmans line thence WxS 222P by Marked trees on Edward Goodricks line thence West 146 Poles By Marked trees in sd Goodricks line to small Gum a Corner thence NW 30 Poles to a Corner tree in Arther Davises line thence NE 78P to Bleakes line to Penny lain road a Corner thence North along Penny lane Road 100 Poles to a Gum a Corner tree Near the head of the long Branch thence down the Various Courses of the sd Branch about ExS and ESE 144 Poles thence along the sd branch about NExE 212 Poles to Gautley Swamp thence about SExE 40 Poles to the Mouth of Miry Branch thence South 78 Poles up the sd Branch to the Beginning]

MILES WELLS of Is. of Wight Co., one Unimproved Lott or parcel of L. Containing half an Acres in sd Co. and on the Town of Smith field laid down in a Platt of sd Town Number 20; 12 Jul 1780, p.615. £250 Current Money of Virginia paid unto Samuel Hardy Gent. Escheator for Is. of Wight Co. ... which sd Lott or half Acres was lately the Property of Messrs. Ozwald & Co. British Subjects & was Sold by sd Samuel Hardy Escheator for the Co. aforesd. unto the sd Miles Walls [sic] aGreeable to two acts of Assembly Passed in 1779 the one Intituld "an act Concerning Escheats and forfeitures from British Subjects the other Intituld an act Concerning Escheators.

THOMAS KING of Is. of Wight Co., 2 Certain Lotts & houses cr parcel of Land Containing half an acre Each in sd Co. and in the town of Smith-field Laid down in the Platt of sd Town No. 67 & 68; 12 Jul 1780, p.616. £7,090 Current Money of Virginia paid unto Samuel Hardy Gent. Escheator for Is. of Wight Co. ... which sd Lotts or parcels of L. was lately the Property of Messers. Ozwald & Co. British Subjects and was sold by sd Samuel Hardy Escheator as aforesd unto sd Thomas King AGreeable to two Acts of Assembly Passed in 1779 the one Intutuld an act Concerning Escheats and forfeitures from British Subjects the other Intuld an act Concerning Escheators.

WOODY BURGE, 100 acs. by Survey 2 Nov 1770 in Pittsylvania Co. on the Brs. of Peters Cr., adj. the old line; 8 Jul 1780, p.617. A.C. of 10 Shill. sterl. [with its Appurtenances to the sd **Boody Burg** and his Heirs for Ever]

HENRY MOBERRY/MARBERRY /MARBRY, 254 acs. by Survey 7 Apr 1775 in Bedford Co. on the Brs. of Otter Riv., Beginning 8 Chains from McClanahans Corner in Pleasants line; adj. Capt. Ewing, Marbry & Pleasant; 12 Jul 1780, p.618. A.C. of 15 Shill. sterl.

LEONARD DELOSURE Ass'ee of BENJAMIN DUNCAN, 131 acs. by Survey 6 Nov 1778 [**Pittsylvania Co.**] on the N Brs. of Tomahock Cr., Crossing Buck Horn Br.; adj. George Smith, James Smith & John Ball; 8 Jul 1780, p.619. A.C. of 15 Shill. sterl.

GEORGE GADDY, 320 acs. by Survey 1 Mar 1771 in Bedford Co. on the Head Brs. of Ivey Cr. on the sides Spurs and top of Flemings Mountain; adj. Nicholas Davis, Anthony & [sd] Davies; 8 Jul 1780, p.620. A.C. of 35 Shill. sterl.

WILLIAM LIPSCOMB ass'ee of JOHN PRICE, 26 acs. by Survey 14 Apr 1752 in Louisa Co. on Both Sides of Rockey Cr.; adj. John Ross, sd Price & Ragland; 8 Jul 1780, p.622. A.C. of 5 Shill. sterl.

WILLIAM MEAD, WILLIAM AUSTIN & ISHAM TALBOT, 294 acs. by Survey 19 Nov 1770 in Pittsylvania Co. on Bare Br., to a Cucumber tree on the Cory Br.; 8 Jul 1780, p.622a. 30 Shill. sterl.

JAMES LYON, 216 acs. by Survey 16 Mar 1768 in Pittsylvania Co. on the North fork of Rossells Cr. [Russells Cr.]; 5 Jul 1780, p.624. A.C. of 25 Shill. sterl.

JOHN KENDRICK, 393 acs. by Survey 12 Nov 1768 in Pittsylvania Co. on Buffaloe Cr., adj. his own lines & Thomas Huff; 8 Jul 1780, p.625. A.C. of 40 Shill. sterl.

ALEXANDER BELL, 400 acs. by Survey 25 Nov 1779 in Norfolk Co., along the Road, adj. James Wilson Dec'd; 13 Jul 1780, p.627. A.C. of 40 Shill. Sterl.

ALEXANDER BELL, 243 acs. by Survey 24 Nov 1779 in Norfolk Co.; 13 Jul 1780, p.627. A.C. of 25 Shill. sterl.

JOHN COLLIAR, 336 acs. by Survey 15 Nov 1779 in Henry Co. on the Brs. of Fishing fork of Leatherwood Cr.; adj. the sd Gravley, and Lomax & Co.; 13 Jul 1780, p.629. A.C. of 35 Shill.

SAMUEL COX & WILLIAM HICKINBOTTOM, 402 acs. by Survey __ Apr 1763 in Halifax Co. on Both Sides Dan Riv., at the foot of the Mountain; 14 Jul 1780, p.630. A.C. of 40 Shill. sterl.

JOHN FOX ass'ee of RICHARD GWYNN, 330 acs. by Survey 3 Aug 1773 in Pittsylvania Co. on the Waters of Sandy Cr., adj. John Kerby & Kennon; 14 Jul 1780, p.631. A.C. of 35 Shill. sterl.

JOHN SADLER Ass'ee of BENJAMIN FITZPATRICK, 400 acs. by Survey 29 Jan 1778 in Fluvanna Co. on Rays Br., adj. P. Napier; 14 Jul 1780, p.632. A.C. of 40 Shill. sterl.

JAMES MAMURDY, 263 acs. by Survey 2 Nov 1762 in Halifax Co. on the Brs. of White oak, to the School House Spring, adj. his former line & Watkins; 7 Jun 1780 in the *4th year of the Commonwealth*, p.633. A.C. of 30 Shill. sterl.

STANHOPE EVANS, 350 acs. by Survey 25 Jan 1769 in Amherst Co. on both sides of Johns Br. a North Br. of Buffaloe Riv., on the North Bank of sd Riv., Beginning at Thomas Corner [Thomas Evans?]; adj. James Freeland, John Fry & Thomas Evans; 14 Jul 1780 in the 5th year of the Commonwealth, p.634, p.635 & p.638. A.C. of 35 Shill. sterl. **into the late Receiver Generals Office**. [The Scribe skipped p.636 & p.637]

JOHN FOX ass'ee of RICHARD GWYNN, 400 acs. by Survey 3 Aug 1773 in Pittsylvania Co. on the Brs. of Sandy Cr., adj. his own line & Kennon; 14 Jul 1780, p.638. A.C. of 40 Shill. sterl.

THOMAS ANDERSON of Dinwiddie, 400 acs. by Survey 1 Dec 1778 in Bedford Co. on the E side of Falling Riv., Beginning near the River Bank at the first Sharp bent above the great Buffaloe foard, adj. Thomas Rodgers & his own line; 14 Jul 1780, p.639. A.C. of 40 Shill. Sterl.

ANTHONY MURRAY Ass'ee of JOHN MURRAY Eldest son and Heir of RICHARD MURRAY Dec'd, 380 acs. by Survey 28 Mar 1764 in Buckingham Co. amongst the Br. of Georges Cr. in the sd Country, adj. Colo. Peter Jefferson Dec'd; 14 Jul 1780, p.640. A.C. of 40 Shill. sterl.

NATHANIEL COCKE Ass'ee of BURWELL GRANT who was Ass'ee of DAVID GRANT, 24 acs. by Survey 27 May 1771 in Halifax Co. on the Brs. of Difficult Cr.; adj. Daniel Wall, Colo. Richard Cocke & John Wall; 14 Jul 1780, p.641. A.C. of 5 Shill. sterl.

HUGH DIVER Ass'ee of JOSEPH BAILEY, 185 acs. by Survey 4 Jul 1773 in Augusta Co. on the E side of black thorn, on a Ridge, adj. Mark Swaldley's or Swadley's Survey & James Hoggs l.; 14 Jul 1780, p.642. A.C. of 20 Shill. sterl.

JOHN DENTON, 19¼ acs. by Survey 18 Apr 1780 in Fluvanna Co. on little Mechunk Cr.; adj. Denton, Allegree & Pleasant; 14 Jul 1780, p 643. A.C. of 5 Shill. sterl.

HUGH INNIS Ass'ee of FRANCIS BUCKNALL, 235 acs. by Survey 26 Apr 1768 in Pittsylvania Co. on James Daniels Mill Cr., adj. Peter Copland Gent. & James Daniel; 14 Jul 1780, p.644. A.C. of 25 Shill. sterl.

DAVID MOSBY DAVIDSON, 112 acs. by Survey 2 Nov 1778 in Bedford Co. on the N side of Seneca Cr. on both sides of Buck-horn Br.; 14 Jul 1780, p.645. A.C of 15 Shill. sterl.

JOSEPH MOTLEY, Gent., 330 acs. by Survey 2 Feb 1774 in Pittsylvania Co. on Shoco Cr.; adj. Terrys order Line, McDaniel, Embry, Calloway & Woodson; 14 Jul 1780, p.646. A.C. of 35 Shill. sterl.

AUGUSTINE BROWN, 324 acs. by Survey 7 Dec 1773 in Henry Co. on Brs. of Peters Cr. & Russells Cr., adj. Jonathan Hansby; 14 Jul 1780, p.647. A.C. of 35 Shill. sterl.

THOMAS DODSON son and Heir at Law of JOSEPH DODSON Dec'd Ass'ee of TIMOTHY STAMPS, 370 acs. by Survey 14 May 1767 in Halifax Co. on the Brs. of the lower Double Creeks; adj. Nash, William Russel, Carter & Wilson; 15 Jul 1780, p.649. A.C. 40 Shill. sterl.

[Margin note: *This Grant was made out when Thos. Jefferson was Governor: he Resignd before it was signd or Seald which is Altered in the name of Benj. Harrison 20th. Augt. 1783*]
RICHARD STITH, 1,400 acs. by an **Inclusive Survey** 25 Mar 1779 in Bedford Co. on Mulberry Cr. and on other East Brs. of Falling Riv., near narrow Passage Br.; adj. John Stap, Dinwiddie, Edward Pharis, Jonas Payne, Read, Goode & Stapp; 20 Aug 1783 in the *8th year of the Commonwealth*, Benjamin Harrison Esquire Governor, p.650. A.C. of £7 sterling. **320 acs. part thereof was Survey'd 20 Jan 1764 William Harris also 420 acs. part thereof was Surveyed for William Harris 9 Apr 1767 the Right of Which is since become Vested in the sd Richard Stith and 666 acs. the Residue Never before Survey'd.**

EDWARD RICHARDS, 230 acs. by Survey 12 Apr 1779 in Henry Co. on the North fork of Chesnut Cr.; adj. Warrain, James Smith, Mason & Archer; 15 Jul 1780, p.652. A.C. of 25 Shill. sterl.

PETER JOHNSON, 246 acs. by Survey 22 Jan 1772 in Pr. Edward Co. on the South fork of Rough Cr., Crossing the County Road Several times, adj. William Black; 15 Jul 1780, p.654. A.C. of 25 Shill. sterl.

GEORGE RUNNOLDS, 200 acs. by Survey 9 Nov 1779 in Henry Co. on the Waters of Muster Br. of Leatherwood Cr., adj. his own line formerly Murrills; 15 Jul 1780, p.655. A.C. of 20 Shill. sterl.

MICHAEL DUNN, 120 acs. by Survey 17 Dec 1778 in Henry Co. on the Brs. of

Snow Cr., Beginning at the head of a Meadow of Black run, Crossing the forks of Guttery run, Crossing Back run, adj. Richard Varnon or Vamon; 14 Jul 1780, p.656. A.C. of 15 Shill. sterl.

DAVID CRENSHAW ass'ee of DAVID PARISH, 238 acs. by Survey 21 Nov 1779 in Goochland Co. along Paynes Road; adj. John Thruston, Paul Mechum, David Parish, David Martin, David Davis, William Prossett & Stephen Davis; 14 Jul 1780, p.658. *£900 Current Money of Virginia paid unto William Harrison Gent. Escheator for Goochland Co. by David Crenshaw David Parish ... being part of a larger tract lately the Property of Jarvis Elam a British Subject and was sold by sd William Harrison Escheator as aforesd unto the sd David Parish A Greeable to two acts of Assembly Passed in 1779 the one Intituld "an act Concerning Escheats and forfeitures from British Subjects the other Intituld "an act Concerning Escheators.*

WILLIAM STROTHER MADISON ass'ee of WILLIAM PRESTON who was ass'ee of HENRY SMITH, 180 acs. by Survey 8 Apr 1773 in Botetourt Co., Beginning on the S side of Paint Bank Valley under Caravans Nob, on the head of a Hollow, on the foot of the Mountain, near a Spring; 15 Jul 1780, p.659. A.C. of 20 Shill. sterl.

WILLIAM STROTHER MADISON Ass'ee of WILLIAM PRESTON who was ass'ee of HENRY SMITH, 24 acs. by Survey 4 Oct 1772 in Botetourt Co. on Potts Cr. a Br. of James Riv., Beginning at a Great Rock Corner to the land of the sd Henry Smith bought of Preston, Crossing the Paid run, leaving Land or Caving Land to a Spanish oak on a hill; 15 Jul 1780, p.660. A.C. of 5 Shill. sterl.

ANTHONY MURRAY ass'ee of JOHN MURRAY Eldest son and Heir at Law to RICHARD MURRAY, 183 acs. by Survey 12 Apr 1765 in Buckingham Co. on the Brs. between little & Great Georges Creeks, adj. Thomas Ballow & his own Line; 15 Jul 1780, p.661. A.C. of 20 Shill. sterl.

THOMAS MAXWELL Ass'ee of sd JOHN GILLIAM, 200 acs. by Survey 17 Nov 1775 in Kentucky Co. on a Cr. which Emptys into the Kentucky about 8 Miles above Boonsborough on the N side, to 2 Sugar trees on a Point, to 2 box elders on the Cr., up the Kentucky Riv., to 2 Sugar trees and a Cherry tree at the foot of a ridge by a draft; 15 Jul 1780, p.663. *in Consideration of Military Service performed by John Gilliam in the late War between Great Britain & France according to the terms of the King of Great Britains Proclamation of 1763.*

THOMAS MAXWELL Ass'ee of sd JOHN GILLIAM, 200 acs. by Survey 18 Nov 1775 in Kentucky Co. on a Cr. which Emptys into the Kentucky on the N side about 8 Miles above Boonsborough, Beginning on the E side the Cr. above a Great Bent, on a flat ridge; 15 Jul 1780, p.664. *in Consideration of Military Service performed by John Gilliam in the late War between Great Britain & France according to the terms of the King of Great Britains Proclamation of 1763.*

RICHARD RANDOLPH, 34 acs. by Survey 10 Mar 1779 in Cumberland Co. on a Br. of Appomatox Riv., near the

Sandy ford of Appamattox Riv., adj. James Anderson & sd Randolph; 15 Jul 1780, p.665. A.C. of 5 Shill. sterl.

CHARLES NUCKLES, 149 acs. by Survey 18 Apr 1774 in Amherst Co. on the Head Br. of Manalys Br. and the Blue ridge, on the Top of the Blue Ridge; adj. Main Burges, William Colborth, John Pannel, David Manaley & William Calbreth; 14 Jul 1780, p.566. A.C. of 15 Shill. Sterl.

TULLY CHOICE, 147 acs. by Survey 5 Mar 1762 in Henry Co. on the fork of Guttery run, Crossing Guttery fork; adj. Hard, Confrey, Tully Choice & Heard; 14 Jul 1780, p.668. A.C. of 15 Shill. sterl.

JOSEPH GRAUBY/GRAULY, 196 acs. by Survey 15 Nov 1779 in Henry Co. on the Grassy fork of the fishing fork of Leatherwood Cr.; adj. his own line, Lomax & Co. [their line], & Akinses line; 14 Jul 1780, p.669. A.C. of 20 Shill. sterl.

WALTER LAMB, 800 acs. by Survey 13 May 1779 in Pittsylvania Co. on the Brs. of Bearskin & on both sides of Keiheys road, up the lick Br.; adj. William Pigg, Hutchings & Bynum; 14 Jul 1780, p.670. A.C. of £4 sterl.

JOHN ELLIS, 407 acs. by Survey 27 Nov 1778 in Henry Co. on the Brs. of Bull run, Jacks Cr. and Tinkey Cr.; adj. John Smith; 14 Jul 1780, p.672. A.C. of £2.S5 sterl.

WILLIAM RYON, 202 acs. by Survey 2 Sep 1779 in Henry Co. on the Brs. of the Grassy fork of Snow Cr., adj. Bradshaw, the sd Ryons own line; 14 Jul 1780, p.673. A.C. of 20 Shill. sterl.

PETER JOHNSTON ass'ee of CHARLES LELBA, 400 acs. by Survey 12 Jan 1773 in Pr. Edward Co. on both Sides of Rough Cr. & on the head Brs. of Sawneys Cr.; adj. James Blacks line, Absolom Fears's line, Stills or Hills line & Patrick Bains line; 14 Jul 1780, p.674. A.C. of 40 Shill. sterl.

JOHN HUGAR/HARGER/HARGAR, 152 acs. by Survey 13 Apr 1779 in Henry Co. on the Waters of the North fork of Chesnut Cr.; adj. Richards line, James Calloway, Mason & Smith; 14 Jul 1780, p.675. A.C. of 15 Shill. sterl.

SAMUEL PHELPS Ass'ee of WILLIAM CHANDLER, 500 acs. by Survey 28 Apr 1752 in Lunenburg Co. on the head of Owl Cr. and Juniper Cr.; adj. Isbell, Hawkins, Pledger, Petty & Jones; 14 Jul 1780, p.677. A.C. of 50 Shill. sterl.

WILLIAM STROTHER MADISON ass'ee of WILLIAM PRESTON who was ass'ee of HENRY SMITH, 268 acs. by Survey 20 Oct 1772 in Botetourt Co. on Potters Cr. a Br. of James Riv., Beginning on the N side of the Cr. by a Glade, by a Gully, by a Draft, along the hill side, adj. the Lands of sd Henry Smith Bought of Preston; 14 Jul 1780, p.678. A.C. of 30 Shill. sterl.

WILLIAM PRESTON Ass'ee of JOHN FLOYD, 250 acs. by Survey 13 Sep 1772 in Botetourt Co. on Potters Cr. a Br. of James Riv., Beginning at a Poplar and Mahogany on the S side of the South fork of the Cr., on a Ridge, adj. Preston; 15 Jul 1780, p.679. A.C. of 25 Shill. sterl.

ROBERT JOHNSTON/JOHNSON, 125 acs. by Survey 9 Dec 1771 in Amherst Co. on the Brs. of Horsleys Cr.; adj.

Rederick McCullock, David Crawford & Lunsford Lamax [Lomax]; 17 Jul 1780, p.680. A.C. of 15 Shill. sterl.

JOHN PETER BONDURANT Ass'ee of PETER BONDURANT, 1,125 acs. by Survey 16 Oct 1755 in Albemarle Co. on the head Brs. of Sharps Cr. [of Slate Riv. now in Buckingham Co.], Crossing Howards road, adj. William Baber; 17 Jul 1780, p.682. A.C. of £5.S15. sterl.

ROBERT JOHNSON, 197 acs. by Survey 8 May 1771 in Amherst Co. on both sides of Peggs Cr. on the Brs. of Thomas's Mill Cr.; adj. William Floyd, Hugh Morris, his own lines & David Davenport; 17 Jul 1780, p.683. 20 Shill. Sterl.

DAVID BELL, 113 acs. by Survey 7 July 1773 in Augusta Co. on the Brs. of the West fork of Black Thorn above Trimbles Survey, to a Bunch of Maples by a Spring; 12 Jan 1780 *in the 4th year of the Commonwealth In Witness whereof the sd Thomas Jefferson Esquire Governor of the Commonwealth of Virginia hath hereunto Set his Hand and Caused the Seal of the sd Commonwealth to be affixed at Williamsburgh*, p.684. A.C. of 10 Shill. [Margin note: **Recorded at Page 254**. [This is a duplicate of his grant on p.254]

Examined Pr. Saml. McCraw.

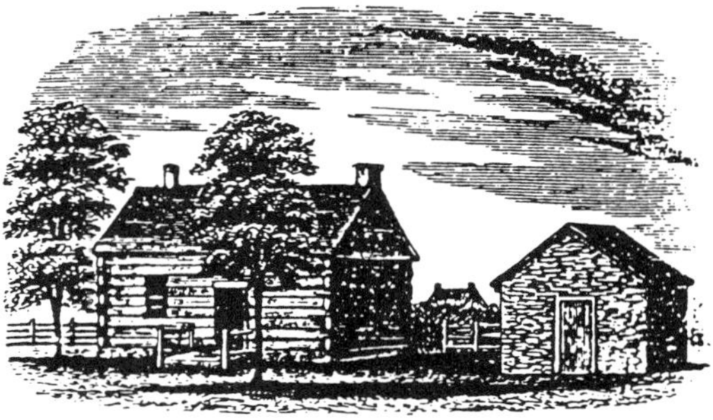

GRANT BOOK B

26 Oct 1779 to 20 July 1780

JACOB CHANEY, 354 acs. Pittsylvania Co. on burches Cr., down Cuthe Cr., crossing buck horn br., adj. Parish & Owen; 26 Oct 1779 *in the 4th year of the Commonwealth, Thomas Jefferson Esq. Governor of the Commonwealth of Virginia Hath hereunto Set his hand and Caused the Seal of the sd Commonwealth to be Affixd. at Williamsburg*, p.1. A.C. of 35 Shill. Sterl. [The number 56879 is at the top and bottom of this grant]

THOMAS & SWENKFIELD HILL, Executores & legatees of ROBT. HILL Dec'd, 468 acs. Henry Co. on the meadow br., crossing a Spring br.; adj. Hill, *the Grassy Hill Company* [their line], Easley or Earley, Callaway, & Swenkfield Hill; 8 Nov 1779, p.1. 50 Shill. Sterl.

JOSEPH AKIN, 154 acs. Hallifax Co. on the brs. of burches Cr.; adj. John Noble, Edmundsen, Hickey & Carter; 8 Nov. 1779, p.2. 15 Shill. Sterl.

HENRY JONES, 152 acs. Pittsylvania Co. on the brs. of Pigg Riv., crossing [Inak] run; adj. James Rentfroe, Isaac Jones & Jacob Brillemon; 8 Nov 1779, p.2. 15 Shill. Sterl.

THOMAS HUTCHINGS & THOMAS JONES, [97] acs. Pittsylvania Co. on the waters of Pigg riv., in the fork of br., adj. Isaac Jones; 8 Nov 1779, p.3. A.C. of 10 Shill. Sterl.

DANIEL SPANGLER Ass'ee of PETER VERDEMAN, 30 acs. in Henry Co. Crossing Pigg Riv., adj. his own line, to a Mahoggany [tree]; 8 Nov 1779, p.3. 5 Shill. Sterl.

WILLIAM MAVITY Ass'ee of WILLIAM McVIATY, 193 acs. Henry Co. on the South fork of Pigg riv., adj. Thomas Hutchings; 8 Nov 1779, p.4. A.C. of 20 Shill. Sterl.

JOHN HUFF, 82 acs. Henry Co. on the South fork of Pigg riv.; adj. James

Rentroe, Huff & Thomas Jones; 8 Nov 1779, p.4. A.C. of 10 Shill. Sterl.

THOMAS HAIL, 50 acs. Pittsylvania Co. on Pigg riv.; adj. Verdeman, Jones & Vardeman; 10 Nov 1779, p.5. A.C. of 5 Shill. Sterl.

DARBY RION, 54 acs. Pittsylvania Co. on the Waters of Pigg Riv.; adj. his Old line, Turpin & Jones; 10 Nov 1779, p.5. A.C. of 5 Shill. Sterl.

THOMAS & SWENFIELD HILL Executors and legatees of ROBERT HILL Dec'd, 378 acs. Henry Co. on the meadow br. and on McDowels br.; 10 Nov 1779, p.6. A.C. 40 Shill. Sterl.

WILLIAM MENIFEE, 212 acs. Henry Co. on both Sides Pigg riv., in a meadow, adj. Callaway; 10 Nov 1779, p.6. A.C. 25 Shill. Sterl.

THOMAS HAIL Ass'ee of WILLIAM YOUNG, 75 acs. Henry Co. on both sides of Pigg Riv.; 10 Nov 1779, p.7. A.C. of 10 Shill. Sterl.

HENRY JONES, 230 acs. Hallifax Co. on the brs. of Pigg riv., crossing Haw br. & Cow br., adj. sd Jones; 10 Nov 1779, p.7. A.C. of 25 Shill. Sterl.

JOHN WILSON, 176 acs. Henry Co. Adj. his Own land he now lives on, on the South fork of black Water riv.; 10 Nov 1779, p.8. 20 Shill. Sterl.

DARBY RION Ass'ee of DANIEL RION, 162 acs. Henry Co., on both Sides of Otter Cr.; 10 Nov 1779, p.8. A.C. of 20 Shill. Sterl.

JAMES POTEETE, 422 acs. Henry Co. on the brs. of Poplar Camp Cr., Crossing Smith Riv.; adj. Rentfroe, & Daniel Rion; 10 Nov 1779, p.9. A.C. of 45 Shill. Sterl.

GEORGE HEARD, 250 acs. Henry Co. on Simmons Cr., on a Ridge; adj. Heards old line, Wittens Order line [his line], & Ward; **to a Grey Rock Mark'd J D 1779**; 10 Nov 1779, p.9. A.C. of 25 Shill. Sterl. [Note: The adj. land may have been surveyed in 1779 by surveyor with initials J.D.; also see Stephen Hierd's 93 acs. Pittsylvania Co. on Timber Ridge in PB 39 p.333]

WILLIAM CANNADAY, 108 acs. Henry Co. / Pittsylvania Co. on riconnet bag Cr., in the fork of the Cr. at the foot of a mountain thence along the Sd Mountain; 10 Nov 1779, p.10. A.C. of 15 Shill. Sterl.

DANIEL SPANGLER, 84 acs. Henry Co. on the brs. of black Water, adj. James Rentfroe & Joseph Byrd; 8 Nov 1779, p.10. A.C. of 10 Shill. Sterl.

JOHN KEMP, 172 acs. Pittsylvania Co. now Henry Co. on the S Side of black water riv., Crossing Camp br., adj. Guin; 10 Nov 1779, p.11. A.C. of 35 Shill. Sterl.

JOHN FUSON, 329 acs. Pittsylvania Co. on Stag Cr.; 10 Nov 1779, p.11. A.C. of 35 Shill. Sterl.

JOHN SUTHERLIN, 215 acs. Pittsylvania Co. on the brs. of Sandy riv., adj. Bostick, Murras, Dillon & Walton; 31 Oct 1779, p.12. A.C. of 25 Shill. Sterl.

JOHN ASHBY, 1,000 acs. Kentucky Co. on the head brs. of bear Grass Cr. a br. of the Ohio, adj. Himbeecher; 10 Nov 1779, p.12. *In consideration of Military Service performed by John Ashby During the late War between Grrat Brittain and France According to the terms of the King of Great Brittains proclamation of 1763.*

JOHN ASHBY, 2,000 acs. Kentucky Co. on the N side of the Kentucky a br. of the Ohio, adj. Hancocke Taylor; 10 Nov 1779, p.13. *In consideration of Military Service performed by John Ashby in the late war between Great Brittain and France according to the terms of the King of Great Brittains proclamation of 1763.*

JOHN SMITH, 573 acs. Pittsylvania Co. on both sides Stewarts Cr. of Sandy Cr.; adj. Barnet Macollough, the sd Macolloug, Joseph Cunningham, sd Johns Smiths former line & James Fulton; 31 Oct 1779, p.13. A.C. of £3 Sterl.

JOHN BOWMAN, ISAAC HITE, ABRAHAM BOWMAN & JOSEPH BOWMAN Ass'ees of the Sd PHILLIP LOVE, 2,000 acs., in Kentuckey Co. on Elk horn Cr., Crossing the main Cr., adj. William Peachy; 10 Oct 1779, p.13. *In consideration of Military Service performed by Phillip Love according to the King of Great Brittains proclamation of 1763.*

WILLIAM PHILLIPS, 3,000 acs. in Kentuckey Co. on the brs. of Elk horn Cr. a North br. of the Kentucky Riv. about 90 Miles from the Ohio Riv. and on the S Side thereof, Beginning at 2 Elms near a Draft Corner to William Prestons land; 17 Oct 1779, p.14. *In consideration of Military Service performed by William Phillips according* *to the terms of the King of Great Brittains proclamation of 1763.*

WILLIAM YOUNG, 250 acs. Henry Co. on Coles Cr. and black water riv., adj. Capt. Dodgett; 10 Nov 1779, p.14. A.C. of 25 Shill. Sterl.

JOHN RAMSEY, 113 acs. Pittsylvania now Henry Co. on Chesnut Cr., crossing a bent of sd Cr., adj. his own line; 10 Oct 1779, p.15. A.C. of 15 Shill. Sterl.

WILLIAM MARRABLE Ass'ee of GARDINER GREEN, 86 acs. by Survey made 30 Apr 1772 in Mecklenburg Co. on the Waters of Buffala; adj. Taylor, John Westmorland, Griffin & Green; 10 Nov 1779, p.15. A.C. of 10 Shill. Sterl.

JOSEPH WALTON, 200 acs. by Survey 17 Dec 1751 in Fluvanna Co. on both Sides bremore Cr. in the fork of James Riv., adj. Good; 10 Nov 1779, p.15. 20 Shill. Sterl.

JOHN SMITH, 153 acs. Pittsylvania Co. on both sides Sandy Riv., adj. John Smith & Cunningham; 31 Oct 1779, p.16. A.C. of 15 Shill.

MARTIN PICKETT ass'ee of sd JOHN LAWSON, 1,000 acs. Kentuckey Co. on the Ohio Riv., Beginning at the mouth of the gut on the bank of the Riv. about 16 Miles below the mouth of the Kentuckey Riv.; 10 Nov 1779, p.16. *In consideration of Military Service performed by John Lawson in the late War between Great Brittain and France according to the terms of the King of Great Brittains proclamation of 1763.*

LEWIS JINKINGS, 335 acs. Henry Co. on Turkey Cr. a North br. of Pigg Riv., down Jacks Cr.; adj. Stegal, & Jenkings line formerly Grays; 10 Nov 1779, p.17. A.C. 35 Shill. Sterl.

ABRAHAM CAMPELL, 250 acs. Pittsylvania Co. on the S brs. of banister Riv.; adj. Walthers line, John Donalson, & Lucks line; 10 Nov 1779, p.17. A.C. of 25 Shill. Sterl.

DAVID PREWITT, 255 acs. by Survey 9 Jan 1764 in Pittsylvania Co. now Henry Co. on both Sides of Camp br. of Snow Cr., adj. William Heard; 10 Nov 1779, p.17. A.C. of 30 Shill. Sterl.

NORTON DICKENSON, 204 acs. Pittsylvania Co. on the brs. of bearskin Cr.; adj. Adkinson & Hughes; to a post white oak in a ruff; 10 Nov 1779, p.18. A.C. of 20 Shill. Sterl.

LEWIS WILLIAMS, 302 acs. Pittsylvania Co. on both Sides of the Head brs. of banister Riv.; adj. Dixan, James Dixen; 10 Nov 1779, p.18. A.C. of 30 Shill. Sterl.

JOHN WILLIS, 391 acs. Henry Co. on the Waters of Hatchet Run; adj. Hill, Willis's other Survey of this Date, and Early & Callaway their line; 10 Nov 1779, p.18. A.C. of 40 Shill. Sterl.

DAVID HUNT, 400 acs. Pittsylvania Co. on the brs. of Straight Stone Cr., adj. James Hunt & Zechariah Wood; 10 Nov 1779, p.19. A.C. of 40 Shill. Sterl.

PETER HOGG ass'ee of HUGH MURPHIE, 317 acs. Augusta Co. on South Mill Cr. a br. of the South br. of Potomack above Woods land; 10 Nov 1779, p.19. A.C. of 35 Shill. Sterl.

WILLIAM McCLELLON, 30 acs. Augusta Co. on a br. of loones Mill Cr., by a Spring, in a Hollow, in a Draught under a Steep Ridge, adj. John McClellon; 10 Nov 1779, p.19. A.C. of 5 Shill. Sterl.

CHARLES WINDHAM, 140 acs. on the S Side of the main black water Sw.; p.20. 15 Shill. Sterl. [This grant was also cancelled after being entered in GB A p.162. The land was in Surry Co., now Sussex Co., on the Black Sw.]

JOSEPH BOLING / BOWLING, 264 acs. Henry Co. on the head of Chesnut Cr. a br. of town Cr., crossing Coles Road, adj. John Donelson; 10 Nov 1779, p.20. A.C. of 30 Shill. Sterl.

THOMAS READ, 370 acs. Charlotte Co. on the N side of Staunton Riv., adj. Johnathan Vermon, James McDavid & Israel Pickins; 12 Nov 1779, p.21. In consideration of the A.C. of 40 Shill. Sterliing paid by Sd Thomas Read into the treasury of this Commonwealth. *whereas by pat. under the Seal of the Colony and Dominion of Virginia bearing Date 1 Mar 1743/44 there was gtd. to William Kennon Junior and Richard Kennon 31,700 in Charlotte Co. formerly Lunenburg [Brunswick Co. PB 23 p.647] which was Granted on Condition of the payment of the Quitrants and of making the Cultivation and Improvements in the said patent Express'd and whereas Richard Treadway in whom the Right and title of 376 acs. part has Since become Vested, had fail'd to pay the Quitrance that were due thereon and Thomas Read had before the late Revolution petitioned the then President of the King of Great Brittains Council of the Said Colony, and had obtained a G. for the Said 376 acs.* [Also see David Caldwell's 1,026 acs. Lunenburgh Co. in PB 34 p.562 & 355 acs. in PB 36 p.578 and James Martin's 137 acs. Charlotte Co. in PB 39 p.397, all part of the 31,700 acs.]

JOHN DICKENSON, 206 acs. Henry Co. on both Sides of Pigg Riv.; 10 Nov 1779, p.21. 25 Shill. Sterl.

JAMES McCLUNG Ass'ee of ROBERT SHAW, 37 acs. Augusta Co. on the Waters of little mary Cr. a br. of James Riv., Crossing a Draught to three Chesnuts on the bank of a deep draught; 10 Nov 1779, p.21. A.C. of 5 Shill. Sterl.

WILLIAM DUVAL, 180 acs. Amherst Co. on the brs. of Lyme Kiln Cr.; adj. James Christian, Henry Bell, Larkin Gatewood & his own line; 10 Nov 1779, p.22. A.C. of 20 Shill. Sterl.

DUDLEY GLASS, 400 acs. Halifax Co. on both Sides of Cow Cr., crossing a br. and the Cr. to the Draughts of bush Cr.; adj. Peter Trible & Isaac Pyne; 18 Oct 1779, p.23. A.C. of 40 Shill. Sterl.

THOMAS DILLARD, JUNIOR, 383 acs. Pittsylvania Co. on Deans br. of Staunton Riv.; 10 Nov 1779, p.23. A.C. of 40 Shill. Sterl.

JAMES MOORE JUNR., 130 acs. Botetourt Co. on a br. of loones Mill Cr. being a br. of James Riv., beginning near his pat. line, near Andrew Woods line; 10 Nov 1779, p.23. A.C. of 15 Shill. Sterl.

THOMAS HAIL, 52 acs. Henry Co. on a br. of Pigg Riv. adj. the land he now lines on; also adj. Early & Callaway; 10 Nov 1779, p.23. A.C. of 5 Shill.

THOMAS BLACK, 318 acs. Henry Co. on Snow Cr. crossing a road; adj. the land he now lives on, William Young & Finney; 10 Nov 1779, p.24. A.C. of 35 Shill. Sterl.

ESUM HANNAN Ass'ee of JOHN BOWMAN, 88 acs. Bottetourt Co. on the waters of roan oak, in a Field; adj. the land of Colo. David Stewart & the tract Sd. Boman lives on; 10 Nov 1779, p.24. A.C. of 10 Shill. Sterl.

JAMES MARTIN, 375 acs. Henry Co. on the brs. of Chesnut Cr., on Coles Road, adj. David Haley; 10 Nov 1779, p.25. A.C. of 40 Shill. Sterl.

ROBERT SHAW, 220 acs. Rockbridge Co. on a Steep bank near the river, in the mouth of a draught, to a Spring; adj. Williamson, Wilson, & Shaws old line; 10 Nov 1779, p.25. A.C. of 25 Shill. Sterl.

ESUM HANNAN Ass'ee of JOHN BOWMAN, 61 acs. Botetourt Co. on Mudlick br. the Water of Roanoak, Beginning in or near to the tract he lives on, to a Spurr, adj. Stewarts land; 10 Nov 1779, p.26. A.C. of 10 Shill. Sterl.

JOHN LOVE, 212 acs. Botetourt Co. between the Said Love and the Brushey Mountain, adj. his line & William Bryan Junr; 10 Nov 1779, p.26. A.C. of 25 Shill. Sterl.

WILLIAM P. PEACHEY, 1,000 acs. in Kentuckey Co. on the Ohio River; adj. Hancok Eustace about 1,541 poles above the mouth of Bear Grass Cr. & David

Robinsons line; 12 Nov 1779, p.27. In consideration of Military Service perform'd by William Peachey in the late Warr between Great Brittain and France according to the terms of Great Brittains proclamation of 1763.

JUDITH GRIFFIN, Daughter of the Said LERAY GRIFFIN Deceas'd, 2,000 acs. in Kentuckey Co. on the Ohio river, about 18 or 20 Miles from the falls; 12 Nov 1779, p.27. In consideration of Military Service perform'd by Leray Griffin in the late warr between Great Brittain and France according to the terms of the King of Great Brittains proclamation of 1763. Beginning at an Ash by two large Rocks by the river Side, two miles below the point of the third Island above the falls and leaving the river S38E 130Poles Crossing two branches to five ash trees near harrods Creek and up Crossing the draughts thereof N30E 630Poles crossing a branch to two ash trees and one Sugar tree near a branch of the sd Creek thence N40W 470Poles to a Lyn ash and Sugar tree at the head of a Gulley in the fork of a branch and Down the Same to the River Opposite the Island, then down the River according to its meanders 640Poles to the first Station

AMOSE RICHARDSON, 292 acs. Henry Co. on the Grassey fork of Snow Cr. and on both Sides thereof; adj. his owns, an Old line & Randolph; 12 Nov 1779, p.28. A.C. of 30 Shill. Sterl.

JOHN PENN Ass'ee of JOSEPH LYELL, 350 acs. Pittsylvania Co. on both Sides of a br. of Cherry Stone Cr., Crossing a large br.; adj. Thomas Hodges, Rigney & Right; 16 Nov 1779, p.28. A.C. of 35 Shill.

JOHN DICKENSON, 650 acs. Henry Co. on the South fork of Story Cr.; adj. Luke Standefer, Smith, James Standefer Junior & [Wreek]s line; 16 Nov 1779, p.29. A.C. £3.S10 Sterl.

JOHN LANE, 400 acs. Bedford Co. on the E Side of the South fork of falling riv. including the mouth of Bull run; adj. Staples, John Wood & Brook; 16 Nov 1779, p.29. A.C. of 40 Shill. Sterl.

THOMAS HODGES/HOGES, 335 acs. Pittsylvania Co. on the brs. of bear Skin Cr.; adj. Edmund Hoges on the road, Emmerson & his Exrs.; 16 Nov 1779, p.30. A.C. of 35 Shill. Sterl.

THOMAS HICKERSON, 342 acs. Henry Co. on Mountain Cr. of Pigg riv., at the road; adj. Coatney Broyles, Heard & Broles; 16 Nov 1779, p.31. A.C. of 35 Shill. Sterl. [Also see Richard Witton's Pittsylvania Co. PB 42 p.642 on Mountain Cr.]

PETER WILSON, 374 acs. Pittsylvania Co. on the N side of white walnut Cr.; adj. William Wilson, Jacob Dean & John Wilson Gent.; 2 Nov 1779, p.31. A.C. of 40 Shill. Sterl.

JOHN SMITH, 327 acs. Pittsylvania Co. on the S brs. of Sandy riv.; adj. Joseph Cunningham, Stell, his old line & his new lines; 20 Oct 1779, p.32. A.C. of £1.S15 Shill. Sterl.

EDMUND HOGES, 365 acs. Pittsylvania Co. on the brs. of bear skin Cr., in a meadow, Crossing the road; adj. sd Hoges former line, Gorman & Mr Cinsey; 2 Nov 1779, p.33. A.C. of 40 Shill. Sterl.

WILLIAM McCLELLON, 97 acs. Botetourt Co. on Loone's mill Cr. a br. of James riv.; 2 Nov 1779, p.34. A.C. of 10 Shill. Sterl.

JAMES TURPIN, 100 acs. Henry Co. on the brs. of black Water and Pigg riv., together with 118 acs. before Surveyed by Thomas Hutchings Containing in the Whole 218 acs.; adj. his former Corner on Hatchett run, Tolbots/Tolbuts line, Heltons or Meltons line, & the Said [Dewerse or Duverse?] line; 2 Nov 1779, p.35. A.C. of 25 Shill. Sterl.

ROBERT ERVING ass'ee of CALEB ERVING, 370 acs. Bedford Co. on the N brs. of Goose Cr.; adj. Beard, Cary, Read & Bunch; 2 Nov 1779, p.36. A.C. of 40 Shill. Sterl.

ROBERT PEDIGON, 362 acs. Henry Co. on the brs. of Reed Cr.; adj. Gordan, Innes & Copland; 2 Nov 1779, p.37. A.C. of 40 Shill. Sterl.

RICHARD ADKINS, 266 acs. Pittsylvania Co. on both sides of bareskin Cr., adj. Owen Adkins; 2 Nov 1779, p.38. A.C. of 30 Shill. Sterl.

JOHN PARSONS, 284 acs. Pittsylvania Co. on the S brs. of Tomahauk Cr., adj. Pat Marham; 2 Nov 1779, p.39. A.C. of 30 Shill. Sterl.

HUGH DONOGHO, 1,227 acs. Augusta Co. on both sides of naked Cr. a br. of the North riv. of Shanando, by a Gulley, by a road; adj. Robert McCutchan, John King, John Seawright, sd Donogho's old line, Gawan Leeper, John McMahan & William Blayr; 10 Nov 1779, p.40. A.C. of £6.S5. sterl. *including a tract of 230 acs. part thereof included in a pat. Gtd. to John Seawright 26 Apr 1742, and another part thereof included in a pat. gtd. to James Leeper 12 Jul 1746, which afterwards became vested in the sd Donogho and one tract of 23 acs. first Gtd. to sd Hugh Donogho by pat. 14 Jul 1769 and also one tract of 116 acs. Gtd. to sd Donogho by pat. 1 Aug 1772 the remaining 400 acs. with 250 adjoining thereto, new and unpatented lands the* **inclusive** *Courses of the whole are bounded as follows [etc.]*

[Margin note: *James Robertson Examined done in the other Book*] [This is a repeat of GB A, p.150]
JAMES ROBERTSON, by survey 28 Jan 1767, 184 acs. Augusta Co. on the South fork of Roanoak riv., along the foot of the Hill to the bottom; 10 Nov 1779, p.43. A.C. of 20 [Shill.]

ISRAEL STANDIFER, 230 acs. Henry Co. on Standifers Cr. a br. of black water Riv., adj. his own line; 10 Nov 1779, p.44. A.C. of 25 Shill. Sterl.

JOHN HARTWEL/HARTWELL, 209 acs. Henry Co. on the N side of Pigg riv. on Robertsons br., adj. Robertson & Callaway; 10 Nov 1779, p.45. A.C. of 25 Shill. sterl.

WILLIAM PEACHY, 2,000 acs. Kentucky Co. in the fork of the Junction of the Ohio & the Kentucky Rivers, Beginning at a beech and Sugar tree on the bank of the Ohio Corner to William Christians land; 10 Nov 1779, p.46. *In consideration of Military Service perform'd by William Peachy as a feild officer in the late warr between Great Brittain & France acording to the terms of the King of Great Brittains proclamation of 1763.*

WILLIAM PEACHY, 2,000 acs. Kentucky Co. on elk horn Cr., adj. Phillip Love; 10 Nov 1779, p.47. *In consideration of Military service performed by William Peachy as a fiel'd officer in the late warr between Great Brittain and France according to the terms of the King of Great Brittains proclamation of 1763.*

SAMUEL McDOWEL, 2,000 acs. Kentucky Co. by survey dated 11 Jul 1775, on the waters of Elk horn Cr. a br. of the Kentucky; 10 Nov 1779, p.48. *In consideration of Military Service perform'd by Samuel McDowel inthe late war between Great Brittain and France according to the terms of the King of great Brittains proclamation of 1763.*

JAMES SOUTHALL, Ass'ee of Sd JOHN HICKMAN, by Survey 13 Jul 1774, 1,000 acs. Kentucky Co. on the N side of Kentucky riv. a br. of the Ohio; adj. at letter A. the SW corner of the Hon; William Byrds land & the NW Corner of Capt. Robert McKenzie at letter C.; 10 Nov 1779, p.49. *In consideration of Military Service perform'd by John Hickman in the late war between great brittain and France according to the terms of the king of Great Brittains proclamation of 1763.*

WILLIAM SUTTON Ass'ee of Sd WILLIAM HENRY, 1,000 acs. Kentucky Co. on the waters of Elk horn Cr. a North br. of Kentucky riv. about 85 miles from the Ohio and on the S Side of the Same, Beginning on the bank of a Small Cr., adj. John Floy'd & Patrick Henry; 10 Nov 1779, p.50. *In consideration of Military service perform'd by William Henry in the late war between Great Brittain and france according to the terms of the king of Great Brittains proclamation of 1763.*

SWINKFIELD HILL, 186 acs. Henry Co. on Pigg Riv., adj. Hills old line & Bates; 10 Nov 1779, p.51. A.C. of 20 Shill. Sterl.

JAMES McCORKLE ass'ee of DANIEL TRIGG who was Ass'ee of sd JOHN BLAGG, by survery 3 Jun 1774 in Kentucky Co. formerly Fincastle on the waters of bearGrass Cr. a br. of the Ohio riv. on the S side of the same; Beginning at at Mulberry, Sugar tree, and Honey Locust, Corner to the land of Alexander Waugh, Finnie and Charleton 800 poles form the Ohio River 1½ miles above the falls; with a line of Finnie & Charleton; crossing a br. of the North fork of the cr. and a br. of the south fork of sd cr.; Crossing the south fork of the Cr. 3 times to a flat ridge; Crossing a br. and the cr. to opposite to & 20 poles from Waugh's corner; 27 Nov 1779, p.52. *In consideration of Military service perform'd by John Blagg in the late war between the king of Great Brittain and France according to the terms of the King of Great Brittains proclamation of 1763.*

JAMES SOUTHALL Ass'ee of Sd JOHN HICKMAN, by survey 13 Jul 1774, 1,000 acs. Kentucky Co. on the N side the Kentucky riv. a br. of the Ohio; adj. another tract of land at the letter A. & the letter & C.; 27 Nov 1779, p.53. *in consideration of military service performed by John Hickman in the late war between Great Brigtain and France according to the terms of the king of Great Brittains proclamation of 1763.*

WILLIAM FORD Ass'ee of JOHN MANN who was Ass'ee of HENRY MARTIN who was ass'ee of DANIEL McRAE, by survey 10 Mar 1777, 380 acs. Albemarle Co. on the S side the Rivanna riv. and on the brs. of Adran's [Adrian's] and Burks creeks, to a long br., to the new road; adj. Henry Martin, John Hopkins & John Haiden; 27 Nov 1779, p.54. A.C. of 40 Shill. sterl.

JOHN LYNE, by survey 28 Apr 1779, 115 acs. King & Queen Co. along Spencers mill road; adj. Thurston, William Halliard, William Thurston, Tureman, Edmund Burkly/Berkly & Steardman; 27 Nov 1779, p.55. A.C. of 15 Shill. sterl.

ZECHARIAH TALIAFERRO Heir at law of sd BENJAMIN dec'd, by survey 3 Apr 1750, 400 acs. Albemarle Co. on the brs. of thrashers cr.; adj. Pearce Wade, John Taliaferro & his own line; 22 Nov 1779, p.56. **A.C. of 40 Shill. sterl. paid into the late receiver Generals office by BENJAMIN TALIAFERO.**

JAMES SOUTHALL & RICHARD CHARLTON ass'ees of sd WILLIAM FINNY, by survey 1 Jun 1774, 6,000 acs. Kentucky Co. formerly Fincastle, on the SE side the Ohio riv., adj. Taylors land above the mouth of bear grass cr. which empties into the Ohio opposite to the head of the falls; 20 Nov 1779, p.57. *In consideration of Military service perform'd by WILLIAM FINNIE in the late war between the king of Great Brittain and France according to the terms of the king of Great Brittains Proclamation of 1763.*

OWEN RUBLE, 164 acs. Henry Co. on the waters of Turners cr., at a path; adj. Andrew Furgason & Thomas Jones; 20 Nov 1779, p.58. A.C. of 20 Shill. Sterl.

Colo. GEORGE LYNE, by survey 27 Apr 1779, 204 acs. King & Queen Co. along the Irish road; adj. Thomas Bland, Robert Groom, Richard Walden, Colo. Richard Cobbin [Corbin], John Dunlairy or Dunlavy, sd Corbin & William Bland; 20 Nov 1779, p.59. A.C. of 20 Shill. Sterl. paid by Colo. GEORGE LYNE.

CUTHBERT BULLET Devisee of sd THOMAS, by survey 24 May 1775, 130 acs. Green Brier Co. formerly Botetourt on the E side the Great Kanhaway and S side Elk riv. in the fork of sd rivers, down the Elk river to a large a Sycamore on the point marked "T,B," [for Thomas Bullet?]; 20 Nov 1779, p.60. *in consideration of military service perform'd by THOMAS BULLET in the late war between Great Brittain and France according to the terms of the king of Great Brittains Proclamation of 1763.*

ZECHARIAH TALIAFERRO heir at Law of sd BENJN. TALIAFERRO, by survey 2 Apr 1750, 400 acs. Albemarle Co. on Franklins cr., adj. James Smith; 20 Nov 1779, p.61. **A.C. of 40 Shill. sterl. paid into the late receiver Generals office by BENJAMIN TALIAFERRO.**

LEONARD THOMPSON Ass'ee of JAMES J. HICKS who was Ass'ee of JOHN BELLAMY, 186 acs. Fluvanna Co. adj. Bellamy; 22 Nov 1779, p.62. A.C. of 20 Shill. Sterl.

DAVID ROBERTSON ass'ee of SAMUEL WHITE who was Ass'ee of JOHN REA, 106 acs. Albemarle Co. on the S side the rivanna riv. and on its brs.; adj. Samuel Taliaferroes line, Henry Martin, John Rea & James Addams; 17 Nov 1779, p.63. A.C. of 15 Shill. sterl.

WILLIAM CHRISTIAN, 1,000 acs. Kentucky Co. on a br. of the Ohio riv. called the Bigg bone cr., including the large Buffaloe lick being about 4 miles from the Ohio riv., near a mud lick, crossing the Great Bone Cr.; 24 Nov 1779, p.64. *In consideration of military service perform'd by William Christian in the late warr between Great Brittain & France according to the terms of the King of Great Brittains proclamation of 1763.*

LUND WASHINGTON Ass'ee of WILLIAM CRAWFORD who was Ass'ee of sd DAVID CANNADY, by survey 1 Feb 1775, 2,000 acs. on the waters of Rackoon Cr. in Ohio Co., on a Ridge, on the N side of the painters Run, adj. Thomas Cherry & Ranking; 24 Nov 1779, p.65. *In consideration of military service perform'd by David Canady in the late war between Great Brittain and France according to the terms of the king of Great Brittains Proclamation of 1763.*

ARTHER CAMPBEL, 1,000 acs. Kentucky Co. on the brs. of Grass cr. a South br. of the Ohio, and about a mile from the same; adj. Harrison, & John Connolly; 24 Nov 1779, p.66. *In consideration of Military service perform'd by Arther Campbel in the late war between Great Brittain and France according to the terms of the king of Great Brittains proclamation of 1763.*

LUND WASHINGTON ass'ee of VALENTINE CRAWFORD and JNO. NEVILLS who was Ass'ee of BENJN. TEMPLE who was Ass'ee of TUNSTALL BANKS the Legl. Representative of the sd WILLIAM BANKS dec'd, by survey 20 Jan 1775, 1,000 acs. Ohio Co. on the main Fork of Shirtees cr. where the mingo path crosses sd cr., Beginning in the Lower End of crages bottom on the bank of the cr. the same being a corner to land known by the name of Bandfields land, adj. sd Banfield's land; 20 Nov 1779, p.67. *In consideration of Military service perform'd by William Banks in the late war between Great Brittain and France according to the terms of the king of Great Brittains proclamation of 1763.*

THOMAS & SWINKFIELD HILL Executors & legators of ROBERT HILL Dec'd, 371 acs. Henry Co. on the S side of Pigg riv., adj. John Furgason & Joseph Bird; 20 Nov 1779, p.69. A.C. of 40 Shill. Sterl.

THOMAS & SWINKFIELD HILL Executors & legatees of ROBERT HILL Dec'd, 266 acs. Henry Co. on Pigg Riv., crossing two Drains; adj. sd Hills old line, Swinkfield Hill, & Callaway & Co.; 22 Nov 1779, p.70. A.C. of 30 Shill. Sterl.

WILLIAM McVEATY/McVETY, 140 acs. Henry Co. on Pigg riv.; adj. Rentfroes Corner, Thomas Jones & Robt. Jones; 22 Nov 1779, p.71. A.C. of 15 Shill. Sterl.

WILLIAM TODD, 400 acs. Pittsylvania Co. on Fly blow cr., on Hickeys or Mickeys Road; adj. Echolls, & Thomas Faris; 10 Nov 1779, p.72. A.C. of 40 Shill. Sterl.

JAMES GEORGE, 329 acs. Pittsylvania Co. on the waters of Allens Cr.; adj. Benjn. Lankford, John George & Pemberton; 15 Nov 1779, p.73. A.C. of 35 Shill.

WILLIAM OWEN, 400 acs. Pittsylvania Co. on the Waters of Dan Riv.; adj. McDaniel, Aris or Acris & Roberts; 18 Nov 1779, p.74. A.C. 40 Shill. Sterl.

GEORGE RUSHER, 77 acs. Bedford Co. on the head brs. of the North fork of Great Br. of Ivy Cr.; adj. Fry and company, John Barker, the Companies line & James Callaway; 10 Nov 1779, p.76. **A.C. of 10 Shill. Sterl. paid into the late receiver Generals office.**

JOHN TALBOT, 154 acs. Bedford Co. on both sides of Beaver Dam Cr. a north br. of Staunton Riv.; 10 Nov 1779, p.77. **A.C. of 15 Shill. Sterl. paid into the late receiver Generals Office.**

MARK COLE, 400 acs. Bedford Co. on both sides of back Run of little Cr.; 10 Nov 1779, p.79. **A.C. of 40 Shill. sterl. paid into the late reciever Generals Office.**

JOHN BOOTH Ass'ee of JOHN CLIBORN who was Ass'ee of JOHN SOLLOMON who was Ass'ee of JOSEPH UNDERWOOD who was Ass'ee of **JOHN BOARD for whom the land was Originally Survey**, 340 acs. Bedford Co. on the North Fork of Merrymans Run; 10 Nov 1779, p.80. **A.C. of 35 Shill. paid into the late receiver Generals Office by JOHN BOOTH.**

MESHACK TURNER, 557 acs. Pittsylvania Co. on the S side of Banister Riv. and on both sides of Byrd Cr.; adj. Joseph Rogers, the order line & sd Turner; 16 Nov 1779, p.82. A.C. of £3. Sterl.

JOHN LAWSON, 277 acs. Pittsylvania Co. on the S side of Staunton Riv., adj. Peter Bennit; 16 Nov 1779, p.83. A.C. of 30 Shill.

JOHN WATSON, 216 acs. Pittsylvania Co. on the S Brs. of Cherry stone Cr.; adj. sd Watson, Lovell & Turner; 16 Nov 1779, p.85. A.C. of 30 Shill. Sterl.

WILLIAM MAPLES, 263 acs. Pittsylvania Co. on both sides the North fork of Cherry Stone Cr.; adj. Hix, Bynum, & John Donelsons Order line; 16 Nov 1779, p.86. A.C. of 30 Shill. Sterl.

EDMUND PAYNE, 425 acs. Pittsylvania Co. on the brs. of the Horse shoe, crossing Sullens br., in the Horse fork, adj. Mustun/Muston & Gray; 13 Nov 1779, p.88. A.C. of 45 Shill. Sterl.

ROBERT ADAMS, 184 acs. Pittsylvania Co. on the waters of the white oak cr., adj. Greenstreet; 16 Nov 1779, p.90. A.C. of 20 Shill. Sterl.

BENJAMIN HOLLAND, 374 acs. Pittsylvania Co. on both sides of the Cat Tail Fork of Sycamore Cr., crossing a fork of the sd fork, adj. Isacc Clements line; 18 Nov 1779, p.91. A.C. of 40 Shill. Sterl.

THOMAS HARDY, 298 acs. Pittsylvania Co. on the Indian Field Br., adj. Grays order line; 13 Nov 1779, p.93. A.C. of 30 Shill. Sterl.

JEREMIAH WARSHAM, 234 acs. Pittsylvania Co. on the brs. of Cherry stone Cr., adj. his old line; 13 Nov 1779, p.94. A.C. of 25 Shill. Sterl.

JOHN COLYER, 95 acs. Pittsylvania Co. on the East fork of the old womans Cr.; 11 Nov 1779, p.96. A.C. of 20 Shill. Sterl.

JESSE PATEY, 46 acs. Pittsylvania Co. on the brs. of Staunton riv., adj. sd Pateys line; 16 Nov 1779, p.97. A.C. of 5 Shill. Sterl.

REUBEN PAYNE, 340 acs. Pittsylvania Co. on both sides of the middle Cr. of banister Riv.; adj. Kennon, Martin & the sd Paynes former line; 15 Nov 1779, p.98. A.C. of 35 Shill. sterl.

JAMES TAYLOR, 371 acs. Pittsylvania Co. on both sides of Great Cherry stone Cr.; 16 Nov 1779, p.100. A.C. of 40 Shill. Sterl.

PETER DYERLY, by survey 2 Jun 1767, 364 acs. Botetourt Co. on Roan Oak Riv., by the Great Road, in a hollow, adj. his Patent Land; 2 Nov 1779, p.101. A.C. of 40 Shill. sterl.

THOMAS DAVIS, 497 acs. Pittsylvania Co. on both sides of Stinking Riv., down Slavary br.; adj. Joseph Johnson, Thomas Farris, Arthur Keesus, Jacob Farris & the sd Davis's old line; 11 Nov 1779, p.103. A.C. of 50 Shill. Sterl.

ISAAC ECKOLS, 261 acs. Hallifax Co. on the S of Staunton riv., crossing Mays Ferry Road, down a Gut; adj. his old line, John Saunders, Joseph Eckols, Charles Bostick & Booker; 18 Nov 1779, p.104. A.C. of 30 Shill. Sterl.

RICHARD ECKOLS, 476 acs. Pittsylvania Co. on the main Fork of Sandy cr.; adj. Parrish, Roger Adkinson & George Musick; 11 Nov 1779, p.106. A.C. of 50 Shill. Sterl.

WILLIAM PHILLIPS Son an heir at Law of RICHARD PHILLIPS Dec'd, by survey 11 Jun 1752, 1,201 acs. Louisa Co. on both sides Cross Sw., by the Side of a Glade of sd Sw.; adj. William Haley, Francis Clark, Venable, Matthew Watson, James Nuckols, Thomas East, Jouet/Jouett, Beverly Randolph, Phillips, Isaac Cole & Clarke; 22 Nov 1779, p.107. A.C. of £6.S5 Sterl. [This land includes the 56 acs. patented by Richard Phillips in PB 25 p.247 dated 12 Jan 1746/47]

SHADRACH TURNER, 327 acs. Pittsylvania Co. on both sides of Green Rock of cherry stone Cr.; 16 Nov 1779, p.110. A.C. of 40 Shill. Sterl.

RICHARD THURMAN, 364 acs. Pittsylvania Co. on the N brs. of Read Cr., adj. sd Thurman; 18 Nov 1779, p.112. A.C. of 40 Shill. Sterl.

BENJAMIN LANGFORD, 400 acs. Halifax Co. on the N side Childry Cr.; adj. John Dyer, Shadrach Trebble & Paler Treble; 19 Nov 1779, p.113. A.C. of 40 Shill. Sterl.

SPENCER SHELTON, 356 acs. Pittsylvania Co. on both sides of Cattail fork of Georges Cr., adj. James Fariss & Armistead Shelton; 13 Nov 1779, p.115. A.C. of 40 Shill. Sterl.

BURWELL BOWDEN, 486 acs. Pittsylvania Co. on the S brs. of Banister riv.; adj. John McGee, the order line,

Donelson & Claybrook; 13 Nov 1779, p.116. A.C. of 50 Shill. Sterl.

ISAAC ECKOLS, 356 acs. Halifax Co. on the S Side of Childry Cr., adj. Benjamin Hubbard; 16 Nov 1779, p.118. A.C. of 40 Shill. Sterl.

JOSHUA STONE, 414 acs. Pittsylvania Co. on Jacobs br. of Stinking Riv., down Slavary br.; adj. Jacob Farris, Childres & Thomas Farris; 13 Nov 1779, p.119. A.C. of 45 Shill. Sterl.

WILLIAM COLLENS, 310 acs. Pittsylvania Co. on Straite Stone Cr., crossing the cr. and camp Br.; adj. Vaughan, James Collens & Shadrach Tribble; 12 Nov 1779, p.121. A.C. of 35 Shill. Sterl.

SAMUEL MEREDITH, by Survey 11 Jul 1774, 2,000 acs. Kentucky Co. on the waters of Elk horn Cr. a br. of Kentucky Riv. and on the N Side thereof being the waters of the Ohio Riv. and about 100 Miles from the Same; Beginning at a large Ash, Elm and Hoopwood in a Cane brake Corner to William Christians land; adj. sd Christian, & Alexander S. Dandridge; 1 December 1779, p.122. *In consideration of Military Service perform'd [by] Samuel Meredith as Captain in the late warr between Great Brittain and France according to the terms of the king of Great Brittains Proclamation of 1763.*

JOHN HANNAH, 120 acs. by Survey 6 Nov 1767 in Rockbridge Co. on Buffalo Cr. in the Fork of James Riv., Crossing sd Cr. to a Valley, adj. James Young & his Old Survey; 1 Dec 1779, p.123. A.C. of 15 Shill. Sterl.

JOHN HANNAH, by survey 4 Nov 1767, 98 acs. Rockbridge Co. on bothsides of Buffaloe Cr. in the Fork of James Riv., adj. his Old survey; 1 Dec 1779, p.125. A.C. of 10 Shill. Sterl.

JOHN HANNAH, 396 acs. by survey 4 Sep 1772 in Rockbridge Co. on both Sides of Buffalo Cr. a br. of James riv. including a Tract of 230 acs. Gtd. by Pat. to sd John Hannah 16 Aug 1756 [Augusta Co. PB 34 p.136], up the Cr. to a Rock in the Cr., over a Grassey Hill, down a Gulley; adj. sd Hannah, John Sumer & James Moore; 1 Dec 1779, p.126. A.C. of 40 Shill. Sterl.

HENRY MILLER ass'ee of MATHIAS CLEEK who was ass'ee of JOHN ALLISON, 400 acs. by Survey 28 Sep 1769 in Augusta Co. in the fork of James Riv., crossing the Great road, adj. James Gilmore; 1 Dec 1779, p.128. A.C. of 40 Shill. Sterl.

ROBERT WEAKLY, by Survey 26 May 1769, 236 acs. Halifax Co. on the brs. of runaway Cr.; adj. Robert Weakley, an Old line & Henry Cross; 1 Dec 1779, p.130. A.C. of 25 Shill.

JOSEPH ROGERS & JOHN SEABERRY Ass'ees of sd WILLIAM PRESTON, by Survey 13 Jul 1774, 1000 acs. Kentucky Co. on the waters of Elk horn Cr. a br. of Kentucky Riv. and about 90 Miles from its Junction with the Kentucky ; Beginning at a buckeye and Elm near a Draft SW corner to William Phillips's Land Just above where Elk horn Cr. divides into Smaller brs., near a Draught; adj. sd Phillips & [Beckley]; 1 Dec 1779, p.131. *In consideration of Military Service perform'd by William Preston in the late war between Great*

Brittain and France according to the Terms of the King of Great Brittains proclamation of 1763.

JOSEPH ROGERS & JOHN SEABERRY Ass'ees of GEORGE SKILLERN who was Ass'ee of JOHN LOGAN who was Ass'ee of JAMES SMITH who was Ass'ee of JOHN SMITH afforesaid, by survey 13 Jul 1774, 1,000 acs. Kentucky Co. on the North Fork of Elk horn cr. a br. of the Kentucky, near a Draft; adj. Vaughan, William Preston & Phillips; 1 Dec 1779, p.133. *In consideration of Military service perform'ed by John Smith in the late war between Great Brittain and France according to the terms of the King of Great Brittains Proclamation of 1763.*

Revd. JOHN CAMERON, by Survey 22 Apr 1755, 360 acs. Mecklenburg Co. on the brs. of Tewahominie & Buffalo Creeks; on Reads & Goods line from A to B, John Griffins Line G to H, & Vaughans line I to A; 1 Dec 1779, p.134. A.C. of 40 Shill. Sterl. paid into the Treasury of this Commonwealth.

WILLIAM THACKSTON Ass'ee of CHARLES CLAY who was Ass'ee of CHARLES LITTLE, 340 acs by Survey 31 Mar 1757 in Pittsylvania Co., crossing Sandy Cr.; adj. Sylvester, Billings, Falling & Little; 1 Dec 1779, p.136. **A.C. of 35 Shill. Sterl. paid by Wm. Thackston into the late receiver Generals Office**.

LAMBOTH DODSON, by Survey 26 Apr 1754, 200 acs. Henry Co. on both sides of the South fork of Mayo Riv., on the Country line [East]; 1 Dec 1779, p.137. A.C. of 20 Shill. Sterl.

ROBERT WEAKLEY, by Survey 7 Mar 1750, 208 acs. Hallifax Co. on both sides of a br. of Runaway Cr., adj. James Laws; 1 Dec 1779, p.139. A.C. of 25 Shill. Sterl.

THOMAS BOWMAN, by Survey 10 Jan 1771, 160 acs. Hallifax Co. on the brs. of by Creek, adj. Travis Tune, the Revd. James Toulis, William Hall & William Powel; 1 Dec 1779, p.140. A.C. of 20 Shill. Sterl.

ROBERT WOODING, by Survey 24 Nov 1755, 4,222 acs. Halifax Co. on the brs. of Hico Riv. and Aarons Cr.; Crossing Siths br., Pinsons Shoal & Buck Shoal (branches of Hico); Crossing Moriss's Cr.; on the North fork of Aarons Cr.; adj. Tally, Colo. Byrd & Peter Overby; 1 Dec 1779, p.141. A.C. of £21.S5 Sterl.

JAMES GREENWAY, by survey 5 Apr 1775, 129 acs. Dinwiddie Co. on the S Side of Sapony Cr.; adj. John Winfield, Goodwyn, John Dixon, Henry Dixon, Thomas Dixon near his Old field, Thomas Dixons Old patent line & Goodwin; 1 Dec 1779, p.144. A.C. of 15 Shill. Sterl. including 208 acs., 79 acs. part thereof being formerly Gtd. to Thomas Dixon by Pat. 16 Aug 1756 [Thomas Dickson's PB 33 p.228] the Residue 129 acs. new Land and never before Gtd. [For Thomas Dixon's Old field land see PB 25 p.199, for Henry Dixon's see PB 24 p.189]

JAMES GREENWAY, by Survey 14 Mar 1777, 350 acs. Dinwiddie Co. on the Head Briahry Br., near the Mill path, in the corn field br. near Baughs Fence, up the Bryary br.; adj. John Sears, Wood Tucker, Winfields Old patent Line &

Perry; 1 Dec 1779, p.146. 40 Shill. Sterl. [For John Sears, see Paul Seares' PB 22 p.365 on the Bryery Br. of the Flat Br. of Stoney Cr.]

ALEXANDER HANNAH Ass'ee of ROBERT YOUNG, by Survey 7 Feb 1767, 130 as. Rockbridge Co. on Buffalo Cr. in the fork of James Riv.; adj. John Hannah, Edward Faire & James Beal; 1 Dec 1779, p.147. A.C. of 15 Shill. Sterl.

JAMES HOPKINS Ass'ee of HENRY SANHEN or LAWHON & WHITE VAUGHAN, by Survey 25 Nov 1773 or 1778, 48 acs. Amherst Co. on the head brs. of Davis's Cr., adj. their Own lines & Josias Wood; 1 Dec 1779, p.149. A.C. of 5 Shill. Sterl.

ROBERT WEAKLY/WEEKLY, by Survey 10 Nov 1772, 450 acs. Halifax Co. on the Draughts of Runaway Cr., Crossing Bookers Road; adj. sd Weekly's old line & Bates; 1 Dec 1779, p.151. A.C. of 45 Shill. Sterl. 140 acs. new and 310 acs. Survey'd 27 May 1767

ROBERT WOODING, by Survey 17 Jun 1767, 554 acs. Halifax Co. on the brs. of Wymes [Wynnes] Cr. and Terrible, adj. sd Wooding, Sparrow, Eckolds & Baird; 1 Dec 1779, p.153. A.C. of 20 Shill. Sterl. Including 398 acs of Old L., 238 acs. Gtd. by Pat. 14 Feb 1761 [PB 34 p.808] and 160 acs. Pr. Date 26 Jun 1765 [26 Jul 1765 in PB 36 p.798].

AUGUSTINE STEEL Ass'ee of MICAJAH TERRIL, by Survey 16 Mar 1769, 400 acs. Amherst Co. on both Sides of the North and South forks of Bollings Cr.; adj. Lynch, & Daniel Burford; 1 Dec 1779, p.155. A.C. of 40 Shill. Sterl.

JOHN DAVIS, by Survey 26 Oct 1770, 90 acs. Amherst Co. on the N brs. of Rutledges Cr.; adj. his own lines, James Mannus, Carter Braxton & Benjamin Higingbotham; 1 Dec 1779, p.157. A.C. of 10 Shill. Sterl.

GILES NANCE, by Survey 26 Mar 1756, 1,574 acs. Halifax Co. on the brs. of Cascade cr. & Sugar Tree Cr., adj. Cox & Clay; 1 Dec 1779, p.158. A.C. of £8 Sterl.

JOHN FLOY'D Ass'ee of CHARLES CUMMINGS who was ass'ee of JAMES COWDEN who was Ass'ee of sd JAMES BUFORD, by Survey 5 Aug 1775, 200 acs. Kentucky Co. near the head of the middle fork of Elkhorn Cr. and Joining a line of the Land measured for John Maxwel; 1 Dec 1779, p.160. *In consideration of Military Service perform'd by James Buford in the late warr between Great Brittain and france according to the Terms of the King of Great Brittains proclamation of 1763.*

HENRY CHILDERS/CHILDRIS Ass'ee of ROBERT JOHNSTON, by survey 14 Apr 1756, 400 acs. Amherst Co. on both Sides Piggs Cr.; adj. his own new line, Hugh Morris & John Burk; 1 Dec 1779, p.161. A.C. of 40 Shill. Sterl.

GEORGE DAVIS Ass'ee of JOSEPH LANE who was Ass'ee of ROBERT JOHNSTON, by Survey 7 Nov 1771, 218 acs. Amherst Co. on the S Side & Joining Cashaw Cr. and on the chesnut mountain, Beginning on the North br. of sd Cr., adj. his own line; 1 Dec 1779, p.163. A.C. of 25 Shill. Sterl.

DAVID CRAWFORD, by Survey 23 Apr 1761, 50 acs. Amherst Co. on the

North br. of Horsalys Cr., on a Ridge, adj. his own Old Line & William Floy'd; 1 Dec 1779, p.164. A.C. of 5 Shill. Sterl.

WILLIAM MADISON Ass'ee of Sd JOHN BOWYER, by Survey 4 Jun 1775, 1,000 acs. Kentucky Co. on a br. of Floyds Cr. about 3 Miles from the Kentucky Riv., adj. Dandridge; 1 Dec 1779, p.165. *In consideration of military Service perform'd by John Bowyer in the late War between Great Brittain and france Accoding to the terms of the king of Great Brittains proclamation of 1763.*

WILLIAM HOGES/HODGES Ass'ee of THOMAS HUBBARD who was Ass'ee of CHARLES FARISS, by Survey 27 Aug 1775, 257 acs. Louisa Co. on the waters of camp Cr.; adj. Richard Morris, Thomas Harlow, Richard White & William Pettit; 1 Dec 1779, p.166. A.C. of 30 Shill. Sterl.

WILLIAM PRESTON Ass'ee of ABRAHAM HITE who was Ass'ee of Sd JOHN SAVAGE, by Survey 15 Jul 1775, 1,000 acs. Kentucky Co. known by the name of the Cave Spring, Beginning on the waters of the South fork of Elk horn Cr. a br. of Kentucky Riv.; 1 Dec 1779, p.167. *In consideration of Military Service performed by John Savage in the late War between Great Brittain and France According to the terms of the King of Great Brittains proclamation of 1763.* [Written as one thousand Seven Acres. The survey is S70°E 440 poles by N20°E 370 poles, which computes to 1,017½ acs.]

HENRY STREET, by Survey 27 Feb 1778, 15 acs. Essex Co. on Dragon Sw., through the Pocoson to the main Dragon Run, adj. John Tayloe Corbin & sd Street; 1 Dec 1779, p.169. A.C. of 5 Shill. Sterl.

WILLIAM FARISS/FARIS, by Survey 21 Dec 1778, 284 acs. Bedford Co. on the S side of entry Cr.; adj. Robert Mitchel, James Mitchel, Dougherty, & Wood Jones; 1 Dec 1779, p.170. A.C. of 30 Shill. Sterl.

AUGUSTINE STEEL ass'ee of JOHN HANSFORD who was Ass'ee of WILLIAM BROWN who was Ass'ee of MICAJAH MEREMAN, by Survey 17 Mar 1767, 125 acs. Amherst Co. on the brs. of Bollings Cr.; adj. Henry Harper, Abraham North, Lynch/Linch, & Micajah Terril; 1 Dec 1779, p.171. A.C. of 15 Shill. Sterl.

JAMES GREENWAY, by Survey 19 Nov 1773, 99¾ acs. Dinwiddie Co. on the N side of Butterwood Cr., on the Side of the main Road, near a Slash, crossing a Road; adj. John Nunnally near his House, Williamson, Maye's corner Cut down at the edge of a small Field, Michel/Mitchel, & Roger Adkinson; 1 Dec 1779, p.173. A.C. of 10 Shill. Sterl. [For Maye's land, see PB 11 p.207 to James Anderson; for Williamson's, see PB 11 p.215 to James Thweat Jr.; also adj. Francis Wyatt's PB 23 p.635]

JOHN TAYLER, by Survey 2 Apr 1772, 184 acs. Bedford Co. on the N Side of Gills Cr., adj. Poteet; 1 Dec 1779, p.174. A.C. of 20 Shill. Sterl.

HARTMAN DORAN, by Survey 16 Apr 1763, 200 acs. Bedford Co. on both Sides the Weary br.; 1 Dec 1779, p.175. A.C. of 20 Shill. Sterl.

WILLIAM KELLY, by Survey 16 Apr 1763, 141 acs. Bedford Co. on the head brs. of Gills Cr.; 1 Dec 1779, p.176. A.C. of 15 Shill. Sterl.

HENRY HARRISON Son and Heir at Law of sd HENRY HARRISON Dec'd, by Survey 2 Jun 1774, 1,000 acs. Kentucky Co. on the S side the Ohio, 2¼ Miles from the Head of the falls, between 2 meadows, adj. Thomas Bowyer & William Fleming; 1 Dec 1779, p.178. *In consideration of Military Service perform'd by Henry Harrison Dec'd in the late war between Great Brittain and France According to the Terms of the King of Great Brittains proclamation of 1763.* [This land was sold for £5 in Surry County Va. Deed Book 12 (1783-1787) p.276 on 1 Oct 1786 as Jefferson Co. Kentucky to Peyton Short of Lincoln District in Kentucky]

GILES ALLEGREE, by Survey 6 Mar 1750, 388 acs. Fluvanna Co. on both Sides of the three Notch'd Road and Joining to Mechunk Cr. on the N Side the Rivanna Riv.; 1 Dec 1779, p.179. A.C. of 40 Shill. Sterl.

JOHN STRANGE Ass'ee of JOHN & DANIEL KING, by Survey 22 Jan 1755, 200 acs. Fluvanna Co. on the N Side the Rivanna Riv. on the brs. of Ballengers cr.; 1 Dec 1779, p180. A.C. of 20 Shill. Sterl.

JOHN TIMBERLAKE, by Survey 15 Jun 1779, 421 acs. Louisa Co. on the brs. of contrary and Christopher Run; adj. Cole, Thompson, Lipscomb, Mitchel, Bond, Poindexter & Spiller; 1 Dec 1779, p.181. A.C. of 45 shil. Sterl. [about 2 lines of the survey is destroyed]

JOHN SHAW, by Survey 3 Oct 1771, 400 acs. Halifax Co. on the brs. of Difficult Cr., on Sarahs Br., Crossing a br. of Hunting Cr.; adj. Ephraim Hill, Lax, Compton, Richard Brown, John Legrand, Lewis, & Joseph Shaw; 1 Dec 1779, p.182. A.C. of 40 Shill. Sterl.

DANIEL KING, by Survey 18 Apr 1777, 231 acs. Fluvanna Co. on the N Side the riv. and on some of the brs. of Ballengers cr., to the Lower Long Br. of sd Cr., on a Ridge; adj. David Bibee, John Strange, Long, William Murril & Henderson; 1 Dec 1779, p.184. A.C. of 25 Shill.

HENRY HARRISON Son and Heir at Law of the sd HENRY HARRISON Dec'd, by Survey 7 Jun 1774, 1,000 acs. Kentucky Co. on the waters of bear Grass Cr. a South br. of the Ohio riv. and about 5 Miles from the same, in a Low place, on a flat Hill Side, adj. John Ware; 1 Dec 1779, p.185. *In consideration of Military Service performed by Henry Harrison Dec'd in the late war between Great Brittain and France According to the terms of the King of Great Brittains proclamation of 1763.* [This land was sold for £5 in Surry County Va. Deed Book 12 (1783-1787) p.279 on 1 Oct 1786 as Jefferson Co. Kentucky to Peyton Short of Lincoln County Kentucky]

WILLIAM HAIDEN/HADEN, by Survey 12 Apr 1779, 364 acs. Fluvanna Co. on the S Brs. of the Rivanna Riv. and on the brs. of Burkes and Cunninghams Creeks, crossing the Road; adj. sd Haden, Lightfoot, John M. Harden & Robert Parsley; 1 Dec 1779, p.187. A.C. of 40 Shill. Sterl.

ZACHARIAH MOREMAN, by Survey 29 Jan 1773, 98 acs. Bedford Co. on the forks of Rock Casle [sic] Cr., on the foot of & upon the NW Side of Candlers Mountain, adj. his own line; 1 Dec 1779, p.188. A.C. of 10 Shill. Sterl.

JAMES FINLEY, by Survey 29 Jan 1773, 328 acs. Bedford Co. on the E Side of & crossing the fork of Dreaming Cr., crossing Rock Castle Cr., adj. John Thompson; 1 Dec 1779, p.189. A.C. of 35 Shill. Sterl.

GEORGE STOVALL JUNR., by Survey 20 Feb 1768, 178 acs. Amherst Co. on both sides of the South fork of Stovals/Stovauls Cr., adj. George Jefferson & Henry Fry; 1 Dec 1779, p.190. A.C. of 20 Shill. Sterl.

GEORGE STOVAL/STOVALL, by Survey 16 Dec 1772, 140 acs. Amherst Co. on the S brs. of Stovalls Cr., up the the South bank of the Wolf br., adj. Robert Ballow & Thomas Richel; 1 Dec 1779, p.191. A.C. of 15 Shill. Sterl.

GEORGE STOVAL, by Survey 1 Dec 1767, 235 acs. Bedford Co. on the Head bs. of Archers Cr., Crossing Grassy br., adj. Lynch & Thompson, 1 Dec 1779, p.193. A.C. of 25 Shill. Sterl.

JAMES STRANGE, by Suvey 28 Sep 1773, 352 acs. Henry Co. on both Sides of Mullins's fork of Bull run & the Head brs. of Bull run, adj. Walton & James Darnel; 1 Dec 1779, p.194. A.C. of 35 Shill.

FRANCIS WHITLOW, by Survey 12 Nov 1771, 400 acs. Halifax Co. on the brs. of Grassy Cr., adj. Randolph & EnRoughty; 1 Dec 1779, p.195. A.C. of 40 Shill. Sterl.

JOHN FLOYD Ass'ee of Sd JOHN DRAPER, by Survey 6 Jun 1774, 1,000 acs. Kentucky Co. on the Waters of bear Grass Cr. an East br. of the Ohio and about 3 or 4 Miles from the falls; crossing the Cr. to a buckeye, Hickory and Walnut near the Cr. by a Buffaloe ford, adj. his own L.; 1 Dec 1779, p.196. *In consideration of Military Service permorm'd by John Draper in the late Warr between Great Brittain and France according to the Terms of the King of Great Brittains proclamation of 1763.*

JOHN FLOY'D ass'ee of WILLIAM PRESTON who was Ass'ee of Sd ALEXANDER WAUGH, by Survey 21 Jul 1774, 1,000 acs. Kentucky Co. on Elk Horn Cr. a North br. of the Kentucky Riv. being the waters of the Ohio Riv. and on the S side thereof, Beginning at 2 Sugar trees and a Honey Locust and Ash by and below the Mouth of a Small Draft on the South bank of the Cr. near a Buffaloe ford, down a small cr.; 1 Dec 1779, p.197. *In consideration of Military Service perform'd by Alexander Waugh in the late War between Great Brittain and France according to the Terms of the King of great Brittains proclamation of 1763.*

JOHN STRANGE Ass'ee of JOHN KING, by Survey 1 Mar 1755, 135 acs. Fluvanna Co. on the N Side of the Rivanna Riv. on the waters of Horsleys Cr., adj. Daniel King; 1 Dec 1779, p.199. A.C. of 15 Shill. Sterl.

ARNOLD TOMMERSON, by Survey 21 Mar 1773, 19 acs. Pr. Edward Co. on the S Side of the East fork of mountain Cr.; adj. Scot, Ligon, & Richard Tommerson; 1 Dec 1779, p.200. A.C. of 5 Shill. Sterl.

NICHOLAS CABELL, by Survey 2 Dec 1773, 227 acs. Amherst Co. on the brs. of Ivy cr. of Rock fish Riv., adj. his own lines & Charles Tyler; 1 Dec 1779, p.201. A.C. of 25 Shill. Sterl.

RICHARD THURMAN, by Survey 1 May 1772, 415 acs. Bedford Co. on both sides of Phelps's old Road on the E side of seneca cr., on the sd road at the mouth of Locust thicket Road, down Seneca Cr. to the bent and up the Hill; adj. Benjamin Gilbert, Neilson, Samuel Gilbert, Welches line, John Michales line & William Brown; 1 Dec 1779, p.202. A.C. of 45 Shill. Sterl.

WILLIAM PRESTON, by Survey 6 Jun 1774, 1,000 acs. Kentucky Co. on the brs. of the Ohio Riv. on the S side the Same, Beginning at 3 beeches in Colo. Birds Line 48 poles from McCorkles upper corner and 1,398 poles from the falls of the Ohio at the mouth of bear Grass cr., by a meadow, with McCorkles line to the Beg.; 1 Dec 1779, p.205. *In consideration of Military Service perform'd by William Preston in the late War between Great Brittain and france according to the terms of the King of Great Brittains proclamation of 1763.*

WILLIAM PRESTON Ass'ee of GEORGE SKILLIEM who was ass'ee of Sd JOHN SMITH, by Survey 29 Jun 1775, 1,000 acs. Kentucky Co. on the brs. of Spring Cr. a br. of the Kentucky Riv., crossing 3 forks of the Cr., adj. Glen & Moffett; 1 Dec 1779, p.206. *In consideration of military Service perform'd by JOHN SMITH as captain in the Late War between Great Brittain and france According to the terms of the King of Great Brittains proclamation of 1763.*

SAMUEL RAGLAND, by Survey 11 Mar 1771, 400 acs. Louisa Co. on the brs. of Cauthans Run and Joining the Lands of Menoah Lastly, Richard Anderson and the Land formerly posses'd by John Dashper; also adj. Brechen, Howard, Anderson in a bottom & Colo. Richard Anderson; 1 Dec 1779, p.207. A.C. of 40 Shill. Sterl.

JAMES TELFORD, by Survey 30 Mar 1773, 72 acs. Rockbridge Co. on the waters of Mary Cr. a br. of James Riv.; on the end of, up and along the Side of, and over the top of a Spur; by a br. and a Path; 1 Dec 1779, p.209. A.C. of 10 Shill. sterl.

ROBERT WILLIAMS, by Survey 18 Oct 1762, 168 acs. Pittsylvania Co. on both sides the East fork of cascade Cr., adj. Charles Clay; 1 Dec 1779, p.210. A.C. of 20 Shill. Sterl.

GEORGE THOMPSON, by Survey 3 Nov 1775, 400 acs. Fluvanna Co. on the N Side the riv. and on the brs. of Horsleys Cr., across a br. of the Rivanna Riv. to another br. of the sd Riv., to Bibees Road, to Bibees race ground, to the race ground path; adj. William Payne, sd George Thompson, John Bernard, Christopher McCrae, Danl. King & Abner Bernard; 1 Dec 1779, p.211. A.C. of 40 Shill. Sterl.

ROBERT WILLIAMS, by Survey 6 Feb 1762, 404 acs. Pittsylvania Co. on the brs. of Toby's Cr., Beginning at the head of a Sorrel Br.; 1 Dec 1779, p.213. A.C. of 40 Shill. Sterl.

JOHN RUTHERFORD ass'ee of sd JOHN MADISON & JOHN WEST JUNIOR, 900 acs. by Survey 10 Apr

1775, in Yohogania Co. on Colepit run a br. of Shirtee cr., on a Ridge, above the Head of a Drain, on the brow of a Hill in the fork of a Drain, near the Top of a Rich Hill; 23 Dec 1779, p.214. *In consideration of Military Service performed by John Madison and John West Junior in the late [war] between Great Brittain and france according to the Terms of the King of Great Brittains proclamation of 1763.*

THOMAS RUTHERFORD OF Berkely Co. Ass'ee of Sd ROBERT RUTHERFORD, 500 acs by Survey 9 Apr 1775 in Ohio Co. on the head brs. of the South fork of Short Cr. a br. of the Ohio, Beginning near the Side of a drain about 80 poles on the E side cf Jacob Pratts Improvement, crossing 3 Drains; 23 Dec 1779, p.216. *In consideration of Military Service perform'd by Robert Rutherford in the late War between Great Brittain and France according to the terms of the King of Great Brittains proclamation of 1763.*

THOMAS RUTHERFORD, 1,000 acs. by Survey 3 Apr 1775 in Yohogania Co. on the Western brs. of Racoon Cr. in the Co. aforesd., Beginning on a Hill about 144 poles on the W Side of the Sd Creek, crossing a br. or drain of cross cr. to a level, on a Dividing ridge; 23 Dec 1779, p.217. *In consideration of Military Service perform'd by Thomas Rutherford in the late War between Great Brittain and France according to the Terms of the King of Great Brittains proclamation of 1763.*

WILLIAM THOMPSON & WILLIAM PRESTON Exrs. of the sd JAMES PATTON Dec'd, by Survey 30 Oct 1747, 440 acs. (*part of an Order of council Granted the said James Patton and others which Said Survey having been Laid before the court of Appeals, is by them Certified to have been Established*), in Augusta Co. on the W Side of Woods Riv.; 23 Dec 1779, p.219. **A.C. of 45 Shill. Sterl. paid into the late Receiver Generals office by James Patton Dec'd.**

ROBERT RUTHERFORD, 2,500 acs. by Survey 7 Apr 1775, in Yohogania Co. on the Western br. of Racoon Cr. in the Co. aforesd., on the Ridge which divides the waters of Racoon Cr. and Cross cr., crossing various Drains, on the N Side of a rich Hill, Crossing a Large br. of Cross cr., on a level, on a Hill near and on the S side of a Drain of Racoon Cr.; adj. James Stephenson, a Tract of Land lately Survey'd for Alexander Wells and Others, & Sd Alexander Wells; 23 Dec 1779, p.220. *in consideration of Military Service perform'd by Robert Rutherford in the late war between Great Brittain and france According to the terms of the King of great Brittains proclamation of 1763.*

WILLIAM THOMPSON & WILLIAM PRESTON Executors of sd JAMES PATTON Dec'd, by Survey 27 Feb 1749, 394 acs. (*part of an order of Council Granted to the Said James Paton and others, which said survey having been laid before the Court of Appeals by them Certified to have been Established*) in Augusta Co. on sinking Br. on the waters of the Missisippie, in a break of a High Ridge, in a Draft; 23 Dec 1779, p.223. **A.C. of 40 Shill. sterl. paid into the late Receiver Generals Office by JAMES PATON Dec'd Ass'ee of JOHN TALOE.**

WILLIAM THOMPSON & WILLIAM PRESTON Exors. of the Sd JAMES PATTON Dec'd, by Survey 10 Mar 1747/8, 170 acs. *(part of an order of Council granted to the sd James Patton and others, which said Survey having been laid before the Court of Appeals, is by them Certified to have been Established)* in Augusta Co. on the forks of Walkers Cr. a br. of new Riv., Beginning at the foot of a Mountain, crossing the south fork & the west fork, crossing the cr. to the Lower end of a point of Rocks on a Hill side; 23 Dec 1779, p.224. **A.C. of 20 Shill. Sterl. paid into the late receiver Generals Office by James Patton Dec'd.**

WILLIAM THOMPSON & WM. PRESTON Exrs. of the Sd JAMES PATTON Dec'd, by Survey 11 Mar 1747/8, 260 acs. *(part of an order of Council Granted the sd James Patton & others, which said Survey having been Laid before the Court of Appeals, is by them Certified to have been Established)*, in Augusta Co. on a br. of the new Riv. call'd Walkers Cr.; Beginning in the Mouth of a Hollow on the W Side of the Cr.; 23 Dec 1779, p.226. **A.C. of 30 Shill. Sterl. paid into the Late Receiver Generals Office by James Patton Dec'd.**

WILLIAM THOMPSON & WILLIAM PRESTON Exrs. of Sd JAMES PATTON Dec'd by Survey 14 Mar 1746/47, 750 acs. *(part of an Order of Council granted to the Said James Patton and Others which Said Survey having been laid before the Court of Appeals, is by them Certified to have been Established)*, in Augusta Co. on the South fork of the Indian Riv., Beginning near a Spring, on a Ridge, in a Valley; 23 Dec 1779, p.227. **A.C. of £3.S15 Sterl. paid into the late Receiver Generals Office by James Patton Dec'd.**

WILLIAM THOMPSON & WILLIAM PRESTON Exrs. of Sd JAMES PATTON Dec'd, by Survey 18 Mar 1747/8, 70 acs. *(part of and Order of Council granted to Said James Patton and Others, which Said survey haveing been laid before the Court of Appeals is by them Certified to have been Established)*, in Augusta Co. on a branch of the new Riv. call'd the Sinking Spring, Beginning at the head of a Draft, crossing a run to a Small bottom; 23 Dec 1779, p.228. **A.C. of 10 Shill. Sterl. paid into the late Receiver Generals Office by James Patton Dec'd.**

JOHN MOORE, by Survey 15 Mar 1749/50, 400 acs. Lunenburg Co. on the brs. of Twittys Cr.; adj. Vaughan from A to B, Frank from C to D, & Jones from E to A; 1 Dec 1779, p.230. 40 Shill. Sterl. [This land was referred to as Turner's in John Sullivant's Charlotte Co. PB 39 p.326 on Stith's Br. & Tyree Glen's (Robert Davis's) PB 33 p.872. For Nehemiah Franks's land on the Horsepen & Twitty's Cr., see his PB 37 p.13 & Abraham Vaughan's PB 36 p.662. Jones's adj. land was also referred to as Bentley's]

FRANCIS PRESTON & JOHN SMITH Ass'ees of FRANCIS SMITH, who was Ass'ee of sd GEORGE ELLIOTT, by Survey 21 May 1774, 200 acs. Kentucky Co. on the Ohio Riv. joining and below the Mouth of Kentucky Riv., Beginning on a Hill Side below the Mouth of little Kentucky; 1 Dec 1779, p.231. *in consideration of Military Service perform'd by George Elliott in the late war between Great Brittain and france According to the terms of the Kings of Great Brittains proclamation of 1763.*

WILLIAM THOMPSON & WILLIAM PRESTON Exrs. of Sd JAMES PATTON Dec'd, by Survey 13 Feb 1746/47, 650 acs. *(part of an order of Council granted the Said James Patton and others, which said Survey having been laid before the court of Appeals by them Certified to have been Established)*, in Augusta Co. on Sinking Cr. a Br. of Woods Riv.; 23 Dec 1779, p.232. **A.C. of £3.S5. Sterl. paid into the late Receiver Generals office by James Patton Dec'd.**

WILLIAM CAMPBELL & WILLIAM PRESTON Exors. of JOHN BUCHANAN Dec'd Ass'ee of sd JAMES PATTON Dec'd, by Survey 19 Feb 1749/50, 720 acs. then in Augusta Co. on Shallow Cr. a br. of the Missisippie *(being part of an Order of council granted to the Said James Patton Dec'd and others, which Said Survey having been laid before the Court of Appeals is by them Certified to have been Establis'd)*, Beginning on the W Side the West br. of sd Cr., in a Vally under a Rocky Ridge then North to a white Oak in a Valley, on the East end of a Ridge by the Edge of a pine Barronee then passing the head of a Large Spring; 23 Dec 1779, p.234. **A.C. of £3.S15 Sterl. paid into the late Receiver Generals office by JAMES PATTON Dec'd Ass'ee of JOHN TAYLOE.**

WILLIAM CAMPBELL & WILLIAM PRESTON Exrs. of JOHN BUCKANNAN who was Ass'ee of Sd JAMES PATTON Dec'd, by Survey 22 Feb 1749/50, 1,946 acs. *(part of an order of council granted the said James Patton and other's which sd Survey having been Laid before the Court of Appeals is by them certified to have been established)*, in Augusta Co. on Woods Riv. and on Shallow Cr. a br. of the middle fork of Indian Riv. at a place call'd **the Saplin grove**, Beginning on the Spur of a Ridge, in a Gully, on a Spur of a Timber Ridge; 23 Dec 1779, p.235. **A.C. of £9.S7.d6 Sterl. paid into the late Receiver Generals Office by JAMES PATTON Dec'd.**

WILLIAM THOMPSON & WILLIAM PRESTON Exrs. of the Sd JAMES PATTON Dec'd, by Survey 15 Mar 1747/8, 280 acs. *(part of an order of council granted the said James Patton and others which Said Survey having been laid before the court of appeals is by them certified to have been establish'd)*, in Augusta Co. on a br. of the new riv. call'd back Cr.; 23 Dec 1779, p.237. **A.C. of 30 Shill. Sterl. paid into the late Receiver Generals Office by JAMES PATTON Dec'd.**

WILLIAM THOMPSON & WILLIAM PRESTON Executors of Sd JAMES PATTON Dec'd, by Survey 16 Nov 1746, 640 acs. *(part of an order of council granted the sd James Patton & Others*; which sd survey having been laid before the Court of Appeals, is by them certified to have been established), in Augusta Co. on the NW side of the Indian Riv., in a Draft; 23 Dec 1779, p.238. **A.C. of £3.S5 Sterl. paid into the late Receiver Generals Office by James Patton Dec'd.**

WILLIAM THOMPSON & WILLIAM PRESTON Executors of Sd JAMES

PATTON Dec'd, by survey 26 Oct 1749, 4,400 acs. (*part of an order of council granted the Sd James Patton and others, which sd Survey having been laid before the Court of Appeals is by them Certified to have been Establish'd*), in Augusta Co. on Woods Riv. at a place Call'ed Tanat [Fanat of Tanfat?] surrounded by the Mountain Nochollow and Glenvar, Beginning on the East point of a High Spur of the Mountain on the N Side of a Small Br., at the head of a Glade, on a ridge, in a Draft, on the W side of a Barren Ridge, on the point of a Ridge near a br.; 23 Dec 1779, p.240. **A.C. of £22 Sterl. paid into the late Receiver Generals Office by James Patton Dec'd.**

WILLIAM THOMPSON & WILLIAM PRESTON Executors of sd JAMES PATTON Dec'd, by Survey 30 Oct 1746, 500 acs. (*part of an order of council granted the sd James Patton and others, which said Survey having been Laid before Court of Appeals by them Certified to have been established)*, in Augusta Co. on the W side of Woods Riv., Beginning at the foot of a high Rocky Hill thence to the Riv. Bank & up the Riv. to a high Bank of the Riv.; 23 Dec 1779, p.243. **A.C. of 50 Shill. Sterl. paid into the late Receiver Generals Office by James Patton Dec'd.**

WILLIAM THOMPSON & WILLIAM PRESTON Executors of the sd JAMES PATTON Dec'd, by Survey 24 Mar 1747/8, 104 acs. (*part of an order of Council granted the said James Patton and Others; which Said Survey having laid before the Court of Appeals is by them Certified to have been establish'd*), in Augusta Co. on both sides of the little Riv., Beginning at the foot of a Mountain on the S side the Riv. thence crossing the Riv.; 23 Dec 1779, p.244. **A.C. of 10 Shill. Sterl. paid into the late Receiver Generals Office by James Patton Dec'd.**

WILLIAM THOMPSON & WILLIAM PRESTON Executors of the sd JAMES PATTON Dec'd, by Survey 9 Feb 1748/9, 220 acs. (*part of an order of council granted the Sd James Patton and others, which said Survey having been laid before the court of appeals is by them Certified to have been established*), in Augusta Co. on a br. of Woods Riv. Call'd Plumb Cr., Beginning on a piney Spurr, on the S side of a Ridge, to a parcel of Rocks near a Br., on the N side of a Ridge; 23 Dec 1779, p.245. **A.C. of 25 Shill. Sterl. paid into the late Receiver Generals Office by James Patton Dec'd Ass'ee of GEORGE ROBINSON.**

WILLIAM THOMPSON & WILLIAM PRESTON Executors of the sd JAMES PATTON Dec'd, by Survey 12 Mar 1747/8 130 acs. (*part of an order of Council Granted the Sd James Patton and others which sd Survey having been laid befoe the Court of Appeals, is by them Certified to have been establish'd)*, then in Augusta Co. on a br. of the new Riv. call'd "the N,W, Branch of Walkers Cr." Beginning at the upper end of a high Bank of Rocky; 23 Dec 1779, p.247. **A.C. of 15 Shill. Sterl. paid into the late Receiver Generals Office by James Patton Dec'd.**

WILLIAM THOMPSON & WILLIAM PRESTON Executors of sd JAMES PATTON, by Survey 14 Feb 1748/9, 495 acs. (*part of an order of Council granted the sd James Patton and other, which sd Survey having been laid before the court of Appeals is by them Certified to have been Establish'd)*, then in Augusta Co. on a Br. of Woods Riv. Call'd Sinking Cr.; 23 Dec 1779, p.248. **A.C. of 50 Shill. Sterl. paid into the late Receiver Generals office by James Patton Dec'd Ass'ee of GEORGE ROBERTSON.**

WILLIAM THOMPSON & WILLIAM PRESTON Executors of Sd JAMES PATTON Dec'd, by Survey 10 Feb 1748/9, 490 acs. *(part of an order of Council granted the Sd James Patton and others, which sd Survey having been laid before the Court of Appeals is by them certified to have been Establish'd)*, in then Augusta Co. on the Waters of Woods Riv.; 23 Dec 1779, p.249. **A.C. of 50 Shill. Sterl. paid into the late Receiver Generals Office by James Patton Dec'd Ass'ee of GEORGE ROBINSON.**

WILLIAM THOMPSON & WILLIAM PRESTON Executors of Sd JAMES PATTON Dec'd, by Survey 14 Feb 1748/9, 304 acs. in then Augusta Co. on a br. of Woods Riv. Call'd Sinking Cr. *(part of an order of council granted the Sd James Patton and others, which sd Survey having been Laid before the Court of Appeals, is by them Certified to have been establish'd)*; 23 Dec 1779, p.250. **A.C. of 30 Shill. Sterl. paid into the late Receiver Generals Office by James Patton Dec'd.**

WILLIAM THOMPSON & WILLIAM PRESTON Exrs. of the sd JAMES PATTON Dec'd, by Survey 9 Feb 1748/49, 119 acs. *(part of an order of council Granted the sd James Patton and others, which sd Survey having been laid before the Court of Appeals is by them Certified to have been Establish'd)*, in then Augusta Co. on the waters of the S side of Woods Riv., Beginning on a naked ridge; 23 Dec 1779, p.251. **A.C. of 15 Shill. Sterl. paid into the late Receiver Generals Office by James Patton Dec'd Ass'ee of GEORGE ROBINSON.**

WILLIAM CAMPBELL & WILLIAM PRESTON Executors of JOHN BUCHANNAN Dec'd who was Ass'ee of sd JAMES PATTON Dec'd, by Survey 21 Feb 1749/50, 1,000 acs. *(part of an order of Council granted the sd James Patton and others, which sd Survey having been Laid before the Court of Appeals is by them certified to have been Establish'd)*, in then Augusta Co. on Shallow Cr., Beginning in a piece of Stony Ground on the E Side the Cr., by a Draft, on the NE Side of a high nob of a Hill; 23 Dec 1779, p.253. **A.C. of £5 Sterl. paid into the late Receiver Generals Office by James Patton Dec'd Ass'ee of JOHN TAYLOE.**

WILLIAM THOMPSON & WILLIAM PRESTON Exors. of Sd JAMES PATTON Dec'd, by Survey 14 Mar 1747/8, 130 acs. *(part of an order of council granted the sd James Patton and others, which Sd Survey having been laid before the Court of Appeals is by them Certified to have been Establish'd)*, in then Augusta Co. on a br. of the new Riv. Call'd Walkers Cr., Beginning on the SE side of the Cr. above the mouth of the second fork, in a hollow, down the Cr. to the foot of a Mountain, along the foot of the Mountain to the Beg.; 23 Dec 1779, p.254. **A.C. of 15 Shill. Sterl. paid into the late Receiver Generals Office by James Patton Dec'd.**

WILLIAM THOMPSON & WILLIAM PRESTON Executors of sd JAMES PATTON Dec'd, by Survey 10 Mar 1747/8, 260 acs. *(part of an order of council Granted the Sd James Patton and others, which sd Survey having been laid before the Court of Appeals is by them certified to have been establish'd)*, in then Augusta Co. on a br. of the new riv. called Walkers Cr.; 23 Dec 1779, p.255. **A.C. of 30 Shill. Sterl. paid into the late Receiver Generals Office by James Patton Dec'd.**

WILLIAM THOMPSON & WILLIAM PRESTON Exrs. of JAMES PATTON Dec'd, by Survey 25 Feb 1748/9, 85 acs. *(part of an order of council granted the sd James Patton and others, which sd Survey having been laid before the Court of Appeals is by them Certified to have been establish'd)*, in then Augusta Co. on the N Side of Woods Riv., at the Mouth of Reed Cr., on the point of a Spurr; 23 Dec 1779, p.256. **A.C. of 10 Shill. Sterl. paid into the late Receiver Generals Office by James Patton Dec'd Ass'ee of GEORGE ROBINSON.**

WILLIAM THOMPSON & WILLIAM PRESTON Exors. of Sd JAMES PATTON Dec'd, by Survey 22 Feb 1748/9, 680 acs. *(part of an order of council Granted the sd James Patton and others, whcih sd Survey having [been] laid before [the Court] of Appeals is by them certified to have been establish'd)*, in then Augusta Co. on the N side of Woods Riv.; 23 Dec 1779, p.258. **A.C. of £3.S10 Sterl. paid into the late Receiver Generals Office by James Patton Dec'd.**

WILLIAM THOMPSON & WILLIAM PRESTON Exrs. of sd JAMES PATTON Dec'd, by Survey 5 Apr 1748, *70 acs.* *(part of an order of council granted the sd James Patton and others, which sd survey having been laid before the court of Appeals, is by them certified to have been establish'd)*, in then Augusta Co. on the E side of the new Riv. at a place Call'd *the Sulpher Spring*, Beginning above a high point of Rocks on the Riv., to a high Bank of Rocks on the Riv.; 23 Dec 1779, p.259. **A.C. of 10 Shill. Sterl. paid into the late Receiver Generals Office by James Patton Dec'd.**

WILLIAM THOMPSON & WILLIAM PRESTON Executors of sd JAMES PATTON Dec'd, by Survey 25 Mar 1748, 87 acs. *(part of an order of council granted the sd James Patton and others, which sd Survey having been laid before the court of appeals, is by them certified to have been Establish'd)*, in then Augusta Co. on the little riv.; 23 Dec 1779, p.260. **A.C. of 10 Shill. Sterl. paid into the late Receiver Generals Office by James Patton Dec'd.**

WILLIAM PRESTON as Heir at Low of JOHN PRESTON who was Ass'ee of sd JAMES PATTON Dec'd, by Survey 28 Feb 1748/9, 2,675 acs. *(part of an order of council granted the Sd James Patton and others, which sd survey having been laid before the court of Appeals is by them Certified to have been establish'd)*, in then Augusta Co. on a Br. of Woods riv. Call'd Peek Cr., on the N Side of a meadow, in a Glade, on the Spurr of a Mountain, on a Spur; 23 Dec 1779, p.262. **A.C. of £13.S17 Sterl. paid into the late Receiver Generals office by James Patton Dec'd.**

WILLIAM CAMPBELL & WILLIAM PRESTON Exrs. of JOHN BUCHANNAN Dec'd who was Ass'ee of sd JAMES PATTON Dec'd, by Survey 17 Feb 1749/50, 1,150 acs. *(part of an order of council granted the sd James Patton Dec'd and others, which sd Survey having been laid before the court of appeals is by them Certified to have been Establish'd)*, in then Augusta Co. on Sinking Br. on the Waters of the Middle br. of the Indian Riv., Beginning at the foot of a Ridge, to 5 White Oak Saplins in Brushey Barrans, on a Saplin Ridge, on a Bushey Ridge near a br.; 23 Dec 1779, p.264. **A.C. of £5.S7.d6 Sterl. paid into the late Receiver Generals Office by James Patton Dec'd.**

MATTHEW ARBUCKLE, 480 acs. by Survey 27 Sep 1771, Rockbridge Co. on the N side of James Riv. and including a Tract of L. gtd. by Pat. to James Arbuckle 5 Sep 1749 containing 400 acs. and now the property of Matthew Arbuckle [Augusta Co. PB 27 p.374, below the Island Ford], by the foot of a hill and edge of a meadow; 5 Jan 1780 *in the 5th year of the Commonwealth*, p.266. 10 Shill. Sterl. [*They didn't wait for the 4th of July to start the new ordinal year. This error was later corrected beginning with Peter Poythress's patent on p.298*]

PATRICK McCONNEL Ass'ee of GEORGE GIBSON, 28 acs. by Survey 19 Feb 1755 in Rockbridge Co. upon a Br. of Buffaloe Cr. Call'd the dry Br., adj. sd Gibsons old Survey; 5 Jan 1780, p.267. A.C. of 5 Shill. Sterl.

JOHN HOWARD Ass'ee of sd WILLIAM BOWYER, by Survey 13 Jul 1774, 1,000 acs. Kentucky Co. on elk horn Cr. a Br. of the Kentucky Riv., adj. Vaughan; 5 Jan 1780, p.268. *in consideration of Military Service perform'd by THOMAS BOWYER in the late Warr between Great Brittain and France According to the terms of the King of Great Brittains proclamation of 1763.*

JOHN SUMNER, by Survey 24 Jun 1775, 2,000 acs. Kentucky Co. on the Waters of elk horn Cr. call'd *Sumners Forest*; 5 Jan 1780, p.269. *In consideration of Military Service perform'd by John Sumner in the late War between Great Brittain and France according to the Terms of the King of Great Brittains proclamation of 1763.*

GEORGE MINOR ass'ee of RICHARD TAYLOR & THOMAS LANIER, by Survey 11 Nov 1754, 336 acs. Mecklenburg Co. on both sides of the Reedy Br., Beginning on the S side the fork below Mitchels Deer pen, in the fork of the Road, adj. Fletcher & Robertson; 5 Jan 1780, p.271. A.C. of 35 Shill. Sterl. [For Fletcher's land, see Joseph Dodson's PB 34 p.717 which was also referred to as John Speed's in GB E p.96 to John Davis. For Robertson's land, see PB 34 p.591 to Nicholas Roberson on Canoe Gutt]

DAVID ROSS ass'ee of sd WILLIAM FLEMING, and to JOHN MAY Ass'ee of sd DAVID ROSS, by Survey 2 Jun 1774, 3,000 acs. Kentucky Co. on the Ohio Riv.; Beginning at a Double Honey Locust, Buckeye and Hoopwood on the South bank of the River, 590 poles below Connelly's lower Corner and about 20 poles above a small Branch and about 5 Miles below the falls; bet. two Meadows; adj. Thomas Bowyer & John Ware; 5 Jan 1780, p.272. *in consideration of Military Service perform'd by William Fleming as Captain in the Virginia Regiment in the late War between Great Brittain and france according to the terms of the King of Gret Brittains proclamation of 1763.*

DANIEL McRAE Ass'ee of THOMAS EVANS, 150 acs. by Survey 7 May 1757 in Albemarle Co. on both sides of Mechams Riv.; adj. Robert McNeely, Archebald Wood & John Dichey; 5 Jan 1780, p.274. 15 Shill. Sterl.

ROBERT CRAWLEY, 275 acs. by Survey 11 Oct 1765, Mecklenburg Co. on Island Cr. and Joining the Land he now lives on, in the Country Line [West], near the Road, also adj. Maynard; 5 Jan 1780, p.275. A.C. of 30 Shill. Sterl. [For his other land, see PB 40 p.725. For Maynard's land, see PB 33 p.627 to John Bracy. Also adj. Robert Mitchel's PB 28 p.526]

JOHN TAYLOR, JUNIOR, by survey 18 Dec 1773, 300 acs. Mecklenburg Co. on the S Side of Roan Oak Riv. and on the Waters of Long Grass, along the Country line [West]; adj. Robertson's Orphans, Lewis's Orphans & Johnson; 5 Jan 1780, p.276. A.C. of 30 Shill. Sterl.

NATHANIEL GIST, 3,000 acs. by Survey Jun 1775 in Kentucky Co. on the N side of the Kentucky on Gist's Cr., the Waters of the Ohio, Joining on the N side of a Tract Surveyed for him; 5 Jan 1780, p.278. *in consideration of Military Service perform'd by Nathaniel Gist in the late War between Great Brittain and France according to the Terms of the King of Great Brittains proclamation of 1763.*

NATHANIEL GIST, Eldest Son and Heir at Law of sd CHRISTOPHER GIST Dec'd, 3,000 acs. by Survey Jun 1775 in Kentucky Co. on the N Side of the Kentucky Riv. a br. of the Ohio and on Gist's Cr. a South Br. of Licking Cr.; 5 Jan 1780, p.279. *in consideration of Military Service perform'd by Christopher Gist in the late War between Great Brittain and France according to the Terms of the King of Great Brittains proclamation of 1763.*

THOMAS GIST, 2,000 acs. by Survey Jun 1775, in Kentucky Co. on Gist's Cr. the Waters of the Ohio; 5 Jan 1780, p.280. *in consideration of Military Service perform'd by Thomas Gist in the late War between Great Brittain and France according to the Terms of the King of Great Brittains proclamation of 1763.*

ALEXANDER STEWART, 99 acs. by Survey 21 Sep 1772 in Botetourt Co. on the Mill Cr. a br. of Craigs Cr. being the Waters of James Riv., on a Ridge; 5 Jan 1780, p.281. A.C. of 10 Shill. Sterl.

JAMES ALLEN, Representative of the Sd JOHN ALLEN Dec'd, by Survey 22 Jul 1776, 2,000 acs. Kentucky Co. on the Waters of the Salt Riv., Beginning in a fork where the North br. is about ten yards Wide, crossing 2 Brs. & the Riv. to the side of a flat Ridge; 5 Jan 1780, p.282. *in consideration of Military Service perform'd by John Allen Dec'd in the late War between Great Brittain and France according to the Terms of the King of Great Brittains proclamation of 1763.*

MARTHA GALBRATH ass'ee of JOHNATHAN WHETLEY, 73 acs. by Survey 17 Dec 1760, in Rockbridge Co. on the S Side of Buffaloe Cr. and the

Short Hill bet. his own and Beals L., Beginning Close by Gathbraths [Galbraths] clear Field; 5 Jan 1780, p.283. A.C. of 10 Shill. Sterl.

ISRAEL CHRISTIAN Ass'ee of sd MONTEAU DEBNAM, 1,000 by Survey 20 Jul 1774, in Kentucky Co. on Elk Horn Cr. a br. of the Kentucky Riv. and about 12 Miles from the same and on the N side thereof; Beginning at an Elm, Hoopwood and Ash on a Ridge in a cane break corner to the of William Christian; crossing 2 Main Brs. of the Cr., by a Draft, on a flat Ridge; 5 Jan 1780, p.284. *in consideration of Military Service perform'd by Monteau Debnam in the late War between Great Brittain and France according to the Terms of the King of Great Brittains proclamation of 1763.*

ALEXANDER STEWART, 190 acs. by Survey 1 Dec 1770, in Botetourt Co. on the S side of Craigs Cr. a br. of James Riv., by a Gulley, in a Gap of the Ridge & along the Ridge, adj. sd Stewart & Hartsough; 5 Jan 1780, p.285. A.C. of 20 Shill. Sterl.

JOHN WALKER Ass'ee of ALEXANDER WALKER, 70 acs. by Survey 28 Jul 1772 in Rockbridge Co. on some of the Head Brs. of Walkers Cr., over a Rise and along the side of a Hill;, by a Gully, crossing a Draft and up another Hill to a large Rock, crossing over the knole of a High Hill and also a Valley; adj. Hugh Kelso, Bordens Patent Line & Anthony Kelly; 5 Jan 1780, p.287. A.C. of 10 Shill. Sterl.

JOHN ALLEN Heir at Law of sd HUGH ALLEN Dec'd, 1,000 acs. by Survey 25 Jun 1776 in Kentucky Co. on the Waters of Clear cr. a Br. of the Kentucky Riv. and lies about 10 Miles from Harwoods Landing and nearly a South course, crossing a Br. and passing a Spring to the Beg., adj. Rollins's L.; 5 Jan 1780, p.288. *in consideration of Military service perform'd by Hugh Allen Dec'd in the late War between Great Brittaina and France according to the Terms of the King of Great Brittains proclamation of 1763.*

HUGH ALLEN, 1,000 acs. by Survey 7 Jun 1774 in Kentucky Co. on the Waters of Bear Grass Cr. a South Br. of the Ohio Riv. and about 5 Miles from the same, by a Draft; adj. Charlton, Southall & Floyd; 5 Jan 1780, p.289. *in consideration of Military Service perform'd by Hugh Allen in the late War between Great Brittain and France according to the terms of the King of Great Brittains proclamation of 1763.*

JAMES PINE Ass'ee of JAMES LOGAN, 58 acs. by Survey 3 Sep 1772 in Rockbridge Co. on a Br. of Buffaloe Cr. the waters of James Riv., Beginning on a Ridge called McCalisters Ridge, on the top of a Ridge call'd Hucklebury Hill, crossing a Deep Valley to the Beg.; 5 Jan 1780, p.290. A.C. of 10 Shill. Sterl.

NATHANIEL BLACKMORE Ass'ee of sd WILLIAM CROMWELL, 300 acs. Augusta Co., Beginning on the E side of Shirtees Cr. by estimation ½ Mile below Frowman's Mill; 22 Mar 1780, p.292. *in Consideration of Military Service perform'd by William Cromwell as a Subaltern in the late War between Great Britain & France according to the Terms of the King of Great Britain's Proclamation of 1763.*

DAVID PATTERSON Ass'ee of JOHN WARD, by Survey 31 Oct 1776, 186 acs. Henry Co. on the Head brs. of Irvens Riv., Beg on the Top of the blue Ridge of Mountains near a Spring, Crossing a Spring br.; *Thomas Jefferson Esqr. Governour of the Commonwealth of Virginia hath hereunto Set his hand and caused the Seal of the sd Commonwealth to be affixed at Williamsburg on 1 May 1780*, p.293. A.C. of £1.S6.d8 Sterl.

THOMAS HINDS Ass'ee of Sd JAMES ROBINSON, by Survey 16 Jul 1774, 1,000 acs. in Kentucky Co. on the N brs. of Kentucky Riv. about 5 Miles East of the head brs. of elk horn Cr. and about 32 Miles from the Kentucky being the waters of the Ohio Riv. on the South side thereof, adj. Patrick Henry; *Thomas Jefferson Esquire Governour of the Commonwealth of Virginia hath hereunto Set his Hand & Caused the Seal of the Sd Commonwealth to be affixed at Williamsburg Richmond on 11 May 1780*, p.294. *in Consideration of Military Service performed by James Robinson in the late War between Great Brittain and France according to the terms of the King of Great Britains proclamation of 1763.*

ANDREW LEWIS, by Survey 16 Apr 1757, 1,200 acs. Greenbrier Co. on the Sink holes above the head of Indian Cr. at the foot of a Mountain that layeth bet. Indian Cr. and Green brier, Beginning near the foot of the Mountain, to a black Oak in a little Sink hole; 18 May 1780, p.295. **A.C. of £6. Sterl. paid into the late Receiver Generals Office by Andrew Lewis.**

ANDREW LEWIS, by Survey 7 Nov 1752, 400 acs. Greenbrier Co. on the head Springs of Indian Cr. near the waters of Green brier, Beginning on a Ridge, near a high bank; *18 May 1780 in the 5th year of the Commonwealth*, p.297. **A.C. of 40 Shill. Sterl. paid into the late Receiver Generals Office by Andrew Lewis.**

PETER POYTHRESS, by Survey made 21 Nov 1774, 173 acs. Pr. Geo. Co. on the S side of black Water Sw.; Beginning at black water Spring, near a Miery Br., in the Eeal root level; adj. Sd Poythress, James Wamack, William Grammer & Edwards Marks; *20 Jun 1780 in the 4th year of the Commonwealth*, p.298. **A.C. Money of 20 Shill. Sterl. paid into the late Receiver Generals office.**

DAVID ROSS & JOHN HOOK, by an **Inclusive Survey** made 1 May 1772, 565 acs. Bedford Co. on both Sides of Little Mill Cr. of Falling Riv. and on both sides of the main road between falling riv. and Little falling riv., on the head of the Suck br.; on Taylors road near a Spring; adj. William Read, Conners line, Joseph Akin & Jones; 14 Jun 1780, p.299. **A.C. of £3 Sterl. paid into the Late receiver Generals.** [This survey includes 300 acs. Bedford Co. to John Simmons in PB 38 p.550 dated 6 Apr 1769; on both sides of little Mill Cr. a small NE Cr. of Falling Riv. and on both sides of Randolph's long Island road, adj. Jones.] [Part of this tract is included in GB 57 p.320 dated 7 Nov 1808, 420 acs. Campbell Co., to John Reid assignee of Charles Martin]

JOHN HERDMAN, by Survey 9 Jul 1773, 119 acs. Augusta Co. on the head brs. of the W of Cooks Cr., at the foot of a Limestone ridge; adj. his other Pattented L., Henry Euing & Harrison;

near Alexander Millers line; 14 Jun 1780, p.301. A.C. of 15 Shill. Sterl.

JONATH WELDON Ass'ee of NATHANIEL HIGHT or HIGHS, by Survey 12 Feb 1766, 804 acs. Halifax Co. on the Brs. of the Lower Double Cr., on a ridge, Crossing a br. of the Double Cr., Crossing Robt. Walters fork; adj. Thomas Watkins, Charles Weatherford & Henry Talley; 14 Jun 1780, p.302. A.C. of 80 Shill. Sterl.

JOHN CAMPBELL Ass'ee of JAMES McALNARY, by Survey 16 Apr 1774, 200 acs. Fincastle Co. in the rich Valley of the Waters of the north fork of Holston riv., adj. the L. formerly John Bakers; 14 Jun 1780, p.304. A.C. of 20 Shill. Sterl.

GEORGE MOFFETT, by Survey 10 Jul 1775, 1,000 acs. Kentucky Co. on the Waters of Elk horn Cr.; 15 Jun 1780, p.305. *in Consideration of Military Service preformed by George Moffett in the late War between Great Britain & France according to the terms of the King of Great Britains proclamation of 1763.*

JOSEPH DOUGLASS Ass'ee of HUGH DOUGLASS, by Survey 6 Feb 1755, 35 acs. Rockingham Co. on the north Riv. Shanando Joining the sd Hugh Douglass' own L. his former Survey; 14 Jun 1780, p.306. A.C. of 5 Shill. Sterl.

JOHN COX, by Survey 20 Mar 1757, 400 acs. Pittsylvania Co. on Mill Cr. of Banister riv.; adj. Hugh Henry, Gray, Stone & [Musteen]; 15 Jun 1780, p.307. A.C. of 40 Shill. Sterl.

JOSIAS JONES, by Survey 24 Mar 1765, 425 acs. Buckingham Co. on both sides of Philips Cr.; adj. his own line, Alexander Smith & James Meredith; 15 Jun 1780, p.309. A.C. of 40 Shill. Sterl.

AARON STEEGALE Ass'ee of GEORGE STEEGALL, by Survey 19 Apr 1775, 4¾ acs. in Lunenburg Co. on the S or upper side of the little Cr. below honey Cr. [Stoney Cr.], adj. his own line & David Moss; 7 Jun 1780, p.310. A.C. of 5 Shill. Sterl. [For his own line, see PB 33 p.928 to James Wray. David Moss's appears to be about 15 missing acs. or part of PB 18 p.367 to James Mice. Also see adj. land in PB 14 p.81 to James & Jeremiah Mice between the Ruine Cr. (Stoney Cr.) and the Little Cr. (Aarons Cr.)]

JOSEPH CABELL, 300 acs. [Buckingham Co.], by Survey Transfered to sd Joseph Cabell 18 Mar 1752, crossing Frisbeys Cr. [of Slate Riv.]; adj. Samuel Stephens, Thomas Jones & Francis Brothers; 15 Jun 1780, p.311. A.C. money of 30 Shill. Sterl. [For Samuel Stephens' see his PB 25 p.484, for Francis Brothers' see Charles Burk's PB 19 p.11]

JOSEPH RICHARDSON, by Survey 5 Apr 1750, 300 acs. Bedford Co. on both sides of Rock castle br. (a South br. of goose Cr.), adj. George Walton; 15 Jun 1780, p.312. A.C. money of 30 Shill. Sterl.

FRANCIS FOSTER ass'ee of SAMUEL WHITE, Heir at Law of JAMES WHITE dec'd, by Survey 3 Feb 1752/53, 400 acs. [Lunenburg Co. now Charlotte Co.] on the Brs. of Twittys Cr. and Ash Camp Cr.; adj. Covinton, Walters line, Reed, Childres & Hutson; 18 Jun 1780, p.314. A.C. of 40 Shill. Sterl. [For Hutson, see

PB 34 p.456 to Joshua Hudson; for Covinton's, see PB 33 p.926 to Henry Isbell; for Walters, see PB 33 p.519 to Thomas Lipscomb]

JOHN BEAZLEY, by survey made 18 Nov 1765, 150 acs. [Amherst Co.] on the N side of Pedlar riv. on the brown mountain; 20 Jun 1780, p.315. A.C. of 20 Shill. Sterl.

JOHN COX, by survey 22 Oct 1748, 400 acs. Pittsylvania Co. on mill Cr.; 7 Jun 1780, p.317. A.C. of 40 Shill. Sterl.

ROBERT HILL, by Survey 26 Nov 1770, 800 acs. Pittsylvania Co. on Fowl ground br. of black water riv. and Leynors br. of Pigg Riv., on Lynous's br., up low Ground br.; 15 Jun 1780, p.318. A.C. of £4 Sterl.

DANIEL LOVELL, by survey 30 Jan 1766, 90 acs. [Pittsylvania Co.] on Great Cherry Stone Cr.; 16 Jun 1780, p.319. A.C. of 10 Shill. Sterl.

JONAS LAWSON, by survey 4 Nov 1774, 252 acs. Pittsylvania Co. on the head brs. of Sandy Cr., crossing a bold br., adj. John Anglin; 12 Jun 1780, p.320. A.C. of 15 Shill. Sterl.

CONRAD HARKEY, by survey 7 Nov 1754, 73 acs. Augusta Co. on both sides of John's Cr. the Waters of James riv., adj. his old Survey; 16 Jun 1780, p.321. A.C. of 20 Shill. Sterl.

HENRY HOLSTON, by Survey 28 Sep 1772, 326 acs. Botetourt Co., Beginning on the N side of Craigs Cr. a br. of James Riv. corner to the land he lives on, adj. the Land he bought of Preston; 10 Jun 1780, p.322. A.C. of 35 Shill. Sterl.

SAMUEL ASKEY, by Survey 27 Oct 1774, 247 acs. Pittsylvania Co. on both sides of Fall cr., adj. John Kerbey; 16 Jun 1780, p.324. A.C. of 25 Shill. Sterl.

PETER SHOEMAKER, by survey 17 Feb 1773, 29 acs. Rockingham Co. on a br. of rocks Cr., adj. his other L., one Samples L. & sd McBride; 16 Jun 1780, p.325. A.C. of 5 Shill. Sterl.

PATRICK NAPIER, by Survey 28 Jan 1780, 100 acs. Fluvanna Co. which was lately the property of Wm. Ainge a Subject of Great Britain and was sold by the sd Thomas Napier Gent. Escheator for the sd Co. unto the sd Patrick Napier, Beginning at his corner; 16 Jun 1780, p.326. *A.C. of £451 Current Money of Virginia paid by Patrick Napier unto Thomas Napier Gent. Escheator for Fluvanna Co. ... by Virtue of and agreeable to two late acts of General Assembly passed in the year 1779. the one entituled an act concerning escheats and forfeitures from British Subjects and the other entituled an act concerning Escheators.*

SYLVANIUS STOCKS [SYLVANUS STOKES], by Survey 28 Oct 1774, 236 acs. Pittsylvania Co. on the N side White Oak Mountain and on the brs. of White oak Cr., crossing Sucks br.; adj. Robert Adams, Kurbeys line on the Mountain, Clay, the sd Tolifaro's old Line; 21 June 1780, p.328. A.C. of 25 Shill. Sterl.

ADAM STEPHENDS/STEVENS Esqr., by Survey 13 Jul 1774, 1,000 acs. Kentucky Co. on the N Side the Kentucky Riv. a br. of the Ohio on Stephens Cr., Beginning about 1,250 poles Easterly from a large Spring the head of Jessamine Cr. being the first Cr.

on the N Side of Kentuckey Riv. about Dicks river at A, with a line of John Wards Land to 2 Sugar Trees and an Ash at B, with the Line of John Pouls on a Hoop Ash, and Hicory to C; 21 June 1780, p.329. *in consideration of Military Service performed by Adam Stephens Esquire as a Field officer in the late War between Great Britain and France according to the terms of the King of great Britains proclamation of 1763.*

THOMAS WALTERS, by survey 5 Nov 1762, 275 acs. Halifax Co. on the brs. of the upper Double Cr., crossing the north fork of sd Cr. and a br., adj. William Weatherford & William King; 21 Jun 1780, p.331. A.C. of 30 Shill. Sterl.

THOMAS READ, by Survey made 10 Apr 1780, 50 acs. Charlotte Co. adj. John Dabney, Redman & Morton; 21 Jun 1780, p.332. A.C. Money of 5 Shill. Sterl. [This land is near the high hills between Wallaces Cr. (Wallace Br.) & Staunton Riv. For John Dabney's land, see the Kennons's 31,700 acs. on Cubb Cr. in PB 23 p.647; for Morton's see PB 25 p.238 to John Middleton and for Redman's see PB 19 p.701 to Richard Randolph]

WILLIAM RUSSELL, by Survey 6 Apr 1779, 274 acs. Pittsylvania Co. on the brs. of Fall Cr. and Burches Cr.; adj. Dodson, Macbee, Samuel Harris & William Walters Corner; 21 Jun 1780, p.333. A.C. of 30 Shill. Sterl.

SAMUEL HARRISS, by Survey 31 Mar 1774, 404 acs. Pittsylvania Co. on both sides of Burches Cr., adj. Kerby/Kerbey, Linch, Givins lines & Robert Walthers Corner; 21 Jun 1780, p.335. A.C. of 40 Shill. Sterl.

SAMUEL HARRISS, by Survey 31 Mar 1774, 400 acs. Pittsylvania Co. on both sides of Burches Cr.; adj. Robert Walthers Corner, Mofses Terry & William Linch; 21 Jun 1780, p.337. A.C. of 40 Shill. Sterl.

JOHN MOORE, by Survey 12 Dec 1771, 48 acs. Botetourt Co. on the Waters of Loonies Cr. a br. of James Riv., by a ridge, in a draft, adj. James Moore; 22 Jun 1780, p.338. A.C. of 5 Shill. Sterl.

SILVANUS STOCKS [STOKES], by Survey 25 Oct 1774, 304 acs. Pittsylvania Co. on the brs. of White oak Cr., adj. Tollifarro's upper line & Greenstreet; 13 Jun 1780, p.340. A.C. of 30 Shill. Sterl.

PETER SAUNDERS, by Survey 6 Nov 1773, 156 acs. Henry Co. on orter Cr. [Otter Cr.]; adj. Smith, his own Line & McGriff; 22 Jun 1780, p.341. A.C. of 20 Shill. Sterl.

LUKE STANDEFER, by Survey 5 Dec 1778 or 1770, 324 acs. Henry Co. on Black Water Riv., adj. his former corner on sd riv. & John Kemp; 22 Jun 1780, p.343. A.C. of 35 Shill. Sterl.

WILLIAM WILSON, by Survey 7 May 1773, 92 acs. Augusta Co. on the North and South forks of Mill Cr. a br. of Jackson's Riv., by a Spring & a Swamp; 22 Jun 1780, p.345. A.C. of 10 Shill. Sterl.

JAMES HICKS, by Survey 10 Apr 1772, 306 acs. Pittsylvania Co. on Beaver Cr.;

adj. Walker, Talbot & Blevens; 22 Jun 1780, p.347. A.C. of 35 Shill. Sterl.

SHADRACH WOODSON, by Survey 11 May 1779, 79 acs. Henry Co. adj. Stephen Leis Land on the Waters of black Water Riv., at the head Spring of a South fork, adj. his own line; 22 Jun 1780, p.349. A.C. of 10 Shill. Sterl.

ZACHARY TAYLOR Heir at Law of HANCOCK TAYLOR Assignee of ALEXANDER WAUGH who was Ass'ee of sd JOHN WALLER, by Survey made 31 May 1774, 1,000 acs. Kentucky Co. on the Ohio Riv. 240 poles above the mouth of Bear grass Cr., adj. James Southall; *22 Jun 1780 in the 4th year of the Commonwealth*, p.350. *in consideration of Military Service performed by John Waller as a Lieutenant in the Second Virginia Regiment during the late War between great Britain and France according to the terms of the King of great Britain's Proclamation of 1763.*

JOHN EVANS HARRISS, by Survey 24 Apr 1772, 250 acs. Mecklenburg Co. on the head brs. of Avents Cr.; adj. Pickett, Buggs, William Penington, Sack Penington, Whitley & Taylor; *21 Jun 1780 in the 5th year of the Commonwealth*, p.352. A.C. of 25 Shill.

ZACHARY TAYLOR, by survey made 17 Jun 1774, 200 acs. Kentucky Co. on a br. of the Kentuckey Riv. which empties at the great crossing; 22 Jun 1780 in the *4th year of the Commonwealth*, p.354. *in consideration of Military Service performed by Zachary Taylor as a Serjeant in the second Virginia Regiment raised during the Late Ware between great Britain and France according to the terms of the King of great Britains proclamation of 1763.*

JAMES FORD, by Survey 8 Dec 1752, 295 acs. Buckingham Co. amongst the brs. of Joshua and Turpins Creeks of Slate Riv., crossing the road; adj. his own lines Thomas Turpin, Captain William Allen by Joshua's Cr. & William Salley; 22 Jun 1780, p.356. A.C. of 30 Shill. Sterl.

JEREMIAH WHITNEY, by Survey 5 Mar 1755, 245 acs. Albemarle Co. on the N side Great Wreck Island Cr., adj. his own line; 23 Jun 1780 in the *5th year of the Commonwealth*, p.358. A.C. of 25 Shill. Sterl. [Buckingham Co., S of the Fluvanna Riv.]

NICHOLAS CURRY Ass'ee of BENJAMIN LOGAN who was ass'ee of sd WILLIAM BELL, by Survey 7 Jun 1775, 200 acs. Kentuckey Co. adj. Madison; 23 Jun 1780, p.360. *in consideration of Military Service performed by William Bell a Serjeant in the Late War between Great Britain and France according to the terms of the King of great Britains Proclamation of 1763.*

JOHN BOYD Ass'ee of ISRAEL CHISTIAN [CHRISTIAN] who was Ass'ee of sd MORDECAI DEBNAM, by Survey 21 Jul 1774, 1,000 acs. Kentuckey Co. on Elk horn Cr. a North br. of Kentuckey and about 20 miles from the same being on the S side the Ohio Riv. and about 90 miles from the Mouth of the Kentuckey Riv., by a Draft, on a flat Ridge, adj. John Draper; 23 Jun 1780, *5th year of the Commonwealth*, p.361. *in consideration of Military*

Service performed by Mordecai Debnam in the late War between great Britain and France according to the Terms of the King of Great Britains Proclamation of 1763.

ROBERT MASON Ass'ee of WILLIAM TREADWAY, by Survey 1 Dec 1770, 1,663 acs. Pittsylvania Co. on Chesnut Cr.; 24 Jun 1780, *5th year of the Commonwealth*, p.363. A.C. of £9 Sterl.

JAMES COLEMAN Ass'ee of NATHANIEL FEILDS, by Survey 24 Feb 1755, 150 acs. Albemarle Co. on both sides a br. called Long Br., on a Ridge, adj. James Angles & John Jennings; 24 Jun 1780, *4th year of the Commonwealth*, p.365. A.C. Money of 15 Shill. Sterl.

SHADRACH WOODSON, by Survey Made 3 Apr 177, 154 acs. Henry Co. on the Waters of black Water Riv., adj. Richard Doggatts old line; 22 Jun 1780, p.367. A.C. Money of 15 Shill. Sterl.

WILLIAM THURMAN, by Survey 23 Nov 1779, 181 acs. Pr. Edward Co. on the brs. of Appamattox Riv., down Whill's br.; adj. his old line, 2 Fenced Corners & James Matthews; 21 Jun 1780, *5th year of the Commonwealth*, p.369. A.C. of 20 Shill. Sterl.

THOMAS TURPIN, JUNIOR, by Survey made 24 Nov 1779, 400 acs. Fluvanna Co. on the S Side of Bryants Road, up sd road agreeable to the Windings thereof, adj. Bryant; 27 Jun 1780, p.371. £2,205 current money of Virginia paid by Thomas Turpin Jur. to Thomas Napier Gent. Escheator for Fluvanna Co. ... *being part of a Larger Tract lately the property of Samuel Martin a British Subject and was Sold by the sd Thomas Napier unto the sd Thomas Turpin jr. agreeable to 2 acts of Assembly passed in 1779 the one entituled an act concerning Escheats and Forfietures from British Subjects the other entituled an act concerning Escheators.* [This l. is part of Capt. John Martin's PB 13 p.164, 6,186 acs. Henrico Co. dated 13 Oct 1727, which included most of John Thornton's 3,600 acs. Henrico Co. dated 6 Nov 1721 in PB 11 p.64]

JOHN DICKINSON, by Survey 4 Nov 1779, 308 acs. by entry transfered to RALPH ELKINS on the Brs. of the north fork of Leatherwood Cr. in Henry Co., adj. Smith; 7 Jul 1780, *5th year of the Commonwealth*, p.372. A.C. of 35 Shill. Sterl.

JAMES BREWER, by Survey 18 Feb 1774, 373 acs. Pittsylvania Co. on both sides of Bold Br. of Cherry Stone Cr.; adj. William Right, John Swinny & Taylor; 7 Jul 1780, p.374. A.C. of 40 Shill. Sterl.

LANDIE RICHARDSON, by survey Oct 1777, 530 acs. **Inclusive** in Louisa Co. on both sides the north fork of Camp Cr.; adj. Richd. Morris, Samuel Bunch & Harlow; 7 Jul 1780, p.376. A.C. of 55 Shill. Sterl.

THOMAS SOWELL, by survey 17 Apr 1777, 400 acs. Fluvanna Co. on the N side the rivanna riv. & on both Sides Ballengers Cr., to Arbors Road, to the three notch'd Road, on the County line, to the hogpen Br.; adj. Randolph, Watson/Wattson, Winston, Thomas Baber jr. & Jno. Strange; 7 Jul 1780, p.377. A.C. of 40 Shill. Sterl.

MARTIN MASON, by Survey 16 Nov 1770, 35 acs. Bedford Co. on the brs. of Troublesome cr.; adj. his own line, Peter Fonk & Price; 8 Jul 1780, p.380. A.C. of 5 Shill. Sterl.

Rev'd. CHARLES CLAY, by Survey 26 Jan 1775, 400 acs. Albemarle Co. on the N side the Fluvanna Riv. and on each side the south fork of Totier/Toteir/Totear Cr. and on the brs. of Ballengers Cr., to John Coles Church road, to the old Irish road, to a br. of the middle Fork of Totear Cr.; adj. Mr John Cole, David Weaver, Abraham Eades Senr. & Nathaniel Watkins; 10 June 1780, p.381. A.C. of 40 Shill. Sterl.

SYLVANUS STOKES, by Survey 25 Oct 1774, 538 acs. Pittsylvania Co. on both sides of the west fork of White Oak Cr., adj. Jonas Lawson; 7 Jun 1780, *4th year of the Commonwealth*, p.384. A.C. of £2.S15 Sterl.

ORLANDER SMITH, by Survey 6 apr 1779, 158 acs. Pittsylvania Co. on the brs. of Fall Cr.; adj. William Russel, Macbee, & the Order line; 7 Jun 1780, p.385. A.C. of 20 Shill. Sterl.

JOHN FOX Ass'ee of RICHARD GWYN, by Survey 22 Aug 1774, 342 acs. Pittsylvania Co. on the waters of Sandy Cr.; adj. Kennon, John King & Joseph Gary; 8 Jul 1780, *5th year of the Commonwealth*, p.386. A.C. money of 35 Shill. Sterl.

WILLIAM JACKSON ass'ee of THOMAS JACKSON, by Survey 30 Mar 1779, 323 acs. Pr. Edward Co. on the brs. of Appamatox Riv. and rough Cr., Crossing little Rough Cr., adj. James Mathews line & Watkins; 8 Jul 1780, p.388. A.C. of 35 Shill. Sterl.

THOMAS SOWELL Ass'ee of PATRICK NAPIER, by Survey 24 Feb 1779, 400 acs. Fluvanna Co. on the N Brs. of Hardware Riv. and Bryery Cr., adj. John Morris & George Hilton; 8 Jul 1780, p.389. A.C. of 40 Shill. Sterl.

JAMES HICKMAN brother and heir at Law to the Sd RICHARD HICKMAN Dec'd, by survey 29 May 1775, 2,000 acs. Kentuckey Co. on Boons Cr., adj. a tract of Land Mark'd for William Robinson; 8 Jul 1780, p.391. *in consideration of Military Service performed by Richard Hickman as a Lieutenant During the late war between Great Britain and France according to the terms of the King of Great Britians Proclamation of 1763.* [Margin note: James Hickman Assignee of Richard Hickman]

WILLIAM RYON Ass'ee of AMBROSE HOLT, 242 acs. by Survey 15 Feb 1769 in Henry Co. on the Grassey fork of Snow Cr., Crossing 2 brs. and a Road, adj. Randolph, to a Chesnut tree Bradshaws [Athun] in his own line; 13 Jul 1780, p.392. A.C. of 25 Shill. Sterl.

ROBERT GREER, 400 acs. by Survey 8 Feb 1775 in Bedford Co. on the W brs. of Cub Cr.; adj. Goode, Read, Moor & John Harvey; 14 Jul 1780, p.394. A.C. of 40 Shill. Sterl.

GEORGE STOVALL, 338 acs. by Survey 2 Dec 1768 in Bedford Co. on the head Brs. of Wreck Island Cr., on Linches Old Road; adj. his own Line, Fleming, & George Stovall Junior; 14 Jul 1780, p.395. A.C. of 35 Shill. Sterl.

WILLIAM MEAD, 200 acs. Bedford Co. at the mouth of Island Cr. on Otter Riv., by the waggon Road, down Island Cr. thence down Otter Riv. to include the said river with a Small Island 80 poles below the said Island Cr. to join Henry Guthreys L. thence up the North br. of the sd Riv., adj. Clement Moberleys old line; 13 Jul 1780, p.397. A.C. of 20 Shill. Sterl. [Included in William Irvine's 430 acs. in GB 32 p.248 dated 26 May 1795]

WILLIAM YOUNG, 642 acs. by Survey 24 Oct 1777 in Pittsylvaria Co. on both Sides of the Cron br. of Pigg Riv.; adj. James Carr, David Potty & the sd Young; 14 Jul 1780, p.399. A.C. of £3.S5 Sterl.

JOHN HOLLOWAY, 250 acs. by Survey 7 Jan 1745 in Pr. Edward Co. in the fork of Sandy Riv., in the low Ground; adj. Thomas Morten, Penix, & Rolin's line; 14 Jul 1780, p.400. A.C. of 25 Shill. Sterl.

GEORGE GADDY, 240 acs. by Survey 1 Mar 1771, Bedford Co. on the west head Brs. of Ivy Cr.; adj. his own Lines, Anthony, Fry and Company, & Callaway; 14 Jul 1780, p.402. A.C. of 25 Shill. Sterl.

NICHOLAS LEWIS, 44 acs. by Survey 15 Oct 1779 in Glouster Co. near the Dragon and on the Road from the dragon Ordinary to King and Queen and adj. the Lands of the sd Nicholas Lewis, John Dillard, John Dixon and Thomas Hall; 15 Jul 1780, p.404. A.C. of 5 Shill. Sterl.

JOHN PAYNE Esq., by Survey made 21 Nov 1779, 231 acs. Goochland Co. on S side Paynes Road; adj. John Thruston, William Cheak & Ansil George; 14 Jul 1780, p.405. in Consideration of the Sum of £401 Current money of Virginia paid unto William Harrison Gent. Escheator for Goochland Co. by John Payne Esq. ... being part of a larger tract lately the property of Jarvis Elam a British Subject and was sold by the sd William Harrison Escheator unto the sd John Payne agreeable to 2 acts of Assembly passed in the year 1779 the one entitled an act concerning Escheats and forfeitures from British Subjects the other entitled an act concerning Escheators.

HENRY HETH, 1,320 acs. by **Inclusive Survey** 18 Apr 1775 in Augusta Co. on a Mountain on the NW side of the North fork of the South br. of Potowmack at a place Known by *the Hunting Grounds* on the brs. of Big Run, to a Maple and Sugar tree by *a haw orchard*, near *Seneca waters*, on a ridge, Crossing Several Spring Brs. to the Beg.; 15 Jul 1780, p.407. A.C. of £6.S15 Sterl.

NEHEMIAH & JOSIAH HARRISON, 636 acs. by **Inclusive Survey** 7 Jul 1773, in Rockingham Co. on the head drafts of Cooks Cr., at the foot of a Lime Stone Ridge, on a Ridge, by a Pond, by a Road, adj. Henry Ewing & his old Corner, near Alexander Miller; 14 Jul 1780, p.409. A.C. of 15 Shill. Sterl. 370 acs part thereof being formerly gtd. to Jeremiah Harrison by Letters Pat. 10 Feb 1748/49 also 135 acs. another part being formerly Gtd. to Jeremiah Harrison by letters pat. 20 Sep 1768 the right and Title of which is since become Vested in the sd Nehemiah & Josiah Harrison and 131 acs. the residue never before gtd.

PHILLIP HUTCHISON, 274 acs. by Survey 26 Feb 17-- in Henry Co. on Buck Br. of Snow Cr., adj. William Heards Old Line & Thomas Prentys Corner at the road; 14 Jul 1780, p.412. A.C. of 30 Shill. Sterl.

ARTHUR EDWARDS Ass'ee of GEORGE WALKER Gent., 1,658 acs. by Survey 26 Oct 1754 in Halifax Co. on the brs. of Snow Cr.; adj. Woodson, Randolph, John Hickey & Owins line; 14 Jul 1780, p.414. A.C. of £8.S10 Sterl.

JOHN SHARP, 155 acs. by Survey 4 Apr 1772 in Bedford Co. on both Sides of black water riv., adj. John Chetwood & John Lumsden; 14 Jul 1780, p.417. A.C. of 20 Shill. Sterl.

GEORGE STOVALL, 202 acs. by Survey 28 Mar 1760 in Bedford Co. on both sides of the long br. a West br. of Stonewall Cr. and Including a bent of Stone wall Cr., Beginning at Christians & Scrugs Corner; 14 Jul 1780, p.419. A.C. of 20 Shill. Sterl.

STEPHEN SENTER, 216 acs. by Survey 25 Nov 1778 in Henry Co. on the brs. of Turkey Cr., Beginning on a Road; adj. William Young, his own lines & Coplands order line; 14 Jul 1780, p.420. A.C. of 25 Shill. Sterl.

JOHN COLES, Gent., 400 acs. by Survey 16 May 1776 in Albemarle Co. on the brs. of Totier/Toteir/Totear and Ballengers Creeks, to Old field Br., to a br. of the middle fork of Toteir Cr., to said Coles Church Road; adj. sd Coles line, Arthur White, Batersby Dec'd, Nathaniel Watkins, Charles Clay ; 14 Jul 1780, p.422. A.C. of 40 Shill. Sterl.

WILLIAM STROTHER MADISON/MADDISON Ass'ee of WILLIAM PRESTON who was Ass'ee of HENRY SMITH, 68 acs. by Survey 20 Oct 1772 in Botetourt Co. on Potts Cr. a br. of James Riv., by a Gulley, adj. the Land sd Henry Smith bought of Preston; 15 Jul 1780, p.425. A.C. of 10 Shill. Sterl.

WILLIAM PRESTON Ass'ee of sd ALEXANDER WAUGH, by Survey 31 May 1774, 1,000 acs. Kentucky Co. on the Ohio Riv. near the Falls, on the point of a Hill near the south fork of beargrass Cr., adj. John Connelly; 17 Jul 1780, p.426. *in Consideration of Military Service perform'd by Alexander Waugh in the late war between Great Britain and France according to the Terms of the King of Great Britains proclamation of 1763.*

WILLIAM PAGE, by Survey 17 Jan 1775, 253½ acs. Albemarle Co. on the brs. of the great Byrd Cr.; adj. Reubin Francis, William Burges, Colo. John Payne & William Clark; 17 Jul 1780, p.428. A.C. of 25 Shill. Sterl.

JOHN NASH, by survey 19 Nov 1778, 322 acs. Pittsylvania Co. on the brs. of Sandy Riv.; adj. Norvell Nash, Arthur Nash & Moseby; 19 Jul 1780, p.430. A.C. of 35 Shill. Sterl.

WILLIAM STROTHER MADISON ass'ee of WILLIAM PRESTON who was Ass'ee of HENRY SMITH, by Survey 8 Apr 1773, 315 acs. Botetourt Co. on the point bank run a br. of Potts Cr., Beginning on the S side the path; 17 Jul 1780, p.432. A.C. of 35 Shill. Sterl.

WILLIAM PRESTON Ass'ee of JOHN FLOYD, 61 acs. by Survey 2 Oct 1772 in Botetourt Co. on Potts's Cr. a br. of James Riv., adj. Prestons Second Survey; 17 Jul 1780, p.433. A.C. of 10 Shill. Sterl.

JOHN ROBINSON Ass'ee of JACOB SALMON, 50 acs. by Survey 5 May 1772 in Botetourt Co. on Dunlop Cr. a br. of James Riv., Beginning on the Cr. by a point of Rocks, to a pine by a place Cal'd *the horsepound*; 14 Jul 1780, p.435. A.C. of 5 Shill. Sterl. 16 acs. part thereof was gtd. to John Dickinson by letters Pat. 13 Aug 1763 [30 Aug 1763 in Augusta Co. PB 35 p.421 to John Dickison] and 34 acs the residue thereof never before Gtd.

ROBERT JOHNSON, 200 acs. by Survey 18 Apr 1768, Amherst Co. on the brs. of Merrewethers Br. of Rockfish Riv., adj. James Martin Junr.; 14 Jul 1780, p.437. A.C. of 30 Shill. Sterl. [Regranted Charles Bridgwater in GB 41 p.143 dated 2 April 1799 surveyed 18 August 1797]

WILLIAM HART of Surry Co., 438 acs. by Survey 10 Jun 1775 in sd Co. on the N side of Black Water Sw. being a Pocoson; adj. Lewis Long, Charles Kea, Anthony Digge, Dionysias Oliver/Olliver, a piece of Kings Land, Richard Drewit, John Brown & Jesse Little; 20 Jul 1780, p.439. A.C. of £2.S5 Sterl. Including 2 Surveys made by Charles Judkins and the sd William Hart 20 Mar 1775.

GEORGE DUDLEY JR., 368¼ acs. by Survey 2 Apr 1774 in Albemarle Co. on E side the Middle Fork of Buck Island Cr.; adj. Colo. Edward Carter, the land formerly Belonging to William Burrus, John Burrus & Charles Christian; 14 Jul 1780, p.442. A.C. of £2 Sterl.

SAMUEL TALIAFERRO, 240 acs. by Survey 20 Mar 1755 in Fluvanna Co. on the SE Side the Rivanna Riv. on the Brs. of Adreans Cr., Crossing Martin Kings Road, adj. James Adams & Hardin Burnley; 20 Jul 1780, p.445. A.C. of 25 Shill. Sterl.

JAMES SCOTT Ass'ee of JESSE CORN, 132 acs. Albemarle Co. by Survey 2 May 1775, on the S side the Rivanna Riv. and on the Waters of Cunninghams Cr., on brs. of the Middle Fork of sd Cr., adj. John Boswell & George Hardwick; 20 Jul 1780, p.446. A.C. of 15 Shill. Sterl.

WILLIAM CALL, 356 acs. by **inclusive Survey** 6 Feb 1775, in Pr. Geo. and Dinwiddie Countys on both Sides of the second Sw., crossing the Southern Fork & the North fork of the second Sw., to a Round Pond; adj. John Phillips near his fence, sd Calls old line of the land he purch'ed of John Aldridge, Boswell Goodwin, William Brown or the heirs of Lewis Parham near Richard Taylors Plantation, & Frances Massenburg Fenn; 20 Jul 1780, p.448. A.C. of 10 Shill. Sterl. 258 acs. part is part of a pat. for 3,647 acs. gtd. to Henry Randolph, James Cock, John Golightly and Soloman Crook by pat. 19 Feb 1690 [19 Apr 1690, PB 8 p.60 then in Charles Citty Co.] the right and title of which is since become vested in the sd William Call and 98 acs. the residue never before gtd.

JOHN COLES, 306 acs. by Survey 16 May 1776, Albemarle Co. on the Small brs. of Totear Cr., to the ware house Road, adj. Richard OGlesby & Arthur White; 20 Jul 1780, p.450. A.C. of 35 Shill. Sterl.

JAMES BARNETT, by Survey 9 Dec 1767, 70 acs. Botetourt Co. on a Small br. of Roanoake, Beginning on the side of a Steep Ridge; 20 Jul 1780, p.452. A.C. of 10 Shill. Sterl.

WILLIAM MURRAY (of the Atholbrose family of Murrays in Virginia), 10,000 acs. by **Inclusive Survey** 2 Dec 1778 in Bedford Co. on the N side of Stanton Riv. on both sides of Whipping Cr. and on the Fork of Hills Cr., up Hills Cr. and the west fork thereof, crossing lick br. and little whipping Cr., up Staunton Riv.; adj. Moses Fergrea, Randolph, William Brown, Bullock, Charles Folbot [Tolbot], & Marshall; 20 Jul 1780 *in the 5th year of the Commonwealth*, p.454-459. A.C. of £26 Sterl. 4,813 acs. part thereof was gtd. to James Murray by letters patent 16 Sep 1765 the right and Title of which is Since become Vested in the sd William Murray and 5,187 acs. the residue never before gtd.

Grant Book C

1 Sep 1780 to 1 Mar 1781

THOMAS THORNHILL, 404 acs. by Survey 20 Apr 1780 in Buckingham Co. on the small brs. of Fluvanna Riv., at Bradleys road, crossing a br. and Jeremiah Whitneys road, in a bottom; adj. Cabell, Thornhills old Line on the edge of the low Grounds, Colo. William Kennon dec'd & George Hilton; 1 Sep 1780, *in the 5th year of the Commonwealth, Thomas Jefferson Esquire Governor of the Commonwealth of Virginia hath hereunto Sett his hand and caused the lesser seal of the said Commonwealth to be affixed at Richmond*, p.1. A.C. of 40 Shill.

WILLIAM ROANE 470 acs. by an **Inclusive Survey** made 13 Jun 1778 in Essex Co., near Warings Mill house, crossing the county road, by a Spring, in the Sw. at the head of the Mill pond; adj. Smith, Waring & Tandy; 19 Oct 1780, p.2. in consideration of the Sum of £8,885 of current money of Virginia paid unto William Young, Gentleman Escheator for Essex Co. by William Roane Esquire. *lately the property of Laurence MacDuff a British Subject and was sold by the sd William Young, Escheator unto the sd William Roane agreeable to 2 acts of Assembly passed in the year 1779 the one Entitled an act cornerning Escheats and forfeitures from British Subjects the other Entitled an act concerning Escheators.*

JOHN ALLOWAY STRANGE, 250 acs. by Survey 27 Jan 1780 in Fluvanna Co. on the Rivanna riv. Including an Island in the run; 19 Oct 1780, p.3. in consideration of the Sum of £600 current money of Virginia paid by John Allaway Strange to Thomas Napier Gent. Escheator for Fluvanna Co. lateley the property of William Ainge a British Subject and was sold by the sd Thomas Napier, Escheator unto the sd John Alloway Strange *agreable to 2 acts of General Assembly passed in 1779 the one Entitled an act concerning Escheats and forfeitures from British Subjects the other Entitled an Act concerning Escheators.*

DANIEL ALLEGRE, ass'ee of WILLIAM BARTON, by Survey made

107

23 May 1777, 325½ acs. Albemarle Co. on the N Side of the Rivanna riv., to the three Notched road, to Valentine Woods Rollings road, to the long br., to Adams's road, to Burges br., adj. Patrick Morton & Giles Allegre; 1 Sep 1780, p.4. A.C. of 35 Shill. Sterl. [This land was also granted to William Barton in GB G p.125 as 325¼ acs. dated 1 Sep 1782]

DANIEL MITCHEL, by Survey made 1 Dec 1756, 395 acs. Hallifax Co. on the brs. of Childres cr., up Snake horn br.; adj. John Treble, Benjamin Hubbard & Charles Bostick; 1 Sep 1780, p.5. A.C. of 40 Shill. sterl.

NOA HARBER, 240 acs. by Survey 7 May 1772 in Halifax Co. on the draughts of Berches cr.; adj. Edmunds, Farmer, Cary, Jones & Narber; 1 Feb 1781, p.6. A.C. of 25 Shill. Sterl.

JOHN ALLOWAY STRANGE, 400 acs. by Survey made 29 Jan 1780 in Fluvanna Co. on both sides of Ballingers cr.; 19 Oct 1780, p.7. £509 current Money of Virginia paid to Thomas Napier Gent. Escheator for Fluvanna Co. ... being lately the property of William Ainge a British Subject and was sold by the sd Thomas Napier Escheator as aforesaid unto the sd John Alloway Strange agreable to 2 acts of Assembly passed in the year 1779 the one Entittled as Act concerning Escheats and forfeitures from British Subjects the other Entittled an act Concerning Escheators.

EDWARD HATCHER, 659 acs. by Survey 17 Mar 1774 in Bedford Co. on Stanton riv., on the road; adj. Greer, Randolph, Forgason & their old lines; 1 Sep 1780, p.8. A.C. of £3.S10 Sterl. including two old Surveys one of 251 acs. on the S side the sd riv. and was Gtd. by pat. to William Haynes and one of 125 acs. on the N side of sd riv. and was Gtd. by Pat. to George Walton the property of all which has since become vested in the sd Hatcher.

JOHN MERRITT, 696 acs. by Survey 3 Mar 1773 in Bedford Co. on north brs. of wreck Island Cr., at a path, at the edge of a meadow; adj. Hunter, David Martin, Rogers, Whitney, & Alexander Steel; 1 Sep 1780, p.10. A.C. of £3.S10. Sterl. ... by virtue of 2 Entries in his own name for 546 acs. and with 150 acs. assigned him by William Page and Surveyed 3 Dec 1767 makes the above mentioned quantity.

ISAAC DYER, 405 acs. by Surv. 12 Dec 1771 in Halifax Co. on the draughts of Chery tree cr., adj. Patrick Hamrick & Adams; 1 Feb 1781, p.12. A.C. of 45 Shill. Sterl.

JOSEPH STREET, 160 acs. by Survey 31 Jan 1772 in Halifax Co. on the brs. of Childress cr.; adj. Charles Bostick, Sullin, Micajah Hampton, John Sanders & Benjamin Hubbard; 1 Feb 1781, p.13. A.C. of £1 Sterl.

ANDERSON FAMBORAH /FAMBOROUGH, 663 acs. Halifax Co. on the brs. of Childrees and Runaway Creeks, crossing Deans path; adj. Benjamin Branham, John Dyer, Thomas Daughty, Henry Cross, Peter Bowman, Norman, & Peter Treble; 1 Feb 1781, p.14. A.C. of £3.S10 Sterl.

THOMAS COMER, 253 acs. by Survey 26 Nov 1771 in Halifax Co. on the southern draughts of Peters cr., adj. Comer & Wall; 1 Feb 1781, p.15. A.C. of 25 Shill. Sterl.

JACOB STALLINGS, 204 acs. by Survey 7 Apr 1762 in Henry Co. on both sides of Balls cr. of Smiths riv., adj. Merrah Webb/Merray Web [his lines]; 1 Feb 1781, p.16. A.C. of £1 Sterl.

EDWARD TUCK, 334 acs. by Survey 9 Dec 1771 in Halifax Co. on the draughts of Buffaloe cr.; adj. Johnson, Templeton, Smith & Norman; 1 Feb 1781, p.17. A.C. of 35 Shill.

DAVID POLLEY, 440 acs. by Survey 23 Oct 1777 in Pittsylvania Co. on both sides of the wide mouth Cr., on a ridge, adj. Jeremiah Ward & Witcher; 1 Feb 1781, p.18. A.C. of 45 Shill. Sterl.

JOSEPH KING, 151 acs. by Survey 12 Nov 1765 in Halifax Co. on little fork of Reedy cr., crossing a bold br., adj. Coplin; 1 Feb 1781, p.19. A.C. of 15 Shill. Sterl.

JEREMIAH WARD, 196 acs. by Survey 21 Oct 1777 in Pittsylvania Co. on the N Side of Pigg riv.; adj. Trip or Fips, & David Ross; 1 Feb 1781, p.21. A.C. of £1 Sterl.

JEREMIAH WARD, 292 acs. by Survey 21 Oct 1777 in Pittsylvania Co. on both sides of the wide mouth cr. and Reedy's cr., adj. David Ross & sd Ward; 1 Feb 1781, p.22. A.C. of 30 Shill. Sterl.

JOHN DICKENSON, 379 acs. by Survey 16 Apr 1779 in Henry Co. on the S side of Pigg riv., Beginning at Choat's corner otherwise Early and Callaways thence with their line; also adj. Hill, Mayfee, Grimitt & Halloway's or Choats line; 1 Feb 1781, p.23. A.C. of 40 Shill. Sterl.

WILLIAM WEAKS, 447 acs. by Survey 1 May 1779 in Henry Co. on the north fork of Story cr.; adj. Mark Coles old Survey, Rentfrow, Early and Callaway, & John Fuson; 1 Feb 1781, p.24. A.C. of £2.S5 sterl.

GEORGE SOUTHERLAND ass'ee of CHARLES DUNKIN, 395 acs. by Survey 15 Nov 1764 in Halifax Co. on the brs. of Dan Riv.; adj. James Duncan, Stone & Dunkin; 1 Feb 1781, p.26. A.C. of 40 Shill. Sterl.

JOHN SANFORD, 212 acs. by Survey 3 Mar 1768 in Pittsylvania Co. on Beards cr., on a fork of the sd cr.; 1 Feb 1781, p.27. A.C. of 25 Shill. Sterl.

WILLIAM FARGUSON, 169 acs. by Survey 3 Jun 1779 in Henry Co on the brs. of the South fork of Pigg riv.; adj. Robert Jones, Cook, David Jones & Henry Jones; 1 Feb 1781, p.28. A.C. of £1 Sterl.

CHARLES BURNETT ass'ee of SHOCKLEY SIMMONS, 188 acs. by Survey 22 Apr 1768 in Henry Co. formerly Pittsylvania on Mulberry Cr., crossing the double fork, down the South fork; 1 Feb 1781, p.29. A.C. of 20 Shill. sterl.

JOHN SWILIVENT ass'ee of THOMAS CARTER, 210 acs. by Survey 2 Dec 1778 in Henry Co. on the S Side of black Water riv., adj. John Goff & Jeremiah Sowsbury; 1 Feb 1781, p.31. A.C. of 25 Shill.

PHILIP RAYLEY, 212 acs. by Survey 6 Feb 1779 in Henry Co. on the brs. of Bull run; adj. John Gooff [Goff], Peter Craggit, Henry Haynes & Huginges Corner; 1 Feb 1781, p.32. A.C. of 25 Shill.

WILLIAM HUNTER, 182 acs. by Survey 8 Dec 1779 in Henry Co. on the North fork of Butram town Cr., Adj. the land whereon he now lives & Mullings corner; 1 Feb 1781, p.33. A.C. of £1 Sterl.

HENRY COX, 374 acs. by Survey 30 May 1767 in Halifax Co. on the brs. of Bulls cr., crossing a bold br., near Hickeys Road, adj. Brumfield; 1 Feb 1781, p.35. A.C. of 40 Shill. Sterl.

DANIEL GOOSBY ass'ee of MILES JENNINGS, 120 acs. by Survey 27 Oct 1769 in Henry Co. (formerly Pittsylvania) on both sides of Mayo Riv., adj. Harbour; 1 Feb 1781, p.36. A.C. of 15 Shill.

JAMES CALLAWAY, 707 acs. by Survey 10 Mar 1779 in Henry Co. on the brs. of Chesnut cr., at the fork of a path; adj. his own lines, Samuel Paterson & Richards; 1 Feb 1781, p.37. A.C. of £3.S15. Sterl.

ISAAC/ISAACK BUTTERWORTH, 350 acs. by Survey 14 Dec 1762 in Halifax Co. on both sides of flat cr., crossing Turnip cr.; 1 Feb 1781, p.38. A.C. of 35 Shill. Sterl.

WILLIAM BURDETT, 242 acs. by Survey 29 Sep 1773 in Pittsylvania Co. on the brs. of little Bull run, adj. Henry Haynes & the sd Smith; 1 Feb 1781, p.39. A.C. 25 Shill. Sterl.

JAMES DANIEL, 400 acs. by Survey 1 Apr 1774 in Pittsylvania Co. on the brs. of Sandy cr.; adj. Adkinsons order line, Melther, Musick & Robert Walther; 1 Feb 1781, p.41. A.C. of £2 Sterl.

FLOYD TANNER ass'ee of BENJAMIN TERRY, 216 acs. by Survey 30 Sep 1746 in Pittsylvania Co. formerly Lunenburg on both sides of John's Run, crossing John Run, along the old road, adj. Dudgeon & Robert Walton; 1 Feb 1781, p.42. A.C. of £1.S5 Sterl.

JOSEPH TERRY SENR., 400 acs. by Survey 10 May 1780 in Pittsylvania Co. on the brs. of Sandy cr.; adj. Henry's order line, Terry, & Lazarus Dodson; 1 Feb 1781, p.43. A.C. of £2 Sterl.

NATHANIEL MURREY, 251 acs. by Survey 29 Feb 1780 in Pittsylvania Co. on the brs. of the double creeks, crossing the upper double cr.; adj. John Malther, Thomas Hardy & John Watkins; 1 Feb 1781, p.44. A.C. of 25 Shill. Sterl.

THOMAS RICHARDS, 118 acs. by Survey 16 Oct 1769 in Pittsylvania Co. on a br. of elk cr., adj. Fisher; 1 Feb 1781, p.46. A.C. of 15 Shill. Sterl.

JOHN ROBERTSON, 148 acs. by Survey 10 Apr 1772 in Pittsylvania Co. on beaver cr., adj. Hickey; 1 Feb 1781, p.47. A.C. of 15 Shill. Sterl.

JAMES YOUNG, 439 acs. by Survey 21 Jan 1769 in Augusta Co. on the North br. of Naked cr., by a Gulley; adj. James Paterson, James Bell, Edward Ervin & James Dickey; 1 Feb 1781, p.48. A.C. of £2.S5. 200 acs. part formerly Gtd. by Pat. to Hugh Campbell 25 Sep 1746 [PB 24 p.426 or p.427] and was by him conveyed to the sd Young, 135 acs also a part of the sd tract which was Gtd. to John Young Senr. by Pat. 12 Jul 1750 [PB 30 p.226] and by him conveyed to sd James Young. [Also see PB 39 p.125 to James Patterson]

JOHN GIBSON, 54 acs. by Survey 17 Mar 1747 in Lunenburg Co. on both sides the north fork of black water riv., Beginning at the cr. where Randolphs line crosses, in a Meadow; 1 Feb 1781, p.51. A.C. of 5 Shill. Sterl.

JOHN HARDIMAN, 619 acs. by Survey 14 Nov 1779 in Buckingham Co. on the S Brs. of Middle Slate riv., adj. Ralph Flours & his old line; 1 Feb 1781, p.52. A.C. of £3.S5. [For his old line, see PB 29 p.264 to John Easly. Also see Ralph Flowers GB D p.694]

JOSEPH TERRY, 429 acs. by Survey 29 Mar 1774 in Pittsylvania Co. on the brs. of Burches cr.; adj. Moor, Shelton, John Partridge & Joseph Terry's former line; 1 Feb 1781, p.53. A.C. of £2.S5. Sterl.

JOHN WADE, 197 acs. by Survey 21 Sep 1774 in Louisa Co. on the waters of Camp cr., on the head of a Glade; adj. Carver, John Moor, Harlor/Harler, Richard Morris, Benjamin Farriss & John Harriss; 1 Feb 1781, p.55. A.C. of £1 Sterl.

ARTHUR JAMESON, 70 acs. by Survey 22 Apr 1780 in Pr. Edward Co. between the waters of Vaughans cr. Spring and Cubs creeks; adj. William Davis, sd Jamesons old lines, Nathaniel Porter & William Baldwin; 1 Feb 1781, p.56. A.C. of 10 Shill. Sterl.

THOMAS OGLISBY, 356½ acs. by Survey 17 Apr 1780 in Buckingham Co. on the brs. of Wreck Island cr. and the fluvanna riv., crossing the long br., at a Ridge page leading to Whitney's Mill, on the Steep point of a hill; adj. Phelps's Mine Survey now the sd Oglisby's, Jeremiah Whitney & Isaac Staples; 1 Feb 1781, p.58. A.C. of 40 Shill. Sterl. [For the Mine Survey see GB A p.486. For Staples's see GB A p.280]

WILLIAM BELL, 217 acs. by Survey 20 Apr 1780 in Augusta Co. on the E side of his other tract his patent land, on a ridge; 1 Feb 1781, p.59. A.c. of 25 Shill. Sterl.

RICHARD TAYLOR, 203 acs. by Survey 18 Nov 1779 in Buckingham Co. on the S Brs. of Middle Slate riv., crossing the Poplar br., crossing Wolfpen br.; adj. Andrew Floures, Francis Amos, Nicholas, & Andrew Flowers; 1 Feb 1781, p.61. A.C. of £1 Sterl.

PETER LEGRAND, 182 acs. by Survey 10 Apr 1780 in Pr. Edward Co. on the brs. of Appomatox riv., adj. Thomas Jackson; 1 Feb 1781, p.62. A.C. of £1 Sterl.

JACOB RUBSAMAN, 5,920 acs. by Survey made 28 Apr 1780 in Bedford Co. on the brs. of Stanton riv. and Goose cr., on the heads of Clift cr., on the west fork of Lawsons cr., by the roads, at a fork of MacDonalds cr., by a path; adj. John Chiles, Talbot, Cleavland & Murphey; 1 Feb 1781, p.64. A.C. of £29.S15 Sterl.

JOHN MORAIN, 413 acs. by Survey 10 Apr 1780 in Pr. Edward Co. on the N side of little rough cr., adj. Thomas Jackson; 1 Feb 1781, p.66. A.C. of 45 Shill.

JOHN TRIMBLE, 73 acs. by Survey 18 Mar 1775 in Augusta Co. on Cabin run a br. of Mill Cr. the Waters of Great Calf pasture, in the Mouth of a draught, to the top of a piny Hill; 1 Feb 1781, p.67. A.C. of 10 Shill. Sterl.

WILLIAM RICKETS, 55 acs. by Survey 25 Apr 1780 in Pittsylvania Co. on the N Side of White Oak Mountain and on the Draughts of the Dry fork of White Oak Cr., adj. Isaac Certain; 1 Feb 1781, p.69. A.C. of 10 Shill. Sterl.

NATHANIEL HENDRICK, 98 acs. by Survey 6 Apr 1757 in Halifax and Pittsylvania Co. on the uper side of Buffloe Cr.; adj. James Collins, Freeman & the sd Partns's old Line; 1 Feb 1781, p.70. A.C. of 10 Shill. Sterl.

HESEKIAH SHELTON, 364 acs. by Survey 6 Dec 1763 in Pittsylvania Co. on the N side of Mayo riv., adj. his Lines & Leeake; 1 Feb 1781, p.72. A.C. of 40 Shill. Sterl.

WILLIAM MITCHELL, 309 acs. by Survey 22 Feb 1770 in Pittsylvania Co. on the brs. of Potters Cr.; adj. the sd Nowlins old line, Edward Wade, John Goade & Alexander Moore; 1 Feb 1781, p.74. A.C. of 35 Shill. Sterl.

JOSEPH ALEXANDER, 172 acs. by Survey 20 Apr 1780 in Rockbridge Co. joining his own, William Alexander and John Cummins along the foot of the South Mountain, Crossing Irish Cr.; 1 Feb 1781, p.76. A.C. of £1 Sterl.

JOHN OLDUM, 97 acs. by Survey 10 Apr 1770 [Pittsylvania Co. or Henry Co.] on the Waters of Leatherwood Cr., adj. Lomax and Companys Order lines; 20 Aug 1783 *in the 8th year of the Commonwealth, Benjamin Harrison Governor of the Commonwealth of Virginia hath hereunto set his hand and Caused the Lesser Seal of the said Commonwalth to be Affixed at Richmond* [The Thomas Jefferson signature has been partially erased], p.78. A.C. of 10 Shill. Sterl. [Margin Note: *This Grant is altered in the Name of Governour Harrison and dated 20th August 1783 because the Grant is as made out and recorded before Signed by Governor Jefferson who resigned before it could be Signd or Seald.*]

ALEXANDER ROBERTSON, 222 acs. by Survey 24 Apr 1753 in Halifax and Pittsylvania Countys on the N side of Pigg Riv., adj. John Kirby & the sd Mullins's former Surveyed Lands; 1 Feb 1781 *in the 5th year of the Commonwealth, Thomas Jefferson Governor*, p.80. A.C. of 25 Shill. Sterl.

NATHANIEL MEDKIFF, 134 acs. by Survey 5 Nov 1769 in Pittsylvania Co. on the Waters of Peters Cr., on a bold br.; 1 Feb 1781, p.81. A.C. of 15 Shill. Sterl.

RALPH SHELTON, SENIOR, 145 acs. by Survey 8 Nov 1768 in Pittsylvania Co. on Matthews Cr.; adj. John, Ralph & Thomas Shelton; 1 Feb 1781, p.83. A.C. of 15 Shill. Sterl.

RALPH SHELTON, SENIOR, 251 acs. by Survey 8 Nov 1768 in Pittsylvania Co. on Matthews Cr., Crossing 2 brs. & the fork of the Cr., in a Meadow; 1 Feb 1781, p.84. A.C. of 25 Shill. Sterl.

WILLIAM McCLENACHAN ass'ee of JAMES BANE, 480 acs. by Survey 15 Feb 1764 in Botetourt Co. formerly Augusta on the Waters of Roanoke, by a Spring, adj. Griffith; 1 Feb 1781, p.86. A.C. of £2.S10. Sterl.

MARTHA GATLIVE Ass'ee of DRURY PUCKETT, 24 acs. by Survey 18 Mar 1768 in Augusta Co. on Craigs cr. a br.

of James riv., on the point of a ridge, by a br. at the foot of the ridge; 1 Feb 1781, p.88. A.C. of 5 Shill. Sterl.

WILLIAM BRYANS, 168 acs. by Survey 29 Apr 1773 in Botetourt Co. Bet. William Bryans Senr. plantation and the Bushy Mountain, on the top of a Mountain; adj. sd Bryans, William Bryans Senr.; 1 Feb 1781, p.90. A.C. of £1 Sterl.

LODOWICK THOMAS, 185 acs. by Survey 29 Sep 1772 in Botetourt Co. on Johns Cr. the Waters of Craigs cr. a br. of James riv., on a ridge, adj. Sowers land; 1 Feb 1781, p.92. A.C. of £1 Sterl.

JOHN TRIMBLE, 202 acs. by Survey 30 Apr 1780 in Rockbridge Co. on the Waters of Buffaloe Cr., on Lusks run, adj. his own land & John Bowyer; 1 Feb 1781, p.93. A.C. of £1 Sterl.

THOMAS FERGUSON, 110 acs. by Survey 20 Apr 1775 in Botetourt Co. on the Waters of Roanoke, Beginning at the foot of the Mountain, with the old Survey Lines, in the draught; 1 Feb 1781, p.95. A.C. of 15 Shill. *including a Survey Containing 50 acs. made for sd Ferguson 3 Feb 1768.*

ROBERT SKEEN, 55 acs. by Survey 2 Nov 1772 in Botetourt Co. on Todds run a Br. of James riv., Crossing three drafts, Crossing the point of a Ridge, adj. his Land; 1 Feb 1781, p.97. A.C. of 10 Shill. Sterl.

JAMES TAYLOR Ass'ee of PETER CONROD, 53 acs. by Survey 24 Sep 1772 in Botetourt Co. on Craigs Cr. a br. of James riv., on a bushy hill, adj. the land he bought of Preston, the Survey he lives on; 1 Feb 1781, p.98. A.C. of 5 Shill. Sterl.

WILLIAM WALKER, 123 acs. by Survey 10 Dec 1771 in Botetourt Co. on Craigs Cr. a br. of James riv., adj. his other tract; 1 Feb 1781, p.100. A.C. of 15 Shill. Sterl.

FIELD ROBINSON, 150 acs. by Survey 28 Mar 1780 in Pittsylvania Co. on both sides the Ceder pond fork of Frying pan Cr.; adj. John Goads Corner now Robinsons, & Charles Goad; 1 Feb 1781, p.102. A.C. of 20 Shill. Sterl.

WILLIAM BAYS, 251 acs. by Survey 26 Dec 1768 in Pittsylvania Co. on the Waters of Gobling town Cr., Beginning on the Topp of a ridge; 1 Feb 1781, p.103. A.c. of 25 Shill. Sterl.

THOMAS PISTOLE, 236 acs. by Survey 3 Mar 1763 in Pittsylvania Co. formerly Halifax on the East fork of fall Cr.; adj. Hardin, & Samuel Harris's Order Line; 1 Feb 1781, p.105. A.C. of 25 Shill. Sterl.

GEORGE CAMPBELL ass'ee of SAMUEL WOODS, BENJAMIN WOODS & ELIZABETH WOODS Heirs of RICHARD WOODS, 145 acs. by Survey 6 Feb 1755 in Rockbridge Co. formerly Augusta upon a Br. of Ruffets Cr., Beginning in the fork of Buffelo Cr. and the Back run; 1 Feb 1781, p.107. A.C. of 15 Shill. Sterl.

CHARLES GOAD, 271 acs. by Survey 27 Mar 1780 in Pittsylvania Co. on the Brs. of Frying pan Cr.; adj. Field Robinson, Peter Bennet & Glasscock; 1 Feb 1781, p.108. A.C. of 30 Shill. Sterl.

SAMUEL CRAWFORD Ass'ee of THOMAS SMITH, 198 acs. by Survey 24 Sep 1766 in Augusta Co. on the Waters of Roanoak, on a ridge, in a Glade, adj. William Tary/Tarry; 1 Feb 1781, p.110. A.C. of £1 Sterl.

ROBERT McELHENY, 150 acs. **including** a former Survey of 102 acs. made for sd McElhony by Survey 27 Feb 1778 in Botetourt Co. on big run a br. of Back Cr.; adj. Samuel McElhony, the old Lines & Walker; 1 Feb 1781, p.111. A.C. of 15 Shill. Sterl.

JOSEPH MASON Ass'ee of JAMES CAGHEY, 95 acs. by Survey 20 Feb 1760 in Augusta Co. on the Waters of Roanoke, Beginning Nigh a line of John Mason's Land on back Cr., adj. John Eager; 1 Feb 1781, p.113. A.C. of 10 Shill. Sterl.

ABRAHAM DICK Ass'ee of JOHN ROBINSON, 65 acs. by Survey 6 May 1772 in Botetourt Co. on Ugleys cr. a br. of Dolaps Cr. a br. of James Riv., on the edge of & Crossing a draft, over the point of a hill, over the point of a ridge, by a path; 1 Feb 1781, p.114. A.C. of 10 Shill. Sterl.

JOHN WITCHER, 304 acs. by Survey 24 Oct 1777 in Pittsylvania Co. on the N Brs. of Pigg Riv., Crossing the Corn Br.; adj. William Adkins, James Carr, William Young, David Polley, William Wetcher, the old Corner & sd John Witcher; 1 Feb 1781, p.116. A.C. of 30 Shill. Sterl.

JOHN CRADDOCK, 125 acs. by Survey 3 Oct 1777 in Pittsylvania Co. on the Brs. of Buffelo Cr., along the County Line [S11½°W]; adj. his own, Nathaniel Hendrick, William London, James Buckly & sd Downey in his former Line; 1 Feb 1781, p.118. A.C. of 15 Shill. Sterl.

PETER BAYS, 50 acs. by Survey 4 May 1780 in Pittsylvania Co. on Gobling town cr., adj. Jeremiah Claunch; 1 Feb 1781, p.120. A.C. of 5 Shill. Sterl.

GEORGE CARTER, 127 acs. by Survey 18 Oct 1769 in Henry Co. (formerly Pittsylvania) on the Bull Mountain a fork of the Mayo riv., Beginning on the sd Cr.; 1 Feb 1781, p.121. A.C. of 15 Shill. Sterl.

LUKE FOLEY, 173 acs. by Survey 23 Nov 1768 in Henry Co. (formerly Pittsylvania) on the draughts of Gobling town cr.; 1 Feb 1781, p.123. A.C. of £1 Sterl.

JOHN GAMMON, 569 acs. by an **inclusive Survey** 26 Mar 1770 in Pittsylvania Co. on the waters of Sandy riv.; 1 Feb 1781, p.124. A.C. of £3 Sterl.

ROTHERICK McDANIEL /MacDANIEL, 398 acs. by Survey 2 Apr 1774 in Pittsylvania Co. on the brs. of Burches cr.; adj. Robert Walther, Samuel Harriss, Dodson, & William Walther; 1 Feb 1781, p.126. A.C. of 40 Shill. Sterl.

JOSEPH RHEABURN, 122 acs. by Survey 5 Jan 1771 in Augusta Co. on the N Side of Middle riv. of Shanando, by a road; adj. his own line, Robert Reid, Smith, Hugh Green & Robert Stephenson; 1 Feb 1781, p.128. A.C. of 15 Shill. Sterl.

JOHN SANFORD, 156 acs. by Survey 2 May 1768 in Pittsylvania Co. on Beards cr., Beginning at a Mahogny tree in the cr.; 1 Feb 1781, p.130. A.c. of £1 Sterl.

SOLOMON DAVIS, 162 acs. by Survey 28 Nov 1769 in Henry Co. (formerly Pittsylvania) on both sides of Pigg riv.; adj. Paterson, & William Frankhum; 1 Feb 1781, p.131. A.C. of 15 Shill. Sterl.

BRYANT KENNEY, 80 acs. by Survey 5 Apr 1775 in Augusta Co. on the N Side of Jennings's Br., at the foot of the Mountain; adj. Michael Hogshead, Robert Mackettrick & Hugh Johnston; 1 Feb 1781, p.133. A.C. of 10 Shill. Sterl.

JOHN ARCHER, 50 acs. by Survey 24 Nov 1774 in Augusta Co. bet. his and Bradshaws branches, near a draft; 1 Feb 1781, p.135. A.C. of 5 Shill. Sterl.

ALEXANDER GARDNER, 400 acs. by Survey 6 Oct 1779 in Augusta Co. Joining his own and Michael Hogsheads L., by a draft, near John Archers Line, also adj. Thomas Brackeys line; 1 Feb 1781, p.136. A.C. of 40 Shill. Sterl.

THOMAS & SAMUEL WILSON, 63 acs. by Survey 20 Nov 1771 in Augusta Co. Joining their own land, their old Survey, on a Steep hill above the South riv.; 1 Feb 1781, p.138. A.C. of £1 Sterl.

JAMES PARKER, 31½ acs. by Survey 19 Apr 1777 in Augusta Co. on the Waters of Mary cr. a br. of the North br. of James Riv., Beginning below a Spring, down a draft; 1 Feb 1781, p.139. A.C. of 5 Shill. Sterl.

GEORGE FINLEY, 35 acs. by Survey 25 Jan 1772 in Augusta Co. on a Small Br. on the S Side of the Middle riv. of Shanandore; adj. his old Line, Edward Breden & William Anderson; 1 Feb 1781, p.141. A.C. of 5 Shill. Sterl.

ANDREW HAMILTON, 186 acs. by Survey 9 Nov 1779 in Augusta Co. on a br. of the Calf pasture on the SW Side of his other land, at the foot of the Mountain; 1 Feb 1781, p.142. A.C. of 20 Shill. Sterl.

DAVID TRIMBLE, 110 acs. by Survey 21 Apr 1780 in Augusta Co. on the E side of the sd David Trimble other tract, Beginning at a Large Sw., adj. Jacob Peck & the Patent line; 1 Feb 1781, p.144. A.C. of 15 Shill. Sterl.

JOSEPH RHEABURN, 238 acs. by Survey 5 Mar 1771 in Augusta Co. on a Br. of Mossey Cr. Called Pudding Spring, Beginning on the W side of sd Spring, Crossing a draft, on a ridge; 1 Feb 1781, p.146. A.C. of 25 Shill.

JAMES KERR, 130 acs. by Survey 14 Oct 1773 in Augusta Co. on the S Side of the Middle riv. of Shenandore, on a high bank, Crossing Meadow run; adj. William Robertson, Edward Ruttledge, sd Kerrs other land & Beverlys line near Christian Cr.; 1 Feb 1781, p.147. A.C. 15 Shill. Sterl.

FREDERICK BURKETT, 97 acs. by Survey 3 Oct 1779 in Augusta Co. on Some Brs. of the Middle riv. of Shanandore, by a road; adj. James Blayr, Samuel Erwing, Samuel Mackee, John Burnside & *the Meeting house land*; 1 Feb 1781, p.149. A.C. 10 Shill. Sterl.

JOHN OLIVER, 150 acs. by Survey 24 Mar 1780 in Augusta Co. on the N Side of Naked cr. joining his other Land, his

Patent land & Anthony Aylor; 1 Feb 1781, p.151. A.C. of 15 Shill. Sterl.

JAMES PATERSON, 56 acs. by Survey 22 Mar 1773 in Augusta Co. Joining the lines of his land on the South riv. a br. of Shenando, crossing a dry Valley, by a draft, also adj. James Craig; 1 Feb 1781, p.153. A.C. of 10 Shill. Sterl.

THOMAS DIXON, 350 acs. by Survey 20 Sep 1779 in Augusta Co. on the N side of Middle riv. of Shenandore; adj. William Patterson, Robert Gibson, James Gamble & Robert Reed; 1 Feb 1781, p.155. A.C. of 35 Shill. Sterl.

JOHN KING, 220 acs. by Survey 30 Oct 1779 in Augusta Co. on Moffets Br., adj. John Archer & Moffet; 1 Feb 1781, p.158. A.C. of 25 Shill. Sterl.

THOMAS BROWN, 190 acs. by Survey 1 Mar 1775 in Augusta Co. on both Sides of Middle riv. of Shenandore; adj. Beverly, & John Philips; 1 Feb 1781, p.159. A.C. of £1 Sterl.

JOHN CAMPBELL, 250 acs. by Survey 28 Mar 1770 in Augusta Co. on Some drafts of the Middle riv., adj. Alexander Walker; 1 Feb 1781, p.160. A.C. of 25 Shill. Sterl.

JOHN TRIMBLE ass'ee of DAVID TRIMBLE, 162 acs. by Survey 21 Apr 1780 in Augusta Co. on the W side of his other tract, also adj. Beverly, by a Spring; 1 Feb 1781, p.162. A.C. of £1 Sterl.

THOMAS LEWIS JUNR., 355 acs. by Survey 28 Apr 1780 in Botetourt Co. on the Bent Mountain Adj. the land that was formerly Leanard Huffs, Beginning at the point of a hill in the fork of a br., by a parcel of Rock, along the Mountain to a Large red Oak near a path; 1 Feb 1781, p.164. A.C. of 40 Shill. Sterl.

SAMUEL ERWIN, 111 acs. by Survey 5 Jan 1771 in Augusta Co. on a Small br. of the Middle riv. of Shanandore, on a ridge; adj. Jane Erwin, Robert Stevenson & the sd Erwins old corner; 1 Feb 1781, p.166. A.C. of 15 Shill. Sterl.

JAMES TEMPLETON, 49 acs. by Survey 13 Jun 1771 in Botetourt Co. Joining the Lines of the Sd Templetons and John Rynolds Patent land on James River Waters, by the great road, thro a thicket of Brush, Crossing 2 drafts; 1 Feb 1781, p.167. A.C. of 5 Shill. Sterl.

FRANCIS EKERT, 148 acs. by survey 6 Apr 1780 in Augusta Co. on a Br. of Jennings Cr.; adj. a tract of Benjamin Tolman, James Armstrong, Charles Erwin & John Beard; 1 Feb 1781, p.169. A.C. of 15 Shill. Sterl.

[Margin Note: *This Grant is founded on Charles Tomkies Military Warrant for five hundred Acres and* **Number one hundred and thirty,** *two Other Grants to Compleat the Quantity mabe found in the Page of this Book 172 for 200 Acres, the Other for 100 acres in the Book D Page 465*]

ISAAC SHELBY Ass'ee of JOHN FOX who was Ass'ee of Sd CHARLES TOMKIES, by Survey made 4 May 1780, 200 acs. Situate in Lincoln formerly Kentucky Co. on the Nob Lick Br. of the Hanging Fork of Dicks Riv., Beginning at 3 Sugar trees about 80 poles from the Sd Nobb Lick Br. on the S Side thereof in a flatt caney peice of Land being a Corner to his own preemtion tract of 1,000 Acres, on the Top of a Ridge; 22

Feb 1781, p.171. *in Consideration of Military Service performed by Charles Tomkies as a Subaltorn Officer in the late War between Great Britain and France according to the Terms of the King of Great Britians Proclamation of 1763.*

ISAAC SHELBY Ass'ee of JOHN FOX who was Ass'ee of Sd CHARLES TOMKIES, by Survey made 4 May 1780, 200 acs. Situate in Lincoln formerly Kentucky Co. on the Waters of the Nob lick Br. of the hanging fork of Dicks riv., Beginning in Some high flat oak land on the S Side of Sd Nob lick Br. being a Corner to his own Settlement tract, near the bank of a Small Spring br. on the S Side thereof, near a Small Br. being a corner to his own 200 Acre tract and on the S Side of the sd Nob lick br., in a line of his preemption tract being a Corner to his 200 Acre tract, passing two beech trees corner to his Settlemt. and preemption tract to the Beg.; 22 Feb 1781, p.172. *in Consideration of Military Service performed by Charles Tomkies as a Subalton Officer in the late War between Great Britain and France According to the terms of the King of Great Britains proclamation 1763.*

EDWARD HARKIN ass'ee of JOHN DIVER who was ass'ee of MOSES TRIMBLE, 200 acs. by Survey 29 Jan 1754 in Augusta Co. in the forks of James riv. and on the S side of the North fork; 1 Feb 1781, p.174. A.C. of £1 Sterl.

THOMAS CONNOLEY, 250 acs. by Survey 1 Mar 1773 in Augusta Co. on Some Small brs. of the Middle riv. of Shanandore, on a road, on a ridge, by a pond; adj. sd Connoley, John Campbell, Alexander Walker, John McMahon, a Survey of Hugh Donoghe, a Survey of Sd Campbels, another Survey of Sd Walkers, & *hocks land*; 1 Feb 1781, p.175. A.C. of 25 Shill. Sterl.

WILLIAM PAXTON Ass'ee of SAMUEL PAXTON, 100 acs. by Survey 14 Feb 1755 in Augusta Co. Joining the Sd Samuel Paxtons old Survey in the fork of James Riv.; 1 Feb 1781, p.178. A.C. of 10 Shill. Sterl.

HUGH ALLEN, 400 acs. by Survey 15 Oct 1773 in Augusta Co. on the SE Side of the Middle riv. of Shenandore, by a road, Crossing a draft, adj. Samuel Hinds land & Harless's lines; 1 Feb 1781, p.179. A.C. of 50 Shill. Sterl.

JOHN TAYLOR Ass'ee of DAVID FRAME, 67 acs. by Survey 11 Dec 1770 in Botetout Co. on Stony run the Waters of James Riv., Beginning on the Side of a Spurr of the Mountain, on a high Spurr of the Mountain, adj. William Caldwells l.; 1 Feb 1781, p.181. A.C. of 10 Shill. Sterl.

PEEDMT. AKIN ass'ee of ROBERT DAVIES who was Ass'ee of WILLIAM AKIN, 156 acs. by Survey 5 Apr 1773 in Botetourt Co. on Johns Cr. a br. of James Riv. Joining the Upper end of William Prestons survey; 1 Feb 1781, p.182. A.C. of £1 Sterl.

THOMAS TOSH, 426 acs. by survey 4 Apr 1772 in Botetourt Co. on the N Side of Roanoke riv., to *an Indian Grave on a high bank*, adj. Tasker Toshes Survey; 1 Feb 1781, p.184. A.C. of 45 Shill. Sterl. **Including** an entry made for Francis Smith and part of Another entry made by Jonathan Tosh a tittle to which entrys the sd Thomas Tosh hath bargained for and got Assignment on.

JOHN GRATTON, 915 acs. by Survey 4 Mar 1773 in Augusta Co. on the S Side of the North riv. of Shanandore at *Brocks Gap*, on a ridge, adj. Nicholas's l.; 1 Feb 1781, p.186. A.C. of 35 Shill. Sterl. 576 acs. part thereof being part of a large tract of l. Gtd. to Benjamin Burton by pat. as may appear by the Same on record in the secretaries office and by several conveyances became the property of the Aforesaid John Gratton and 339 acs. the other part thereof being new Unpatented l.

JOHN McNUTT/MacNUTT, 175 acs. by Survey 27 Nov 1772 in Botetourt Co. Joining Lines with the lines of his now William Paxton James Templeton and John Smileys l. in the forks of James Riv.; Beginning by the Mouth of a run near the N river [North river]; up a draft, by the great road; 1 Feb 1781, p.188. A.C. of £1 Sterl.

ARTHUR CONOLLY/CONNOLEY, 530 acs. by an **inclusive Survey** 9 Jan 1772 in Augusta Co. on a Small br. of the Midle riv. of Shenandore; adj. John Campbell, the sd Conelly, Alexander Walker, George Crawford, Samuel Henderson, Cohorn & Sd Johnston; near Patrick Crawfords line; 1 Feb 1781, p.191. A.C. of 25 Shill. Sterl. including a tract of 280 acs. first Gtd. sd Conelly by Pat. 27 Jun 1764 and 35 acs. being part of a tract of 230 acs. first Gtd. William Johnson by pat. 12 May 1770 and was by him conveyed to Sd Connolly by deed of lease and release the remaining 215 acs. nevert Gtd. before.

JOHN SALMON, 375 acs. by Survey 17 May 1780 in Henry Co on Jourdans cr., adj. sd Salmons old line; 1 Feb 1781, p.193. A.C. of 40 Shill. Sterl.

MARCUS CUBB, 77 acs. by Survey 19 Apr 1780 in Augusta Co. on the NW Side of his other tract, by a Great road; adj. Casper Sylin, John Patterson & Sd Cubb; near Eanos Jones; 1 Feb 1781, p.194. A.C. of 10 Shill. Sterl.

JOHN LOWRY ass'ee of WILLIAM SHANNON, 77 acs. by Survey 26 Feb 1768 in Augusta Co. on a Small br. of the North riv. of Shenandore, by a draft, adj. his old Lines; 1 Feb 1781, p.196. A.C. of 10 Shill. Sterl.

HUGH CAMBRIL, 281 acs. by Survey 21 Mar 1778 in Henry Co. on Turkey pen br.; adj. James Strongs line, John Mays line & Edmund Edwards line; 1 Feb 1781, p.197. A.C. of 30 Shill. Sterl.

GEORGE WALTON, 1,850 acs. by Survey 29 Oct 1754 in Halifax Co. on both sides of the South fork of Mayo riv. on the brs. of Russells cr., crossing a fork of the South fork of sd riv., adj. Callaham; 1 Feb 1781, p.198. A.C. of £9.S5 Sterl.

STEPHEN GOGGIN, 375 acs. by Survey 21 Jan 1773 in Bedford Co. on the east Brs. of flat Cr.; adj. Hammon, Russell & Irvine; 1 Feb 1781, p.200. A.C. of 40 Shill. Sterl.

STEPHEN GOGGIN JUNR., 144 acs. by Survey 15 Mar 1774 in Bedford Co. on Butterys Br.; adj. Mitchel, Randolph & Walton; 1 Feb 1781, p.202. A.C. of 15 Shill. Sterl.

JOHN CAFRE, 110 acs. by Survey 1 Dec 1763 in Halifax Co. on both Sides the

South fork of Bull Cr., adj. Bayes C. & James Nowlin; 1 Feb 1781, p.203. A.C. of 15 Shill. Sterl.

SAMUEL WALLACE, 93 acs. by Survey 22 May 1778 in Pr. Edward Co. on the S Side of Appomatox riv.; adj. Zachariah Robinson, Robert Peek, Morgan & Baldwin; 1 Feb 1781, p.204. A.C. of 10 Shill. Sterl.

LEONARD CRUTCHER ass'ee of HICKERSON BARKSDALE who was ass'ee of DAVID McCORMACK, 398 acs. by Survey 24 Sep 1770 in Buckingham Co. on both Sides of the white oak br. on the N Side of Holadays riv., Crossing the Country road, adj. William Gilliam & William MacCormack; 1 Feb 1781, p.205. A.C. of 40 Shill. Sterl.

RICHARD ADAMS, by Survey 4 Mar 1780, 377 acs. Henry Co. on the Brs. of Green Cr., adj. Archelous Hughes new Survey & Randolph; 1 Feb 1781, p.207. A.C. of 40 Shill. Sterl.

CHRISTOPHER HOUR, 280 acs. by survey 15 Apr 1780 in Rockingham Co. on the dry fork of Smiths cr., on a ridge, on the E Side of sd drafts, adj. Townsend Mathews & Reubn. Harrison; 1 Feb 1781, p.208. A.C. of 30 Shill. Sterl.

JOHN DICKENSON, 180 acs. by Survey 31 Mar 1780 in Henry Co. on the Muster Br. of Leatherwood Cr.; adj. Stephens, Barnard, Francis Cox & Runnolds; 1 Feb 1781, p.209. A.C. of £1 Sterl.

JESSE WALKER Ass'ee of THOMAS BENGE, 48 acs. by Survey 26 Aug 1760 in Albemarle Co. on the head of a North br. of Moores cr.; adj. William Terril Lewis, & the line of Joel and John Lewis; 1 Feb 1781, p.211. A.C. of 5 Shill. Sterl.

SABERET CHOAT, 30 acs. by Survey 8 Apr 1769 in Pittsylvania Co. on both Sides of Pigg riv., adj. Lenous; 1 Feb 1781, p.212. A.C. of 5 Shill. Sterl.

WILLIAM AMOSE, 299 acs. by surv. 17 Mar 1780 in Henry Co. on sycamore Cr.; adj. Harbour, & Thomas Morrison; 1 Feb 1781, p.213. A.C. of 30 Shill. Sterl.

WILLIAM DUNN ass'ee of BENJAMIN ALLEN, 20 acs. by Survey 25 Apr 1780 in Botetourt Co. on the Waters of Roanoake Joining the stone house land, by a Gully at the foot of a Mountain, to a Spurr of Sd Mountain; 1 Feb 1781, p.215. A.D. of 5 Shill. Sterl.

EZEKIEL KENDRICK, 112 acs. by Survey 12 Dec 1772 in Pr. Edward Co. adj. Hurt, Angelas line, Bostick, John Arnold & Harris; 1 Feb 1781, p.216. A.C. of 15 Shill. Sterl.

THOMAS REEVES, 300 acs. by Survey 11 Apr 1780 in Rockingham Co. on the NW Side of long Meadow; adj. the l. of the sd Thomas Reeves, the l. which Brewer Reeves purchased from Valentine Siveir, & Michl. Holsingers l.; with Brewers line [a line of Brewer Reeves Survey] and passing his corner a Stake near a Sink hole; 1 Feb 1781, p.217. A.C. of 30 Shill. Sterl.

WILLIAM WILSON, 411 acs. by Survey 10 Mar 1780 in Henry Co. on both sides of Spoon cr., adj. Philip Buzzard; 1 Feb 1781, p.219. A.C. of 45 Shill. Sterl.

JAMES DICKEY & DAVID HENDERSON ass'ee of JOHN

DICKENSON who was ass'ee of ZOPHER CARPENTER who was ass'ee of THOMAS KELLY & JAMES LAIRD, 90 acs. by Survey 31 Oct 1772 in Botetourt Co. on Snake run a br. of Dunlaps Cr. being the Waters of James riv.; 1 Feb 1781, p.220. A.C. of 10 Shill. Sterl.

WILLIAM GRAGG, by Survey made 10 Dec 1774, 64 acs. Augusta Co. on the N Side of Seneca Cr., adj. his old Line; 1 Feb 1781, p.221. A.C. of 10 Shill. Sterl.

ADAM LACKEY, 70 acs. by Survey 3 May 1780 in Henry Co. on Rock castle Cr., adj. Walton; 1 Feb 1781, p.223. A.C. of 10 Shill. Sterl. [Cucumber trees, a Poplar, Black Gums, Chesnut trees, a Hickory & a Cinnamon tree were used as Survey markers]

JOHN SALMON, 363 acs. by Survey 4 Dec 1779 in Henry Co. on the Grasey fork of Warf Mountain cr., adj. Jourdan; 1 Feb 1781, p.224. A.C. of 40 Shill. Sterl.

RICHARD KERBY, 358 acs. by Survey 15 Mar 1780 in Henry Co. on Sycamore cr., adj. his own line & Thomas Monrow or Morrow; 1 Feb 1781, p.225. A.C. of 40 Shill. Sterl.

HENRY BARKSDALE, 142 acs. by Survey 7 Apr 1780 in Henry Co. on the brs. of Reedy Cr. and Rock run, adj. John Rowland & Randolph; 1 Feb 1781, p.227. A.C. of 15 Shill. Sterl.

JOHN CAMERON/CAMMERON, 213 acs. by Survey 15 Apr 1780 in Henry Co. on the Nobusiness fork of Mayo Riv., adj. Cogers old line Now Runnolds; 1 Feb 1781, p.228. A.C. of 25 Shill. Sterl.

GEORGE ADAM BRIGHT, 400 acs. by Survey 14 Mar 1776 in Augusta Co. on Mary cr. a br. of the North br. of James riv., adj. Thomas Boyd; 1 Feb 1781, p.229. A.C. of 40 Shill. Sterl.

JOHN DICKENSON, 219 acs. by Survey 3 Jun 1780 in Henry Co. on both Sides of Pigg riv.; adj. Grays and Waltons corner on the N Side of Sd riv., William Hodges Sorrell wood and pointers at the Mouth of a br. & his own line; 1 Feb 1781, p.231. A.C. of 25 Shill. Sterl.

WILLIAM HAYES, 112 acs. by Survey 18 May 1780 in Henry Co. in the fork bet. the North and South Mayo Rivers, with the Country line [West], adj. Labmert Dotson; 1 Feb 1781, p.233. A.C. of 15 Shill. Sterl.

WILLIAM FRAME, 150 acs. by Survey 27 Sep 1780 in Augusta Co. on some brs. of Naked cr.; joining three lines of his old tract, James Gambles line, Alexander Curry & Andrew Wicomb; 1 Feb 1781, p.234. A.C. of 15 Shill. Sterl.

ZACHARIAH NEAL, 72 acs. by Survey 15 Mar 1780 in Bedford Co. on the long br. of Auslin Cr.; adj. Asberry, Hatcher & his own line; 1 Feb 1781, p.236. A.C. of 10 Shill. Sterl. [Regranted sd Neal in GB 12 p.319 dated 8 Aug 1787, on the long br. of Austin Cr. adj. Ashberry]

ZACHARIAH SMITH, 261 acs. by Survey 17 May 1780 in Henry Co. on the Waters of the Mayo [Riv.], crossing fall cr., with the Country line 415 poles, adj. Philip Angling & Smith; 1 Feb 1781, p.237. A.C. of 30 Shill. Sterl. [The survey computes to 278.1 acs. with the closure line - the Country line - being N89.23°W 415.3 poles]

BENJAMIN HANDCOCK Ass'ee of ABNER BARNARD, 206 acs. by Survey 6 May 1780 in Henry Co. on Sycamore cr., adj. Ward; 1 Feb 1781, p.239. A.C. of 25 Shill. Sterl.

ROBERT DINWIDDIE, 92 acs. by Survey 1 Sep 1769 in Augusta Co. Joining his own land [the old Survey] in *Vander Pools Gape*; 1 Feb 1781, p.240. A.C. of 10 Shill. Sterl.

HENRY MILLER, 593 acs. by Survey 6 May 1780 in Augusta Co. bet. the lands formerly Walton Trimbles and John MacDugalls on Some brs. of the North riv. of Shenandore; 1 Feb 1781, p.241. A.C. of £3 Sterl.

ARCHELAUS HUGHES, 304 acs. by survey 3 Mar 1780 in Henry Co. on Green Cr., adj. Waltons order line; 1 Feb 1781, p.243. A.C. of 30 Shill. Sterl.

SAMUEL JOHNSTON, 350 acs. by surv. 15 Nov 1779 in Henry Co. on the Grassy fork of the fishing fork of Leatherwood cr.; adj. his own, Garrot Burch & Short; 1 Feb 1781, p.244. A.C. of 35 Shill. sterl.

THOMAS SPRAGGINS, 215 acs. by survey 9 Feb 1760 in Halifax Co. on the E brs. of Catawbo Cr.; adj. James Bates his line, Spraggins former line & James Nerrell; 1 Feb 1781, p.245. A.C. of 25 Shill. Sterl.

BREWER REEVES, 324 acs. by survey 11 Apr 1780 in Rockingham Co. on the NW side of the long Meadow bet. the lands he purchased of Valentine Sever and Michael Holsingers land, to a Stake near a Sink hole; 1 Feb 1781, p.247. A.C. of 35 Shill. Sterl.

ROBERT DINWIDDIE, 86 acs. by Survey 20 Jul 1773 in Augusta Co. adj. to this own land on the head of Jacksons riv., adj. his old survey & William Myias; 1 Feb 1781, p.248. A.C. of 10 Shill. Sterl.

WILLIAM SPRAGGINS, 400 acs. by Survey 5 Dec 1752 in Halifax Co. on the head brs. of Cattawba Cr., adj. Bates & Watkins; 1 Feb 1781, p.249. A.C. of 40 Shill. Sterl.

FRANCIS TUCKER, 384 acs. by survey 24 Oct 1771 in Halifax Co. on the draughts of Bluewing, on the County line [East], Crossing a road and a ridge of Rocks, adj. George Moore & Richard Andrews; 1 Feb 1781, p.251. A.C. of 40 Shill. Sterl.

JOSEPH CANTERBERRY JUNR. Ass'ee of RICHARD McCARY, by Survey made 13 Dec 1773, 174 acs. in Amherst Co. on the Brs. of the Dutch Cr.; adj. his own, Walter King, William Tiller & Thomas Hopper; 1 Feb 1781, p.252. A.C. of 20 Shill. Sterl.

ASHFORD NAPIER, 96 acs. by survey 2 May 1775 in Albemarle Co. on the S side of the Rivanna riv. and on the S side the North fork of Cunninghams Cr., Crossing a br. of the Middle fork of Cunningham Cr., adj. sd Napier & John Tandy; 1 Feb 1781, p.253. A.C. of 10 Shill. Sterl.

LUKE WALDROPE Ass'ee of WILLIAM GILL, 400 acs. by Survey 5 Oct 1772 in Halifax Co. on the fork of Bluewing, crossing little bluewing; adj. Seat, Atkinson, Richard Andrews, William Gill Senior, Sizemore & Childries line; 1 Feb 1781, p.255. A.C. of 40 Shill. Sterl.

WILLIAM GLIDEWELL, 325 acs. by Survey 30 Mar 1773 in Halifax Co. on the draughts of Bluewing and Seths br.; adj. Hutchings, Harrison, Gledewell & Maurey [Mausey?]; 1 Feb 1781, p.256. A.C. of 35 Shill. Sterl.

JOSEPH GLENN Ass'ee of ANDREW FELT who was Ass'ee of WILLIAM GILL JUNR., 400 acs. by Survey 5 Oct 1772 in Halifax Co. on the fork of Bluewing, crossing little bluewing; adj. Childries line, Stiles, Fontaine, Mausey & Glidewell; 1 Feb 1781, p.258. A.C. of 40 Shill. Sterl.

BENJAMIN BOXLEY, 757 acs. by Survey 2 Nov 1773 in Halifax Co. on the draughts of Peters and Willis's creeks; adj. Edward Wade, Comer, Roberts, Harriss, Liggins, Seldon & Mead; 1 Feb 1781, p.259. A.C. of £4 Sterl.

JOSIAH SMITH, by Survey 15 Apr 1780, 302 acs. Henry Co. on the Brs. of Stones Cr., adj. Jacob Cogar; 1 Feb 1781, p.260. A.C. of 30 Shill. Sterl.

GEORGE HILTON ass'ee of RICHARD FLETCHER GREGORY, 50 acs. by Survey 6 Apr 1761 in Albemarle Co. on both sides a North br. of fishing Cr., adj. John Joslin & William Cabell; 1 Feb 1781, p.262. A.C. of 5 Shill. Sterl.

WILLIAM SMITH, 353 acs. by Survey 8 Mar 1780 in Henry Co on Russels br. and South Mayo riv., Beginning on the N side of Russells Cr., adj. James Mankin,; 1 Feb 1781, p.263. A.C. of 35 Shill. Sterl.

WILLIAM HOBSON, 400 acs. by survey 22 Oct 1771 in Halifax Co. on the brs. of Mayo, adj. John Childries & Byrds lines; 1 Feb 1781, p.264. A.C. of 40 Shill. Sterl.

GEORGE MOFFET, 200 acs. by survey 15 Apr 1780 in Augusta Co. on the W Side of his other l., Beginning near a road Sd Moffetts C., also adj. Anderson; 1 Feb 1781, p.265. A.C. of £1 Sterl.

JOHN CARREL, 373 acs. by Survey 31 Mar 1773 in Halifax Co. on the head of Seths Br.; adj. Harrison, Hutchings & Mutter; 1 Feb 1781, p.266. A.C. of 40 Shill. Sterl.

JOHN CARREL, 410 acs. by Survey 31 Mar 1773 in Halifax Co. on Seths br. and NW Side of Feilds order, Crossing the Hay stack br.; adj. John Tally, Hutchins, Fields Order line, Crook & Mutter; 1 Feb 1781, p.267. A.C. of 45 Shill. Sterl.

MACAJER/MICAJER TERREL, 124 acs. by survey 7 Nov 1766 and in Pittsylvania Co. on both sides of Rockcastle Cr., along the Mountain Side, adj. Walton; 1 Feb 1781, p.269. A.C. of 15 Shill. Sterl.

WILLIAM GOODE Ass'ee of JOSEPH GILL SENIOR, 401 acs. by Survey 7 Oct 1772 in Halifax Co. on the draughts of Bluewing Cr., down Shears br.; adj. Joseph Gill, Maury [Manry?], Stiles & Clift; 1 Feb 1781, p.270. A.C. of 40 Shill. Sterl.

MATTHEW PATTON, 17 acs. by Survey 7 Sep 1774 in Augusta Co. on the W Side of Jacksons riv., adj. his old l.; 1 Feb 1781, p.271. A.C. of 5 Shill. Sterl.

FRANCIS HOLLEY, 310 acs. by Survey 15 Mar 1773 in Bedford Co. on the head brs. of Auslins Cr.; adj. Woodward, his own line & John Holley; 1 Feb 1781, p.272. A.C. of 35 Shill. Sterl.

MICHAEL WERON, 250 acs. by Survey 8 May 1774 in Augusta Co. on Some drafts of Linwells Cr., by a path, adj. Elihu Mosey & Massey; 1 Feb 1781, p.274. A.C. of 25 Shill. Sterl.

MICHAEL WERON, 100 acs. by survey 2 Feb 1761 in Augusta Co. on the E Side of Linvells cr. betwixt two tracts of his land, on a ridge, to a large Hickory near a Rockey hill; 1 Feb 1781, p.275. A.C. of 10 Shill. Sterl.

JOHN POAGE/POAG, 85 acs. by Survey 1 Jun 1768 in Augusta Co. now Rockbridge Joining his own Land, Crossing a br. of Mackeys run; 1 Feb 1781, p.276. A.C. of 10 Shill. Sterl.

JOHN STURDIVANT, 16¾ acs. by Survey 25 Feb 1772 in Pr. Geo. Co. adj. John Lovesay, Edward Davenport, William Lovesay & sd Sturdivant; 1 Feb 1781, p.277. A.C. of 5 Shill. Sterl.

EPHRAIM McDOWELL/MacDOWEL, 200 acs. by Survey 13 Mar 1774 in Bedford Co. on the N brs. of Reedy cr. a West br. of falling riv.; adj. Isaac Davis, McRandle, Aker & Bolling; 1 Feb 1781, p.278. A.C. of £1 Sterl.

JOHN RAMSEY, 42 acs. by Survey 6 Apr 1780 in Augusta Co. on a br. of the South riv. on both Sides of Rockfish road; 1 Feb 1781, p.280. A.C. of 5 Shill. Sterl.

DULTON LAYNE, 642 acs. by survey 11 Apr 1780 in Henry Co. on horse pasture Cr., adj. Randolphs Cos. line [his line] & James East; 1 Feb 1781, p.281. A.C. of £3.S5 sterl.

PATRICK SINATE Ass'ee of GEORGE WALDRUM, 68 acs. by survey 19 Dec 1771 in Rockingham Co. formerly Augusta on a little Mountain Called Clay hill on the E side of Sheltons land on the South br. of Powtomack, Beginning by a buch of Linns and a Hickory by a spring, on a ridge; 1 Feb 1781, p.282. A.C. of 10 Shill. Sterl.

WILLIAM JONES Ass'ee of JOHN SIMMONS who was Ass'ee of ABRAHAM [ACRES], 496 acs. by survey 2 Feb 1764 in Bedford Co. on E brs. of falling riv., on Johnsons br., crossing Simmons br., adj. his own [Jones's] lines; 1 Feb 1781, p.284. A.C. of 50 Shill. Sterl. [For sd William Jones's other land see Lunenburg Co. PB 34 p.94 to Thomas Jones & Thomas Jones Junr.]

JESSE ATKERSON, 280 acs. by survey 3 Mar 1780 in Henry Co. on the S Side of North Mayo riv., crossing a road; adj. his line, Bradley Smith & Taylor; 1 Feb 1781, p.285. A.C. of 30 Shill. Sterl.

JOHN FINLEY, 49 acs by Survey 7 Apr 1780 in Augusta Co. on the South Mountain in Woodes Gap; 1 Feb 1781, p.286. A.C. of 5 Shill. Sterl.

JOHN HENDERSON, JUNIOR, 49 acs. by survey 25 Mar 1767 in Amherst Co. on the N brs. of the Middle fork of Piney riv.; 1 Feb 1781, p.287. A.C. of 5 Shill. Sterl.

THOMAS TURK, 150 acs. by Survey 17 Apr 1780 in Augusta Co. on the S side of a Small br. of the South riv. of shenandore, adj. sd Turks pattent land & Kennerlys land; 1 Feb 1781, p.289. A.C. of 15 Shill. Sterl.

WILLIAM BALL, 130 acs. by Survey 15 Mar 1775 in Bedford Co on the S Side of Stanton Riv., on a high ridge, on a Clift on sd Riv., adj. Spradlin & Day; 1 Feb 1781, p.290. A.C. of 15 Shill. Sterl.

SAMUEL PHILIPS Ass'ee of THOMAS HUNTON, 279 acs. by survey 27 Dec 1780 in Rockingham Co. formerly Augusta on the Western br. of Linwells Cr., on a ridge; 1 Feb 1781, p.291. A.C. of 30 Shill. Sterl.

WILLIAM HAMILTON Ass'ee of ROBERT MacNAIR, 83 acs. by survey 8 Jun 1769 in Augusta Co. adj. to his own Land in the fork of James Riv. & David McCord on the Cr.; 1 Feb 1781, p.292. A.C. of 10 Shill. Sterl.

ARCHIBALD HOPKINS, 134 acs. by survey 21 Mar 1780 in Rockingham Co. on a br. of Muddy Cr. on the NE side of the land he lives on; 1 Feb 1781, p.294. A.C. of 15 Shill. Sterl.

JAMES CAMPBELL, 90 acs. by Survey 26 Dec 1754 in Bedford Co. on the brs. of Beaver Cr., crossing a large br. & the Main br.; 1 Feb 1781, p.295. A.C. of 10 Shill. Sterl.

JOHN WARE, 394 acs. by Survey 17 Mar 1770 in Pittsylvania Co. on the brs. of Dann riv., Along the Country line [West]; adj. John Wilson, Thomas Owen & John Ware; 1 Feb 1781, p.297. A.C. of 40 Shill. Sterl.

SAMUEL JOHNSTON/JOHNSON, 410 acs. by Survey 5 Nov 1779 in Henry Co. on the brs. of Leatherwood Cr.; adj. Garrot Birches/Burches line, Lomax and Compys line, Shorts line, his own lines, Delosairs line & Lomax and Coys. line; 1 Feb 1781 *in the 5th year of the Commonwealth, Thomas Jefferson Esquire Governor*, p.298. A.C. of 45 Shill. Sterl.

[Margin note: *This Grant was altered in the name of Governour Harrison and dated 20th. August because the Grant was made out and recorded before signed by Governour Jefferson who resigned before it Could be sign'd or Seal'd.*]

SAMUEL JAMESON Ass'ee of ABSALOM BROWN, 153 acs. by Survey 20 Mar 1773 in Albemarle Co. on some of the S brs. of Moremans riv.; adj. John MacCulloch, John Rodes, Benjamin Huntsman & James Wherry; 20 Aug 1783 *in the 8th year of the Commonwealth, Benjamin Harrison Esquire Governor*, p.300. A.C. of 15 Shill. Sterl.

JAMES CAMPBELL, 300 acs. by Survey 12 Mar 1775 in Bedford Co. on the N Side of Stanton riv., adj. Weaver & Cooper; 1 Feb 1781 *in the 5th year of the Commonwealth, Thomas Jefferson Esquire Governor*, p.302. A.C. of 30 Shill. Sterl.

OBADIAH OVERBY, 266 acs. by Survey 6 Nov 1770 in Halifax Co. on the North fork of Aarons Cr., on Watry br.; adj. Joseph Gill, Peter Overby Senr. [Said Senior Overbys line], Peter Overby Junior, Hencock, Sizemore, & Joseph Gill Junior; 1 Feb 1781, p.303. A.C. of 30 Shill. Sterl.

WILLIAM HODGES, 93 acs. by Suvey 19 Dec 1764 in Henry Co. formerly

Pittsylvania on Pigg Riv.,; adj. Paterson; 1 Feb 1781, p.305. A.C. of 10 Shill. Sterl.

WILLIAM DINWIDDIE, 149 acs. by Survey 31 Mar 1780 in Augusta Co. on the head brs. of Jacksons Riv.; 1 Feb 1781, p.307. A.C. of 15 Shill. Sterl.

BENJAMIN HUDDLESTONE Ass'ee of ALEXANDER MITCHEL, 274 acs. by survey 7 Mar 1758 made for STEPHEN CHENAULT who Sold it to MATHEW COX of whom the Said Alexander Mitchel recovered it by a Caveat 10 Jun 1773 in Buckingham Co. formerly Albemarle on both sides of Childres Cr. of Bollings Cr.; adj. Colo. John Fry, Casson, & Francis Marshal; 1 Mar 1781, p.308. A.C. of 30 Shill. Sterl. [For Francis Marshal's land see PB 30 p.87 to Zachevrel Whitebread. Also see adj. PB 42 p.616 to William Garland]

DANIEL GAINES & HUGH ROSE, Gentlemen, Ass'ee of sd Daniel Gaines as tenants in Common and not as Joint Tenants, 38 acs. by Survey for sd Daniel Gaines 1 Apr 1774 in Amherst Co. on the S side and Joining Mobleys cr. and bounded by the Variation of the Magnetic from true Meridian of N1°W; adj. James Freeland dec'd & William Megginson; 1 Mar 1781, p.309. A.C. of 5 Shill. Sterl.

DANIEL GAINES & HUGH ROSE, Gentlemen, as ass'ee of sd Daniel Gaines who was Ass'ee of WILLIAM MEGGINSON as tenants in Common and not as Joint tenants, 92 acs. by survey made for sd William Megginson 29 Mar 1771 in Amherst Co. on the N side and Joining Mobleys cr., up the north br. of Mobleys cr.; adj. George Hilton, his own line & Robert Freeland; 13 Mar 1781, p.311. A.C. of 10 Shill. sterl.

[Margin note: *Joseph Jones Dinwiddie 1 Lott Escheated Examd.*]
Colo. JOSEPH JONES as Ass'ee of sd WILLIAM CLAIBAN, a Certain tenement or parcel of l. in Dinwiddie Co. in the town of Peters burg on the N side of the Street adjoining the Tenement late the property of William Cunningham and Co.; 13 Mar 1781, p.312. *in Consideration of the Sum of £7,050 Current money of Virginia paid unto Kennon Jones Gent. escheator for Dinwiddie Co. by William Claiban Gent. ... which sd tenement was lately the property of George Younger and Co. British Subjects and was sold by the sd Kennon Jones as aforesd unto* **sd William Claiborne** *and by him Assigned to sd Joseph Jones agreable to two Acts of Assembly passed in the year 1779 the one Intittled an Act concerning Escheats and forfeitures from British Subjects the other Intittled an Act concerning escheators.*

[Margin note: *John Grammar 1 Lott Escheated Examd.*]
JOHN GRAMMAR, a Certain lot or parcel of land containing One Acres in Dinwiddie Co. And in the new town of Peters burg laid down in a platt of Sd town **Number 19**; 13 Mar 1781, p.313. *in Consideration of the Sum of £2,215 Current money of Virginia paid unto Kennon Jones Gent. Escheator for Dinwiddie Co. ... which sd lott or One Acre was lately the property of Daniel Fraser a British Subject And was Sold by the sd Kennon Jones escheator as aforesaid unto the sd John Grammar Agreable to two Acts of Assembly passed in 1779 the one Intittled an Act*

concerning escheats and forfeitures from British subjects the other Intittled an Act concerning escheators.

JOHN GRIGSBY Ass'ee of ROBERT POAG who was Ass'ee of JOHN POAG, 80 acs. by Survey 12 Mar 1764 in Augusta Co. in the fork of James Riv. Joining to John Poags [old] Survey, to 2 Hickories on a Gravelly hill; 1 Feb 1781, p.314. A.C. of 10 Shill. Sterl.

JOHN GRIGSBY Ass'ee of JOHN POAG, 28 acs. by survey 26 Mar 1768 in Augusta Co. in the south fork of James riv. Joining the Sd John Poags land, his old survey & Samuel MClures land; 1 Feb 1781, p.316. A.C. of 5 Shill. Sterl.

NICHOLAS HARPER, 36 acs. by Survey 31 Mar 1772 in Augusta Co. on the S side of the south br. of Patowmack; 1 Feb 1781, p.317. A.C. of 5 Shihll. Sterl.

GABRIEL COIL [and his heirs forever], 12 acs. by survey 2 May 1766 in Rockingham Co. (formerly Augusta) Joining the land he lives on at the south Br. of Potowmack above Sheltons [tract], on the side of a Ridge, adj. *her old line*; 1 Feb 1781, p.318. A.C. of 5 Shill. Sterl.

ABEL GRIFFITH, 316 acs. by Survey 4 May 1780 in Augusta Co. on the North side of Mossey Cr. and Joining a tract of his own and Thomas Reads; 1 Mar 1781, p.319. A.C. of 35 Shil. Sterl.

CONROD SMITH Ass'ee of JONATHAN HILYARD, 235 acs. by Survey 3 May 1771 in Rockingham Co. formerly Augusta between Smiths Cr. and the long Meadow, Along a ridge; 1 Mar 1781, p.320. A.C. of 25 Shill.

JOHN GRUBB Ass'ee of ASHFORD NAPIER, 247 acs. by Survey 26 Apr 1775 in Albemarle Co. on the S Side the Rivanna riv. and on the N Side the North fork of Cunningham Cr.; adj. sd Napier, one Sandage, William Kenney, Sd Kinney & John Haden; 1 Feb 1781, p.321. A.C. of 25 Shill. Sterl.

JOHN BOWMAN, 50 acs. by Survey 27 Apr 1771 in Botetourt Co. on Roanoke; Beginning at a Box Elder Mulberry and Buck eye at the Mouth of his Mill Stream thence up the river; adj. David Bryan & Evans; 1 Mar 1781, p.323. A.C. of 5 Shill. Sterl.

JOSIAH SMITH, 189 acs. by survey 10 Apr 1780 in Henry Co. on the brs. of Horse pasture Cr.; adj. Cameron, sd Smith, Hughes, Wimbush & Randolph; 1 Feb 1781, p.325. A.C. of £1 Sterl.

MICHAEL WERON, 400 acs. **an inclusive Survey** bearing date 20 Sep 1771 in Augusta Co., Crossing a draft, adj. Another tract of his land & Jacob Jeron; 1 Feb 1781, p.326. A.C. of 25 Shill. Sterl. 150 acs. of which was Gtd. to sd Michael Weron by pat. 12 May 1770, the remaining 250 never Gtd. before.

ROBERT WILEY, 29 acs. by Survey 30 Mar 1780 in Augusta Co. on Jacksons riv.; 1 Feb 1781, p.328. A.C. of 5 Shill. Sterl.

JOHN SIMMONS, 177 acs. by survey 5 Feb 1769 in Pittsylvania Co. on the Waters of Beaver Cr., Beginning on a bold br. of the aforesd Cr.; 1 Feb 1781, p.329. A.C. of £1 Sterl.

RALPH LOFTUS Ass'ee of JARED ERWIN, 51 acs. by Survey 22 Apr 1767 in Rockingham Co. formerly Augusta on a draft of Brieary br., adj. John MaVaes line & his old line; 1 Feb 1781, p.330. A.C. of 5 Shill. Sterl.

JOHN MILLS, 242 acs. by survey 28 Nov 1772 in Botetourt Co. on the S Side the Beaver Dam a br. of Looneys Mill Cr. being the Waters of James Riv., in the edge of a Meadow, near a Spring, adj. Stephen Rentfroes Survey; 1 Feb 1781, p.332. A.C. of 25 Shill. Sterl.

ANDREW RAMSEY, 146 acs. by survey 5 Apr 1780 in Augusta Co. bet. the land of John [**Dallas**] and the south Mountain on a br. of the south riv.; 1 Feb 1781, p.333. A.C. of 15 Shill. Sterl.

THOMAS SPENCER, 196 acs. by Survey 3 May 1780 in Rockingham Co. on Beaver Cr. a br. of the North riv. of Shenandore Near the Mouth of the sd Cr.; adj. Henry Millers land formerly Hendersons, Olifers line - Olivers land, & Abraham Smiths land formerly Morriss's; 1 Feb 1781, p.334. A.C. of £1 Sterl.

WILLIAM COMMACK Ass'ee of WILLIAM WALLACE who was Ass'ee of LUDOWVICK THOMAS, 100 acs. by Survey 3 Apr 1773 in Botetourt Co. Bet. two Mountains on the Northeast br. of Johns Cr.; adj. Casper Server & Colo. Preston; 1 Mar 1781, p.336. A.C. of 10 Shill. Sterl.

JAMES RIDGWAY, 400 acs. by Survey 30 Oct 1753 in Pittsylvania Co. formerly Halifax on both sides of Brush Cr., Crossing two forks of Sd Cr., adj. Thomas Dandy; 1 Mar 1781, p.338. A.C. of £2 Sterl.

JOHN SLAUGHTER, 400 acs. **more or less** in Culpepper Co. Broomfield parrish in the Gourd Vine fork of Rappahanock riv., on a ridge, adj. Colo. John Slaughter, Green & Serjeant; 1 Mar 1781, p.339. *in Consideration of the Sum of £7,000 paid by John Slaughter unto Joseph Wood Escheator for Culpepper Co. ... late the property of John Serjeant a British Subject and was Sold by the said Joseph Wood unto the aforesaid John Slaughter agreable to two Acts of Assembly passed in 1779 the one Intitiled an Act Concerning Escheats and forfeitures from British Subjects the Other Intittled an Act Concerning Escheators.*

SAMUEL HODGES AND OTHERS, 194 acs. by survey 4 Jun 1768 in Norfolk Co., adj. a Corner of Sevills and Nicholls thence Along their line; 1 Mar 1781, p.341. A.C. of £1 Sterl.

RICHARD JONES, 87 acs. by survey 26 May 1780 in Norfork [sic] Co., Along the road that leads to Bear Quarter; 1 Mar 1781, p.342. A.C. of 10 Shill. Sterl.

JOHN MOSLEY HADEN, 338½ acs. by survey 11 Apr 1780 in Fluvanna Co. on the brs. of Cunningham and Burks Cr. and the south brs. of the Rivanna riv., Crossing Rusks Cr.; adj. Joseph Haden, Lightfoot, William Haden & Ingland; 1 Mar 1781, p.343. A.C. of 35 Shill. Sterl.

JOHN BIBEE, 182 acs. by survey 20 Apr 1780 in Fluvanna Co. on the N side the Rivanna Riv. on the brs. of Ballingers Cr., adj. John Strange & John Martin; 1 Mar 1781, p.345. A.C. of £1 Sterl.

HENRY SMITH, 74 acs. by survey 11 May 1780 in Norfolk Co. adj. George Smith, Thomas Woodard, Daniel Sivel & William Nicholas; 1 Mar 1781, p.346. A.C. of 10 Shill. Sterl.

JAMES DILLARD, 400 acs. by Survey 17 Dec 1772 in Amherst Co. on the S brs. of Porrige Cr. and the head of a North br. of stovals Cr.; adj. David Christian Dec'd, & Terisha Turner [his lines]; 1 Mar 1781, p.348. A.C. of £2 Sterl.

WILLIAM FORD Ass'ee of THOMAS ATKINSON who was Ass'ee of WILLIAM HARRIS, 130 acs. by Survey 5 Nov 1762 in Bedford Co. on the N side of Goose Cr., down Back Cr., adj. Hendrickson; 1 Mar 1781, p.350. A.C. of 15 Shill. Sterl.

WILLIAM WARD, 160 acs. by Survey 11 Apr 1775 in Augusta Co. on a br. of black Thorn, on the side of a Mountain, adj. Christopher Eye & his land; 1 Mar 1781, p.351. A.C. of £1 Sterl.

RICHARD RUNNOLDS, 150 acs. by survey 10 Dec 1758 in Henry Co. formerly Pittsylvania on Smiths riv.; 1 Mar 1781, p.353. A.C. of 15 Shill. Sterl.

GRIMES HALCON, 554 acs. by survey 26 Nov 1772 in Pittsylvania Co. on the brs. of Chesnut Cr., adj. James Martin & Thomas Ramsey; 1 Mar 1781, p.354. A.C. of 55 Shill. Sterl.

GEORGE HAIRSTONE, 354 acs. by Survey 3 Nov 1753 in Halifax Co. on both Sides **Join crack Cr.**; 1 Mar 1781, p.356. A.C. of 35 Shill. Sterl.

JAMES DILLARD, 99 acs. by survey 17 Feb 1768 in Amherst Co on both Sides of Porrige Cr.; adj. Richard Peter, his own line & Robert John's line; 1 Mar 1781, p.357. A.C. of 10 Shill. Sterl.

JOHN BYBEE, 185 acs. by survey 16 Apr 1780 in Fluvanna Co. on little MyChunk Cr. and North Waters of the rivanna riv.; adj. James Adams, Allegree & Gilbert; 1 Mar 1781 p.359. A.C. of £1 Sterl.

DANIEL SMITH, 232 acs. by survey 10 Dec 1779 in Henry Co. on the round About br. of Butramtown Cr., adj. his old line; 1 Mar 1781, p.361. A.C. of 25 Shill. Sterl.

ANDREW DUNN, 183 acs. by survey 12 Mar 1769 in Pr. Edward Co. on the brs. of Mill and Sawneys Creeks; adj. Quarles, Mills & Mathews; 1 Mar 1781, p.362. A.C. of £1 Sterl.

JOHN STRANGE, 195 acs. by survey 15 Apr 1780 in Fluvanna Co. on the brs. of Horsley and Ballingers Cr. and N brs. of the rivanna riv., Crossing Martin Kings road; adj. John Strange, Martin, Allen & Clasby; 1 Mar 1781, p.364. A.C. of £1 Sterl.

ABRAHAM PENN, 150 acs. by survey 24 Mar 1749 in Henry Co. formerly Halifax on both sides of Beaver Cr.; 1 Mar 1781, p.366. A.C. of 15 Shill. Sterl.

JAMES BLACKLEY, 578 acs. by **an Inclusive Survey** bearing date 18 Apr 1780 in Pittsylvania Co. on both sides of the Strawberry Cr. and wet Sleave; on Wetsleave Cr.; adj. Chamberlain, Adam Lacky, Watkins & White; 1 Mar 1781, p.367. A.C. of £3.S10 Shill. Sterl.

JOHN STRANGE, 235 acs. by survey 14 Apr 1780 in Fluvanna Co. on the brs. of little My chunk Cr. and N Brs. of Rivanna riv., Crossing Martin Kings Road; adj. Clasby, Strange, Robert Abrams line [Robert Adams?], Denton,

Norton & Smithson; 1 Mar 1781, p.369. A.C. of 25 Shill. Sterl.

JOHN FARISS, 400 acs. by survey 9 Apr 1779 in Bedford Co. on the N brs. of Molleys Cr.; 1 Mar 1781, p.371. A.C. of 5 Shill. Sterl. 368 acs. of which was Gtd. by pat. to Robert Means and properly Conveyed to Sd John Fariss the residue 32 acs. not Gtd. before.

JOHN BRUCE, 400 acs. by survey 28 Apr 1780 in Charlotte Co. adj. Stith, Moseley, Harkin, Blankes Corner & Allen; 1 Mar 1781, p.373. A.C. of £2 Sterl. [N of Staunton Riv. on Cargill's Cr., W of Bluestone Cr.; for Allen's land see PB 34 p.674 to David Wimpee; for Stith's land see PB 33 p.998 to John Powell; for Harkins & Moseley's see PB 29 p.435 to William Byrd]

JOHN EASTHEART, 105 acs. by survey 17 Apr 1780 in Rockbridge Co. upon the south Mountain Joining of David Taylors land, on the Dividing line of Rockbridge Co. and Amherst Co.; 1 Mar 1781, p.375. A.C. of 15 Shill. Sterl.

JOHN HAMMON, 203 acs by survey 27 Jan 1779 in Fluvanna Co. on the N brs. of Hardware riv.; adj. Bryant, Hammon & Ray; 1 Mar 1781, p.376. A.C. of £1 Sterl.

JOHN DAUN, 335 acs. by survey 6 Feb 1764 in Bedford Co. on the E brs. of falling riv. and on head brs. of Dutchmans br.; adj. Harriss & Read; 1 Mar 1781, p.378. A.C. of 35 Shill. Sterl.

MOSES CUNNINGHAM Ass'ee of DAVID LOGGON who was Ass'ee of ANDREW ELDER, 46 acs. by survey 19 Nov 1772 in Botetourt Co. Joining a line of Aaron Collins [Aaron Colliers?] Survey on the Waters of Buffaloe Cr. a br. of James Riv., Crossing a draft to the top of a hill; 1 Mar 1781, p.380. A.C. of 5 Shill. Sterl.

BENJAMIN THACKER, 252 acs. by survey 20 Mar 1778 in Fluvanna Co. on the Waters of the bold br., on a ridge, Crossing Bens br., Crossing a road and a prong of the bold br., near a ridge path; adj. Bethel, Askew, Taylor, Hix, Ballamy & Applebury; 1 Mar 1781, p.381. A.C. of £1.S5 Shill. Sterl.

JOSEPH FITZPATRICK, 265 acs. by Survey 25 Apr 1755 in Albemarle Co. on the S side the rivanna riv. on the brs. of Napiers and Carys Creeks, Crossing Woodsons road, adj. Benjamin Woodson & Hugh Rigby; 1 Mar 1781, p.384. A.C. of 30 Shill. Sterl.

AARON COLLIER, 60 acs. by survey 18 Nov 1771 in Botetourt Co. Joining lines with the land of Andrew Elder and the Sd Aaron Collier in the forks of James Riv., Crossing a draft; 1 Mar 1781, p.385. A.C. of 10 Shill. Sterl.

JAMES DILLARD, 30 acs. in Amherst Co. on the head of Cut Shin br. on the N Side of Porrage Cr. by survey 17 Mar 1763, adj. Joseph Mayo & James Christian; 1 Mar 1781, p.387. A.C. of 5 Shill. Sterl.

RICHARD DAVENPORT, 40 acs. by survey 7 Dec 1778 in Albemarle Co. on the S side the rivanna riv. and on the Waters of the south fork of Hardware; adj. Nicholas Hammer, William Hitchcock & George Ubank; 1 Mar 1781, p.388. A.C. of 5 Shill. Sterl.

PAUL BECK, 459 acs. by Survey 4 Jun 1779 in Henry Co. adj. sd Robert Jones, Abraham Jones & Henry Jones; 1 Mar 1781, p.390. A.C. of 40 Shill. Sterl. 96 acs. part thereof was gtd. to Robert Jones by Pat. 20 Jun 1772 [Pittsylvania Co. PB 40 p.665 on brs. of Pigg Riv.] and 363 acs. the residue never before gtd.

JOSEPH TERRY, SENIOR, 580 acs. by **an inclusive survey** bearing date 7 May 1772 in Halifax Co. and Pittsylvania Co. on Jeremys fork [Jeremiahs fork of Birches Cr.?]; adj. Davidson, Dodson, Griffin, Parish, Clancy & his old line; 1 Mar 1781, p.392. A.C. of £3 sterl.

RICHARD BROWN, 362 acs. by survey 12 Jun 1779 in Pittsylvania Co. on the brs. of Shocko Cr.; adj. sd Brown, Claybrook, John Ferrill, the Order line [Terrys Order line] & William Williams; 1 Mar 1781, p.394. A.C. of 40 Shill. Sterl.

GEORGE FREEDLY Ass'ee of JOHN ARMONTROUT who was Ass'ee of LAURENCE BELL, 105 acs. by survey 8 Nov 1770 in Augusta Co. Bet. Smiths Cr. and the Mountain, adj. his Patent land, near his House; 1 Mar 1781, p.396. A.C. of 15 Shill. Sterl.

PATRICK NAPIER, 31 acs. by survey 17 Mar 1778 in Fluvanna Co. Adj. the land whereon he lives, Rutherford, Bryant & Scott; 1 Mar 1781, p.398. A.C. of 5 Shill. Sterl.

REUBEN PAYNE, 337 acs. by survey 21 Apr 1780 in Pittsylvania Co. on Banister Riv., Crossing Middle Cr.; adj. sd Payne, Shelton & Simmons; 1 Mar 1781, p.399. A.C. of 35 Shill. Sterl.

RICHARD WATTS, 460 acs. by survey 6 Mar 1778 in Bedford Co. on Prathars run a south br. of Stanton riv., down south br., down sd Prathers run by a Mill, adj. Callaway & Gill; 1 Mar 1781, p.401. A.C. of 50 Shill. Sterl.

JOHN POLLEY/POLLY, 63 acs. by survey 26 Apr 1754 in Henry Co. formerly Halifax on the S side of the south fork of the Maryo riv. [Mayo Riv.]; 1 Mar 1781, p.403. A.C. of 10 Shill. Sterl.

JOHN PEMBERTON, 250 acs. by Survey 15 Apr 1780 in Pittsylvania Co. on the brs. of Stanton riv.; adj. John Patrick, Cornelius Mchany & Hancock; 1 Mar 1781, p.404. A.C. of 25 Shill. Sterl.

WILLIAM KING Ass'ee of JOHN McVAE, 236 acs. by survey 7 Mar 1771 in Augusta Co. on the S Side of the North riv. of Shenandore, on a ridge, adj. David Williams; 1 Mar 1781, p.406. A.C. of £1.S5 Sterl.

JOHN KELLY Ass'ee of WILLIAM SAMS? JUNR., 88 acs. by survey 18 Apr 1768 in Henry Co. formerly Pittsylvania on Smiths riv., Crossing Drag Cr.; 1 Mar 1781, p.407. A.C. of 10 Shill. Sterl.

THOMAS ROBERTS, 379 acs. by survey 27 Nov 1772 in Pittsylvania Co. on both [sides] the Middle fork of town Cr., adj. Joseph Bird on the E side the sd fork in the low Grounds; 1 Mar 1781, p.409. A.C. of £2 Sterl.

BENJAMIN BRISTO, 104 acs. by survey 30 Apr 1768 in Henry Co. on Gobling town Cr., on a fork of sd Cr., adj. Gray; 1 Mar 1781, p.411. A.C. of 10 Shill. Sterl.

JOHN KELLY, 94 acs. by survey 22 May 1780 in Pittsylvania Co. on the druaghts of Straight stone and Buffelow Creeks; adj. John Collins line, Francis Lucks line, James Mitchels line & Nat Hendricks line; 1 Mar 1781, p.413. A.C. of 10 Shill. Sterl.

SOLOMON DAVIS, 202 acs. by survey 3 Jun 1780 in Henry Co. on the S side of Pigg Riv., adj. Smith & Grunmet; 1 Mar 1781, p.414. A.C. of £1 Sterl.

JOHN PELFRY, 121 acs. by Survey 14 Apr 1772 in Pittsylvania Co. on both sides Smiths riv.; 1 Mar 1781, p.416. A.C. of 15 Shill. Sterl.

GEORGE TAYLOR, 254 acs. by survey 1 Mar 1780 in Henry Co. on the S Side of North Mayo riv., Crossing a road; adj. his own line, Bradley Smith & Jenning's line; 1 Mar 1781, p.418. A.C. of 25 Shill. Sterl.

ABRAHAM MILLER ass'ee of JACOB FRANCIS, 74 acs. by survey 3 Sep 1772 in Botetourt Co. on Buck run a br. of Craigs Cr. being the Waters of James riv., adj. Jacob Trout, Trouts Survey; 1 Mar 1781, p.420. A.C. of 10 Shill. Sterl.

CHARLES CHRISTIAN JUNR. Ass'ee of JOHN OWNBY JUNR. who was Ass'ee of JOHN MAYFIELD, 116 acs. by survey 18 Feb 1775 in Amherst Co. in the south br. of Buffaloe riv., at Parks road; adj. Henry Gilbert, Charles Christian, John Ownby Junr., Joseph Wilches line & John West; 1 Mar 1781, p.421. A.C. of 15 Shill. Sterl.

RALPH FLOWERS, 150 acs. by survey 12 Nov 1;772 in Buckingham Co. on both sides the Middle fork of Slate riv., adj. his own line & William Jones; 1 Mar 1781, p.423. A.C. of 15 Shill. Sterl.

WILLIAM FITZPATRICK ass'ee of WILLIAM REDIFORD, 400 acs. by Survey 14 Mar 1761 in Albemarle Co. on the heads of the S brs. of Cunningham and Brier Creeks, adj. Benjamin Bryant & John Brumet; 1 Mar 1781, p.424. A.C. of £2 Sterl.

WILLIAM OWENS Ass'ee of THOMAS **JAMES OR JAMERSON?**, 173 acs. by survey 4 Dec 1771 in Albemarle Co. on both sides of Lickinhole run Among the great Mountains, Crossing Lickinghole run, adj. his own & William MacCord; 1 Mar 1781, p.426. A.C. of £1 Sterl.

CHARLES PATTERSON/PATTESON, 296 acs. by survey 24 Mar 1773 in Buckingham Co. on both sides Nothing br. of Wreck Island Cr.; adj. his own lines, James **Harvey?** & Benjamin Witt; 1 Mar 1781, p.428. A.C. of 30 Shill. Sterl.

JOHN PORTER, 3 acs. by survey 16 Apr 1780 in Rockbridge Co. Joining his own land on the North riv.; 1 Mar 1781, p.429. A.C. of 5 Shill. Sterl.

HUGH BARBEY/BARBY, 37 acs. by survey 13 Aug 1780 in Rockbridge Co. in the fork of James Riv. Joining of James Gilmore, his Son Hugh Barby and himself; 1 Mar 1781, p.430. A.C. of 5 Shill. Sterl.

ABRAHAM INGRAM Ass'ee of MATHEW PATTON who was Ass'ee of JAMES DINWIDDIE who was heir at law of JOHN DINWIDDIE dec'd, 115 acs. by survey 30 Aug 1769 in Augusta Co. upon a br. of Jackson riv. above

Vanderpooles Gape and Above David Frames land; 1 Mar 1781, p.431. A.C. of 15 Shill. Sterl.

BARTLET GUIN, 400 acs. by survey 1 Dec 1769 in Halifax Co. on the head Brs. of Terrible, Bradleys and Spider Creeks, Beginning at Thomas Hornsbys Corner Near the Millstone road, in the fork of a Br. of Spider Cr. near Bookers road, Crossing a small branch of said Road, on Peter Bryans line to the head of the south fork of Bradleys Cr.; 1 Mar 1781, p.433. A.C. of £2 Sterl.

THOMAS LESLEY, 144 acs. by survey 2 Jun 1780 in Augusta Co. adj. Borden, David Steel, John Boyd & Thomas Boyd; 1 Mar 1781, p.435. A.C. of 15 Shill. Sterl.

CHARLES PATTERSON/PATTESON, 68 acs. by survey 12 Apr 1780 in Pr. Edward Co. on the S side of Appomatox Riv., adj. John Patterson & James Wright; 1 Mar 1781, p.436. A.C. of 10 Shill. Sterl.

RICHARD NAPIER. 199¾ acs. Albemarle Co. on both sides Smiths br.; adj. Joseph Fitzpatrick Junior, Henry Martin & Benjamin Bryant; 1 Mar 1781, p.438. A.C. of £1 Sterl.

RICHARD LEE, 400 acs. by Survey 14 Mar 1771 in Buckingham Co. on both Sides of the south fork of Holladay Riv., Crossing the road, adj. John Arnold; 1 Mar 1781, p.440. A.C. of £2 Sterl.

JOSEPH TROTTER Ass'ee of JOHN SCOTT, 112 acs. by survey 16 Apr 1780 in Augusta Co. Joining John Scott, Beverly Manner and the said Joseph Trotter, by a road; 1 Mar 1781, p.441. A.C. of 15 Shill. Sterl.

PETER WRIGHT, 36 acs. by survey 15 Apr 1773 in Botetourt Co. on Jacksons riv. and Joining a place of his own, on a Steep hill Above his old line, on his own line near **his still House**, to the old place, Crossing a ridge to the riv.; 1 Mar 1781, p.443. A.C. of 5 Shill. Sterl.

WILLIAM YOUNG, 379 acs. by survey 24 Nov 1778 in Henry Co. on the fish fork of Snow Cr., at Pigg river road, adj. the sd Youngs Corner of an old survey formerly Archelaus Greyham, Crossing the said [first] fork; 1 Mar 1781, p.445. A.C. of £2 Sterl.

THOMAS NAPIER Ass'ee of GEORGE GIBSON who was heir at law of GILBERT GIBSON, 150 acs. by survey 16 Jun 1761 in Fluvanna Co. formerly Albemarle on the Upper Side of Ballingers Cr., adj. Gilbert Gibson; 1 Mar 1781, p.446. A.C. of 15 Shill. Sterl.

MARY ANN JONES, 400 acs. by survey 25 Mar 1780 in Amherst Co. on both sides of the south br. of Hatt Cr. the Variation of the Magnetic from the true Meredian being N15W; Beginning at pointers Corner to Number One in Colo. John Roses line; Crossing Racoon Cr. and Hatt Creek road; adj. Robert Barnett & John Rose Esqr.; 1 Mar 1781, p.448. *in Consideration of the Sum of £200 Current Money of Virginia paid by Mary Ann Jones unto David Shepherd Escheator for Amherst Co. ... which sd tract or parcel of land was lately the property of Walter King, Esquire a British Subject and was Sold by the sd David Shepherd unto the sd Mary Ann Jones Agreable to two Acts of Assembly passed in 1779 the one Intitled an Act Concerning Escheats and forefeitures from British Subjects the other Intitled an Act Concerning Escheators.*

WILLIAM YOUNG, 330 acs. by survey 17 Mar 1769 in Henry Co. formerly Pittsylvania on the Waters of Snow Cr., on the road, adj. James Koff; 1 Mar 1781, p.450. A.C. of 35 Shill. Sterl.

FRANCIS ERVIN, 230 acs. by survey 19 May 1780 in Rockingham Co. on the SE side of the North riv. of Shanido and on the N side the land he lives on, Beginning near a road Corner to his Patent land, also adj. Samuel Ervins land & John Davis's survey; 1 Mar 1781, p.451. A.C. of 25 Shill. Sterl.

ANDREW ARMSTRONG, 298 acs. by Survey 20 Nov 1772 in Botetourt Co. near a large Spring, on a ridge; adj. the land of the sd Andrew Armstrong, sd Armstrongs Survey; 1 Mar 1781, p.453. A.C. of 30 Shill. Sterl. 148 acs. of which was surveyed for Israel Christian the 3rd day of Apr 1772 and the remaining 150 acs. surveyed for Thomas Armstrong 4 Apr 1772 both of which Surveys were Assigned to the sd Andrew Armstrong.

WILLIAM READ, 53 acs. by Survey 28 Apr 1768 in Henry Co. formerly Pittsylvania on both sides black berry Cr.; 1 Mar 1781, p.455. A.C. of 5 Shill. Sterl.

HENRY FEE or Tee, 152 acs. by Survey 2 Nov 1780 in Henry Co. on the N side of the south Mayo Riv.; 1 Mar 1781, p.456. A.C. of 15 Shill. Sterl.

GEORGE THOMSON Ass'ee of JESSE BURTON, 190 acs. by survey 18 Mar 1780 in Fluvanna co. on the N brs. of Fluvanna Riv., to pointers in a ridge path, adj. Jesse Burton; 1 Mar 1781, p.458. A.C. of £1 Sterl.

ANDREW REA, 102 acs. by survey 15 May 1780 in Henry Co. on the Grassey fork of Smiths riv., adj. Jesse Willingham; 1 Mar 1781, p.459. A.C. of 10 Shill. sterl.

JAMES GRIGSBY Ass'ee of WILLIAM GIBSON, 59 acs. by Survey 23 Nov 1779 in Rockbridge Co. on the Waters of Buffaloe Cr., on the top of *Whiskey hill*, in the bent of Buffaloe, adj. sd William Gibson old Survey; 1 Mar 1781, p.461. A.C. of 10 Shill. Sterl.

ISHAM HODGES, 193 acs. by survey 3 Jun 1780 in Henry Co. on Chesnut Cr.; adj. his old line, Robert Grimmitt & Samuel Patterson; 1 Mar 1781, p.462. A.C. of £1 Sterl.

JOHN NEVILLS, 334 acs. by survey 16 Mar 1780 in Henry Co. on Sycamore Cr.; adj. Thomas Morrisons old Line, Luke Follies line & Ward; 1 Mar 1781, p.464. A.C. of 35 Shill. Sterl.

JOHN RICHARDSON, 259 acs. by survey 12 Apr 1780 in Henry Co. on the Waters of Horse pasture Cr., adj. Walton Otherwise Laynes line & Randolph and Companys line; 1 Mar 1781, p.466. A.C. of 30 Shill. Sterl.

THOMAS LOCKHART, 453 acs. by survey 14 Apr 1780 in Henry Co. on the brs. of North Mayo Riv.; 1 Mar 1781, p.467. A.C. of 45 Shill. Sterl.

MILES JENNINGS, 474 acs. by survey 1 Mar 1780 in Henry Co. on the N Side of

Mayo riv., adj. Randolph and Jourdan [their line] & his own line; 1 Mar 1781, p.469. A.C. of 5 Shill. Sterl.

DAVID DICK Ass'ee of JAMES ROBINSON who was Ass'ee of JACOB SALMON, 70 acs. by survey 10 Apr 1773 in Botetourt Co. on Ugleys Cr. Joining a Survey of John Dickensons; 1 Mar 1781, p.471. A.C. of 10 Shill. Sterl.

GARRATT/GARRAT MOAR, 238 acs. by survey 1 Apr 1780 in Henry Co. on the first Bold Br. of Leatherwood Cr., adj. Walter Dunn; 1 Mar 1781, p.473. A.C. of 25 Shill. Sterl.

BOOTH WOODSON, 400 acs. by survey 25 Mar 1752 in Albemarle Co. in the fork of James Riv. on the brs. of Cary Cr., adj. Roger Carrell & Thomas Snelson; 1 Mar 1781, p.474. A.C. of £2 Sterl.

JAMES ROUSEY, 76 acs. by survey 17 Apr 1770 on the S brs. of Buffaloe riv. in Amherst Co. adj. his own lines, John Mayfield, Carter Braxton, Moses Higginbotham, James Rousey & William Gatewood Junior; 1 Mar 1781, p.475. A.C. of 10 Shill. sterl.

JAMES THOMSON, 126 acs. by survey 28 Apr 1780 in Amherst Co. in the hundred of Said County on the N brs. of the south fork of Ruckers run; adj. William Cabell Esquire, the property of Walter King Esquire of Great Britain & the sd Cabell; 1 Mar 1781, p.477. A.C. of 15 Shill. Sterl. by Virtue of an Entry made by William Bibb 28 May 1764 and by him transferred to the sd James Thomson.

JAMES WELLS, 400 acs. by survey 9 Mar 1780 in Amherst Co. on both sides of the south fork of Ruckers run and bounded by the Variation of the Magnetic from the true Meridian being N15W, at pointers Corner to Number 12 in the patent line and with its line; 1 Mar 1781, p.479. in Consideration of the Sum of £1,400 Current Money of Virginia paid by James Wells unto David Shepherd Escheator for Amherst Co. ... which tract was lately the property of Walter King a British Subjects and was Sold by the Aforesaid David Shephead unto the said James Wells agreable to two Acts of General Assembly passed in the year 1779 the one Intittled an Act Concerning Escheats and forfeitures from British Subjects the other Intittled an Act Concerning Escheators.

WILLIAM DUIGUID, 338 acs. by survey 6 Sep 1756 in Albemarle Co. on the N brs. of the Bent Cr. adj. James Freeland; 1 Mar 1781, p.481. A.C. of 35 Shill. Sterl.

JOSEPH MARTIN, 400 acs. by survey 8 Mar 1766 in Pittsylvania Co. formerly Halifax on the head Draughts of Cherry stone Cr.; 1 Mar 1781, p.482. A.C. of £2 sterl.

JAMES JOHNSON, 143½ acs. by Survey 10 Apr 1777 in Lunenburg Co. on the brs. of Reedy Cr.; adj. Trent, Williams, his own line, Hazlewood & Walker; 1 Mar 1781, p.484. A.C. of 15 Shill. Sterl.

PETER DAY Ass'ee of ROBERT WRIGHT, 196 acs. by survey 1 Dec 1772 in Buckingham Co. on the brs. of Wreck Island Cr., adj. Thomas Doss & Elex. Smith; 1 Mar 1781, p.485. A.C. of £1 Sterl.

JAMES MANKING, 140 acs. by survey 13 Mar 1768 in Henry Co. formerly

Pittsylvania on Rossells Cr.; 1 Mar 1781, p.486. A.C. of 15 Shill. Sterl.

JAMES TAIT, 181 acs. by Survey 3 Apr 1780 in Surry Co. near the upper Chip Oaks Cr. and bounded by the Variation of the Magnetic N70E; adj. Colo. William Allen, William Cocke, Philip Birt Dec'd & Thomas Sorsby; 1 Mar 1781, p.488. *in Consideration of the Sum of £3,348.S10 Current Money of Virginia paid by James Tait unto James Belsches Gent. Escheator for Surry Co. ... which Tract or parcel of Land was lately the property of Richard Oswald a British Subject and was Sold by the said James Belshes unto the aforesaid James Tait Agreable to two Acts of Assembly passed in the year 1779 the one Intittled an Act Concerning Escheats and forefeitures from British Subjects the other intittled an Act Concerning Escheators.*

JOHN REEVES Ass'ee of CHRISTOPHER WAGGONER, 400 acs. by survey 14 Jul 1772 in Augusta Co. on the head Brs. of the long Meadow a br. of the North br. of Shenandore, by said Meadow, adj. Thomas Bryants land; 1 Mar 1781, p.490. A.C. of £2 Sterl. including 19 acs. Gtd. to Reuben Harrison by Pat. 20 Sep 1751.

JAME MELTON, 430 acs. by survey 21 Nov 1765 in Henry Co. formerly Pittsylvania on the draughts of Leatherwood Cr., in the fork of sd Cr., adj. Lomax; 1 Mar 1781, p.491. A.C. of 45 Shill. Sterl.

JOHN MARR, 404 acs. by survey 22 Mar 1770 in Pittsylvania Co. on Beens Cr.; adj. Chadwell, Constant Perkins & Wilson; 1 Mar 1781, p.492. A.C. of £2 Sterl.

JOHN MARR, GEORGE HAIRSTON & THOMAS BEDFORD, 126 acs. by survey 14 Dec 1773 in Henry Co. formerly Pittsylvania on the S side Smiths Riv., Crossing a bold br.; 1 Mar 1781, p.494. A.C. of 15 Shill. Sterl.

NICHOLAS DARNELL, 204 acs. by survey 17 Nov 1755 in Henry Co. formerly Halifax on both sides of the south fork of Sandy Riv.; 1 Mar 1781, p.495. A.C. of £1 Sterl.

JOHN DIXSON, 494 acs. by survey 15 Oct 1772 in Bedford Co. on the head brs. of Naked Cr., adj. Archibald Campbell; 1 Mar 1781, p.497. A.C. of 50 Shill. Sterl.

DANIEL McBRIDE, 278 acs. by survey 17 Nov 1779 in Henry Co. on the Waters of Leatherwood Cr.; adj. Lomax and Company, & Rigers line; 1 Mar 1781, p.498. A.C. of 30 Shill. Sterl.

ALEXANDER McCLURE, 280 acs. by survey 24 Apr 1780 in Rockbridge Co. Joining David McClures patent line; 1 Mar 1781, p.500. A.C. of 30 Shill. Sterl.

JOHN PEEBLES, 88 acs. by survey 23 May 1780 in Augusta Co. on a small North br. of the cow pasture, to two white Oak Saplins in Stony Ground, on the side of a Steep hill, on the side of the Mountain, at the head of a Spring; 1 Mar 1781, p.501. A.C. of 10 Shill. Sterl.

DAVID IRBY, 370 acs. by survey 19 May 1780 in Pittsylvania Co. on the N brs. of Stinking Riv., Crossing Steep br., Crossing a Bent of sd riv.; adj. Joseph Echols line, Green Street his lines &

Lightfoot; 1 Mar 1781, p.502. A.C. of £2 Sterl.

BENJAMIN FITZPATRICK, 400 acs. by survey 17 Mar 1778 in Fluvanna Co. on a bank or Steep hillside, on a Slash Side; adj. John Scott, sd Fitzpatrick, Hancock & Cooper; 1 Mar 1781, p.504. A.C. of £2 Sterl.

JACOB PECK, 189 acs. by survey 17 Apr 1780 in Augusta Co. on a small br. of the Middle riv. of Shenandore and Joining John Finleys land on the SE Side, also adj. David Trimble & William Anderson; 1 Mar 1781, p.506. A.C. of £1 Sterl.

JOHN DICKENSON, 420 acs. by survey 8 Sep 1779 in Henry Co. on Pigg riv., down Chesnut Cr.; adj. Dickensons line, Isham Hodges line, Samuel Patersons line, sd Pattersons C. of Another Survey & Grays line; 1 Mar 1781, p.507. A.C. of 45 Shill. Sterl.

WILLIAM BURKE, Ass'ee of JAMES EPPERSON who was Ass'ee of DAVID EPPESON, 120 acs. by survey 14 Nov 1755 in Louisa Co. in Fredrickvills parish on the Spurs of the Great Mountains and on both sides the Middle fork of Buck Mountain Cr., Beginning near a large Rock on the N Side the sd fork, on the side of the Mountain, to a Cherry tree Amongs Rocks, in the flat of the Cr.; 1 Mar 1781, p.509. A.C. of 15 Shill. Sterl.

RICHARD PHILLIPS/PHILIPS, 185 acs. by survey 19 May 1780 in Albemarle Co. on the S Side the Rivanna riv. and on the Waters thereof; adj. Thomas Carr, the road heading to the sd Carrs Mill, Martin Hawkins, the road leading a Cross Ivy Cr., & Joseph Burnett; 1 Mar 1781, p.511. A.C. of £1 Sterl.

BENJAMIN KINLEY, 178 acs. by survey 22 Mar 1780 in Rockingham Co. on the E side of Muddy Cr., in a Hollow; adj. his former tract, his old Line & Hopkins survey; 1 Mar 1781, p.513. A.C. of £1 Sterl.

JAMES TURPINE, 225 acs. by survey 8 May 1779 in Henry Co. on the brs. of Hatchet run and Pigg riv., crossing a road; adj. Henry Jones, Rentfrow, Turpin & Holton; 1 Mar 1781, p.514. A.C. of 20 Shill. sterl.

HUGH DIVER, 210 acs. by survey 18 May 1780 in Rockingham Co. on the N side of the North riv. of Shanandore, by a pond, in a draft, on a hill above Harts Meadow; adj. Millers land formerly Hendersons, Silas Hart & sd Divers Patent land; 1 Mar 1781, p.516. A.C. of 25 Shill. Sterl.

OWEN WEST, 517 acs. by **an inclusive survey** 29 Mar 1780 in Pittsylvania Co. on the south fork of Stinking riv., adj. sd Wests new line; 1 Mar 1781, p.518. A.C. of 55 Shill. Sterl. 233 acs of which was surveyed 20 Oct 1766 the remaining 284 acs. Surveyed 16 Nov 1774.

JOHN PATTESON, 347 acs. by survey 19 Nov 1772 in Buckingham Co. on the W Brs. of Davis Cr.; adj. William Clerk, Thomas Still, Mayes old line & James Burnet; 1 Mar 1781, p.520. A.C. of 35 Shill. Sterl.

HUGH DIVER, 170 acs. by survey 18 May 1780 in Rockingham and Augusta Counties on the W side of Mossey Cr.; adj. Henry Millers land formerly Ervins,

John Davis's Survey, sd Davis's Survey in a line of his land formerly [McCranires], John Diver & Thomas Reed; 1 Mar 1781, p.521. A.C. of £1 Sterl.

ELIZABETH THEEDS [and her Heirs forever], 161 acs. by survey 21 Mar 1778 in Albemarle Co. on the S Side the rivanna Riv. and on the brs. of Ivy Cr., to the Baptist road [several times]; adj. John Shiflet, Stephen Phillips, Samuel Ray, Alexr. Mackie & Joseph Burnett; 1 Mar 1781, p.523. A.C. of £1 Sterl.

JOHN JONES, 46 by survey 25 Nov 1752 in Sussex Co. formerly Surry on the N side of Nottoway riv.; adj. William Harper, the sd Jones & Peter Green dec'd; 1 Mar 1781, p.525. A.C. of 5 Shill. Sterl.

BENJAMIN KINLEY, 255 acs. by survey 23 Mar 1780 in Rockingham Co. on the North West Br. of the Head of Linvels Cr. Called Anthonys Springs, near a road, adj. his other survey & Townsend Mathewes's land; 1 Mar 1781, p.526. A.C. of 30 Shill. Sterl.

WILLIAM YOUNG Ass'ee of WILLIAM STUGALL or STEEGALL, 138 acs. by survey 11 Apr 1765 in Pittsylvania Co. formerly Halifax on both sides Snow Cr.; 1 Mar 1781, p.528. A.C. of 15 Shill. Sterl.

[Margin note: *This Grant was altered in the Name of Governour Harrison and dated 20th August 1783 because the Grant was made out and recorded before Signed by Governour Jefferson who resigned before it could be signed or Seald*]

JAMES PARISH Ass'ee of WILLIAM SAMFORD, 403 acs. by Survey 28 Nov 1754 in Lunenburg Co. on the Brs. of the Great Cr.; adj. Stephen Candles [Caudles] upper Corner a Gum on a small branch at A.; 20 Aug 1783, *8th year of the Commonwealth*, Benjamin Harrison Esquire Governor, p.529. A.C. of £2 Sterl. [This land appears to be on the head waters of Waqua Cr., the Great Cr. & Cedar Cr. on the Brunswick Co. line. Also see PB 34 p.362 to Stephen Caudle]

DANIEL WADE, 103 acs. by survey 29 Apr 1775 in Henrico Co. on each side the road Called Pounceys tract; adj. Ware, Going, Ben Johnson, William Row, George Jude & Rockett; 1 Mar 1781, p.531. A.C. of 10 Shill. Sterl.

JAMES GAMBLE, 200 acs. by survey 14 Jun 17872 in Augusta Co. on the head Brs. of Naked Cr. bet. the Lines of his own and William Frames L., by a road; 1 Mar 1781, p.532. A.C. of £1 Sterl.

WILLIAM PAXTON, 235 acs. by Survey 15 Apr 1780 in Rockbridge Co. on the North fork of James riv., on McNutts run, down the North Riv., at the fork of a draft; adj. his own, Ned Harkin, Dreadens old Corner & William Ramsey; 1 Mar 1781, p.533. A.C. of 25 Shill. Sterl.

JOSEPH WEST, 415 acs. by survey 23 May 1780 in Pittsylvania Co. on the Waters of Straught stone Cr. [Straight stone Cr.]; adj. Thomas Dillard, William Chick, Edmond Kings old line, James Dillard & Major Dillard; 1 Mar 1781, p.536. A.C. of 45 Shill. Sterl.

NATHANIEL ANDERSON Ass'ee of GEORGE ANDERSON, 305 acs. by survey 21 Mar 1752 in Fluvanna Co. formerly Albemarle on both sides the Midle fork of Cary Cr. in the fork of James Riv.; adj. Roger Carroll, Ben Woodson, Miles Cary & Robert Furbish; 1 Mar 1781, p.537. A.C. of 35 Shill. Sterl.

JOHN BREADEN Ass'ee of ROBERT GRAY, 70 acs. by Survey 27 Oct 1779 in Augusta Co. on a br. of Back Cr. in the south Mountain, to a Steep bank; 1 Mar 1781, p.539. A.C. of 10 Shill. Sterl.

JOHN PATTESON, 170 acs. by survey 17 Nov 1772 in Buckingham Co. on the Brs. of Davids Cr. on the E side, Beginning in a Springey place; adj. Nicholas Maynard, Thomas Mathews & his own line; 1 Mar 1781, p.540. A.C. of £1 Sterl.

URIAH GARTIN, 86 acs. by survey 13 or 30 May 1780 in Rockingham Co. on the E side of the Dry Riv. a br. of the North Riv. of Shenandore, near the edge of a Meadow; adj. his land, James Shanond, & Benjamin Harrison land formerly Edwards's; 1 Mar 1781, p.542. A.C. of 10 shill. Sterl.

HENRY DILLIAN, 300 acs. by survey 21 Nov 1780 in Henry Co. on Strouds Cr., adj. his own & James East; 1 Mar 1781, p.543. A.C. of 30 Shill. Sterl.

JOHN OLD Ass'ee of WILLIAM HAMNER, 194 acs. by survey 20 Apr 1772 in Albemarle Co. on some of the N brs. of the North fork of Hardware riv., adj. his own Line & Peter McHauley; 1 Mar 1781, p.545. A.C. of £1 Sterl.

JOHN RUSH Ass'ee of THOMAS JOHNSON who was Ass'ee of JACOB HUTT, 196 acs. by survey 17 Mar 1775 in Bedford Co. on Beaverdam Cr., adj. sd Hutts old Line; 1 Mar 1781, p.546. A.C. of £1 Sterl.

BENJAMIN FARISS, 150 acs. by survey 6 Nov 1770 in Louisa Co. on both sides of Bunches Cr., on the N side of Clarks road, adj. Hopkins & Morriss; 1 Mar 1781, p.548. A.C. of 15 Shill. Sterl.

JOHN EWINS, 27 acs. by survey 24 Mar 1780 in Rockingham Co. on the head br. of Lenvils Cr. Joining his own and Browns land, Beginning on the Grant line, near Sampleses land, near a br. Corner to Browns and saidd Ewins Cab. Tract, adj. John Blains land being part of the said Grant land; 1 Mar 1781, p.550. A.C. of 5 Shill. Sterl.

JOEL BLANKINSHIP, 170 acs. by survey 12 Apr 1774 in Bedford Co. on the N side of Goose Cr., adj. Simon Hencock & Mead; 1 Mar 1781, p.551. A.C. of £1 Sterl.

DAVID JONES, 240 acs. by Survey 25 Mar 1751 in Sussex Co. formerly Surry on the S side of Black Water Sw., on the side of the Court house road, down the black Sw., up Tomkins Meadow br.; adj. the sd Jones [his new Survey], John Goodwin, William Bagbey, William Saunders/Sanders, John Tomkins, Benjamin Barker & Henry Barker; *In witness whereof the said Thomas Jefferson Governor of the Commonwealth of Virginia hath herunto Set his hand and Caused the Lesser seal of the said Commonwealth to be Affixed at Richmond on 1 Mar 1781, in the 5th year of the Commonwealth*, p.553-555. in Consideration of the A.C. of 25 Shill. Sterl. paid by David Jones into the treasury of this Commonwealth. [This land was referred to as James Boisseau Jones's in Jarrard's PB 41 p.364]

Finis

Grant Book D

20 Jul 1780 to 10 Apr 1781

JOHN ROBERTSON/ROBINSON, 69 acs. by Survey 7 Nov 1767 in Botetourt Co. on a small br. of the North fork of Roanoak, along the ridge, adj. William Inglish/Inglis; 20 Jul 1780 *in the 5th year of the Commonwealth*, Thomas Jefferson Esq. Governor, p.1. A.C. of 10 Shill.

THOMAS LOMAX, Esq., 485 acs. By Survey 29 Sep 1778 in Essex Co. Consisting of Water, land and Marsh on port Tobacco and Mediels Bay [or Meditts Bay] on Rappahannock Riv., through a marsh, up and along the sd River Marsh and shore to a valley Commonly Known and called by the appellation of *Gravelly walk*, along the edge of the sunken Ground, adj. Thomas Lunsfords pat ; 20 Jul 1780, p.1. A.C. of £2.S10.

WILLIAM THOMPSON & WILLIAM PRESTON Exors. of JAMES PATTON Dec'd, 200 acs. by Survey 9 Nov 1773 in Montgomery Co. on Toms cr., by a path, adj. John Adams & Jacob Lingole, to a white Oak in the naked Land; 20 Jul 1780, p.2. A.C. of 20 Shill. Sterl. whereas by one pat. under the seal of the Commonwealth and dominion of Virginia bearing date 20 Jun 1753 gtd. James Paton 7,500 acs. on the waters of Woods Riv. then in Augusta Co. [PB 32 p.178] now in Montgomery Co. and whereas *Michael Kinder* in whom the right and title of 200 acs. part has since become vested hath failed to pay quitrents as to the sd 200 acs. and William Thompson and William Preston Exors. of James Patton Dec'd made humble suit to our late Lieutenant Governor and Commander in Chief and hath obtained a g. for the same.

THOMAS WALKER, 400 acs. Louisa Co. & Albemarle Co. on Great Cr. and the brs. thereof, adj. Benjamin Johnson & Timothy Dolton; 20 Jul 1780, p.4. A.C. of 40 Shill. Sterl. whereas by pat. 5 Jul 1751 gtd. Nicholas Oliver in Louisa Co. [PB 29 p.447] and whereas the sd Nicholas Oliver hath failed to pay quitrents and *Walker Taliaferro* have made humble suit to our Late Governor and Commander in Chief of our Colony and Dominion and hath obtained a G. for the same right and title whereof he hath assigned to Thomas Walker Gent. [Near Machunk Cr., see adj. Hanover Co.

PB 14 p.477 to Timothy Dalton and PB 16 p.21 to Benjamin Johnson]

THOMAS FLOWER, 327 acs. by Survey 30 Nov 1772 in Henry Co. Formerly Pittsylvania on the head of Runnett bagg a br. of Ervin Riv., Beginning on the Top of the main Mountain, to a Cu[cu]mber Tree; 20 Jul 1780, p.5. A.C. of 35 Shill. Sterl.

JAMES SPEED, 397 acs. by Survey 23 Sep 1772 in Charlotte Co. on the brs. of Twitteys and the Horse pen Creeks; adj. Cheatham, Bedford & his own line; 20 Jul 1780, p.6. A.C. of 40 Shill. Sterl. [For Cheatham's see PB 33 p.5 to John Hall, for his own see PB 37 p.43 to John Sansom]

JAMES GREEN, 354 acs. by Survey made for Joshua Hix of whom he recover'd it by Caveat before the late Governour and Council bearing date 27th day of [blank] 1747 in Lunenburgh Co. on the head of the little cr. above stoney cr., on a path; adj. Thomas Knight, James Mize, John Wright, Solomon Wright, Walton, & John Parker; 20 Jul 1780, p.7. A.C. of 35 Shill. Sterl.

THOMAS FLOWER, 930 acs. by Survey 15 Nov 1772 in Henry Co. formerly Pittsylvania on both Sides of Flat Cr. of Smith Riv., up the South fork, crossing the upper Rich Run, on a Spur of Bull mountain, down Rich Run, adj. Butterworth & Ward; 20 Jul 1780, p.8. A.C. of £4.S15 Sterl.

JOHN CANEFAX, 254 acs. by Survey 8 Nov 1770 in Bedford Co. on the N Side of Staunton Riv., to a ledge of Rocks near the lower end of a Small Island, up Dennys Road; adj. his own, John Brown & James Talbot; 20 Jul 1780, p.10. A.C. of 25 Shill. Sterl.

THOMAS ARTHER, 824 acs. by Survey 20 Nov 1776 in Bedford Co. on the S brs. of Magotty Cr., Beginning at a glade, on the Road; adj. Grimes, Polley, & Robert Mead; 20 Jul 1780, p.11. A.C. of £4.S5 Sterl.

MATTHEW SHAWDON Ass'ee of WILLIAM ARMSTRONG, 180 acs. by Survey 10 Feb 1755 in Botetourt Co. formerly Augusta on the waters of Catawber, by the road on a hill, adj. [Clyert] & James Mitchell; 20 Jul 1780, p.12. A.C. of 20 Shill. Sterl.

JOSEPH GREEN, 641 acs. by Survey 13 Mar 1772 in Bedford Co. on the S side of Staunton Riv.; adj. Standifer, Acquilla Greer & his own line; 20 Jul 1780, p.13. A.C. of £3.S5 Sterl.

JOHN ANTHONY, 1,300 acs. by Survey 2 Mar 1779 in Bedford Co. on the S brs. of Otter riv., on Johnsons Mountain & a road; adj. his old patent, Quarles & Irvine; 20 Jul 1780, p.14. A.C. of £6.S10 Sterl.

WILLIAM BRADSHAW, 275 acs. by Survey 16 Mar 1779 in Bedford Co. on Marimon Run, adj. Holland & Hunt; 20 Jul 1780, p.15. A.C. 30 Shill. Sterl.

JAMES GATEWOOD, 324 acs. by Survey 4 Dec 1766 in Bedford Co. on both Sides of Cheese Cr., on a ridge; adj. Fry and Company [the Companys line], Tullus/Tullos, Samuel Brown & Barker; 20 Jul 1780, p.16. A.C. of 35 Shill. Sterl.

PETER BRADSHAW, 365 acs. by Survey 16 Mar 1779 in Bedford Co. on

Merimons Run, on the road on the dark hollow, adj. the old line & Hunt; 20 Jul 1780, p.17. A.C. of 40 Shill. Serl.

WILLIAM LEWIS, 383 acs. by Survey 6 Mar 1780 in Pittsylvania Co. on the brs. of the dowble cr., crossing the county line; adj. Nim Scott, John Hall, Jonathan Hill, Dodson, Lewis, John Moore, Payne, Jarrott Gross & William Richardson; 20 Jul 1780, p.18. A.C. 40 Shill. Sterl.

JOSEPH DOUGLASS, 400 acs. by Survey 26 Mar 1772 in Rockingham Co. formerly Augusta on the N side of the North Riv. of Shanandore, adj. Abraham Smith & Hugh Douglass; 20 Jul 1780, p.19. A.C. of 40 Shill. Sterl.

ROGER ATKINSON ass'ee of RICHARD ANDREWS, 209 acs. by Survey 25 Oct 1771 in Hallifax Co. on the draughts of Bluewing, crossing Mulberry br., adj. John Gill & Roger Atkinson; 20 Jul 1780, p.21. A.C. of 25 Shill. Sterl.

CHARLES McLAUGHLIN, 500 acs. by Survey 15 Nov 1772 in Bedford Co. on both sides of Otter riv.; adj. Evans, Kay, Milam, his own, Harmon, Banister & Frigus; 20 Jul 1780, p.21. A.C. of £2.S10.

THOMAS RAFFERTY, 200 acs. by Survey 25 Jan 1764 in Bedford Co. on the E Side of Falling riv.; adj. Darby Conners, Booker & Mitchell; 20 Jul 1780, p.23. A.C. of 20 Shill. Sterl.

ROGER ATKINSON ass'ee of JAMES ROBERTS, gent., 2,935 acs. by Survey 5 Jun 1766 in Pittsylvania Co. formerly Hallifax on both Sides of Johns Run of Sandy Cr., adj. James Terry & Astin; 20 Jul 1780, p.24. A.C. of £8 Sterl. **paid into the late receiver Generalls office**. 400 acs. part was gtd. Nathaniel Terry by pat. 20 Aug 1759 [PB 34 p.417], 400 acs. part was gtd. John Hanna by pat. 16 Aug 1756 [PB 34 p.107], 100 acs. part is part of 400 acs. Gtd. Hugh Miller Gent. by pat. 15 May 1755 [3,320 acs. in PB 32 p.558], 400 acs. part was gtd. William Trigg by pat. 16 Aug 1756 [PB 34 p.95], 75 acs. part is part of 7,050 acs. Gtd. Nathaniel Terry by pat. 31 Oct 1759 [PB 33 p.660] the right and Title of which said Several Tracts of Land is since become vested in the sd Roger Atkinson and 1,560 acs. the residue was never before gtd. but only Survey'd for Nathaniel Terry in Two Survey's one of 800 acs. and the other of 760 acs. the right and Title of which is since become vested in the sd Roger Atkinson.

OBADIAH HENRY TRENT, 284 acs. by Survey 27 Apr 1771 in Bedford Co. on both sides of Trough br., adj. Randolph & Peburn; 20 Jul 1780, p.26. A.C. of 30 Shill. Sterl. 284 acs. being part of Woodson and Companys order of Council for 20,000 acs. Gtd them by Pat. 14 Jun 1749.

BRYAN McDONALD, 600 acs. by Survey 20 Aug 1772 in Botetourt Co. on the waters of Roanoke And James Riv., Beginning on a high ridge near Cloyds land; adj. Cloyd, Allison & Armstrong; 20 Jul 1780, p.27. A.C. of 40 Shill. Sterl. 161 acs. part is part of 218 acs. gtd. Bryan McDonald by pat. 10 Mar 1756 and 58 acs. part is part of 150 acs. gtd. John Armstrong by pat. 16 Sep 1765 also 19 acs. part i spart of 95 acs. Gtd. John Armstrong by pat. 16 Sep 1745 the right and Title of Which sd several tracts of L. is since become vested in the sd Bryan

McDonald and 352 acs. the residune never before gtd. 120 acs. part thereof was Surveyd for David Miller 2 Oct 1753 which was assigned to the sd Bryan McDonald by the sd David Miller 5 Mar 1763.

JOHN WARD, 100 acs. by Survey 4 Nov 1766 in Henry Co. formerly Hallifax on the Ast Side of Sycamore Cr.; 20 Jul 1780, p.29. A.C. of 10 Shill. Sterl.

JONATHAN PHILLIPS, 267 acs. by Survey 21 Feb 1775 in Pittsylvania Co. on the brs. of Potters Cr., on a ridge, along and up Pigg river Road, adj. Barnet/Barenett; 20 Jul 1780, p.30. A.C. of 30 Shill. Sterl.

SAMUEL PATTERSON, 124 acs. by Survey 6 Mar 1765 in Halifax Co. in the fork between Pigg Riv. and Chesnut Cr., adj. Steegal & Reaves; 20 Jul 1780, p.31. A.C. of 15 Shill. Sterl.

ROGER ATKINSON Gent., 12,957 acs. by Survey 1 Mar 1765 in Pittsylvania Co. formerly Halifax on Cain Cr. and the brs. Thereof, along the Country line [East], up Sandy Cr., on the East fork of Fawl cr., down Hendricks Cr.; adj. Cargill, Airs, Stamps, Thomas Pistol, Green, & Nathaniel Terry, Gent.; 20 Jul 1780, p.32. A.C. of £53 Sterl. **paid into the late receiver Generals office**. 250 acs. part Gtd. John Cargill by pat. 15 Dec 1749 [PB 29 p.89], 315 acs. part gtd. John Cargill by pat. 14 Feb 1761 [PB 34 p.817], 170 acs. part gtd. John Cargill by pat. 1 Jun 1750 [PB 30 p.92], 400 acs. part gtd. Benjamin Lawless by pat. 15 Jul 1760 [PB 34 p.583], 383 acs. part gtd. James Hogan by pat. 10 Sep 1760 [PB 34 p.713], 436 acs. part gtd. Samuel Harriss by pat. 15 Jul 1760 [PB 34 p.640], 400 acs. part gtd. Nathaniel Terry by pat. 29 Jul 1765 [26 Jul 1765 in PB 36 p.823], the right and Title of which sd several Tracts of Lands is since become vested in the sd Roger Atkinson and 10,603 acs.the residue never before gtd.

JOHN FITZPATRICK, 900 acs. by Survey 11 Jul 1773 in Bedford Co. on both sides of Mollys Cr., crossing Molleys Cr., at a Gulley; adj. William Manley near the lower meadow br., Heath, Smither, William Bryan, Robert Means, William Read, Dickerson, Thomas Brown, Ajonadal Read & John Simmons; 20 Jul 1780, p.36. A.C. of £2 Sterl. 500 acs. part is part of 3,150 acs. Gtd. John Ornsby Clerk by pat. 5 Feb 1757 [PB 34 p.174 on Molly's alias Bryery Cr.] the right and title of which is since become vested in the sd John Fitzpatrick and 400 acs. the residue never before gtd.

THOMAS ARMSTRONG, 140 acs. by Survey 11 Nov 1761 in Augusta Co. on the N side of Jennings's br. joining the land Sd Armstrong now lives on, Beginning at his old Servey, with Edmiston's line, on a ridge; 20 Jul 1780, p.37. A.C. of 15 Shill. Sterl.

JOHN WARD, 128 acs. by Survey 2 Dec 1768 in Henry Co. formerly Pittsylvania on the draughts of Rock castle cr., along a mountain; 20 Jul 1780, p.38. A.C. of 15 Shill. Sterl.

ROBERT WILLIAMS, 172 acs. by Survey 28 May 1767 in Halifax Co. on the brs. of Brush Cr., crossing two forks of sd cr.; adj. John Steen, Dyers or Dyus line, Prewit, Sullivan & Smith; 20 Jul 1780, p.39. A.C. of 20 Shill. Sterl.

JOHN WARD, Gent., 327 acs. by Survey 11 Nov 1769 in Henry Co. formerly Pittsylvania on Runnett bagg cr., on the Top of a main Mountain, to a Cucumber tree; 20 Jul 1780, p.40. A.C. of 35 Shill. Sterl.

JOHN WARD, 138 acs. by Survey 5 Dec 1768 in Henry Co. formerly Pittsylvania on the draughts of [Wajion and Joninausk] Creeks, on the top of a ridge; 20 Jul 1780, p.42. A.C. of 15 Shill. Sterl.

WILLIAM JAMESON ass'ee of TULLEY CHOICE, 350 acs. by Survey 4 Mar 1762 in Pittsylvania Co. formerly Halifax on the brs. of Keatons Cr., on a Spur of Chesnut mountain, Crossing the North fork of Burets Cr., adj. David Wilson; 20 Jul 1780, p.43. A.C. of 35 Shill. Sterl.

JEREMIAH EARLEY & JAMES CALAWAY, 40 acs. by Survey 17 Apr 1779 in Henry Co. it being Mores entry nobb by some cald the bald nobb, adj. Hill & Swinkfield Hill; 20 Jul 1780, p.44. A.C. of 5 Shill. Sterl.

GEORGE GREEN ass'ee of WILLIAM EAKON, 170 acs. by Survey 7 Apr 1773 in Botetourt Co. on the North fork of Potts Cr., adj. William Preston; 20 Jul 1780, p.45. A.C. of 20 Shill. Sterl.

MALACHI DEMUL, 93 acs. by Survey 28 Jan 1771 in Botetourt Co. on Craigs Creeks a br. of James Riv., Crossing the Cr. and Gap run, at the foot of a Ridge, adj. John Sewer or Saver; 20 Jul 1780, p.46. A.C. of 10 Shill. Sterl.

JOHN WARD, 278 acs. by Survey 8 Dec 1768 in Henry Co. formerly Pittsylvania on the head of the South br. of the Middle fork of Jacks Cr., Beginning at the top of the blew Ridge at the Head of the afforesd Cr.; 20 Jul 1780, p.47. A.C. of 30 Shill. Sterl.

GILBERT HAROLD/HEAROLD, 264 acs. by Survey 19 Mar 1780 in Bedford Co. on the N side of Ivey Cr., on the side of the Creek Hill, on an Old Path; adj. Tate, Christopher Lynch, & Wayles; 20 Jul 1780, p.48. A.C. of 30 Shill. Sterl. by Virtue of an Entry made 27 Jul 1766 by JOHN FROST and Assigned to sd Gilbert Harold.

JOHN DUNCAN, 126 acs. by Survey 15 Dec 1769 in Amherst Co. on the brs. of Pedler Riv., adj. David Burk & Robert Johnson; 20 Jul 1780, p.50. A.C. of 15 Shill. Sterl.

WILLIAM MATTHEWS Ass'ee of ROBERT DAVIS, 380 acs. by Survey 20 Apr 1773 in Amherst Co. on the Brs. of Thomas's Mill Cr. and the N Brs of Otter Cr.; adj. James Kitchen, John Hogg, Robert Johnston & Hugh Morris; 20 Jul 1780, p.51. A.C. of 40 Shill. Sterl.

WILLIAM DAVANPORT, 196 acs. by Survey 16 Feb 1770 in Bedford Co. on both sides of the North fork of the south fork of Cub Cr., near the County Line, adj. Richardson; 1 Sep 1780, p.53. A.C. of 20 Shill. Sterl.

JACOB KEY, 100 acs. by Survey 21 Dec 1778 in Bedford Co. on the N side of Entry Cr., down Sandy Br.; adj. William Fariss/Farris, Wood Jones, Daniel Mitchell, Creddel, & Robert Mitchell; 1 Sep 1780, p.54. A.C. of 10 Shill.

EUCLID WILLS ass'ee of JOHN HALL GLOVER who was ass'ee of THOMAS

LANE who was ass'ee of RICHARD STITH, 400 acs. by Survey 6 Dec 1774 in Bedford Co. on both sides of Little whipping cr., over the Cr. to an Ivy Clift, adj. Samuel Gaulding & Dougherty; 1 Sep 1780, p.55. A.C. of 40 Shill. Sterl.

JONATHAN RICHARDSON, 430 acs. by Survey 7 Apr 1778 in Bedford Co. on Gills cr., at the Mouth of Long br., by a Path, adj. Pate; 1 Sep 1780, p.56. A.C. of 45 Shill. Sterl.

VALENTINE STEARMAN ass'ee of JOHN SMITH, 400 acs by Survey 27 Dec 1754 in Lunenburg Co. on the brs. of Heatt cr. [Hatt cr.]; adj. John Cunningham, Daniel Mitchell, Given & his own line; 1 Sep 1780, p.57. A.C. of 40 Shill. Sterl.

JAMES DOSS, 231 acs. by Survey 1 Mar 1770 in Pittsylvania Co. on the Brs. of Staunton riv., on the head of Childres's cr.; 1 Sep 1780, p.58. A.C. of 25 Shill. Sterl.

GEORGE ALLEN, 287 acs. by Survey 1 Apr 1780 in Pittsylvania Co. on the brs. of Allens Cr. and Little strait stone cr.; adj. sd Allen, William Pollard, Daugherty, & William Batterson; 1 Sep 1780, p.58. A.C. of 30 Shill. Sterl.

JACOB RUBSEMEN, 30 acs. by Survey 23 Mar 1780 in Pittsylvania Co. on Staunton Riv., adj. Benjamin Tarrance & John Goad; 1 Sep 1780, p.59. A.C. of 5 Shill. Sterl.

ISHAM TALBOT, 683 acs. by Survey 17 Nov 1766 in Bedford Co. on the East brs. of Beaver dam Cr., adj. Stith; 1 Sep 1780, p.60. A.C. of £3.S10.

JOHN DIXON, 200 acs. by Survey 23 Mar 1775 in Bedford Co. on the S side of Goose Cr., Beginning on a high clift on sd Cr., down Island br., down sd cr. to a fish dam, adj. his old Lines & Hackworth; 1 Sep 1780, p.62. A.C. of 20 Shill. Sterl.

ANDREW HAIRSTONE, 400 acs. by Survey 13 Jan 1773 in Bedford Co. on the head brs. of Dogwood br.; adj John Dale, Stith, Heath & Arnold; 1 Sep 1780, p.63. A.C. of 40 Shill. Sterl.

DANIEL FRIEL, 77 acs. by Survey 30 Sep 1779 in Augusta Co. on the W side of his other Tract, also adj. James Bell; 1 Sep 1780, p.64. A.C. of 10 Shill. Sterl.

JAMES SLONE, 156 acs. by Survey 3 Apr 1772 in Bedford Co. on Ellots br. a North br. of Magot cr.; 1 Sep 1780, p.65. AC. of 20 Shill. Sterl.

WILLIAM JUSTICE, 160 acs. by Survey 1 Oct 1773 in Pittsylvania Co. on Pigg Riv and Jonakin Cr.; adj. Conway, Richardson & Justice; 1 Sep 1780, p.66. A.C. of 20 Shill. Sterl.

WILLIAM BURGESS, 240 acs. by Survey 30 Sep 1779 in Augusta Co. on a br. of Middle riv. between Walter Trimble and John Trimble's Land and the North Mountain, also adj. Jeremiah Friel; 1 Sep 1780, p.67. A.C. of 25 Shill. Sterl.

WILLIAM SIMPSON, 100 acs. by Survey 1 May 1780 in Bedford Co. on E brs. of South fork of Falling riv.; adj. Campbell, the old Line of Wathen and Jennings, Dixon, & Terancis Line; 1 Sep 1780, p.68. A.C. of 10 Shill. Sterl.

MARY READ, 125 acs. by Survey 1 May 1772 in Halifax Co. on the S brs. of Banister Riv., crossing a road; adj. Givins, Randolph & Bird; 1 Sep 1780, p.69. A.C. of 15 Shill. Sterl.

WALTER ADY/ADEY Ass'ee of JOHN UNDERWOOD, 45 acs. by Survey 4 Dec 1766 in Bedford Co. on both sides of Gills Cr., adj. Starkey; 1 Sep 1780, p.70. A.C. of 5 Shill. Sterl.

MATTHEW EDMISTON, 91 acs. by Survey 11 Feb 1775 in Augusta Co. on the N side of Jenning's br.; adj. James Campbell, John Hogshead & Guin Edmiston; 1 Sep 1780, p.70. A.C. of 10 Shill. Sterl. *bounded by the Variation of the Magnetic from the true Meridian it being 1° East.*

EDWARD ROBERTSON Ass'ee of GEORGE JONES, 204 acs. by Survey 5 Jan 1773 in Bedford Co. on W brs. of Turnip Cr.; adj. Roach, Given, & Robert Smith; 1 Sep 1780, p.72. A.C. of 20 Shill. Sterl.

ANTHONY PATE, 640 acs. by Survey 1 Apr 1778 in Bedford Co. on the South brs. of of Gills cr.; adj. his [Patent Line], Richardson & Charter; 1 Sep 1780, p.73. A.C. of £3.S5 Sterling.

JOHN HICKEY or KICKEY, 468 acs. by Survey 20 Apr 1768 in Henry Co. on the Grasey Fork of Batterrem town Cr.; 1 Sep 1780, p.74. A.C. of 50 Shill. Sterl.

JARREL FITZGERRAL, 76 acs. by Survey 16 Mar 1772 in Bedford Co. on the brs. of Little cr., adj. Johnson & Lewis; 1 Sep 1780, p.75. A.C. of 20 Shill. Sterl. paid by JARRET FITZGARREL into the Treasury of this Commonwealth.

ROBERT HALL, 100 acs. by Survey 16 Apr 1763 in Bedford Co. on the head brs. of Gills cr.; 1 Sep 1780, p.76. A.C. of 10 Shill. Sterl.

FRANCIS GARDNER, 136 acs. by Survey 28 Oct 1774 in Augusta Co. on the NW side of his land, also adj. John Wood; 1 Sep 1780, p.77. A.C. of 15 Shill. Sterl.

THOMAS CLARK, 366 acs. by Survey 18 Feb 1772 in Pittsylvania Co. on the waters of Stinking Riv.; adj. Joseph Fariss, Gudger & Clever; 1 Sep 1780, p.78. A.C. of 40 Shill. Sterl.

JOHN GIVENS JUNR., 97 acs. by Survey 6 Jan 1773 in Augusta Co. on the S side of the Middle Riv. of Shanandore; adj. his old C., William Lamb & Benjamin Yearley; 1 Sep 1780, p.79. A.C. of 10 Shill. Sterl.

WILLIAM WRIGHT, 280 acs. by Survey 10 Mar 1775 in Bedford Co. on Griffith's Mountain; adj. Griffith, Ray & Murphey; 1 Sep 1780, p.80. A.C. of 30 Shill. Sterl. it being part of an Order of Council Granted Walton for 10,000 acs.

ANDREW MANN, 430 acs. by Survey 2 Mar 1773 in Bedford Co. on the N brs. of wreck Island cr.; adj. James Phelps, Stovall & David Martin; 1 Sep 1780, p.81. A.C. of 45 Shill. Sterl.

JOHN WILLIAMS, 390 acs. by Survey 6 May 1780 in Lunenburg Co. on the brs. of Meherrin riv.; adj. Thomas Payson, Sd. Williams Old Line & the sd Passons; 1 Sep 1780, p.82. A.C. of 40 Shill. Sterl.

JAMES CHRISTIAN, 250 acs. by Survey 7 Feb 1767 in Amherst Co. on both Sides of Christians Mill cr., adj. his own Line; 1 Sep 1780, p.83. A.C. of 25 Shill. Sterl.

PEYTON SMITH, 160 acs. by Survey 2 Oct 1773 in Pittsylvania Co. on Pigg Riv.; adj. Justice, Conway, Mullines C. & Kerby; 1 Sep 1780, p.84. A.C. of 20 Shill. Sterl.

ISHAM TALBOT, 900 acs. by Survey 15 Nov 1766 in Bedford Co. on both sides of Keiths Cr., adj. Walton; 1 Sep 1780, p.85. A.C. of £4.S10 Sterl. [This land is on waters of Beaverdam Creek. See plat in Bedford Co. Surveyors Records p.390, surveyed by James Talbot Asst. Surveyor to Richard Stith Surveyor]

MATTHEW TALBOT, 120 acs. by Survey 15 Dec 1762 in Bedford Co. on the S side of Staunton Riv.; 1 Sep 1780, p.86. A.C. of 15 Shill. Sterl.

MATTHEW TALBOT, 388 acs. by Survey 13 Apr 1770 in Bedford Co. on both sides of Sinrells Cr.; adj. Wilson & Hill his corner Mahoggony on Little Linvells cr.; 1 Sep 1780, p.87. A.C. of 40 Shill. Sterl.

WALTER ADEY, 201 acs. by Survey 10 Apr 1770 in Bedford Co. on the N brs. of Black water riv., adj. Maxey; 1 Sep 1780, p.88. A.C. of 20 Shill. Sterl.

WILLIAM DUNLAP, 70 acs. by Survey 12 Feb 1773 in Augusta Co. on the S side of the Middle Riv. of Shanandore; adj. John Dixon, James Ker & Bover line; 1 Sep 1780, p.90. A.C. of 10 Shill. Sterl.

WILLIAM MEAD & ISHAM TALBOT, 300 acs. by Survey 10 Sep 1767 in Bedford Co. on crooked cr.; 1 Sep 1780, p.91. A.C. of 30 Shill. Sterl.

ROBERT McKITTRICK/McKETTRICK /McKETTERICK, 98 acs. by Survey 29 Oct 1774 in Augusta Co. on some brs. of the Middle riv., adj. his old c.; 1 Sep 1780, p.92. A.C. of 10 Shill. Sterl. *bounded by the Variation of the Magnectic from the true Meridian it being 1°E.*

ALEXANDER CURRY ass'ee of ANDREW McCOMB, 40 acs. by Survey 24 Dec 1772 in Augusta Co. on naked Cr., adj. his old line; 1 Sep 1780, p.93. A.C. of 5 Shill. Sterl.

WILLIAM WRIGHT, 63 acs. by Survey 16 Mar 1772 in Bedford Co. on Magotty Cr., adj. Charles Vincent & Miller; 1 Sep 1780, p.94. A.C. of 10 Shill. Sterl.

SAMUEL McCROCLE/McCORKLE Ass'ee of JAMES ALLISON, 50 acs. by Survey 22 Feb 1768 in Augusta Co. on the fork of James riv., to a Stoney knowel, adj. to his own Land/Survey & James Tremble/Trimble; 1 Sep 1780, p.95. A.C. of 5 Shill. Sterl.

JOHN TRIMBLE as heir at Law of JAMES TRIMBLE dec'd, 145 acs. by Survey 26 Oct 1767 in Augusta Co. upon the back cr. a br. of James Riv.; 1 Sep 1780, p.96. A.C. of 15 Shill. Sterl.

JAMES STANDEFORD, 224 acs. by Survey 18 Apr 1769 in Henry Co. formerly Pittsylvania, on Storey cr.; 1 Sep 1780, p.97. A.C. of 25 Shill. Sterl.

WILLIAM DAVIS, 327 acs. by Survey 10 Jun 1779 in Henry Co. on Storey Cr.;

adj. his old Line, Hill & Dilingham; 1 Sep 1780, p.97. A.C. of 35 Shill. Sterl.

PETER GEARHEART, 240 acs. by Survey 3 Mar 1774 in Bedford Co. on the S side of the North fork of Blackwater; adj. Mason, & John Rentfro; 1 Sep 1780, p.98. A.C. of 25 Shill. Sterl.

SHADRACK TURNER, 306 acs. by Survey 7 Dec 1779 in Henry Co. adj. his own lines on the brs. of Butrams town cr.; 1 Sep 1780, p.100. A.C. of 35 Shill. Sterl.

GEORGE SMITH, 404 acs. by Survey 5 Nov 1778 in Pittsylvania Co. on the N brs. of Tomahawk Cr., adj. sd Smith; 1 Sep 1780, p.101. A.C. of 40 Shill. Sterl.

HESEKIAH SHELTON, 344 acs by Survey 6 Dec 1773 in Pittsylvania Co. on the N side of Mayo Riv.; 1 Sep 1780, p.102. A.C. of 35 Shill. Sterl.

SAMUEL YOUNG, 66 acs. by Survey 13 Apr 1780 in Mecklenburg Co. on little Cr.; 1 Sep 1780, p.102. A.C. of 10 Shill. Sterl.

ALEXANDER MOUNTGUMERY Ass'ee of ROBERT MOUNTGUMERY who was ass'ee of WILLIAM BROWN, 162 acs. by Survey 25 Apr 1771 in Botetourt Co. on Cross cr. a br. of Back Cr. being the Waters of Roan Oak, adj. his own L.; 1 Sep 1780, p.103. A.C. of £1 Sterl.

WILLIAM BLAIR, 61 acs. by Survey 30 Mar 1780 in Augusta Co. on the North br. of Naked Cr. betw. sd Blairs and Hugh Donoho's Lines; 1 Sep 1780, p.104. A.C. of 10 Shill. Sterl.

MARY GREGORY, 188 acs. by Survey 8 Apr 1774 in Augusta Co. on back cr. and br. of Jacksons riv. Betw. hers and James Cunninghams L.; 1 Sep 1780, p.105. A.C. of 20 Shill. Sterl. *bounded by the Variation of the Magnectic from the true Meridian it being 1°E.*

JEREMIAH EARLEY, 63 acs. by Survey 12 Dec 1772 in Bedford Co. on the N side of Goose Cr.; adj. Thomas Liftwick, his own Line & Dixon; 1 Sep 1780, p.106. A.C. of 10 Shill. Sterl.

WILLIAM MOORE, 75 acs. by Survey by Survey 23 Apr 1780 in Rockbridge Co. adj. David Moores old Line & Wilsons old Line; 1 Sep 1780, p.107. A.C. of 10 Shill. Sterl.

JAMES ANDERSON, 76 acs. by Survey 1 Apr 1780 in Augusta Co. Joining Andrew McComb, John Blair, William and Samuel Anderson and William Young's Land; 1 Sep 1780, p.108. A.C. of 10 Shill. Sterl.

GEORGE BOSWELL, 182 acs. by Survey 7 Apr 1780 in Rockingham Co. at the foot of the Mountain at a place called *Madisons Gap*, down the run at the Entrance of Madisons Gap; 1 Sep 1780, p.109. A.C. of 20 Shill. Sterl.

BENJAMIN BRAWNER, 165 acs. by Survey 15 Apr 1774 in Pittsylvania Co. on Elk horn Cr.; adj. Chiswell, Winder & Stewart; 1 Sep 1780, p.110. A.C. of £1 Sterl.

SAMUEL LAWRENCE, 54 acs. by Survey 20 Nov 1772 in Botetourt Co. joining the lines of John Hamack's his own and James Halls lands on the waters of Buffalo Cr. a br. of James Riv., with the Line of John Hannah, crossing a draught; 1 Sep 1780, p.110. A.C. of 5 Shill. Sterl.

GEORGE McDONEL/McDonal ass'ee of JOSHUA McCORMACK, 80 acs. by Survey 15 Jan 1772 in Botetourt Co. on the North br. of Roan Oak Riv., Beginning on a high Ridge on the W side of the Tract he lives on; 1 Sep 1780, p.111. A.C. of 10 Shill. Sterl.

CHRISTOPHER BRACKFEILD/ BRACKFIELD ass'ee of JACOB BRACKFEILD, 39 acs. by Survey 24 Sep 1772 in Botetourt Co. on the N side of Craigs Cr. a br. of James Riv.; adj. the Land he lives on; 1 Sep 1780, p.112. A.C. of 5 Shill. Sterl.

WILLIAM TAYLOR Ass'ee of ALEXANDER FORBES who was ass'ee of THOMAS BUFORD who was Ass'ee of HENRY BUNCH, 97 acs. by Survey 7 Dec 1767 in Bedford Co. on the N brs. of Goose Cr., adj. Christian; 1 Sep 1780, p.113. A.C. of 10 Shill. Sterl.

ISHAM TALBOT JUNR., 192 acs. by Survey 4 Dec 1778 in Henry Co. on both sides of Little Bull run, adj. William Greer; 1 Sep 1780, p.114. A.C. of 20 Shill. Sterl.

DAVID IRVINE, 126 acs. by Survey 9 Nov 1779 in Bedford Co. on the north Fork of Otter Riv., down Sawpit br., adj. Wain; 1 Sep 1780, p.115. A.C. of 15 Shill. Sterl.

WILLIAM CURVEY ass'ee of JOHN NICHOL, 400 acs. by Survey 19 Sep 1755 in Augusta Co on a draught of Mossey Cr. *at a place Called whitestone*, Beginning near a a path; 1 Sep 1780, p.116. A.C. of 40 Shill. Sterl.

JOHN WATKINS Ass'ee of JAMES RICHEY, 40 acs. by Survey 22 Aug 1772 in Botetourt Co. on Craigs Cr. a br. of James Riv. opposite to Kyseers bottom, adj. Tillevier; 1 Sep 1780, p.117. A.C. of 5 Shill. Sterl.

JACOB CHANEY, 400 acs. by Survey 2 Mar 1780 in Pittsylvania Co. on the brs. of Jeremy's Fork and berches cr. and the head brs. of Tobys Cr.; adj. George Dodson, Stomp, John Bennet & Davidson; 1 Sep 1780, p.118. A.C. of £2 Sterl.

JAMES HUSTON & JAMES TRIMBLE, 300 acs. by Survey 3 Mar 1767 in Augusta Co. *and known by the Name of Chalk banks* on a Small br. of the North br. of James riv., Near Nul McGleasters Line; 1 Sep 1780, p.119. A.C. of 10 Shill. Sterl.

WILLIAM BLAIR, 18 acs. by Survey 31 Mar 1780 in Augusta Co. adj. Andrew Honeman, Robert McCutchen, Traime [Fraime] & Robert McKutchen; 1 Sep 1780, p.120. A.C. of 5 Shill. Sterl.

JOHN McDUGAL, 85 acs. by Survey 4 May 1780 in Augusta Co. on the N side of Mossey Cr. joining his other tract and William Ralstons; 1 Sep 1780, p.121. A.C. of 10 Shill. Sterl.

AZARIAH SHELTON ass'ee of JAMES GREEN LEA, 122 acs. by Survey 1 Nov 1770 in Pittsylvania Co. on Mathis's Cr., adj. John Parr; 1 Sep 1780, p.122. A.C. 15 Shill. Sterl.

JOHN OWEN SULLIVEN/SULLIVAN ass'ee of HUGH MEANS, 82 acs. by

Survey 21 Sep 1772 in Botetourt Co. on Craigs Cr. a br. of James riv. *at a place called the hunting Ground*; 1 Sep 1780, p.123. A.C. of 10 Shill. Sterl.

JOHN MOORE Ass'ee of WILLIAM HARRIS, 400 acs. by Survey 1 Dec 1763 in Bedford Co. on both sides of polecat br. and on other W brs. of the South fork of Falling Riv.; adj. Brooks, Peter Daniel, Rosser & Staples; 1 Sep 1780, p.124. A.C. of 40 Shill. Sterl.

DAVID ROGERS, 154 acs. by Survey 16 Mar 1768 in Henry Co. on the North fork of Russells Cr.; adj. Rogers, & George Carter; 1 Sep 1780, p.125. A.C. of 15 Shill. Sterl.

WILLIAM BLACK, 151 acs. by Survey 17 Mar 1769 in Pr. Edward Co. on the South fork of Rough Cr.; 1 Sep 1780, p.126. A.C. of 15 Shill. Sterl.

JOHN BARNETT, 148 acs. by Survey 7 Sep 1764 in Pittsylvania Co. on Potters Cr.; 1 Sep 1780, p.127. A.C. of 15 Shill. Sterl.

JAMES CHRISTIAN, 400 acs. by Survey 8 Feb 1770 in Amherst Co. on the brs. of Limekiln Cr., to the South fork & the Middle fork of Lyme Kiln cr., adj. James Christian & Henry Bell; 1 Sep 1780, p.128. A.C. of 40 Shill. Sterl.

ABSALOM RAMEY, 163 acs. by Survey 2 Feb 1780 in Pittsylvania Co. on the Draughts of Streight Stone Cr., down Camp br.; adj. William Collings, Tribble, Gilbert Hunt, Donelson, & John Ballenger; 1 Sep 1780, p.130. A.C. of 20 Shill. Sterl. it being a resurvey on a Survey formerly made by Thomas Hutchings 19 Apr 1774 which was found to be Erronious.

JOHN CHILES, 200 acs. by Survey 5 Mar 1775 in Bedford Co. on Lawsons br., crossing Loveing Fork of Lawsons cr., down Cliffts Cr., on Cody's Cr., adj. Woodson; 1 Sep 1780, p.131. A.C. of 20 Shill. Sterl.

MICHAEL REAL, 178 acs. by Survey 8 Jun 1779 in Henry Co. on Nicholas's cr., adj. Thomas Jones & John Jones; 1 Sep 1780, p.132. A.C. of 20 Shill. Sterl.

JACOB ATKINS, 404 acs. by Survey 5 May 1779 in Henry Co. on the S brs. of Pigg riv. near the head of the North fork of Story cr. on a nobb called Jones's Nobb; 1 Sep 1780, p.133. A.C. of 40 Shill. Sterl.

HENRY BARNS, 115 acs. by Survey 18 Nov 1772 in Halifax Co. on Cherry tree cr., adj. Nowlin & Hicks; 1 Sep 1780, p.134. A.C. of 15 Shill. Sterl.

JEREMIAH WHITE, 98 acs. by Survey 18 Apr 1780 in Pittsylvania Co. on the brs. of Sweetings fork of Sandy cr., crossing the road; adj. Williams, the sd White, Dudgeon, Henry McDaniel & Claybrook; 1 Sep 1780, p.135. A.C. of 10 Shill. Sterl.

JAMES BAGS Ass'ee of ALEXANDER BAGS, 63 acs. by Survey 20 Nov 1779 in Rockbridge Co. on Buffalo Cr.; 1 Sep 1780, p.136. A.C. of 10 Shill. Sterl.

ROBERT STOCKTON, 244 acs. by Survey 29 Apr 1768 in Pittsylvania Co. on Nicholas's Cr.; 1 Sep 1780, p.137. A.C. of 25 Shill. Sterl.

HENRY HARTLESS Ass'ee of ROBERT EDMUSTON, 170 acs. by Survey 1 Mar 1775 in Augusta Co. on the waters of Irish Cr. of James Riv., Beginning on a Spur, along a ridge; 1 Sep 1780, p.138. A.C. of £1 Sterl.

ROBERT WRIGHT Ass'ee of WILLIAM CLARKSON, 160 acs. by Survey 25 Nov 1758 in Bedford Co. on the E brs. of Stone Wall cr.; adj. Joseph Bellew/Ballew; 1 Sep 1780, p.139. A.C. of 20 Shill. Sterl.

WILLIAM DEVAN, 404 acs. Pittsylvania Co. on both sides of the west Sleaves Cr., crossing little Cr.; adj. Chamberlaine, White & Leak; along the Order line crossing West Sleave to the Beg.; 1 Sep 1780 p.140. A.C. of 40 Shill. Sterl.

JAMES SCARBOROUGH Ass'ee of ROWLAND HORSELY BURKS, 173 acs. by Survey 10 Apr 1767 in Bedford Co. on the head brs. of Otter riv.; 1 Sep 1780, p.141. A.C. of 20 Shill. Sterl.

MOSES SWENNY/SWENNEY, 130 acs. by Survey 18 Feb 1774 in Pittsylvania Co. on the brs. of the middle fork of cherry Stone; adj. Hix, & Charles Rigney; 1 Sep 1780, p.142. A.C. of 15 Shill. Sterl.

EDWARD TATUM, 43 acs. by Survey Dec 1773 in Pittsylvania Co. on the brs. of Peters cr., Beginning cn sd Tatum's Spring br., on the Waggon Road, adj. Jonathan Hanly; 1 Sep 1780, p.143. A.C. of 5 Shill. Sterl.

WILLIAM DURRETT, 360 acs. by Survey 7 Mar 1780 in Pittsylvania Co. on the brs. of the double Cr., adj. Nimrod Scott & William Harrisson; 1 Sep 1780, p.144. A.C. of 40 Shill. Sterl.

JOHN HAGOOD, 412 acs. by Survey 17 Nov 1772 in Halifax Co. on Cherry Tree Cr.; adj. Nowlin, Cockerham, Smith, Norman & Lucas; 1 Sep 1780, p.145. A.C. of 45 Shill. Sterl.

WILLIAM DEVAN, 327 acs. by Survey 19 Apr 1770 in Pittsylvania Co. on Banister riv., on the Court house road [Court house road], adj. William Cook; 1 Sep 1780, p.146. A.C. of 35 Shill. Sterl.

HENRY BROWN, 470 acs. by Survey 24 Feb 1770 in Pittsylvania Co. on the waters of Streight Stone Cr., crossing Camps br.; adj. Evans, Willcox & Vance; 1 Sep 1780, p.147. A.C. of 50 Shill. Sterl.

CONRAD KESTER Ass'ee of JOHN COMPTON, 115 acs by Survey 15 aPR 1762 Rockingham Co. formerly Augusta Co. on the three lick br. in *Brock's Gap*, Beginning on the side of a Spurr, in a Draft; 1 Sep 1780, p.148. A.C. of 15 Shill. Sterl.

JOHN GEORGE, 272 acs. by Survey 12 Aug 1772 in Pittsylvania Co. on the west fork of Allens Cr.; adj. Daniel Morgan, William Doss & Baker; 1 Sep 1780, p.149. A.C. of 30 Shill. Sterl.

JOSIAH TURNER, 326 acs. by Survey 7 Dec 1779 in Henry Co. on Butramtown Cr., on the South fork; adj. Shadrack Turner, Turner's old line; 1 Sep 1780, p.150. A.C. 35 Shill. Sterl.

SAMUEL HEMPHIT/HUMPHIT, 125 acs. by Survey 15 Nov 1770 in Augusta Co. on the east draught of Cook's Cr., adj. his Patent Land & Harrison's line; 1 Sep 1780, p.152. A.C. of 15 Shill. Sterl.

PETER GARLAND, 31 acs. by Survey 19 Apr 1775 in Lunenburg Co. on the N side of Meherrin riv., up Stoney Cr.; adj. John Rhodes, Parham, & William Turner; 1 Sep 1780, p.153. A.C. of 5 Shill. Sterl.

DAVID ELLILNGTON, 104 acs. by Survey 6 May 1780 in Lunenburg Co. on the brs. of Meherrin Riv., adj. his own c.; 1 Sep 1780, p.154. A.C. of 10 Shill. Sterl.

WILLIAM TAYLOR Ass'ee of ISAAC BROWN Heir at Law to ISRAEL BROWN dec'd, 366 acs. by Survey 16 Aug 1748 in Lunenburg Co. on the head brs. of Beaverpond fork of flat rock cr., in a slash, down Beaverpond Cr.; adj. Edloe, Edward Brodnor [Broadnax] & James Davis; 1 Sep 1780, p.155. A.C. of 40 Shill. Sterl.

MICHAEL KELLY, 395 acs. by Survey 15 Mar 1773 in Pittsylvania Co. on Nicholas's Cr. & crossing Daniel's Run; 1 Sep 1780, p.156. A.C. of 40 Shill. Sterl.

NATHANIEL HUNTER Ass'ee of JAMES STANDEFORD, 196 acs. by Survey 10 Apr 1769 in Pittsylvania Co. on black water Riv., adj. Haile's line & the sd Standeford; 1 Sep 1780, p.157. A.C. of 20 Shill. Sterl.

JAMES STANDEFORD, 400 acs. by Survey 6 Nov 1773 in Pittsylvania Co. formerly Henry on the waters of Otter Cr., on Nicholas's cr., adj. Peter Sanders; 1 Sep 1780, p.158. A.C. of 40 Shill. Sterl.

STEPHEN HEARD, 170 acs. by Survey 11 Dec 1778 in Henry Co. on black water riv., on a clift at the sd Riv., crossing Poplar Camp Cr., adj. William Heards old line & Hallaway; 1 Sep 1780, p.159. A.C. of 20 Shill. Sterl.

ROBERT PRUNTEY ass'ee of WILLIAM COOK, 76 acs. by Survey 31 Mar 1769 in Henry Co. formerly Pittsylvania on the waters of Pigg Riv.; 1 Sep 1780, p.160. A.C. of 10 Shill. Sterl.

JOHN FORGUSON, 229 acs. by Survey 20 Oct 1773 in Henry Co. formerly Pittsylvania on both sides of jumping br. of Story Cr.; 1 Sep 1780, p.161. A.C. of 25 Shill. Sterl.

ABNER ECHOLDS, 177 acs. by Survey 13 Nov 1773 in Henry Co. formerly Pittsylvania Co. on the North fork of Gobling Town cr., adj. Tilmon Harbour & Callaway; 1 Sep 1780, p.162. A.C. of 20 Shill. Sterl.

ABNER ECHOLDS, 160 acs. by Survey 12 Nov 1773 in Henry Co. formerly Pittsylvania on both sides of Gobling Town Cr., adj. Callaway & Tittle; 1 Sep 1780, p.163. A.C. of 20 Shill. Sterl.

JOSIAH WATKINS, 411 acs. by Survey 13 Nov 1779 in Henry Co. on Savil Cr., down sd Cr. to the Mouth and cross the other fork; adj. Clay's order line & George F. Harriss's Line; 1 Sep 1780, p.165. A.C. of 45 Shill. Sterl.

FRANCIS GRIMES, 272¾ acs. by Survey 10 Nov 1773 in Henry Co. formerly Pittsylvania on both sides of Gobling Town Cr., adj. Tittle & Tilues lines; 1 Sep 1780, p.166. A.C. of 30 Shill. Sterl.

WILLIAM FORGUSON, 93 acs. by Survey 13 Oct 1773 in Henry Co.

formerly Pittsylvania on the South fork of Pigg Riv.; adj. James Renffrow, Richard Huff & the sd Forguson; 1 Sep 1780, p.167. A.C. of 10 Shill. Sterl.

RICHARD RAGEN, 170 acs. by Survey 15 Jan 1771 in Rockingham Co. formerly Augusta on the head of the East draft of Cooks Cr.; adj. his Patent line, John Harrison & Sheltman; 1 Sep 1780, p.168. A.C. of 20 Shill. Sterl.

JAMES BRAMMER, 64 acs. by Survey 24 Nov 1768 in Pittsylvania Co. on Joinerack Cr., on a ridge; 1 Sep 1780, p.169. A.C. of 10 Shill. Sterl.

JOHN FARGUSON, 66 acs. by Survey 15 Apr 1779 in Henry Co. on Pigg Riv., adj. his line & Cole; 1 Sep 1780, p.170. A.C. of 10 Shill. Sterl.

JAMES INGRAM, 289 acs. by Survey 12 Nov 1773 in Pittsylvania Co. on the waters of Gobling Town Cr.; adj. Hailey, Claunche's line & Foley; 1 Sep 1780, p.171. A.C. of 30 Shill. Sterl.

MATTHIAS GABERT Ass'ee of NATHANIEL EVINS who was Ass'ee of JAMES EDMISTON, 116 acs. by Survey 5 Mar 1762 in Augusta Co. upon the Buffelo Hill opposite to the Mouth of Buffelo Cr.; 1 Sep 1780, p.172. A.C. of 15 Shill. Sterl.

ALEXANDER STEEL/STELL, 150 acs. by Survey 22 Nov 1770 in Bedford Co. on brs. of falling riv., adj. Bolling & his own lines; 1 Sep 1780, p.174. A.C. of 15 Shill. Sterl.

JOHN DIXON, 91 acs. by Survey 8 Sep 1779 in Augusta Co. on some small brs. on the NW side of the Middle riv. of Shanandore, in a draft; adj. John Allison, Andrew McClure, Kerr's old c. & sd Dixons old Line; 1 Sep 1780, p.175. A.C. of 10 Shill. Sterl.

JOHN FORGUSON, 275 acs. by Survey 20 Oct 1773 in Henry Co. formerly Pittsylvania on the brs. of Pigg Riv., crossing fall br., adj. his Line; 1 Sep 1780, p.176. A.C. of 30 Shill. Sterl.

HENRY HERRYFORD, 390 acs. by Survey 27 Nov 1749 in Halifax Co. on both sides of Polecat Cr.; 1 Sep 1780, p.177. A.C. of 40 Shill. Sterl. [paid into the Treasury of this Commonwealth]

CHRISTOPHER HUTCHINGS, 2,462 acs. by Survey 22 Sep 1773 in Pittsylvania Co. on Banister Riv. and Bearskin Cr., on Hickeys road & Piggs road, on Polecat Cr.; adj. Chamberlain, Echolds, Nuckolds, Finney & Echols; 19 Oct 1780, p.179. A.C. of £10 Sterl. 532 acs. part formerly Gtd. to Richard Echols by pat. 20 Aug 1748 the property of which has since become vested in the sd Christopher Hutchings.

JOSEPH DENTON, 449 acs. by Survey 6 Apr 1770 in Pittsylvania Co. on the waters of Bea's cr., Beginning at the head of the middle fork of the aforesd Cr., adj. Watkins; 1 Sep 1780, p.181. A.C. 45 Shill. Sterl.

DANIEL LOVELL Ass'ee of HENRY HALL, 200 acs. by Survey 25 Mar 1779 in Pittsylvania Co. on the brs. of Strawberry Cr., on the Long br., adj. Joshua Cantrell & Mosses Johnson; 1 Sep 1780, p.182. A.C. of 20 Shill. Sterl.

WILLIAM EASLEY, 365 acs. by Survey 7 Feb 1774 in Pittsylvania Co. on the waters of Banister Riv., on Turkey br.; adj. Leak, Robertson & Chamberlain; 1 Sep 1780, p.184. A.C. of 40 Shill. Sterl.

THOMAS DOSS, 220 acs. by Survey 6 Feb 1767 in Pittsylvania Co. on the brs. of the Long br. of the Timbered fork of white thorn Cr.; adj. Hugh Innes, Sibley & Innise's line; 1 Sep 1780, p.185. A.C. of 25 Shill. Sterl.

GEORGE CLOPTON, 90 acs. by Survey made for WILLIAM LAIN 12 Oct 1758 *and by him forfeited by being returned as an Insolvent by the Sheriff of the County and since Sold by the Surveyor to the sd George Clopton*, in Hanover Co. and parish of Saint Paul, down Troopers br. to the Mouth in black Cr.; adj. Sheldrake Brown, Roger Shackelford, John Tucker & Shildrakes Brown; 19 Oct 1780, p.186. A.C. of 10 Shill. Sterl. [Probably part of PB 9 p.602 to Francis Clarke, 282 acs. New Kent Co.]

FRANCIS COX, 278 acs. by Survey 9 Nov 1779 in Henry Co. on the brs. of the Muster br. of leatherwood Cr.. Beginning at George Runnolds's c. thence with his formerly Murrels old line; also adj. Lomax and Company's order Line, his own line, Pinkard, & sd Runnolds new line; 1 Sep 1780, p.187. A.C. of 30 Shill. Sterl.

JAMES SHOCKLEY, 348 acs. by Survey 3 Dec 1777 in Pittsylvania Co. on both sides of the long br. of Little Turkey Cock, adj. sd Shockley & Copeland; 1 Sep 1780, p.189. A.C. of 35 Shill. Sterl.

THOMAS CORBEN, 136 acs. by Survey 29 Jan 1767 in Pittsylvania Co. on the S brs. of Banister riv. and Shock Cr.; 1 Sep 1780, p.190. A.C. of 15 Shill. Sterl.

WILLIAM LONDON, 300 acs. by Survey 10 Dec 1771 in Halifax Co. on the draughts of Buffaloe, crossing the County line, on the County line [N10°E]; adj. Hendrick, Johnson, Smith & Coleman; 1 Sep 1780, p.191. A.C. of 30 Shill. Sterl.

WILLIAM PEAK, 165 acs. by Survey 2 Dec 1777 in Pittsylvania Co. on both sides of Little Turkey Cock Cr., adj. James Shockley; 1 Sep 1780, p.192. A.C. of 20 Shill. Sterl.

ROBERT OAR, 310 acs. by Survey 16 Dec 1771 in Pittsylvania Co. on Tomahawk Cr., adj. Elliott; 1 Sep 1780, p.193. A.C. of 35 Shill. Sterl.

JAMES WATSON, 107 acs. by Survey 2 Mar 1780 in Pittsylvania Co. on the Draughts of the double Cr. and Burches Cr.; adj. John Bennett, Hardy & Stamp; 1 Sep 1780, p.194. A.C. of 15 Shill. Sterl.

JESSEY KEESEY, 250 acs. by Survey 28 Jan 1767 in Pittsylvania Co. on both sides of Old womans Cr., crossing a fork and the other fork; 1 Sep 1780, p.195. A.C. of 25 Shill. Sterl.

JOHN WALKER, 250 acs. by Survey 28 Feb 1769 in Pittsylvania Co. on the rifle br. of Pigg riv.; 1 Sep 1780, p.196. A.C. of 25 Shill. Sterl.

JOHN MORTON, 735 acs. by Survey 14 Apr 1770 in Pittsylvania Co. on the waters of Sandy Riv.; adj. John Morton, Mitchell, & Samuel Shields; 1 Sep 1780, p.197. A.C. of £3.S15. Sterl.

[Margin note: *This Grant was altered in the name of Governour Harrison and dated 19th August because the Grant was*

made out and recorded before Signed by Governour Jefferson who resign'd before it could be signd or Seald.]
ROBERT CAMPBELL, 206 acs. by Survey 4 Apr 1780 in Rockingham Co. betw. the South riv. and the South Mountain, in Swampy Ground, Beginning in a line of Glaves l., to a pine supposed near Joseph Hannah's l., also adj. George Boswell; 19 Aug 1783, p.199. A.C. of 25 Shill. Sterl.

BENJAMIN SMITH Ass'ee of DANIEL SMITH, 200 acs. by Survey 25 May 1769 in Rockingham Co. formerly Augusta bet. his and James Wrights Lines on some brs. of Smith's Cr.; 1 Sep 1780, p.200. A.C. of 20 Shill. Sterl.

WILLIAM MATTHEWS, 160 acs. by Survey 24 Nov 1774 in Augusta Co. on the SW side of his other Land in the forks of Moffetts br., on a ridge, also adj. Adam Reabourn; 1 Sep 1780, p.201. A.C. of 20 Shill. Sterl. *bounded by the Magnetic Variation from the true Meredian of 1°E.*

JOHN FRAZIER, 62 acs. by Survey 11 Apr 1780 in Rockingham Co. adj. William Hook, Matthew Thompsons old place, Kern & Frazers own L.; 1 Sep 1780, p.203. A.C. of 10 Shill. Sterl.

WILLIAM MATTHEWS, 400 acs. by Survey 26 Nov 1774 in Augusta Co. on the N side of Moffetts br., on a ridge, adj. his old Lines; 1 Sep 1780, p.205. A.C. of 40 Shill. Sterl.

JAMES ANDERSON, SENIOR, 137 acs. 5 Dec 1772 in Augusta Co. on the head spring of the long Glade, crossing the spring br.; adj Samuel Currey, sd Anderson & sd Curry; 1 Sep 1780, p.206. A.C. of 10 Shill. Sterl. 50 acs. part thereof was gtd. to the sd James Anderson by Pat. 10 Sep 1755 and 87 acs. the residue never before gtd.

WILLIAM HOOK ass'ee of WILLIAM CAMPBELL, 60 acs. by Survey 5 Dec 1769 in Rockingham Co. formerly Augusta on Stoney Lick run a br. of the North riv. of Shanandoah, adj. Matthew Thompson & Hook; 1 Sep 1780, p.207. A.C. of 10 Shill. Sterl.

DAVID BERRY, 54 acs. by Survey 24 Nov 1768 in Augusta Co. on the East br. of Muddy Cr., Beginning at a large Stone by his old c., also adj. Ben Kinley; 1 Sep 1780, p.209. A.C. of 5 Shill. Sterl.

GEORGE HARTER Ass'ee of MARTIN WETZELL, 54 acs. by Survey 26 Feb 1773 in Augusta Co. on *Wests Gap* above the Land he lives on, Beginning by a Gully, near a Line of Thomas Wests Land; 1 Sep 1780, p.210. A.C. of 5 Shill. Sterl.

MARTIN WETSELL, 25 acs. by Survey 1 Mar 1773 in Augusta Co. on *West's Gap*, Beginning on the N side of the Tract he Lives on; 1 Sep 1780, p.211. A.C. of 5 Shill. Sterl.

THOMAS CAMPBELL, 150 acs. by Survey 12 Dec 1774 in Augusta Co. on the Hickory Level on the N side of Seneca Cr. a br. of the North fork of the South Brack of Patowmack, adj. William Gragg; 1 Sep 1780, p.212. A.C. of 15 Shill. Sterl.

ANDREW HUDLOW, 34 acs. by Survey 12 Apr 1780 in Rockingham Co. Beginning on the S side of Stoney Lick run on a Line formerly Robert Scott's, by a br. Supposed to be in a line of another of Scotts tracts; 1 Sep 1780, p.213. A.C. of 5 Shill. Sterl.

JAMES OLIVER, SENIOR, 200 acs. by Survey 11 Dec 1771 in Halifax Co. on the draughts of Cherry tree, adj. Coleman; 1 Sep 1780, p.214. A.C. of 20 Shill. Sterl.

GEORGE SHAVER Ass'ee of GEORGE KEPLINER, 133 acs. by Survey 25 Feb 1773 in Augusta Co. on *Wests Gap* on a br. called George's run, on a ridge; 1 Sep 1780, p.215. A.C. of 15 Shill. Sterl.

ADAM BIBLE ass'ee of JAMES LAWREY, 145 acs. by Survey 23 Feb 1773 in Augusta Co. on hungry run in *Brocks Gap*, Beginning near Adam Bybles Land, adj. James Logan; 1 Sep 1780, p.217. A.C. of 15 Shill. Sterl.

NICHOLAS BOSS ass'ee of ANTHONY AYLER who was Ass'ee of JACOB PERSINGER, 250 acs. by Survey 5 May 1768 in Rockingham Co. on the N side of the North riv. of Shendandore, adj. his old Tract; 1 Sep 1780, p.218. A.C. of 25 Shill. Ster.

THOMAS BRYANT, 54 acs. by Survey 19 Sep 1771 in Augusta Co. on the W side of Lenvills Cr., on a ridge; adj. his old Line, Jacob Gum, Cornelius Bryant & Thomas Bryant; 1 Sep 1780, p.219. A.C. of 5 Shill. Sterl.

THOMAS BEGGS, 98 acs. by Survey 22 Feb 1773 in Augusta Co. in *Rocks Gap*, Beginning on the S side Toads or Touds Hill, adj. his old Line; 1 Sep 1780, p.220. A.C. of 10 Shill. Sterl.

THOMAS BRYANT, 350 acs. by Survey 17 Jul 1772 in Augusta Co. on the head brs. of the Long Meadow a br. of the North fork of Shannandore, Beginning on the SE side of Matthias Leches Land, crossing a draught of sd Meadow, on a ridge; 1 Sep 1780, p.221. A.C. of 35 Shill. Sterl.

The Heirs of HUGH MERCER dec'd who was ass'ee of JAMES DUNCANSON who was ass'ee of sd JOSEPH BLEDSOE, 2,000 acs. by Survey 28 Jun 1774 in Kentucy Co. formerly Fincastle on the Waters of Elk Horn Cr., the waters of the Ohio, adj. Charles Lewis; 1 Sep 1780, p.222. *in consideration of Military Service performed by Joseph Bledsoe as Ensign in the Second Virginia Regiment in the late war between Great Britain and France according to the terms of the King of Great Britains Proclamation in 1763.*

JOHN QUARLES, 400 acs. by Survey 2 Mar 1779 in Bedford Co. on both sides of Verdeman's Mountain Road on head of brs. of Johnson's Cr. and Irvines Cr., Beginning on John Talbots Line near the head of Callaway's Camp cr.; 1 Sep 1780, p.223. A.C. of £2 Sterl.

JOHN WARD, 215 acs. by Survey 30 Nov 1768 in Pittsylvania Co. on the waters of Gills cr., along a Mountain, adj. Hendrick; 1 Sep 1780, p.224. A.C. of 25 Shill. Sterl.

DANIEL DRISKILL as Ass'ee of part of an Entry made in the name of THOMAS WATKINS dated 5 Mar 1754 for 400 acs., 300 acs. by Survey 12 Apr 1780 Bedford Co. on the E side of Falling riv., at the Mouth of Island br., across the sd riv. near Michael Pruits Mill dam, on the East bank of the Riv. thence up passing the End of the Mill dam, up Dog Cr., adj.

Low Todd & Watkins; 1 Sep 1780, p.225. A.C. of 30 Shill. Sterl.

MATTHEW TALBOT, 430 acs. by Survey 10 Mar 1775 in Bedford Co. on the brs. of Lenvells Cr., near the red banks, adj. his old c. & Thomas Payne; 1 Sep 1780, p.227. A.C. of £2.S5 Sterl.

BENJAMIN GILBERT, 215 acs. by Survey 18 Sep 1778 in Bedford Co. on the NW side of Phelps's old road on brs. of Seneca Cr., Beginning on the sd Road at the Mouth of Locust Thicket Old road; adj. Neilson, & William Brown; 1 Sep 1780, p.228. A.C. of 25 Shill. Sterl.

JOHN TALBOT, 770 acs. by Survey 4 Mar 1780 in Bedford Co. on the head of Amose's br., crossing the Road, on Leftwich's Road; adj. Butler, Matthew Talbot, Pratt & Niman; 1 Sep 1780, p.229. A.C. of £4 Sterl.

JOHN TALBOT, 367 acs. by Survey 5 Feb 1780 in Bedford Co. on the N side of Stanton riv., adj. Woodson & Walden; 1 Sep 1780, p.231. A.C. of 40 Shill. Sterl.

JOHN LYNCH, 3,000 acs. by Virtue of 7 Entries made by WILLIAM FERRELL and Assigned to John Lynch, by Survey 3 Feb 1779 in Bedford Co. on both sides of Black Water Cr. and Fishing Cr., up a Steep high hill, up Ferry Road, down Meeting house br., between a Spring br. and a Road, down Joes br., on a high ridge above fishing cr., down the Fluvanna riv.; adj. Christopher Lynch, Tate, Benjamin Clark, Micajah Clark, David Ferrell, William Johnson, & Winston; 1 Sep 1780, p.232. A.C. of £12.S10 Sterl. 540 acs. part of the sd 3,000 acs. was formerly Gtd. by Pat. [This 3,000 acs. is included in GB 28 pp.591-593, 3,453 acs. in Campbell & Amherst Counties, unto sd John Lynch dated 23 July 1793]

JOHN MURPHEY Ass'ee of GABRIEL TERRELL, 309 acs. by Survey 9 Apr 1770 in Bedford Co. on the N side of Goose Cr.; adj. Holligan, Green, Arther & Murphey; 1 Sep 1780, p.235. A.C. of 35 Shill. Sterl.

THOMAS HELM, 220 acs. by Survey 2 May 1780 in Bedford Co. including the Pilot Mountain, on an Ivy Hill; adj. Nathaniel Patterson, Bolling, Wathan and Jennings Old Lines, Helm, & William Dinwiddie; 1 Sep 1780, p.236. A.C. of 25 Shill. Sterl.

[Margin note: *This Grant was altered in the name of Governour Harrison and dated 20th August 1783 because the Grant was made out and recorded before Signed by Governour Jefferson who resigned before it Could be Sign'd or Seald*]

JOHN BUFORD Ass'ee of WILLIAM VAUGHAN, 144 acs. by Survey 18 Mar 1775 in Bedford Co.; adj. Brown, Pate, Thomas Pate & Nuquan/Nuqan; 1 Sep 1780, p.238. A.C. of 15 Shill. Sterl. *[For Nuquan's land, see GB 33 p.591 dated 21 Apr 1796 granted Elias Atkinson by an Old Military Warrant & LOTW #976 issued 16 May 1783, by Survey 27 June 1794. The plat of Nuquan's land is in Bedford Surveyors Records p.333: 130 acs. surveyed 18 March 1775 for Richard Nugan by WMead Asst to Richard Stith Survr. and also in Bedford Surveyors Records p.521, 130 acs. surveyed 27 June 1794 by Wm Cavenaugh Asst. to Wm. Callaway S.B.C for Elias Adkison Assignee of Charles M.*

Talbot by Virtue of LOTW #976 Granted to John Whain 16 May 1780]

SAMUEL JACK ass'ee of DAVID WRIGHT who was Ass'ee of ARCHIBALD ROBERTSON who was Ass'ee of GEORGE WALTON the Executor of ROBERT WALTON dec'd, 304 acs. by Survey 26 Jun 1767 in Bedford Co. on the brs. of Little Otter Riv. on a ridge of rocks thence along the old Lines, up the dividing br.; adj. Talbot & McLaughlin; 30 Nov 1780, p.239. A.C. of 30 Shill. Sterl. *being part of 20,000 acs. granted 14 Jun 1749 by Order of Council to Woodson and Company.*

JAMES DIXON Ass'ee of WILLIAM LAMME, 120 acs. by Survey 20 Mar 1771 in Bedford Co. on both sides of the main br. of the South fork of Beaver Cr. on and upon the NE side and End of the Long Mountain, down New London road; adj. Campbell, & James Winters Line; 1 Sep 1780, p.240. A.C. of 15 Shill. Sterl.

ALEXANDER DAVIDSON, 400 acs. by Survey 3 Mar 1773 in Bedford Co. on N brs. of wreck Island Cr., at a path; adj. Mann, Phelps, Martin, Merritt, & Hunters Old Lines; 1 Sep 1780, p.241. A.C. of £2 Sterl.

MATTHEW TALBOTT, 397 acs. by Survey 10 Mar 1775 in Bedford Co. on the brs. of Lenvills Cr., by a Lick, adj. his old Line & Booker; 1 Sep 1780, p.243. A.C. of £2 Sterl.

JOHN WOOLLOMS ass'ee of PRESTON GILBERT, 300 acs. by Survey 17 Nov 1779 in Bedford Co. on the E side of Seneca Cr., up Rockey br. to just below the Mouth of Pheasants br., at a path; adj. Thomas East, James Vest, Randolph, William Vest & John Templeton; 1 Sep 1780, p.244. A.C. of 30 Shill. Sterl.

JOHN WARD, 277 acs. by Survey 30 Oct 1769 in Henry Co. on the waters of Jacks Cr., Beginning on the main Top of the Mountain; 1 Sep 1780, p.245. A.C. of £1.S10.

[The next 4 grants, as well as William Spencer's 365 acs. in GB A p.397, are divisions of the 28,528 acs. in Albemarle Co. PB 29 p.99 to Walter King dated 1 Jun 1750]

JOSEPH CABELL Esquire, 2,200 acs. **by an Inclusive survey** made 20 Mar 1780 in Amherst Co. on both sides of Ruckers run, crossing Bobbs Cr. & the Court house road; adj. No.6 in the Patent Line, Number 16, the old dividing line, Number 14, Number 13, Lunsford Lomax Esquire & Number 9; 19 Oct 1780, p.247. in consideration of the Sum of £14,575 Current Money of Virginia paid to David Shepherd Gent. Escheator for Amherst Co. ... being part of a larger tract Lately the Property of John Harmer esquire a British Subject and was Sold by the sd David Shepherd Escheator as aforesaid unto the sd Joseph Cabell agreeable to two Acts of Assembly passed in the year 1779 the one Intitled an Act Concerning Escheats and forfeitures from British Subjects the other Intitled an Act Concerning Escheators. bounded by the Variation of the Magnetic from the true Meridian of 15' West.

WILLIAM CABELL Esquire, 2,380 acs. **by an Inclusive Survey** made 13 Mar

1780 in Amherst Co. on both sides of Ruckers run, Crossing the Court house Road; adj. No. 1 in the Patent line, Number 5, Number 8, Number 11, Number 12, Lunsford Lomax Esquire & Number 1; 19 Oct 1780, p.248. in Consideration of £18,425 Current Money of Virginia paid to David Shepherd Gent. Escheator for Amherst Co ... being part of a larger Tract lately the property of John Harmer Esquire a British Subject and was Sold by the sd David Shepherd Escheator unto the sd William Cabell agreeable to two Acts of Assembly psssed in the year 1779 the one Intituled An Act Concerning Escheats and Forfeitures from British Subjects the other Intituled an Act Concerning Escheats.. bounded by the Variation of the Magnetic from the true Meridian of 15' West.

WILLIAM CRESP, 640 acs. **by Inclusive Survey** made 21 Mar 1780 in Amherst Co. on the S Brs. of Ruckers Run; adj. William Alford, the Patent Line, Number 17, No. 15, Number 3, Number 2 & the old Line dividing line; 19 Oct 1780, p.250. in Consideration of £920.S4 Current Money of Virginia paid to David Shepherd Gent. Escheator for Amherst Co. ... being part of a larger tract lately the property of John Harmer and Walter King Esquires British Subjects and was Sold by the sd David Shepherd Escheator unto the sd William Cresp agreeable to two Acts of Assembly psssed in the year 1779 the one Intituled An Act Concerning Escheats and forfeitures from British Subjects the other Entituled an Act Concerning Escheats.

WILLIAM CABELL Esquire, 1,970 acs. **by an Inclusive Survey** made 4 Mar 1780 in Amherst Co. on the S brs. of Ruckers Run, crossing the South fork of sd Ruckers Run & crossing the Court House Road; adj. George Blain, William Cabell Esqr., Edmond Wilcox, Number 12, the Patent Line, Number 9, the Old Dividing Line, Number 4 & William Bibb; 19 Oct 1780, p.252. in Consideration of £8,715 Current Money of Virginia paid to David Shepherd Gentleman Escheator for Amherst Co. ... being part of a larger Tract Lately the Property of Walter King Esquire a British Subject and was Sold by the said David Shepherd Escheator unto the sd William Cabell agreeable to two Acts of Assembly passed in the year 1779 the one Intituled an Act Concerning Escheats and forfeitures from British Subjects the other Intituled an Act Concerning Escheators ... bounded by the Variation of the Magnetic from the true Meridian of 15' West.

WILLIAM McCLUNEY, 135 acs. by Survey 16 Jan 1773 in Bedford Co. on E brs. of Seneca Cr.; adj. Brown, Neilson & Stith; 1 Sep 1780, p.254. A.C. of 15 Shill. Sterl.

FRANCIS THORP, 1,264 acs. by Survey 14 Apr 1775 in Bedford Co. on North fork of Goose Cr., by the Suck [Br.]; adj. Davis, Randolph's Old Line, Mills Lines, Mill's Dividing Line & Thorp's and Buford's Dividing Line; 1 Sep 1780, p.255. A.C. of £4.S10 Sterl. including 150 acs. Surveyed for William Hayes and 80 as. part of Randolphs Survey made by Order of Council.

ALEXANDER DOBBINS, 32 acs. by Survey 23 Nov 1770 in Bedford Co. on both sides of the Main head br. of Wreck Island Cr.; adj. his own Line, James Carson & Thomas Carson; 1 Sep 1780, p.257. A.C. of 5 Shill. Sterl.

WILLIAM McCAMISH Ass'ee of ALEXANDER STEEL who was Ass'ee of JOHN McMANAMY, 326 acs. by Survey 6 Nov 1771 in Bedford Co. on the head brs. of Little wreck Island Cr., on a Ridge, at the Edge of Meadow Ground; adj. Hunter, Oglesby, Coleman & Whitney; 1 Sep 1780, p.259. A.C. of 35 Shill. Sterl.

SAMUEL CURREY, 35 acs. by Survey 12 Mar 1770 in Augusta Co. on the head of Long Glades a br. of the North Riv. of Shanandore; adj. James Anderson & his old C. & John Young; 1 Sep 1780, p.260. A.C. of 5 Shill. Sterl.

JOHN WESTBROOK FORGASON, 300 acs. by Survey 4 Apr 1778 in Bedford Co. on the N brs. of Blackwater Riv., adj. Walton; 1 Sep 1780, p.261. A.C. of 30 Shill. Sterl.

WILLIAM EWING, 300 acs. by Survey 10 Oct 1777 in Bedford Co. on the South fork of Otter Riv.; adj. Charles Ewing, Robert Ewing & his other Survey; 1 Sep 1780, p.262. A.C. of 30 Shill. Sterl.

DAVID WRIGHT, 1,316 acs. by Survey 27 Apr 1771 in Bedford Co. on both sides of Stoney fork, up Shoulder Camp Cr.; adj. Jacob Piburn, Woodson, Prather, Callaway, George Walton & Morgin; 1 Sep 1780, p.264. A.C. of £6.S15 Sterl. *being part of Woodson's and Company's Order of Council for 20,000 acs. Granted 14 Jun 1749.*

JOHN LANE, JUNIOR, 400 acs. by Survey 8 Feb 1779 in Bedford Co. on W brs. of the South fork of Falling Riv.; adj. Peter Daniel, John Roberts, Weathan, Andrew Hairstone, Heath, Robertson & Pursley; 1 Sep 1780, p.266. A.C. of 40 Shill. Sterl.

JAMES GATES, 362 acs. by Survey 20 Dec 1770 in Bedford Co. on both sides of Little falling Riv., on Sullavan's/Sullavants Br.; adj. Charles Cobb, William Thompson, John Irvin & the dividing line; 1 Sep 1780, p.267. A.C. of 40 Shill. Sterl. 200 acs. part thereof formerly Gtd. John Campbell the property of Which has since become Vested in the sd James Gates, 162 acs. being the Residue thereof and not before Gtd.

JOHN CALLAWAY Ass'ee of JOHN RENTFRO, 393 acs. by Survey 15 Feb 1773 in Bedford Co. on the North fork of Black water Riv., adj. the Pat. Line & Jessey Rentfroes Line; 1 Sep 1780, p.269. A.C. of £2 Sterl. Including 113 acs. before Gtd. to Richard Randolph by Pat.

THOMAS YUILLE, 1,180 acs. by Survey 10 Dec 1772 in Bedford Co. on the N side of Otter Riv. on both side of Troublesome Cr., at Shoal's br.; adj. the Old Lines of the Patent for 226 acs., William Arther, the Line of the patent for 280 acs., Meads and Talbots c., & Henry Davis; 1 Sep 1780, p.270. A.C. of £3.S10 Sterl. 201 acs. which 473 acs. Surveyed 26 Mar 1767 & Amounts to 674 acs. not before Patented which with 226 acs. Gtd. to John Phelps by Pat. 12 Jul 1742, and 280 acs. Gtd. to John Phelps by Pat. 30 Jul 1750 and properly Conveyed & Amounts to the above Mentioned quantity of 1,180 acs.

JEREMIAH EARLEY, 500 acs. by Survey 16 Feb 1775 in Pittsylvania Co. on both sides of Sycamore Cr., crossing the Cattail fork, adj. James Faris; 1 Sep 1780, p.273. A.C. of £2.S10 Sterl.

JOHN GIBSON, 338 acs. by Survey 11 Nov 1771 in Bedford Co. on the N brs. of Black water Riv., on Lick Br.; adj. Mason, & Joseph Rentfroe; 1 Sep 1780, p.274. A.C. of 35 Shill. Sterl.

THOMAS LOGWOOD Ass'ee of ROBERT CLARK who was Ass'ee of JAMES BRYANT who was Ass'ee of WILLIAM BRYAN who was Ass'ee of THOMAS WOOD, 270 acs. by Survey 2 Apr 1766 in Bedford Co. upon the Main Ledge of Mountains including the head brs. of the North fork of Otter Riv., Beginning near the Old Apple Orchard, to a Mahogany near a Spring of Jenning's Cr.; 1 Sep 1780, p.276. A.C. of 30 Shill. Sterl. *paid into the Treasury of this Commonwealth.*

THOMAS LOGWOOD, 458 acs. by Survey 18 Apr 1765 in Bedford Co. on the forks of the North fork of Otter Riv., Beginning on the South fork of sd North fork, to the Sawpit br.; 1 Sep 1780, p.277. A.C. of £2.S10 Sterl. *paid into the Office of the Late receiver General.*

WILLIAM TRIGG, 360 acs. by Survey 19 Mar 1773 in Bedford Co. on Jones's Cr. a br. of Otter riv., adj Boyd; 1 Sep 1780, p.279. A.C. of 40 Shill. Sterl. *paid into the Treasury of this Commonwealth.* Including 142 acs. part thereof which was formerly Surveyed for Andrew Jones.

JOHN MERRITT, 430 acs. by Survey 10 Mar 1772 in Bedford Co. including the head of Stonewall Cr., crossing Reedy br.; adj. Thomas Martin, David Martin & George Rodger's Line; 1 Sep 1780, p.280. A.C. of 45 Shill. Sterl.

[Margin note: *This Grant was made out when Thomas Jefferson was Governor and was Omitted being Signd, therefore it is Oble'd to be Altered in the Name of Ben Harrison*]
SAMUEL HAIRSTON, 300 acs. by Survey 31 Mar 1772 in Bedford Co. on brs. of Beaver Cr., on the W side of Coopers Mountain, on a point of Rocks on the S end of the sd Mountain, on the E side of sd Mountain, Beginning at Brown's and Lynch's dividing corner; 1 Sep 1780, p.282. A.C. of 30 Shill. Sterl.

JOHN CLEAVER, 440 acs. by Survey 15 Jan 1773 in Pittsylvania Co. on the South and Middle fork of Stinking Riv., adj. John Barber; 1 Sep 1780, p.283. A.C. of £2.S5 Sterl.

JOHN JONES, 433 acs. by Survey 6 Jun 1780 in Mecklenburg Co. on the Brs. of Aarons Cr.; adj. sd Jones, Atkinson, Revd. John Cameron & Rudd; 1 Sep 1780, p.284. A.C. of £2.S5 Sterl.

WILLIAM HAYNES, 193 acs. by Survey 26 Nov 1778 in Henry Co. on the N brs. of Pigg Riv. on a br. Called Dinner Cr., adj. an Old Line; 1 Sep 1780, p.286. A.C. of £1 Sterl.

JOHN SMITH, 604 acs. by Survey 12 Mar 1779 in Bedford Co. on the N side of black water Riv., on the Road; adj. his old c., Markham, Clay, Holland; down the sd Riv. as it Meanders including 185 acs. old patented land now his property; 1 Sep 1780, p.287. A.C. of £3 Sterl. including 250 acs. transferred from James Standefer to sd John Smith.

JAMES HUNTER, 480 acs. by Survey 9 Mar 1775 in Bedford Co. on E brs. of Seneca Cr.; adj. Murray, Read, Ornsby,

& James Linsey; 1 Sep 1780, p.288. A.C. of £2.S10 Sterl.

SARAH LEWIS, 230 acs. by Survey 12 Dec 1770 in Rockingham Co. on the South Riv. of Shanendo and the South Mountain; 1 Sep 1780, p.290. A.C. of 25 Shill. Sterl.

THOMAS MASSIE Ass'ee of JOHN DICKENSON, 83 acs. by Survey 17 Oct 1772 in Botetourt Co. on the N side of the Land he bought of Seely *in the falling Spring Valley* on the waters of James Riv., on a Ridge; 1 Sep 1780, p.291. A.C. of 10 Shill. Sterl.

THOMAS MASSIE Ass'ee of JOHN DICKINSON, 125 acs. by Survey 27 Oct 1772 in Botetourt Co., Beginning on the SE side of the Land bought of Seely *in the falling Spring Valley* being the waters of James Riv., in a draught, on a Spur of the Mountain; 1 Sep 1780, p.292. A.C. of 15 Shill. Sterl.

DAVID ROBINSON/ROBERTSON, 27 acs. by Survey 8 Jun 1769 in Augusta Co. on the N side of the North fork of Shanandore, Beginning on the point of a Rockey hill, by a draught; adj. John Bear, Philip Dealey & Isaac Robinson; 1 Sep 1780, p.293. A.C. of 5 Shill. Sterl.

JACOB SHEETZ ass'ee of JOHN STEPHENSON, 25 acs. by Survey 4 Apr 1780 in Augusta Co. on the SE side of his old tract; adj. the old Lines, the old patent Line; 1 Sep 1780, p.295. A.C. of 5 Shill. Sterl. it being the land recovered by the sd John Stephenson before the Late Council held 15 Jun 1774 of William Blair.

ROBERT EWING, 700 acs. by Survey 10 May 1777 in Bedford Co., by a Spring, adj. Mabry/Mabery & Randolph; 1 Sep 1780, p.296. A.C. of £3.S10 Sterl. including a Survey made by William Callaway in the rough spurs of the Mountain.

DANIEL FRENCH, 463 acs. by Survey 10 Apr 1775 in Bedford Co. on Griffith Cr., on the Road; adj. Griffith, Walton, Arther, Potty or Polly his Lines, & Howel; 1 Sep 1780, p.298. A.C. of £2.S10 Sterl. 140 acs. part thereof was formerly Surveyed for John Murphey the residue thereof being part of Meads Order of Council.

WILLIAM MEAD & ISHAM TALBOT, 1,144 acs. by Survey 15 Nov 1769 in Bedford Co. on both sides of Maggotty Cr., adj. George Johnson & Mckahey; 1 Sep 1780, p.300. A.C of £5.S15 Sterl.

JAMES CAMPBELL, 265 acs. by Survey 25 Feb 1779 in Rockbridge Co.; adj. Matthew Robertson, the Patent Lines, McClure & McClurle; 1 Sep 1780, p.303. A.C. of 30 Shill. Sterl.

MICAJAH WHEELER, SENIOR, 105½ acs. by Survey 11 Apr 1780 in Albemarle Co. on the waters of one of the head brs. of Moore's Cr., at the W end of a Mountain; adj. Joseph Bullen, Thomas Collin, Micajah Wheeler, Thomas Merriwether, William Gooche & Henry Wood; 1 Sep 1780, p.304. A.C. of 15 Shill. Sterl.

WILLIAM ROBERTSON, 390 acs. by Survey 5 Apr 1775 in Bedford Co. on the W side of Falling riv., up the hill on the S side of Hickory Cr., in the head of a Valley; adj. Blaickley, Garrett, & John Bailey; 1 Sep 1780, p.306. A.C. of 40 Shill. Sterl.

PATRICK NAPIER Ass'ee of ASHFORD NAPIER, 73½ acs. by survey 18 Mar 1778 in Fluvanna Co. adj. Bryant, Haden & Champion; 1 Sep 1780, p.307. A.C. of 10 Shill. Sterl.

MATTHEW TALBOT, 1,062 acs. by Survey 12 Apr 1770 in Bedford Co. on both sides of Lenvils/Lenvills Cr. a South br. of Stanton Riv., adj. Haythes Line; 1 Sep 1780, p.308. A.C. of £5.S10 Sterl.

SAMUEL SHROSBERRY, 470 acs. by Survey 12 Apr 1774 in Bedford Co. on the brs. of Beaverdam Cr.; adj. Walton, John Finley, William Bramblett & Talbot; 1 Sep 1780, p.310. A.C. of 25 Shill. Sterl. 470 acs. as to Include two Tracts one of 239 acs. the other of 231 acs.

GUY SMITH, 300 acs. by Survey 9 Mar 1774 in Bedford Co. on the S Brs. of Otter Riv., along the old Line; 1 Dec 1780, p.312. A.C. of 30 Shill. Sterl.

ALEXANDER HENDERSON of Fairfax Co., 2 certain Lots or parcels of Land containing ½ an Acre in the town of Colchester Numbered in the Plan of the Town 5 and 38; bounded by Fairfax street on the S, by the River Occaquan on the W, by Lots Number 2 and 4 on the N, and by Lot Number 14 on the E; 19 Oct 1780, p.313. *in consideration of the sum of £6,600 Current Money of Virginia paid unto Hector Ross Gentleman Escheator for Fairfax Co. being Lateley the property of Glasford and Henderson Subjects of Great Britain and was Sold by the sd Hector Ross Gentleman Escheator for the sd Co. unto the sd Alexander Henderson with Lots and Houses and Appurtenances Appurtaining the sd Lot being lately the Propety of Glasford and Henderson by Virtue of an agreeable to two late Acts of General Assembly passed in 1779 the one Entitled an Act Concerning Escheators and forfeitures from British Subjects and the other Intituled an Act concerning Escheators.*

ROBERT DICK, 3 certain Lotts or parcels of L. containing ½ an Acres Each in the Town of Colchester, part thereof is a Lot and Houses numbered in the Plan of the sd Town 15; Bounded by Essex street on the S, by Number 12 belonging to Mr Hector Ross on the W, by the Back line of the town on the N, and by Lott Number 17 belonging to Colo. Peter Wagener on the E; and the other part is the Lots Numbered in the Plan of the sd Town 6 and 42 bounded by Lot Number 7 belonging to Mr. William Bayley on the S, by the river Occaquan on the W, by Fairfax street on the N, and by Lot Number 21 belonging to Mr. William Bayley on the E; 19 Oct 1780, p.314. *in consideration of the sum of £15,200 current Money of Virginia paid unto Hector Ross Gentleman Escheator for Fairfax Co. by Robert Dick of Blansburg in the State of Myraland [Bladensburg Maryland]. of which Lots being lately the property of David Dalyell and company Subjects of Great Britian and was sold by the sd Hector Ross Gentleman Escheator for the sd Co. unto the sd Robert Dick with Lots and Houses and Appurtenances Appurtaining to the sd Lots late the property of David Dalyell and Company by Virtue of and agreeable to two Acts of General assembly passed in 1779 the one Entitled an Act concerning Escheats and forfeitures from British Subjects and the other Entitled an Act concerning Escheators.*

JOHN JONES, 478 acs. by Survey 6 Jun 1780 in Mecklenburg Co. on the Brs. of Aaron's cr., adj. Smith & Rudd; 1 Sep 1780, p.315. A.C. of £2.S10 Sterl.

SAMUEL YONGUE/YOUNG, 308 acs. by Survey 17 Mar 1772 in Mecklenburg Co. on the forks of Little Mine Creeks; adj. James Sparrow, Rances Clark, Merritt Bland & Lancier [Lanier]; 11 Dec 1780, p.316. A.C. of 35 Shill. Sterl.

TALIAFERRO CRAIG Ass'ee of JOHN BOWMAN, 285 acs. by Survey 6 Oct 1780 in Botetourt Co. on the S side of Roan Oak joining the Lands of Thomas Carney; 11 Dec 1780, p.317. A.C. of 30 Shill. Sterl.

TALIAFERRO CRAIG Ass'ee of JOHN BOWMAN, 325 acs. by Survey 6 Oct 1780 in Botetourt Co. on the S side of Roan Oak near Tash's Meadow; 11 Dec 1780, p.318. A.C. of 35 Shill. Sterl.

PATRICK NAPIER, 243 acs. by Survey 23 Feb 1779 in Fluvanna Co. on the N Brs. of Hardware Riv.; adj. sd Napier, Sadler, Hammon/Hammond & Bryant; 1 Sep 1780, p.319. A.C. of 25 Shill. Sterl.

MARTIN WETSALL/WETSELL, 50 acs. by Survey 26 Feb 1773 in Augusta Co. on the upper South fork in *Wests Gap*, Beginning in a flat place on the S side of a Survey of Thomas West, on a Ridge & a flat; 1 Sep 1780, p.320. A.C. of 5 Shill.

JOHN HOOE Gentleman, 476 acs. **by an Inclusive Survey** 1 Oct 1780 in Prince William Co. in the head of a Valley, on Reeves br., to the Edge of an Old Field, on the Road, down a Steep Valley, down Occoquan Riv. & up Raines's spring Br.; adj. Thomas Stone, George Rain, James Whaley, John Hammett, John Reeve, Bradfield, Colo. Ewell & the sd Rainie; 11 Dec 1780, p.321. *in consideration of the sum of £4,800 Current Money of Virginia paid unto Henry Peyton Escheator for Prince William Co. by John Hooe Gentleman. Lately the property of Henry Ellison a British Subject and was lately sold by the sd Henry Peyton Escheator as aforesd unto the sd John Hooe Agreeable to two Acts of Assembly passed in 1779 the one Entitled an Act Concerning Escheat[s] and forfeitures from British Subjects the other Entitled an Act Concerning Escheators.*

JOHN HANCOCK, 147 acs. by Survey 27 Mar 1780 in Fluvanna Co. on the Brs. of the South fork of Cunningham's Cr.; adj. Ross, Cole, Amos & Fraser; 1 Sep 1780, p.323. A.C. of 15 Shill. Sterl.

JOHN LEMON, 225 acs. by Survey 2 May 1774 in Augusta Co. on the W side of Brock's Cr., Beginning near the foot the Mountain, on a Ridge; adj. John Thomas, John Philp's Survey, sd Phip's Line, Samuel Cormer & Micael Ford; 1 Sep 1780, p.324. A.C. of 25 Shill. Sterl.

JOHN MINOR, 200 acs. in Caroline Co. by the Main Road; adj. Jonathan Johnson, John Gough, Chowning, Hacket/Hackett, Chew[n]ing & Quarles; 11 Dec 1780, p.325. *in consideration of £4,175 Current Money of Virginia paid unto Edmund Pendleton Junr. Escheator for Caroline Co. lately the property of Richard Goodall a British Subject and was Sold by the sd Edmond Pendleton Escheator aforesd unto the sd John Minor agreeable to two Acts of assembly passed in the year 1779 the one Entitled an Act concerning Escheats and forfeitures from British Subjects the other Entitled an Act Concerning Escheators.*

JOHN PICKETT, 400 acs. Caroline Co. in the hundred of South River, on a Level & a hill, adj. Rogers's back Line; 11 Dec 1780, p.326. *£3,100 current Money of Virginia paid unto Edmund Pendleton junior Gentleman Escheator for Caroline Co. lately the property of Cunningham and Company British Subjects and was Sold by the sd Edmund Pendleton Escheator as aforesd unto the sd John Pickett agreeable to two Acts of Assembly passed in the year 1779 the one Intitled an Act Concerning Escheats and forff[ei]tures from British Subjects the other Intitled an Act concerning Escheators.*

MACE PICKETT, 339 acs. by Survey 2 May 1766 in Caroline Co. and Parish of Drysdale, near Mace Picketts Corn fi[e]ld, a Long the Road; adj. the Patent Line, Thomas Pickett & Daniel; near Crouches's; 11 Dec 1780, p.327. A.C. of 35 Shill. Sterl. it being Surplus Land as Appears by the Survey within the bounds of a patent Granted to William Wakeling and Edward Merick for 1,014 acs. 26 Apr 1704 and which he also claims by a conveyance from the sd Wakeling and Merick to his father and from his father to him. [See Essex Co. PB 9 p.597 to Edward Merrick & Wm. Wakeling on the S side of Rappahannock Riv. & W side of Little Tuckahoe Br. of Mattapony Riv. which was adj. to K. & Q. Co. PB 9 p.721 to Col. James Tayor & Mr. John Baylor on brs. of Morocosick Cr. & brs. of Beverly's Run which 1,000 acs part was regranted to William Daniel Junior in Caroline Co. PB 32 p.405]

WILLIAM FLEMING Esquire, 500 acs. by Survey 20 Jun 1779 in Botetourt Co. on both sides of Glade Cr. and on Tinker Cr., near an old Cabbin, on the Point of a Ridge, near Willsons Cabbin, by a road; adj. an old Survey, the Concluding Line of Skillerns Survey, Armstrongs Land, Daniel McNeills Land & McNeills field; 11 Dec 1780, p.328. A.C. of 5 Shill. Sterl. 75 acs. part thereof was gtd. by Pat. to John Askins 10 Sep 1755 and 85 acs. part thereof was gtd. by Pat. and 350 acs. part thereof was gtd. to George Skillern by Pat. 12 May 1770 which Last Tract Included part of the former the Right and Title of which Land is since become Vested in the sd William Fleming and the residue never before granted.

WILLIAM EVANS, 130 acs. by Survey 18 Oct 1773 in Henry Co. formerly Pittsylvania Co. on both sides the North fork of Chesnut Cr., adj. Robert Mason & Ramsey; 11 Dec 1780, p.330. A.C. of 15 Shill. Sterl.

JOHN HUFF, 308 acs. by Survey 7 May 1779 in Henry Co. on the waters of Turners Cr. and brs. of Pigg Riv.; adj. James Rentfrow, Jones, Andrew Farguson, Reubil, William Young & Huff; 11 Dec 1780, p.331. A.C. of 35 Shill. Sterl. [to a Mahogany tree]

JOHN LYNCH ass'ee of MICAJAH TERRILL, 99 acs. by Survey 18 Mar 1769 in Amherst Co. on the N side and joining the Fluvanna Riv.; adj. Miles Buford/Burford, Joseph Anthony & Charles Lynch; 1 Sep 1780, p.332. A.C. of 10 Shill. Sterl.

THOMAS NELSON, 164 acs. by Survey 1 Feb 1779 in Henry Co. formerly

Pittsylvania on the Draughts of Smiths Riv., adj. Martin Webb; 11 Dec 1780, p.333. A.C. of 20 Shill. Sterl.

JOHN FARGUSON, 230 acs. by Survey 15 Apr 1779 in Henry Co. on the S side of Pigg Riv., down Stoney Cr.; adj. Hill, William Davis, the sd Road's now Fargusons C., a cherry tree on Stoney Creek Near his Mill & his own Line; 11 Dec 1780, p.334. A.C. of 25 Shill. Sterl.

JOHN FARGUSON, 300 acs. by Survey 16 Mar 1774 in Bedford Co. on N Brs. of Blackwater Riv., adj. Maxeys Lines & Souths Lines; 11 Dec 1780, p.335. A.C. of 30 Shill. Sterl.

HENRY YOUNG ass'ee of WILLIAM HUSTON, 263 acs. by Survey 9 Mar 1778 in Pr. Edward Co. on the Brs. of Falling Cr.; adj. McBride, Robert Martin, Hay's line, Chaffin, Donavant, Frazier & Coleman; 11 Dec 1780, p.336. A.C. of 30 Shill. Sterl.

DARBY RYON, 370 acs. by Survey 30 Apr 1779 in Henry Co. on the Brs. of Pigg riv.; adj. Henry Jones, Ryons own Line, Robert Jones, Thomas Jones & Hill; 11 Dec 1780, p.337. A.C. of 40 Shill. Sterl.

DARBY RYON, 268 acs. by Survey 6 May 1779 in Henry Co. on Pigg Riv. and other Brs. thereof, on Whistling hill, at a Rock on a Ridge; adj. Miller Dogget, Mavity, Hill, & John Bohannan; 11 Dec 1780, p.339. A.C. of 30 Shill. Sterl.

JOSEPH LANKFORD, 325 acs. by Survey 23 Apr 1756 in Pittsylvania Co. formerly Halifax on Brush Cr.; adj. Thomas Dendy, Charles Farris & Robert Sim; 11 Dec 1780, p.340. A.C. of 35 Shill. Sterl.

WILLIAM ROUTON Ass'ee of ARCHER ALLEN, 342 acs. in Charlotte Co. formerly Lunenburg on the Brs. of Cub Cr.; adj. Allen, Lovel, Wallace & Duggan; 11 Dec 1780, p.341. A.C. of 35 Shill. Sterl. by Survey made for Christopher Almond 25 Mar 1751 of whom the sd Archer Allen recovered it on a Caveat before the late Council 9 Jun 1773. [For Allen's land, see PB 28 p.617 to Samuel Allen & for Lovel's land see PB 41 p.31 to Edward Robertson]

RICHARD PRICE ass'ee of WILLIAM TOWNS who was ass'ee of STEPHEN WADE, 215 acs. by Survey 27 Apr 1773 in Halifax Co. on the Draughts of Stanton; adj. Foushee, Hunt & Nowlin; 11 Dec 1780, p.342. A.C. of 25 Shill. Sterl.

WILLIAM NEALEY ass'ee of WILLIAM MADISON, 356 acs. in Botetourt Co. on the Bent Mountain at a place known by the name of *chesnut neck* on the South fork of Roan Oak; 1 Sep 1780, p.343. A.C. of 40 Shill. Sterl.

ROBERT GORDON ass'ee of SAMUEL & PHILIP GOODE, 670 acs. by Survey 1 Apr 1775 in Bedford Co. on W brs. of Little falling Riv.; adj. Burnley, Venable & Goode; 1 Sep 1780, p.344. A.C. of £3.S10 Sterl.

NATHANIEL COCK ass'ee of JAMES FARRES, 350 acs. by Survey 29 Nov 1774 in Pittsylvania Co. on both sides of the North fork of George's Cr., along his Line; 1 Sep 1780, p.345. A.C. of 35 Shill. Sterl.

PEYTON WADE, 167 acs. by Survey 22 Oct 1777 in Pittsylvania Co. on the N Brs. of Pigg Riv.; adj. his Line, Robert Daulton, William Adkinson & the sd Ward; 1 Sep 1780, p.346. A.C. of 20 Shill. Sterl.

DAVID WRIGHT, 604 acs. by Survey 25 Mar 1771 in Bedford Co. on the S side of Little Otter Riv.; adj. Grundy, Roundtree, Randolph, Callaway, Quarles, Talbot & McLoughlin; 1 Jan 1781, p.347. A.C. of £3 Sterl. being part of Woodson's and Company's Order of Council for 2,000 acs. Gtd. 14 Jun 1749.

JOHN WARD, 100 acs. by Survey 29 Nov 1779 in Pittsylvania Co. on the draughts of Roscastle Cr., adj. Kendrick; 1 Sep 1780, p.348. A.C. of 10 Shill. Sterl.

JAMES COX, 310 acs. by Survey 18 Nov 1778 in Pittsylvania Co. on both sides of Morrisons br. of Sandy, at the fork of the road, adj. King; 1 Sep 1780, p.349. A.C. of 35 Shill. Sterl.

JOHN WEBSTER, 120 acs. by Survey in Bedford Co. on the North Fork of Blackwater, adj. Mason & Rentfroe; 1 Sep 1780, p.350. A.C. of 15 Shill. Sterl.

JOHN FERRILL, 400 acs. by Survey 16 Apr 1774 in Pittsylvania Co. on both sides of Bird Cr. & Main Bird Cr., adj. Terry's Order Line; 1 Sep 1780, p.350. A.C. of 40 Shill. Sterl.

JEREMIAH SHELTON, 154 acs. by Survey 9 Mar 1768 in Pittsylvania Co. on the North fork of Mayo riv.; 1 Sep 1780, p.351. A.C. of 15 Shill. Sterl.

ISHAM EDWARDS, 174 acs. by Survey 13 Jan 1769 in Henry Co. on the brs. of Clout Cr., adj. William James; 1 Sep 1780, p.352. A.C. of 20 Shill. Sterl.

BENJAMIN WOODSON, 33 acs. by Survey 30 Jan 1778 in Fluvanna Co. on the brs. of Rackoon cr. and S brs. of Revanna Riv., on Napier's Road, adj. sd Woodsons Lines; 1 Sep 1780, p.353. A.C. of 5 Shill. Sterl.

JOHN MORGAN, 400 acs. by Survey 1 Apr 1762 in Halifax Co. on the brs. of Cashade Cr., adj. John Rice & Russell; 1 Sep 1780, p.353. A.C. of £2 Sterl.

NATHANIEL SHREWSBURY, 266 acs. by Survey 8 Mar 1773 in Bedford Co. on the heads of Beaver dam Cr., adj. Shrewsberry & Bluford; 1 Sep 1780, p.354. A.C. of 30 Shill. Sterl.

WILLIAM MARTIN ass'ee of JEREMIAH STONE who was Ass'ee of MATTHEW TALBOT, 250 acs. by Survey 11 Apr 1770 in Bedford Co. on both sides of Gills Cr.; adj. Haynes Line, Benjamin Greer & Hays; 1 Sep 1780, p.355. A.C. of 25 Shill. Sterl.

NATHANIEL MAMON ass'ee of HENRY WILLIAMS who was Ass'ee of JOHN HARVEY, 383 acs. by Survey 27 Jan 1775 in Halifax Co. on the South fork of Cubb cr.; 1 Jan 1781, p.356. A.C. of 40 Shill. Sterl.

GEORGE EARNEST Ass'ee of JOHN RENTFRO, 245 acs. by Survey 18 Apr 1763 in Bedford Co. on both sides of Balls br., up Bells br. aforesaid; 1 Sep 1780, p.357. A.C. of 25 Shill. Sterl.

WILLIAM WATSON, 233 acs. by Survey 26 Feb 1772 in Albemarle Co. on the Little Mountains on the head of a br.

called Doltons br.; adj. William Ragland, Thomas Mann Randolph, Martin Key & the Land formerly Dalton's; 1 Sep 1780, p.358. A.C. of 25 Shill. Sterl.

JOHN DEPRIEST, 400 acs. by Survey 8 Mar 1780 in Amherst Co. on the south fork of Ruckers Run, on the North br. of sd fork; adj. Number 11, Edmund Wilcox, Lucas Powel, the Patent Line & Number 10; 19 Oct 1780, p.359. *in consideration of the Sum of £3,000 Current Money of Virginia paid to David Shepherd Gentleman Escheator for Amherst Co. and being part of a Larger Tract Lately the Property of Walter King Esquire a British Subject and was sold by the sd David Shepherd Escheataor as aforesd unto the sd John Depriest agreeable to two Acts of Assembly passed in the Year 1779 the one Entitled an Act Concerning Escheats and forfeitures from British Subjects the other Entitled an Act Concerning Escheators which sd Tract or Parcel of Land is bound by the Variation of the Magnetic from the true Meridian being N15'W.* [Regranted John Dupriest in GB G p.157 dated 1 Sep 1782, both being part number 12 of Walter King's PB 29 p.99]

JOEL WALKER ass'ee of ANDREW GROBBS [GRUBBS], 165 acs. by Survey 2 Mar 1756 in Bedford Co. on Elk Island Cr.; 1 Sep 1780, p.360. A.C. of 20 Shill. Sterl.

THOMAS THORNILL, 250 acs. by Survey 22 Feb 1764 in Buckingham Co. on both sides of Stephens's Cr., up Davids Cr.; adj. Thomas Stephens, his own Line & Robert Kylers's line; 1 Sep 1780, p.360. A.C. of 25 Shill. Sterl.

THOMAS WALTERS, 318 acs. by Survey 24 Apr 1780 in Halifax Co. on the brs. of Stanton Riv.; adj. John Walters Lines of his new Survey, Watkins's line formerly Mary Coles, Treadway, Cobb, & Joel Watkins; 1 Feb 1781, p361. A.C. of 35 Shill. Sterl.

DANIEL MITCHELL, 275 acs. by Survey 8 Dec 1769 in Halifax Co. on the Brs. of Bull Cr., up Heikey's Road, adj. his old Lines & George Trible; 1 Feb 1781, p.362. A.C. of 30 Shill. Sterl.

VINSON SPROUCE, 107 acs. by Survey 19 Nov 1760 in Albemarle Co. on the N brs. of Ballengers Cr., Crossing a water Course; 1 Sep 1780, p.363. A.C. of 15 Shill. Sterl.

JOHN THOMPSON, 363 acs. by Survey 2 Dec 1756 in Halifax Co. on the Brs. of Childrys Cr., Crossing Heikeys Road, to a pine Just over Hickeys Road; adj. Hugh Prewit, Joseph Mayes, Charles Bostick, Daniel Humphris, John Trimble & John Gillington; 1 Feb 1781, p.363. A.C. of 40 Shill. Sterl.

WILLIAM MARTIN, 400 acs. by Survey 6 Dec 1770 in Halifax Co. on the Lower side of Childree Cr.; adj. Joseph Collins, his old Line, Mouldin, Streets former Lines, Bayses Line & Peter Tribel; 1 Feb 1781, p.364. A.C. of 40 Shill. Sterl.

DARBY RION, 270 acs. by Survey 8 Nov 1753 in Halifax Co. on both sides of Wiggon Cr. adj. Harbord; 1 Feb 1781, p.365. A.C. of 30 Shill. Sterl.

JAMES ARNOLD, 212 acs. by Survey 28 Nov 1771 in Halifax Co. on the draughts of Stewarts Cr., up Boyds Road, adj. Wall & Scoggin; 1 Feb 1781, p.366. A.C. of 25 Shill. Sterl.

JOHN WARD, 320 acs. by Survey 28 Feb 1775 in Pittsylvania Co. on both sides of Chiles's Cr., adj. James Doss; 1 Feb 1781, p.367. A.C. of 35 Shill. Sterl.

JEREMIAH WARD, 141 acs. by Survey 20 Oct 1777 in Pittsylvania Co. on the S side of Pigg Riv.; adj. John Waldrope's/Waldrops line. Bennet & Goad; 1 Feb 1781, p.367. A.C. of 15 Shill. Sterl.

THOMAS HOPE, 332 acs. by Survey 26 Mar 1780 in Halifax Co. on the S side of Difficult Cr.; adj. Pride, Burchets old Lines & Wade; 1 Feb 1781, p.368. A.C. of 40 Shill. Sterl.

ALEXANDER RUDDER, 387 acs. by Survey 28 Apr 1774 in Lunenburg Co. in the Long br., down Flatrock Cr., adj. Stephen Edmards Broadnan & the Patent Line; 1 Feb 1781, p.369. A.C. of 5 Shill. Sterl. 344 acs. part thereof was formerly Gtd. by Pat. to William & Richard Gill [Brunswick Co. PB 29 p.98] the residue not before Ptd. [also see PB 31 p.740 to Stephen Edward Broadnax]

SWINFIELD HILL, 130 acs. by Survey 7 May 1753 in Halifax Co. on the N Brs. of Pigg Riv. and on the S of [a] *Mountain called the Grassey Hill*; 1 Feb 1781, p.370. A.C. of 15 Shill. Sterl. [also as SWINGFIELD HILL]

JOHN KENDRICK/KINDRICK, 250 acs. by Survey 2 Nov 1778 in Pittsylvania Co. on Smiths Riv., Crossing Buffesons Cr., to a Cinnamon tree on a Br. of Smith's Riv. Opposite Thomas Harbours Corner on Smith's Riv.; adj. Thomas Huff, Thomas Hough & Thiffs Lines; 1 Feb 1781, p.371. A.C. of 25 Shill. Sterl.

JOHN STUART, 225 acs. by Survey 11 Jan 1779 in Henry Co. on Black water Riv., adj. Jessey Clay & Daniel Ward; 1 Feb 1781, p.372. A.C. of 25 Shill. Sterl.

WALTER MAXEY, 228 acs. by Survey 16 Apr 1768 in Henry Co. formerly Pittsylvania on Smith's Riv., adj. John Reivs on the Riv.; 1 Feb 1781, p.373. A.C. of 25 Shill. Sterl.

ISAAC CLOUD, 175 acs. by Survey 28 Nov 1766 in Henry Co. on both sides of Elk Cr., along the Country Line [East], crossing a fork sd Cr.; 1 Feb 1781, p.374. A.C. of £1 Sterl.

WILLIAM MAVITY, 285 acs. by Survey 1 May 1779 in Henry Co., crossing the North fork of Sotry Cr.; adj. William Weak, John Fuson & Phillip Sheridan; 1 Feb 1781, p.375. A.C. of 30 Shill. Sterl.

FRANCES & JANE HOPKINS, 780 acs. by Survey 25 Nov 1772 in Pittsylvania Co. on the Brs. of Town Cr. and Chesnut Cr., on Turners Road, adj. David Haley; 1 Feb 1781, p.376. A.C. of £4 Sterl.

JOSHUA SHORE PRICE, 193 acs by Survey 11 Oct 1773 in Pittsylvania Co. on the draughts of Blackwater Riv., adj. Randolph; 1 Feb 1781, p.377. A.C. of £1 Sterl.

SAMPSON STEPHENS, 200 acs. by Survey 9 Nov 1779 in Henry Co. on the Brs. of the Muster br. of Leatherwood Cr.; adj. George Runnold, an old Line & William Bernard; 1 Feb 1781, p.378. A.C. of £1 Sterl.

ROBERT PEDIGROW/PODIGROW, 395 acs. by Survey 17 Nov 1779 in Henry Co. on the Brs. of Leatherwood

Cr.; adj. Daniel McBride, Reger [Rogers], Talbot, Gordon, & Lomax and Company; 1 Feb 1781, p.379. A.C. of 40 Shill. Sterl.

HENRY DILLIAN, 535 acs. by Survey 4 Dec 1779 in Henry Co. on Strouds Cr. a fork of Warf Mountain Cr.; adj. Jourdan, Randolph, & Jordan; 1 Feb 1781, p.380. A.C. of 55 Shill. Sterl.

WILLIAM SWANSON Ass'ee of NATHAN SWANSON, 309 acs. by Survey 28 Nov 1778 in Henry Co. on the Brs. of Bull Run; adj. William Haynes's old Line & George Waltons old Line; to a white Oak Stump in old Mr. Swansons plantation a Corner of his land thence with his otherwise Haynes's line; 1 Feb 1781, p.381. A.C. of 35 Shill. Sterl.

PHILIP SHERIDAN, 362 acs. by Survey 30 Apr 1779 in Henry Co. on the North fork of Story Cr., adj. John Fuson, to a Mahogany tree; 1 Feb 1781, p.382. A.C. of £2 Sterl.

HENRY TERRY, 356 acs. by Survey 28 Feb 1780 in Pittsylvania Co. on Sandy cr.; adj. David Terry, James Terrys Order line, King & Walker; 1 Feb 1781, p.384. A.C. of 40 Shill. Sterl.

JAMES RAY, 194 acs. by Survey 11 Apr 1768 in Henry Co. formerly Pittsylvania Co. on Little Marrowbone Cr., adj. Randolph; 1 Feb 1781, p.385. A.C. of £1 Sterl.

JONATHAN HENBEY/HANBEY, 36 acs. by Survey 4 Dec 1773 in Henry Co. formerly Pittsylvania on both sides of Peters Cr., adj. the sd Hanbey; 1 Feb 1781, p.386. A.C. of 5 Shill. Sterl.

JAMES PARBARY, 162 acs. by Survey 17 Dec 1775 in Pittsylvania Co. on the head brs. of Read Cr., on the Top of Chesnut Mountain, adj. McGee; 1 Feb 1781, p.386. A.C. of £1 Sterl.

MOSES VINCENT, 159 acs. by Survey 13 Mar 1777 in Pittsylvania Co. on the brs. of Sandy Riv., adj. the old Line & John Smith; 1 Feb 1781, p.387. A.C. of £1 Sterl.

JOHN ADAMS, 319 acs. by Survey 22 Apr 1780 in Pittsylvania Co. on Banister Riv., near the Road, Crossing the Rockey Br.; adj. Robert Martin, John Short & the sd Adams old Line; 1 Feb 1781, p.389. A.C. of 35 Shill. Sterl.

JOHN PHILPOTT, 250 acs. by Survey 17 Apr 1772 in Pittsylvania Co. on the S Side of Smiths riv.; 1 Feb 1781, p.390. A.C. of 25 Shill. Sterl.

JOHN SMITH, 150 acs. by Survey 22 Mar 1780 in Pittsylvania Co. on Stanton Riv., adj. John Chiles C. & the sd Smiths former Line; 1 Feb 1781, p.391. A.C. of 15 Shill. Sterl.

JAMES STANDERFER, SENIOR, 374 acs. by Survey 1 May 1779 in Henry Co. on Story Cr., adj. James Standerfer Junior & Standerfer's old Survey; 1 Feb 1781, p.392. A.C. of £2 Sterl.

JOSEPH CUNNINGHAM, 284 acs. by Survey 16 Dec 1777 in Pittsylvania Co. on the Brs. of Sandy Riv., adj. sd Joseph Cunningham & Sparks Line; 1 Feb 1781, p.393. A.C. of 30 Shill. Sterl.

WILLIAM PROCISE, 310 acs. by Survey 9 Feb 1774 in Pittsylvania Co. on both sides of Bearskin Cr., on a Ridge, adj. Richard Adkinson; 1 Feb 1781, p.394. A.C. of 35 Shill. Sterl.

MOSES AYRES, 260 acs. by Survey 24 Mar 1775 in Pittsylvania Co. on the Brs. of Double Cr.; adj. Thomas Sandridge, Bird, Payne, Nim Scott & Walthers line; 1 Feb 1781, p.395. A.C. of 30 Shill. Sterl.

JAMES CALLAWAY, 390 acs. by Survey 5 Apr 1769 in Pittsylvania Co. on the waters of Blackwater riv., adj. his C.; 1 Feb 1781, p.397. A.C. of 40 Shill. Sterl.

JAMES BOYD, 156 acs. by Survey 24 Nov 1779 in Buckingham Co. on both sides of the Middle br. of Slate Riv.; adj. Thomas Heads dec'd now Richard Williams's; near the top of Slate river mountain; 1 Feb 1781, p.397. A.C. of £1 Sterl.

GEORGE MOORE, 325 acs. by Survey 11 Jan 1773 in Pr. Edward Co. on Jennings's Cr.; adj. Hill, Soloman Fear & John Morrow; 1 Feb 1781, p.398. A.C. of 35 Shill. Sterl.

GEORGE HOOPER, 200 acs. by Survey 12 Dec 1771 in Buckingham Co. on the Ridges and North Draughts of Willises Riv.; adj. Mr John Nicho.as, Epperson, Nathaniel Jefferus or Jefferees C., his own Line & John Fry; 1 Feb 1781, p.399. A.C. of £1 Sterl. [For his own Line see Albemarle Co. PB 27 p.152 to Joseph Hooper]

JEREMIAH JAMES, 85 acs. by Survey 24 Mar 1780 in Surry Co. on the N side of Black Water Sw., on the East Edge of the Burch Island road, up the Said Main Road & up the long br.; adj. William Cox, John James, William Lane's forward and after Line, Benjamin Spratly/Spratley & James's own Line; 1 Feb 1781, p.400. A.C. of 10 Shill.

JACOB RUBSAMON, 175 acs. by Survey 17 Apr 1753 in Pittsylvania Co. formerly Halifax on the S side of Stanton and Pigg Rivers; adj. John Adams, James Bobbit, Leonard Tarrence; 1 Feb 1781, p.401. A.C. of £1 Sterl.

HENRY SAVIGE, 54 acs. by Survey 24 Mar 1780 in Surry Co. on the N side of Black Water Sw.; adj. his own L., William Edwards & Willis Smith; 1 Feb 1781, p.403. A.C. of 5 Shill. Sterl.

WILLIAM THOMPSON, 358 acs. by an **Inclusive Survey** bearing date 1 Mar 1774 in Pittyslyvania Co. on the Brs. of Potters Cr.; adj. Nowlin, Raysois Line, Coffey & the sd Thompson; 1 Feb 1781, p.404. A.C. of 40 Shill. Sterl.

JOHN TULLY, 302 acs. by Survey 24 Mar 1763 in Pittsylvania Co. on the brs. of Harpen Cr., on a Naked hill, adj. Thomas Godfry & James Slone; 1 Feb 1781, p.405. A.C. of 30 Shill. Sterl.

JAMES TRIMBLE, 250 acs. by Survey 23 Nov 1772 in Botetourt Co. on the NW side of the Camp Mountain on a br. of Long Entry Cr. a br. of James Riv., Beginning at the foot of a Spur, below a Spring, up a Steep Mountain, down the side of a mountain and Crossing a Cr., on a Ridge in a Gap of the Mountain, by a Rockey druaght; 1 Feb 1781, p.406. A.C. of 25 Shill. Sterl.

JAMES DOWNNEN, 400 acs. by Survey 21 Apr 1753 in Pittsylvania Co. formerly Halifax on the Glady fork of frying pan

Cr., adj. John Goards old Line & new Line; 1 Feb 1781, p.407. A.C. of 40 Shill. Sterl.

JOHN STRANGE, 182 acs. by Survey 9 Apr 1762 in Pittsylvania Co. formerly Halifax on the Glady fork of Sandy Riv., Crossing the Road, adj. his old Line; 1 Feb 1781, p.408. A.C. of 20 Shill. Sterl.

JESSE DODSON, 84 acs. by Survey 12 Mar 1765 in Pittsylvania Co. formerly Halifax on the brs. of Burches Cr., adj. Henry Order Line & Terry; 1 Feb 1781, p.410. A.C. of 10 Shill. Sterl.

ARMSTEAD SHELTON, 360 acs. by Survey 12 Feb 1773 in Pittsylvania Co. on the South fork of timber Cr. of white Thorn Cr.; 1 Feb 1781, p.410. A.C. of 49 Shill. Sterl.

JOHN RAGSDALE, 787 acs. by Survey **inclusively made** 5 Dec 1761 in Lunenburg Co. down Bears Element Cr.; adj. Matthews, Cock, his own Line, Winston & Thomas Mucklehonney; 1 Feb 1781, p.411. A.C. of 45 Shill. Sterl. 342 acs. being part of the sd tract and was formerly Gtd. by Pat. to Thomas Mcklehonney by pat. 1 Oct 1747 [Brunswick Co. PB 28 p.218 to Thomas Mucklehoney]. [Adj. PB 28 p.83 to Richard Cocke, PB 34 p113 to Charles Gee, PB 31 p.563 to William Wallace, PB 31 p.724 to John Lowry & his own PB 40 p.631]

GEORGE CARTER, 190 acs. by Survey 19 Oct 1770 in Henry Co. formerly Pittsylvania on the Bull Mountain [Cr.] of Mayo Riv., down the Cr., adj. sd Carters Line; 1 Feb 1781, p.413. A.C. of 20 Shill. Sterl.

JOSEPH DENNIS, 112 acs. by Survey 9 May 1770 in Bottetourt Co. on the W end of the short hill in the fork of James Riv., by a run; 1 Feb 1781, p.414. A.C. of 15 Shill. Sterl.

WILLIAM LEWIS, 170 acs. by Survey 13 Apr 1763 in Bottetourt Co. in the Gap that leads from Sweet Spring to Second creek in the South fork of Dunlops cr. and Joining the upper end of his Land, up the Spurs of the Mountain; 1 Feb 1781, p.416. A.C. of £1 Sterl.

JAMES HALL, 83 acs. by Survey 18 Mar 1779 in Rockbridge Co. on Buffalo cr. in the fork of James Riv., adj. John Wilson & Halls old Survey; 1 Feb 1781, p.417. A.C. of 10 Shill. Sterl.

JOSEPH MASON, 110 acs. by Survey 21 Apr 1775 in Bottetourt Co. on back Cr. between Masons old place, John Bowmans and Samuel Montgomery's Survey; 1 Feb 1781, p.417. A.C. of 15 Shill. Sterl.

JAMES PERRY, 120 acs. by Survey 13 Feb 1769 in Augusta Co. in the fork of James Riv. adj. the sd James Perry's own Land, his own Survey; in the head of a draft, on a barren hill, also adj. Renicks old c.; 1 Feb 1781, p.418. A.C. of 15 Shill. Sterl.

JOSEPH MASON, 63 acs. by Survey 21 Apr 1775 in Bottetourt Co. on the Waters of Back cr. between Masons old place and Samuel Montgomery, on a Ridge; 1 Feb 1781, p.420. A.C. of 10 Shill. Sterl.

ALEXANDER BAGGS, 114 acs. by Survey 14 Nov 1772 in Bottetourt Co. Joining Lines with his own and the Land of John Matthews and James Simpson on the waters of James Riv., on the top of a ridge, Cross a draft to the top of a hill, Crossing three draughts to a hill side; 1 Feb 1781, p.421. A.C. of 15 Shill. Sterl.

SAMUEL REED, 76 acs. by Survey 20 Oct 1772 in Bottetourt Co. on Back Cr. a br. of Roanoke, adj. the tract he Lives on, in a bottom; 1 Feb 1781, p.422. A.C. of 10 Shill. Sterl.

WILLIAM WALKER, 165 acs. by Survey 15 Oct 1772 in Bottetourt Co. on the South fork of Pattersons Cr. a br. of James Riv., Beginning near Crawfords Line; 1 Feb 1781, p.423. A.C. of £1 Sterl.

ANTHONY STREET, WILLIAM HAWKINS JUNIOR & ARCHIBALD BLAIR, Brother and heir at Law of JOHN BLAIR dec'd devisee of the sd JAMES BLAIR dec'd, 5,000 acs. in Lunenburg Co. on both sides of Elk Cr., up Gibsons br., on Callaways Road, adj. Randolph & William Callaway; 1 Feb 1781, p.425. £20 sterl. paid into the Treasury of this Commonwealth.
Whereas by one Pat. under the Seal of our late Colony and Dominion of Virginia 4 Oct 1753 was gtd. to Joseph Walton [PB 31 p.415] which sd Tract or parcel of Land was gtd. on Condition of paying the Quitrents and Cultivating and Improveing as in the pat. is expressed and Whereas the sd Joseph Walton hath failed to pay such Quitrents and Anthony Street and Wm. Hawkins Junior made Humble Suit to the Honourable the Lieutenant Governor and Commander in chief of the sd Colony and Dominion of Virginia under the Regal Government and obtained a Certificate from the General Court for the same 23 Apr 1765 and by their Assignment have desired that a Pat.

may Issue in their names and in the name of James Blair jointly thereof.

WILLIAM WALKER, 250 acs. by Survey 21 Sep 1772 in Bottetourt Co. on the waters of Craigs Cr. a br. of James Riv., Beginning on a hill side near the Mill cr., on the top of a mountain; 1 Feb 1781, p.427. A.C. of 25 Shill. Sterl.

WILLIAM NEELY Ass'ee of ROBERT ALSUP, 138 acs. by Survey 11 Jun 1771 in Bottetourt Co. on the brs. of Back Cr. the waters of Ronoak, on a hill side by the fall of a run; 1 Feb 1781, p.428. A.C. of 15 Shill. Sterl.

SAMUEL LYLE, 250 acs. by Survey 11 Mar 1779 in Rockbridge Co. in the forks of James Riv., in the head of a deep hallow; adj. John McCorkel, the old Patent Line, Matthew Elder, John Paxton, Barnabas Rely & sd Releys Line; 1 Feb 1781, p.429. A.C. of 25 Shill. Sterl.

JEREMIAH KEESEE ass'ee of DAVID MITCHELL, 386 acs. by Survey 15 Nov 1774 in Pittsylvania Co. on the middle fork of Stinking Riv.; adj. Thomas Farris/Farres; 1 Feb 1781, p.431. A.C. of 40 Shill. Sterl.

CHARLES DUNKIN, 282 acs. by Survey 18 Mar 1779 in Pittsylvania Co. on the Brs. of the open Ground fork of Beens Cr.; adj. James Dunkin, McGuff, Perkins Line & Dunkins former Line; 1 Feb 1781, p.432. A.C. of 30 Shill. Sterl.

JOHN GRIGGS, 347 acs. by Survey 13 Apr 1780 in Rockbridge Co. adj. John Trimble, Alexander Smily, John Bowyer & sd Smely/Smeley; 1 Feb 1781, p.433. A.C. of 35 Shill. Sterl.

WILLIAM CRAWFORD, 133 acs. by Survey 28 Sep 1779 in Augusta Co. on the top of the North Mountain about two Miles S of dry branch Gap, on the top of a Ridge; 1 Feb 1781, p.435. A.C. of 15 Shill. Sterl.

GEORGE McDONALD Ass'ee of JOSHUA McCORMICK, 110 acs. by Survey 10 Nov 1767 in Augusta Co. on both sides of the North br. of Roanoke and being part of the tract of Land whereon Daniel McCormick now Lives, on a Rockey hill, along the Patent Line & the Mountain, adj. Smith; 1 Feb 1781, p.436. A.C. of 15 Shill. Sterl.

SAMUEL McELHENNY, 375 acs. by Survey 27 Feb 1778 in Bottetourt Co. on big run a br. of back Cr., and including part of a Survey made for Robert McElheny 20 Apr 1775, to a Double Dogwood and Swith Wasel corner to the old Survey, adj. the old Lines, on a dry Run, Crossing the old Survey; 1 Feb 1781, p.437. A.C. of 40 Shill. Sterl.

JAMES SNODGRASS, 250 acs. by Survey 18 Sep 1772 in Botetourt Co. on the S side of Catabo Cr. a br. of James Riv., Beginning by the C. of his patent L. on a ridge, adj. the l. of William Snodgrass; 1 Feb 1781, p.438. A.C. of 25 Shill. Sterl.

ROBERT ARMSTRONG, 230 acs. by Survey 7 Apr 1780 in Augusta Co. on a small br. of Jenning's br.; James Elliott, John Elliott & William Crawford; 1 Feb 1781, p.439. A.C. of 25 Shill. Sterl.

JAMES POTEEAT, 295 acs. by Survey 14 Sep 1779 in Pittsylvania Co. on Smiths Riv., down white Oak Cr.; 1 Feb 1781, p.441. A.C. of 30 Shill. Sterl.

THOMAS BAGGS ass'ee of ALEXANDER BAGGS, 48 acs. by Survey 20 Nov 1779 in Rockbridge Co. on the waters of Buffaloe cr. on the forks of James Riv.; adj. sd Baggs old Survey, Thomas Baggs & the said Posey's Line; 1 Feb 1781, p.442. A.C. of 5 Shill. Sterl.

JAMES DALZELL, 110 acs. by Survey 12 Apr 1779 in Botetourt Co. on the Waters of Catawbo, on a hill near a road, on the E side of a draft; adj. Colo. Preston, Alderson, & James Johnston; 1 Feb 1781, p.443. A.C. of 15 Shill. Sterl.

MOSES DUNLAP ass'ee of FRANCIS SMITH, 360 acs. by Survey 4 Jun 1767 in Augusta Co. on Roanoke Riv., by the foot of a mountain, on a ridge, in a hallow, by the road, adj. Peter Dyerly & Isaac Taylor; 1 Sep [Feb] 1781, p.444. A.C. of 40 Shill. Sterl.

JOHN RAMEY, 290 acs. by Survey 10 May 1780 in Pittsylvania Co. on the brs. of Allens and Buffaloe creeks, crossing the Long br.; adj. Joseph Farriss, James George, sd Ramey, Absolom Ramey, Daugherty, James Buckley & William Allen; 1 Feb 1781, p.446. A.C. of 30 Shill. Sterl.

JOHN POAGE, 340 acs. by Survey 9 Nov 1779 in Augusta Co. on the head br. of falling springs, Beginning near George Kings Line; adj. William Anderson, Sampson Matthews Line & William Lewis's L.; 1 Feb 1781, p.447. A.C. of 35 Shill. Sterl.

SAMUEL VANCE, 150 acs. by Survey 7 Jul 1774 in Augusta Co. on Little back Cr. a br. of Jacksons riv. above the Land where he Lives; 1 Feb 1781, p.448. A.C. of 15 Shill. Sterl.

JOHN PARKS, 198 acs. by Survey 21 Oct 1772 in Augusta Co. Joining the Lines of his own and the Land of John Keys on the waters of Mary cr. a br. of James Riv., through the bush to the top of a rise, down the rise and up a draft, along the side of a hill and crossing a Spur to a Sink hole; 1 Feb 1781, p.449. A.C. of 20 Shill. Sterl.

WILLIAM LEWIS, 200 acs. by Survey 17 Oct 1774 in Augusta Co. on the head drafts of falling Spring a br. of the Middle riv. of Shanandore; adj. John King, Beverleys Manor Line; 1 Feb 1781, p.451. A.C. of £1 Sterl.

LACOSTA BRUMFIELD & COMPANY, 2 Lotts or parcels of L. and houses thereon in the Town of F[r]edricksburg Numbered in the plan of the town No. 15 and 16 and Bounded by Carolina, Sophia, and Hanover Streets and by Lotts No. 13 and 14; 1 Feb 1781, p.452. in consideration of the Sum of £40,200 current Money of Virginia paid unto Charles Washington Gentleman Escheator for Spotsylvania Co. by Lacoste Brumfield and company. which sd Lotts were Lately the Property of Ritchie & Company Subjects of great Britain and was Sold by the Sd Charles Washington Gentleman Escheator for the Co. aforesaid unto the sd Lacosta Brumfield and Company by Virtue of and agreeable to two Acts of General assembly passed in the year 1779 and Entitled an Act concerning Escheators and forfeitures from british Subjects and the other entitled an Act concerning Escheators. to the sd Lacoste Brumfield and Company and their heirs forever.

SAMUEL REDDY & JAMES TAYLOR, 2 Lotts with the houses thereon belonging in the Town of F[r]edricksburg and Numbered in the plan of the sd town 33 and 34 bounded by Caroline, Prusia and Princess Anne Streets and by the Lotts Numbered 35 & 36; 1 Feb 1781, p.453. in consideration of £41,100 current Money of Virginia paid to Charles Washington Esqr. Escheator for Spotsylvania Co. which Sd Lotts and Tenements were lately the Property of Cockran and Company Subje[c]ts of Great Britain and was Sold by the sd Charles Washington to the sd Samuel Reddy and James Taylor by Virtue of and agreeable to two Acts of General assembly pased in 1779. The one Intitled an Act Concerning Escheats and Forfeitures from British Subjects, the other Intitled an Act Concerning Escheators, with their Appurtenances.

Genl. GEORGE WEEDON, 300 acs. more or less by Certificate bearing Date 7 Sep 1780 in Spotsylvania Co. on fall hill near the Said town; bounded on one side by a tract of L. belonging to sd Weedon, by another side a tract of L. belonging to Mr. William Thompson which Said Thompson purchased of Allen Wiley; by another side a tract of L. belonging to Col. Edward Carter, and by another side a tract of L. belonging to Mr. Grayson a British Subject; 1 Feb 1781, p.454. £7,500 Current Money of Virginia paid to Charles Washington Escheator for Spotsylvania Co. and was Sold by the sd Charles Washington Escheator as aforesd unto the Said Genl. George Weedon agreeable to two Acts of Genl. Assembly passed in the year 1779 one Intitled an Act concerning Escheats and forfeitures from British Subjects and the other Intitled an Act concerning Escheators with its Appurtenances.

JAMES CURRY, 69 acs. by Survey 18 May 1780 in Augusta Co. on the NW side of his other tract; adj. Thomas Waddell, Robert Lewis, near sd Laws Cr. & Thomas Waddle; 1 Feb 1781, p.455. A.C. of 10 Shill. Sterl.

THOMAS WADDLE, 66 acs. by Survey 17 May 1780 in Augusta Co. on the NW side of his other tract; adj. James Curry, Thomas Waddle & Joseph Waddle; 1 Feb 1781, p.457. A.C. of 10 Shill. Sterl.

JOHN WARMSLEY/WARSLEY, 384 acs. by Survey 2 Dec 1767 in Rockbridge Co. formerly Augusta on the Mole hill a draft a br. of Looks cr., adj. Daniel Harrison; 1 Feb 1781, p.458. A.C. of 40 Shill. Sterl.

WILLIAM STARNET/STARNEL ass'ee of CHARLES PHILIPS who was Ass'ee of WILLIAM McGILL, 43 acs. by Survey 2 Sep 1760 in Augusta Co. on the S side of Buffaloe br., adj. William McGill & David Stewart; 1 Feb 1781, p.459. A.C. of 5 Shill. Sterl.

THOMAS FOSH, 120 acs. by Survey 10 Apr 1750 in Augusta Co. on Roanoke riv., with the Patent Line; 1 Feb 1781, p.460. A.C. of 15 Shill. Sterl. being part of a tract of L. Gtd. to Tasker Fosh by Pat. 20 Sep 1748 [PB 28 p.386 to Tasker Tosh, 200 acs. crossing Goose Cr.].

DANIEL McNARE, 525 acs. by Survey 9 Feb 1775 in Augusta Co. on both sides of the Middle riv. & Jennings br., on the N side of a high rock, near a draft, adj. George Moffet/Moffett; 1 Feb 1781, p.461. A.C. of 55 Shill. Sterl. including 174 acs. a part of 400 acs. first Gtd. by Sd Daniel McNare by Pat. 10 Jun 1740 the other 351 acs. never before Gtd.

[Margin note: *This Grant is founded upon a Settlement right for 400 Acres Granted to the said Shilby by the Commissioners of the Kentucky District & a preemption Warrant for 1000 Acres No. 18*]

ISAAC SHELBY, 1,400 acs. by Survey made ther rights Mentioned and dated 4 May 1780 in Lincoln Co. formerly Kentuckey on the waters of nob Lick a br. of the Hanging fork of Dicks Riv.; Beginning for the settlement tract of 400 acs. about 1¼ Mile SE of the Nobb Lick, to the S Bank of Nobb Lick Br. of the hanging fork, on the top of a high Clift of Rocks, to some flat Oak Land corner to his own 200 acs. tract, adj. his own Preemption tract;
the Preemption tract of 1,000 acs. adj. to the above Settlement & his own 200 acs. tract, to a Flat Caney Piece of Land on the S side of the sd Nobb Lick Br. of the Hanging Fork, on the Point of a Low Ridge;
22 Feb 1781, p.463. A.C. of £2 Sterl. unto the Treasury of this Commonwealth upon a Setlement Right of 400 acs. obtained by him from the Commissioners of the Kentuckey destrict and a Preemption Warrant adjoining such Settlement, issued to the sd Isaac Shelby 7 Feb 1780 which Warrant is of the No. 18.

[Margin note: *This Grant is founded on Charles Tomkies Military Warrant for 500 Acres and No. 130. two other Grants to compleate the Quantity will be found in the Book C, Pages 171 & 172*]

ISAAC SHELBY/SHILBY ass'ee of JOHN FOX who was ass'ee of sd CHARLES TOMKIES, 100 acs. by Survey made 4 May 1780 in Lincoln Co. formerly Kentuckey on the Waters of the Nob Lick Br. of the hanging fork of

Dicks Riv., Beginning in some high flatt Oak Land on the S side of the sd Nob Lick br. of the Hanging fork, adj. his own settlement Tract, on a high Clift of Rocks on the S bank of sd Nobb Lick br.; 22 Feb 1781, p.465. in consideration of Military Service Performed by Charles Tomkies as a Subaltern officer in the Late War between Great Britian and France according to the terms of the King of Great Britains Proclamation of 1763.

JAMES WARD ass'ee of JAMES McKEACHY who was ass'ee of THOMAS EAGAR who was ass'ee of JOHN EAGER, 140 acs. by Survey 25 Feb 1767 in Augusta Co. on the waters of Roanoke, on a ridge, by a road, adj. James Coghey; 1 Feb 1781, p.466. A.C. of 15 Shill. Sterl.

ABSALOM RAMEY, SENIOR, 330 acs. by Survey 12 Apr 1756 in Pittsylvania Co. formerly Halifax on the brs. of Allens cr.; 1 Feb 1781, p.467. A.C. of 35 Shill. Sterl.

JOHN RISK ass'ee of JOHN YOUNG, 156 acs. by Survey 2 Nov 1772 in Botetourt Co. Joining the Lines of John Young and Andrew Hayes's L. on the waters of Buffaloe Cr. a br. of James Riv.; also adj. Bordins Patent Line & sd John Youngues Lines; 1 Feb 1781, p.468. A.C. of £1 Sterl.

WILLIAM PERIGEN/PEREGEN, 300 acs. by Survey 11 May 1774 in Augusta Co. on the head of the west draft of Cooks Cr., on a ridge; adj. Jeremiah Harrisson, Jeremiah Regan, John Harrisson & Henry Ewing; 1 Feb 1781, p.469. A.C. of 30 Shill. Sterl.

PATRICK BAISON Ass ee of LEWIS GARRETT who was Ass'ee of JOSEPH DAVIS, 250 acs. by Survey 28 Feb 1778 in Botetourt Co. on the N side of the South Mountain, adj. the old Survey Lines, on the foot & a Spur of the Mountain, on the dividing ridge; 1 Feb 1781, p.471. A.C. of 25 Shill. Sterl. including a Survey made for Sd Joseph Davis 20 Apr 1775.

DAVID SRUM as Ass'ee of HENRY COLLIER, 186 acs. by Survey 20 Feb 1775 in Rockingham Co. formerly Augusta on the head brs. of Cortesses Run a br. of Shanandore Riv.; adj. his old c., William Lamb & sd Collier; 1 Sep [Feb] 1781, p.472. A.C. of 20 Shill. Sterl.

WILLIAM BATTERSON/BETTERSON, 434 acs. by Survey 1 Apr 1780 in Pittsylvania Co. on the waters of Allens cr.; adj. John Ballenger, Daugherty, George Allen, Lankford, Henderson, & John Buckley; 1 Feb 1781, p.473. including 46 acs. Surveyed for Thomas Davis 24 Feb 1770 and transferred to sd Betterson.

SAMUEL ERWIN, 167 acs. by Survey 1 Jul 1773 in Augusta Co. on both sides of the middle riv. of Shanandore, Beginning by the riv. near the Mouth of a draft; adj. James Allen, Barbara Smith, Robert Reed & William Oldham; 1 Feb 1781, p.475. A.C. of 10 Shill. Sterl. including 50 acs. Gtd. William Hamilton by Pat. 20 Jul 1768 and 47 acs. being part of a tract of 230 acs. Gtd. sd William Hamilton by pat. 29 May 1760 the remaining 70 acs. not before Surveyed.

JOHN BEARD, 923 acs. by Survey 10 Feb 1775 in Augusta Co. on both sides of Jennings br., crossing a Spring br., on a ridge; adj. James Campbell, Matthew

Edmiston, John Archer, George Moffett & Beards old C.; 1 Feb 1781, p.476. A.C. of 35 Shill. Sterl. including a tract of 183 acs. gtd. Thomas Bea[r]d by Pat. 10 Feb 1741 an 24 and 70 acs. both Gtd. to Sd John Beard by pat. 3 Aug 1771 also including 290 acs. Gtd. George Moffett by Pat. 1 Mar 1773 the Residue being 346 acs. new L. never Gtd.

EZEKIAH HOLLAND Ass'ee of JOHN HOLLAND who was ass'ee of JOHN BAKER, 226 acs. by Survey 24 Jan 1755 in Albemarle Co. on the N side the Rivanna riv. on both sides the Bird cr.; adj. his own Line, Timothy Lee & the Late Secretary Carter; 1 Feb 1781, p.479. A.C. of 25 Shill. Sterl.

JOHN DANIEL, 300 acs. by Survey 22 Apr 1780 in Henry Co. on both sides of bigg Dan riv., adj. Belcher; 1 Feb 1781, p.480. A.C. of 30 Shill. Sterl.

JAMES DICKEY & DAVID HENDERSON assignees of JOHN DICKENSON who was Ass'ee of ZOPHAN CARPENTER who was ass'ee of JAMES LAIRD, 19 acs. by Survey 2 Nov 1772 in Botetourt Co. on Snake run a br. of Dunlops Cr. being the waters of James Riv.; 1 Feb 1781, p.481. A.C. of 5 Shill. Sterl.

ROBERT BAKER, 205 acs. by Survey 4 Mar 1780 in Henry Co. on the waters of Green Cr., adj. Waltons otherwise Thomas Lows Line; 1 Feb 1781, p.482. A.C. of 25 Shill. Sterl.

FRANCIS HOLLY/HOLLEY, 140 acs. by Survey 15 Mar 1773 in Bedford Co. on the W side of Nobusiness Mountain; adj. Irwin, Cobb & Irvine; 1 Feb 1781, p.483. A.C. of 15 Shill. Sterl.

EZEKIAH HOLLAND Ass'ee of HENRY NASH, 400 acs. by Survey 28 Mar 1777 in Albemarle Co. on the N Side of Rivanna riv. and on the waters of the Great Byrd, to Kents br. a br. of the Great Bird aforesd; adj Hezekiah Holland, sd Nash, Peter Ross & Glasby; 1 Feb 1781, p.484. A.C. of 40 Shill. Sterl.

JEREMIAH SIMPSON, 367 acs. by Survey 30 Aug 1780 in Pittsylvania Co. formerly Halifax on a br. of the double Cr.; 1 Feb 1781, p.486. A.C. of 40 Shill. Sterl.

THOMAS JOHNSON, 27½ acs. by Survey 8 Dec 1779 in Hanover Co. on the N side of Chickahomy sw., down Turkey hill br. to an Elbow in the br., in the Low grounds of Chickahomony Sw.; 1 Feb 1781, p.487. A.C. of 5 Shill. Sterl.

ROBERT BAKER, 155 acs. by Survey 4 Mar 1780 in Henry Co. on Green Cr. Waters; adj. Walton, & Archeleus Hughe's new Line; 1 Feb 1781, p.488. A.C. of £1 Sterl.

PHILIP THOMAS, 47 acs. by Survey 7 Mar 1780 in Pittsylvania Co. on the brs. of Sandy Cr.; adj. William Derret, John Payne, Robert Williams, Lewis, & Birds Order Line; 1 Feb 1781, p.489. A.C. of 5 Shill. Sterl.

JOHN DINWIDDIE, 201 acs. by Survey 3 Apr 1780 in Augusta Co. on the East fork of Jacksons riv. Joining Ashtons tract, on a ridge; 1 Feb 1781, p.489. A.C. of £1 Sterl.

JOHN RAMEY, 400 acs. by Survey 19 Apr 1755 in Halifax Co. on the head brs. of the path fork of Buffaloe cr., crossing the Main br. of the Sd path fork, adj. Thomas Daughtey; 1 Feb 1781, p.491. A.C. of 40 Shill. Sterl.

THOMAS GRIFFITH, 135 acs. by Survey 14 Mar 1780 in Brunswick Co. on the S side of Meherrin Riv., up Plumb tree; adj. Edward Travis, Wall, Harwell, & Thomas Harrison; 1 Feb 1781, p.492. A.C. of 15 Shill. Sterl. [Plumb tree probably a br. of Poplar Cr.]

SAMUEL JOHNSTON, 272 acs. by Survey 30 Mar 1780 in Henry Co. on the waters of Leatherwood cr., on a Spur of Turkey Cock Mountain; adj. his Line, Dickenson & Willis or Wills; 1 Feb 1781, p.493. A.C. of 30 Shill. Sterl.

MICHAEL SELLARS, 106 acs. by Survey 13 Apr 1780 in Rockingham Co. on the W side of Smiths Cr., on the Point of a ridge, adj. Daniel Smith's Survey; 1 Feb 1781, p.494. A.C. of 15 Shill. Sterl.

JAMES WADDELL, 139 acs. by Survey 18 Mar 1780 in Augusta Co. Joining Beverleys Mannen on the S side of the South riv.; 1 Feb 1781, p.495. A.C. of 15 Shill. Sterl.

ADAM LACKEY, 900 acs. by Survey 2 May 1780 in Henry Co. on the head of Smiths riv., Dann Riv. and Rock castle; 1 Feb 1781, p.496. A.C. of £4.S10 Sterl.

ISAAC KINKLE/KINKEL/KINKELL Ass'ee of JAMES CUNNINGHAM, 85 acs. by Survey 28 Oct 1773 in Rockingham Co. formerly Augusta on the SE side of the North fork of the South br. of Potawmack at *Sugar Lick Gap*; 1 Feb 1781, p.497. A.C. of 10 Shill. Sterl.

JOHN SALMON, 81 acs. by Survey 17 May 1780 in Henry Co. on the brs. of Marrow bone Cr., adj. Harmour; 1 Feb 1781, p.498. A.C. of 10 Shill. Sterl.

JAMES DICKEY & DAVID HENDERSON Ass'ee of JOHN DICKENSON who was Ass'ee of ZOPHAR CARPENTER who was ass'ee of THOMAS KELLY and JAMES LAIRD, 400 acs. by Survey 2 Nov 1772 in Botetourt Co. on Snake run a br. of Dunlops cr. being the waters of James Riv., in a draft; 1 Feb 1781, p.499. A.C. of 40 Shill. Sterl.

RICHARD DICKONS, 594 acs. by Survey 15 Apr 1780 in Henry Co. on a cr. called Greys cr., adj. Greys Order Line; 1 Feb 1781, p.500. A.C. of £3 Sterl.

ISHAM HODGES, 249 acs. by Survey 3 Jun 1780 in Henry Co. on the brs. of Chesnut cr., adj. his own Line & Dickenson; 1 Feb 1781, p.501. A.C. of 25 Shill. Sterl.

WILLIAM WILSON, 175 acs. by Survey 18 Apr 1780 in Augusta Co. on the waters of Jacksons riv., in [the] mouth of a Gully, adj. [his] own tract; 1 Feb 1781, p.502. A.C. of 20 Shill. Sterl.

MICHAEL DICKEY, 73 acs. by Survey 2 Oct 1780 in Augusta Co. on some drafts of a br. of the North riv. of Shanandore on the NE side of his other L. his old Patent Line, also adj. James Hendersons L. & John Hinds Line; 1 Feb 1781, p.503. A.C. of 1 Shill. Sterl.

JOHN PIGG, 238 acs. by Survey 26 Apr 1780 in Pittsylvania Co. on both sides of Great Baraskin cr. and Little Baraskin cr., adj. the sd Piggs former Line & Bynom; 1 Feb 1781, p.504. A.C. of 25 Shill. Sterl.

JOHN LIGON, 135 acs. by Survey 21 Mar 1780 in Halifax Co. on Rockey br., crossing a bold br., on a ridge; adj. Waldon, Jones & Ligon; 1 Feb 1781, p.505. A.C. of 15 Shill. Sterl.

ADAM DUNLAP, 185 acs. by Survey 12 Nov 1773 in Augusta Co. on a br. of the Middle riv. of Shanandore; adj. his old Lines, Beverleys Line & James Kennerley; 1 Feb 1781, p.506. A.C. of 20 Shill. Sterl.

JAMES TAYLOR, 422 acs. by Survey 15 Apr 1780 in Henry Co. on the South fork of Nobusiness fork of Mayo; 1 Feb 1781, p.507. A.C. of 45 Shill. Sterl.

SAMUEL JOHNSON, 90 acs. by Survey 17 Mar 1772 in Henry Co. formerly Pittsylvania on the waters of Leatherwood cr., on the road, adj. Short & Lomax; 1 Feb 1781, p.508. A.C. of 10 Shill. Sterl.

JORDAN ANDERSON, 63½ acs. by Survey 6 Mar 1780 in Pr. Edward Co. on the brs. of falling cr.; adj. John Anderson, Bries and Hills Line, Stone & William Thaxton; 1 Feb 1781, p.508. A.C. of 10 Shill. Sterl.

CHRISTOPHER GRIFFITH /GRIFFETH, 90 acs. by Survey 28 May 1778 in Bedford Co. on the head brs. of South fork of Falling riv. on both sides of the main road, on the foot of a Long Mountain, adj. Richard Stith; 1 Feb 1781, p.509. A.C. of 10 Shill. Sterl.

ROBERT PEDIGROW, 206 acs. by Survey 4 Apr 1780 in Henry Co. on Beavers cr.; adj. Smith, Barnard & Barnett; 1 Feb 1781, p.510. A.C. of 25 Shill. Sterl.

THOMAS GLASS, 230 acs. by Survey 9 Oct 1772 in Halifax Co. on the draughts of Bluewing; adj. Street, Glidewell & Gills late Survey; 1 Feb 1781, p.511. A.C. of 25 Shill. Sterl.

SAMUEL JOHNSON Ass'ee of MOSES HODGES, 77 acs. by Survey 7 Feb 1774 in Pittsylvania Co. on Turkey br. of Banister Riv.; adj. Treadwell, Leak & Chamourlain; 1 Feb 1781, p.512. A.C. of 10 Shill. Sterl.

DANIEL GLASS Ass'ee of GEORGE MINOR, 334 acs. by Survey 30 Mar 1773 in Halifax Co. adj. Thomas Glass, Gledewell, Seth Petty Pool, Pooles Line, Mutter, Fields order Line & Gill; 1 Feb 1781, p.513. A.C. of 35 Shill. Sterl.

THOMAS ANDERSON, 10 acs. & 70 Poles by survey 28 Nov 1772 in Dinwiddie Co. adj. John Booth, his own Line & John Jones; 1 Feb 1781, p.514. A.C. of 5 Shill. Sterl.

CHARLES STOKES, 203 acs. by Survey 4 Mar 1754 in Halifax Co. on the brs. of Stuarts cr., adj. his own Line & Richard Wall; 1 Feb 1781, p.515. A.C. of £1 Sterl.

THOMAS SPRAGGINS, 220 acs. by Survey 1 Dec 1772 in Halifax Co. on the draughts of Childrie and Catawba creeks, crossing Bookers road; adj. Hunt, Street & Tinsley; 1 Feb 1781, p.515. A.C. of 25 Shill. Sterl.

JOHN ALLEN Ass'ee of DAVID DICK or DIEK, 60 acs. by Survey 21 Apr 1773 in Augusta Co. adj. the lines of Beverleys land on the Little Calf Pasteur a br. of James Riv., up a draft; 1 Feb 1781, p.516. A.C. of 10 Shill. Sterl.

HENRY MILLER, 518 acs. by Survey 4 May 1780 *and including a hill of Iron ore containing 118 acs.* in Augusta Co. on some drafts of the North riv. of Shanandore between the Land formerly John Trimbles and John McCarneys [also as MacCarney], by a Lick, on a ridge; 1 Feb 1781, p.517. A.C. of £2 Sterl. [Apparently there was no cost for the hill of Iron ore]

THOMAS PAXTON, 30 acs. by Survey 18 May 1763 in Augusta Co. upon the North br. of James Riv. adj. his own L., his old Survey; 1 Feb 1781, p.519. A.C. of 5 Shill. Sterl.

JOHN FIELDER ass'ee of THOMAS BELL, 43 acs. by Survey 13 Sep 1769 in Prince Edward Co. on the S side of Appomatox riv.; adj. Peak, Venable & Lancaster; 1 Feb 1781, p.520. A.C. of 5 Shill. Sterl.

JOSEPH BYBEE ass'ee of JOHN BYBEE, 274 acs. by Survey 18 Apr 1780 in Fluvanna Co. on both sides little Mychunk cr. and the North br. of the Rivanna Riv., adj. Robertson; 1 Feb 1781, p.521. A.C. of 30 Shill. Sterl.

JOHN SKIDMORE, 290 acs. by Survey 11 Apr 1775 in Augusta Co. on the SE side of Crab apple bottom, near the foot of the Mountain; 1 Feb 1781, p.522. A.C. of 30 Shill. Sterl.

AUGUSTINE PRICE, 170 acs. by Survey 29 Apr 1780 in Rockingham Co. Beginning at two pines said to be in a line of Franciscor [Francisco's] land; also adj. Peter Miller, the land formerly Jacob Persingers, & Ergebrignt; 1 Feb 1781, p.523. A.C. of £1 Sterl.

JOHN POAGE, 85 acs. by Survey 1 Jun 1768 in Rockbridge Co. formerly Augusta adj. his own Land in the fork of James Riv., Beginning in his old survey, by the great road; 1 Feb 1781, p.524. A.C. of 10 Shill. Sterl.

JOSEPH LANNIAM ass'ee of RICHARD McCARRY who was Ass'ee of WILLIAM FILLER, 98 acs. by Survey 18 Nov 1772 in Amherst Co. on the brs. of Dutch Cr. between the two tops of the Marrow bone Mountain; 1 Feb 1781, p.525. A.C. of 10 Shill. Sterl.

WILLIAM SHELTON, 20½ acs. by Survey 19 Oct 1779 in Albemarle Co. on the S side Mechums riv. and on the waters thereof, adj. John Gillum/Gilliam & James Coleman; 1 Feb 1781, p.525. A.C. of 5 Shill. Sterl.

AMBROSE JONES, 95 acs. by Survey 6 Feb 1769 in Pittsylvania Co. on a bold br. of Leatherwood Cr., adj. Copland; 1 Feb 1781, p.526. A.C. of 10 Shill. Sterl.

THOMAS TURK, 292 acs. by Survey 8 Apr 1780 in Augusta Co. adj. his own Land and Charles Teeses Land between the South Riv. and South Mountain; 1 Feb 1781, p.527. A.C. of 30 Shill. Sterl.

JOSIAH SMITH, 343 acs. by Survey 14 Apr 1780 in Henry Co. on Mayo Riv., adj. Jordan/Jourdan; 1 Feb 1781, p.528. A.C. of 35 Shill. Sterl.

[Margin note: *This Grant was altered in the name of Governour Harrison and dated 20th August because the Grant was made out before recorded before sign'd by Governour Jefferson who resign'd before it could be Signd of Seal'd*]

DAVID RALSTON, 48 acs. by Survey 22 Mar 1780 in Rockingham Co. on the E side of the south br. of Lenvils cr.; adj. Leonard Harris, Daniel Slover, his own L. & Coplin; 20 August 1783 in the 8th year of the Commonwealth, Benjamin Harrison Governor of the Commonwealth of Virginia, p.529. A.C. of 5 Shill. Sterl.

WILLIAM FLORNEY ass'ee of JAMES HARRIS who was ass'ee of JOHN McVIA, 113 acs. by Survey 22 Apr 1767 in Rockingham Co. formerly Augusta between beaver Cr. and Brier Br., adj Henry Black; 1 Feb 1781, p.530. A.C. of 15 Shill. Sterl.

HENRY TATE, 172 acs. by Survey 7 Apr 1780 in Henry Co. on the brs. of Smiths Riv., adj. Randolph & Chigley; 1 Feb 1781, p.531. A.C. of £1 Sterl.

RICHARD HARVIE, 137 acs. by Survey 16 Jun 1780 in Albemarle Co. on the side of the Rivanna Riv. and its brs., *on the road leading from Charlotsville to Thomas Carrs Mill*, to the North fork of Meadow cr.; adj. sd Richard Harvie, Nicholas Lewis, George Gilmer & Martin Hawkin's Line; 1 Feb 1781, p.532. A.C. of 15 Shill. Sterl.

GEORGE HARSTON & Co.: JOHN MARR AND THOMAS BEDFORD, 584 acs. by Survey 6 Apr 1780 in Henry Co. at a place called *the timber Level*, crossing a br. and a road; adj. Powers and Company, & Mordecai Hoards corner formerly Randolphs and Companys Line; 1 Feb 1781, p.533. A.C. of £3 Sterl.

WILLIAM BRADLEY ass'ee of sd JOHN MILLER BELL, a Certain Lott or parcel of Land containing ½ an Acre in the Town of Fairfax in Culpeper Co.; 12 Mar 1781, p.534. *in consideration of the Sum of £5,750 Current Money of the Commonwealth of Virginia paid by John Miller Bell to Joseph Wood Escheator for Culpeper Co. Lately the Property of Andrew Cockran and Company British Subjects and was Sold by the sd Joseph Wood Escheator as aforesd unto the sd John Miller Bell and by him assigned to the sd William Bradley agreeable to two Acts of assembly passed in the year 1779 the one Intitled an Act Concerning Escheats and forfeitures from British Subjects the other Intitled an Act concerning Escheators.*

FRANCIS HODGE Ass'ee of FRANCIS CRAVEN, 151¾ acs. by Survey 29 Sep 1779 in Albemarle Co. on the S side Rivanna Riv. and on some of the N brs. of Moore's cr.; adj. Nathaniel Haggard, Joseph Woodson & William Terrell Lewis; 1 Feb 1781, p.535. A.C. of 15 Shill. Sterl.

JAMES CAMPBELL, 98 acs. by Survey 18 Mar 1768 in Bedford Co. on brs. of the South fork of Beaver Cr., on a road, on Naked hill, adj. his own Line & Rutherford; 1 Feb 1781, p.536. A.C. of 10 Shill. Sterl.

WILLIAM SHELTON, 92½ acs. by Survey 20 Oct 1779 in Albemarle Co. on the S side Mechums riv. and on the waters thereof; adj. John Gillum/Gillium, Gamiliel Bailey, John Ellingon, Josiah Wallace & William Shelton; 1 Feb 1781, p.537. A.C. of 10 Shill. Sterl.

JOHN MILLS, 116 acs. by Survey 28 Nov 1772 in Botetourt Co. on the S side of James Riv.; adj. Joseph Looneys Survey, Looney's old Tract & sd Mills other tract; 1 Feb 1781, p.538. A.C. of

15 Shill. Sterl. [Included with John Mills's other 38 acs. part of Robert Luney's 250 acs. in PB 21 p.20 dated 30 Jul 1742 in an inclusive survey of 325 acs. to John Mills in GB 3 p.122, dated 22 June 1786, on Loony's Cr. and James Riv. adj. Captain William Crow and Andrew Boyd]

JOHN HOPKINS, 96 acs by Survey 26 May 1780 in Rockingham Co. and Hampshire Co. on the W side of the South br. of Powtomack, Beginning on the side of a Mountain and on the N side of red cr.; adj. Wolfs Land formerly Sheltons Tract, & George Kiles Line (part of sd Sheltons Tract); 1 Feb 1781, p.539. A.C. of 10 Shill. Sterl.

INGLE BOYER, 316 acs. by Survey 30 Mar 1780 in Rockingham Co. on the W side of Smiths Cr.; adj. John Armentrouts L., Hogus L., sd Hagues, a tract of Reuben Harrisson L. & William Hintons Survey; 1 Feb 1781, p.540. A.C. of 35 Shill. Sterl.

WILLIAM JETER JUNR., 401 acs. by Survey 11 Nov 1756 in Lunenburg Co. on the brs. of Little cr. [of Ledbetter's Cr.], adj. Bolton & Shelton; 1 Feb 1781, p.541.   A.C. of 40 Shill. Sterl. [Surrounded by PB 28 p.592 to Ralph Shelton, PB 35 p.203 to Edmund Belsher, PB 30 p.46 to Young Stokes & Henry Stokes & PB 34 p.244 to Robert Boulton]

DAVID PATTERSON, 165 acs. by Survey 11 Mar 1773 in Buckingham Co. on both sides of Sycamore Island cr., on the bank of the North fork of sd Cr., adj. his own and Samuel Spencer; 1 Feb 1781, p.542. A.C. of £1 Sterl.

ROBERT MATTHEW, 23 acs. by Survey 27 Mar 1780 in Rockingham Co. on the South fork of Lenvills cr.; adj. Coplins Line, David Ralstons Survey & Leonard Herrin; 1 Feb 1781, p.543. A.C. of 5 Shill. Sterl.

WILLIAM STOKES, 9½ acs. by Survey 8 Mar 1777 in Lunenburg Co. on the brs. of Reedy cr.; adj. Dozer, his own Line & Abanathey; 1 Feb 1781, p.544. A.C. of 5 Shill. Sterl.

ARCHELIUS HUGHES, 315 acs. by Survey 14 Apr 1780 in Henry Co. on Mill cr. of Mayo riv., to a post Oak in a Quarry of rocks, adj. his old Line; 1 Feb 1781, p.545. A.C. of 35 Shill. Sterl.

BENJAMIN PETTY POOLE/POOL, 346 acs. by Survey 6 May 1773 in Halifax Co. on the draughts of Aarons cr., on the South fork of Morrifs cr.; adj. sd Petty Pooles Line, Smith & Pryor; 1 Feb 1781, p.546. A.C. of 35 Shill. Sterl.

MICHAEL WARIN, 120 acs. by Survey 14 Apr 1780 in Rockingham Co. between the head of McCoyes and the Long Meadow Drafts, Beginning on the face of a Stoney ridge, crossing a Draft, adj. sd Warins patent Line & Brients Line; 1 Feb 1781, p.547. A.C. of 15 Shill. Sterl.

JOHN NEWKAM, 64 acs. by Survey 20 May 1780 in Albemarle Co. on the S side of the rivanna riv. and on the Meadows cr.; adj. John Abner, Martin Hawkin & George Gilmer; 1 Feb 1781, p.548. A.C. of 10 Shill. Sterl.

JOSEPH PULLIAM, 400 acs. by Survey 2 Feb 1771 in Halifax Co. on the Brs. of difficult Cr.; adj. Aaron Williams, sd Pulliams old Lines, Richard Wall, Daniel

Wall & John Tucker; 1 Feb 1781, p.549. A.C. of 40 Shill. Sterl.

KENNETH McCOLLIN, 31 acs. by Survey 26 Oct 1771 in Botetourt Co. Joining the Land of Stapleton on the S brs. of Roanoke; 1 Feb 1781, p.551. A.C. of 5 Shill. Sterl.

JOSEPH DOUGLASS, 17 acs. by Survey 18 May 1780 in Rockingham Co. Opposite to the head of fishers cr., in a hollow, adj. John Mcloyes Land & his Land formerly Boyds; 1 Feb 1781, p.552. A.C. of 5 Shill. Sterl.

JOHN RAMSEY, 74 acs. by Survey 5 Apr 1780 in Augusta Co. between his own Land and the South Mountain and a br. of the South riv.; 1 Feb 1781, p.552. A.C. of 10 Shill. Sterl.

JAMES McGILL, 220 acs. by Survey 19 May 1780 in Rockingham Co. on the S side of the North Riv. of Shanandore, by the road; adj. the land he lives on, his patent Land, Francis Ervin, & John Davies's Survey; 1 Feb 1781, p.553. A.C. of 25 Shill. Sterl.

JOSEPH DOUGLASS, 58 acs. by Survey 19 May 1780 in Rockingham Co. on the head drafts of Fiers Spring, adj. his Land formerly Boyds & a Line of his other tract; 1 Feb 1781, p.554. A.C. of 10 Shill. Sterl.

WILLIAM WARD Ass'ee of CHRISTOPHER EYE, 35 acs. by Survey 27 Mar 1772 in Augusta Co. on Black Thorn a br. of the South br. of Powtomack, adj. his old Tract; 1 Mar 1781, p.555. A.C. of 5 Shill. Sterl.

Colo. WILLIAM THORNTON, 800 acs. in Culpeper Co. on a high Point near the riv., to the Edge of Wrights Mountain, on the side of a mountain, up white Walnut run; adj. Colo. John Slaughter, Green & Col. John Thornton; 1 Mar 1781, p.556. A.C. *Sum of £15,300 paid unto Joseph Wood Escheator for Culpeper Co. Late the Property of John Sarjeant a British Subject and was Sold by the sd Joseph Woodson unto the aforesd William Thornton agreeable to two Acts of Assembly passed in the year 1779 the one Entitled an Act concerning Escheats and forfeitures from British Subjects the other Entitled an Act concerning Escheators.*

~~THOMAS~~ THEOPHILUS CHERRY & JOSEPH BALLENTINE, 111 acs. by Survey 2 Jun 1780 in Norfolk Co. adj. John Campbells Lands; 1 Mar 1781, p.558. A.C. of 15 Shill. Sterl.

PHILIP RYAN, 108 acs. by Survey 15 Apr 1780 in Pittsylvania Co. on the brs. of Streight Stone cr.; adj. Cornelius McHaney, William Chick, Hubbard & Collins; 1 Mar 1781, p.559. A.C. of 15 Shill. Sterl.

MOSSER GRIMES, 71 acs. by Survey 27 Apr 1780 in Norfolk Co. adj. sd Mosser Grimes L.; 1 Mar 1781, p.560. A.C. of 10 Shill. Sterl.

ROBERT LANGLEY Ass'ee of JULIAS NICHOLAS, 400 acs. by Survey 29 Oct 1754 in Lunenburg Co. on the Huckelberry br. of Great Cr. of Roanoke; adj. William Riddle, Julias Nicholas & William Nance; 1 Mar 1781, p.561. A.C. of £2 Sterl. [For William Riddle's see PB 29 p.487 to Joseph Hickman, for William Nance's see PB 33 p.223, also adj. PB 14 p.80 to Robert Hicks]

WILLIAM SERJEANT Ass'ee of JAMES PULLAM who was Ass'ee of JOHN

HELM, 320 acs. by Survey 24 Nov 1768 in Bedford Co. on both sides of Rough fork of Seneca Cr.,; adj. Aquela Gilbert [his Line] & Murray; 1 Mar 1781, p.562. A.C. of 35 Shill. Sterl.

JOHN STRANGE, 391 acs. by Survey 13 Apr 1780 in Fluvanna Co. on the waters of Ballengers Cr. and the N waters of Rivanna riv., crossing Martin Kings road and South road, adj. Daniel King & John Strange; 1 Mar 1781, p.563. A.C. of £2 Sterl.

JAMES MURPHEY Ass'ee of PETER COPELAND, 51 acs. by Survey 9 Feb 1769 in Pittsylvania Co. on the draughts of Daniels Mill cr., adj. his old Line & Bucknels Line; 1 Mar 1781, p.564. A.C. of 5 Shill. Sterl.

JAMES PREWIT, 400 acs. by Survey 9 Dec 1771 in Halifax Co. on the draughts of cow cr., crossing Hickeys road, crossing Cherry tree, adj. Adams & Tyins; 1 Mar 1781, p.565. A.C. of £2 Sterl.

JOHN JONES, 391 acs. by Survey 7 Jun 1779 in Henry Co. on the brs. of Turners cr. and Nicholasses Cr., adj. Thomas Jones; 1 Mar 1781, p.566. A.C of £2 Sterl.

TURNER RICHARDSON, 41½ acs. by Survey 16 Apr 1780 in Fluvanna Co. on the Brs. of Raccoon Cr. and S brs. of the Rivanna Riv., adj. Stone & Cockran; 1 Mar 1781, p.567. A.C. of 5 Shill. Sterl.

PETER COPELAND, 300 acs. by Survey 25 Apr 1768 in Pittsylvania Co. on Little beaver Cr., adj. his Order Line; 1 Feb 1781, p.568. A.C. of 30 Shill. Sterl.

RICHARD NUTT, 306½ acs. by Survey 26 Apr 1780 in Fluvanna Co. on the brs. of Careys Cr. and S brs. of the Rivanna Riv.; adj. Mayo, Nutt & Strange; 1 Mar 1781, p.569. A.C. of 35 Shill. Sterl.

ANTHONY ASKEW, 400 acs. by Survey 4 Feb 1778 in Fluvanna Co. on the brs. of Ballenger's Cr. and N brs. of the Rivanna riv.; adj. Taylor, Bellomy, Moore, Robinson, Robertson, Eads Line & Bethel; 1 Mar 1781, p.570. A.C. of £2 Sterl.

JAMES DOSS, 42 acs. by Survey 14 Mar 1780 in Bedford Co. on the N side of Staunton riv. adj. Canefax/Canifax & Alford; 1 Mar 1781, p.571. A.C. of 5 Shill. Sterl.

WILLIAM OWEN Ass'ee of THOMAS JAMES, 37 acs. by Survey 17 Nov 1767 in Albemarle Co. on the Top of a mountain on the blue ridge called the Bucks elbow, by a Spring, adj. William McCord; 1 Mar 1781, p.572. A.C. of 5 Shill. Sterl.

JOHN SCOTT, JUNIOR, 158 acs. by Survey 17 fEB 1779 in Fluvanna Co. on the waters of Cunninghams cr. and S brs. of Rivanna Riv., crossing the Secretaries road/Secretary's road; adj. Benjamin Fitzpatrick, Scott, Patrick Napier, Richard Nutt & Ross; 1 Mar 1781, p.573. A.C. of £1 Sterl.

[Margin note: *This Grant was altered in the name of Governour Harrison and dated the 20th. August 1783 because the Grant was not made out and recorded before Signed by Governour Jefferson who resign'd before it Could be Signed or Seald*]

WILLIAM McGEHEE, SENIOR, 204 acs. by Survey 23 Apr 1774 in Albemarle Co. partly on *the white Oak bottom*; adj. Giles Allegree, Charles Christian & John Burrass/Burruss; 20 Aug 1783 in the 8th year of the Commonwealth, p.575. A.C. of £1 Sterl.

WILLIAM RUSSELL heir of the sd HENRY RUSSELL, 2,000 acs. by Survey 12 Jul 1774 in [Kentucky] County formerly Fincastle on a N br. of Kentuckey riv. about 94 Miles from the Ohio Riv. and on the S side thereof, on a rise, adj. Alexander Spotswood's Dandridge Land; 1 Mar 1781, p.576. *in consideration of Military service Performed by Henry Russell as a Subaltern in the Late war and by Virtue of the King of Great Britains Proclamation of 1763 and Lord Dunmores Warrant.*

ABRAHAM DOOLY ass'ee of ISHAM TALBOT, 425 acs. by Survey 3 Jun 1772 in Botetourt Co. on Jennings cr.; 1 Mar 1781, p.577. A.C. of 45 Shill. Sterl. Including a Survey of sd Abraham Dooley of 80 acs.

MAJOR CHILDRESS, 108 acs. by Survey 15 Apr 1780 in Pittsylvania Co. on the brs. of streight stone Cr., adj. Francis Luck & Cornelius Machany; 1 Mar 1781, p.578. A.C. of 15 Shill. Sterl.

PALIKAH SHELTON, 109 acs. by Survey 14 Mar 1768 in Pittsylvania Co. on the South forks of Russels cr., adj. Walton; 1 Mar 1781, p.579. A.C. of 15 Shill. Sterl.

SAMUEL HUBBARD Ass'ee of DAVID ROBINSON, 234 acs. by Survey 23 Feb 1769 in Bedford Co. on both sides of a S br. of Bear cr. and including the head; adj. William Pursley, James Robinson & Daniel; 1 Mar 1781, p.580. A.C. of 25 Shill. Sterl.

HENRY KELLAM, 800 acs. more or Less in Pr. Anne Co. and Lynhaven Par., Beginning on a cove of the riv. dividing this L. from the L. of Mrs. Tenants, on the road side, adj. Mr. Walker; 1 Mar 1781, p.581. *in consideration of the Sum of £34,400 current Money paid by Henry Kellam unto Thomas R. Walker Gentleman Escheator for Princess Anne Co. ... Lately the Property of John Saunders a British Subject and was sold by sd Thomas R. Walker Escheator aforesd unto Henry Kellam agreeable to two Acts of Assembly passed in 1779 the one Intitled an Act conerning Escheats and forfeitures from British Subjects and the other Intitled an Act Concerning Escheators.*

JOHN SIMMONS, 638 acs. by Survey 3 Dec 1779 in Henry Co. on the Grassey Cr. of Smith's Riv., crossing the sd Grassy fork, adj. John Rowland; 1 Mar 1781, p.582. A.C. of £3.S5 Sterl.

JAMES SHARD, 432 acs. by Survey 3 Mar 1780 in Henry Co. and Mayo Waters, up the North Mayo Riv.; adj. James Roberts, George Taylor & Hughe's Line; 1 Mar 1781, p.583. A.C of 45 Shill. Sterl.

THOMAS HARRISS, 996 acs. by **an Inclusive Survey** 11 May 1775 in Pr. Geo. Co. on the E side of Black water Sw., in the Middle of the Cat Tail br., down the main run of sd Cat Tail; adj. Morrisson, Robert Hunnicut & Barnaby Syke's c.; 1 Mar 1781, p.584. A.C. of £2

Sterl. 600 acs. of which being old Land the residue 396 new Land.

GEORGE HARSTON, 442 acs. by Survey 24 Nov 1779 in Henry Co. on the waters of Smith's Riv., Beginning at a Road; 1 Mar 1781, p.585. A.C. of 45 Shill. Sterl.

THOMAS CHOWNING, 185 acs. by Survey 1 Feb 1769 in Henry Co. formerly Pittsylvania on Smiths Riv., Drag cr. and Turkey cock Cr., adj. James Elkin & Gilley; 1 Mar 1781, p.586. A.C. of £1 Sterl.

JESSE WILLINGHAM, 135 acs. by Survey 15 May 1780 in Henry Co. on the brs. of Marrow bone cr., adj. Andrew Rea; 1 Mar 1781, p.587. A.C. of 15 Shill. Sterl.

JOHN SIMS, 172 acs. by Survey 2 Mar 1780 in Henry Co. on both sides of South Mayo Riv., Beginning at Fontain's C. on the Country Line at Guilford and Surry Counties, crossing crooked Cr., with the Country Line [West], also adj. Walton; 1 Mar 1781, p.588. A.C. of £1 Sterl.

JOHN WILSON, 80 acs. by Survey 9 Nov 1780 in Pittsylvania Co. on the brs. of Dann Riv. on the N side, crossing the still house br.; adj. sd Wilsons old Lines, John Stones Line now sd Wilsons, & Silvesters Adams [his] Line; 1 Mar 1781, p.589. A.C. of 10 Shill. Sterl.

JAMES HAGGARD, 235 acs. by Survey 18 Apr 1780 in Fluvanna Co. on the brs. of great Mychunk cr. and N brs. of the Rivanna riv.; adj. Bybee, Gilbert, Clark, Howard, Priddy & Allegree; 1 Mar 1781, p.590. A.C. of 25 Shill. Sterl.

WILLIAM BROOKS, 204 acs. by Survey 26 Feb 1756 in Bedford Co. on both sides of the South fork of Falling Riv., adj. Wathen; 1 Mar 1781, p.591. A.C. of £1 Sterl.

WILLIAM MOSS, 390 acs. by Survey 8 Jan 1777 in Bedford Co. on the N brs. of Phelps cr.; adj. Dougherty, McCown & Pruit; 1 Mar 1781, p.592. A.C. of £2 Sterl.

JOHN COLYER ass'ee of JOHN CONWAY, 351 acs. by Survey 17 Mar 1772 in Henry Co. formerly Pittsylvania on the brs. of Leatherwood Cr.; adj. James Bliver, Bolling, Christopher Bolling, Lomax & Blevin; 1 Mar 1781, p.593. A.C. of 35 Shill. Sterl.

BENJAMIN KINLEY, 208 acs. by Survey 23 Mar 1780 in Rockingham Co. on Anthonys Spring a br. of Lenvills cr., near a Sink hole, near a Glade; adj. Townsend Matthews's Land, Ervins well place & sd Ervins c.; 1 Mar 1781, p.594. A.C. of 25 Shill. Sterl.

CARY HARRISON Ass'ee of JOHN TAYLOR, 204 acs. by Survey 21 Mar 1760 in Bedford Co. on both sides of Slippery Gut a small S cr. of Fluvanna Riv., Beginning on sd Cr. at a great Stone; 1 Mar 1781, p.595. A.C. of £1 Sterl.

THOMAS RODGERS, 380 acs. by Survey 17 Mar 1779 in Charlotte and Bedford Counties on both sides of Turnup Cr.; adj. Rodgers, Mason, Watkins & John Phelp's Lines; 1 Mar 1781, p.596. A.C. of £1 Sterl. 200 acs. of which was Gtd. to the sd Thomas Rodgers by Pat. 20 Sep 1748 [204 acs.

Lunenburg Co. in PB 28 p.440] the Residue 180 acs. new land.

RICHARD RUNNOLDS, 312 acs. by Survey 18 Mar 1780 in Henry Co. on Smiths Riv., up Rock castle cr.; adj. sd Runnolds's own Old Line, Matthew Small, Elizabeth Crowly [his Line?], Valentine Mayo, & Hutchings's and Company's Line; 1 Mar 1781, p.598. A.C. of 35 Shill. Sterl.

JOHN MITCHELL, 379 acs. by Survey 12 Nov 1779 in Henry Co. on the brs. of Rockey br. of Sandy Riv.; adj. Samuel Moseley, Thomas Callaway & his old Line; 1 Mar 1781, p.599. A.C. of £2 Sterl.

HENRY SUMPTER, 1,494 acs. by Survey 7 Apr 1780 in Henry Co. on Rock Run and Ramseys cr. Waters; adj. Randolph and Company's Line, his old Line, & Hairston and Companys new Line; 1 Mar 1781, p.600. A.C of £7.S10 Sterl.

NICHOLAS CONNER, 504 acs. by Survey 10 Mar 1773 in Buckingham Co. on both sides of the middle fork of Slate Riv., adj. his own Line; 1 Mar 1781, p.601. A.C. of 50 Shill. Sterl.

DANIEL CRENSHAW Ass'ee of SILVANUS WALKER who was heir at Law of TANDY WALKER, 300 acs. by Survey 21 Nov 1748 in Lunenburg Co. on both sides the South fork of Juniper Cr., adj. Ellis; 1 Mar 1781, p.602. A.C. of 30 Shill. Sterl. [For Ellis's land, see PB 34, p.278 to James Roberts. Also see adj. land in PB 34, p.471 to Joseph Williams executor of Thomas Williamson; PB 36, p.645 to Thomas Nance; PB 36, p.646 to Reps Osborne; and GB F, p.430 to George Walton]

SILAS WHORLEY/WHORLY ass'ee of THOMAS DOSS, 92 acs. by Survey 30 Nov 1772 in Buckingham Co. on the Brs. of Wreck Island cr., crossing Stovals road; adj. his own Line, William Duiguid, William Gilliam & Charles Witt; 1 Mar 1781, p.603. A.C. of 10 Shill. Sterl.

RALPH FLOWERS, 332 acs. by Survey 16 Nov 1779 in Buckingham Co. on the S brs. of Middle Slate riv. and on both sides of Pick Skin Road; adj. his old Line, John Hardiman, Capt. John Moseley & Thomas Jones; 1 Mar 1781, p.604. A.C. of £2 Sterl.

JOHN RICHARDSON, 129 acs. by Survey 15 May 1780 in Henry Co. on the brs. of Marrow bone Cr., adj. John Hardman/Hardiman; 1 Mar 1781, p.605. A.C. of 15 Shill. Sterl.

JOHN WIMBISH, 400 acs. by Survey 9 Feb 1774 in Pittsylvania Co. on Bearskin cr., adj. Roberts; 1 Mar 1781, p.606. A.C. of £2 Sterl.

JEMMY & JOHN JAMES, 400 acs. by Survey 12 Nov 1753 in Henry Co. formerly Halifax on both sides Turkey cock Cr., Beginning in a fall of sd cr., cross Rackoon br.; 1 Mar 1781, p.606. A.C. of 40 Shill. Sterl.

JOHN WIMBISH, 300 acs. by Survey 9 Feb 1774 in Pittsylvania Co. on Little cr.; 1 Mar 1781, p.607. A.C. of 30 Shill. Sterl.

DAVID CHADWELL, 110 acs. by Survey 13 Dec 1773 in Henry Co.

formerly Pittsylvania on the S side of Smiths Riv., adj. his Lines; 1 Mar 1781, p.608. A.C. of 15 Shill. Sterl.

DAVID HUNT, 174 acs. by Survey 8 Feb 1775 in Pittsylvania Co. on the Brs. of Streight Stone Cr.; adj. James Jones, John Jones, Brown, & George Keesee; 1 Mar 1781, p.609. A.C. of £1 Sterl.

CORNELIUS HILYARD, 200 acs. by Survey 2 May 1771 in Rockingham Co. formerly Augusta on Smiths cr.; 1 Mar 1781, p.610. A.C. of £1 Sterl.

DAVID McCLOURE/McCLURE, 390 acs. by Survey 22 Apr 1780 in Rockbridge Co. on the Great pond & by the Little pond; 1 Mar 1781, p.611. A.C. of 40 Shill. Sterl.

PETER WRIGHT, 176 acs. by Survey 29 Oct 1772 in Botetourt Co. on James Riv., Beginning on the Riv. Just below Kincades Land; 1 Mar 1781, p.612. A.C. of £1 Sterl. including 64 acs. formerly Gtd. by Pat. to sd Peter Wright.

JAMES GRIGSBY/GRIGGSBY Ass'ee of JAMES CORBET, 73 acs. by Survey 15 Mar 1779 in Rockbridge Co. in the Forks of James Riv.; adj. Samuel Braford, James Corbet, Joseph Walker & Wood; 1 Mar 1781, p.613. A.C. of 10 Shill. Sterl.

FRANCIS GILLEY, 444 acs. by Survey 18 Apr 1768 in Henry Co. formerly Pittsylvania on Turkey Cock cr.; 1 Mar 1781, p.614. A.C. of 45 Shill. Sterl.

FRANCIS KERBY Ass'ee of JOSIAH KERBY, 584 acs. by Survey 30 Nov 1778 in Henry Co. on the Pole Cat br. of Pigg Riv. on Owens Cr., adj. Walter Maxey & Davis; 1 Mar 1781, p.616. A.C. of £3 Sterl.

ROBERT BOLTON, 1,319 acs., 1,176 acs. by Survey 25 Nov 1778 exclusive of 143 acs. Gtd. by pat. to William Young and now Transferred to the sd Robert Bolton, in Henry Co. on both sides of Snow Cr., at the road; adj. Copeland, his own old Line, Stephen Senter & Copelands Order Line; 1 Mar 1781, p.617. A.C. of £6 Sterl.

JOHN RUNYAN, 98 acs. by Survey 26 Feb 1773 in Rockingham Co. in *Brocks Gap* on both sides of Turners Cr.; 1 Mar 1781, p.618. A.C. of 10 Shill. Sterl.

JOHN JUDD Ass'ee of MORRIS MacKENNY, 39 acs. by Survey 20 Mar 1780 in Brunswick Co. adj. John Jones, Joshua Hightower, John Fisher, John Latimer, Jack Latimer & Judds old Line; 1 Mar 1781, p.619. A.C. of 5 Shill. Sterl. [N of Waqua Cr. near Possum Quarter Br.]

THOMAS HOLLINGSWORTH, 52 acs. by Survey 28 Apr 1768 in Henry Co. formerly Pittsylvania Co. on both sides Blackberry Cr.; 1 Mar 1781, p.620. A.C. of 5 Shill. Sterl.

WILLIAM HENCOCK Ass'ee of DAVID DURHAM, 400 acs. by Survey 1 Jan 1773 in Pr. Edward Co. on the heads of Sawners Cr.; adj. Emry, Jenning & Porter; 1 Mar 1781, p.621. A.C. of £2 Sterl.

CHARLES CLAY, 121 acs. by Survey 25 Mar 1780 in Bedford Co. on the Brs. of Elk cr.; adj. his own Line, Forguson, Rowland, Burton & Cobb; 1 Mar 1781, p.622. A.C. of 15 Shill. Sterl.

THOMAS CHOWNING, 200 acs. by Survey 20 Mar 1778 in Henry Co. on the Brs. of Turkey Cock Cr. of Smiths Riv., crossing a Large Br. of Turkey Cock, adj. James Bowling & Webb; 1 Mar 1781, p.623. A.C. of £1 Sterl.

OWEN WEST, 45 acs. by Survey 14 Jun 1780 in Pittsylvania Co. on the brs. of Streight Stone Cr., on the road; adj. Thomas Dillard, Hubbards old Line & Edward King; 1 Mar 1781, p.624. A.C. of 5 Shill. Sterl.

HENRY HALL, 146 acs. by Survey 24 Apr 1780 in Pittsylvania Co. on the brs. of Cherry stone cr., adj. Thomas Hardy; 1 Mar 1781, p.624. A.C. of 15 Shill. Sterl.

JOHN CALFERRY, 223 acs. by Survey 14 Dec 1754 in Bedford Co. formerly Albemarle on both sides of Beaver Cr. on the S side of the Fluvanna Riv., adj. John Harey [Harvey]; 1 Mar 1781, p.625. A.C. of 25 Shill. Sterl.

LEWIS CIRCLE, 300 acs. by Survey 3 Jun 1774 in Augusta Co. on the E side of Smiths cr., on a ridge, adj. Andrew Huland & John Philips; 1 Mar 1781, p.626. A.C. of 30 Shill. Sterl.

DAVID RODES/ROADS, 66 acs. by Survey 19 Mar 1773 in Albemarle Co. on the side of Jameson's Mountain and waters of Rockey Cr., near a dry br., on the Top of a mountain, adj. William Crafford; 1 Mar 1781, p.628. A.C. of 10 Shill. Sterl.

EDMUND WINSTON, 250 acs. by Survey 13 Feb 1773 in Bedford Co. on the S Sides of Fluvanna riv., on the top of a high ridge, down Joe's br., adj. his own old Lines; 1 Mar 1781, p.629. A.C. of 25 Shill. Sterl.

JOHN THOMAS, 126 acs. by Survey 6 Apr 1779 in Pittsylvania Co. on the Brs. of fall cr.; adj. Smith, the order Line & John Walton; 1 Mar 1781, p.630. A.C. of 15 Shill. Sterl.

JOSIAS COFFER, 94 acs. by Survey 10 Apr 1771 in Bedford Co. on the brs. of Elk cr.; adj. Joshua Earley, Jocob Early & his own Line; 1 Mar 1781, p.631. A.C. of 10 Shill. Sterl.

JAMES MATTHEWS, 110 acs. by Survey 19 Mar 1771 in Buckingham Co. on the head of Davids Cr., adj. William Still; 1 Mar 1781, p.631. A.C. of 15 Shill. Sterl.

JOHN WELSH, 1 Lott in Spotsylvania Co. in the town of Fredericksburg and Numbered in the plan of sd town 257 and bounded by Caroline and Paussia [Prussia] Streets and by Lotts numbered 267, 256 and 266; 10 Apr 1781, p.633. *in Consideration of the Sum of £10,100 Current Money of Virginia unto Charles Washington Escheator for Spotsylvania Co. which sd lott was lately the property of William Wims a Subject of Great Britain and was Sold by the sd Charles Washington escheator as aforesd unto the sd John Welsh agreable to two Acts of Assembly passed in the year 1779 the one entittled an Act concerning escheats and forefeitures from British Subjects the other entittled An Act concerning Escheators.*

JOSEPH HAWKINS Ass'ee of AUSTIN BURNLEY who was Ass'ee of JAMES HILL who was Ass'ee of THOMAS LEWIS, 191 acs. by Survey 18 Apr 1771 in Botetourt Co. on the brs. of Glade Cr. being the waters of Roanoke, adj. Baptist Armstrong; 1 Mar 1781, p.634. A.C. of £1 Sterl.

WILLIAM TABLER & CHRISTIAN VINEYARD Ass'ee of JOHN MacADOW/McADOW, 115 acs. by Survey 2 May 1774 in Botetourt Co. on the waters of Wolf cr. Joining the Survey the sd McAdow lives on, on a ridge; 10 Apr 1781, p.635. A.C. of 15 Shill. Sterl.

JOHN WILSON, 174 acs. by Survey 2 Feb 1769 in Henry Co. formerly Pittsylvania on Smiths Riv.; adj. his old line, Lomax & Web; 1 Mar 1781, p.636. A.C. of £1 Sterl.

THOMAS STILL heir at Law of WILLIAM STILL who was Ass'ee of JOSEPH HAMMON, 1,000 acs. by Survey 2 Apr 1754 in Albemarle Co. on both sides of Davids and fish pond creeks, Beginning on the N side of Bairds road, adj. Philip Mayo & his own line; 1 Mar 1781, p.637. A.C. of £5 Sterl. [This land is near the Appamattox Ridge, see sd Mayo's PB 31 p.653 dated 10 Sep 1755]

JAMES DILLARD, 400 acs. by Survey 17 Mar 1763 in Amherst Co. on both sides of Porrige cr.; adj. his own line, James Christian, Edward Cottrell & Joseph Mayo; 1 Mar 1781, p.638. A.C. of £2 Sterl.

MILES JENNINGS, 453 acs. by Survey 17 May 1780 in Henry Co. on Mayo Riv., crossing a road; adj. his own line, Daniel Goodsby, William Hayes line, Lambeth Dotson, Bradley Smith & Jesse Atkeison; 1 Mar 1781, p.639. A.C. of 45 Shill. Sterl.

ABEL GRIFFITH ass'ee of JAMES McCOY, 160 acs. by Survey 15 Jun 1762 in Augusta Co. on the N side of Mossey cr. and Joining the sd James McCoys land, by a path, near a road, also adj. Minters land; 1 Mar 1781, p.640. A.C. of £1 Sterl.

WILLIAM SOWELL/SOWEL, 96½ acs. by Survey 1 Apr 1775 in Albemarle Co. on the N Side the Fluvanna Riv. on the little Mountains in the south Garden and on a br. of South Hardware, adj. Jeremiah White & Charles Hudson; 1 Mar 1781, p.641. A.C. of 10 Shill. Sterl.

WALTER CROW, 216 acs. by Survey 15 Apr 1780 in Rockingham Co. on the heads of a draft of Lenvills cr. on the E side of the land he lives on, Beginning in a meadow, crossing a draft; adj. the Patent Land, Leonard Herrins Survey, Jerry Raggin, sd Ragins line & Eversole; near a Corner of Fraziers land & near a Corner of Curries land; 1 Mar 1781, p.643. A.C. of 25 Shill. Sterl.

WILLIAM CORNET ass'ee of JOSEPH PAINE who was ass'ee of THOMAS BOAZ, 72 acs. by Survey 15 Mar 1771 in Buckingham Co. on both sides the North fork of Holliday Riv., crossing the two Main brs. of the Aforesd riv., adj. Thomas Boaz his own line [GB D p.725]; 1 Mar 1781, p.645. A.C. of 10 Shill. Sterl.

JOSEPH WEST, 404 acs. by Survey 13 Jun 1780 in Pittsylvania Co. on the brs. of Straight Stone and Maggotty creeks; adj. Benjamin Gudger, Anderson, Stephen Clement, William Short, Robert Brewis, Keesee, John Barrett, William Duning & Thomas Clark; 1 Mar 1781, p.646. A.C. of £2 Sterl.

GEORGE HARSTON ass'ee of ELISHA WALLING, 467 acs. by Survey 24 Nov 1779 in Henry Co. on the N side of Smiths riv., crossing Mill cr., adj. Randolphs order otherwise the sd Harstons old line & Copelands line; 1 Mar 1781, p.647. A.C. of 50 Shill. Sterl.

JAMES BUCHANNAN, 128 acs. by Survey 1 Jul 1772 in Botetourt Co. Joining the lines of his own and John Bowyers l. on the waters of Buffaloe cr. a br. of James Riv., by a point of Rocks, on a hill Side by the great road, by the Mouth of a draft, up the Spurr of a hill, cross the run and two Gulleys to below the head of a Spring; 1 Mar 1781, p.649. A.C. of 15 Shill. Sterl.

WILLIAM JOHNSON, 245 acs. by Survey 7 Jun 1780 in Albemarle Co. on the S side the Rivanna riv. and on its waters, to the road leading from Charlotts ville to Thomas Carrs Mill, to a new road leading to the Barracks, on a N br. of Meadow cr.; adj. sd Johnson, Samuel Carr dec'd, Richard Harvie, Martin Hawkins, Thomas Carr & Rober[t] Adams; 1 Mar 1781, p.651. A.C. of 25 Shill. Sterl. including 90 acs. formerly Surveyed.

BENNET HENDERSON, 247 acs. by Survey 10 Jun 1780 in Albemarle Co. on some of the S brs. of Hardware riv. and Among the little Mountains Adj. the South Garden, on the top of a mountain; adj. his own line, William Moore, Thomas Martin, Thomas Tadlock & James Boyd; 1 Mar 1781, p.654. A.C. of 25 Shill. Sterl.

HENRY ALLEY, 111 acs. 109 poles by Survey 20 May 1780 in Pr. Geo. Co. on both sides of the great Br. of Warwick Sw., near the head of the Wolf pit br., on the S side of the Bull br.; adj. sd Alleys own line, Samuel Lee, James Baugh & Peter Roser [Rosser]; 1 Mar 1781, p.657. A.C. of 15 Shill. Sterl.

ALEXANDER CAMPBELL, 177 acs. by Survey 4 Mar 1780 in Rockbridge Co., crossing the great road to a large white oak near a large Spring; adj. Colo. Samuel MacDowel, Bordens old Patent line, James Lyle, sd Campbell & Matthew Donald; 1 Mar 1781, p.659. A.C. of £1 Sterl.

JOSEPH WILLIAMS, 414 acs. by Survey 18 Nov 1774 in Pr. Geo. Co. on the N side of the Second Sw., in Whortleberry Sw.; adj. the lands of Benjamin Fernando, Isham Baugh, Daniel Sturdivant, Thweat, John Baird, William Call & John Baugh; 1 Mar 1781, p.661. A.C. of 45 Shill. Sterl.

JOHN SMITH, 150 acs. by Survey 4 May 1780 in Rockingham Co. on the SW side of Bever cr., crossing a road to a pine near a pond; adj. sd Smith, Josiah Shipman & James Divers; 1 Mar 1781, p.662. A.C. of 15 Shill. Sterl.

WILLIAM SHARPS, 93 acs. by Survey 26 Oct 1769 in Pittsylvania Co. on the Middle fork of Mayo riv.; 1 Mar 1781, p.664. A.C. of 10 Shill. Sterl.

MARY WEBB, 56 acs. by Survey 16 Apr 1768 in Pittsylvania Co. on Smiths riv. and Marrowbone cr., adj. John Rice; 1 Mar 1781, p.665. A.C. of 10 Shill. Sterl.

JOEL HURT, 152 acs. by Survey 22 May 1780 in Pittsylvania Co. on the draughts of Straight stone and Buffaloe creeks; adj. Nat Hendricks, William Pollard &

James Mitchel; 1 Mar 1781, p.666. A.C. of 15 Shill. Sterl.

RALPH SHELTON JUNR., 78 acs. by Survey 1 Apr 1763 in Henry Co. formerly Halifax on both sides of Dann Riv., at the foot of a Mountain thence along the same; 1 Mar 1781, p.667. A.C. of 10 Shill. Sterl.

ISAAC CHANDLER ass'ee of JOHN FIELDS, 134 acs. by Survey 1 Dec 1772 in Buckingham Co. on the brs. of Wreck Island Cr., adj. James Beckham & Thomas Doss; 1 Mar 1781, p.668. A.C of 15 Shill. Sterl.

CHARLES COX, 271 acs. by Survey 30 Jan 1769 in Henry Co. formerly Pittsylvania on turkey pen br.; 1 Mar 1781, p.669. A.C. of 30 Shill. Sterl.

LEONARD HERRIN, 88 acs. by Survey 22 Mar 1780 in Rockingham Co. on the drafts of the South br. of Lenvils cr., to a Stake in a field; adj. Walter Crow, sd Herrin & John Crow; 1 Mar 1781, p.670. A.C. of 10 Shill. Sterl.

[Margin note: *This Grant was altered in the name of Governour Harrison and dated the 20th of August because the Grant was made out and recorded before Signed by Governour Jefferson who resign'd before it Could be Signed or Sealed*]

REUBEN HARRISON Ass'ee of JACOB DICKENSON, 277 acs. by Survey 30 May 1769 in Augusta Co. on some drafts of Smiths cr., Beginning on the E side of a Great road opposite to Reuben Harrisons land; 20 Aug 1783, p.671. A.C. of 30 Shill. Sterl.

JOHN SKIDMORE, 63 acs. by Survey 13 Oct 1772 in Rockingham Co. formerly Augusta on the E side of the South br. of Powtomack, Beginning at the foot of the Mountain, with a ridge, adj. John Conrad & sd Skidmore; 1 Feb 1781, p.672. A.C. of 10 Shill. Sterl.

CHARLES COX, 271 acs. by Survey 30 Jan 1769 in Henry Co. formerly Pittsylvania on Turkey pen br.; 1 Mar 1781, p.674. A.C. of 30 Shill. Sterl.

CHARLES COGBILL, 30 acs. by Survey 3 May 1780 in Chesterfield Co. Beginning on the W side of Timbury, down sd Timsbury; adj. Thomas Stratton, John Walthel/Wathal, William Wathal, William or Henry Walthals line, & sd Cogbill; 1 Mar 1781, p.675. A.C. of 5 Shill. Sterl.

PETER COPLAND, 625 acs. by an **inclusive Survey** 10 Feb 1769 in Pittsylvania Co. on Wins Cr. of Preed cr., adj. his order line; 1 Mar 1781, p.677. A.C. of £3.S5 Shill. Sterl.

STEPHEN GRIMES, 88 acs. by Survey 17 Apr 1780 in Albemarle Co. on the S side Totear cr. and on its brs.; adj. Thomas Tilman, John Lewis, Phelps, & John Tooley; 1 Mar 1781, p.678. A.C. of 10 Shill. Sterl.

OWEN WEST, 385 acs. by Survey 24 May 1780 in Pittsylvania Co. on the brs. of Straight stone cr.; adj. John West, Thomas Dillar & sd Wests formerly line; 1 Mar 1781, p.680. A.C. of £2 Sterl.

GEORGE HILTON, 270 acs. by Survey 4 May 1780 in Augusta Co. on the fourth hundred on both sides of Bare br., on Buck mountain; adj. his own, William Horsely/Horseley, James Pamplin & Samuel Allen; 1 Mar 1781, p.681. A.C.

of 30 Shill. Sterl. *by virtue of an Entry made by Peter Biby 26 Jul 1769 and by him transferred to sd Hilton.*

JOHN WILLS/WELLS, 300 acs. in Henry Co. formerly Pittsylvania; 10 Apr 1781, p.683. *in Consideration of the Sum of £900 Current money paid by John Wells unto Abraham Penn escheator for Henry Co. late the property of James Smith a Subject of Great Britian and Sold by the Sd Abraham Penn Escheator unto the sd John Wells agreable to two Acts of Assembly passed in 1779 the one Intittled an Act concerning escheats and forfeitures from British Subjects the other Intittled an Act concerning Escheators.*

JACOB SHEETZ ass'ee of JOHN STEVENSON, 396 acs. by Survey 22 Dec 1774 in Augusta Co. on a Small br. of Naked cr., crossing 2 Spring brs.; adj. his old C., Robert McCutchens & John King; 1 Mar 1781, p.685. A.C. of 5 Shill. Sterl. 300 acs. part thereof was Gtd. John Stevenson by pat. 20 Sep 1748, 54 acs. also part thereof was Gtd. to sd Stevenson by pat. 27 Jun 1764 and 42 acs. the residue never before Gtd. bounded by the variation of the Magnetic from the true Meridian of 1° east.

JOHN HAWKINS, 400 acs. by Survey 22 Mar 1780 in Amherst Co. on the S brs. of Ruckers run, at Spencers road; adj. Number 11, Walter King & Number 13; 1 Mar 1781, p.687. in Consideration of the Sum of £1,700 Current money paid by John Hawkins unto David Shepherd Gent. Escheator for Amherst Co. lately the property of John Harmer a British Subject and Sold by the Aforesd David Shepherd unto the sd John Hawkins agreable to two Acts of Assembly passed in 1779 the one Intittled an Act concerning Escheats and forefeitures from British Subjects the other intittled an Act concerning Escheators. bounded from the tru Meridian being N15W [N15'W].

OBADIAH HUDSON, 84 acs. by Survey 8 Apr 1763 in Pittsylvania Co. formerly Halifax on both sides of little Dann riv., adj. Bell; 1 Mar 1781, p.689. A.C. of 10 Shill. Sterl.

WILLIAM ROANE, 45 acs. being low Grounds made by Piscataway Sw. by Survey 15 Aug 1774 in Essex Co., Beginning near the Main Run of sd Sw., along the edge of the high land of Benjamin Coughland including the low gounds of the aforesd Sw., on the edge of Vincent Colemans high land including the low Grounds of the aforesd Sw., crossing the Sw. that divides Colemans from Latany's land, to the extreme part of an Island in the low Grounds of a Sw. called Balls Sw., with the line of Aforementioned Roanes land, with Samuel Allens line; 1 Mar 1781, p.691. A.C. of 5 Shill. Sterl.

JOHN ARNOLD ass'ee of PATRICK BURNS, 185 acs. by Survey 18 Aug 1777 in Pr. Edward Co. on both sides of Rough cr., adj. Charles Simmons; 1 Mar 1781, p.693. A.C. of £1 Sterl.

JOHN CRAWFORD, 363½ acs. by Survey 6 May 1780 in Rockingham Co. on both sides Brira br., in a Hollow, on a red bank; adj. sd Crawford, Welden, James Divers, Thomas King, Donelsons survey & Malcoms l.; 1 Mar 1781, p.695. A.C. of £2 Sterl.

INGLE BOYER, 56 acs. by Survey 31 Mar 1780 in Rockingham Co. on the

Mountain run a br. of Smiths cr.; adj. John Harrison, Armantrouts l., sd Armantrouts last survey & Robert Dickeys Survey; 1 Mar 1781, p.697. A.C. of 10 Shill. Sterl.

WILLIAM PATTESON, 224 acs. by Survey 18 Nov 1772 in Buckingham Co. on the brs. of Davids cr., in the Church road; adj. his own line, Nicholas Maynard, William Clerk & James Burnet; 1 Mar 1781, p.698. A.C. of 25 Shill. Sterl.

WILLIAM CURETON, 53 acs. & 132 poles 14 Nov 1774 in Pr. Geo. Co. on both Sides the trading br., along the County line of Sussex [N58°E]; adj. his own old line, William Griffin & Thomas Ambrose; 1 Mar 1781, p.700. A.C. of 5 Shill. Sterl. [For sd Griffin's see PB 21 p.228 to Samuel Griffir., for Thomas Ambrose's see PB 39 p 108 to James Pittillo. Also adj. PB 22 p.185 to Thomas Tadlock & PB 17 p.422 to Richard Tatum]

BRADLEY SMITH, 244 acs. by Survey 17 May 1780 in Henry Co. on the brs. of Mayo Riv.; adj. George Taylor, Henry Fee, Jesser Atkerson & sd Smiths formerly line; 1 Mar 1781, p.702. A.C. of 25 Shill. Sterl.

ARCHIBALD HOPKINS, 128 acs. by Survey 21 Mar 1780 in Rockingham Co. on the E side of Muddy cr., near a line of Shanklins land in a line of his patent land; 1 Mar 1781, p.704. A.C. of 15 Shill. Sterl.

WILLIAM ANDERSON, 210 acs. by Survey 17 Apr 1780 in Augusta Co. on the SE side of his other tract and Joining Eanos Jones's land, on a ridge, near Moffets line, by John Anderson's road & by Moffets path; 1 Mar 1781, p.706. A.C. of 25 Shill. Sterl.

INGLE BOYER, 200 acs. by Survey 30 Mar 1781 in Rockingham Co. on the W side of Smiths cr.; adj. Reuben Harrisons l., Laurence Bells open line, a survey of William Kinton & Boyers Survey; 1 Feb 1781, p.708. A.C. of £1 Sterl.

AMBROSE KINGE Ass'ee opf JOHN WINGO who was Ass'ee of PETER HAMMOND who was Ass'ee of JAMES ROSS, 167 acs. by Survey 1 Dec 1757 in Pr. Edward Co. on the N side of Rough cr., Beginning at the mouth of a large br. on sd cr.; 1 Mar 1781, p.710. A.C. of £1 Sterl.

JOSEPH GRIMES, 250 acs. by Survey 18 Mar 1780 in Fluvanna Co. [and Albemarle Co.] on the S Brs. of Hardware riv., Crossing the County line into Albemarle, adj. John Morriss's line; 1 Mar 1781, p.712. A.C. of 25 Shill. Sterl.

GRIFFIN PEART, 2,000 acs. by Survey 30 Jun 1774 in Fincastle Co. on Elk horn cr. the waters of Ohio, by a Small cr., adj. Charles Lewis; 1 Mar 1781, p.714. *in Consideration of Military Service performed by Griffin Peart as an Ensign in the late war between Great Britain and France and agreable to the Governors warrant and his Majesties proclamation of Oct 1763.*

ROWLAND HORSELY BIRK, 199 acs. by Survey 7 May 1768 in Henry Co. formerly Pittsylvania on Gobling town cr.; 1 Mar 1781, p.715. A.C. of £1 Sterl.

JOSIAH HODGES, 173 acs. by Survey 17 Oct 1766 in Henry Co. formerly

Pittsylvania on both sides of Pigg riv., adj. Richard Whitton; 1 Mar 1781, p.717. A.C. of £1 Sterl.

THOMAS STITH & MARY READ the sd MARY READ Ass'ee of CLEMENT READ and the sd CLEMENT READ AND THOMAS STITH Ass'ees of GEORGE LOVEL, 162 acs. by Survey 18 Nov 1756 in Lunenburg Co. on the brs. of Turnip cr. adj. Francis Grimes & William Rogers; 1 Mar 1781, p.719. A.C. of £1 Sterl.

THOMAS STITH & MARY READ the Sd Mary Read as ass'ee of CLEMENT READ, 219 acs. by Survey 18 Mar 1756 in Lunenburg Co. on both Sides of a great bear cr.; adj. Nathaniel Venable, Abraham Venable & John McNeese; 1 Mar 1781, p.721. A.C. of 25 Shill. Sterl.

THOMAS STITH & MARY READ the Sd Mary Read as Ass'ee of CLEMENT READ, 390 acs. by Survey 28 Jan 1755 in Lunenburg Co. on the south fork of Cub cr., adj. Harvey and Nicks their line; 1 Mar 1781, p.722. A.C. of 40 Shill. Sterl.

THOMAS STITH & MARY READ the Sd MARY READ being Ass'ee of CLEMENT READ, 180 acs. by Survey 19 Mar 1756 in Lunenburg Co. on both Sides of Turkey cock br., adj. David Jones & Francis Grimes; 19 Aug 1783, 8th year of the Commonwealth, Benjamin Harrison Governor, p.724. A.C. of £1 Sterl.

WILLIAM CORNET Ass'ee of JOSEPH PAINE Ass'ee of THOMAS BOAZ, 158 acs. by Survey 19 Mar 1771 in Buckingham Co. on both sides the North fork of Hallidays Riv., crossing the County road; 1 Mar 1781, p.725. A.C. of £1 Sterl.

SAMUEL HARRIS, 310 acs. by Survey 19 Nov 1779 in Pittsylvania Co. on the brs. of fall cr., in the fork of finns br.; adj. Abia Clay, Cheatham, sd Harriss's former lines, Cargill & Walton; 1 Mar 1781, p.727. A.C. of 35 Shill. Sterl.

JOHN POAGE, 150 acs. by Survey 28 Feb 1754 in Rockbridge Co. formerly Augusta, on the road; adj. his own land his old Survey, Jacob Pattons land, Richard Mathews & John Allison; 1 Mar 1781, p.729. A.C. of 15 Shill. Sterl.

ALEXANDER & WILLIAM ROBERTSON, 78 acs. by Survey 22 Dec 1780 in Augusta Co.; adj. the lands of Thomas Stephenson, James Allen Senior, Mathew Robertson, Beverly, King, George Poage & Stuart; 1 Mar 1781, p.731-732. A.C. of 10 Shill. Sterl.

PALITIAH SHELTON, 310 acs. by Survey 15 Oct 1770 in Henry Co. formerly Pittsylvania on the South fork of Russells cr., adj. Robert Walton & David Rogers; 1 Mar 1781, p.731a-732a. A.C. of 35 Shill. Sterl.

HENRY RAWLINGS ass'ee of JOSHUA CANTRIL, 110 acs. by Survey 28 Apr 1780 in Pittsylvania Co. on the brs. of Strawberry cr., adj. Thomas Boaz & Robert Ralston; 1 Mar 1781, p.732a-733. A.C. of 15 Shill. Sterl.

JOHN MILLAR Ass'ee of JOHN HICKLIN who was Ass'ee of JAMES BURNSIDES, 75 acs. by Survey 12 Dec 1767 in Augusta Co. Adj. James Burnsides land in Bull pasture, William Martin & his old line; 1 Mar 1781, p.734. A.C. of 10 Shill. Sterl.

GEORGE MALLOW, 185 acs. by Survey 13 May 1780 in Rockingham Co. at the foot of the peeked Mountain; adj. Snider, his own land & Hermon; 1 Mar 1781, p.735. A.C. of £1 Sterl.

JOHN BROWN ass'ee of JAMES VEST, 354 acs. by Survey 15 Mar 1780 in Bedford Co. on the N Side of Stantoun riv., on James Talbots br., up Dennys road, crossing a large br., on the bank of the fork of Cattamcunt br.; adj. Cannefaxes lines, Alford, Thomas Vest & James Martin; 1 Mar 1781, p.737. A.C of 35 Shill. Sterl.

JAMES DIVER, 585 acs. by Survey 5 May 1780 in Rockingham Co. on brira br., near a pond, near a road; adj. Henry Millers land formerly Hendersons, Iseah Shipmans land, John Smiths Survey & sd Divers patent land; 1 Mar 1781, p.739. A.C. of £1 Sterl. 400 acs. of which was formerly Gtd. by Patent to sd Diver the residue 185 acs. New unpatented land.

BENNET HENDERSON, 346 acs. by Survey 9 Jun 1780 in Albemarle Co. on the waters of Rock fish riv. and among the little mountains; adj. the South Garden, Nathaniel Haggard, John Tooll/Tool & Robert Page; 1 Mar 1781, p.742. A.C. of 35 Shill. Sterl.

GEORGE THOMPSON Ass'ee of JESSE BURTON, 400 acs. by Survey 17 Mar 1780 in Fluvanna Co. on the N brs. of the Fluvanna riv. on Damson cr., adj. William Burtons line on the old Court house road, crossing the road; 1 Mar 1781, p.744. A.C. of £2 Sterl.

JESSE HEARD, 183 acs. by Survey 6 May 1779 in Henry Co. on the N Side of Pigg riv., on a ridge; adj. Hill, Darby Rion, John Bohannan & Cook; 1 Mar 1781, p.746. A.C. of £1 Sterl.

JOHN HENRY Ass'ee of JACOB HELM, by two Entries 530 acs. by Survey 26 Feb 1778 in Botetourt Co. on the waters of Back cr., Beginning by the path up the Bent Mountain, on a ridge, on the top of the good Spurr, on the Bent Mountain; 1 Mar 1781, p.748. A.C. of 55 Shill. Sterl.

CHARLES CHRISTIAN, JUNIOR Ass'ee of JOHN ROUSEY, 130 acs. by Survey 23 Apr 1770 in Amherst Co. on the brs. of Rockey Run and Buffaloe riv.; adj. sd Charles Christian, John Mayfield, John Fry & John Ownby Junior; 1 Mar 1781, p.750. A.C. of 15 Shill. Sterl.

CASPER SYLEN, 178 acs. by an **Inclusive Survey** 18 Apr 1781 in Augusta Co., in a Gully, by a great road, by the great road, on the top of a ridge; adj. Sd Sylen, Eanos Jones, Lewis Mowras line & Marcus Cub; 1 Mar 1781, p.751. A.C. of 10 Shill. Sterl. 100 acs. of which being part of a tract of 195 acs. first Gtd. to Robert Boyd by pat. 10 Mar 1756 [PB 32 p.702] and by Several conveyances became the property of the sd Casper Sylen.

JOHN HENDERSON JUNR., 366 acs. by Survey 14 Apr 1772 in Albemarle Co. on both sides Bisket Run; adj. his own lines, the land formerly James Davis's, & James Jones; 1 Mar 1781, p.753. A.C. of £2 Sterl.

WILLIAM DAVIS assignee of ANDERSON BRYAN, 400 acs. by Survey 6 May 1775 in Albemarle Co. on the S Side the Rivanna River and on some of the head brs. of Cunningham and

Briery creeks, to a head br. of Cunningham cr., to Bremore road, adj. William Fitzpatrick; 1 Mar 1781, p.755. A.C. of £2 Sterl.

ROBERT WILEY, 117 acs. by Survey 29 Mar 1780 in Augusta Co. on the N Side of his other tract on Jacksons riv., Beginning on the S Side of the dry br., at the foot of a Mountain, on a ridge, adj. sd Wileys patent line; 1 Mar 1781, p.757. A.C. of 15 Shill. Sterl.

JOHN WEST, 276 acs. by an **Inclusive Survey** 23 May 1780 in Pittsylvania Co. 150 acs. of which lyes on the brs. of Straight Stone cr. and the other 126 acs. on Deans br. of Straight Stone Surveyed 27 Feb 1770 for THOMAS HUTCHINGS and transferred to the Sd John West, adj. Thomas Dillard & Major Dillard; 1 Mar 1781, p.759. A.C. of 30 Shill. Sterl.

CHAMPION NAPIER Ass'ee of ASHFORD NAPIER, 151¾ acs. by Survey 28 Apr 1775 in Albemarle Co. on the S Side the Rivanna Riv. and on the N Side the North fork of Cunningham cr., to Hyrun br.; adj. the land the Sd Ashford Napier purchased of William Kinney, old marked lines & Sandages line; 1 Mar 1781, p.761. A.C of 15 Shill. Sterl.

JOHN & JOSEPH FARRAR Ass'ees of ASHFORD NAPIER, 400 acs. by Survey 25 Apr 1775 in Albemarle Co. on the S Side the Rivanna riv. and on the N Side the North fork of Cunningham cr.; adj. the l. Sandage purchased of Harden Bur[n]ley, sd Ashford Napier, George Thompson the Younger & John Haden; 1 Mar 1781, p.763. A.C. of £2 Sterl.

DANIEL HANKINS, 282 acs. by Survey 19 Mar 1770 in Pittsylvania Co. on the Waters of Dann Riv., crossing little Wolf Island Cr. three times, in the fork of the cr., crossing the east fork, adj. Owens & Sd Dunkins's line; 1 Mar 1781, p.766. A.C. of 30 Shill. Sterl.

THOMAS ROGERS, 330 acs. by Survey 27 Mar 1756 in Lunenburg Co. on the brs. of Turnip cr.; adj. George Pattillo, William Stanfiel & John Smith ; 1 Mar 1781, p.767. A.C. of 35 Shill. Sterl.

SERAIAH STRATTON, 160 acs. by Survey 25 May 1780 in Rockingham Co. on both Sides of the south br. of Powtomack between the tracts of Samuel Seidmore deceast land, Beginning on the Side of a Mountain, crossing a deep Hollow; 1 Mar 1781, p.770. A.C. of £1 Sterl.

BRYAN McDEARMANROE /MacDEARMANROE, 300 acs. by Survey 11 Apr 1780 in Pr. Edward Co. on both sides Rough cr., at the Mouth of the bold br.; adj. Ambrose Hinge, sd MacDearmanroe, Lovel, Arnold & Watkins; 1 Mar 1781, p.772. A.C. of 30 Shill. Sterl.

JOHN HAWKINS, 400 acs. by Survey 22 Mar 1780 in Amherst Co. on the S brs. of Ruckers run, crossing the Court house road; adj. Number 12, Walter King & Lomax; 1 Mar 1781, p.774. *in Consideration of the Sum of £5,030 Current Money of Virginia paid into David Shepherd Escheator for Amherst Co. lately the property of John Harmer a British Subject and was Sold by the Said David Shepherd agreable to two Acts of Assembly passed in the year 1779 the one Intittled an Act concerning Escheats and forfeitures from British Subjects the other Intittled an act Concerning Escheators.*

bounded by the Variation of the Magnetic from the true Meridian being N15W.

JOHN FONTAINE, 109 acs. by Survey Apr 1780 in Henry Co. on the waters of Smiths riv. and Leatherwood cr.; Boulding, Leatherwood order line & Smiths river order line; 1 Mar 1781, p.775. A.C. of 15 Shill. Sterl.

THOMAS STITH & MARY READ the Sd MARY READ as Ass'ee of CLEMENT READ, 436 acs. 11 Mar 1756 in Lunenburg Co. on the E brs. of Cubb cr., down the little cr. ; adj. Thomas Duggins, Samuel Allen, Thomas Williams, Thomas Willis, Samuel Moore, John Marshal & Nathaniel Christian; 1 Mar 1781, p.777. A.C. of 45 Shill. Sterl.

MARY READ & WILLIAM GOODE the Sd MARY READ as Ass'ee of CLEMENT READ, 362 acs. by Survey 14 Mar 1755 in Mecklenburg Co. formerly Lunenburg on the brs. of Buffaloe cr.; adj. Capt. Smith, White, William Vaughan, John Griffin & Stith; 1 Mar 1781, p.779. A.C. of £2 Sterl. [For John Griffin's land, see PB 35 p.118 to Abraham Wells]

GEORGE BAXTER Ass'ee of SAMUEL HERONS, 97 acs. by Survey 27 Jan 1760 in Augusta Co. on the head brs. of Johns Run a br. of Linvels cr., at the foot of the Mountain; 1 Mar 1781, p.780. A.C. of 10 Shill. Sterl.

JOHN RAY, 234 acs. by Survey 30 Oct 1770 in Augusta Co. on the W side of Smiths cr., adj. Harrison & Ewin; 1 Mar 1781, p.782. A.C. of 25 Shill. Sterl.

PATRICK NAPIER Ass'ee of THOMAS POTTER, 400 acs. by Survey 16 Dec 1780 in Albemarle Co. on the S Side the Rivanna riv. and on Some of the brs. of Buck Island cr., on plum tree br. & Martin Kings road, adj. McCowen & Francis Bishop; 1 Mar 1781, p.784. A.C. of 2 Sterl.

JOHN McGILL/MacGILL, 242 acs. by Survey 19 Apr 1780 in Rockingham Co. on the N Side of the North riv. of Shenandore, in a draft; adj. his Patent land, James Murry, William Herrin & Snoddin; 1 Mar 1781, p.786. A.C. of 25 Shill. Sterl.

GEORGE BAXTER ass'ee of EPHRAIM LOVE, 153 acs. by Survey 11 Jan 1763 in Augusta Co. on the North fork of Joes Cr. bet. said Loves patented land and the North Mountain, adj. Daniel Harrison & sd Love; 1 Mar 1781, p.788. A.C. of 15 Shill. Sterl.

CHARLES SHOULS, 312 acs. by Survey 14 Apr 1780 in Rockingham Co. on the W Side of the Dry fork of Smiths cr. and including the land he lives on; adj. Reuben Harrison & Coffmans Survey; to two pines amongst a parcel of Rocks; 1 Mar 1781, p.789. A.C. of 35 Shill. Sterl.

JOSEPH SMITH, 114 acs. by Survey 14 May 1780 in Rockingham Co. on the E Side of the Dry Riv., adj. his own land, his patent land, & Andrew Johnsons land, Beginning on a high hill; 1 Mar 1781, p.791. A.C. of 15 Shill. Sterl.

BENJAMIN HUGHES ass'ee of ASHFORD NAPIER, 261 acs. by Survey 26 Mar 1780 in Fluvanna Co. on the brs. of Cunningham Cr.; adj. William Fitzpatrick, Dickerson, Burnly, & Ashford Napier; 1 Mar 1781, p.792. A.C. of 30 Shill. Sterl.

RICHARD NUTT, 223½ acs. by Survey 27 Apr 1780 in Fluvanna Co. on the N brs. of the Rivanna Riv., adj. Strange & Richard Nutt; 1 Mar 1781, p.794. A.C. of 25 Shill. Sterl.

JOSEPH LAYMAN Ass'ee of JAMES ALCORN, 80 acs. by Survey 21 Jul 1779 in Botetourt Co. on back cr. a br. of James riv. Joining the sd Alcorns old Survey and the land of John Johnson; 10 Apr 1781, p.795. A.C. of 10 Shill. Sterl.

HUGH DONOHO, 268 acs. by Survey 1 Mar 1781 in Augusta Co. on the S side of Rankins land on naked cr., beginning at the mouth of sd cr., by a road, to a pine on a rock, on the top of a ridge, near Campbel's line, adj. Rankin & sd Donoho; 10 Apr 1781, p.797. A.C. of 30 Shill. Sterl.

ANTHONY SMITH, 440 acs. by Survey 10 Apr 1780 in Henry Co. on Horse pasture and Mayo Waters, crossing two brs. and a road; adj. Hughes's and Wimbushes [their] line, Josiah Smiths line formerly Randolphs and Co[s] line, & sd Smiths own line; 10 Apr 1781, p.799. A.C. of 45 Shill. sterl.

DANIEL NEWMAN, 205 acs. by Survey 12 Apr 1780 in Henry Co. on Stones cr., adj. Jacob Cogar; 10 Apr 1781, p.800. A.C. of 25 Shill. Sterl.

JOHN BROWN, 73 acs. by Survey 23 Nov 1768 in Rockingham Co. on the head brs. of Linvels cr.; adj. his other land, Robert Patterson & John Gordon; 10 Apr 1781, p.802. A.C. of 10 Shill. Sterl.

ISABEL LAPSLEY, 50 acs. by Survey 23 Nov 1779 in Rockbridge Co. at the Bent of Buffelo cr. in the forks of James Riv., Beginning at the mouth of Arthur McClures br., on the N side of Whiskey hill; 10 Apr 1781, p.803. A.C. of 5 Shill. Sterl.

STEPHEN HEARD, 397 acs. by Survey 20 Jan 1781 in Henry Co. on the Meadow br. and foul ground br., adj. Lumsden; 10 Apr 1781, p.805. A.C. of £2 Sterl.

JAMES ROBERTS, 346 acs. by Survey 8 Apr 1768 in Pittsylvania Co.; adj. Read, Thomas Jones & Daniel Prewet; 10 Apr 1781, p.806. A.C. of 35 Shill. Sterl.

JOHN DAVIS, 44 acs. by Survey 25 Nov 1780 in Augusta Co. on a Small br. of back cr. opposite to Cunninghams land, Beginning on the side of a ridge, near a Gap; 10 Apr 1781, p.808. A.C. of 5 Shill. Sterl.

ZEPHENIAH NEAL, 80 acs. by Survey 16 Feb 1781 in Bedford Co. on the S brs. of Otter Riv.; adj. Allin, Haynes, Jones & McRaw; 10 Apr 1781, p.809. A.C. of 10 Shill. Sterl.

JOHN MARR ass'ee of JOHN FREDERICK MILLER, 142 acs. by Survey 13 Apr 1780 in Henry Co. on the S side of North Mayo riv.; 10 Apr 1781, p.811. A.C. of 15 Shill. Sterl.

JOSEPH BENET ass'ee of GODFREY BUMGARDNER, 127 acs. by Survey 14 Dec 1771 in Rockingham Co. formerly Augusta on the SE side of the north fork of the South br. of Powtomack, on a ridge; 10 Apr 1781, p.812. A.C. of 15 Shill. Sterl.

JOSEPH LAYMAN ass'ee of JAMES ALCORN, 30 acs. by Survey 31 Jul 1779 in Botetourt Co. on back cr. a br. of James Riv., adj. his own Survey; 10 Apr 1781, p. 814. A.C. of 5 Shill. Sterl.

ISAAC KELLY ass'ee of JAMES NICHOLAS, 20 acs. by Survey 6 May 1772 in Botetourt Co. on a br. of Looneys Mill cr. the waters of James riv.; adj. Herbinson, Simpson & Woods; 10 Apr 1781, p.815. A.C. of 5 Shill. Sterl.

HAMAN CRITZE, 200 acs. by Survey 19 Dec 1780 in Henry Co. on both sides of Spoon cr., adj. Barrett & Keetin; 10 Apr 1781, p.816. £1 Sterl.

HAYMAN CRITZE, 48 acs. by Survey 19 Dec 1780 in Henry Co. on Spoon cr., adj. Robert Barrett & his own old Lines; 10 Apr 1781, p.818. A.C. of 5 Shill. sterl.

WILLIAM HALBERT, 486 acs. by Survey 4 Mar 1780 in Henry Co. on Russells cr. Waters, adj. his own Line & John Parr; 10 Apr 1781, p.320. A.C. of 50 Shill. Sterl.

BARTLET RENALDS, 367 acs. by Survey 13 Apr 1780 in Henry Co. on Stones cr.; 10 Apr 1781, p.821. A.C. of £2 sterl.

JOHN BURNS, 100 acs. by Survey 5 Jan 1781 in Augusta Co. on *Jennings Gap*, crossing the great road and a br. to a bank, with John Poages line to a ridge; 10 Apr 1781, p.823. A.C. of 10 Shill. sterl.

BENJAMIN HAWKINS ass'ee of ROBERT HOOKER, 309 acs. by Survey 11 Apr 1780 in Henry Co. on stones cr., adj. William Taylor; 10 Apr 1781, p.825. A.C. of 35 Shill. Sterl.

JAMES LEATHERDALE, 70 acs. by Survey 30 Mar 1780 in Botetourt Co. on the waters of Looneys Mill cr. a br. of James Riv. and Joining the land of Jeremiah Jenkins, Mathew Wilson/Willson, Samuel Crawford and his [own] patented land; 10 Apr 1781, p.827. A.C. of 10 Shill. Sterl.

JOHN BALL, 233 acs. by Survey 9 Apr 1768 in Pittsylvania Co. on the waters of Pye Cr.; 10 Apr 1781, p.828. A.C. of 25 Shill. Sterl.

THOMAS MORRISON, 180 acs. by Survey 16 Mar 1780 in Henry Co. near a br. of Sycamore cr., adj. his own line; 10 Apr 1781, p.830. A.C. of £1 Sterl.

WILLIAM BOYD, 40 acs. by Survey 9 Feb 1781 in Bedford Co. on the north fork of Otter riv., on a road, adj. James Boyd & his own lines; 10 Apr 1781, p.831. A.C. 5 Shill. sterl.

JOHN NEWMAN, 182 acs. by Survey 13 Apr 1780 in Henry Co. on stones cr., adj. Daniel Newman & Jacob Cogar or Cagar; 10 Apr 1781, p.833. A.C. of £1 Sterl.

JOHN SMITH, 188 acs. by Survey 22 Aug 1772 in Botetourt Co. on Craigs cr. a br. of James Riv., Beginning near Carling Spring Survey; 10 Apr 1781, p.835. A.C. of £1 Sterl.

ROBERT STARRETT/STARRET, 50 acs. by Survey 3 Oct 1780 in Augusta Co. on back cr. Joining his other land on the NW side, also adj. Andrew Alexander; 10 Apr 1781, p.836. A.C. of 5 Shill. Sterl.

GEORGE HOAL, 270 acs. by Survey 22 Jun 1780 in Augusta Co. on the NW side of his own and Isaac Gums land on Crab apple, at the foot of the Mountain; 10 Apr 1781, p.838. A.C. of 30 Shill. Sterl.

HENRY THOMAS ass'ee of JOHN LIGGIN who was Son and heir of JOSEPH LIGGIN dec'd, 179 acs. by Survey 15 Apr 1758 in Albemarle Co. on both sides the South br. of Rock Island cr. on the S Side the Fluvanna riv.; 10 Apr 1781, p.839. A.C. of £1 Sterl.

NEHEMIAH PRAYTHER, 160 acs. by Survey 14 Apr 1780 in Henry Co. on the brs. of the Mayo, adj. Thomas Stockton; 10 Apr 1781, p.840. A.C. of £1 Sterl.

ROBERT GRAG, 68 acs. by Survey 29 Sep 1780 in Augusta Co. on the white oak Bottom in the North fork of the North riv. of Shenando, by the bank of the riv.; 10 Apr 1781, p.842. A.C. of 10 Shill. Sterl.

ROGERT GRAG, 70 acs. by Survey 28 Sep 1780 in Augusta Co. on North br. of Skidmore Run a br. of the North riv. of Shenandore; 10 Apr 1781, p.844. A.C. of 10 Shill. Sterl.

ROBERT GRAG, 37 acs. by Survey 28 Sep 1780 in Augusta Co. near Thorny br. Joining John Stunkard and John Bings land; 10 Apr 1781, p.845. A.C. of 10 Shill. Sterl.

GEORGE CLARK, 150 acs. by Survey 24 May 1774 in Augusta Co. on the head brs. of Smiths cr.; adj. David Leard, Robert Sample, William Ham & George Carpenter; 10 Apr 1781, p.847. A.C. of 15 Shill. Sterl.

JOHN BROWN ass'ee of ROBERT PATTERSON, 75 acs. by Survey 12 Feb 1755 in Rockingham Co. on the waters of Linvells Mill cr. and on the S Side the Sd Robert Pattersons patent land; 10 Apr 1781, p.848. A.C. of 10 Shill. Sterl.

AUGUSTINE BROWN, 162 acs. by Survey 19 Apr 1780 in Henry Co. on the waters of Peters cr., with the Country line or County Line [West], adj. Woody Burges C.; 10 Apr 1781, p.850. A.C. of £1 Sterl.

JANE MULDWICK, 22 acs. by Survey 20 Jul 1779 in Botetourt Co., Beginning by a bank and by a ford of James Riv., to a large rock on the riv. bank, Joining her own land her old Survey; 10 Apr 1781, p.851. A.C. of 5 Shill. Sterl.

JOHN BERRY, 398 acs. by Survey 3 Oct 1780 in Augusta Co. on Mills cr. a br. of back cr. near Robert Stuarts land, on the N Side of a Spur; 10 Apr 1781, p.853. A.C. of £2 Sterl.

FREDERICK STEELL, 85 acs. by Survey 30 Nov 1780 in Augusta Co. on the S Side of the South riv. of Shenandore, adj. his and Ben Yearlys lands; 10 Apr 1781, p.854. A.C. of 10 Shill. Sterl.

JAMES HARRIS, 77 acs. by Survey 13 Mar 1756 in Alblemarle Co. on the N Side Moremans riv., adj. John Jameson & John Mullin; 10 Apr 1781, p.856. A.C. of 10 Shill. Sterl.

PETER HEAL, 160 acs. by Survey 23 Apr 1780 in Augusta Co. on the SE of his other tract in Crab Apple, adj. Cougers line, near sd Heals line; 10 Apr 1781, p.857. A.C. of £1 Sterl.

JOSEPH SKIDMORE, 19 acs. by Survey 26 Aug 1769 in Augusta Co. on the N side of the south br. of Powtomack, Beginning on the N side of his Mill cr. on a br.; 10 Apr 1781, p.859. A.C. of 5 Shill. Sterl.

JOHN CABELL Ass'ee of CHARLES PATTESON who was Ass'ee of WILLIAM FLOWERS, 120 acs. by Survey 21 Mar 1771 in Buckingham Co. on the head of the North fork of Davids cr., adj. Charles Patteson & Thomas Blakey; 10 Apr 1781, p.860. A.C. of 15 Shill. Sterl.

JAMES EAST, 286 acs. by Survey 11 Apr 1780 ini Henry Co. on the S Side of Horse pasture cr., adj. his own line & Watson; 10 Apr 1781, p.862. A.C. of 30 Shill. Sterl.

GEORGE POOR, 351 acs. by Survey 28 Apr 1780 in Henry Co. on Fusys forks, with the Country line [West], adj. Shelton; 10 Apr 1781, p.863. A.C. of 35 Shill. Sterl.

WILLIAM GALLOWAY, 400 acs. by Survey 5 Sep 1772 in Botetourt Co. on the S Side of James Riv. and opposite to the Mouth of the Cow pasture riv., Beginning in a place called *the Barrens*, along the Mountain; 10 Apr 1781, p.865. A.C. of £2 Sterl.

JOHN MOSELEY, 405 acs by Survey 4 May 1780 in Buckingham Co. on the E brs. of Slate riv., crossing three brs. and Moseleys road; adj. Charles Moseley, William Hensley & Allen Tys line; 10 Apr 1781, p.866. A.C. of 45 Shill. Sterl.

WILLIAM ROBINSON, 60 acs. by Survey 6 May 1766 in Augusta Co. on a Small br. of Roanoke, Bg. in a Valley above the head of a Spring; 10 Apr 1781, p.868. A.C. of 10 Shill. Sterl.

JOHN McCLARA, 214 acs. by Survey 20 Sep 1774 in Louisa Co. and parish of Fredricksville on the waters of Beaverdam and Camp creeks; adj. John McClara, David Ross, Elijah Graves, Andrew Greenhorn & Becknal Alverson; 10 Apr 1781, p.870. A.C. of 25 Shill. Sterl.

JOHN SLAVAN, 191 acs. by Survey 1 Apr 1780 in Augusta Co. Joining Roger Patton and Robert Dinwiddie on the head of Jacksons riv.; 10 Apr 1781, p.871. A.C. of £1 Sterl.

WILLIAM GALLOWAY, 48 acs. by Survey 26 Oct 1770 in Botetourt Co. on the W side of Jacksons riv. Joining his own patent land; 10 Apr 1781, p.873. A.C. of 5 Shill. Sterl.

FREDRECK FULKERSON, 189 acs. by Survey 17 May 1780 in Henry Co. on the N side of South Mayo Riv.; adj. his own formerly Waltons line, & Roberts's line; 10 Apr 1781, p.874. A.C. of £1 Sterl.

JAMES MANKIN, 290 acs. by Survey 7 Mar 1780 in Henry Co. on both Sides of Russells cr., crossing a br. and Fary's fork; 10 Apr 1781, p.876. A.C. of 30 Shill. Sterl.

ABRAHAM INGRAM, 176 acs. by Survey 31 Mar 1780 in Augusta Co. on the head brs. of Jacksons riv., adj. William Lewis & Roger Patton; 10 Apr 1781, p.878. A.C. of £1 Sterl.

JOHN KERBY, SENIOR, 111 acs. by Survey 12 Feb 1780 in Albemarle Co. on the E side of Buck Island cr., to the New road leading to Charlotts ville, adj. Valentine Wood & Milburn Hogg; 10 Apr 1781, p.879. A.C. of 15 Shill. Sterl.

JAMES ROBERTS, 302 acs. by Survey 3 Nov 1774 in Pittsylvania Co. on the brs. of Sandy cr., crossing a bold br., adj. John Anglin & Jones Lawson; 10 Apr 1781, p.881. A.C. of 30 Shill. Sterl.

DEBERIX GILLUM, 202 acs. by Survey 12 Apr 1780 in Henry Co. on the N brs. of North Mayo riv.; adj. Randolph, Harman and Kings line, sd Randolphs and Co^s line; 10 Apr 1781, p.883. A.C. of £1 Sterl.

DAVID HARMON, 125 acs. by Survey 14 Dec 1771 in Augusta Co. on Sugar lick run on the SE side of the North fork of the South br. of Powtomack, on a ridge; 10 Apr 1781, p.885. A.C. of 15 Shill. Sterl.

JAMES ROBERTS, 232 acs. by Survey 8 Apr 1768 in Pittsylvania Co. on Sandy riv.; adj. Daniel Prewit, William Lovel & Aaron Airs line; 10 Apr 1781, p.886. A.C. of 25 Shill. Sterl.

THOMAS HAMILTON, 198 acs. by Survey 13 Apr 1780 in Henry Co. on the waters of Stones cr., adj. Jacob Cogars line; 10 Apr 1781, p.888. A.C. of £1 Sterl.

HAYMAN CRITZE, JUNIOR, 347 acs. by Survey 19 Dec 1780 in Henry Co. on Mill cr., adj. Archelaus Hughes; 10 Apr 1781, p.890. A.C. of 35 Shill. Sterl.

HAYMAN CRITZE, 210 acs. by Survey 19 Dec 1780 in Henry Co. on the brs. of Mill cr., adj. Hughes's old line & new line; 10 Apr 1781, p.891. A.C. of 25 Shill. Sterl.

JOHN ROSS, 184 acs. by Survey 10 May 1780 in Henry Co. on the S side of Smiths riv., adj. Turner; 10 Apr 1781, p.893. A.C. of £1 Sterl.

ABRAHAM FRAZER, 266 acs. by Survey 10 Mar 1780 in Henry Co. on Spoon cr., adj. James Dickenson & William Wilson; 10 Apr 1781, p.895. A.C. of 30 Shill. Sterl.

JAMES BELL, 38 acs. by Survey 6 Feb 1781 in Augusta Co. on the long Glade; adj. his other land, Henry Miller & Ervin; 10 Apr 1781, p.896. A.C. of 5 Shill. Sterl.

NICHOLAS SIBERT, 180 acs. by Survey 28 Jul 1780 in Augusta Co. on the E side of his other land on Straight cr. a br. of the South br. of Powtomack, by a Laurel Bank, adj. his c.; 10 Apr 1781, p.898. A.C. of £1 Sterl.

JOHN GRISHAM, JUNIOR, 350 acs. by Survey 11 Mar 1780 in Henry Co. on Spoon Cr., adj. John Grisham & Parr; 10 Apr 1781, p.900. A.C. of 35 Shill. Sterl.

JAMES EAST, 670 acs. by Survey 11 Apr 1780 in Henry Co. on the N Side of Bigg pasture cr., adj. John Watson; 10 Apr 1781, p.902. A.C. of £3.S10 Sterl.

RICHARD ADAMS, 434 acs. by Survey 14 Apr 1780 in Henry Co. on the waters of Mill cr., adj. Hayman Critze & sd Adams's own old line; 10 Apr 1781, p.903. A.C. of 45 Shill. Sterl.

PHILIP BUZZARD, 383 acs. by Survey 10 Mar 1780 in Henry Co. on the waters of Spoon cr., adj. Abraham Frazer & William Wilson; 10 Apr 1781, p.905. A.C. of £2 Sterl.

HUGH GARVIN, 280 acs. by Survey 10 May 1780 in Bedford Co. on the N brs. of wreck Island Cr., Along Stovals road; adj. Stovall, Mann & McBride; near sd Garvins fence; 10 Apr 1781, p.907. A.C. of 30 Shill. Sterl.

HENRY PARR, 445 acs. by Survey 9 Mar 1780 in Henry Co. on the brs. of the south Mayo riv., crossing a road 3 times, to a paw paugh tree in his old line; 10 Apr 1781, p.909. A.C. of 45 Shill. Sterl.

JOHN PARR, SENIOR, 148 acs. by Survey 6 Mar 1780 in Henry Co. on Mayo Riv., at a road, adj. his old line; 10 Apr 1781, p.911. A.C. of 15 Shill. Sterl.

DANIEL NEWMAN, 442 acs. by Survey 12 Apr 1780 in Henry Co. on Stones cr., to a red Bud bush on Jacob Cogars line; 10 Apr 1781, p.913. A.C. of 45 Shill. Sterl.

WILLIAM CROW, 120 acs. by Survey 9 Apr 1773 in Botetourt Co. on the waters of James riv., down the Cr. [Looneys Mill Cr.]; 10 Apr 1781, p.915. A.C. of 15 Shill. Sterl.

HUGH GREEN, 145 acs. by Survey 29 Dec 1769 in Augusta Co. on Some Small brs. of the middle Riv. of Shenandore, on a ridge; adj. Robert Stevenson, Thomas Stevenson & John Poage; 10 Apr 1781, p.916. A.C. of 15 Shill. Sterl.

JOHN PARR SENR., 391 acs. by Survey 6 Mar 1780 in Henry Co. on the N side of the south Mayo riv., cross a road, adj. his old line; 10 Apr 1781, p.918. A.C. of £2 Sterl.

JAMES LYON, 360 acs. by Survey 20 Apr 1780 in Henry Co. on the brs. of Russels cr., adj. his own line & Palitiah Shelton; 10 Apr 1781, p.920. A.C. of £2 Sterl.

THOMAS ADAMS, 428 acs. by Survey 14 Apr 1780 in Henry Co. on Mill cr., adj. Richard Adams; 10 Apr 1781, p.921. A.C. of 45 Shill. Sterl.

NICHOLAS SIBERT, 72 acs. by Survey 29 Jul 1780 in Augusta Co. on a Small br. of the south br. of Powtomack and a place known by the name of *Cliftens hole*; 10 Apr 1781, p.923. A.C. of 10 Shill. Sterl.

WILLIAM SCOTT, 120 acs. by Survey 22 Feb 1768 in Amherst Co. on both sides of Ishams br., adj. John Ballow; 10 Apr 1781, p.924. A.C. of 15 Shill. Sterl.

JOHN CABELL, 341 acs. by Survey 22 Feb 1769 in Buckingham Co. on both sides of Mims cr. and on the Spurs of Slate river Mountain, crossing Migginsons road, adj. Cabell & Walton; 10 Apr 1781, p.926. A.C. of 35 Shill. Sterl.

WILLIAM PERKINS, 492 acs. by Survey 2 May 1780 in Henry Co. on poplar Camp cr., adj. Charles Thomas & John Brammer; 10 Apr 1781, p.928. A.C. of 50 Shill. Sterl.

DANIEL ROSS, 260 acs. by survey 10 May 1780 in Henry Co. on the N side of Smiths Riv., crossing Beards cr., up Nichols's cr., adj. his line; 10 Apr 1781 *in the 5th year of the Commonwealth, Thomas Jefferson Esq. Governor*, p.930. A.C. of 30 Shill. Sterl.

GRANT BOOK E

1 May 1775 to 1 February 1781

[The first 38 pages of Grant Book E were Colonial Government Patents, dated 1 May 1775 to 15 Mar 1776, and were published in Volume VII after Patent Book 42]

CHARLES LOVELL/LOVEL, 211 acs. Pr. Edward Co. on the lower side of Rough Cr., adj. Black & Fear; 1 May 1775 *in the 15th year of our Reign, George the third, John Earl of Dunmore our Lieutenant and Governor General of our sd Colony and Dominion at Williamsburg Under the seal of our aforesd Colony*, p.1. 25 Shill.

BENJAMIN BRETT, 139 acs. Brunswick Co. adj. William Johnson & Randle; 1 May 1775, p.2. 15 Shill. [Between Quarrel Sw. & Rockey Run]

CHARLES CLAY, 340 acs. Halifax Co. on Sandy Cr. of Dan Riv.; adj. Silvester, Billings, Falling & Little; 1 May 1775, p.3. 35 Shill.

THOMAS SCOTT JUNR., 393 acs. Pittsylvania Co. on both sides of the East fork of Cascade Cr., adj. Clay & Russell; 1 May 1775, p.4 £2.

JOHN COX, 400 acs. Pittsylvania Co. on the Glady fork of Sandy Riv., to Pointers in a naked ruff, adj. Gray & Yarrington; 1 May 1775, p.4. £2.

JOHN ARMOUR FENDLEY, 215 acs. Bedford Co. on the head Brs. of the North fork of Beaver dam Cr., adj. Walton; 1 May 1775, p.5. £1.S5.

JOHN FISHER, 360 acs. Halifax Co. on the head of Peters Cr., crossing Boyd's Road and Irby's Road, adj. Comer; 1 May 1775, p.6. £2.

THOMAS DOSWELL, 78 acs. Amherst Co. on the fork mountain of Tye riv.; 1 May 1775, p.7. £1.

WILLIAM SPIERS, 148 acs. Albemarle Co. on the head of Moores Cr.; 1 May 1775, p.7. 15 Shill.

WILLIAM WHITEHEAD, 129 acs. Southampton Co. up the Run of the

Little sw.; adj. Anne Brookes [her Lines], Edmund Day, the sd Whitehead, Samuel Atkinson, Sarah Crocker [her Lines] & John Barrow; 1 May 1775, p.8. 15 Shill. [N of Meherrin Riv.]

THOMAS HOPE, 315 acs Halifax Co. on Difficult Cr., crossing the new Road; adj. Morefield, Robertson, Hunt, Nowlin, Wade, Wades Mill tract; 1 May 1775, p.9. £1.S15.

ISHAM REAVIS, 181 acs. Brunswick Co. adj. Ledbeter & Jones; 1 May 1775, p.10. £1.

ELEAZER CLAY, 123 acs. Chesterfield Co. adj. Tiller; 1 May 1775, p.11. 15 Shill.

THOMAS DOSWELL, 204 acs. Amherst Co. on the N brs. of the South fork of Tye riv., to Pointers of Ivy in a br. adj. his own Lines; 1 May 1775, p.11. £1.

FRANCIS IRBY, 400 acs. Pittsylvania Co. on Fly blow Cr., adj. Echoles & Anderson; 1 May 1775, p.12. £2.

JOSHUA ABSTEN, 260 acs. Pittsylvania Co. on the waters of Sycamore Cr., adj. sd Absten & Holland; 1 May 1775, p.13. £1.S10.

JABEZ NORTHINGTON, 224 acs. Mecklenburg Co. adj. the Lands of John Brown Junr., Thomas Nance, Fowler, Floid & John Brown Senr.; 1 May 1775, p.14. £1.S5. [S of Avents Cr.]

WILLIAM LONDON, 174 acs. Halifax Co. on the Brs. of Runaway Cr., adj. Henry Cross & Robert Davis; 1 May 1775, p.15. £2.

THOMAS HUGART, 95 acs. Augusta Co. on Wilson's mill Cr. a br. of Jacksons Riv.; 1 May 1775, p.15. 10 Shill.

WILLIAM ALEXANDER, 75 acs. Augusta Co. crossing Irish Cr., Beginning by a spring on the Cr., adj. Joseph Alexander; 1 May 1775, p.16. 10 Shill.

ROBERT HILL, 125 acs. Augusta Co. on the dry Riv., Beg. at the foot of a bank, on the Edge of a Bottom thence along the hillside, adj. Oneal's Survey; 1 May 1775, p.17. 15 Shill.

JOHN FARRAR, 95 acs. Mecklenburg Co. on the brs. of Allens Cr.; adj. Lundy, Mallet, Hawkins & Blackwelder; 1 May 1775, p.18. 10 Shill.

JOHN TUGGLE, 82 acs. Amherst Co. on the N brs. of Ruckers run; adj. his own lines, John Mountgomery, John Loving Junr., Abraham Seay Junr. & Lunsford Lomax; 1 May 1775, p.18. 10 Shill.

THOMAS LEWELLIN, 62 acs. Sussex Co. on the S side of Nottoway Riv., on the County Line which divides Surry from Brunswick [N12°E, now dividing Sussex Co. from Greensville Co.]; adj. Isaac Oliver, Colo. Richard Cock & Lawrence House dec'd; 1 May 1775, p.19. 10 Shill.

WILLIAM SIKES, 31½ acs. Norfolk Co. in the Green sea; 1 May 1775, p.20. 5 Shill.

JOHN TAYLOE CORBIN, 26 acs. King & Queen Co. on the Dragon sw., Beginning on maple sw. in the Lowgrounds of the Dragon sw., up the Dragon to the Causeway at the Bridge and along the same to the high Land, down and along the Lowgrounds; 1 May 1775, p.21. 5 Shill.

ELY GRIFFIN, 60 acs. Nansemond Co. adj. Kedah Raby & James Raby; 1 May 1775, p.22. 10 Shill.

RICHARD LAMKIN, 244 acs. Halifax Co. on the brs. of Difficult Cr., adj. Wilson Mattox & William McCrery; 1 May 1775, p.22. £1.S5.

THOMAS DICKSON, 400 acs. Halifax Co. on both sides of sandy Cr. of Banister Riv., adj. Robert Sweeting & Lane; 1 May 1775, p.23. £2.

RICHARD NAPIER, 166 acs. Albemarle Co. on the S Brs. of the Rivanna Riv., down the Horse shoe br.; adj. Patrick Napier, George Dudley, Creasy, & Bouth Napier; 1 May 1775, p.24. £1.

JOSEPH BILLUPS, 450 acs. Lunenburg Co. on the head brs. of dry Cr.; adj. Johnson, Oliver, Boulton, Billup, Hardy & Flake; 1 May 1775, p.25. £2.S5.

BETTY KIRKLAND, 600 acs. Brunswick Co. in the fork of Bedingsfields Cr., down the middle fork of Bedingfield Cr.; adj. Haris [Harris], Price & Brewer; 1 May 1775, p.26. £3. Whereas by pat. 5 Feb 1753 gtd. William Brewer containing 1,718 acs. [1,781 acs. in PB 32, p.30] And Whereas *Betty & William Kirkland* in whom the Right and title of 600 acs. part is since become vested hath failed to pay Quitrents as to 600 acs. and *Gideon Harris* hath made humble to the Late President of our Council & Commander in Chief and hath obtained a G. for the same which he hath assigned unto Betty Kirkland.

EDMUND TAYLOR, 400 acs. Mecklenburg Co. on both sides of Mitchel's fork of Bluestone Cr., adj. Miller; 1 May 1775, p.28. £2. Whereas by pat. 19 Jul 1757 [19 May 1757] gtd. unto John Wilbourn [PB 33, p.360] in Mecklenburg formerly Lunenburg Co. and whereas the sd John Wilbourn have failed to pay Quitrents and Timothy Smith hath made humble suit to our Late Lieutenant Governor and Commander in Chief and hath obtained a G. for the same.

ANTHONY STREET, 214 acs. Lunenburg Co. on polecat Cr.; adj. Thos. Scott, Ben Burchett, Jones Sikes, Valentine Brown, Mason, William Smithson & John Smithson; 1 May 1775, p.29. £1.S5. Whereas by Pat. 10 Apr 1751 gtd. unto Abraham Cocke [PB 29, p.366] one Certain tract or parcel of Land Containing 5,450 acs. Lunenburg Co. And Whereas Peter Cocke in whom the right of 200 acs. part thereof is since become vested hath failed to pay the Quitrents of the sd 200 acs. which upon a resurvey is found to contain 214 acs. and *Sylvanus Walker* hath made humle Suit to our Lieutenant & Governor General and hath obtained a G. for the same which he hath Assigned unto Anthony Street.

EDMUND TAYLOR, 400 acs. Mecklenburg Co. on the Brs. of Bluestone Cr., along Hogans Road, on the middle fork, adj. Stith & Cox; 1 May 1775, p.30. £2. Whereas by Pat. 12 May 1759 gtd. unto Joshua Worsham [PB 34, p.306] in Mecklenburg formerly Lunenburg Co. And Whereas the sd Joshua Worsham hath failed to pay Quitrents and *Timothy Smith* hath made humble suit to our Late Lieutenant Governor and Commander in Chief and hath obtained a G. for the same which he hath assigned unto Edmund Taylor.

LITTLEBURY ROBINSON, 693 acs. Brunswick Co. on the N side of Fountains; adj. Wyche, Clark & Freeman; 1 May 1775, p.32. £2. 418 acs. part was gtd. sd Robinson by pat. 10 Sep 1767 [PB 37, p.207], 104 acs. other part was gtd. to Henry Wych by Pat. 25 Sep 1762 [PB 35, p.75] the right & title whereof is since become vested in the sd Littlebury Robinson and 171 acs. the Residue never before gtd.

CHARLES RUDDER, 369⅓ acs. Norfolk Co.; adj. Thomas Nash Senior, Thomas Nash, John Jameson, Samuel Barrington, Hugh McCoy & Jonathan Stokes; 1 May 1775, p.34. 40 Shill.

WILLIAM WHITLOCK & SARAH his wife, 311 acs. Nansemond Co. adj. Thomas Norflet, Summer's Manor plantation, to a small Gutt & the Riv.; 1 May 1775, p.35. for 2 lbs. tobacco for every Acre of sd Land Whereas by Inquisition indented taken in Co. 4 Jan 1774 by virtue of a Warrant directed to John Gregory our Escheator for sd Co. It appears that *Edward Jordan* Late of sd Co. died seized of 2 tracts or parcels of Land containing 311 acs. in sd Co. which is found to escheat to use from the sd Edward Jordan And Whereas *Sarah Jordan* now the wife of William Whitlock before the Intermarrige made humble Suit to our Lieutenant and Governor General & obtained a G. for the same.

GEORGE WATKINS, 1,204 acs. Pittsylvania Co. crossing the Hazle run; adj. Terry, Chiswell, Weakley, Medkiff & Chaney; 15 Mar 1776 *in the 16th year of our Reign, George the third, John Earl of Dunmore our Lieutenant and Governor General of our sd Colony and Dominion at Williamsburg*, p.37-38. £6. Whereas by Pat. 30 Aug 1763 Gtd. John Robinson Esq. [PB 35, p.345] containing 7,384 acs. in Halifax Co. now Pittsylvania And Whereas *William Stokes* Exor. &c of *Robert Wade decd.* in whom the right of 1,200 acs. part thereof is Since become Vested hath failed to pay the Quitrents of and To Cultivate & Improve the sd 1,200 acs. Which upon a Resurvey is found to Contain 1,204 acs. and George Watkins hath made humble Suit to our late Governor of our sd Colony and Dominion and hath Obtained a G. for the same.

[*The preceding entry was the final patent issued under the Seal of the Colony and Dominion of Virginia.*]

Grant Book E, pp.38–929
14 Jul 1780 to 1 Feb 1781

JOSEPH SMITH, Assignee of JAMES PRUNTY, 170 acs. by Survey bearing date 12 Mar 1765, in Pittsylvania Co. on the head of Dittoes Cr., adj. Charles Below; 14 Jul 1780 and of the Commonwealth the 5th, *In witness whereof Thomas Jefferson Esq. Governor of the Commonwealth of Virginia hath hereunto Set his hand and Caused the Seal of the sd Commonwealth to be Affixed at Richmond*, p.38. for the Ancient Composition of 20 Shillings Sterling paid into the Treasury of this Commonwealth by Joseph Smith.

JOHN LEWIS, 2,000 acs. by Survey 30 Jun 1774 in Kentuckey Co. on Elk Horn Cr. the Waters of Ohio, adj. Leroy

Griffin & Hugh Mercer; 14 Jul 1780, p.39. *in Consideration of Military Service performed by John Lewis According to the terms of the King of Great Britains Proclamation of 1763.*

ANDREW LEWIS, Esquire, 2,000 acs. by Survey 8 Jul 1775 in Kentuckey Co. on Sinking Cr. about 8 or 9 Miles from Kentucky River and nearly a North Course from Harwoods Landing, by a draught, on a Rise; 17 Jul 1780, p.39. *in Consideration of Military Service performed by Andrew Lewis Esquire According to the terms of the King of Great Britains Proclamation of 1763.*

ANDREW LEWIS, Esquire, 3,000 acs. by Survey the 1st day of July 1774 in Kentucky Co. on Elk horn Cr. a br. of the Kentuck being the Waters of the Ohio; Crossing a Buffaloe Road, a br. & Elk horn Cr.; adj. John Lewis; 14 Jul 1780, p.40. *in Consideration of Military Service performed by Andrew Lewis Esquire According to the terms of the King of Great Britains Proclamation of 1763.*

ANDREW LEWIS, Esquire, as ass'ee of MATTHEW ROBERT & GEORGE HARNES, 100 acs. by Survey 4 Nov 1774 in Greenbrier Co. on the NE side of the Great Kanawa about 5 Miles above the Mouth on the lower side of Rock Castle Run, to a double Lynn [tree] by some Large Rocks; 14 Jul 1780, p.41. *in Consideration of Military Service performed by George Harnes & William Roberts According to the terms of the King of Great Britains Proclamation of 1763.*

CHARLES LEWIS's Sons JOHN LEWIS, ANDREW LEWIS & CHARLES LEWIS to whom he devised the same by his Last Will & Testament, 2,000 acs. by Survey 28 Jun 1774 in Kentuckey Co. on the Waters of Elk horn a br. of the Kentuckey Riv.; adj. the Lands of Griffin Peart, John Ashley & Hugh Mercer; 14 Jul 1780, p.42. *in Consideration of Military Service performed by Charles Lewis According to the terms of the King of Great Britains Proclamation of 1763.*

GEORGE WASHINGTON & ANDREW LEWIS, 250 acs. by Survey 26 May 1775 in Greenbrier Co. on the E side of the Great Kanhawa Including the buring Springs, Beginning by a Noal by a Run, by the Path; 14 Jul 1780, p.43. *in Consideration of Military Service performed by George Washington & Andrew Lewis Esquire According to the terms of the King of Great Britains Proclamation of 1763.*

ALEXANDER BLAINE/BLANE, 94 acs. by Survey 22 Mar 1775 in Albemarle Co. on the little Mountain and the Waters of the Cove Cr., in the Tabacco House Br., on the side of a mountain; adj. the sd Blaine/Blane, Charles Martin & John Thurmon; 14 Jul 1780, p.44. A.C. of 10 Shill.

THOMAS BOWYER, 1,000 acs. by Survey date 2 Jun 1774 in Kentuckey Co. near the Falls of the Ohio; adj. John Connelly, Charles Warrantstaff & Arthur Campbell; 14 Jul 1780, p.45. *in Consideration of Military Service performed by Thomas Bowyer, Gent. According to the terms of the King of Great Britains Proclamation of 1763* and also of the A.C. of £5 Sterl. paid into the Treasury of this Commonwealth.

MATTHEW RITCHIE & WILLIAM BRUCE ass'ee of BURTON LUCAS, 1,307 acs. by Survey 28 Jan 1775 in Yohogania Co. on the Waters of Shirtees Cr., Beginning on a Ridge; adj. Rankins, William Price & Marcus Stephinson; 20 Jul 1780, p.46. *in Consideration of Military Service performed by Barton Lucas According to the terms of the King of Great Britains Proclamation of 1763.*

ROBERT JOHNSTON, 328 acs. by Survey 14 Dec 1769, in Amherst Co. on the Brs. of Horsleys Cr., adj. Charles Ellis's Orphans [their Lines]; 20 Jul 1780, p.47. A.C. of 35 Shill. Sterl.

WILLIAM PRESTON, Ass'ee of JOHN FLOYD & HENRY SMITH, 120 acs. by survey 1 Oct 1772 in Botetourt Co. on Palls Cr. [Potts Cr.?] a Br. of James Riv., Beginning at the lower End of William Preston first Survey, near a High Bank, Crossing the Cr. to a Steep Rockey Bank; 20 Jul 1780, p.48. A.C. of 15 Shill. Sterl.

JOHN HOGG, Ass'ee of ROBERT JOHNSTON, 392 acs. Albemarle Co. by Survey 14 Apr 1756 on the S side of Maple Cr., adj. John Burk & William Stephenson; 20 Jul 1780, p.49. A.C. of 40 Shill. Sterl.

ROBERT ELLIOT, 87 acs. by Survey 12 Nov 1767 in Botetourt Co. on a Br. of the South fork of Roanoke, to the Cr. at the head of a small Island, on the point of a Spur, in a Gully; 20 Jul 1780, p.50. A.C. of 10 Shill. Sterl.

WILLIAM DIZMANG/DISMANG, 239 acs. by Survey 22 Jan 1774 in Lunenburg Co. on the Brs. of the Haw Br.; adj. Nicholas Callaham, Edlow & Degraffenriedt; 20 Jul 1780, p.50. A.C. of 25 Shill. Sterl.

CHARLES YANCEY, 360 acs. by Survey 25 Sep 1768 in Mecklenburg Co. on the brs. of Grassey Cr.; adj. the Country Line [East], Franklin, Allen & sd Yancey; 20 Jul 1780, p.51. A.C. of £2 Sterl.

THOMAS MAXWELL Ass'ee of the said JOHN GILLIAM, by Survey 18 Nov 1775, 200 acs. in Kentucky Co. on a Br. which empties into the Kentucky on the N side about 8 Miles above Boonsborough, by a Draft; 20 Jul 1780, p.52. *in Consideration of Military Service performed by John Gilliam in the late War between Great Britain and France according to the Terms of the King of Great Britains proclamation of 1763.*

JOHN ROBINSON, by Survey 5 Jul 1767, 83 acs. Botetourt Co. on Den Run a Br. of Roanoke, down the River Bank and passing the Mouth of sd Run to the foot of a high Mountain, adj. Thomas Evans; 20 Jul 1780, p.53. A.C. of 10 Shill. Sterl.

JOHN ROBINSON, by Survey 18 Jan 1772, 200 acs. Botetourt Co. on the Brs. of Ingles Mill Cr. being the Waters of Roan Oke, adj. another of this Surveys; 20 Jul 1780, p.54. A.C. of 20 Shill. Sterl.

JOHN ROBINSON, by Survey 20 Jan 1772, 115 acs. Botetourt Co. on the head Brs. of Ingles Mill Cr. being the Waters of Roanoke; 20 Jul 1780, p.55. A.C. of 15 Shill. Sterl.

JAMES BURNSIDES ass'ee of JOHN McCLENACHAN who was Ass'ee of

HENRY WILLIAMS, 1,000 acs. by Survey 2 Apr 1774 in Greenbrier Co. on Indian Cr. a br. of New Riv.; adj. Thomas Stewart, sd Burnsides, John Cantley, John Patterson & John Handley; 20 Jul 1780, p.56. *in Consideration of Military Service performed by Henry Williams According to the terms of the King of Great Britains Proclamation of 1763.*

JANE POUND, by Survey 29 Apr 1773, 400 acs. Halifax Co. on the drafts of Peters Cr., up the North fork of sd Cr., up Boyds Ferry Road; adj. Daniel Wall, Cole, David Wall, Dunkley & Comer; 20 July 1780, p.58. A.C. of 40 Shill. Sterl.

WILLIAM THOMPSON & WILLIAM PRESTON Executors of JAMES PATTON dec'd, 320. acs. by Survey 9 Nov 1779 in Montgomery Co. on Toms Cr. a br. of New Riv., with the Patent Lines, to a Stake on a Barran hill, on a Ridge, adj. George Sharps Land; 20 Jul 1780, p.59. 35 Shill. Sterl. whereas by one Patent under the Seal of our Colony and Dominion of Virginia bearing date 20 Jun 1753 Gtd. to James Patton Containing 7,500 acs. on the Waters of Woods Riv. then in Augusta Co. [PB 32 p.178] now Montgomery Co. and whereas Hardness Sharp and George Sharp his Eldest son and heir at Law in whom the right and title of 320 acs. part is since become Vested hath failed to pay Quitrents as to the sd 320 acs. and William Thompson and William Preston Exors. of James Patton dec'd made humble suit to our Late Lieutenant Governor and Commander in chief and hath obtained a grant for the same.

WILLIAM THOMPSON & WILLIAM PRESTON Exors. of JAMES PATTON dec'd, by Survey 10 Nov 1779, 290 acs. Montgomery Co. on Toms Cr. a br. of New Riv., by a Path, on a Ridge; adj. Michael Kinders Land, William Byers Land, John Cooks Line & Jacob Lingells line; 20 Jul 1780, p.61. A.C. of 30 Shill. Sterl. Whereas by one Patent 20 Jun 1753 gtd. James Patton containing 7,500 acs. on the Waters of Woods Riv. then in Augusta Co. [PB 32 p.178] now Montgomery Co. and whereas Conrad Kinder in whom the right and title of 290 acs. part is since become Vested hath failed to pay Quitrents as to the said 290 acs. and William Thompson and William Preston Exors. of James Patton dec'd made humble Suit to our late Lieutenant Governor and Commander in Chief and hath obtained a grant for the same.

DAVID McCLENACHAN Ass'ee of WILLIAM McCLENACHAN eldest son and heir at Law to JOHN McCLENACHAN Dec'd, by Survey 23 Dec 1754, 100 acs. in Botetourt Co. formerly Augusta on a Br. of Buffaloe Cr. a Br. of Roanoke; adj. Tobias Smith, Reaves & Snodgras; 20 Jul 1780, p.62. A.C. of 10 Shill. Sterl.

WILLIAM THOMPSON & WILLIAM PRESTON Executors of JAMES PATTON dec'd, 210 acs. by Survey 10 Nov 1779 in Montgomery Co. on Toms Cr. a br. of New Riv., by a path; adj. Michael Kinder, Prices Land, Lortons Line & Jacob Harmon's line; 20 Jul 1780, p.63. A.C. of 25 Shill. Sterl. Whereas by one Patent under the Seal of our Colony and Dominion of Virginia bearing date 20 Jun 1753 gtd. to James Patton 7,500 acs. on the Waters of Woods Riv. then in Augusta Co. [PB 32 p.178] now Montgomery Co. and whereas John Adams in whom the right and title of 210 acs. part is Since become Vested hath failed to pay Quitrents as to the sd 210 acs. and William Thompson and William Preston Exors. of James Patton dec'd Made humble Suit to our Late Lieutenant Governor and Commander in Chief and hath Obtained a G. for the same.

JOHN ARMSTRONG, by Survey 10 Jul 1776, 200 acs. in Kentucky Co. formerly Fincastle on a Br. of Licking Cr.; 20 Jul 1780, p.64. in Consideration of Military Service performed by John Armstrong as a Sergeant during the Late War between Great Britain and France according to the terms of the King of Great Britains Proclamation of 1763.

WILLIAM THOMPSON & WILLIAM PRESTON Executors of JAMES PATTON dec'd, 285 acs. by Survey 20 Nov 1779 in Montgomery Co. on Toms Cr. a br. of the New Riv., on a ridge, adj. Martin Loys Land, with the Patent Line and the Line of a former Survey; 20 Jul 1780, p.65. A.C. of 30 Shill. Sterl. Whereas by one Patent under the Seal of our Colony and Dominion of Virginia 20 Jun 1753 gtd. to James Patton containing 7,500 acs. on the Waters of Woods Riv. then in Augusta Co. [PB 32 p.178] now in Montgomery Co. and whereas George Sharp in whom the right and title of 285 acs. part thereof is Since become Vested hath failed to pay Quitrents as to the sd 285 acs. and William Thompson and William Preston Exors. of James Patton dec'd made humble Suit and hath Obtained a G. for the same.

RICHARD HIGHT Ass ee of WYATT WILLIAMS Heirs at Law of JOHN WILLIAMS Dec'd and also Ass'ee of ISAAC BROWN Heir at Law of ISRAEL BROWN Dec'd, 393 acs. by Survey 28 Feb 1750/51 made for the sd John Williams and Israel Brown in Lunenburg Co. on the head of Crooked Run and Stoney Cr., adj. Ussery & Brown; 20 Jul 1780, p.67. A.C. of 40 Shill. Sterl. [This land was referred to as Williams's & Brown's in PB 32 p.503 to George Green. Also see adj. land in PB 30 p.490 to John Ussery, PB 37 p.183 to Joseph Lyell & PB 37 p.732 to David Garland] [The Grant is duplicated on p.81]

DAVID ROBINSON, 1,000 acs. by Survey 16 May 1776 in Fincastle Co. now Kentuckey on a br. of the Kentuckey Riv. which empties about 4 or 5 Miles below Boonsborough; 20 Jul 1780, p.68. in Consideration of Military Service Performed by David Robinson According to the terms of the King of Great Britains Proclamation of 1763 also of the Ancient Composition of £5 Sterl. paid into the Treasury of this Commonwealth.

JOHN ROBINSON, by **Inclusive Survey** bearing Date 9 Nov 1767 and Contains 133 acs. the other bearing Date 10 Mar 1772 and Contains 51 acs. in all 184 acs. in Botetourt Co. on a Small Br. of Ingles Mill Cr. called Ceder Run a br. of Roanoke, Beginning by a Br. near the Land of William Handley, on a Ridge, adj. Madly's Land; 20 Jul 1780, p.69. A.C. of 20 Shill. Sterl.

SACKVILL BREWER as ass'ee of JAMES EAST, 382 acs. by survey 12 Aug 1773 in Pittsylvania Co. on the Brs. of Horse pasture Cr.; adj. Joseph Camron, Randolph, & Neal ONeal; 20 Jul 1780, p.70. A.C. of 40 Shill. Sterl.

JOHN ROBINSON, 92 acs. by Survey 20 Jan 1772 Botetourt Co. on the Brs. of Ingles Mill Cr. being the waters of Roanoke, Beginning in the Road Leading from Drapers to Hanns Meadow; 20 Jul 1780, p.72. A.C. of 10 Shill. Sterl.

JOHN ARMSTRONG, 350 acs. by **an Inclusive Survey** 21 Aug 1772 in Botetourt Co. on the Waters of Roanoke, at the head of a Spring, along the Mountain; adj. McDonald, Preston & Snodgrass; 20 Jul 1780, p.72. A.C. of 35 Shill. Sterl. 57 acs. part thereof being part of a pat. for 218 acs. formerly Gtd. Bryan McDonald Senior 10 Mar 1756 [Augusta Co. PB 34 p.12] the Right and Title of which is since become vested in sd John Armstrong and 76 acs. part thereof being part of a pat. for 95 acs. formerly Gtd. by pat. to the sd John Armstrong 16 Sep 1765 [Augusta Co. PB 36 p.889] and 92 acs. part being part of a pat. for 150 acs. formerly Gtd. to sd John Armstrong 16 Sep 1765 [Augusta Co. PB 36 p.878] and 125 acs. the Residue never before gtd.

JAMES SPEED, 397 acs. by Survey 23 Sep 1772 in Charlotte Co. on the Brs. of Twittys Cr. adj. Magabeys Line; 20 Jul 1780, p.74. A.C. of 40 Shill. Sterl.

JOHN MAGEE, 35 acs. by Survey 17 Mar 1768 in Botetourt Co. formerly Augusta on the Waters of Catawbo Cr. a br. of James Riv., Beginning by a br. at the foot of a Ridge, to a Rocky Point of a Ridge, adj. Donilly; 20 Jul 1780, p.75. A.C. of 5 Shill.

JOHN ROBINSON, 64 acs. by Survey 7 Nov 1767 in Botetourt Co. on a Br. of the North fork of Roanoke; 20 Jul 1780, p.75. A.C. of 10 Shill. Sterl.

ALEXANDER SNODGRASS ass'ee of JOHN WITHERS who was Ass'ee of JAMES McMILLAN, 135 acs. by Survey 9 Jun 1767 in Botetourt Co. formerly Augusta on a small br. of Catawbo a Br. of James Riv., on a Ridge, adj. John Donnilly / Donilly; 20 Jul 1780, p.76. A.C. of 15 Shill. Sterl.

STEPHEN HEARD, 1,245 acs. by Survey 9 Dec 1778 in Henry Co. on the brs. of Camp br. and Cedar Run between Pigg Riv. and Blackwater Riv.; Crossing Ceder Run & poplar Camp Cr.; adj. Heards old Line, Isham Belcher & Wittons order Line; 20 Jul 1780, p.77. A.C. of £6.S5 Sterl.

JOHN ROBINSON, 110 acs. by Survey 6 Jun 1767 in Botetourt Co. formerly Augusta on the Waters of Roanoke Joining the Land whereon he dwells, also adj. Ingles's Line; 20 Jul 1780, p.79. A.C. of 15 Shill. Sterl.

JAMES MEADOR, 303 acs. by Survey 15 Apr 1774 in Bedford Co. on Jumping Run; adj. Walton, Wallox & Talbot; 20 Jul 1780, p.80. A.C. of 30 Shill. Sterl. [Regranted to William Board in GB 46 p.559 dated 11 Dec 1800]

RICHARD HIGHT Ass'ee of WYATT WILLIAMS & ISAAC BROWN, the said Wyatt Williams being Heir at Law to JOHN WILLIAMS dec'd and the said ISAAC BROWN being Heir at Law to ISRAEL BROWN dec'd, 393 acs. by Survey 28 Feb 1750/51, in Lunenburg Co. on the head of Crooked run and Stoney Cr., adj. Usery & Brown; 20 Jul

1780, p.81. A.C. 40 Shill. Sterl. [This grant is a duplicate of p.67]

WILLIAM BUTLER, 490 acs. by Survey 22 Mar 1775 in Bedford Co. on the Brs. of Crab Orchard and Back Creeks, to the Road; adj. Talbot, William Austin & his old Lines; 20 Jul 1780, p.82. A.C. of £2.S10 Sterl.

CHRISTOPHER IRVINE, 290 acs. by Survey 8 Nov 1775 in Bedford Co. on the S side of Cattail Spring Br. and on both sides of Watry Br. being West Brs. of Flat Cr.; adj. Anthony, Russell, & John Callaway near a high land pond; 20 Jul 1780, p.83. A.C. of 30 Shill. Sterl.

BUCKLEY WALKER, 200 acs. by Survey 8 Mar 1775 in Bedford Co. on both sides of Black water Road between the Brs. of Flat Cr. and Troublesome Cr.; adj. Gaddy, his own Line, Thompson, David Irvine & Nathaniel Winston; 20 Jul 1780, p.84. A.C. of 20 Shill. Sterl.

HENRY EDSON, 424 acs. by Survey 15 Nov 1770 in Bedford Co. on both sides of Otter Riv., on the sd River Bank Just below the Mouth of Flintstone Cr., adj. Phelps; 20 Jul 1780, p.85. A.C. of 30 Shill. Sterl. 124 acs. part formerly gtd. to John Abston by Letters patent 17 May 1759 [PB 33 p.564] the right and title thereof is since become vested in the sd Henry Edson and 300 acs. the residue never before granted.

JOHN BOOTH, 286 acs. by Survey 28 Apr 1778 in Bedford Co. on both sides of Stanton Riv.; adj. Yarbroug, Randolph, Talbot & Bradshaw; 20 Jul 1780, p.87. A.C. of 30 Shill. Sterl.

JOHN WEBSTER GILBERT, 360 acs. by Survey 15 Mar 1770 in Bedford Co. on West br. of Seneca Cr., adj. his own Lines & Gordon; 20 Jul 1780, p.88. A.C. of 40 Shill. Sterl.

CHARLES SIMMONS, 37 acs. by Survey 13 Mar 1771 in Bedford Co. on W Brs. of Falling Riv., crossing 2 Small Brs.; adj. Davis, his own Line & Bolling; 20 Jul 1780, p.89. A.C. of 5 Shill. Sterl.

JAMES GREER, 290 acs. by Survey 6 Apr 1772 in Bedford Co. on the N side of Staunton Riv., by the Point of an Island, down & Crossing the Riv.; adj. William Greer, Walton & his own lines; 20 Jul 1780, p.90. A.C. of 30 Shill. Sterl. [Written as JAMES GREER twice & JAMES GREEN once]

THOMAS HUNT, 304 acs. by Survey 18 Mar 1774 in Bedford Co. on the S side of Stanton Riv.; adj. Bradshaw, John Hailes Lines & Mead; 20 Jul 1780, p.91. A.C. of 30 Shill. Sterl.

WILLIAM McPIKE, 304 acs. by Survey 10 Mar 1755 in Bedford Co. on both sides of black water Riv.; 20 Jul 1780, p.92. A.C. of 30 Shill. Sterl.

SAMUEL LANGDON, 160 acs. by Survey 6 Nov 1771 in Bedford Co. on the Brs. of Griffiths Cr. adj. Bounds's Line; 20 Jul 1780, p.93. A.C. of 20 Shill. Sterl.

PETER HOLLAND, 210 acs. by Survey 16 Mar 1779 in Bedford Co. on Meriman Run, on the Road, adj. his own Lines & Dividing Line; 20 Jul 1780, p.94. A.C. of 25 Shill. Sterl.

ABNER MARKHAM, 180 acs. by Survey 14 Apr 1778 in Bedford Co. on the N Brs. of Black water Riv., adj. Farlor; 20 Jul 1780, p.95. A.C. of 20 Shill. Sterl.

JOHN DAVIS, 400 acs. by Survey 8 Apr 1769 in Mecklenburg Co. adj. the Tract whereon he Lives at Kings ford and on the N side Rowanoak Riv.; adj. John Spead, Mitchell, Isaac Mitchell & Speed; 20 Jul 1780, p.96. A.C. of 40 Shill. Sterl.

ROGER ATKINSON Gent., 400 acs. by Survey 25 Oct 1771 in Halifax Co. on the Draughts of Bluewing, on the Country Line [East], Crossing a Road; adj. Herbert Hawkins Line, Atkinsons Western Line & William Gills East Line; 20 Jul 1780, p.97. A.C. of 40 Shill. Sterl.

ROGER ATKINSON Gent. Ass'ee of JOSEPH GILL, 400 acs. by Survey 17 Oct 1772 in Halifax Co. on the Draughts of Aarons Cr., adj. Street; 20 Jul 1780, p.98. A.C. of 40 Shill. Sterl.

JONATHAN RICHARDSON, 80 acs. by Survey 1 nov 1771 in Bedford Co. on both sides of Gills Cr., down pates Br., adj. Charles Cox; 20 Jul 1780, p.99. A.C. of 10 Shill. Sterl.

ROGER ATKINSON Gent. Ass'ee of ARCHIBALD ROBERTSON who was ass'ee of the Heirs of ROBERT WALTON dec'd, 384 acs. by Survey 10 Mar 1752 in Pittsylvania formerly Lunenburg Co. on both sides of Cane Cr., adj. Cargil; 20 Jul 1780, p.100. A.C. of 40 Shill. Sterl.

THOMAS ARTHUR, 197 acs. by Survey 16 Feb 1773 in Bedford Co. on the Little Cr. (a Br. of Griffiths Cr.); adj. his own Line, Doggel & Mead; 20 Jul 1780, p.101. A.C. of 20 Shill. Sterl.

ROBERT BABER, 150 acs. by Survey 10 Dec 1772 in Bedford Co. on the S side of Otter Riv., adj. his own Lines & John Talbot; 20 Jul 1780, p.102. A.C. of 15 Shill. Sterl.

JOHN WELCH, 400 acs. by Survey 7 Feb 1771, 304 acs. which with 96 acs. formerly Survey'd amounts to 400 acs., in Bedford Co. on the N side of Seneca Cr., up Rogers Br., down Phelps old Road; adj. his own Line, Samuel Gilbert, John Michael & David Mosley Davidson; 20 Jul 1780, p.103. A.C. of 40 Shill. Sterl.

JOHN WARD Gent., 111 acs. by Survey 10 Nov 1769 in Henry Co. formerly Pittsylvania on Turkey co[c]k Cr.; 20 Jul 1780, p.104. A.C. of 15 Shill. Sterl.

RICHARD BAILEY ass'ee of JAMES CHITWOOD, 445 acs. by Survey 21 Dec 1762 in Bedford Co. on both sides of Black Water Riv.; 20 Jul 1780, p.105. A.C. of 45 Shill. Sterl.

JOHN FARMER Ass'ee of WILLIAM BURFORD Ass'ee of ISHAM TALBOT Ass'ee of JOHN WALLOX, 420 acs. by Survey 9 Apr 1755 in Bedford Co. on both sides of Jumping Run, adj. Richard Stith; 20 Jul 1780, p.106. A.C. of 45 Shill. Sterl.

STEPHEN PANKEY as Ass'ee of JOHN EDMONDS, 200 acs. by Survey 2 Apr 1774 in Pittsylvania Co. on the Brs. of

Birches Cr.; 20 Jul 1780, p.107. A.C. of 20 Shill. Sterl.

JOHN WARD, 89 acs. by Survey 28 Oct 1766 in Henry Co. formerly Halifax on both sides of Buffaloe a Cr. of the Irwin Riv., Crossing two Bold Brs., adj. sd John Wards old Line; 20 Jul 1780, p.108. A.C. of 10 Shill. Sterl.

JAMES STEWARD, 400 acs. by Survey 21 Mar 1769 in Pittsylvania Co. on Chesnut Cr., Crossing a fork of the aforesd Cr., adj. his own Line; 20 Jul 1780, p.109. A.C. of 40 Shill. Sterl.

JONATHAN DAVIS, 120 acs. by Survey 8 Apr 1765 in Halifax Co. on both sides of Chesnut Cr., adj. Thomas Hall; 20 Jul 1780, p.110. A.C. of 15 Shill. Sterl.

SAMUEL PATTERSON, 155 acs. by Survey 15 Oct 1773 in Pittsylvania Co. on Doe Cr., adj. his own Lines & Choats Lines; 20 Jul 1780, p.111. A.C. of 20 Shill. Sterl.

JOSEPH ANTHONY, 550 acs. by Survey 5 Dec 1771 in Bedford Co. on the Head Brs. of Beaver Cr. including the Maple Pond at the head of a fork of Seneca Cr., crossing the Otter River Road, near the main Br., adj. Mary Read [her Lines] & Clements Lines; 20 Jul 1780, p.112. A.C. of 15 Shill. Sterl. *400 acs. part thereof was gtd. to the sd Joseph Anthony [& Robert Bumpass] by Letters Pat. 20 Jun 1772 [PB 40 p.726 which was a regrant of Albemarle Co. PB 34 p.18 to James Johnson] and 150 acs. the residue never before gtd.*

CHARLES LYNCH, 3,480 acs. by Survey 3 Nov 1773 in Bedford Co. on the N side of Staunton Riv. on the upper side of Otter Riv. including Briery Cr., Beginning at the Mouth of sd Otter Riv. thence up the same to Just above the Mouth of Wash arse Cr., on the top of the Ridge between the Heads of Lynches Cr. and Briery Cr. thence down the Ridge between two Creeks, down a small Br.; 20 Jul 1780, p.113. A.C. of £9.S5. Sterl. *1,379 acs. part thereof is part of 3,344 acs. gtd. sd Charles Lynch by Pat. 20 Sep 1759 [PB 33 p.641 which included his Brunswick Co. PB 19 p.1068 & PB28 p.252 which included his PB 19 p.1037 & PB 19 p.1130], 81 acs. part gtd. sd Charles Lynch by Pat. 20 Sep 1759 [Lunenburg Co. PB 33 p.640], 167 acs. part gtd. to Jonathan Jennings by Pat. 10 Sep 1767 [PB 37 p.168] the right and title of which is Since become vested in the sd Charles Lynch and 1,853 acs. the residue never before gtd., 454 acs. part was Surveyed for Charles Lynch 14 Nov 1770, 240 acs. part was Surveyed 14 Nov 1770 and 1,159 acs. was Seperately surveyed for the sd Charles Lynch by Virtue of three entries Assigned by Jonathan Jennings.*

WILLIAM TOMPSON, 400 acs. by Survey 17 Mar 1773 in Pittsylvania Co. on both sides of Chesnut Cr.; adj. Grayham, Callaway, Robert Hill, Thomas Hutchings & sd Graham; 20 Jul 1780, p.115. A.C. of 40 Shill. Sterl.

WILLIAM ARMSTRONG, 328 acs. by Survey 27 Oct 1774 in Augusta Co. on Pine run a br. of Jennings's br. [a Br. of Catheys Riv.], to a pine on a bank; adj. Samuel Morra, Robert Mckettrick, Robert Armstrong & John Kirk; 20 Jul 1780, p.116. A.C. of 15 Shill. Sterl. *200 acs. part thereof is part of 400 acs. gtd. James Ball by Letters Pat. 1 Dec*

1740 [PB 19 p.817 to James Bell in that part of Orange Co. called Augusta] the right and title of which is since become vested in the sd William Armstrong, 14 acs. part was gtd. the sd William Armstrong by Letters Pat. 3 Aug 1771 [PB 40 p.618] and 114 acs. the residue never before gtd.

WILLIAM CALL, Gent., 250 acs. by Survey 1 May 1775 in Pr. Geo. Co. between and on Each side of Black Water Sw. and the Fox Br., crossing the Hog br., on the head of the middle Slash, crossing the heads of the Fox br., on the Long br.; adj. Theophilus Feild, sd Calls old Line, William Brown, Richard Stewart, his or the Heirs of Lewis Parham [their Lines], Francis Massenburg Fenn, the Land sd Call Purchased of Abraham Tucker & the Land he Purchased of James Pittillow; 20 Jul 1780, p.118. A.C. of 15 Shill. Sterl. *100 acs. part was gtd. to Abraham Tucker by Letters Pat. 20 Sep 1751 [PB 31 p.49] the right and title of which is since become vested in the sd William Call and 150 acs. resdiue never before gtd. it being only Entered with the Surveyor of the County by Samuel Gordon and by Alexander Gordon Heir of sd Samuel Assigned to the sd William Call.*

SAMUEL RUNKLE Ass'ee of GEORGE MOFFET, 160 acs. by Survey 9 Feb 1775 in Augusta Co. on the N side of Jennings Br., adj. **Daniel McNaris?** & John Beard; 20 Jul 1780, p.120. A.C. of 20 Shill. Sterl.

JOHN WARD, Gent., 87 acs. by Survey 5 Nov 1766 in Henry Co. formerly Halifax on the Brs. of the Flat Cr. of the Irvine Riv., Crossing Rich Run; 20 Jul 1780, p.121. A.C. of 10 Shill. Sterl.

ROBERT WILLIAMS, 30 acs. by Survey 12 Oct 1762 in Pittsylvania Co. on both sides the South fork of Sandy Riv., adj. Wade; 20 Jul 1780, p.122. A.C. of 5 Shill. Sterl.

JOHN WARD, Gent., 135 acs. by Survey 6 Nov 1773 in Henry Co. formerly Pittsylvania on the North fork of Turkey Cock Cr. and the Brs. of Runnettbagg, adj. Robert Harston; 20 Jul 1780, p.123. A.C. of 15 Shill. Sterl.

SAMUEL PATTERSON, 126 acs. by Survey 29 Nov 1769 in Pittsylvania Co. on the North fork of doe Cr.; 20 Jul 1780, p.124. A.C. of 15 Shill. Sterl.

SAMUEL PATTERSON, 552 acs. by Survey 29 Nov 1769 in Pittsylvania Co. on Doe Cr., on a fork of sd Cr., adj. his old Line; 20 Jul 1780, p.125. A.C. of £2.S15 Sterl.

JOHN WARD, Gent., 333 acs. by Survey 5 Mar 1770 in Pittsylvania Co. on the Waters of Stanton Riv., Crossing Tinkers Cr.; 20 Jul 1780, p.126. A.C. of 35 Shill. Sterl.

JOHN POAGE, 200 acs. **by an Inclusive Survey** 16 Jun 1772 in Augusta Co. on a Gap of the North Mountain known by the name of Jennings Gap, crossing Jennings Br., adj. Robert McKittrick; 20 Jul 1780, p.127. A.C. of 20 Shill. Sterl.

JOHN WARD, Gent., 217 acs. by Survey 22 Nov 1773 in Henry Co. formerly Pittsylvania on the head Brs. of Wagion Cr., on the Top of Main

Mountain; 20 Jul 1780, p.128. A.C. of 25 Shill. Sterl.

JOHN WARD, Gent., 206 acs. by Survey 28 Oct 1766 in Pittsylvania Co. formerly Halifax on both sides of Buffaloe Cr., adj. John Kendrick; 20 Jul 1780, p.129. A.C. of 25 Shill. Sterl.

JOHN WARD & JOHN CALLOWAY, Gentlemen, 1,170 acs. by Survey 15 Nov 1773 in Henry Co. formerly Pitsylvania on both sides of Smiths Riv., Beginning on the S side of [Fointerack] Cr.; adj. Daniel Rion, Daniel Campbell, Luke Folue, Bartley Folue & James Poteete; 20 Jul 1780, p.130. A.C. of £6 Sterl.

JOHN WARD, Gent., 200 acs. by Survey 6 Nov 1773 in Henry Co. Formerly Pittsylvania on both sides of Smiths Riv., down Runetbag Cr., adj. Clonches Line & the sd Ward; 20 Jul 1780, p.132. A.C. of 20 Shill. Sterl.

THOMAS MANN RANDOLPH, JOHN HARMER & WALTER KING, Esquire, 1,155 acs. by Survey 17 Mar 1748/49 in Henry Co. formerly Lunenburg on both Sides of the North fork of Mayo Riv., along their former Line; 31 Jul 1780, p.133. A.C. of £6 Sterl.

THOMAS MANN RANDOLPH, JOHN HARMER & WALTER KING, Esquire, 890 acs. by Survey 16 Mar 1748/49 in Henry Co. formerly Lunenburg on Jordans Cr. and its Brs., adj. their Line; 31 Jul 1780, p.134. A.C. of £4.S10 Sterl.

JOHN WARD, Gent., 318 acs. by Survey 5 Nov 1773 in Henry Co. formerly Pittsylvania Co. the S side of Runnetbag Cr. of Smiths Riv., adj. Chiles Line & Harstons Line; 20 Jul 1780, p.135. A.C. of 35 Shill. Sterl.

JAMES TAYLOR, 63 acs. by Survey 5 Nov 1779 in Rockbridge Co. in the forks of James Riv. On the Waters of Buffaloe Cr.; 20 Jul 1780, p.136. A.C. of 10 Shill. Sterl.

GARROT GROCE, 125 acs. by Survey 14 May 1767 in Pittsylvania Co. formerly Halifax on the Brs. of the upper double Cr., adj. William Payne Senior & Bird; 20 Jul 1780, p.137. A.C. of 15 Shill. Sterl.

EDWARD CHOAT JUNR., 253 acs. by Survey 13 Oct 1772 in Henry Co. formerly Pittsylvania on the South fork of Doe Run; 20 Jul 1780, p.138. A.C. of 25 Shill. Sterl.

The Heirs of PAUL CHILDS Dec'd, 146 acs. by Survey 6 Dec 1768 in Pittsylvania Co. on the Waters of Wogion Cr., adj. Harbour; 20 Jul 1780, p.139. A.C. of 15 Shill. Sterl.

JAMES CALAWAY & JEREMIAH EARLEY Ass'ee of FRANCIS BIRD who was Ass'ee of JOSEPH BIRD, 240 acs. by Survey 20 Apr 1769 in Pittsylvania Co. on the S side of Pigg Riv.; 20 Jul 1780, p.139. A.C. of 25 Shill. Sterl.

GARROT GROCE, 312 acs. by Survey 2 Apr 1774 in Pittsylvania Co. on the Brs. of Birches Cr.,; adj. Joseph Terry; 20 Jul 1780, p.140. A.C. of 30 Shill. Sterl.

EDWARD CHOAT, 485 acs. by Survey 18 Mar 1773 in Henry Co. formerly Pittsylvania on Doe Cr., adj. his own

Line; 20 Jul 1780, p.141. A.C. of £2.S10. Sterl.

ARCHIBALD GRAYHAM / GRAHAM, 900 acs. by Survey 11 May 1774 in Henry Co. formerly Pittsylvania on Chesnut Cr.; adj. Smith, Standefor, Robert Hill & Hanken; 20 Jul 1780, p.142. A.C. of £4.S10. Sterl.

WILLIAM STEGALL, 190 acs. by Survey 11 Dec 1764 in Pittsylvania Co. formerly Halifax on both sides of Turkey Cr. of Pigg Riv.; 20 Jul 1780, p.143. A.C. of 20 Shill. Sterl.

SAMUEL WOODS Ass'ee of OWEN HERNDON, 82 acs. by Survey 4 Mar 1774 in Amherst Co. on the S Brs. of Rockfish Riv.; adj. James Herd, David Doak & John Campbell; 20 Jul 1780, p.143. A.C. of 10 Shill. Sterl.

GEORGE TAYLOR, 70 acs. by Survey 9 Nov 1779 in Rockbridge Co. on the Waters of Buffaloe Cr. in the forks of James Riv. on the N side of the Short Hill, to two black Oaks on a Step, adj. Alexander Ligget; 20 Jul 1780, p.144. A.C. of 10 Shill. Sterl.

SMITH WEBB, 129 acs. by Survey 12 Apr 1769 in Henry Co. formerly Pittsylvania on Doe Cr., adj. his own Line; 20 Jul 1780, p.145. A.C. of 15 Shill. Sterl.

JEREMIAH EARLEY & JAMES CALAWAY, 374 acs. by Survey 9 Oct 1773 in Henry Co. formerly Pittsylvania on both sides of peeping Cr. of Pigg Riv., Crossing the Chappel Br. to the Road, to a Chestree Chesnut Tree; 20 Jul 1780, p.146. A.C. of 40 Shill. Sterl.

JOHN PAYNE, 388 acs. by Survey 23 Mar 1775 in Pittsylvania Co. on the Brs. of Sandy Cr., on the Road, adj. William [Durrell] & Wynn; 20 Jul 1780, p.147. A.C. of 40 Shill. Sterl.

BENJAMIN HOLLAND, 114 acs. by Survey 5 Dec 1763 in Pittsylvania Co. formerly Halifax on both sides of Sycamore Cr., adj. Calaway; 20 Jul 1780, p.147. A.C. of 15 Shill. Sterl.

EDWARD CHOAT, 295 acs. by Survey 25 Oct 1773 in Henry Co. formerly Pittsylvania on the S Brs. of Pigg Riv., crossing the double Brs., on Holloways Road, adj. John Holloway & James Smith; 20 Jul 1780, p.148 & p.149. A.C. of 30 Shill. Sterl.

JOHN MURCHIE, ½ Acre, one Lott or Parcel of Land in Chesterfeild Co. in the Town of Manchester Laid down in a platt of the sd Town Number 238, adj. the lands of the Honble. Archibald Cary Esquire &c.; 20 Jul 1780, p.149. in Consideration of the Sum of £17,000 Current Money of Virginia paid unto Jessee Cogbill Escheator for Chesterfeild Co. by John Murchie... *which was the Property of William Cuningham and Co. British Subjects and was sold by the sd Jesse Cogbill Escheator as aforesd unto the sd John Murchie Agreable to two Acts of Assembly passed in the year 1779 the One Intituled an Act Concerning Escheats and Forfeitures from British Subjects the other Intituled an Act Concerning Escheators.*

JAMES WHITE, 242 acs. by Survey 8 Feb 1775 in Chesterfeild Co., to the Court House Road; adj. Joseph Hardeway, Richard Perdue, James Baugh, John Graves & Francis Mann; 20

Jul 1780, p.150. A.C. of 25 Shill. Sterl. Whereas by one Pat. 5 Jun 1746 gtd. unto John Hatchett Containing 796 acs. in Chesterfeild Co. formerly Henrico [PB 25 p.107 to John Hatchet Junior on the S side Sappony Road and Crossing Worsham's Br.] and whereas John Hatchett & Charles Stuart in whom the right and title of 242 acs. part is since become Vested hath failed to pay Quitrents as to the sd 242 acs. and James White made humble Suit to our late Lieutenant Governor and Commander in Chief and hath obtained a G. for the same.

JEREMIAH EARLY and Company, 1,196 acs. by Survey 27 Apr 1779 in Henry Co. on the Brs. of Black water and Pigg Riv., Beginning on the Waters of the Meadow Br., Crossing two brs. of Maple Sw., near Hills Powder Mill; adj. Hill, John Savarywoods old Line, John Lumsden, John Heard, Early and Calaways Line, & Hills new Survey; 20 Jul 1780, p.152. A.C. of £6 Shill. Sterl.

JEREMIAH EARLY & JAMES CALAWAY, 1,057 acs. by Survey 17 Apr 1779 in Henry Co. on Pigg Riv. and the North Brs. thereof, crossing a Cr. and a Road, Crossing Hills Powder Mill br.; adj. Swenkfeild Hills new Survey, Bates, James Calaway, Robertson, & John Heard; 20 Jul 1780, p.153. A.C. of £5.S10. Sterl.

JEREMIAH EARLY & JAMES CALAWAY, 2,256 acs. by Survey 3 Mar 1779 in Henry Co. on the brs. of Pigg Riv. and Black water; adj. Manyfee, Hail, Vardiman, Cock, Donelsons Otherwise Early and Calaways line, Coles Otherwise Early and Calaways Line, & Farguson; 20 Jul 1780, p.154. A.C. of £11.S10 Sterl.

GEORGE TAYLOR, 100 acs. by Survey 5 Nov 1779 in Rockbridge Co. bet. Longs and James Harriss's Land on Buffaloe Cr. in the forks of James Riv., Beginning on the N side of the Short Hill; 20 Jul 1780, p.156. A.C. of 10 Shill. Sterl.

JEREMIAH EARLEY & JAMES CALAWAY, 533 acs. by Survey 5 Mar 1779 in Henry Co. on the S Brs. of Pigg Riv.; adj. William Manyfee Line where John Furgasons Line Crosses it, Another Survey of sd Furgasons on Stony Cr. Waters, & William Maryfee [sic]; 20 Jul 1780, p.157. A.C. of £2.S15. Sterl.

GEORGE TAYLOR, 92 acs. by Survey 5 Nov 1779 in Rockbridge Co. on the waters of Buffaloe Cr. in the forks of James Riv. at a place called *Richmans Draft*, on the N side of a Hill above the head of the Richmans Draft; 20 Jul 1780, p.158. A.C. of 10 Shill. Sterl.

THOMAS RUDD Ass'ee of HENRY TURPIN, 5 acs. by Survey 29 Mar 1780 in Chesterfield Co. on Spring Run, along the sd Spring; adj. William Purdue, James Rudd & James Gill; 20 Jul 1780, p.159. A.C. of 5 Shill. Sterl.

WILLIAM ROWLETT Ass'ee of JOHN HUMPHRIES, 400 acs. by Survey 14 Mar 1775 in Mecklenburg Co. on the waters of Laytons Cr., to a Maple in a Sw.; adj. Keiton, Marrable & sd Humphries Line; 20 Jul 1780, p.160. A.C. of 40 Shill. Sterl.

WILLIAM ROWLETT Ass'ee of JOHN HUMPHRIES, 272 acs. by Survey 14

Mar 1775 in Mecklenburg Co. on the Waters of Laytons Cr.; adj. Keiton, Marrable & Crowder; 20 Jul 1780, p.160. A.C. of 30 Shill. Sterl.

MICHAEL MORRISON, 48 acs. by Survey 2 Dec 1772 in Amherst Co. on the N Brs. of Hickory Cr., adj. his own Line; 20 Jul 1780, p.161. A.C. of 5 Shill. Sterl.

JOHN BATES, 200 acs. by Survey 28 Nov 1769 in Halifax Co. on the Upper side of the North fork of Bradley Cr., near Bookers Road, adj. Edward Hodges C. & Wades Line; 20 Jul 1780, p.162. A.C. of 20 Shill. Sterl.

JOHN WATHALL, 8 acs. by Survey 29 Mar 1780 in Chesterfield Co., adj. sd Wathall & William Nunally; 20 Jul 1780, p.163. A.C. of 5 Shill. Sterl.

THOMAS STOVALL, 242 acs. by Survey 9 Oct 1765 in Halifax Co. on the Draughts of little Reedy Cr.; adj. his own, William Owen, John Nichols Line, Thomas Treadaway, Richard Owen, Henry Owen & Thomas Clark; 20 Jul 1780, p.163. A.C. of 25 Shill. Sterl.

CHARLES SKIDWELL Ass'ee of ROBERT BOYLES, 360 acs. by Survey 18 Mar 1773 in Bedford Co. on the Brs. of Otter Riv., adj. Boyd & Sharp; 20 Jul 1780, p.164. A.C. of 40 Shill. Sterl.

JOHN OWEN, 320 acs. by Survey 23 Mar 1770 in Pittsylvania Co. on the Brs. of Dan Riv., on the Road; adj. sd John Owen, Adkinson, Thomas Wyn & Roberts Line; 20 Jul 1780, p.165. A.C. of 35 Shill. Sterl.

DUDLEY GLASS,, 400 acs. by Survey 5 Dec 1769 in Halifax Co. on the head Brs. of Bradleys Cr. and on both sides of Bookers Road, on the North fork of sd Cr.; adj. Peter Bryan, Micajah Hampton, Edmund Hodges, John Bates, Davis & Collier; 20 Jul 1780, p.166. A.C. of 40 Shill. Sterl.

SAMUEL PAXTON, 145 acs. by Survey 16 Apr 1765 in Augusta Co. near the Falls; adj. Bordens patent Line, Joseph Alexander, Samuel Paxton; 20 Jul 1780, p.167. A.C. of 15 Shill.

THOMAS BUFORD, 1,297 acs. by Survey 7 May 1771 in Bedford Co. on both sides of Bore Auger Cr., on the Top of a little Mountain; adj. the Pat. line, Charles Tate, Bramble & Walton; 20 Jul 1780, p.168. A.C. £6 Sterl. *136 acs. part thereof was gtd. to John Mills by Pat. 10 Jul 1767 [PB 37 p.35] the right and title of which is Since become vested in the said Thomas Buford and 1,161 acs. the Residue never before gtd.*

BENJAMIN ARTHUR, 250 acs. by Survey 10 Nov 1773 in Bedford Co. on E Brs. of Flat Cr., at the Road; adj. Christopher Irvine Clendening, the old line of Mead and Talbot, his own Line, John Machen & Clendening; 20 Jul 1780, p.170. A.C. 25 Shill. Sterl.

JEREMIAH WALTON, 400 acs. by Survey 23 Apr 1757 in Pittsylvania Co. formerly Halifax on the Brs. of Fly Blow Cr., adj. Goram Brown & Francis Anderson; 20 Jul 1780, p.171. A.C. 40 Shill. Sterl.

JAMES BUFORD, 235 acs. by Survey 14 Mar 1780 in Bedford Co. on the S Brs. of the North fork of Otter Riv., Crossing Lils Br., adj. Key & his own lines; 20 Jul 1780, p.172. A.C. 25 Shill. Sterl.

GASPER HOUSE ass'ee. of HUGH WOODS 426 acs. by Survey 2 Nov 1773 in Henry Co. formerly Pittsylvania Co. on the North fork of Grassey fork of Chesnut Cr., on Coles Road; adj. James Martins old Line, James Martian Afforesaid; 20 Jul 1780, p.172. A.C. 45 Shill. Sterl.

JAMES BATES, 400 acs. by Survey 5 Dec 1772 in Halifax Co. on draughts of Catawbo, on the Falls Br., crossing five Brs. of Catawbo (including the main); adj. Chandler, Spraggins Line, Earley & Abney; 20 Jul 1780, p.174. A.C. 40 Shill. Sterl.

BENJAMIN DAVIS, 740 acs. by Survey 7 Dec 1767 in Bedford Co. on the N side of Goose Cr., up Reads br. & Goose Cr.; adj. Callaway, Read & Bramblett; 20 Jul 1780, p.175. A.C. of £3.S15 Sterl.

ROBERT HODGES, 193 acs. by Survey 8 Sep 1779 in Henry Co. on Chesnut Cr., on a Clift of sd Cr.; adj. Samuel Patterson, Grimmett, Stewart & Davis; 20 Jul 1780, p.176. A.C. of 20 Shill. Sterl.

NATHAN GLYNN, 307 acs. by Survey 20 Apr 1757 in Halifax Co. on the draughts of Stinking Riv., adj. William May & Lightfoot; 20 Jul 1780, p.178. A.C. of 35 Shill. Sterl.

WILLIAM GOEN, 240 acs. by Survey 20 Mar 1762 in Bedford Co. on both sides of Island Cr., adj. Walton; 20 Jul 1780, p.178. A.C. of 25 Shill. Sterl.

THOMAS TUNSTALL/TUNSALL in trust for the use of the Estate of ROBERT ROBERTSON HUNT dec'd, 400 acs. by Survey 6 Oct 1750 in Halifax Co. on both sides of Reedy Cr.; 20 Jul 1780, p.179. A.C. of 40 Shill. Sterl.

HUDSON BLANKENSHIP, 170 acs., by Survey 10 Mar 1780 by Virtue of an Entry made by WILLIAM CANDLER 28 Jun 1763 and by him Assigned to sd HUDSON BLANKINSHIP, in Bedford Co. on Brs. of Rock Castle Cr.; adj. his own Lines, Moorman, John Lynch & Nowel Blankenship; 20 Jul 1780, p.180. A.C. of 20 Shill. Sterl.

FRANCIS MOORE PETTY, 469 acs. by Survey 8 Feb 1774 in Pittsylvania Co. on the Lick Br. of Green Rock Cr., adj. Turner; 20 Jul 1780, p.181. A.C. of £2.S10.

POLSER SMELSER, 560 acs. by Survey 5 Apr 1775 in Bedford Co. adj. his own Lines on South fork of Goose Cr. **including 160 acs. of Ptd. Land**, on Clove Cr.; adj. Randolphs old Line, Pierce & Walton; 20 Jul 1780, p.182. A.C. of £3.S12 Shill. Sterl. [Note the payment of the full 72 shillings for 720 acs. even though part of the land was already patented]

JAMES BOYD, 300 acs. by Survey 18 Mar 1773 in Bedford Co. on the Brs. of Otter Riv., down Stoney Run, Crossing a Fork of the sd Run; 20 Jul 1780, p.183. A.C. of 30 Shill. Sterl.

THOMAS BLANTON ass'ee of WILLIAM BOWIN, 38 acs. by Survey 17 Apr 1771 in Botetourt Co. on the S side Glade Cr. a Br. of Roan oke, adj. Rice Bowen; 20 Jul 1780, p.184. A.C. of 5 Shill.

THOMAS ASBURY/ASBERRY ass'ee of DANIEL ONEIL, 150 acs. by Survey

15 Dec 1770 in Bedford Co. on the N Brs. of Otter Riv.; adj. Richey, Turmon, Boyd, Dooley & Ritchey; 20 Jul 1780, p.185. A.C. of 15 Shill. Sterl.

ISAAC COLES Gent., 380 acs. by Survey 1752 in Halifax Co. on both sides of Ellis's Cr.; adj. Abney, Roy, Baughan & his own Lines; 20 Jul 1780, p.186. A.C. of 40 Shill. Sterl.

FRANCIS MOORE PETTY, 95 acs. by Survey 8 Feb 1774 in Pittsylvania Co. on the waters of Greenrock Cr.; adj. Washam, Turner & the sd Pettys former lines; 20 Jul 1780, p.187. A.C. of 10 Shill. Sterl.

ROBERT CHURCH, 185 acs. by Survey 6 Apr 1779 in Bedford Co. on a br. of Goose Cr., on McFalls Mountain, adj. sd Church & Talbot; 20 Jul 1780, p.188. A.C. 20 Shill. Sterl.

THOMAS BLANTON ass'ee of REICE BOWIN, 67 acs. by Survey 17 Feb 1768 in Botetourt Co. formerly Augusta on the Waters of Glade Cr. a Br. of Roan Oke, Beginning on a Hill side by the Great Road and near his patent Line, by a Draft, on a Ridge, Crossing the Panther Hollow; 20 Jul 1780, p.189. A.C. of 10 Shill. Sterl.

ELIJAH HUNT, 239 acs. by Survey 14 Dec 1765 in Halifax Co. on the S side of little Childreys Cr., crossing Cow Br., adj. John Sulling; 20 Jull 1780, p.189. A.C. of 25 Shill. Sterl.

THOMAS CAMPBELL, 246 acs. by Survey 23 May 1777 in Bedford Co. on the Widdows Mountain adj. William Buford's line, on McBrides, down McBride Br. to the fork; 20 Jul 1780, p.190. A.C. of 25 Shill. Sterl.

MARY ECKOLDS, 151 acs. by Survey 10 Dec 1767 in Bedford Co. on both sides of Bore Auger Cr., on Raccoon Br. a W Br. of the sd Cr.; 20 Jul 1780, p.191. A.C. of 15 Shill. Sterl.

JOHN SHARP, 123 acs. by Survey 17 Nov 1772 in Bedford Co. on a Br. of Otter Riv., adj. his own Line; 20 Jul 1780, p.192. A.C. of 15 Shill. Sterl.

JOHN WARE ass'ee of JOHN PETER CORN, 254 acs. by Survey 7 Feb 1755 in Fluvanna Co. formerly Albemarle on the N side of Hardware Riv. and on its Brs.; adj. Henry Trent, John Henry & John Trent; 20 Jul 1780, p.193. A.C. of 25 Shill. Sterl.

FRANCIS MOORE PETTY ass'ee of JOHN GWIN, 854 acs. by Survey 16 Feb 1749 [1749/50] on the brs. of Turnip Cr., on Austons Br., adj. Thomas Williams & Harris; 20 Jul 1780, p.194. A.C. of £4.S5 Sterl. [Probably surveyed as Lunenburg Co. now Charlotte Co.]

JOHN WATSON Ass'ee of THOMAS ROBERTSON, 165 acs. by Survey 24 Nov 1779 in Pr. Edward Co. on the Brs. of Rough Cr., on the Road, near the North fork of sd Cr.; ; 20 Jul 1780, p196. A.C. of 20 Shill. Sterl.

JOSEPH BLANKENSHIP, 185 acs. by Survey 17 Mar 1775 in Bedford Co. on the Brs. of Beaver dam Cr., Beginning at Hutts [Huffs?] new corner in the old Line, adj. Thomas Pate; 20 Jul 1780, p.197. A.C. of 20 Shill. Sterl.

JOHN BAKER, 117 acs. by Survey 4 Oct 1771 in Halifax Co. on the Brs. of Difficult Cr., Crossing Browns Path; adj. Compton, Morehead & Brown; 20 Jul 1780, p.198. A.C. of 15 Shill. Sterl.

STEPHEN BATES, 348 acs. by Survey 2 May 1757 in Halifax Co. on the Brs. of Buckskin Cr., Crossing Fuquas Road, adj. Joseph Shaw & Cole; 20 Jul 1780, p.199. A.C. 35 Shill. Sterl.

JEREMIAH SAULSBURY / SAULSBUREY, 36 acs. by Survey 15 Mar 1763 in Halifax Co. on the S side of Staunton Riv., on the Side of Smiths Mountain, adj. Randolph; 20 Jul 1780, p.200. A.C. of 5 Shill. Sterl.

JOHN EDWARDS ass'ee of HENRY SMITH, 150 acs. by Survey 10 Apr 1768 in Bedford Co. on a W Br. of Goose Cr., adj. Hays; 20 Jul 1780, p.201. A.C. of 15 Shill. Sterl.

WILLIAM HALL, SENIOR, 230 acs. by Survey 10 Jan 1771 in Halifax Co. on both sides of Adams's Spring Br. and draughts of By Cr.; adj. William Powell, the Reverend James Foulis, Adams, Robert Wooding & Robert Hall; 20 Jul 1780, p.202. A.C. of 25 Shill. Sterl.

THOMAS TUNSTALL (in Trust) for the use of the Estate of ROBERT ROBERTSON HUNT Dec'd, 400 acs. by Survey 24 Feb 1750 in Halifax Co. on the Brs. of Reedy Cr.; adj. his own, John Owen & Henry Owen; 20 Jul 1780, p.203. A.C. of 40 Shill. Sterl.

FRANCIS READ, 720 acs. by Survey 13 Nov 1780 in Bedford Co. on both sides of Mountain Cr., adj. McGehee; 20 Jul 1780, p.204. A.C. of 40 Shill. Sterl.

320 acs. part thereof was gtd. sd Francis Read by Letters Pat. 10 Sep 1767 [PB 37 p.108] and 400 acs. the residue never before gtd.

MICHAEL GILBERT, 231 acs. by Survey 18 Feb 1780 in Pittsylvania Co. on both sides of Jonakin Cr., adj. Henry Conway; 20 Jul 1780, p.205. A.C. of 25 Shill. Sterl.

ROBERT COWAN, 130 acs. by Survey 7 Apr 1779 in Bedford Co. on the N side of Black Water Riv., on Dunkins Mill Run; adj. Randolphs old Line, Walton, & Walter Edey; 20 Jul 1780, p.206. A.C. of 15 Shill. Sterl.

ELIJAH HUNT, 404 acs. by Survey 12 Mar 1756 in Halifax Co. on the Head of Bates's Br., Crossing Just below the Great Meadow on sd br., Crossing Mayes's Ferry Road & Mayes's Road, adj. Abraham Abney; 20 Jul 1780, p.207. A.C. of 40 Shill. Sterl.

WILLIAM BATES & SAMUEL BATES as ass'ee of JAMES BATES, 450 acs. by Survey 29 Oct 1750 in Halifax Co. on the Cuttawbo Cr., up the Falls Br.; adj. James Hunt, Joseph Hunt, John Bates, Dennit Abney, Watkins, & Abraham Abneys old Line; 20 Jul 1780, p.208. A.C. of £2.S5 Sterl.

STEPHEN MITCHELL, 380 acs. by Survey 1 Dec 1768 in Bedford Co. on both sides of Possum Cr., on the Top & Side of Coopers Mountain, adj. his own Line & James's; 20 Jul 1780, p.210. A.C. of 40 Shill. Sterl.

JOHN DICKENSON, 690 acs. by Survey 12 Feb 1763 in Halifax Co. on the S Brs. of Staunton Riv.; adj. his own

Lines, Radford Maxey Gentleman, Walter Cole Gentleman, John Walters, James Cobb, Robert Cobb & Randolph; 20 Jul 1780, p.211. A.C. of £3.S10 Sterl. 400 acs. part thereof was Assigned to him by Ambrose Cobbs.

JAMES BATES, 682 acs. by **Inclusive Survey** 4 Dec 1772 in Halifax Co. on the Draughts of Catawbo, Crossing Hunts Road & Several Brs.; adj. McMahon, Brown, Jones, Phelps & Abney; 20 Jul 1780, p.212. A.C. of £3.S10 Sterl.

ROBERT WOODING, 285 acs. by Survey 25 Mar 1755 in Halifax Co. on the Brs. of Difficult Cr., adj. Robert Wade & Hunt; 20 Jul 1780, p.214. A.C. of 30 Shill. Sterl.

JOHN WALL, 400 acs. by Survey 5 Mar 1752 in Halifax Co. on the Brs. of Tobys Cr. and Burches Cr., adj. Waller & Weatherford; 20 Jul 1780, p.215. A.C. of 40 Shill. Sterl.

FLEMING BATES, 610 acs. by Survey 12 Mar 1771 in Pittsylvania Co. on the Brs. of Fawl Cr., crossing Floods Cr.; adj. Brown, Lawless, Jones, & Gorom Brown; 20 Jul 1780, p.216. A.C. of £3.S5 Sterl.

THOMAS TUNSTALL Ass'ee of JOHN EAST, 352 acs. by Survey 8 Jan 1766 in Pittsylvania Co. formerly Halifax on the Draughts of Stinking Riv., adj. Keese & Cox; 20 Jul 1780, p.217. A.C. of 40 Shill. Sterl.

HENRY BUFORD, 438 acs. by Survey 6 May 1771 in Bedford Co. on the N Brs. of Bore Auger Cr., adj. Hayes; 20 Jul 1780, p.218. A.C. of 45 Shill. Sterl.

THOMAS TUNSTALL, 310 acs. by Survey 18 Feb 1772 in Pittsylvania Co. on the waters of Stinking Riv., adj. Joseph Fariss & Eckol's Line; 20 Jul 1780, p.219. A.C. of 35 Shill. Sterl.

EDWARD WARE, 54 acs. by Survey 16 Mar 1773 in Amherst Co. on the N Brs. of Horsleys Cr.; adj. his own, Solomon Carter, William Cabell & Peter Carter; 20 Jul 1780, p.220. A.C. of 5 Shill. Sterl.

JOSIAH ELLIS, 32 acs. by Survey 28 Oct 1766 in Amherst Co. on the S side and Joining Pedlar Riv., adj. his own Line & Samuel Burcks's; 20 Jul 1780, p.221. A.C. of 5 Shill. Sterl.

ARCHIBALD BURDEN, 145 acs. by Survey made for Richard Elliot who was an Insolvent and Sold by the Surveyor to the said Archibald Burden bearing date 3 Dec 1765 in Amherst Co. on the N Brs. of Horsleys Cr.; adj. Peter Carter & Henry McGuffey or McGaffey; 20 Jul 1780, p.222. A.C. of 15 Shill. Sterl.

HENRY HARPER Ass'ee of WILLIAM MUSTERD, 37 acs. by Survey 10 Apr 1766 in Amherst Co. on the N Brs. of Hat Cr.; adj. Colo. John Rose, Benjamin Denny & Abraham Smith; 20 Jul 1780, p.223. A.C. of 5 Shill. Sterl.

WILLIAM SMITH Ass'ee of THOMAS SMITH who was Ass'ee of ROBERT JOHNSTON, 120 acs. by Survey 13 Nov 1771 in Amherst Co. on the S side and Joining Otter Cr., adj. his own Line; 20 Jul 1780, p.224. A.C. of 15 Shill. Sterl.

JAMES MARTIN Ass'ee of JOHN TULLY who was Ass'ee of JOSEPH EDWARDS who was Ass'ee of JOHN

HIX, 90 acs. by Survey 21 Nov 1767 in Amherst Co. on both Sides of Pedlar Riv., adj. his own Line & John Blan [Bland?]; 20 Jul 1780, p.225. A.C. of 10 Shill. Sterl.

GEORGE McDANIEL JUNR. Ass'ee of ANGUS McDANIEL, 82 acs. by Survey 14 Mar 1768 in Amherst Co. on the N Brs. of Pedlar Riv., Beginning on the point of the Brown Mountain; 20 Jul 1780, p.226. A.C. of 10 Shill. Sterl.

RODERICK McCULLOCK, 11 acs. by Survey 15 Apr 1773 in Amherst Co. on the N Brs. of Horseleys Cr.; adj. his own Lines, Isaac Wright, William Haynes & David Crawford; 20 Jul 1780, p.227. A.C. of 5 Shill. Sterl.

JOHN DUNCAN, 265 acs. by Survey 12 Mar 1767 in Amherst Co. on the Brs. of the Cornfield Br., adj. his own Line & John Bryan; 20 Jul 1780, p.228. A.C. of 30 Shill. Sterl.

FRANCIS WEST Ass'ee of CHARLES TYLER, 182 acs. by Survey 16 Oct 1753 in Amherst Co. formerly Albemarle on the Brs. of Swan and Gilberts Creeks, adj. Colonel William Mayo, Samuel Spencer; 20 Jul 1780, p.229. A.C. of 20 Shill. Sterl.

JAMES MARTIN Ass'ee of JOHN TULLY who was Ass'ee of JOSEPH EDWARDS who was Ass'ee of JOHN HIX, 77 acs. by Survey 17 Mar 1762 in Amherst Co. on the S Side and Joining Pedlar Riv.; 20 Jul 1780, p.230. A.C. of 10 Shill. Sterl.

FRANCIS WEST, 110 acs. by Survey 6 May 1773 in Amherst Co. on the Brs. of Mayes Cr. or Mayos Cr., adj. Moses Gowen & his own Lines; 20 Jul 1780, p.231. A.C. of 15 Shill. Sterl.

JOHN CHILDRESS / CHILDRES ass'ee of WILLIAM HIX, 320 acs. by Survey 19 Nov 1767 in Amherst Co. on both Sides of Pedlar Riv., at Roberts's Cr.; 20 Jul 1780, p.232. A.C. of 35 Shill. Sterl.

WILLIAM PRYOR, JUNIOR Ass'ee of WILLIAM PRYOR, SENIOR, 247 acs. by Survey 7 Apr 1770 in Amherst Co. on the Brs. of the Inchanted Cr., crossing the North fork & South fork of sd Cr.; 20 Jul 1780, p.233. A.C. of 25 Shill. Sterl.

WILLIAM MATTHEWS Ass'ee of ROBERT DAVIS who was Ass'ee of JAMES KITCHEN, 136 acs. by Survey 20 Apr 1773 in Amherst Co. on the N Brs. of Otter Cr., adj. his own Line & John Hogg; 20 Jul 1780, p.234. A.C. of 15 Shill. Sterl.

ZEDEKIAH SHOEMAKER Ass'ee of WILLIAM PRYOR, SENIOR, 229 acs. by Survey 12 Apr 1771 in Amherst Co. on both sides of the Irish Cr.; 20 Jul 1780, p.235. A.C. of 25 Shill. Sterl.

JOHN BROWN, JUNIOR, 182 acs. by Survey 5 Mar 1773 in Amherst Co. on both sides the Inchanted Cr. of Pedlar Riv., adj. William Pryor & Daniel Burford; 20 Jul 1780, p.236. A.C. of 20 Shill. Sterl.

THOMAS GRISSUM, 123 acs by Survey 4 Nov 1767 in Amherst Co. on the Brs. of Harris's Cr., adj. David Buford Junior; 20 Jul 1780, p.237. A.C. of 15 Shill. Sterl.

JOHN BROWN, 120 acs. by Survey 7 Apr 1763 in Amherst Co. on the S side of Pedlar Riv. and on both sides of Browns Cr., adj. his own Lines; 20 Jul 1780, p.239. A.C. of 15 Shill. Sterl.

WILLIAM FORBUS, 82 acs. by Survey 1 May 1770 in Amherst Co. on both sides of Cox's / Coxes Cr. of Tye Riv., adj. Nicholas Morran & James Coffey; 20 Jul 1780, p.240. A.C. of 10 Shill. Sterl.

WILLIAM CRIBBIN, 115 acs. by Survey 25 Feb 1761 in Amherst Co. at the foot and on the S side the blue Ridge; adj. John McNelley, Colo. Chiswell & Burrow Kinkead; 20 Jul 1780, p.241. A.C. of 15 Shill. Sterl.

JACOB SMITH, 33 acs. by Survey 16 Mar 1767 in Amherst Co. on the S Brs. of Buffaloe Riv., adj. his own Line & Edmund Powel; 20 Jul 1780, p.242. A.C. of 5 Shill. Sterl.

WILLIAM CALBRETH, 180 acs. by Survey 29 Mar 1773 in Amherst Co. on the brs. of Cribbons and Manallys Branches and on the S side of the Blue Ridge; adj. David Manally, Menes Burger & John Manally; 20 Jul 1780, p.243. A.C. of 20 Shill. Sterl.

JOSEPH WITTSHIRE, JUNIOR, ass'ee of MATTHEW WHITE & ELIZABETH WHITE devisees of JAMES WARREN who was ass'ee of DANIEL TOLLESON, 187 acs. by Survey 3 Mar 1756 in Amherst Co. formerly Albemarle on Tollesons br., adj. John Warren, Carter Braxton & James Chrishan [Christian]; 20 Jul 1780, p.244. A.C. of 20 Shill. Sterl.

LUKE PANNEL, 134 acs. by Survey 20 Apr 1771 in Amherst Co. on the Brs. of Rodes's Cr., adj. Thomas Pannel; 20 Jul 1780, p.245. A.C. of 15 Shill. Sterl.

EDMUND FRANKLIN ass'ee of WILLIAM BROWN, 252 acs. by Survey 14 Mar 1771 in Bedford Co. on Brs. of Cub Cr. and Falling Riv., at a Path, upon Beards Mountain; adj. Harris, Hays, his own Lines & Wooldridge; 20 Jul 1780, p.246. A.C. of 25 Shill. Sterl.

JOHN HARRIS, 93 acs. by Survey 22 Apr 1780 in Albemarle Co. on the N side of the Fluvanna Riv. and on some of the brs. of Totear Cr., adj. William Battersby deced, sd Scot and Battersby, & Robert Moreman; 20 Jul 1780, p.247. A.C. of 10 Shill. Sterl.

JOHN RUCKER, 200 acs. by Survey 17 Mar 1773 in Bedford Co. on Buck Mountain; adj. Gaddy, Crews, Woodroof & his own Lines; 20 Jul 1780, p.249. A.C. of 20 Shill. Sterl.

WILLIAM CREASY ass'ee of NICHOLAS HAYS, 200 acs. by Survey 11 Mar 1773 in Bedford Co. on E Brs. of Falling Riv., near Beards Road; adj. Hays, Beard, William Lee, John Callwell & Franklin; 20 Jul 1780, p.250. A.C. of 20 Shill. Sterl.

JOHN WHITLEY ass'ee of PEARCE WADE, 100 acs. by Survey 14 Apr 1755 in Albemarle Co. on a br. of Stone House Cr.; adj. Richard Powel, Howard Cash & Jeremiah Wade; 20 Jul 1780, p.251. A.C. of 10 Shill. Sterl.

THOMAS POWEL, 354 acs. by Survey 19 Mar 1765 in Amherst Co. on the brs. of Horsleys Cr. and Puppies Cr.; adj. his own Lines, Charles Taliaferroes Lines,

Edward Ware & Peter Carter; 20 Jul 1780, p.252. A.C. of 35 Shill. Sterl.

WILLIAM LOVING Ass'ee of JOHN LOVING, 20 acs. by Survey 7 Nov 1770 in Amherst Co. on the N Brs. of Ruckers Run, adj. William Loving & George Purvis; 20 Jul 1780, p.253. A.C. of 5 Shill. Sterl.

DAVID MONTGOMERY / MOUNTGOMERY, 98 acs. by Survey 10 Apr 1772 in Amherst Co. on the N Brs. of the North fork of the Dutch Cr., adj. his own & William Tiller; 20 Jul 1780, p.254. A.C. of 10 Shill. Sterl.

JOHN MERRIT Ass'ee of TIMOTHY FINNY who was ass'ee of DANIEL BURFORD, 124 acs. Amherst Co. on the N brs. of Harrises Cr.; adj. his own and John Burford their Lines, Joshua Fowler, Robert Warren dec'd, Alexander McCaul, Moses Higginbotham, John Hardwick, George Carrington & John Thomas's Orphans Line; 20 Jul 1780, p.255. A.C. of 20 Shill. Sterl.

JOSEPH EDWARDS Ass'ee of ISON MATLOCK, 350 acs. by Survey 16 Mar 1780 in Amherst Co. on both sides of the Brown Mountain Cr. a North Br. of Pedlar Riv., on the Top of the Brown Mountain, adj. John Beazley & John Blane; 20 Jul 1780, p.257. A.C. of 35 Shill. Sterl.

FRANCIS WEST, 70 acs. by Survey 19 Dec 1768 in Amherst Co. on the Brs. of Mayss Cr. [Mayos Cr.], adj. Docter William Cabell & William Ray; 20 Jul 1780, p.258. A.C. of 10 Shill. Sterl. [This appears to be a revised version of PB 42 p.697 dated 5 Jul 1774]

JAMES NEVIL, 69 acs. by Survey 30 Apr 1773 in Amherst Co. on the Brs. of the South fork of Rock fish Riv., adj. his own Lines & Cornelius Thomas; 20 Jul 1780, p.259. A.C. of 10 Shill. Sterl.

THOMAS SOWELL ass'ee of JOSEPH MORRIS, 50 acs. by Survey 25 Apr 1768 in Amherst Co. on the N Brs. of Hickory Cr., adj. Daniel Ross; 20 Jul 1780, p.260. A.C. of 5 Shill. Sterl.

GABRIEL PENN, 32 acs. by Survey made for Robert Whitton 8 Mar 1762 of whom the sd Gabriel Penn recovered it by a Caveat before the Late Governor and Council 16 Jun 1764, in Amherst Co. on the Head Brs. of Beaver Cr. on the E side of Tobacco Row Mountain, adj. his own Lines; 20 Jul 1780, p.261. A.C. of 5 Shill. Sterl.

JOHN ROBERTS, 164 acs. by Survey 3 Dec 1768 in Amherst Co. on the S brs. of Pedlar Riv., adj. John Brown; 20 Jul 1780, p.262. A.C. of 20 Shill. Sterl.

THOMAS PHILLIPS, 182 acs. by Survey 3 Apr 1767 in Amherst Co. on the N side and Joining Tye Riv.; 20 Jul 1780, p.263. A.C. of 30 Shill. Sterl. [10 Shill. too much]

THOMAS SOWELL ass'ee of DANIEL ROSS, 46 acs. by Survey 22 Apr 1768 in Amherst Co. on the N Brs. of Hickory Cr., with the County Line [S25°E], adj. his own Lines; 20 Jul 1780, .264. A.C. of 5 Shill. Sterl.

JOHN MERRITT Ass'ee of BOYCE EIDSON, 300 acs. by Survey 22 Feb 1768 in Amherst Co. on the N Brs. of Stovals Cr., at Stovals Road, adj. Joseph

Crews & George Jefferson; 20 Jul 1780, p.266. A.C. of 30 Shill. Sterl.

PHILIP THURMOND ass'ee of WILLIAM PRYOR, SENIOR, 90 acs. by Survey 17 Nov 1767 in Amherst Co. on the head of the South Brs. of Pedlar Riv., on the Top of the Blue Ridge thence along the Ridge, adj. his own Lines; 20 Jul 1780, p.267. A.C. of 10 Shill. Sterl.

PETER CARTER, 50 acs. by Survey 13 May 1771 in Amherst Co. on the brs. of Horsleys Cr.; adj. his own, William Cabell & Joseph Edwards; 20 Jul 1780, p.268. A.C. of 5 Shill. Sterl.

ROBERT CHRISTIAN, 279 acs. by Survey 14 Mar 1770 in Amherst Co. on both sides of Lime Kiln Cr.; adj. James Christian, his own Lines, John Christian & Larkin Gatewood; 20 Jul 1780, p.269. A.C. of 30 Shill. Sterl.

DAVID MOUNTGOMERY, 40 acs. by Survey 2 Mar 1770 in Amherst Co. on the Brs. of Davis's Cr., adj. his own Lines & David Montgomery Junr.; 20 Jul 1780, p.271. A.C. of 5 Shill. Sterl.

AMBROSE RUCKER, 375 acs. by Survey 14 Mar 1774 in Amherst Co. on the S brs. of Harris's Cr., on the Top of the Tobacco Row Mountain, adj. Robert Johnston, William Pendleton & Henry McDaniel; 20 Jul 1780, p.272. A.C. of 40 Shill. Sterl. *bounded by the Variation of the Magnetic from the true Meridian being N1°W.*

WILLIAM TYRE, 180 acs. by Survey 19 Nov 1773 in Amherst Co. on the N side and Joining Tye Riv., adj. Nicholas Cabell; 20 Jul 1780, p.273. A.C. of 20 Shill. *the Variation of the Magnetic from the true Meridian being now N1°W.*

EDWARD WILCOX [also as EDMUND WILCOX] Ass'ee of JOHN HARGOVE, 20 acs. by Survey 24 Feb 1774 in Amherst Co. on the S side and Joining Tye Riv., adj. his own Line; 20 Jul 1780, p.275. A.C. of 5 Shill. Sterl. bounded *by the Variatiion of the Magnetic from the true Meridian being N1°W.*

STEWARD BALLOW, 340 acs. by Survey 7 Apr 1775 in Amherst Co. on both sides of the Middle fork of Pedlar Riv., at the sd Fork just below a Great falls, adj. William Higginbotham & George McDaniel; 20 Jul 1780. p.276. A.C. of 35 Shill. *bounded by the Valuation of the Magnetic from the true Meridian being N15'W.*

JOSIAH ELLIS ass'ee of ROBERT JOHNSTON, 98 acs. by Survey 29 Oct 176 in Amherst Co. on the S side of Pedlar Riv.; adj. Josiah Ellis, Joel Watkins, Corn[e]lius Thomas & Samuel Burks; 20 Jul 1780, p.277. A.C. of 10 Shill. Sterl.

GEORGE McDANIEL, 165 acs. by Survey 9 Jun 1774 in Amherst Co. on the S brs. of Harris's Cr.; adj. Duncan Graham, John Houchins & Nicholas Davis; 20 Jul 1780, p.278. A.C. of 20 Shill. Sterl. *bounded by the Variation of the Magnetic from the true Meridian being N1°W.*

JOHN DIGGES ass'ee of OWEN HERNDON, 400 acs. by Survey 23 Mar 1772 in Amherst Co. on the S Brs. of Hatt Cr.; adj. Thomas Mann Randolph, Jane Sheilds & John Shields; 20 Jul 1780, p.280. A.C. of 40 Shill. Sterl.

CHARLES DAVIS devisee of NATHANIEL DAVIS, 124 acs. by Survey 18 Mar 1774 in Amherst Co. on the brs. of Thomas's Mill Cr.; adj. Cornelius Thomas, Nicholas Davis, his own Lines & Hugh Morris; 20 Jul 1780, p.281. A.C. of 15 Shill. Sterl. *bounded by the Variation of the Magnetic from the true Meridian being N1°W.*

WILLIAM CLARK, 72 acs. by Survey 15 Apr 1775 in Amherst Co. on the head Brs. of Pedlar Riv. and on the blue Ridge, Beginning on the Top of the Blue Ridge, adj. Walter Power with the Ridge; 20 Jul 1780, p.282. *A.C. of 10 Shill. Sterl. the Variation of the Magnetic from the true Meridian being N15"W.*

JAMES MATHEWS, 90 acs. by Survey 8 Apr 1775 in Amherst Co. on both sides of Swaping Camp Cr., adj. James Smith & Neill Campbell; 20 Jul 1780, p.283. *A.C. of 10 Shill. Sterl. bounded by the Variation of the Magnetic from the true Meridian being N15'W.*

ANGUS McDANIEL, 250 acs. by Survey 10 Mar 1775 in Amherst Co. on the South fork of Nicklestons Run and the head the S Brs. of Pedlar Riv., adj. David Moor & James Frazier; 20 Jul 1780, p.284. A.C. of 25 Shill. Sterl. *bounded by the Variation of the Magnetic from the true Meridian being N15'W.*

ANGUS McDANIEL, 110 acs. by Survey 10 Mar 1775 in Amherst Co. on the North fork & South fork of Nicklestons Run, adj. David Moor & William Taylon or Taylor; 20 Jul 1780, p.286. A.C. of 15 Shill. Sterl. *bounded by the Variation of the Megnetic from the true Meridian being N15'W.*

ABRAHAM WARWICK, 50 acs. [Amherst Co.] adj. the late Hugh Willoughby, & Enoch Nash; 20 Jul 1780, p.287. A.C. of 5 Shill. Sterl. *by Survey the Variation of the Magnetic from the true Meridian being N1°W.*

JOHN CHRISTIAN, 400 acs. by Survey 20 Jan 1769 in Amherst Co. on Both Sides of the Great Br.; adj. his own Line, Drury Christian, Robert Christian, & Robert Christians Orphans Line; 20 Jul 1780, p.288. A.C. of 40 Shill. Sterl.

DAVID MONTGOMERY, JUNIOR, Ass'ee of WILLIAM MARTIN who was Ass'ee of ANN NEAL, 58 acs. 14 Feb 1763 in Amherst Co. on the Brs. of the North fork of the Dutch Cr., in a Spur of the Rocky Mountain, adj. her own Line & Colo. Lomax; 20 Jul 1780, p.289. A.C. of 10 Shill. Sterl.

AMBROSE TOMLINSON ass'ee of PHILIP WALKER, 154 acs. by Survey 6 Nov 1765 in Amherst Co. on both sides the North fork of Buffaloe Riv.; 20 Jul 1780, p.290. A.C. of 15 Shill. Sterl.

HENRY MARTIN Ass'ee of ABRAHAM WARWICK who was ass'ee of RICHARD HARVIE, 92 acs. by Survey 14 Apr 1772 in Amherst Co. on the Brs. of the Dutch Cr.; adj. Hugh Willoughby dec'd, Abraham Warwick, Daniel Corner & William Tiller; 20 Jul 1780, p.291. A.C. of 10 Shill. Sterl.

RICHARD HARRISON ass'ee of JOHN TENISON who was ass'ee of JOHN HOUTCHIN, 114 acs. by Survey 25 Apr 1770 in Amherst Co. on the N Brs. of Pedlar Riv. and on the S Brs. of Harris's Cr., adj. his own Line; 20 Jul 1780, p.292. A.C. of 15 Shill. Sterl.

JACOB PHILLIPS ass'ee of GEORGE TAYLOR, JUNIOR, 144 acs. by Survey 16 Nov 1770 in Amherst Co. on the N Brs. of the South fork of Pedlar Riv., adj. Adam Reid; 20 Jul 1780, p.293. A.C. of 15 Shill. Sterl.

JOSEPH EDWARDS ass'ee of JOHN HIX, 320 acs. by Survey 18 Mar 1768 in Amherst Co. on the N Brs. of Pedlar Riv., adj. Charles Blan; 20 Jul 1780, p.295. A.C. of 35 Shill. Sterl.

JAMES MATHEWS, 230 acs. by Survey 17 Feb 1773 in Amherst Co. on the S Brs. of the Dutch Cr. and on the head of the South fork of Rockfish Riv.; adj. his own Lines, Thomas Jopling, John Harmer, John Gregory & Theoderick Webb; 20 Jul 1780, p.296. A.C. of 25 Shill. Sterl.

JOHN STAPLES, Eldest Son and Heir at Law of SAMUEL STAPLES dec'd, 128 acs. by Survey 25 Apr 1771 in Amherst Co. on the N Brs. of the Dutch Cr., adj. his own Line & William Fitzpatrick; 20 Jul 1780, p.297. A.C. of 15 Shill. Sterl.

WILLIAM CRIBBIN, 53 acs. by Survey 29 Mar 1773 in Amherst Co. on the South fork of Pattons Br., adj. Garland & his own lines; 20 Jul 1780, p.298. A.C. of 5 Shill. Sterl.

JAMES NOWLIN ass'ee of JOSEPH LANE, 279 acs. by Survey 10 Apr 1771 in Amherst Co. on the N side and Joining the Fluvanna Riv., up Otter Cr.; adj. his own Lines, Nathaniel Davis & Benjamin Stinnet Junr.; 20 Jul 1780, p.299. A.C. of 30 Shill. Sterl.

DAVID MEREWETHER, 50 acs. by Survey 27 Mar 1770 in Amherst Co. on the Brs. of Taylors Cr.; adj. his own Lines, Edward Moseby, Roger Casey & William Mountgomery; 20 Jul 1780, p.301. A.C. of 5 Shill. Sterl.

JOSEPH HIGGINBOTHAM, 290 acs. by Survey 14 Apr 1775 in Amherst Co. on the S brs. of the Middle fork of Pedlar Riv., adj. Walter Power & his own Lines; 20 Jul 1780, p.302. A.C. of 30 Shill. Sterl. *the Variation of the Magnetic from the true Meridian being N15'W.*

JOHN DIGGES ass'ee of WILLIAM MORRISON JUNR., 53 acs. by Survey 5 Dec 1772 in Amherst Co. on the N Brs. of Buck Cr., adj. John Mountgomery & John Digges; 20 Jul 1780, p.303. A.C. of 5 Shill. Sterl.

FREDERICK HUFMAN, 77 acs. by Survey made for JOSEPH KING who was an Insolvent and sold by the Surveyor to the said Frederick Hufman, in Amherst Co. on the S brs. of the Middle fork of Pedlar Riv.; 20 Jul 1780, p.304. A.C. of 10 Shill. Sterl.

JOSEPH DILLARD ass'ee of GEORGE WINTHAM who was ass'ee of BENJAMIN PENDLETON who was ass'ee of WILLIAM RAMSEY, 134 acs. by Survey 27 Nov 1772 in Amherst Co. on the Brs. of Kings Cr. of Little Piney Riv.; 20 Jul 1780, p.305. A.C. of 15 Shill. Sterl.

JOHN JARVIS, 99 acs. by Survey 9 Apr 1770 in Amherst Co. on the S Brs. of Pedlar Riv.; 20 Jul 1780, p.306. A.C. of 10 Shill. Sterl.

JAMES FRAZIER, 366 acs. by Survey 11 Apr 1775 in Amherst Co. on the S

Brs. of the middle fork of Pedlar Riv., adj. Joseph King & his own Line; 20 Jul 1780, p.307. A.C. of 40 Shill. Sterl. *the Variation of the Magnetic from the true Meridian being N15'W.*

WILLIAM CAMDEN ass'ee of HENRY CHILDERS, 170 acs. by Survey 4 May 1771 in Amherst Co. on the S Brs. of Pedlar Riv., on the Top of the Blue Ridge and with it; 20 Jul 1780, p.309. A.C. of 20 Shill. Sterl.

EDWARD WARE, 250 acs. by Survey 9 Apr 1763 in Amherst Co. on the Brs. of Puppies Cr. and on the Tobacco Row Mountain, adj. his own Lines; 20 Jul 1780, p.310. A.C. of 25 Shill. Sterl.

WILLIAM CLARKE, 46 acs. by Survey 5 Nov 1766 in Amherst Co. on the Head Brs. of the South fork of Pedlar Riv., on the Top of the Blue Ridge; 20 Jul 1780, p.311. A.C. of 5 Shill. Sterl.

CHARLES ISON ass'ee of THOMAS ROBERTSON, 122 acs. by Survey 17 Nov 1770 in Amherst Co. on the S Brs. of Pedlar Riv., adj. Walter Power & Alexander Bagg; 20 Jul 1780, p.312. A.C. of 15 Shill. Sterl.

JOSEPH HUNTER ass'ee of EDWARD WYATT who was ass'ee of JOHN ROBINSON, 141 acs. by Survey 5 May 1772 in Botetourt Co. on Delaps Cr. a br. of Jackson Riv.; Beg on the NE side of the Cr. and along a Stoney ground, along the side of a Steep hill, to a Large Buck Eye at foot of a Hill, to two Lynns on a Steep bank, Crossing a loop of the Cr.; 20 Jul 1780, p.313. A.C. of 15 Shill. Sterl.

JOSEPH HIGGINBOTHAM ass'ee of ALEXANDER DUGGIN, 110 acs. by Survey 15 Apr 1775 in Amherst Co. on the S Brs. of Pedlar Riv.; adj. Angus McDaniel, William Taylor, Joseph King & James Frazier; 20 Jul 1780, p.315. A.C. of 15 Shill. Sterl. *bounded by the Variation of the Magnetic from the true Meridian being N15'W.*

CHARLES YANCEY / YANCY, 132 acs. by Survey 27 Mar 1772 in Amherst Co. on the Head Brs. of Hickory and Taylors Cr.; adj. Edward Moseley, George Douglass, William Maxwell & Charles Evans; 20 Jul 1780, p.316. A.C. of 15 Shill. Sterl.

WILLIAM AARON, Heir at Law of DANIEL AARON dec'd, 150 acs. in Amherst Co. formerly Albemarle Co. on both sides of Cabells Mill Cr.; 20 Jul 1780, p.317. A.C. of 15 Shill. Sterl.

FRANCIS MEREWETHER, 99 acs. by Survey 25 Mar 1772 in Amherst Co. on the N Brs. of Rock fish Riv. on the Side of the Pilot Mountain; adj. Alexander Henderson, Alexander Patten & Samuel Murrel; 20 Jul 1780, p.318. A.C. of 10 Shill. Sterl.

JOHN STAPLES, Heir at Law of SAMUEL STAPLES dec'd, 17 acs. by Survey 16 Dec 1773 in Amherst Co. on the Brs. of the Dutch Cr., adj. his own Line & William Fitzpatrick; 20 Jul 1780, p.320. *A.C. of 5 Shill. Sterl. bounded by the Variation of the Magnetic from the true Meridian being N1°W.*

JONATHAN DAVIS, 530 acs. by Survey 18 Sep 1779 in Henry Co. on the Waters of Chesnut Cr.; adj. Stewart, Paterson & Robert Hodges Line; 20 Jul 1780, p.321. A.C. of £2.S15 Sterl.

Capt. JOHN DAWSON, 146 acs. by Survey 26 Apr 1773 in Amherst Co. on the N Brs. of Rock fish Riv. and on both sides of Hickory Cr.; adj. John Sorrel, his own Line & William Morrison; 20 Jul 1780, p.322. A.C. of 15 Shill. Sterl.

DAVID MEREWETHER Ass'ee of EDWARD MOSELY, 26 acs. by Survey 23 Mar 1775 in Amherst Co. on the Brs. of Taylors Cr., at a Large Rock, adj. his own Lines; 20 Jul 1780, p.323. A.C. of 5 Shill. Sterl. *bounded by the Magnetic from the true Meridian being N15'W.*

JONATHAN JOHNSTON / JOHNSON, 350 acs. by Survey 16 Mar 1769 in Amherst Co. on both sides of the Falls Cr., adj. Edward Bolling; 20 Jul 1780, p.324. A.C. of 35 Shill. Sterl.

JONATHAN JOHNSON / JOHNSTON, 340 acs. by Survey 9 Mar 1770 in Amherst Co. on the Brs. of the Falls and Bollings Cr.; adj. his own Lines, Abraham North, Micajah Moreman & Henry Harper; 20 Jul 1780, p.325. A.C. of 35 Shill. Sterl.

WILLIAM HIGGINBOTHAM, 154 acs. by Survey 12 Apr 1775 in Amherst Co. on both sides of the North fork of Pedlar Riv., adj. his own Lines; 20 Jul 1780, p.327. A.C. of 15 Shill. Sterl. *bounded by the Variation of the Magnetic from the true Meridian being N15'W.*

WILLIAM CAMDEN ass'ee of WILLIAM HIX, 74 acs. by Survey 5 Apr 1771 in Amherst Co. on the Brs. of Huffs Cr.; adj. his own Lines, George McDaniel and Battle Harrison their Line, Thomas Gooldsby & John Childers; 20 Jul 1780, p.328. A.C. of 10 Shill. Sterl.

THOMAS LAYNE, 385 acs. by Survey 20 Apr 1775 in Amherst Co. on the N brs. of Tye Riv., on the Top of Berrys Mountain and with it; adj. William Tyre, Arthur Robinson & Samuel Spencer; 20 Jul 1780, p.329. A.C. of 40 Shill. Sterl. *bounded by the Variation of the Magnetic from the true Meredian being N15'W.*

WILLIAM MATHEWS ass'ee of ROBERT DAVIS, 250 acs. by Survey 17 Mar 1774 in Amherst Co. on the S side and Joining Dancing Cr., adj. Joseph Cabell & Robert Payton; 20 Jul 1780, p.331. *A.C. of 25 Shill. Sterl. bounded by the Variation of the Magnetic from the ture Meridian being N1°W.*

WILLIAM HORSLEY, 300 acs. by Survey 26 Mar 1774 in Amherst Co. on the N Brs. of the Fluvanna Riv.; adj. John Hornsby, James Freeland dec'd, George Hilton & his own Lines; 20 Jul 1780, p.332. A.C. of 30 Shill. Sterl. *bounded by the Variation of the Magnetic from the true Meridian being N1°W.*

WILLIAM HORSLEY, 275 acs. by Survey 23 Mar 1774 in Amherst Co. on both sides of Elk Island Cr.; adj. Robert Horsley, Charles Perron, Drury Christian, James Freeland dec'd & George Hilton; 20 Jul 1780. p.334. A.C. of 30 Shill. Sterl. *bounded by the Variation of the Magnetic from the true Meridian being N1°W.*

JOHN McDANIEL, 324 acs. by Survey 10 Apr 1775 in Amherst Co. on the Brs. of Brown Mountain Cr. and the N Brs. of Pedlar Riv.; adj. Angus McDaniel, Neil/Neill Campbell, David Moore & Joseph Edwards; 20 Jul 1780, p.335.

A.C. of 35 Shill. Sterl. *bounded by the Variation of the true Meridian being N15'W.*

WILLIAM HORSLEY, 245 acs. by Survey 15 Mar 1775 in Amherst Co. on the Brs. of Owens and Elk Island Creek; adj. his own Lines, George Hilton & William Megginson; 20 Jul 1780, p.337. A.C. of 25 Shill. *bounded by the Variation of the Magnetic from the true Meridian being N15'W.*

WILLIAM HORSLEY, 250 acs. by Survey 26 Mar 1774 in Amherst Co. on the N Brs. of the Fluvanna Riv.; adj. James Freeland dec'd, his own Lines & George Hilton; 20 Jul 1780, p.338. A.C. of 25 Shill. Sterl. *bounded by the Variation of the Magnetic from the true Meridian being N1°W.*

ALEXANDER KELLY, 195 acs. by Survey 7 Dec 1774 in Bedford Co. on E Brs. of Whipping Cr., adj. John Drinkwater & Marshall; 1 Sep 1780 in the fifth year of the Commonwealth, p.340. A.C. of 20 Shill. Sterl.

JAMES DINWIDDIE, 154 acs. by Survey 7 Mar 1765 in Bedford Co. on both Sides of the North fork of Mulberry Cr. on East Br. of Falling Riv., adj. his own Line & McRandle, 1 Sep 1780, p.341. A.C. of 20 Shill. Sterl.

JOHN RICHARDSON, 192 acs. by Survey 11 Mar 1779 in Bedford Co. on both Sides of Wards Road including the head of Wainwrights grave Branch, on the brow of a hill over a Branch S77°E 170 poles Crossing Wain Writes grave Branch, adj. his own Lines; 1 Sep 1780, p.342. A.C. of 20 Shill. Sterl.

MATTHEW PETTYCREW, 165 acs. by Survey 20 Nov 1770 in Bedford Co. on both Sides the Main Road on the Ridge between the Brs. of the Falling Riv. and the Brs. of Wreck Island Cr.; adj. Adams, Bolling & Radcliff; 1 Sep 1780, p.343. A.C. of 20 Shill. Sterl.

ROBERT CLARK, 213 acs. by Survey 9 May 1777 in Bedford Co. on Mcfalls Mountain, on a Path, adj. John Ewing; 1 Sep 1780, p.344. A.C. of 25 Shill. Sterl.

JAMES BOARD / BOAD, 268 acs. by Survey 8 Apr 1755 in Bedford Co. on the Ridge between Jumping Run and Beaver dam Cr. including heads of Brs. of each, adj. Richard Stith; 1 Sep 1780, p.345. A.C. of 30 Shill. Sterl.

GEORGE JONES, 304 acs. by Survey 8 May 1777 in Bedford Co. on E Brs. of Whipping Cr.; adj. Lane, Thomas Lane, Gaulding & Marshall; 1 Sep 1780, p.346. A.C. of 30 Shill. Sterl.

ROBERT ADAMS, JUNIOR, 220 acs. by **Inclusive Survey** 4 Nov 1773 in Bedford Co. on the head Brs. of Lynch's Cr., upon the Top of the Ridge between the heads of Lynch's Briery and Irvines Creeks, at Pocket Road; adj. Charles Lynch, the Old Lines & Irvine; 1 Sep 1780, p.347. A.C. of 55 Shill. Sterl.

JAMES STEWART (assignee of JOHN LANE Son of JOHN), 170 acs. by Survey 6 Apr 1776 in Bedford Co. on W Brs. of Little Falling Riv.; adj. Rogers, Garrett, Wallace & McElroy; 1 Sep 1780, p.349. A.C. of 20 Shill. Sterl.

BENJAMIN GILBERT, 240 acs. by Survey 19 Mar 1780 in Bedford Co. on W Brs. of Seneca Cr., Beginning on the

Creek at Phelps old Road Ford; adj. the old Lines of Witton, his own Lines & David Terrell; 1 Sep 1780, p.350. A.C. of 25 Shill. Sterl.

WILLIAM THOMPSON, 274 acs. by Survey 22 Feb 1774 in Bedford Co. at the head of Falling Riv. on both sides of New London Road, to his Corner Just Over Beards Road; adj. his own Lines, Patterson, Callwell, & William Lee; 1 Sep 1780, p.351. A.C. of 30 Shill. Sterl.

ROBERT GARREL / GARRELL, 135 acs. by Survey 7 Dec 1763 in Bedford Co. on the N side of Staunton Riv., down Bowmans Cr., adj. Winford & Pendleton; 1 Sep 1780, p.352. A.C. of 15 Shill. Sterl. [The plat of this land, now in Campbell Co., is in Bedford Co. Surveyors Records p.41 surveyed by Richard Stith, Surveyor, for Robert Garrett. For Pendleton's land, see PB 41 p.366 to Alexander Womack]

JAMES SNOW, 167 acs. by Survey 9 Nov 1768 in Bedford Co. on both sides of Crab apple tree Br.; adj. Aquila Gilbert, Gilbert his Line; 1 Sep 1780, p.353. A.C. of 15 Shill. Sterl.

THOMAS LESTER, 130 acs. by Survey 18 Sep 1778 in Bedford Co. on the head Brs. of Whipping Cr., on Phelps old Road at the Mouth of locust thicket Oald Road, down Phelps Road, adj. William Brown commonly Called the line of the Locust Thickett Land, to Locust Thicket road aforesaid thence down the South Thickett Road; 1 Sep 1780, p.354. A.C. of 15 Shill. Sterl.

VINCENT GLASS, 254 acs. by Survey by Survey 22 Mar 1774 in Bedford Co. on W Brs. of Falling Riv.; adj. Andrew Cook, Hylton, his own Lines & Tanner; 1 Sep 1780, p.355. A.C. of 25 Shill. Sterl.

MOSES HELM, 40 acs. by Survey 10 Mar 1767 in Bedford Co. on and upon the N Side of the Pilot Mountain, upon an Ivy Hill, adj. his own Line & Wathen; 1 Sep 1780, p.357. A.C. of 5 Shill. Sterl.

JOHN BOUGHTON, 60 acs. by Survey 15 May 1780 in Bedford Co. on W Brs. of Little Falling Riv.; Beginning at Ross and Hooks and Jacob Barners Corner on Taylors Road at a Spring, up Thompsons Path, up Taylors Road being Barners Line; adj. Ross and Hooks line, Akins, his own Lines; 1 Sep 1780, p.358. A.C. of 10 Shill. Sterl.

THOMAS OGLEBY, 125 acs. by Survey 18 Mar 1767 in Bedford Co. on W Brs. of Wreck Island Cr., adj. his own Line; 1 Sep 1780, p.359. A.C. of 15 Shill. Sterl.

THOMAS OGLEBY, 46 acs. by Survey 5 Nov 1771 in Bedford Co. on N Brs. of Wreck Island Cr., adj. his own Lines & Coleman; 1 Sep 1780, p.360. A.C. of 5 Shill. Sterl.

ROBERT PUCKETT / PUCKET ass'ee of ROBERT GARRETT, 268 acs. by Survey 20 Dec 1777 and is part of 368 acs. Surveyed for the sd Garrett 7 Dec 1763 in Bedford Co. on E Brs. of Whipping Cr.; adj. William Marshall, Low Todd & Barlow; 1 Sep 1780, p.361. A.C. of 30 Shill. Sterl.

WILLIAM VEST, 220 acs. by Survey 1 Dec 1772 in Bedford Co. on the N Side of Staunton Riv. on both Sides of Seneca Cr. and Buck Br. Including the Mouth of the Cr. and br.; adj. Randolph, & John Woolloms; 1 Sep 1780, p.362. A.C. of 25 Shill. Sterl.

AJONADAB READ/REED, 220 acs. by Survey 3 Mar 1708 [1780] in Bedford Co. on both Sides of Phelps's old Road, on both Sides of Deep Br.; adj. William Hutcheson, John Drinkwater, his own Line, Terrell & Hammock; 1 Sep 1780, p.364. A.C. of 25 Shill. Sterl. part of an Entry assigned to the Said Ajonadab Read made by John Fitzpatrick for 400 acs. the 24th of Mar 1779

SAMUEL HENDERSON, 212 acs. by Survey 4 Mar 1774 in Bedford Co. on the North fork of black water riv., adj. Isaac Rentfro & Henderson; 1 Sep 1780, p.365. A.C. of 25 Shill. Sterl.

WILLIAM CHILDERS, 70 acs. by Survey 1 Dec 1772 in Bedford Co. on both sides of Seneca Cr., at a Path, adj. Francis Callaway & William Vest; 1 Sep 1780, p.366. A.C. of 10 Shill. Sterl.

JOHN TALBOT, 1,110 acs. by Survey 10 Apr 1780 in Bedford Co. on Glady Br. of Goos[e] Cr., on [a] Road; adj. Mead, Irby, William Leftwich, Randolphs old Line, Overstreet, Butler, M Talbots old Corner, Newman & Haile; 1 Sep 1780, p.367. A.C of £5.S15 Sterl.

JOSEPH TERENCE, 200 acs. by Survey 15 Jan 1774 in Bedford Co. on W Brs. of Naked Cr.; adj. Harry Terrell, Wathen and Jennings; Patterson & Dixson/Dixon; 1 Sep 1780, p.369. A.C. of 20 Shill. Sterl.

DRURY HARDAWAY ass'ee of Mrs. MARY READ of Charlotte Co., 350 acs. by Survey 18 Feb 1755 in Bedford Co. on the head Brs. of Little falling Riv., adj. Samuel Goode; 1 Sep 1780, p.371. A.C. of 35 Shill. Sterl.

WILLIAM CALLAWAY, 460 acs. by Survey 10 May 1771 in Bedford Co. on the Flat top Mountain; adj. Cary, Bunch & Ewing; 1 Sep 1780, p.372. A.C. of 50 Shill. Sterl.

WILLIAM MEAD, 4,228 acs. by Inclusive Survey 10 Mar 1770 in Bedford Co. on both Sides of Goose Cr., crossing Mill Cr.; to Maple Br., Rock cassel Cr., Meadow Br., Glady Br. & Difficult Cr.; adj. Hencock, Morgan, Randolph, Walton, Joseph Richardson, Tinley, Mead, Talbot, Newman, Irby, Overstreet, Donohoo & Turner; 1 Sep 1780, p.373. A.C. of £21.S5 Sterl. *453 acs. part thereof was Surveyed for John Mead the right and title of which is since become vested in the sd William Mead and also 875 acs. part thereof was Surveyed for the sd William Mead and 2,900 acs. the residue never before Surveyed.*

NICHOLAS HAYS, 954 acs. by Survey 15 Mar 1771 in Bedford Co. on E Brs. of Falling Riv., at a Path, on Beards Mountain; adj. his own Lines, Simmons, & Edmund Franklin; 1 Sep 1780, p.377. £4.S15.

RICHARD STITH, 1,200 acs. by Survey 3 May 1754 in Bedford Co. on the Head Brs. of the South fork of Falling Riv., at a small Br. near the Main Road; adj. Samuel Branch, Thomas Harris, the old Lines of Ornsby, & Wathen and Jennings their Lines; 1 Sep 1780, p.379. A.C. of £6 Sterl. *part of 8,000 acs. gtd. by Order of Council 27 Apr 1748 to John Hall George Walton and James Johnson on the head Brs. of Falling Riv. and Wreck Island Cr. of James Riv. the Main Bulk of which hath been Otherwise directed and disposed of, the Right and title of the said 1,200 acs. is since become Vested in the Said Richard Stith.*

JOSEPH AKIN, 384 acs. by Survey 21 Mar 1775 in Bedford Co. on both Sides of Dutchmans Br., with the Main Ridge, at a pond; adj. Samuel Morris, Charles Taylor, Terrell; 1 Sep 1780, p.381. A.C. of 40 Shill. Sterl.

RICHARD STITH, 1,100 acs. by Survey 27 Nov 1777 in Bedford Co. on both sides of Goose Cr. and both sides of Lick fork of Enuck's Cr. including the Tops of Two little Mountain named Harpeth and Shalum from the Top of Harpeth to the Top of Shalum is S30°E, on a Small Br. of Bore Auger Cr., across Goose Cr. and up the Bank and high Steep Hill; adj. Quarles, Charles Tate [at a Large Rock] & Parker; 1 Sep 1780, p.382. A.C. of 30 Shill. Sterl. *800 acs. part thereof was granted to Richard Stith by Letters Patent 1 Mar 1772 [1 Aug 1772 in PB 40 p.818] and 300 acs. the residue was assigned to him by William Callaway and William Mead and never before granted.*

JOHN & WILLIAM CALLAWAY, 800 acs. by Survey 8 May 1771 in Bedford Co. on Wilsons Mountain, adj. Porter; 1 Sep 1780, p.384. A.C. of £4 Sterl.

RICHARD STITH, 1,150 acs. by Survey 22 Feb 1775 in Bedford Co. on both sides Jumping Run, Crossing a fork of sd Run; adj. the old Patent Lines, James Board & Talbot; 1 Sep 1780, p.386. A.C. of 20 Shill. Sterl. *965 acs. part thereof was Gtd. to sd Richard Stith by Letters Pat. 10 Jul 1767 [PB 37 p.53 which included Acquila Gilbert's 420 acs. in PB 34 p.757 dated 26 Sep 1760] and 185 acs. the residue never before Gtd.*

HARDEN EVANS ass'ee of JOHN PREEDLE who was ass'ee of BENJAMIN GILBERT, 384 acs. by Survey 28 Feb 1779 in Bedford Co. on the W side of Hills Cr. and on both Sides of Cheese Cr., adj. Gordan; 1 Sep 1780, p.388. A.C. of 40 Shill. Sterl.

HENRY DAVIS, 560 acs. by Survey 9 Dec 1772 in Bedford Co. on the E side of Otter Riv. on both sides of Flintstone Cr., at a Spring, adj. Henry Edson; 1 Sep 1780, p.389. A.C. of £3 Sterl.

SAMUEL HENDERSON, 205 acs. by Survey 3 Mar 1774 in Bedford Co. on the North fork of Blackwater, Crossing sd Fork to a Road; 1 Sep 1780, p.390. A.C. of 25 Shill. Sterl.

JOHN FORBES ass'ee of WILLIAM JAMES, 346 acs. by Survey 9 Apr 1772 in Bedford Co. on S Brs. of Possum Cr. including the head of a Br. of Beaver Cr.; adj. his own Lines, Chandler, Charles Caffry & Lynch; 1 Sep 1780, p.391. A.C. of 35 Shill. Sterl.

CHARLES CAFFRY JUNR., 200 acs. by Survey 7 Nov 1777 in Bedford Co. on E Brs. of Beaver Cr. on both sides of the main Road, on a Spur of the long Mountain thence off across the Spurs and Valleys thereof to the Second Corner pine, adj. Samuel Hairston; 1 Sep 1780, p.393. A.C. of 20 Shill. Sterl.

JOHN CARSON, 420 acs. by Survey 11 Mar 1754 in Bedford Co. on naked Cr.

and on Brs. of Bull Br.; adj. McMurtry, Patterson, Wathen and Jennings their Line & Manly; 1 Sep 1780, p.394. A.C. of 45 Shill. Sterl.

JOHN ROBERTS, 137 acs. by Survey 16 Mar 1772 in Bedford Co. on the head Brs. of Little Cr., adj. William Roberts; 1 Sep 1780, p.396. A.C. of 15 Shill. Sterl.

WILLIAM SPENCER / SPENSER, 540 acs. by Survey 2 Oct 1775 in Bedford Co. on Griffiths Cr.; adj. his own Line, Arthur, Griffith, Anderson, Bome or Borne & Murphey; 1 Sep 1780, p.397. A.C. of 55 Shill. Sterl. *Part of Meads Order of Council.*

JOHN BRYAN, 80 acs. by Survey 15 Jan 1773 in Bedford Co. on the S Brs. of Molleys Cr., adj. Ornsby [the old Lines] & Douglas; 1 Sep 1780, p.399. A.C. of 10 Shill. Sterl.

LITTLEBURY APPERSON, 400 acs. by Survey 22 Nov 1779 in Halifax Co. on the Brs. of Runaway and Childrys Cr., on a Ridge, Crossing a Small Br. and Tribles Road, to a Small Meadow; adj. Davis, Daughaty, & John Dyer; 1 Sep 1780, p.400. A.C. of 40 Shill. Sterl.

ROBERT CLARK and the Heirs of GEORGE CALLAWAY dec'd, 550 acs. by Survey 30 Nov 1773 in Bedford Co. on both sides of Island Cr.; adj. Ward, Hailes/Hails Line, Mead & Sampson; 1 Sep 1780, p.401. A.C. of 55 Shill. Sterl.

ROBERT GARRETT, 454 acs. by Survey 6 Apr 1776 in Bedford Co. on both sides of Falling Riv., across the River 3 poles; adj. William Rogers, James Stuart, Thomas Rogers, William Matthews & Robertson; 1 Sep 1780, p.403. A.C. of 45 Shill. Sterl.

JAMES ADAMS, 270 acs. by Survey 4 Apr 1780 in Bedford Co. on N Brs. of Staunton Riv., down the Pocket Road; adj. Robert Adams & Smith; 1 Sep 1780, p.404. A.C. of 30 Shill. Sterl.

LEONARD BALLOW, 649 acs. by Survey 11 Nov 1766 in Bedford Co. on both Sides of Bore Auger Cr., Shoccos Cr. & on Goose Cr.; adj. Callaway, Bramblitt, Welch & Talbot; 1 Sep 1780, p.405. A.C. of £3.S5 Sterl. [to a Mahoggany Tree on Bore Auger Cr.]

BENJAMIN TANNER, 162 acs. by Survey 8 Mar 1765 in Bedford Co. on the North (or East) side of Falling Riv., Beginning at the Mouth of a Small Br. the next above Rattle Snake br.; 1 Sep 1780, p.407. A.C. of 20 Shill. Sterl.

JOSEPH AKIN, 260 acs. by Survey 6 Mar 1778 in Bedford Co. on W brs. of Little Falling Riv. on both sides of the Main Road, across Ivy Fork; adj. his own, Ross and Hook [their Lines], Morris, William Simmons & Harris; 1 Sep 1780, p.408. A.C. of 25 Shill. Sterl.

SAMUEL GAULDING, 200 acs. by Survey 20 Nov 1771 in Bedford Co. on both sides of the North Fork of Little whipping Cr., near the head Br. of the sd Fork, at an Ivy Clift; adj. Todd, Marshall & Daugherty; 1 Sep 1780, p.409. A.C. of 20 Shill. Sterl.

WILLIAM MATTHEWS (as Assignee of JOHN BAILY), 400 acs. by Survey 5 Apr 1775 in Bedford Co. on the W side of Falling Riv. on both sides of Hickory Cr.; adj. Barrett, Mason, Garrett & his own Lines; 1 Sep 1780, p.411. A.C. of 40 Shill. Sterl.

WILLIAM SINGLETON, 600 acs. by Survey 13 Apr 1780 in Bedford Co. on Brs. of Hatt Cr. and Dog Cr. and other brs. of Falling Riv., up the Bank of a Fork of Hatt Cr.; adj. James Zachary, Thurston, Todd, Sturman, Booker, Thomas Rafferty, Mitchell, & David Hutcheson; 1 Sep 1780, p.412. A.C. of £3 Sterl. *part thereof is part of an Entry made by John Smith 23 Dec 1754 and by him Assigned to sd William Singleton and part thereof is part of an Entry made by Thomas Rogers 10 Jan 1769 and by him Assigned to sd William Singleton.*

JAMES McRANDLE ass'ee of ISAAC DAVIS, 400 acs. by Survey 13 Mar 1777 in Bedford Co. on both Sides of Mountain Run; adj. his own Line, Patterson, Campbell, Simmons & Bolling; 1 Sep 1780, p.414. A.C. of 40 Shill. Sterl.

WILLIAM MARSHALL Ass'ee of ROBERT GARRETT, 100 acs. by Survey 20 Dec 1777 in Bedford Co. on E Brs. of Whipping Cr.; adj. his own Lines, Low Todd & Barlour; 1 Sep 1780, p.416. A.C. of 10 Shill. Sterl. *part of 368 acs. Surveyed for Robert Garrett 7 Dec 1763.*

ARCHIBALD CAMPBELL, 300 acs. by Survey 27 Oct 1752 in Lunenburg Co. on the head brs. of Naked Cr.; adj. Bolling, & Wathen and Jennings [their Lines]; 1 Sep 1780, p.417. A.C. of 30 Shill. Sterl.

CHARLES RORK, 1,045 acs. by **Inclusive Survey** 16 Feb 1773 in Bedford Co. on the Brs. of Beaver Cr. and Archers Cr., on Rorks Mountain; adj. William Rutherford, Caffry, Thomas Mawkin, Baskerville & Lynch; 1 Sep 1780, p.418. A.C. of £5.S5 Sterl.

BENJAMIN WATKINS, 138 acs. by Survey 12 mar 1777 in Bedford Co. on head Brs. of falling Riv. and Brs. of wreck Island Cr.; adj. Campbell, Bolling & Dixson; 1 Sep 1780, p.420. A.C. of 15 Shill. Sterl.

PETER HOLLAND, 159 acs. by Survey 31 Mar 1772 in Bedford Co. on the Waters of Little Indian Run; adj. his own the Patent Line, Hail & Meader; 1 Sep 1780, p.421. A.C. of 20 Shill. Sterl.

JAMES RADCLIFF, 240 acs. by Survey 21 Nov 1770 in Bedford Co. on both Sides of the main Ridge betw. the Brs. of falling Riv. and Brs. of wreck Island Cr., Crossing the Road; adj. Pettycrew, Bolling, his own Lines, Carson & Steel; 1 Sep 1780, p.423. A.C. of 25 Shill. Sterl.

MICHAEL JONES, 235 acs. 21 Dec 1778 in Bedford Co. on E brs. of Little Falling Riv., at the head of Stoney br.; adj. Wood Jones, Key, Caldwell, Thompson, & Daniel Mitchell; 1 Sep 1780, p.424. A.C. of 25 Shill. Sterl.

JAMES DIXON, 340 acs. by Survey 15 Dec 1773 in Bedford Co. on brs. of White Marsh and Brs. of Golloways Br., up Rosser Road; adj. his own Lines, Golloway, Wilson & Chiles; 1 Sep 1780, p.425. A.C. of 35 Shill. Sterl.

JOHN GIVENS / GIVINS, 188 acs. by Survey 6 Apr 1770 in Pittsylvania Co. on the Long Br. of Sandy Riv., adj. John

Grisham & Watkins; 1 Sep 1780, p.427. A.C. of 20 Shill. Sterl.

THOMAS ARTHUR, 154 acs. by Survey 24 Mar 1775 in Bedford Co. on the N Brs. of Goose Cr., on Toms Br.; adj. John Arthur Junr., Ferrell & Arthurs old Lines; 1 Sep 1780, p.428. A.C. of 15 Shill. Sterl.

CHRISTOPHER JOHNSON, 50 acs. by Survey 17 Nov 1770 in Bedford Co. on both Sides of Doughertrys Road; adj. Dougherty, his own Line, Wayles, & Fry and Company; 1 Sep 1780, p.429. A.C. of 5 Shill. Sterl.

THOMAS JONES, 270 acs. by Survey 15 Dec 1773 in Bedford Co. on the S side of Reedy Cr. and other W Brs. of Falling Riv.; adj. his own Lines, Gollaway, Thompson, Wilson, James Dixson & Gallaway; 1 Sep 1780, p.430. A.C. of 30 Shill. Sterl.

JOHN DAVIS, 289 acs. by Survey 27 Feb 1779 in Henry Co. on Owens Cr. of Pigg Riv., up the South fork; adj. his own Land, Josiah Kerby & Jessey Kerby; 1 Sep 1780, p.432. A.C. of 30 Shill. Sterl.

JOHN DRINKWATER Ass'ee of JOHN FITZPATRICK who was Ass'ee of CHARLES TALBOT, 400 acs. by Survey 3 Mar 1780 by Virtue of an Entry made by Charles Talbot on 22 Sep 1754 in Bedford Co. on both Sides of Deep Br. (Adjoining Bullocks Lines), also adj. Read & Terrell; 1 Sep 1780, p.433. A.C. of 40 Shill. Sterl.

ROBERT HUGHES / HUGHS, 540 acs. by Survey 7 Mar 1775 (including two Surveys) in Bedford Co. on S Head Brs. of Beaver Cr. on both Sides of Irvins Road, near a Meadow Ground, including the Brushy Mountain; adj. Hilton, Daugherty, Irvin, & John Leikh; 1 Sep 1780, p.435. A.C. of 55 Shill. Sterl.

BENJAMIN ECHOLS, 400 acs. by Survey 1 Apr 1774 in Pittsylvania Co. on the Brs. of Sandy Cr.; adj. King, Adkinsons Order Line & George Musick; 1 Sep 1780, p.436. A.C. of 40 Shill. Sterl.

JOHN SNOW, 300 acs. by Survey 11 Mar 1779 in Bedford Co. on both sides of Wards Ferry Road on Heads of E Brs. of Troubleson Cr. [Troublesome Cr.]; adj. John Richardson, Harris, Mauray /Marray & his own Lines; 1 Sep 1780, p.437. A.C. of 30 Shill. Sterl.

JOHN STONE JUNR., 134 acs. by Survey 14 Mar 1770 in Pittsylvania Co. on Sandy Cr.; adj. John Stone Senr., Bostick & Walton; 1 Sep 1780, p.438. A.C. of 15 Shill. Sterl.

JOHN SHIELDS, 345 acs. by Survey 29 Apr 1780 in Pittsylvania Co. on the Brow of Sandy Riv.; adj. Thomas Robertson, sd Shields Old Line & William Shields New line; 1 Sep 1780, p.439. A.C. of 35 Shill. Sterl.

MATTHEW SPARKES / SPARKS, 305 acs. by Survey 13 Mar 1778 in Pittsylvania Co. on the Brs. of Sandy Riv., Crossing Callael fork of beens Cr.; adj. William Wilson, Richardson, Denton, Nehemiah Norton & the sd Watson [Wilson]; 1 Sep 1780, p.441. A.C. of 35 Shill. Sterl.

STARLING CATO / SARLING CATO, 164 acs. by Survey 3 May 1780 in

Pittsylvania Co. on the Brs. of Mountain Cr., on the Road; adj. Thomas Smith, Charles Burton, sd Catos former Line & Vincent; 1 Sep 1780, p.442. A.C. of 20 Shill. Sterl.

THOMAS OWEN, 334 acs. by Survey 26 Mar 1770 in Pittsylvania Co. on the S side of Sandy Riv.; adj. John Gammon & Bolling; 1 Sep 1780, p.443. A.C. of 35 Shill. Sterl.

JOHN WILSON, 440 acs. by Survey 5 May 1780 in Pittsylvania Co. on both sides of Great Cherrystone Cr.; adj. Robert Wooding, Hix, & James Watson; 1 Sep 1780, p.445. A.C. of 45 Shill. Sterl.

CHARLES JOHNSON (as Assignee of THOMAS DAUGHERTY), 175 acs. by Survey 31 Mar 1779 in Bedford Co. on E Brs. of Flat Cr., on the Ridge betw. the Waters of Flat Cr. and Beaver Cr., near Irvins Road; adj. Goggin, Irvin, Hairston, Edmeston & Hughs / Hughes; 1 Sep 1780, p.446. A.C. of 20 Shill. Sterl.

WILLIAM SUTTON, 743 acs. by Survey 5 Apr 1770 in Pittsylvania Co. on the Brs. of Dan Riv.; adj. Nicholas Perkins, Snowden Kirlland, William York, Samuel Harris, Sweeting & John Cargell; 1 Sep 1780, p.448. A.C. of £3.S15 Sterl.

JOHN GOVER, 282 acs. by Survey 13 Apr 1770 in Pittsylvania Co. on the Waters of Sandy Riv., adj. Hargate; 1 Sep 1780, p.449. A.C. of 30 Shill. Sterl.

JOHN STYLES Ass'ee of JOHN CHILDRES, 400 acs. by Survey 22 Oct 1771 in Halifax Co. on the Brs. of dry Cr., Crossing a Road, adj. Joseph Gill Senr. & Byrd; 1 Sep 1780, p.450. A.C. of 40 Shill. Sterl.

THOMAS SPARKS, 137 acs. by Survey 28 May 1780 in Pittsylvania Co. on the Brs. of Strawbery Cr., adj. Adam Larky, McGehee, & Jonathan Thomas; 1 Sep 1780, p.451. A.C. of 15 Shill. Sterl.

JOHN FULTON, 248 acs. by Survey 12 Dec 1777 in Pittsylvania Co. on both Sides of Little Stuarts Cr. of Sandy Riv., adj. James Boaz & Frances Mabary [his Line]; 1 Sep 1780, p.452. A.C. of 25 Shill. Sterl.

JOSEPH GILL, SENIOR, 400 acs. by Survey 27 Oct 1771 in Halifax Co. on Hico Riv., Crossing Shoars Br.; adj. sd Gill, Byrd, another Tract of sd Gills & Clift; 1 Sep 1780, p.453. A.C. of 40 Shill. Sterl.

JAMES BURNETT / BURNET, 172 acs. by Survey 31 Mar 1770 in Pittsylvania Co. on the Waters of Sandy Riv.; adj. sd Burnet, & John Oaks; 1 Sep 1780, p.455. A.C. of 20 Shill. Sterl.

ASHLEY JOHNSON Ass'ee of MICAJAH TERREL, 74 acs. by Survey 28 Nov 1754 in Bedford Co. Formerly Albemarle on the S Side of the Fluvanna Riv. on the Brs. of Fishing Cr., adj. Micajah Terril; 1 Sep 1780, p.456. A.C. of 10 Shill. Sterl.

MARK MATTENLY, 604 acs. by Survey 17 Mar 1779 in Pittsylvania Co. on the Brs. of Sandy Riv.; adj. Perkins, Richardson, William Walson, Givens, Gammon, & Charles Dunkin; 1 Sep 1780, p.457. A.C. of £3 Sterl.

JOHN HENDRICK / HENDRICKS, 345 acs. by Survey 10 Mar 1770 in Amherst Co. on the Brs. of Stovalls Cr., adj. George Jefferson & Alexander McCaul; 1 Sep 1780, p.459. A.C. of 35 Shill. Sterl.

SAMUEL SHEILDS / SHIELDS, 340 acs. by Survey 14 Apr 1770 in Pittsylvania Co. on the Waters of Sandy Riv., adj. John Morton & Elizabeth Read; 1 Sep 1780, p.460. A.C. of 40 Shill. Sterl.

SYLVESTER ADAMS ass'ee of WILLIAM MUNKOUS, 487 acs. by Survey 16 Mar 1770 in Pittsylvania Co. on the Brs. of Sandy Cr.; adj. Wilson, Stokes & the sd Munkous former Line; 1 Sep 1780, p.461. A.C. of 50 Shill. Sterl.

JOHN ANGUS (as Assignee of JOHN ROGERS JUNR. who was Assignee of JOHN CHILDRES, 395 acs. by Survey 3 Oct 1772 in Halifax Co. on Little Blewing / Bluewing; adj. Stiles, Sizemore & Gill; 1 Sep 1780, p.463. A.C. of 40 Shill. Sterl.

GROSS SCRUGGS as Ass'ee of JOHN PARTREE BURK, 126 acs. by Survey 10 Apr 1767 in Bedford Co. on the E Brs. of Goose Cr., adj. his own Line the Patent Line; 1 Sep 1780, p.464. A.C. of 15 Shill. Sterl.

BRAXTON MABRY, 306 acs. by Survey 9 Jan 1778 in Pittsylvania Co. on the Brs. of Shocko Cr.; adj. Hugh Henry, David Walker, Willis, & David Givins; 1 Sep 1780, p.465. A.C. of 15 Shill. Sterl. *200 acs. part thereof is part of a Survey of 306 acs. made for Robert Sweeting the right and Title of which is Since become Vested in the sd Braxton Mabry.*

BALLENGER WAID, 94 acs. by Survey 11 Mar 1774 in Amherst Co. on both Sides of Clarks Cr., adj. Nicholas Davis, his own Line & Nicholas Davies; 1 Sep 1780, p.466. A.C. of 10 Shill. Sterl. *bounded by the Variation of the Magnetic from the True Meridian being N1°W.*

JOHN LYNCH, 380 acs. by Survey 12 Nov 1779 in Bedford Co. on the W Side of Rockcastle Cr., on Lynch's Road, Crossing Rock Castle Cr. Several times, up Russells Road, up Winstons Road to a Bent; adj. Robert Clark, his own Lines & Mooreman; 1 Sep 1780, p.467. A.C. of 40 Shill. Sterl. *part of an Entry made by him the sd John Lynch 28 May 1768.*

WILLIAM JOHNSON, 80 acs. by Survey 10 Mar 1780 in Bedford Co. on E Brs. of Fishing Cr., upon the foot of the W side of Candlers Mountain; adj. David Ross, John Lynch & his own Lines; 1 Sep 1780, p.469. A.C. of 10 Shill. Sterl. *part of an entry made by him the sd William Johnson 25 Sep 1770.*

JOHN SMITH, 344 acs. by Survey 3 May 1780 in Pittsylvania Co. on Sandy Riv., on the Road; adj. Thomas Smith, his old Lines & John Fulton; 1 Sep 1780, p.470. A.C. of 35 Shill. Sterl.

NEHEMIAH NORTON, 314 acs. by Survey 26 Mar 1770 in Pittsylvania Co. on the waters of Sandy Riv., adj. Givan & Watson; 1 Sep 1780, p.472. A.C. of 35 Shill. Sterl.

SYLVESTER ADAMS (as assignee of PETER HUSTON who was Assignee of WILLIAM SOUTHERLAND), 204 acs. by Survey 12 Jan 1764 in Pittsylvania

Co. formerly Halifax on the N Brs. of Dan Riv., Beginning in the Draughts of Stones Spring Branch, adj. Wilson & Stone; 1 Sep 1780, p.473. A.C. of 20 Shill. Sterl.

REUBIN FRANCIS, 238½ acs. by Survey 2 June 1777 in Albemarle Co. on the N side of the Rivanna Riv. and on the S Side Kents br., to a South fork of sd br.; adj. Henry Nash, Peter Ross & Edmerson; 1 Sep 1780, p.474. A.C. of 30 Shill. Sterl.

LEWIS WILLIAMS, 222 acs. by Survey 13 Mar 1778 in Pittsylvania Co. on both Sides of Open Ground Fork of Been Cr., adj. Constant Perkins & Parkins; 1 Sep 1780, p.475. A.C. of 25 Shill. Sterl.

JOHN KITCHEN, 135 acs. by Survey 28 Mar 1770 in Bedford Co. on W Brs. of Stonewall Cr., on Cattail Br.; adj. Stovall, Kitchen & McBride; 1 Sep 1780, p.476. A.C. of 15 Shill. Sterl.

RICHARD TIMBERLAKE, 50 acs. by Survey 9 Mar 1780 in Bedford Co. on the S Side of Ivy Cr., at a bent of the Cr.; adj. Wayles, Wilkerson & Clark; 1 Sep 1780, p.477. A.C. of 5 Shill. Sterl. by Virtue of an Entry made By the Said Richard Timberlake 30 Jan 1769.

JOHN FULTON, 284 acs. by Survey 13 Dec 1777 in Pittsylvania Co. on the Brs. of Steuarts Cr., Crossing the Long Br.; adj. James Boaz, Barnetts McCullough, the sd Fultons Lines, Smith, Vincent & McCollough; 1 Sep 1780, p.479. A.C. of 30 Shill. Sterl.

SYLVESTER ADAMS Ass'ee of THOMAS OWEN, 400 acs. by Survey 17 Mar 1770 in Pittsylvania Co. on the waters of Dan Riv., Crossing Little Wolf Island cr.; adj. sd Owen, Charles Duncan & William Shelton; 1 Sep 1780, p.480. A.C. of 40 Shill. Sterl.

BUTLER STONE STREET, 133 acs. by Survey 19 Apr 1768 in Henry Co. formerly Pittsylvania on Both sides of Leatherwood Cr., adj. Merry Webb; 1 Sep 1780, p.481. A.C. of 15 Shill. Sterl.

GEORGE ADAMS, 277 acs. by Survey 6 Apr 1770 in Pittsylvania Co. on the Long Br. of Sandy Riv.; 1 Sep 1780, p.482. A.C. of 30 Shill. Sterl.

JOHN PAYNOR ass'ee of NATHAN ADAMS who was Ass'ee of JOHN TALIAFERRO, 271 acs. by Survey 15 Mar 1774 in Pittsylvania Co. on Sandy Cr., adj. Keerby; 1 Sep 1780, p.483. A.C. of 30 Shill. Sterl.

THOMAS SMITH, 101 acs. by Survey 14 Mar 1778 in Pittsylvania Co. on the N side of Sandy Riv.; adj. John Smith; 1 Sep 1780, p.484. A.C. of 10 Shill. Sterl.

JOHN STONE, 262 acs. by Survey 11 Jan 1764 in Pittsylvania Co. formerly Halifax on both Sides of his Spring Br., on a fork of the Rockey Br.; adj. Nathan Bostick, John Bostick & sd John Stones former Line; 1 Sep 1780, p.485. A.C. of 20 Shill. Sterl.

WILLIAM EVANS ass'ee of BENJAMIN CLEMENTS who was ass'ee of THOMAS DILLARD and ISAAC CLEMENTS, 315 acs. by Survey 27 Feb 1775 in Pittsylvania Co. on both Sides of Ralphs Br. of Sycamore Cr., on Whealers Br., adj. Loving, & John Roberson; 1 Sep 1780, p.487. A.C. of 35 Shill. Sterl.

WILLIAM SMITH, 244 acs. by Survey 27 Jan 1769 in Pittsylvania Co. on both Sides of Sycamore Cr., Crossing both forks of Whealers Br., Crossing a Bent of the Cr., adj. John Smith & Robertson; 1 Sep 1780, p.488. A.C. of 25 Shill. Sterl.

JOHN WARD ass'ee of JOHN RODGERS, 400 acs. by Survey 5 Apr 1780 in Bedford Co. on the N side of Staunton Riv., down Buck Br., adj. Joseph Eades & William Vest; 1 Sep 1780, p.489. A.C. of 40 Shill. Sterl. *by Virtue of an Entry made 25 Feb 1750 by John Rogers and by him Assigned to the sd John Ward.*

JOHN BOUGHTON ass'ee of JOHN CHAMBERS, 100 acs. by Survey 15 May 1780 in Bedford Co. on the head Brs. of Agers Br. of Little Falling Riv., **on the Road from Barners Mill to Ross and Hooks Store**, at a Spring, on the Store Road aforesaid, adj. Francis Barner & Conners; 1 Sep 1780, p.491. A.C. of 10 Shill. Sterl. *part of an Entry of 400 acs. made 15 May 1769 by James Boyd and by him assigned to William Thompson and by him Assigned the sd John Chambers.* [This 100 acs. was regranted to John Boughton in GB 57 p.309 dated 9 Nov 1808, by survey 1 Jul 1806, 100 acs. Campbell Co. and delivered to Mr John Dabney 6 Feb 1809; adj. Samuel Day & sd Boughton; on the **road from Reid's store to Boughton's Mill**]

HENRY DAVIS, 738 acs. by Survey 26 Mar 1767 in Bedford Co. on both Sides of Otter Riv., up Troublesome Cr., on Sholes Br., to a Willow Oak on the foot of Flintstone Hill; adj. Thomas Yuille, Henry Edson & David Irvine; 1 Sep 1780, p.492. A.C. of £3.S5 Sterl. *124 acs. part thereof is part of 350 acs. Gtd. by Letters Pat. to John Phelps 10 Jan 1748 the right and title of which is since become Vested in the sd Henry Davis and 254 acs. part thereof was Surveyed for the sd Henry Davis 8 Dec 1772 and 360 acs. the residue never before Surveyed.*

JOHN RAFFERTY, 104 acs. by Survey 22 Nov 1771 in Bedford Co. on the W forks of Bowmans Cr.; adj. Talbot, Pendleton, Pruit & Garrett; 1 Sep 1780, p.494. A.C. of 10 Shill. Sterl.

JOHN DAVIS, 167 acs. by Survey 17 Mar 1769 in Pittsylvania Co. on the Piney fork of Owens Cr.; 1 Sep 1780, p.495. A.C. of 20 Shill. Sterl.

WILLIAM DAVIS, 149 acs. by Survey 18 Apr 1752 in Pittsylvania Co. on both Sides of Story Cr. of Pigg Riv., adj. his old Line; 1 Sep 1780, p.496. A.C. of 15 Shill. Sterl.

JOSEPH PATTERSON, 215 acs. by Survey 24 Apr 1774 in Bedford Co. on Shoulder Camp Cr., on Pyburns Mountain; adj. William Mead Junr., Holland, Embrough & Hollands Mountain Line; 1 Sep 1780, p.497. A.C. of 25 Shill. Sterl.

JOHN MASON, 95 acs. by Survey 18 Mar 1779 in Bedford Co. on W Brs. of Turnip Cr., at Austins Br.; adj. Gwin, John Willson / Wilson, his own Lines & Rogers; 1 Sep 1780, p.499. A.C. of 10 Shill. Sterl.

MOSES GREEN, 400 acs. by Survey 10 Nov 1776 in Bedford Co. on the N side of Black water Riv. adjoining Doggetts

Land, down half way Br., adj. Dogget & Thomson; 1 Sep 1780, p.500. A.C. of 40 Shill. Sterl.

RICHARD PARSLEY / PARSLY, 200 acs. by Survey 13 Feb 1769 in Henry Co. on Beaver Cr., adj. Walkers order Line; 1 Sep 1780, p.501. A.C. of 20 Shill. Sterl.

JESSE CLAY, 154 acs. by Survey 3 Apr 1772 in Bedford Co. on both Sides of Black water Riv., adj. Carter; 1 Sep 1780, p.503. A.C. of 15 Shill. Sterl.

JOHN JOHNSTON Ass'ee of BENJAMIN GRIFFITH, 54 acs. by Survey 19 Dec 1762 in Bedford Co. on both Sides of the North fork of Griffiths Cr.; 1 Sep 1780, p.504. A.C. of 5 Shill. Sterl.

BENJAMIN BROWN, 55 acs. by Survey 1 Nov 1779 in Augusta Co. and Joining his other Land on the Middle Riv. of Shanandore, also adj. Thomas Brown & John Frisl / Friel; 1 Sep 1780, p.505. A.C. of 10 Shill. Sterl.

THOMAS GOLLAHER, 290 acs. by Survey 18 Jan 1774 in Bedford Co. on both Sides of Miry Cr. and on other E Brs. of Falling Riv.; adj. Charles Cobb, Wallace, Thomas Rogers & Read; 1 Sep 1780, p.506. A.C. of 30 Shill. Sterl.

LEWIS DEUPREE, 400 acs. by Survey 19 Dec 1774 in Charlotte Co. adj. Norris, Roberts, Hunt, Barns & Evans; 1 Sep 1780, p.507. A.C. of 40 Shill. Sterl.

WILLIAM READ, 370 acs. by Survey 10 May 1779 in Bedford Co. on the E Side of Falling Riv. on both Sides of Suck Br., Beginning on the Riv. a little below the Old Rod Ford; adj. George Cock, his own Line & Nicholas Conner; 1 Sep 1780, p.508. A.C. of 40 Shill. Sterl.

CHARLES COBBS Ass'ee of CHARLES GAUSNEL, 100 acs. by Survey 18 Jan 1774 in Bedford Co. including heads of Brs. of Falling Riv. and Little [Falling] Riv.; adj. McCord, Wallace & his own Lines; 1 Sep 1780, p.509. A.C. of 10 Shill. Sterl.

WILLIAM MARTIN, 200 acs. by Survey 2 Apr 1778 in Bedford Co. on the S Brs. of Gills Cr., adj. Talbot; 1 Sep 1780, p.511. A.C. of 20 Shill. Sterl.

RICHARD LITTLEPAGE, 200 acs. by Survey 21 Dec 1779 in Bedford Co. on E Brs. of Little Falling riv., on Rices Road, in the Feild between Craddles and Littlepage; adj. Robert Mitchel, Abraham Irvine, William Thompson & Irvin; 1 Sep 1780, p.512. A.C. of 20 Shill. Sterl.

JOHN HARTWELL, 80 acs. by Survey 4 Apr 1778 in Bedford Co. on Merrymans Run, on a Path, along the Ridge, adj. Greer; 1 Sep 1780, p.513. A.C. of 10 Shill. Sterl.

JAMES DIXSON, 50 acs. by Survey 17 Feb 1773 in Bedford Co. on E head Brs. of the South Fork of Falling Riv., Crossing a Large Br.; adj. his own Lines, Lax, & Wathen and Jennings [their Line]; 1 Sep 1780, p.514. A.C. of 5 Shill. Sterl.

WILLIAM DAVIS, 400 acs. by Survey 21 Oct 1773 in Pittsylvania Co. on the Brs. of Pigg Riv. and on Story Cr., Crossing Coles Br., adj. James

Handeford & the sd William Davis; 1 Sep 1780, p.515. A.C. of 40 Shill. Sterl.

AARON LEVINSTON / LEVISTON Ass'ee of WILLIAM WRIGHT, 156 acs. by Survey 27 Mar 1772 in Bedford Co. on the S Brs. of Maggotty Cr., adj. Moses Ray; 1 Sep 1780, p.516. A.C. of 20 Shill. Sterl.

HENRY CONWAY, 266 acs. by Survey 1 Oct 1773 in Pittsylvania Co. on Johneykin Cr., adj. Richardson; 1 Sep 1780, p.517. A.C. of 30 Shill. Sterl.

WILLIAM MEAD & ISHAM TALBOT, 432 acs. by Survey 15 Nov 1762 in Bedford Co. on the S Side of Staunton Riv., adj. Bradshaw & Meadow; 1 Sep 1780, p.518. A.C. of 45 Shill. Sterl.

JOHN THOMPSON, 184 acs. by Survey 12 Apr 1774 in Bedford Co. on Beaver dam Cr. a North Br. of Stanton Riv., adj. Thomas Pate & Talbot; 1 Sep 1780, p.519. A.C. of 20 Shill. Sterl.

DANIEL RAMEY, 159 acs. by Survey 19 Apr 1768 in Henry Co. on the Waters of Smiths Riv., adj. Randolphs order Line & William Alexander; 1 Sep 1780, p.521. A.C. of 20 Shill Sterl.

HENRY BELL, 340 acs. by Survey 29 Apr 1751 in Albemarle Co. on the head Brs. of Porrage Cr.; adj. Daniel Gains, Mr Braxton, John Christian, Henry Teneson, Edward Eidson, Joseph Magann & the sd Gaines; 1 Sep 1780, p.522. A.C. of 35 Shill. Sterl.

LODWICK TUGGLE (as assignee of PARKER ATKINSON), 175 acs. by Survey 1 Mar 1762 in Pittsylvania Co. on the S side of Pigg Riv.; adj. Francis Kerbey; 1 Sep 1780, p.523. A.C. of 20 Shill. Sterl.

ROBERT CURRY ass'ee of DAVID NALY, 400 acs. by Survey 9 Sep 1771 in Augusta Co. on the draughts between Long Glade and Mossey Cr.; 1 Sep 1780, p.524. A.C. of 40 Shill. Ster.

JOSEPH WEBSTER, 44 acs. by Survey 7 Nov 1765 in Halifax Co. on both sides of Smiths Riv.; 1 Sep p1780, p.525. A.C. of 5 Shill. Sterl.

THOMAS VEST, 312 acs. by Survey 2 Dec 1772 in Bedford Co. on Brs. of Green Spring Cr., Swan Cr. and Cattamount Falls Br., on Dennys Road, Crossing a br. of Gum Spring Cr., adj. Dudly & Pilis [his] Line; 1 Sep 1780, p.526. A.C. of 35 Shill. Sterl.

SAMUEL HAIRSTON, 287 acs. by Survey 29 Nov 1752 in Lunenburgh Co. on the Brs. of Seneca Cr., in a Meadow; adj. Murray, Ornsby, Nelson & Murry; 1 Sep 1780, p.527. A.C. of 30 Shill. Sterl.

THOMAS LOGWOOD, 220 acs. by Survey 11 Nov 1779 in Bedford Co. on the Top of the Main Blue Ledge; Beginning at the head of a Br. of the North fork of Otter Riv., on the Top of the Mountain (whereby Extreem Cold the trees None Exceed ten feet high); 1 Sep 1780, p.529. A.C. of 25 Shill. Sterl.

DAVID STEEL, 38 acs. by Survey 25 Nov 1779 in Rockbridge Co. on Bufflellow Cr. below the fork; 1 Sep 1780, p.530. A.C. of 5 Shill. Sterl.

JOSHUA WYNNE JUNR., 325 acs. by Survey 5 May 1779 in Bedford Co. on both Sides of Shepherds Cr. and on other

E Brs. of Falling Riv., adj. George Cock & William Read; 1 Sep 1780, p.531. A.C. of 35 Shill. Sterl.

SAMUEL RUNKLE, 126 acs. by Survey 21 Apr 1780 in Augusta Co. on Kirks Br. of the Middle Riv. Shanandore and on the N side the land he Lives on; adj. Charles [Eyvers], James Tremble & sd Runkles pattent Line; 1 Sep 1780, p.532. A.C. of 15 Shill. Sterl.

TOLLY DAVITT, 43 acs. by Survey 29 Apr 1780 in Augusta Co. Joining a tract of his own NE side; 1 Sep 1780, p.533. A.C. of 5 Shill. Sterl.

THOMAS ARTHUR / ARTHER, 112 acs. by Survey 29 Sep 1779 in Bedford Co. on Griffiths Cr.; adj. his Line, Spencer on a Dividing Line, Doggel & Rentsfrd; 1 Sep 1780, p.534. A.C. of 15 Shill. Sterl.

WILLIAM BUTLER, 200 acs. by Survey 2 Mar 1779 in Bedford Co. on the Brs. of Crab Orchard Cr., on a Road, adj. his own Lines & Talbot; 1 Sep 1780, p.535. A.C. of 20 Shill. Sterl.

JESSE SANDERS, 392 acs. by Survey 5 May 1780, Lunenburg Co. on the Brs. of Meherrin Riv.; adj. Burwell, Erskin & Dupries Lines; 1 Sep 1780, p.536. A.C. of 40 Shill. Sterl.

ISHAM TALBOT, 320 acs. by Survey 18 Nov 1766 in Bedford Co. on the W Brs. of Beaverdam Cr., adj. Simmons; 1 Sep 1780, p.537. A.C. of 35 Shill. Sterl.

MATTHEW TALBOT, 370 acs. by Survey 10 Apr 1754 in Bedford Co. on both sides of Crab Orchard Cr., adj. his own Line & Mead; 1 Sep 1780, p.539. A.C. of 40 Shill. Sterl.

JAMES BELL, 85 acs. by Survey 3 May 1770 in Augusta Co. on a Small Br. of the Middle Riv. of Shanendore, on a Ridge, adj. his own Lines & James Phillips; 1 Sep 1780, p.540. A.C. of 10 Shill. Sterl.

WILLIAM BOHANNAN, 300 acs. by Survey 3 May 1779 in Henry Co. on the head Brs. of Butramtown Cr., adj. Key & his own Line; 1 Sep 1780, p.541. A.C,. of 30 Shill. Sterl.

ISHAM TALBOT, 727 acs. by Survey 12 Nov 1766 in Bedford Co. on the S side of Goose Cr., down Hayses run from the head & down Shoco Cr., adj. Welch & Bramblett; 1 Sep 1780, p.542. A.C. of £3.S15 Sterl.

ROBERT MEAVEATY, 68 acs. by Survey 5 May 1758 in Pittsylvania Co. on Snows fork of Otter Cr.; 1 Sep 1780, p.543. A.C. of 10 Shill. Sterl.

WILLIAM CHRISTIAN, 47 acs. by Survey 21 Jan 1759 in Amherst Co. on both sides of Lime Kill Cr., Crossing the South fork of sd Cr., adj. his own Line; 1 Sep 1780, p.544. A.C. of 5 Shill. Sterl.

MARTHA BAUGH / BOUGH, 85 acs. & 78 poles by Survey 14 Mar 1777 in Dinwiddie Co. and Bristol Par. on the Northern Brs. of Stoney Cr., Beginning at the Mouth of Corn feild Br. where it empties into the Briary Br., to the Mouth of a Small Br. running near her corn feild where we Began, adj. Agness Perry & Bough her own old Line; 1 Sep 1780, p.545. A.C. of 10 Shill. Sterl. *[For her old line see PB 23 p.901 to Thomas*

Baugh; for Agness Perry's land see PB 14 p.346 to John Moreland (John Moreley), all East of Flat Br. of Stoney Cr.]

ISHAM TALBOT, 270 acs. by Survey 17 Nov 1766 in Bedford Co. adj. Walton; 1 Sep 1780, p.546. A.C. of 30 Shill. Sterl.

ISHAM TALBOT, 120 acs. by Survey 10 Jul 1768 in Bedford Co. on both sides of the North fork of Otter Riv., down Sawpets Br., adj. Keeny; 1 Sep 1780, p.547. A.C. of 15 Shill. Sterl.

ISHAM TALBOT, 163 acs. by Survey 18 Nov 1766 in Bedford Co. on the N Brs. of Staunton Riv., adj. Weaver & Simmons; 1 Sep 1780, p.549. A.C. of 20 Shill. Sterl.

WILLIAM WRIGHT, 174 acs. by Survey 16 Mar 1774 in Bedford Co. on the S side of Maggoty Cr., adj. Randolph & Johnson, to a Mahogany tree on a Br.; 1 Sep 1780, p.550. A.C. of 20 Shill. Sterl.

HENRY CONWAY, 400 acs. by Survey 1 Oct 1773 in Pittsylvania Co. on the Draughs of Johnaykin Cr.; adj. his own line, Grayham, Keerly & Richardson; 1 Sep 1780, p.551. A.C of 40 Shill. Sterl.

ADAM CLEMENT, 102 acs. by Survey 31 Mar 1773 in Bedford Co. on head Brs. of Beaver Cr.; adj. Hylton, Anthony & his own Lines; 1 Sep 1780, p.552. A.C. of 10 Shill. Sterl.

[Margin note: *"NB This Grant was made out under the administration of Governor Jefferson it was altered in the name of Governor Harrison as it was not signed before Governor Jefferson resigned"*]

JAMES CRAINE ass'ee of SILVANUS STOKES, 312 acs. by Survey 27 Oct 1774 in Pittsylvania Co. on the Brs. of Fall Cr., on Banister Mountain, adj. John Donelson; 1 Jan 1782 in the 6th year of the Commonwealth, p.553. A.C. of 35 Shill. Sterl. paid by James Craine. In Witness whereof the said Thomas Jefferson hath hereunto set his hand and Caused the Seal of the said Commonwealth to be Affixed at Richmond [not signed].

JAMES CHRISTIAN, 253 acs. by Survey 6 Feb 1757 in Amherst Co. on both Sides of Christians Mill Cr., adj. his own Lines; 1 Sep 1780, p.554. A.C. of 25 Shill. Sterl.

SAMUEL FOX, 119 acs. by Survey 5 Jun 1779 in Henry Co. on Little Otter Cr., adj. Christopher Choat; 1 Sep 1780, p.555. A.C. of 15 Shill. Sterl.

SAMUEL HAMMELTON (ass assignee of SAMUEL MILLER), 25 acs. by Survey 28 Aug 1772 in Botetourt Co. joining the Lines of George Daugherty and John Sprouts Land on the forks of James Riv., Crossing two draughts; 1 Sep 1780, p.556. A.C. of 5 Shill. Sterl.

WILLIAM HAINSER Ass'ee of JAMES BOYLE who was ass'ee of JOHN ROBERTSON, 60 acs. by Survey 28 Aug 1772 in Botetourt Co. on dunlaps Cr. a Br. of James Riv.; 1 Sep 1780, p.557. A.C. of 10 Shill. Sterl.

ROBERT HILL, 313 acs. by Survey 4 May 1753 in Henry Co. formerly Halifax on both sides of Pigg Riv.; 1 Sep 1780, p.558. A.C. of 35 Shill. Sterl.

WILLIAM TALBOT, 385 acs. by Survey 2 Dec 1778 in Bedford Co. on the Forks of Hills Cr. and on the E Brs. of Seneca Cr., upon the top of Seneca Hill; adj. Murray, William Brown, Randolph & Gilbert; 1 Sep 1780, p.559. A.C. of 40 Shill. Sterl.

JAMES STANDEFORD, 127 acs. by Survey 18 Apr 1759 in Pittsylvania Co. on Nicholas's Cr., crossing a Br. and a fork of the sd Cr.; 1 Sep 1780, p.560. A.C. of 15 Shill. Sterl.

CAPT. THOMAS JONES, 393 acs. by Survey 7 Jun 1779 in Henry Co. on Turners Cr. and Nicholas's Cr., adj. his own Line; 1 Sep 1780, p.561. A.C. of 40 Shill. Sterl.

JOHN GRIMMET, 800 acs. by Survey 21 Oct 1773 in Henry Co. formerly Pittsylvania on the S side of Pigg Riv.; adj. Callaway, & Robert Hill; 1 Sep 1780, p.562. A.C. of £4 Sterl.

WILLIAM SMITH, 332 acs. by Survey 21 Feb 1775 in Pittsylvania Co. on the Brs. of Potters Cr., on the Road; adj. Barnett, Morrison, & Jonathan Philips; 1 Sep 1780, p.564. A.C. of 35 Shill. Sterl.

JOHN CAROLILE, 50 acs. by Survey 30 Apr 1773 in Augusta Co. joining the Lines of his own Land on the Bull pasture Riv.; 1 Sep 1780, p.565. A.C. of 5 Shill. Sterl.

CHARLES DONNELY, 75 acs. by Survey 26 Apr 1773 in Augusta Co. joining his own Land on Stewarts Cr. a Br. of the Cow pasture, Beginning by a Gap of a Hill, up a draughts, along a Bank, Crossing a Spring; 1 Sep 1780, p.566. A.C. of 10 Shill. Sterl.

ROBERT POAGE, 67 acs. by Survey 29 Dedc 1772 in Botetourt Co. on back Cr. a br. of Roanoak, Beginning at the Mouth of a Br. a Little above his old Survey; 1 Sep 1780, p.567. A.C. of 10 Shill. Sterl.

JAMES OLIVER, 311 acs. by Survey 30 Apr 1780 in Augusta Co. on the S Side of Naked Cr. and ajoining his other Tract; also adj. Hugh Donoho, John Searight & Anthony Aylor; 1 Sep 1780, p.568. A.C. of 35 Shill. Sterl.

HENDRY OLDHOUSER (as Assignee of STEPHEN ARNOLD who was Assignee of DANIEL GOODWIN), 170 acs. by Survey 27 Oct 1767 in Augusta Co. upon the head of Possum Cr. in the South Mountains; 1 Sep 1780, p.569. A.C. of 20 Shill. Sterl.

THOMAS TRIMBLE ass'ee of JOSEPH LONG, 98 acs. by Survey 8 May 1759 in Augusta Co. upon Buffles Cr.; 1 Sep 1780, p.570. A.C. of 10 Shill. Sterl.

JAMES LAWLESS, 138 acs. by Survey 2 Nov 1774 in Pittsylvania Co. on the head Brs. of Fall Cr., on the top of white Oak Mountain, in the head of a Glade, adj. Charles Clay; 1 Sep 1780, p.571. A.C. of 15 Shill. Sterl.

WILLIAM HANDY, 90 acs. by Survey 18 Mar 1770 in Bedford Co. on the W Brs. of Orucks Cr., adj. William Austin & Cabbel; 1 Sep 1780, p.572. A.C. of 10 Shill. Sterl.

HENRY NEAVELLS, 85 acs. by Survey 30 Apr 1780 in Rockbridge Co. near the foot of the South Mountain of the S side, adj. John Bowyer; 1 Sep 1780, p.573. A.C. of 10 Shill. Sterl.

THOMAS FARMER, 174 acs. by Survey 3 Mar 1779 in Bedford Co. on W Brs. of Johnsons Cr. and on Spurs of Johnstons Mountain, adj. his own & Wests dividing Corner; 1 Sep 1780, p.573. A.C. of 20 Shill. Sterl.

JOHN TRIMBLE as Heir at Law of JAMES TRIMBLE Dec'd, 128 acs. by Survey 26 Nov 1772 in Botetourt Co. joining the Lines of his own Land in the Forks of James Riv., on the top of a Hill near the Line of Samuel McCorkels Land; 1 Sep 1780, p.574. A.C. of 15 Shill. Sterl.

JEREMIAH WARD, 100 acs. by Survey 16 Apr 1753 in Pittsylvania Co. on the first Bold Br. that Makes out of the Frying Pan Cr., adj. Robert Walton & James Bobbet; 1 Sep 1780, p.575. A.C. of 10 Shill. Sterl.

JOHN HAYNES Ass'ee of THOMAS RAMSEY, 145 acs. by Survey 2 Mar 1754 in Botetourt Co. formerly Augusta on Burdins run a Br. of Cawtaba the Waters of James Riv., Beginning on a Barrin Ridge Corner to Burdens Entry, on the Spur of a Mountain, by a Sink hole; 1 Sep 1780, p.576. A.C. of 15 Shill. Sterl.

THOMAS TOSH Ass'ee of ELIZABETH the wife of JAMES HOWELL, 85 acs. by Survey 22 Dec 1771 in Botetourt Co. on the N Side of Masons Cr. a Br. of Roanoake, adj. John Griffiths Tract; 1 Sep 1780, p.577. A.C. of 10 Shill. Sterl.

WILLIAM DAVIS, 400 acs. by Survey 24 Apr 1780 in Pittsylvania Co. on the Brs. of Banister Riv. and Chery Stone Cr., adj. Thomas Hardy & Finnys Order Lines; 1 Sep 1780, p.578. A.C. of 40 Shill. Sterl.

JAMES WARD Ass'ee of JAMES McKEACHEY who was Ass'ee of THOMAS EDGER, 83 acs. by Survey 26 Mar 1772 in Botetourt Co. on a S Br. of Roan Oak, adj. John Ager; 1 Sep 1780, p.579. A.C. of 10 Shill. Sterl.

BARTLEY FOLEY, 78 acs. by Survey 24 Nov 1768 in Pittsylvania Co. on Joinerack Cr.; 1 Sep 1780, p.580. A.C. of 10 Shill. Sterl.

JOHN BLAIR, 60 acs. by Survey 12 Jun 1769 in Augusta Co. on the E Side of the Long Glade a Br. of the North Riv. of Shanondore; adj. Alexander Blair, William Frame & James Blair; 1 Sep 1780, p.581. A.C. of 10 Shill. Sterl.

JOEL MEADOR, 60 acs. by Survey 13 Mar 1774 in Bedford Co. on Stanton Riv., Beginning at his C. on the Riv.; 1 Sep 1780, p.582. A.C. of 10 Shill. Sterl.

GILBERT HAROLD, 270 acs. by Survey 15 Mar 1775 in Bedford Co. on the N Brs. of Stanton Riv., Beginning at Pates Path; 1 Sep 1780, p.583. A.C. of 30 Shill. Sterl.

THOMAS THORNILL, 70 acs. by Survey 22 Feb 1754 in Buckingham Co. on the W Side of Davis Cr.; adj. his old Line & William Staples New Line; 1 Sep 1780, p.584. A.C. of 10 Shill. Sterl.

AUSTIN SMITH, 125 acs. by Survey 15 Mar 1757 in Albemarle Co. in the Coves of the Ragged Mountain at the head of a Br. of Mores Cr.; adj. Robert Edges Corner, William Terrel Lewis & the sd

Edgers Line; 1 Sep 1780, p.584. A.C. of 15 Shill. Sterl.

EDWARD HATCHER, 250 acs. by Survey 18 Mar 1774 in Bedford Co. on the S Brs. of Staunton Riv., on Tick Cr.; adj. Walton, James Greer & John Greer; 1 Sep 1780, p.585. A.C. of 25 Shill. Sterl.

GEORGE CARTER, 53 acs. by Survey 10 Nov 1768 in Henry Co. on the North fork of the North fork of the Mayo Riv.; 1 Sep 1780, p.586. A.C. of 5 Shill. Sterl.

LUKE FOLEY, 146 acs. by Survey 13 Dec 1768 in Henry Co. and on Gobblingtown Cr.; 1 Sep 1780, p.587. A.C. of 15 Shill. Sterl.

GEORGE CARTER, 200 acs. by Survey 17 Mar 1768 in Henry Co. on Russells Cr., adj. Hanby/Hanbey; 1 Sep 1780, p.588. A.C. of 20 Shill. Sterl.

JAMES GRAY Ass'ee of JACOB JACKSON, 44 acs. by Survey 21 Mar 1771 in Botetourt Co. on Craigs Cr. a Br. of James Riv. joining the Land formerly Hartsoughs, to a Spruce pine on the Bank of the Cr. opposite Potts Feild; 1 Sep 1780, p.589. A.C. of 5 Shill. Sterl.

GEORGE BOSWELL, 220 acs. in Rockingham Co. between the Land he Lives on and the Mountains, Beginning in a Line of his own Land and running with the Line of a Survey made for Hugh Donoho, on a Bank near Lewis's Land; 1 Sep 1780, p.590. A.C. of £2.S5 Sterl. [should have been only 25 Shill.]

JACOB COX & JOHN CANTWELL, 293 acs. 7 Nov 1770 in Henry Co. on the S side of the South Mayo, adj. Fontain & Walton; 1 Sep 1780, p.591. A.C. of 30 Shill. Sterl.

JOSEPH SLADON, 400 acs. by Survey 6 Mar 1752 in Pittsylvania Co. on the Brs. of Double Creeks; adj. Henry Taylor, Walters, & Henry Tally; 1 Sep 1780, p.592. A.C. £2 Sterl.

JOSEPH WRIGHT, 57 acs. by Survey 13 Dec 1762 in Bedford Co. on the N Brs. of Staunton Riv., adj. his own Lines; 1 Sep 1780, p.592. A.C. of 10 Shill. Sterl.

JOHN HALL, 153 acs. by Survey 1 Mar 1780 in Pittsylvania Co. on the Brs. of Doubles Cr.; adj. Thomas Hardy, George Roberts, Nimrodd Scott, the sd Halls former Line & Nathaniel Murrey; 1 Sep 1780, p.593. A.C. of 15 Shill. Sterl.

ALEXANDER BAGS, 40 acs. by Survey 24 Nov 1779 in Rockbridge Co. in the fork of James Riv.; adj. said Bags old Line, Robert McCalpin & Widow Spences Corner Locust thence Spencers Lines; 1 Sep 1780, p.594. A.C. of 5 Shill. Sterl.

JOHN HUSTON, 70 acs. by Survey 3 Aug 1769 in Augusta Co. upon a Draught of Colliers Cr. in the fork of James Riv., adj. John Sommor / Sommer; 1 Sep 1780, p.595. A.C. of 10 Shill. Sterl. paid by John Huston *into the Treasury of this Commonwealth.*

JOHN CHILDS, 400 acs. by Survey 23 Oct 1752 in Bedford Co. on the W side of Reedy Cr. and on a br. of the Same Called white Marsh Br.; adj. Bolling,

Rutherford & Dixon; adj; 1 Sep 1780, p.596. A.C. of 40 Shill. Sterl. paid by John Childs *into the Office of the late Receiver General.*

CHARLES DUNKIN, 390 acs. by survey 17 Mar 1779 in Pittsylvania Co. on the Brs. of Sandy Riv., on the Road, on the Mill road; adj. Constant Purkins near the Pilot pine, Gammon, Chadwell, & Perkins Line to the Pilot pine; 1 Sep 1780, p.597. A.C. of 40 Shill. Sterl. paid by Charles Dunkin *into the Treasury of this Commonwealth.*

MICHAEL CLARDY, 367 acs. by Survey 2 Nov 1773 in Halifax Co. on the draughts of Peters Cr., down the Main Br. of sd Cr.; adj. Mead, the Pine on which Edward Wades and Cargills Lands; 1 Sep 1780, p.598. A.C. of 40 Shill. Sterl.

ROBERT GORDAN Ass'ee of SAMUEL GOODE who was Ass'ee of WILLIAM SPICER, 474 acs. by Survey 17 Mar 1772 in Bedford Co. on the head Brs. of Beaverpond Br., Beginning near the Main head, adj. Burnley; 1 Sep 1780, p.599. A.C. of £2.S10 Sterl.

JAMES HUTCHISON Ass'ee of William Hutcheson, 150 acs. by Survey 22 Apr 1755 in Augusta Co. on the Waters of Catawba ajoining his own L.; also adj. Samuel McRoberts, James Neely & sd Hutchesons L.; 1 Sep 1780, p.600. A.C. of 15 Shill. Sterl.

JAMES STANDEFER, 411 acs. by Survey 4 May 1779 in Henry Co. on the head Brs. of the South fork of Story Cr., on a Ridge, adj. Luke Standefer; 1 Sep 1780, p.601. A.C. of 45 Shill. Sterl.

JAMES HALL (as Assignee of THOMAS BATES), 85 acs. by Survey 14 Oct 1751 in Augusta Co. upon Beffelo Cr., on a Spur of the Mountain, adj. John Long; 1 Sep 1780, p.602. A.C. of 10 Shill. Sterl.

JOHN OWEN SULLIVEN / SULLEVEN (as Assignee of HUGH MEANES), 113 acs. by Survey 20 Aug 1772 in Botetourt Co. on the N side of Craigs Cr. a Br. of James Riv., adj. William Crow; 1 Sep 1780, p.602. A.C. of 15 Shill. Sterl.

JOEL STOW, 192 acs. by Survey 17 Dec 1777 in Pittsylvania Co. on both sides of Vals fork of Strawber; adj. Joel Stow, Cantrell & Edward Adkins; 1 Sep 1780, p.603. A.C. of 20 Shill. Sterl.

JACOB GARRETT, 400 acs. by Survey 13 Nov 1771 in Halifax Co. on the S side of Willies Cr., adj. Randolph & Wade; 1 Sep 1780, p.604. A.C. of 40 Shill. Sterl.

JAMES FLANNIKIN, 360 acs. by Survey 20 Mar 1780 in Pittsylvania Co. on the Brs. of Kents and Falling Cr., Crossing Several Brs. of Kents Cr. & three Brs. of falling Cr., adj. sd Flannakins old Line; 1 Nov 1780, p.605. A.C. of 40 Shill. Sterl.

WILLIAM WALKER, 63 acs. by Survey 11 Dec 1770 in Botetourt Co. on Barbers Cr. a Br. of James Riv. joining and about the Land of Isaac Ballenger; 1 Sep 1780, p.606. A.C. of 10 Shill. Sterl.

SAMUEL MARTAIN / MARTIN, 400 acs. by Survey 19 Apr 1770 in Pittsylvania Co. on the Waters of

Tommahawk Cr.; 1 Sep 1780, p.607. A.C. of 40 Shill. Sterl.

WILLIAM EVANS, 349 acs. by Survey 16 Dec 1773 in Pittsylvania Co. on both sides of the Muddy fork of Chesnut Cr., Beginning on the N side of Chesnut Mountain, adj. Woods Line; 1 Sep 1780, p.608. A.C. of 35 Shill. Sterl.

GEORGE SMITH, 144 acs. by Survey 17 Feb 1774 in Pittsylvania Co. on the Brs. of harping Cr., adj. his own Line; 1 Sep 1780, p.609. A.C. of 15 Shill. Sterl.

JOHN BLAIN, 19 acs. by Survey 25 Nov 1763 in Augusta Co. on the S side of the long Glade between the said Blairs and John Andersons Land, on the side of a Ridge, also adj. James Blair; 1 Sep 1780, p.610. A.C. of 5 Shill. Sterl.

ISHAM SOLOMAN, 87 acs. by Survey 16 Oct 1769 in Henry Co. on Elk Cr., adj. Bells order; 1 Sep 1780, p.610. A.C. of 10 Shill. Sterl.

ROBERT ADAMS, 310 acs. by Survey 22 Apr 1780 in Pittsylvania Co. on the Brs. of Banister Riv., on the rockey Br.; adj. Thomas Hardy, Donelson, Burwell Bowden, & Finneys Order Line; 1 Sep 1780, p.611. A.C. of 35 Shill. Sterl.

JOHN WRIGHT, 40 acs. by Survey 15 Nov 1766 in Bedford Co. on both sides of Beaverdam Cr., adj. his own Line; 1 Sep 1780, p.612. A.C. of 5 Shill. Sterl.

WILLIAM GREGORY, 50 acs. by Survey 8 Apr 1774 in Augusta Co. on back Cr. between two Tracts of his Lands; 1 Sep 1780, p.613. A.C. of 5 Shill. Sterl.

PETER CLAYWELL Ass'ee of HENRY EIDSON, 182 by Survey 10 Nov 1773 in Bedford Co. on the Ridge between Flat Cr. and Troublesome Cr.; adj. the Old Lines of Mead and Talbot, Arther & Yuille; 1 Sep 1780, p.614. A.C. of 20 Shill. Sterl.

JOHN BALL, 284 acs. by Survey 5 Nov 1778 in Pittsylvania Co. on the N Brs. of Tomahawk Cr., adj. George Smith & sd John Balls line; 1 Sep 1780, p.615. A.C. of 30 Shill. Sterl.

ADAM ERGABRIGHT Ass'ee of EDWARD YOUNG and JAMES SMITH Ass'ee of JOHN GIVEN, 80 acs. by Survey 15 Nov 1770 in Rockingham Co. formerly Augusta on back draft a Br. of Cooks Cr., adj. Hemphil; 1 Sep 1780, p.616. A.C. of 10 Shill. Sterl.

JOHN SHELTMAN, 80 acs. by Survey 12 Nov 1770 in Rockingham Co. formerly Augusta on a Br. of Cooks Cr., adj. his patent Land; 1 Sep 1780, p.617. A.C. of 10 Shill. Sterl.

CHARLES FINCH, 203 acs by Survey 12 Apr 1758 in Pittsylvania Co. on the Brs. of Marrowbone Cr., adj. Randolphs order Line & Hubbord; 1 Sep 1780, p.618. A.C. of 20 Shill. Sterl.

LEONARD GEARHEART, 338 acs. by Survey 4 Mar 1774 in Bedford Co. adj. Henderson; 1 Sep 1780, p.619. A.C. of 35 Shill. Sterl.

JOHN JONES, 110 acs. by Survey 30 Oct 1755 in Henry Co. formerly Pittsylvania on both sides of the South fork of Pigg Riv.; 1 Sep 1780, p.620. A.C. of 15 Shill. Sterl. [Survey pointers include an Ironwood tree (hornbeam) and a Mahoggany tree]

JOHN BIBE, 82 acs. by Survey 22 Oct 1755 in Henry Co. formerly Halifax on both sides of Daniels Mill Cr. of Black Water Riv., to a Mahagonny Tree thence to a Locust at the foot of the Mountain; 1 Sep 1780, p.621. A.C. of 10 Shill. Sterl.

JOHN WILLIS, 222 acs. by Survey 10 Jan 1775 in Pittsylvania Co. on the Brs. of Black Water Riv., adj. Francis Bird & Hetton; 1 Sep 1780, p.623. A.C. of 25 Shill. Sterl.

CHARLES FINCH, 58 acs. by Survey 13 Apr 1768 in Pittsylvania Co. on the warf Mountains; 1 Sep 1780, p.624. A.C. of 10 Shill. Sterl.

DANIEL SMITH, 190 acs. by Survey 28 Nov 1772 in Henry Co. formerly Pittsylvania on both sides of Buttramtown Cr., adj. George Reaves; 1 Sep 1780, p.625. A.C. of 20 Shill. Sterl.

JAMES SHOCKLEY, 412 acs. by Survey 2 Nov 1777 in Pittsylvania Co. on both sides of Little Turkey Cock, adj. his old Lines; 1 Sep 1780, p.626. A.C. of 45 Shill. Sterl.

THOMAS PASSONS, 400 acs. by Survey 5 May 1780 in Lunenburg Co. on the Brs. of the Meherrin Riv.; 1 Sep 1780, p.627. A.C. of 40 Shill. Sterl. [adj. GB D p.82 to John Williams]

JONES JONES heir at law to JOHN ARMSTED VOLLINTINE alias JONES, 68 acs. by Survey 2 Mar 1775 in Lunenburg Co. on the Brs. of Kettlestick Cr., adj. Jeremiah Morgan & Edward Ragsale; 1 Sep 1780, p.628. A.C. of 10 Shill. Sterl. [For Jeremiah Morgan's see PB 29 p.90 to Mason Bishop & for Edward Ragsdale's see GB A p.278 to Mason Bishop]

HENRY SUMTER, 278 acs. by Survey 7 Oct 1759 in Henry Co. formerly Pittsylvania Co. on the Waters of Smiths Riv., adj. Woodson & Randolph; 1 Sep 1780, p.628. A.C. of 30 Shill. Sterl.

WILLIAM BOHANNAN, 174 acs. by Survey 16 Oct 1777 in Henry Co. formerly Pittsylvania on Town Cr.; 1 Sep 1780, p.629. A.C. of 20 Shill. Sterl.

MICHAEL KELLY, 70 acs. by Survey 16 Mar 1773 in Henry Co. formerly Pittsylvania Co. on the draughts of Nicholas's Cr., adj. his Line; 1 Sep 1780, p.630. A.C. of 10 Shill. Sterl.

HENRY RISER Ass'ee of GEORGE ARMANTROUT, 85 acs. by Survey 1 May 1771 in Augusta Co. on the S side of Smiths Cr., along a Ridge, adj. Lawrence Bell; 26 Jun 1783 *in the 7th year of the Commonwealth*, p.631. A.C. of 10 Shill.

THOMAS & SWINKFIELD HILL Executors and legatees of ROBERT HILL dec'd, 159 acs. by Survey 27 Apr 1779 in Henry Co. on both sides of black water Riv., adj. John Stephenson; 1 Sep 1780, p.632. A.C. of 20 Shill. Sterl.

JAMES STANDEFORD, 177 acs. by Survey 17 Oct 1772 in Henry Co. formerly Pittsylvania Co. on the Brs. of Storey Cr.; 1 Sep 1780, p.633. A.C. of 20 Shill. Sterl.

JESSE CLAY, 142 acs. by Survey 11 Jan 1779 in Henry Co. and Parish of

Saint Patrick on black Water Riv., adj. Stephen Heard & the sd Clays old Line; 1 Sep 1780, p.634. A.C. of 15 Shill. Sterl.

JAMES MAYO Ass'ee of WILLIAM AMOS, 130 acs. by Survey 23 Nov 1761 in Albemarle Co. on the N side of the South fork of Cunninghams Cr., on the Hill of the sd Cr.; adj. George Hilton, Richard Melton, Arthur Cooper & George Hilton Junr.; 1 Sep 1780, p.635. A.C. of 15 Shill. Sterl.

WILLIAM HOOK JUNR., 112 acs. by Survey 12 Apr 1780 in Rockingham Co. Beginning on the S Side of his field, in a hollow; adj. L. formerly Robert Shanklins, Hudlows Lines, Robert Hook Junr., James Hook, Perkey & Hooks own L.; 1 Sep 1780, p.636. A.C. of 15 Shill. Sterl.

JAMES EDWARDS, 142 acs. by Survey 16 Nov 1773 in Henry Co. formerly Pittsylvania on the Brs. of Smiths Riv., adj. Daniel Rion & James Poteet; 1 Sep 1780, p.637. A.C. of 15 Shill. Sterl.

ROBERT SINCLAIR, 244 acs. by Survey 7 May 1771 in Bedford Co. on the N Brs. of Bore Auger Cr., adj. Charles Tate; 1 Sep 1780, p.638. A.C. of 25 Shill. Sterl.

THOMAS JONES, 147 acs. by Survey 30 Oct 1766 in Henry Co. formerly Halifax on both sides of Turners Cr. of Pigg Riv., adj. his former Line; 1 Sep 1780, p.639. A.C. of 15 Shill. Sterl.

DAVID SRUM Ass'ee of HENRY COLLIER, 186 acs. by Survey 20 Feb 1775 in Rockingham Co. formerly Augusta on the head Brs. of Corteses Run a Br. of Shanandore Riv., near William Lambs Line, adj. sd Collier; 1 Sep 1780, p.640. A.C. of 20 Shill. Sterl.

VALNTINE SEVEYOR, 386 acs. by Survey 5 June 1759 in Augusta Co. on the S side the Long Meadow between Smiths and Linvells Creeks, adj. his L.; 1 Sep 1780, p.641. A.C. of 40 Shill. Sterl.

JEREMIAH RAGEN Ass'ee of DAVID FRAZER who was Ass'ee of DANIEL SMITH who was Ass'ee of SOLOMAN TURPIN, 220 acs. by Survey 27 May 1769 in Rockingham Co. formerly Augusta on the E side of Walter Crons Land on some drafts of Linvells Cr., Beginning on the S side of a Ridge, near a road; 1 Sep 1780, p.642. A.C. of 25 Shill.

GEORGE REAVES, 138 acs. by Survey 28 Nov 1772 in Henry Co. formerly Pittsylvania on both sides of Butram Town Cr., at the Mouth of & on a Br. of Hickeys Mill Cr., adj. Childs; 1 Sep 1780, p.643. A.C. of 15 Shill. Sterl.

FRANCIS THORPE Ass'ee of JAMES BUFORD, 620 acs. by Survey 2 Mar 1772 in Bedford Co. on both sides of Buffalow Cr.; adj. his own, Austin, Robinson & the Pat. Line; 1 Sep 1780, p.645. A.C. of 35 Shill. Sterl. Including 195 acs. Gtd. to John Harvey by pat. 30 Jul 1742 [Brunswick Co. PB 20 p.426] also 91 acs. Gtd. Stephen White by pat. 23 May 1763 [PB 35 p.172].

SAMUEL GATES ass'ee of BENJAMIN HUBBARD who was Ass'ee of WILLIAM SMITH, 354 acs. by Survey 27 Jan 1779 in Pittsylvania Co. on Matrimony Cr., along the Country Line

[West]; 1 Sep 1780, p.646. A.C. of 35 Shill. Sterl.

THOMAS HAIL, 200 acs. by Survey 5 May 17__ in Henry Co. on Pigg Riv.; adj. his own Line, Mavity, & Thomas Jones; 1 Sep 1780, p.647. A.C. of 20 Shill. Sterl.

JOHN COGER, 33 acs. by Survey 23 Oct 1759 in Pittsylvania Co. on Cogers Cr.; 1 Sep 1780, p.648. A.C. of 5 Shill. Sterl.

JOSHUA RENTFROE, 110 acs. by Survey 14 Oct 1773 in Henry Co. formerly Pittsylvania on the Brs. of Black Water Riv., adj. his sd Rentfroes Line & William Cook; 1 Sep 1780, p.649. A.C. of 15 Shill. Sterl.

GEORGE REIVES, 106 acs. by Survey 13 Dec 1773 in Henry Co. formerly Pittsylvania on both Sides of Smiths Riv., adj. William Cox & Adams. 1 Sep 1780, p.650. A.C. of 15 Shill. Sterl. 52 acs. part thereof being formerly Surveyed for Christopher Bolling the Right and Title of which has Since become Vested in the sd George Reives.

JOSEPH ELLIS, 230 acs. by Survey 11 Oct 1773 in Pittsylvania Co. on both sides of Fly blow Cr. of black water Riv., Crossing the main fork of sd Cr. to a fork, adj. Joseph Ellis; 1 Sep 1780, p.651. A.C. of 25 Shill. Sterl.

JAMES ELKINS, 149 acs. by Survey 18 Nov 1768 in Pittsylvania Co. on the North fork of Rock castle Cr.; 1 Sep 1780, p.652. A.C. of 15 Shill. Sterl.

BARTHOLOMEY FOLIER, 219 acs. by Survey 23 Nov 1758 in Henry Co. on the Draughts of Smiths Riv.; 1 Sep 1780, p.653. A.C. of 25 Shill. Sterl.

DANIEL SMITH, 10 acs. by Survey 19 Nov 1773 in Pittsylvania Co. on Otter Cr., adj. his former Line; 1 Sep 1780, p.654. A.C. of 5 Shill. Sterl.

WILLIAM HAYNES, 110 acs. by Survey 26 Nov 1778 in Henry Co. on the Grassy Fork of Bull Run; 1 Sep 1780, p.655. A.C. of 15 Shill. Sterl.

JOHN SMALL, 188 acs. by Survey 18 Nov 1773 in Henry Co. formerly Pittsylvania on the Brs. of Gills Cr. and Rock castle Cr.; adj. Walton, John Nevel & Ward; 1 Sep 1780, p.657. A.C. of 20 Shill. Sterl.

ADAM RADAR / REDAR, 200 acs. by Survey 6 Mar 1773 in Rockingham Co. formerly Augusta on the N side of the North fork of Shanandore, to 2 black Oaks and a Hickory in a Sink, by a Road, adj. his old Line; 1 Sep 1780, p.658. A.C. of 20 Shill. Sterl.

SAMUEL MOSELY, 215 acs. by Survey 9 Apr 1752 in Pittsylvania Co. formerly Halifax on the Brs. of Sandy Riv., adj. his former Lines; 1 Sep 1780, p.659. A.C. of 25 Shill. Sterl.

EDMOND EDWARDS, 263 acs. by Survey 12 May 1768 in Henry Co. formerly Pittsylvania Co. on Stewards Cr.; 1 Sep 1780, p.660. A.C. of 30 Shill. Sterl.

WILLIAM ALLEN, 190 acs. by Survey 23 Feb 1770 in Pittsylvania Co. on the Waters of Allins Cr.; adj. Thomas Henderson, Daugherty, & Ben Langford; 1 Sep 1780, p.661. A.C. of 20 Shill. Sterl.

JAMES DOROUGH, 206 acs. by Survey 13 Jan 1778 in Pittsylvania Co. on the Brs. of Tomahawk Cr., adj. John Ball; 1 Sep 1780, p.662. A.C. of 25 Shill. Sterl.

ROBERT BRUAS, 247 acs. by Survey 28 Apr 1762 in Pittsylvania Co. formerly Halifax on both sides of a main Br. of Streight Stone Cr., adj. John Jones; 1 Sep 1780, p.663. A.C. of 25 Shill. Sterl.

JOHN DRINKWATER, 195 acs. by Survey 7 Dec 1774 in Bedford Co. on E Brs. of Whipping Cr., adj. Alexander Kelly & Marshall; 1 Sep 1780, p.664. A.C. of 20 Shill. Sterl.

EPHRAIM WETCHER, 400 acs. by Survey 31 Mar 1775 in Pittsylvania Co. on the Brs. for Rudys Cr.;,adj. David Polly, Ross, Thomas Ramsey & sd Wetcher; 1 Sep 1780, p.666. A.C. of 40 Shill. Sterl.

JOHN SWENNY / SWENNEY & JOSEPH MAPLES, 357 acs. by Survey 17 Feb 1774 in Pittsylvania Co. on both Sides of C[h]erry Stone Cr., Crossing two fork of Sd Cr.; adj. John Donelson, sd Donnelson; 1 Sep 1780, p.667. A.C. of 40 Shill. Sterl.

ALEXANDER LACKEY, 480 acs. 14 Aug 1779 in Pittsylvania Co. on both sides of the roaring fork of Cherry Stone cr.; adj. Hicks, Regney, & John Watson; 1 Sep 1780, p.669. A.C. of £2.S10 Sterl.

JOHN BENNETT, 424 acs. by Survey 14 Feb 1766 in Pittsylvania Co. formerly Halifax on the Brs. of the double Creeks, adj. John Madding; 1 Sep 1780, p.670. A.C. of 45 Shill. Sterl.

WILLIAM PAYNE, 250 acs. by Survey 18 Feb 1780 in Pittsylvania Co. on the Brs. of White thorn Cr.; adj. William Pace, Gordin & sd Paynes former Line; 1 Sep 1780, p.671. A.C. of 25 Shill. Sterl.

SAMUEL MOSELY / MOSELEY, 114 acs. by Survey 19 Nov 1778 in Pittsylvania Co. on the S Brs. of the South fork of Sandy Riv.; adj. his own Line, Young, & Fuller Harris; 1 Sep 1780, p.673. A.C. of 15 Shill. Sterl.

JOHN McCLAIN, 435 acs. by Survey 12 Nov 1764 in Halifax Co. on both Sides of Rutledges Cr., Crossing four Brs., adj. Samuel Bynum; 1 Sep 1780, p.674. A.C. of 45 Shill. Sterl.

GEORGE LANDSDOWN, 103 acs. by Survey 5 Apr 1780 in Halifax Co. on the S Side of Banister Riv., in a Br. of Elk horn Cr.; adj. George Moore, John Logan, John Laws & Cargill; 1 Sep 1780, p.675. A.C. of 10 Shill. Sterl.

ROBERT OAR, 452 acs. by Survey 16 Dec 1771 in Pittsylvania Co. on Tomahawk Cr.; adj. Roberts, Elliot, Tully Choice, Savories Line & Jefferson; 1 Sep 1780, p.676. A.C. of 45 Shill. Sterl.

THOMAS GARDENER, 398 acs. by Survey 17 Mar 1772 in Pittsylvania Co. on the Waters of Beaver Cr.; 1 Sep 1780, p.678. A.C. of 40 Shill. Sterl.

JESSEE TAYLOR of Fairfax Co., ¼ of an Acre being One half of ½ an Acre Lott with a Large Store House thereon Number 114 in the Plan of the Town of Alexandria; Bounded on the North by King Street on the East by PM Street on the South by Lott Number 112 the Property of General Washington on the

West by Baldwins Dades half of Said Lott Number 114; 19 Oct 1780, p.679. £21,000 Current Money of Virginia paid unto Hector Ross Gent. Escheator for Fairfax Co. by Jessee Taylor of sd Co. being one full Moiety or half of Lott Number 114 the said Lott being *Lately the Property of John Goodrich a Subject of Great Britain and was sold by the said Hector Ross Gent. Escheator for the said Co. unto the sd Jessee Taylor with Store Houses and Appurtenances Appurtaining to the said Lott late the property of John Goodrich by Virtue of an Agreable to two Late Acts of General Assembly passed in the year 1779 the one Entitled an Act Concerning Escheats and forfeitures from British Subjects and the other Entitled an Act concerning Escheators.*

THOMAS PAYNE, 240 acs. by Survey 15 Mar 1774 in Pittsylvania Co. on the Brs. of Mill Cr.; adj. David Haley, Reuben Payne, Gray, & sd David Hayley; 1 Sep 1780, p.680. A.C. of 25 Shill. Sterl.

ROBERT CAROLILE, 65 acs. by Survey 30 Apr 1773 in Augusta Co. Joiniing his own Land on the Bull Pasture, Beginning on a bank thence up a draft, above a Spring; 1 Sep 1780, p.681. A.C. of 10 Shill. Sterl.

JAMES RANKIN Ass'ee of ANDREW NICKLES, 145 acs. by Survey 5 Oct 1779 in Augusta Co. adj. his other Tract on the S side on a Br. of the middle Riv. of Shanadore, also adj. John Nicholls C. & William Mathews Line; 1 Sep 1780, p.683. A.C. of 15 Shill. Sterl.

ANTHONY AYLOR, 115 acs. by Survey 23 Mar 1780 in Augusta Co. Joining his other Tract on the N side, his Patent Line; 1 Sep 1780, p.684. A.C. of 15 Shill. Sterl.

WILLIAM HUNTER, JUNIOR, ¼ Acre a certain Lott or parcel of L. being one half of ½ an Acre Lott with two Wooden Houses and an old Stable thereon Number thirty three in the Plan of the Town of Alexandria Situated on the West by Lott Number 34 the Property of William Ramsey Esquire on the North by part of Lott Number 33 the Property of Robert Adams Esquire, and on the South by Lot Number 38 the Property of Messrs. Carson and Muir (deceased); 19 Oct 1780, p.685. £1,000 Currant Money of Virginia paid unto Hector Ross Gent. Escheator for Fairfax Co. by William Hunter Junior. *late the Property of Colin Dunlop and son and Company Subjects of Great Britain and was sold by the said Hector Ross Gent. Escheator for the sd Co. unto the sd William Hunter with Houses and Appuprtenances Appurtaining to the said Lot late the Property of Colin Dunlop and Son and Company by Virtue of an Agreeable to two Late Acts of General Assembly passed in 1779 the one Entitled an Act Concerning Escheats and forfeitures from British Subjects and the other Entitled an Act Concerning Escheators.*

WILLIAM BLAIR, 69 acs. by Survey 31 May 1780 in Augusta Co. Joining Jacob [Shitze] George Sommon and Robert McCutchens Land, by a Road; also adj. Stephenson & Fraim; 1 Sep 1780, p.687. A.C. of 10 Shill. Sterl.

WILLIAM NALLE, 150 acs. by Survey 21 Apr 1780 in Rockingham Co. between Maggots and L. formerly

Boughmans on the Hawksbill in a narrow Valley between two Mountains, Beginning on the E side of the Cr. at the Point of a Spur of the Mountain near a C. of Boughmans L., Crossing the Cr. to the Side of the Oposite Mountain, at the bottom of the Mountain in the Edge of the Low Grounds near the L. of Hans Maggot; 1 Sep 1780, p.688. A.C. of 15 Shill. Sterl.

JOHN CAPLENGER Ass'ee of DANIEL SMITH who was Ass'ee of THOMAS WEST, 60 acs. by Survey 13 Dec 1754 in Rockingham Co. formerly Augusta on the N side the North Riv. of Shanando in a Place Called *Wests Gap*, adj. his Pattent land; 1 Sep 1780, p.689. A.C. of 10 Shill. Sterl.

JOHN HARPER, 96 acs. by Survey made for JANE REABURN to whom he is Married, bearing date 6 Nov 1771 in Augusta Co. on some small Brs. of the North Riv. of Shanandore, in a draft; adj. Joseph Lindon, Thomas McMahon, Jacob Campbell & Thomas Rankin; 1 Sep 1780, p.691. A.C. of 10 Shill. Sterl.

GEORGE McNEAL Ass'ee of JOHN BRIGGS, 46 acs. by Survey 25 Feb 1773 in Rockingham Co. formerly Augusta in *Wests Gap*, Beginning near a Corner of John FitzWaters Land by the Br., on a Mountain, down sd Br. to the forkes; 1 Sep 1780, p.692. A.C. of 5 Shill. Sterl.

JOHN HAMOND, 45 acs. by Survey 11 May 1771 in Augusta Co. on the foot of the peeked Mountain, adj. Nicholas & Price; 1 Sep 1780, p.693. A.C. 5 Shill. Sterl.

THOMAS BOGGS, 40 acs. by Survey 22 Feb 1773 in Augusta Co. on the N Side of his other L. in *Brocks Gap*; 1 Sep 1780, p.694. A.C. of 5 Shill. Sterl.

JOHN COMPTON, 93 acs. by Survey 24 Feb 1773 in Augusta Co. on Cove run in *Brocks Gap*; 1 Sep 1780, p.696. A.C. of 10 Shill. Sterl.

GEORGE HARTER, 82 acs. by Survey 23 Feb 1773 in Augusta Co. on Hungry run in *Brocks Gap*, Beginning by a Gully, adj. James Lowry / Lowrey & Adam Byble; 1 Sep 1780, p.697. A.C. of 10 Shill. Sterl.

JOHN FITZ WATER, 23 acs. by Survey 25 Feb 1773 in Augusta Co. on *West Gap*; adj. John Keplener, a tract of Thomas Wests L. & Kepliner; 1 Sep 1780, p.698. A.C. of 5 Shill. Sterl.

CONROD CUSTARD, 40 acs. by Survey 19 Feb 1773 in Rockingham Co. in *Brocks Gap* on the W side of Tunis's Cr., Beginning near his old Line; 1 Sep 1780, p.699. A.C. of 5 Shill. Sterl.

HENRY TOUP Ass'ee of JOHN KEPLINER, 52 acs. by Survey 26 Feb 1773 in Augusta Co. on some Small Brs. in *Wests Gap* above the Land where he Lives, on a ridge, adj. his own & Martin Wetsall; 1 Sep 1780, p.700. A.C. of 5 Shill. Sterl.

ROBERT ALLEN, 195 acs. by Survey 14 Apr 1780 in Fluvanna Co. on both Sides of Horsely Cr. and North Waters of Rivanna Riv., Beginning at a Pile of Rocks Stones in sd Allens Line and Smithsons; 1 Sep 1780, p.702. A.C. of 20 Shill. Sterl.

JOHN KEPLINGER SENR. ass'ee of DANIEL SMITH who was ass'ee of

THOMAS WEST, 74 acs. by Survey 14 Jan 1753 in Augusta Co. on the forks of Shanendore in *Brocks Gap* joining the upper end of John McDonalds upper Survey, in a Draught; 1 Sep 1780, p.703. A.C. of 10 Shill. Sterl.

JOHN ROBERTS, 350 acs. by Survey 25 Feb 1773 in Bedford Co. on S Brs. of the South fork of falling Riv.; adj. Harris, Wathen, & Peter Daniel; 1 Sep 1780, p.704. A.C. of 35 Shill. Sterl.

ROBERT CAMPBLE, 14 acs. by Survey 25 Mar 1780 in Augusta Co. between his and Thomas Fraims L., near a road; 1 Sep 1780, p.705. A.C. of 5 Shill. Sterl.

WILLIAM NICHOLES, 56 acs. by Survey 8 Oct 1765 in Halifax Co. on Reedy Cr. adj. Thomas Owen, John Nicholes, Thomas Treadway & John Owen; 1 Sep 1780, p.707. A.C. of 10 Shill. Sterl.

HENRY HERNSBERG, 30 acs. by Survey 19 Apr 1780 in Rockingham Co. between his own Kerllys and the lands of Peter Fish and Daniel Sinks, on a Ridge, up Shanando Riv., adj. Kirtly/Kirtley; Beginning in Kirttys Line; 1 Sep 1780, p.708. A.C. of 5 Shill. Sterl.

WILLIAM GREGORY, 104 acs. by Survey 10 Oct 1772 in Augusta Co. on back Cr. a br. of Jacksons Riv., Beginning on the E side of the Cr. above William Cunninghams L.; 1 Sep 1780, p.709. A.C. of 10 Shill. Sterl.

JAMES BRADSHAW, 76 acs. by Survey 29 Apr 1773 in Augusta Co. Joining his own L. on a Br. of the bull Pasture Riv., below a Spring, by a draft; 1 Sep 1780, p.710. A.C. of 10 Shill. Sterl.

JOHN GIBSON Ass'ee of WILLIAM RENTFRO, 140 acs. by Survey 18 Apr 1763 in Bedford Co. on both sides of Black water Riv., adj. Rentfro; 1 Sep 1780, p.712. A.C. of 15 Shill. Sterl.

JOHN JOHNSON Ass'ee of GEORGE JOHNSTON, 201 acs. by Survey 11 Nov 1769 in Bedford Co. on both sides of Maggotty Cr., adj. Patrick Johnson; 1 Sep 1780, p.713. A.C. of 20 Shill. Sterl. *into the Treasury of this Commonwealth.*

ROBERT WILLIAMS Ass'ee of ELIJAH KING, 325 acs. by Survey 29 Jul 1773 in Pittsylvania Co. on Sweating's fork; adj. his former Line, Keerbey, Challiss & the sd King; 1 Sep 1780, p.714. A.C. of 35 Shill. Sterl. *unto the late Receiver General of Virginia.*

ROBERT WILLIAMS Ass'ee of ELIJAH KING, 400 acs. by Survey 29 Jul 1773 in Pittsylvania Co. on Sweating's fork, adj. his former Line & Challiss; 1 Sep 1780, p.716. A.C. of £2 Sterl. *unto the late Receiver General of Virginia.*

ROBERT WILLIAMS (as Assignee of ELIJAH KING), 400 acs. by Survey 29 Jul 1773 in Pittsylvania Co. on Sweating's fork, crossing the big br. several times and the north fork of sd fork, adj. Challiss; 1 Sep 1780, p.717. A.C. of 40 Shill. Sterl. *unto the late Receiver General of Virginia.*

[Margin notes: **William Brown 1750 New 5300 old Examd.**
(Survey Recorded in Book No. 1 page 369)]

WILLIAM BROWN, 7,050 acs. by Survey 30 Oct 1771 in Bedford Co. on both Sides of Whipping Cr., Little Whipping and Lick Cr. including their heads on the E Side of Seneca Cr. and on brs. of Molleys Cr., Crossing Buckhorn Br.; adj. the old Lines of Ornsby, Heaths Corner Near Phelp's Road, Neilson & Gilbert; 1 Sep 1780, p.718. A.C. of £35.S5 Sterl. *(373 acs. with 400 acs., and 104 acs. being two Tracts Surveyed for William Harris; 385 acs. Surveyed for Benjamin Gilbert; 175 acs. Surveyed for Thomas Gilbert, and 300 acs. Surveyed for John Michael; all being part thereof and properly Assigned, 5,300 acs. being the Residue thereof which was Gtd. by order of Council to, and Surveyed for Matthew Talbot, by him Assigned to William Clinch by William Clinch Assigned to Edmund Ruffin; and by Edmund Ruffin Assigned to the sd William Brown. [William Clinch paid £26.S10 for the 5,300 acs. in his PB 29 p.353 dated 3 Nov 1750.*

The Heirs of HUGH MERCER dec'd., 5,000 acs. by survey made 9 May 1774 in Kentuckey Co. formerly Fincastle on the Ohio Riv., Beginning on the Bank of Locust Cr.; 1 Sep 1780, p.721. *in Consideration of Military Service performed by Hugh Mercer in his Life time, as Colonel of the third Battallion of the Pensylvania Regiment in the late War between Great Britain & France according to the terms of the King of Great Britains Proclamation of 1763.*

The Heirs of HUGH MERCER Dec'd who was ass'ee of sd JAMES DUNCANSON, 1,000 acs. by Survey 11 May 1774 in Kentuckey Co. formerly Fincastle on the Ohio Riv., Beginning about 6 Miles above the Big Meame Riv., at the Point of a Ridge; 1 Sep 1780, p.722. *in Consideration of Military Service performed by James Duncanson as Luietenant in the Second Virginia Regiment in the Late War between Great Britain and France According to the terms of the King of Great Britains Proclamation of 1763.*

The Heirs of HUGH MERCER dec'd who was ass'ee of sd JAMES DUNCANSON, 1,000 acs. by Survey 1 Jun 1774 in Kentuckey Co. formerly Fincastle on the Ohio Riv.; adj. James Southall, Richard Charleton & Hancock Eustace; 1 Sep 1780, p.723. *in Consideration of Military Service performed by James Duncanson as Lieutenant in the Second Virginia Regiment in the Late War between Great Britain & France According to the terms of the King of Great Britains Proclamation of 1763.*

The Heirs of Hugh MERCER dec'd who was ass'ee of sd GEORGE WEEDON, 3,000 acs. by Survey 4 Jun 1774 in Kentuckey Co. formerly Fincastle, Beginning on the Bank of the Ohio Riv. about 16 or 17 Miles above the falls of the Ohio, to the Edge of a Hill near Harwoods Cr.; 1 Sep 1780, p.724. *in consideration of Military Service performed by George Weedon as Captain Lieutenant in the Second Virginia Regiment in the late Ware between Great Britain and France According to the terms of the King of Great Britains Proclamation of 1763.*

CHRISTOPHER DEJARNETT, 127¾ acs. which with 53¼ acs. formerly Patented making in the whole 181 acs. by Survey 19 Dec 1775 in Pr. Edward Co. on the Main Road, up Ellingtons fork being the out bounds of the Patent Land, along Floyed Tanners Line to *the Rackoon tract*, adj. Peter Jones & Hamlin; 1 Sep 1780, p.725. A.C. of 15 Shill. Sterl. *into the Late Receiver Generals Office.*

THOMAS BOULDEN JUNR. Ass'ee of PAUL CARRINGTON, 436 acs. Charlotte Co. formerly Lunengburgh on both Sides of Terrys Run; adj. John Griffith, James Murphey, James Rutherford, Robert Weakley, Randolph, James Hevit, Hunt, Liddercale & Richard Austen; 1 Sep 1780, p.726. A.C. of £2.S10 Sterl. Paid *into the Late Receiver Generals office* by Thomas Boulden junr. Whereas by Pat. under the Seal of the Colony and Dominion of Virginia bearing date 10 Jul 1767 Gtd. Thomas Boulden which was Gtd. on Condition of the Payment of His Majestys Quitrent and of Making the Cultiv. and improv. and Whereas Thomas Boulden Junr. in Whom the Right and title of the Sd Land has Since become Vested had failed to pay the quitrents that were due thereon and Paul Carrington had before the late Revolution Petitioned the then President of the King of Great Britains Councel of the sd Colony and had Obtained a Grant for the sd 436 acs.

THOMAS WALKER, 3,155 acs by Survey Oct 1752 in Greenbrire Co. to the Westward of Green Brire Riv. lying on Walkers Riv. and some brs. thereof, Beginning on the W side of Clear Cr. a br. of sd Riv.; Crossing the Riv., Muddy Cr., Meadow Run, & Savana Cr. from a flat; 1 Sep 1780, p.728. A.C. of £16 Sterl. paid by Thomas Walker *into the Treasury of this Commonwealth.* (including 7 tracts of 400 acs. each and one more of 355 acs.)

RICHARD STITH, 1,150 acs. by Survey 22 Nov 1777 in Bedford Co. on both sides of Stoney fork of Goose Cr., on Pates Road, to the top of Pyburns Mountain; adj. William Buford, Peter Holland, Basham or Baskam, Walton, William Board, Talbot & Payne; 1 Sep 1780, p.731. A.C. of £5.S15 Sterl. (by Virtue of two Entries made in his own Name and one in the Name of Lidal Bacon made According to Law)

ISREAL BURNLEY, 900 acs. by Survey 7 Feb 1775 in Bedford Co. on both sides of Beaver Pond br. and on other W brs. of Little falling Riv., crossing the South fork & North fork of sd br.; adj. his own Lines, Goodes Lines & Venable; 1 Sep 1780, p.733. A.C. of £4.S10. (146 acs. part thereof Surveyed for Philemon Manuel on 10 Feb 1767 and by him Assigned to the Sd Burnley and by Virtue of Two entries made in his own Name for 754 acs. the Residue thereof)

DAVID IRVINE, 870 acs. by Survey 3 Nov 1773 in Bedford Co. on the S side of Otter Riv. on both sides of Irvines Cr. including the Mouth of the Cr., near the Road, on a br. of Irvins Cr.; adj. the Patent Lines the Old Line, John Talbot & Charles Lynch; 1 Sep 1780, p.734. A.C. of 35 Shill. Sterl. (320 acs. part thereof formerly Gtd. to sd David Irvine by Pat. 12 May 1759. 550 acs. the Residue thereof not before Gtd.)

JOHN RODGERS / ROGERS Ass'ee of JAMES MITCHELL, 382 acs. by Survey 8 Feb 1770 in Bedford Co. on E brs. of Little Falling Riv., near Tantraugh br.; adj. John Irvine, Robert Mitchell &

Daugherty; 1 Sep 1780, p.736. A.C. of £2. Sterl.

WILLIAM STURMAN or STEERMAN, 240 acs. by Survey 28 Sep 1747 in Bedford Co. on the Lower Brs. of falling Riv., adj. Booker; 1 Sep 1780, p.737. A.C. of 25 Shill. Sterl.

THOMAS LOGWOOD, 540 acs. by Survey 10 Nov 1779 in Bedford Co. on the North fork of Otter Riv.; adj. his old Lines, Irvines Old Line & Callaway; 1 Sep 1780, p.738. A.C. of £2.S15 Sterl.

THOMAS HEATH, 220 acs. by Survey 15 Jan 1773 in Bedford Co. on W Brs. of Molleys Cr.; adj. Gabriel Smitther's C., Brown, his own Lines & Smithers's Lines; 1 Sep 1780, p.739. A.C. of 25 Shill. Sterl.

DAVID IRVINE, 404 acs. by Survey 8 Mar 1775 in Bedford Co. on the Head brs. of Troublesome Cr. on both sides of *the Main fish day Road*, adj. Nathaniel Winston & John Thompson; 1 Sep 1780, p.741. A.C. of 40 Shill. Sterl.

JOHN McCLUNY Ass'ee of SAMUEL HAIRSTON, 285 acs. by Survey 31 Mar 1779 in Bedford Co. on brs. of Beaver and flat Creeks, at the Edge of a Meadow, crossing the Meadow Br., crossing New London Road; adj. Edmeston, Hairston, Gilliam, Steerman, Goggin & Edmiston; 1 Sep 1780, p.742. A.C. of 30 Shill. Sterl.

JAMES CALLAWAY, 127 acs. by Survey 3 Nov 1762 in Bedford Co. on both Sides of Mobberly's Branch (a north branch of Stanton River), adj. William Verdaman Jur. & Eckole's Line; 1 Sep 1780, p.743. A.C. of 15 Shill. Sterl.

WILLIAM BROWN ass'ee of ISHAM TALBOT, 381 acs. by Survey 10 Dec 1767 in Bedford Co. on both Sides of Cates Cr., adj. Weaver & Finley; 1 Sep 1780, p.744. A.C. of £2 Sterl.

LOW TODD, 122 acs. by Survey 1 Aug 1775 (51 acs. part thereof being part of Stanton River) in Bedford Co. on the N Side of Stanton River, on a Stoney Pint [Point], down the River (being Parham Bookers Line) to a white Oak below a large high remarkable Rock, across the River to a bunch of Sycamores below Rocks on the N Side of the River, along the bank of the River being Randolphs Line; adj. Randolph, Pruit, & Parham Booker; 1 Sep 1780, p.745. A.C. of 15 Shill. Sterl.

CHARLES TAYLOR, 314 acs. by Survey 19 Dec 1770 in Bedford Co. on both sides of the Dutchmans br. on the fork thereof and including the head of the North fork of the same, at a pond near sd br., adj. Samuel Morris; 1 Sep 1780, p.747. A.C. of 35 Shill. Sterl.

PATRICK HENRY Esqr., 949 acs. by Entrys by Survey made 1 Apr 1780 in Henry Co. on Smiths Riv. and Leatherwood Waters; adj. Lomax & Company, Dugger, Thomas Wilson, John Reas, Webb, & Baileys otherwise Robertsons Lines; 28 Nov 1780, p.748. A.C. of £4.S15 Sterl.

[Margin note: *This grant not being Signed by the Governor, A new one Issued the 1st day of September 1780 and Recorded in Book No. 20, Page 602*] JOHN MILLS Ass'ee of ALEXANDER EVANS, 185 acs. by Survey 3 Mar 1768 in Augusta Co. on the waters of Back Cr. a br. of James Riv., on a Stoney Point, by a Spring, on a Ridge, adj. his Pat. L.; 21 Sep 1780, p.750. A.C. of 20 Shill. Sterl. [Thomas Jeffersons supposed signature is at the end of the grant]

GEORGE HACKWORTH, 256 acs. by Survey 8 Apr 1772 in Bedford Co. on the S side of Goose Cr., on McDaniels br.; 1 Sep 1780, p.751. A.C. of 30 Shill. Sterl. Including (25 acs. being part of 125 acs. Gtd. to Thomas Price by Pat. bearing date 27 Sep 1753)

MATTHEW TALBOT ass'ee of JOSHUA BARTON, 129 acs. by Survey 28 Mar 1769 in Pittsylvania Co. on Pigg Riv., adj. his Old Line; 1 Sep 1780, p.752. A.C. of 15 Shill. Sterl.

JEREMIAH RUST ass'ee of MARY READ, 458 acs. by Survey 31 Mar 1755 in Bedford Co. on the head brs. of Molleys Cr. and beaver Cr.; adj. Ornsbys old Lines, his own Line & Shearses or Shearees [his] Line; 1 Sep 1780, p.753. A.C. of 50 Shill. Sterl.

JOHN RAFFERTY, 154 acs. by Survey 12 Apr 1780 in Bedford Co. on the E side of Falling Riv., up Dog Cr. [from the Mouth] being Driskills Line, along Todds Line & Sturmans Lines to his Corner Stump (near Raffertys house); 1 Sep 1780, p.754. A.C. of 15 Shill. Sterl.

ANDREW HAIRSTONE, 400 acs. by Survey 8 Nov 1779 in Bedford Co. on W brs. of the South fork of Falling Riv., crossing broad br. to pointers on the Brow of the Hill, near a Path; adj. his own Line, Weathen & Arnold; 1 Sep 1780, p.755. A.C. of £2. Sterl.

MICHAEL PRUIT / PREWIT, 460 acs. by Survey 26 Jan 1764 in Bedford Co. on the S side of Falling Riv.; adj. Winford, his own lines, Booker & Randolph; 1 Sep 1780, p.756. A.C. of 50 Shill. Sterl.

CHRISTOPHER IRVINE CLENDENING, 90 acs. by Survey 10 Nov 1773 in Bedford Co. on E brs. of flat Cr., at a Spring, adj. Machen & his own c.; 1 Sep 1780, p.758. A.C. of 10 Shill. Sterl.

JOHN McCLUNY Ass'ee of SAMUEL HAIRSTONE, 235 acs. by Survey 25 Aug 1775 in Bedford Co. on head brs. of Beaver Cr., Crossing the Meadow Ground; adj. Hylton, Clement, Hughes Lines, Daugherty & Edmeston; 1 Sep 1780, p.759. A.C. of 25 Shill. Sterl.

FRANCIS THORP ass'ee of JOHN ROBERTSON, 794 acs. by Survey 3 Mar 1772 in Bedford Co. on both Sides of Buflow Cr.; adj. Buford, Joseph White head, his own Lines & Austin; 1 Sep 1780, p.760. A.C. of 65 Shill. Sterl. *(126 acs. being part there of was formerly by Pat. Gtd. to John Wainright [Lunenburgh Co. PB 31 p.518 on Buffalo Cr. a N Br. of Otter Riv. dated 10 Jul 1755], 48 acs. also being a part of the Same was Gtd. by Pat. to William Harvey [PB 33 p.624 dated 27 Aug 1759])*

JONES READ, 346 acs. by Survey 11 Apr 1765 in Bedford Co. on the S brs. of Otter Riv.; adj. McGlaughlin, Banister, Callaway & Walton; 1 Sep 1780, p.762. A.C. of 35 Shill. Sterl.

ANTHONY DEBRAEL / DIBRAEL, 415 acs. by Survey 13 Mar 1773 in

Buckingham Co. on a br. of Waltons Fork of Slate Riv., adj. Miles Gibson & his own Line; 1 Sep 1780, p.763. A.C. of 45 Shill. Sterl.

ANTHONY DUBREL, 400 acs. by Survey 30 Nov 1749 in Albemarle Co. on the N brs. of Slate Riv.; adj. Benning, John Bondurant & Anthony Benning; 1 Sep 1780, p.764. A.C. of 40 Shillings Sterl.

BENJAMIN HARRISON ass'ee of JNO. McCLURE, 300 acs. by Survey 14 Jul 1772 in Augusta Co. on both sides of the North Riv. of Shennendore, Crossing into a bent of the Riv., up Dry Riv.; adj. Hugh Duglas, John Logan, John McGill, William Heron & Maurius or Maurices Line; 1 Sep 1780, p.765. A.C. of 30 Shill. Sterl. *(130 acs. part thereof which was formerly Gtd. to sd McClure by Pat. 5 Sep 1762 the Residue thereof not before Gtd.)*

MICHAEL PREWIT / PRUIT, 860 acs. by Survey 21 Nov 1771 by Virtue of 2 Entries entred in Bedford Co. on the brs. of Falling Riv., Phelp's and Bomans Creeks, at Rogers's Path, at a road; adj. his own lines, Rafferty, Hugh McCown, Walton, Daugherty, Samuel Gaulding, Robert Garrett, Pendleton & Winford; 1 Sep 1780, p.766. A.C. of £4.S10 Sterl.

HUMPHREY CRIDDLE, 360 acs. by Survey 21 Dec 1778 in Bedford Co. on both sides of Millstone br. an E br. of Little falling Riv., to Sandy br. a N br. of Entry Cr.; adj. Thompson near the falling, Robert Mitchell, Daniel Mitchell & Caldwell; to a Locust in the feild between Criddle and Littlepages; 1 Sep 1780, p.768. A.C. of £2 Sterl.

THOMAS FAILING, 120 acs. by Survey 9 Mar 1775 in Bedford Co. on a Ridge Betw. the forks of Seneca Cr., adj. James Hunter & Read; 1 Sep 1780, p.769. A.C. of 15 Shill. Sterl.

THOMAS EAST, 415 acs. by Survey 5 May 1779 in Bedford Co. on both sides of Senaca Cr., Beginning at the Mouth of Rockey Br. on the E side of Seneca Cr., at a Path, adj. Gilbert; 1 Sep 1780, p.770. A.C. of 25 Shill. Sterl. *(190 acs. part thereof was formerly Gtd. by Pat. to Charles Talbot and properly Conveyed) the Residue thereof not before Gtd.*

JONES WYNNE, 370 acs. by Survey 12 Feb 1779 in Bedford Co. on both sides of Falling Riv., Beginning on the E Side of the Riv. Opposite to Sandy Point, Crossing Rockey br., up a br. out at the Head over the Ridge, on an Old Path, near Lick Cr.; adj. Read, Cock, Richard Stith & Harry Terrell; 1 Sep 1780, p.771. A.C. of 40 Shill. Sterl.

CHARLES TALBOT, 400 acs. by Survey 3 Dec 1778 in Bedford Co. on the E side of Whipping Cr., over nusery br., up Mire br.; adj. his own Old Lines, Samuel Seegar, Pennell, Lane & Marshall; 1 Sep 1780, p.773. A.C. of 40 Shill. Sterl.

ANDREW HAIRSTONE, 400 acs. by Survey 8 Nov 1777 in Bedford Co. on both Sides of Burnt bridge br. and on both Sides of the Main Road to New London, near and upon the Spurs of the Long Mountain, adj. Charles Caffrey & Hylton; 1 Sep 1780, p.774. A.C. of £2 *into the Treasury of this Commonwealth.*

RICHARD KERBY Ass'ee of THEOPHELUS LACY, 367 acs. by

Survey 22 Mar 1769 in Pittsylvania Co. on the N brs. of the North fork of Sandy Cr., on a Ridge, adj. William Asten & Kennon; 1 Sep 1780, p.775. A.C. of 40 Shill. Sterl. *into the Late Receiver Generals Office.*

[Margin note: *This Grant was Altered in the Name of Governor Harrison and dated the 1st January 1780 Because the Grant was made out & Recorded before Signed by Governor Jefferson who Resigned before it Could be Signed or Sealed*] ROBERT PEDIGOW, 1,214 acs. by Survey made 16 Nov 1779 in Henry Co. on the Brs. of Leatherwood and Talbots Cr.; adj. his own, Lomax and Company, Ephraim Gordan, Hickey, Burnett, Garner & Smith; 1 Jan 1782 in the 6th year of the Commonwealth, p.776. A.C. of £6.S5 Sterl. paid by Robert Pedigow *into the Treasury of this Commonwealth.* [Signed by Benjamin Harrison]

JOSHUA AGEE, 144 acs. by Survey 7 Apr 1779 in Bedford Co. on the S Side of Stanton Riv., on Dunkins Mill Run; adj. Cowan, Walter Edey, Hatcher & Maxey; 1 Sep 1780, p.779. A.C. of 15 Shill. Sterl.

SAMMY LAMKIN MOORE Ass'ee of WILLIAM HARRIS, 420 acs. by Survey 1 Dec 1763 in Bedford Co. on both Sides of Pole Cat Br. including the head (being a West Br. of the South fork of Falling Riv.); adj. Rosser, John Moore & Peter Daniel; 1 Sep 1780, p.780. A.C. of £2.S5.

THOMAS DOUGHERTY, 290 acs. by Survey 12 Sep 1774 in Bedford Co. on Head brs. of Hat Cr., Crossing a Fork, over a small Br., near an old Road; adj. Josiah Campbell, his own Lines, George Jones, Barns, & Wood Jones; 1 Sep 1780, p.782. A.C. of £1.S10 Sterl.

ISREAL / ISRAEL CHRISTIAN, 352 acs. by Survey 11 Mar 1773 in Bedford Co. on the head of Bore Auger and Beaverdam Creeks, along the County Line, adj. Hays; 1 Sep 1780, p.783. A.C. of 35 Shill. Sterl.

ABRAM PRICE Ass'ee of THOMAS NAPIER, 150 acs. by Survey 19 Mar 1767 in Albemarle Co. on both sides of Shepherds Cr.; adj. Lacy / Lacey, Harden / Hardin Burnley, & Charles Bond; 1 Sep 1780, p.785. A.C. of 15 Shill. Sterl.

ANN CORNELIUS, 202 acs. by Survey 16 Apr 1753 in Pittsylvania Co. on both sides of Buck Br. of Frying Pan Cr.; 1 Sep 1780, p.786. A.C. of 20 Shill. Sterl.

THOMAS EDWARDS, 315 acs. by Survey 31 Jan 1769 in Henry Co. on the draughts of touslout Cr., adj. William Edwards & James; 1 Sep 1780, p.787. A.C. of 35 Shill. Sterl.

WILLIAM DIVER Ass'ee of BENJAMIN DENNY, 190 acs. by Survey 10 Apr 1767 in Amherst Co. on the Brs. of Ruckers run; adj. William Bibb, Lawrence Sudderth & Colo. Lunsford Lomax; 1 Sep 1780, p.788. A.C. of 20 Shill. Sterl.

JOHN McMAHAN, 330 acs. by Survey 20 Feb 1775 in Augusta Co. on the dividing Ridge betw. the Brs. of the Middle and North rivers, nearly with Margaret Frames Line, adj. Walker; 1 Sep 1780, p.780. A.C. of 35 Shill. Sterl.

JAMES DILLARD, 98 acs. by Survey 8 Dec 1766 in Amherst Co. on the N brs.

of Porrage Cr.; adj. James Christian, Edward Cottril & Richard Peter; 1 Sep 1780, p.791. A.C. of 10 Shill. Sterl.

WILLIAM CRAWFORD, 90 acs. by Survey 7 Nov 1779 in Augusta Co. on the dry br. of the Middle Riv. of Shannandore in the North Mountain, by a Road; 1 Sep 1780, p.793. A.C. of 10 Shill. Sterl.

SAMUEL HAIRSTONE, 265 acs. by Survey 25 Jun 1774, in Bedford Co. on both sides of the North fork of Seneca Cr.; adj. Neilson, his own Lines, the old Lines of Ornsby, & Douglas; 1 Sep 1780, p.794. A.C. of 30 Shill. Sterl. formerly Surveyed for THOMAS LENOX who is absconded and by the Sheriff returned insolvent.

ROBERT LINSEY / LINDSEY, 285 acs. by Survey 16 Jan 1773 in Bedford Co. on both sides and including the head of Plum Br. (a W Br. of Mollys Cr.); adj. Ager, Neison, Lenox, Douglas & the old Lines of Ornsby; 1 Sep 1780, p.796. A.C. of 30 Shill. Sterl.

BENJAMIN GRIFFETH, 230 acs. by Survey 16 Feb 1773 in Bedford Co. on both sides of Black Water Riv., on the Road, adj. John Anderson & his own c.; 1 Sep 1780, p.797. A.C. of 25 Shill. Sterl.

ANDREW TURNER Ass'ee of THOMAS MIDDLETON who was Ass'ee of MOSES WATKINS, 424 acs. by Survey 4 Mar 1773 in Bedford Co. on S Brs. of Wreck Island Cr., near a Large Br.; adj. James Phelps, Stovall, Bolling, Hunter, Dobyns & Carson; *In Witness whereof the sd Thomas Jefferson Governor of the Commonwealth hath hereunto Set his hand, and Caused the Lesser Seal of the sd Commonwealth to be Affixed at Richmond*, 1 Sep 1780, p.799. A.C. of £2.S5 Sterl.

[Margin note: *When this Grant was made out, Thomas Jefferson was Governor. the Grant was not Granted by him therefore the Grant was made out in Benjamin Harrisons Name*]
JAMES REYNOLDS, 238 acs. by Survey 2 Mar 1764 in Bedford Co. on S Brs. of the South fork of Falling Riv., at a Spring; adj. Brooks, Weathen, Edmeston, Tweedy & Harris; *In witness whereof the sd Benjamin Harrison Governor of the Commonwealth hath hereunto Set his hand, and Caused the Lesser Seal of the sd Commonwealth to be Affixed at Richmond, 20 Aug 1783 in the 8th year of the Commonwealth*, p.801. in Consideration of the Ancient Composition of 25 Shill. Sterl.

[Margin note: *When this Grant was made out Thomas Jefferson was Governor. the Grant was not Sgnd. by him therefore the Grant must be made out in Ben Harrisons name*]
SAMUEL HAIRSTONE, 550 acs. by Survey 7 Nov 1777 Made by Virtue of two Entries in his own Name, in Bedford Co. on the E side of Beaver Cr., near Long Mountain thence a Cross the Spurs and Valleys of the Mountain, crossing a Br. and the Main Road, on the Cr. at the old Mill Place, adj. his Old & New Patent Lines; *In Witness whereof the sd Thomas Jefferson Governor of the Commonwealth hath hereunto Set his hand, and Caused the Lesser Seal of the sd Commonwealth to be Affixed at Richmond; 1 Sep 1780 in the 5th year of the Commonwealth,* p.802. A.C. of £2.S15. Sterl.

WILLIAM SHEILDS, **by Inclusive Survey** made 28 Apr 1780, 300 acs. in Pittsylvania Co. on the Brs. of Sandy Riv., near the Road, adj. Samuel Sparks Line & Thomas Robertson; 1 Sep 1780, p.804. A.C. of 35 Shill. Sterl.

JACOB RUBSAMAN, 935 acs. **Inclusively** by Survey 22 Mar 1780 in Pittsylvania Co. on Stanton Riv.; adj. John Talbot, William Ward, William Bennet, John Lawson & John Chiles Line; 1 Sep 1780, p.806. A.C. of £4.S15. Sterl.

JOHN WILLSON, 148 acs. by Survey 18 Mar 1779 in Bedford Co. on Brs. of Turnip Cr. on both Sides of the road to Charlotte; adj. Gwin, John Mason, Rogers & Smith; 1 Sep 1780, p.808. A.C. of 15 Shill. Sterl.

JAMES SLONE, 677 acs. by Survey 24 Nov 1776 in Bedford Co. on Maggotty Cr.; adj. Apshear, Grimes Line, Marley & Thomas; 1 Sep 1780, p.809. A.C. of £3.S10 Sterl. including 220 acs. for which a G. was formerly issued.

WILLIAM MOORE, 130 acs. by Survey 26 Apr 1780 in Rockbridge Co. on Marys Cr.; adj. Daniel Miller & Willsons Old Patent Line; 1 Sep 1780, p.811. A.C. of 15 Shill. Sterl.

[Margin note: *This Grant was altered in the Name of Governour Harrison and dated 20th of August 1783 because the Grant was made out & recorded before Signed by Governour Jefferson who resigned before it could be isgned or Sealed*)
WILLIAM SMITH, 139 acs. by Survey 13 Oct 1769 in Henry Co. formerly Pittsylvania on Little Peters Cr.; *In witness whereof the sd Benjamin Harrison Governor of the Commonwealth of Virginia hath hereunto set his hand and caused the Lesser Seal of the sd Commonwealth to be Affixed at Richmond,* 20 Aug 1783, p.813. A.C. of 15 Shill. Sterl.

GEORGE CARTER, 344 acs. by Survey 13 Oct 1770 in Henry Co. formerly Pittsylvania on the South Mayo Riv., adj. sd Carters old Line; 1 Sep 1780, p.814. A.C. of 35 Shill. Sterl.

JOSIAH MAXEY, 455 acs. by Survey 10 Mar 1778 in Bedford Co. on the Waters of Gills Cr.; adj. Mead, Greer, South [his Line] & Maxey; 1 Sep 1780, p.815. A.C. of £2.S10 Sterl. *into the Treasury of this Commonwealth.*

FRANCIS GRAHAM, 140 acs. by Survey 7 Aug 1767 in Botetourt Co. formerly Augusta on Carvins Cr. a Br. of Roan Oak, Crossing Carvans Cr., adj. sd Grahams Line & the Land of John Robinson; 11 Dec 1780, p.817. A.C. of 15 Shill. Sterl. *into the Late Receiver Generals Office.*

WILLIAM HERBERT of the Town of Alexander [Alexandria], ½ an Acre in the Town of Alexandria Numbered in the Plan of the town 300; bounded by Oronooko Street on the South a Lot of Robert Adam on the West Potowmac River on the North and a Lot of Richard Conways on the East; 19 Oct 1780, p.818. in Consideration of the Sum of £10,700 Current Money of Virginia, paid unto Hector Ross Gent. Escheator for Fairfax Co. by William Herbert of the Town of Alexander [sic]. being *Lately the Property of William Hicks a Subject of Great Britain and was Sold by the sd*

Hector Ross Gent. Escheator for the sd Co. unto the sd William Herbert with Lot and Houses and Appurtenances Appurtaining to the said Lot Late the Property of William Hicks by Virtue of an Agreable to two Late Acts of General Assembly passed in 1779 the one Entitled an Act Concerning Escheats and forfeitures from British Subjects and the other Entitled an Act Concerning Escheators.

JOHN CAMERON, 300 acs. by Survey 5 Jun 1780 in Mecklingburg Co. on the Brs. of Buffaloe and Arons Cr.; adj. Atkinson, Benjamin Jones, John Shotwell & sd Camerons Line; 1 Sep 1780, p.819. A.C. of 30 Shill. Sterl. *paid into the Treasury of this Commonwealth.*

SAMUEL YOUNG Ass'ee of CUNROD MESSERSMITH, 55 acs. by Survey 18 Feb 1769 in Mecklinburg Co. on the South fork of Allens Cr.; adj. sd Young, Jeffreis, Hoopery & Boyd; 1 Sep 1780, p.821. A.C. of 10 Shill. Sterl.

JAMES BLANTON, 314 acs. by Survey 5 Nov 1773 it being the Land recovered by Joshua Mabry of Gabriel Harden before the late Council the 10th of Jun 1772, by him Assigned to sd James Blanton, in Mecklenburg Co. on the Brs. of Great Cr.; adj. Lambert, Field, Donalds Lines & Stephen Jones; 11 Dec 1780, p.822. A.C. of 35 Shill. Sterl.

[Margin note: *This Grant was altered in the name of Governour Harrison and dated 20th. August 1789 because the Grant was made out and records before Signed by Governour Jefferson who resigned before it Could be Sign'd or Seald*]

JOHN OLLIVER, 97 acs. by Survey 12 Mar 1772 in Mecklenburg Co. on the Brs. of Allens Cr.; adj. Mrs. Hughes, Richard Willis, Crowder & sd John Olliver; *In witness whereof the sd Benjamin Harrison Governor of the Commonwealth of Virginia hath heretunto Set his hand and Causes the Lesser Seal of the sd Commonwealth to be Affixed at Richmond, 20 Aug 1780 [1789] in the 8th year of the Commonwealth,* p.823. A.C. of 10 Shill. Sterl.

ROBERT YANCY, 400 acs. by Survey 5 Jun 1780 in Mecklenburg Co. on the Brs. of Buffalo and Aarons Creks; adj. the Reverend John Cameron, John Parish, Griffin, James Griffin & John Stanback; 11 Dec 1780 *in the 5th year of the Commonweath,* p.824. A.C. of £2 Sterl.

WILLIAM LUCAS, 275 acs. by Survey 16 Mar 1772 in Mecklenburg Co. on the Waters of Dockayes and Flat Creeks; adj. Matthew Perham, sd Lucas, Mabry, Cuningham & Robert Lark; 11 Dec 1780, p.826. A.C. of 30 Shill. Sterl.

JAMES RANKIN Ass'ee of ANDREW & ROBERT NICHOLLS, 270 acs. by Survey 25 Nov 1774 in Augusta Co. on the N side of Moffets Br., near the old Line; 1 Sep 1780, p.827. A.C. of 30 Shill. Sterl. *bounded by the Variation of the Magnetic from the true Meridian it being 1° East.*

RICHARD NUTT, 400 acs. by Survey 26 Apr 1780 in Fluvanna Co. on the Brs. of Cary Cr. and S Brs. of the Rivanna Riv.; adj. Hughes / Hughs, Riddle,

Mandley & the sd Nutts Line; 1 Sep 1780, p.828. A.C. of 40 Shill. Sterl.

JESSEE BURTON, 11½ acs. by Survey 17 Mar 1780 in Fluvanna Co. on the N side of Fluvanna Riv., on a ridge, down the river from the Mouth of Driver Cr., adj. Martin Key; 1 Sep 1780. p.829. A.C. of 5 Shill. Sterl.

WILLIAM LAMME ass'ee of JOHN MADISON JUNIOR, 500 acs. by Survey 18 Jun 1772 in Rockingham Co. formerly Augusta on the East fork of Cooks Cr., at a Spring, Crossing a Meadow, adj. John Craven & Joseph Craven; 11 Dec 1780, p.830. A.C. of 20 Shill. Sterl. paid by Willaim Lamme *into the Late Receiver Generals Office. 141 acs. part thereof is part of 200 acs. gtd. Robert Cravens by Pat. 10 Feb 1748/49 [Augusta Co. PB 27 p.115 including Dyes Meadow] and 200 acs. part thereof was gtd. to John Madison by Pat. 10 Jul 1766 [Augusta Co. PB 36 p.957] the right and title of which Lands is since become Vested in the sd William Lamme and 159 acs. the Residue never before gtd.*

JOHN NICHOLAS, 44 acs. by Survey 15 Apr 1767 in Augusta Co. on the N side of Moffetts Br., in a Gully, adj. the Land whereon he Lives; 1 Sep 1780, p.832. A.C. of 5 Shill. Sterl. *into the Tresasury of this Commonwealth.*

ROBERT MAYO Ass'ee of JOHN TOMMERSON who was Ass'ee of ANGUS FORBUS, 54 acs. by Survey 18 Mar 1771 in Amherst Co. on the S Brs. of Davisis Cr.; adj. his own Lines, Benjamin Childers & William Forbus; 1 Sep 1780, p.833. A.C. of 5 Shill. Sterl.

Messrs. WILLIAM GREEN, CLUVERIUS COLEMAN & BENJAMIN WHITEHEAD Ass'ees of sd MATTHEW MARRABLE, 400. acs. Mecklenburg Co. on a Br. of Allens Cr., on the Road; adj. Humphries Line, Atkerson, McQues Line & Whitehead; 11 Dec 1780, p.835. in Consideration of the Sum of £6,080 Current Money of Virginia paid unto Clausel Clausel Escheator for Mecklenburg Co. by Matthew Marrable. *Lately the Property of Andrew Cockran, William Cunningham and Company British Subjects and was Sold by the sd Clousel Clousel Escheator as aforesaid unto the sd Matthew Marrable and by him Since Sold to the sd Messrs. William Green Cleveruis Coleman and Benjamin Whitehead Agreable to two Acts of Assembly passed in the year 1779 the one Entitled an Act Concerning Escheats and forfeitures from British Subjects the other Intitled an Act Concerning Escheators.*

WILLIAM LEWIS, 100 acs. by Survey 29 Apr 1780 in Botetourt Co. at the Gap of Peters Mountain near the Sweet Springs and on the Waters of Dunlaps Cr. a Br. of James Riv., by a Gully; 1 Sep 1780 *in the 5th year of the Commonwealth*, p.836. A.C. of 10 Shill. Sterl.

[Margin note: *This Grant was altered in the name of Governour Harrison and dated 20th. August 1783 becaused the Grant was made out and recorded before Signed by Governour Jefferson who resigned before it could be signd or Seald*]

THOMAS MEDKIFF, 129 acs. by Survey 2 Dec 1773 in Henry Co. formerly Pittsylvania Co. the Brs. of

Peters Cr., adj. his old Lines; 20 Aug 1780 in the 8th year of the Commonwealth, p.838. in Consideration of the Ancient Composition of 15 Shill. Sterl. In Witness whereof, the said Benjamin Harrison Governor of the Commonwealth of Virginia hath hereunto set his hand, and Caused the Lesser Seal of the said Commonwealth to be Affixed at Richmond.

JOHN TENNANT Ass'ee of WILLIAM WOODFORD, 2,000 acs. by Survey 28 May 1774 in Jefferson Co. on the Ohio Riv., Beginning about 12 miles above the Falls of the Ohio Corner to Hugh Mercers thence down the Riv., Opposite to the upper end of a Large Island; 11 Dec 1780 in the 5th year of the Commonwealth, p.839. Signed by Thomas Jefferson. *In Consideration of Military Service performed by William Woodford in the Late War between Great Britain and France According to the terms of the King of Great Britains Proclamation of 1763.*

ROBERT GELCHRIST/GILCHRIST, ½ an Acre in the Town of Port Royal Numbered in the Plan of the said Town Twenty in Caroline Co.; 11 Dec 1780, p.841. in Consideration of the Sum of £6,622 Current Money of Virginia paid unto Edmund Pendleton Junior Gent. Escheator for Caroline Co. by Robert Gelchrist Esquire. being *Lately the Property of John Gray and Company Subjects of Great Britain and was sold by the said Edmund Pendleton Escheator as aforesaid unto the said Robert Gilchrist with the Appurtenances Appurtaining to the said Lot by Virtue of an Agreable to 2 Late Acts of General Assembly passed ian 1779 the one Entitled an Act Concering Escheats and forfeitures from British Subjects and the other Entitled an Act Concerning Escheators.*

RICHARD TAYLOR Ass'ee of JAMES LEWIS, 400 acs. by Survey 22 Sep 1766 in Mecklenburg Co. on the S side of Roanoak riv. on the waters of Long Grass Sw.; adj. sd James Lewis, Mecheaux, Johnson & Taylor; 11 Dec 1780, p.842. A.C. of £2 Sterl. *325 acs. part thereof was Surveyed for James Lewis father of the said James Lewis 9 Nov 1761. [For Johnsons's Line see PB 34 p583 to John Johnson on the Country Line and brs. of Great Nut Bush Cr.]*

MILES JENNINGS, 400 acs. by Survey 9 Nov 1770 in Pittsylvania Co. on Jennings Cr., on Jacks Br., adj. Randolphs Order Line; 1 Sep 1780, p.843. A.C. of £2. Sterl.

JOEL RAGLAND, 160 acs. by Survey 7 May 1779 in Henry Co. on a Br. of Pigg Riv. Called Turners Cr., adj. Robert Jones & Mavily; 11 Dec 1780, p.844. A.C. of 20 Shill. Sterl.

JOEL RAGLAND, 441 acs. by Survey 4 jun 1779 in Henry Co. on the Brs. of Pigg Riv., Beginning at a Large Br. Called Turners Cr. near the Mouth of a South Br., up the North fork to another fork thence up the South fork, on a Ridge; adj. Jones, & William Mavily; 11 Dec 1780, p.845. A.C. of £2.S5 Sterl.

JOHN MURPHEY, 337 acs. by Survey 14 May 1779 in Henry Co. on the Waters of Pigg Riv. Near the Great Mountain; adj. Joseph Hals Line, the sd Hails Line; 11 Dec 1780, p.846. A.C. of 35 Shill. Sterl.

THOMAS GOODE of Chesterfield Co., 214 acs. Mecklenburg Co. Bounded as followeth "by and between the Lands of Thomas Eastland James Holloway and John Davis it being the Lands Conveyed to the said Andrew Johnston Jr. by John Lynch"; 11 Dec 1780, p.848. £6,621 Current Money of Virginia paid unto Clausel Clausel Gent. Escheator for Mecklenburg Co. by Thomas Goode of Chesterfield Co. *Lately the Property of Andrew Johnston Junr. a British Subjects and was sold by sd Clausel Clausel Escheator as foresaid unto sd Thomas Goode agreeable to 2 Acts of Assembly passed in the year 1779, the one Entitled an Act Concerning Escheats and forfeitures from British Subjects the other Entitled an Act Concerning Escheators.* [Probably part of Michael Johnston's 262 acs. Lunenburg Co. in PB 33 p.719]

GEORGE CONROD Ass'ee of MATTHIAS McGLAMMERY, 590 acs. by Inclusive Survey 2 Nov 1770 in Rockingham Co. formerly Augusta on Smiths Cr., adj. Harrison & Needham; 11 Dec 1780, p.849. A.C. of £3 Sterl. *Including a Survey of 400 acs. and the other of 190 acs.*

GEORGE CONROD Ass'ee of DAVID TATE who was Ass'ee of JOHN ROBINSON, 380 acs. by Survey 13 Apr 1773 in Botetourt Co. on the head Springs of the South fork of Dunlaps Cr., on the dividing Ridge, down the Gap that Leads from the Sweet Springs to Second Creek, near the run and a Spring, up the Spurs of the Mountain; 11 Dec 1780, p.850. A.C. of 40 Shill. Sterl.

JOHN BRAMMER, 248 acs. by Survey 9 Nov 1769 in Henry Co. formerly Pittsylvania on white Oak Cr.; 11 Dec 1780, p.851. A.C. of 25 Shill. Sterl.

RICHARD MACOY, 377 acs. by Survey 4 Apr 1769 in Henry Co. formerly Pittsylvania on Brs. of Black water Riv., along a Mountain, near a Meadow; 11 Dec 1780, p.852. A.C. of 40 Shill. Sterl.

PHILIP THOMAS, 212 acs. by Survey 3 Dec 1779 in Henry Co. on Smiths Riv., adj. Harstone & his old Line; 11 Dec 1780, p.853. A.C. of 25 Shill. Sterl.

THOMAS AVENT, 19 acs. by Survey 9 Oct 1770 in Sussex Co. on the N side of the three Creeks; adj. Colo. David Mason, Joseph Tharp & Avents old line; 11 Dec 1780, p.855. A.C. of 5 Shill. Sterl.

WILLIAM ROBINSON, JUNIOR, 372 acs. by Survey 27 Mar 1780 in Brunswick Co. on the Road, down a Slash, in a Meadow; adj. William Robinson Senr., John Doby, Avent, Brewer, Hill & Gowin; 11 Dec 1780, p.856. A.C. of 20 Shill. Sterl. *45 acs part thereof is part of a Pat. for 1,485 acs gtd. to Nicholas Brewer by Pat. 5 Jul 1751 [PB 29 p.441 on the Lower Side of Beaver Pond Cr.] and 130 acs. part thereof was gtd. to William Wise by Pat. 1 Oct 1747 [PB 28 p.223 on the head of Cattail Cr.] the right and title of which is since become Vested in sd William Robinson and 200 acs. the residue never before gtd.*

PAUL HARTWELL, 22 acs. by Survey 11 Feb 1775 in Brunswick Co. up Bull Run, adj. John Moore & Thorp; 11 Dec 1780, p.857. A.C. of 5 Shill. Sterl. [Bull Run is a br. of the Great Cr. below the Fort. It was referred to as Bull Br. in

Joseph Tharp's PB 31 p.448 & as Great Br. in William Wesson's PB 35 p.70]

HOWELL ADAMS ass'ee of THOMAS ADAMS, 53 acs. by Survey 5 Jan 1763 in Southampton Co. in Nottoway Par., in the County line dividing Southampton from Sussex [S60°W], down Iveys Meadow, up Plowmans br., adj. Thomas Adams; 11 Dec 1780, p.858. A.C. of 5 Shill. Sterl.

JOHN JOHNSON, 354 acs. by Survey 26 Oct 1762 in Brunswick Co. up White Oak Cr.; adj. Hines, his own old line, Morgan, Keley, Edward Wisson & Coxey; 11 Dec 1780, p.859. A.C. of 35 Shill. Sterl.

NATHANIEL MABRY, 48 acs. by Survey 28 Feb 1772 in Brunswick Co. adj. his own line, Morris, & Robert Powell; 11 Dec 1780, p.860. A.C. of 5 Shill. Sterl. [Near Hicks Br.; for his own lines, see James Bilberry's PB 32 p.94]

JOHN TRIMBLE / TREMBLE, 130 acs. by Survey 2 Mar 1775 in Augusta Co. on a Ridge called the Painter Mountain on the Waters of Irish Cr. being the waters of James Riv., in a flatt; 1 Sep 1780, p.861. A.C. of 15 Shill. Sterl.

JOHN TRIMBLE, 74 acs. by Survey 1 Mar 1774 in Augusta Co. on a Ridge between some of the Southermost brs. of Irish Cr. the waters of James Riv.; 1 Sep 1780, p.862. A.C. of 10 Shill. Sterl.

JOHN PARKS, 94 acs. by Survey 20 Oct 1772 in Augusta Co. Joining Lines with the Land of William Chambers on the waters of Mary Cr. a br. of James Riv., crossing two draughts twice, down the Sugar tree draught; 1 Sep 1780, p.863. A.C. of 10 Shill. Sterl.

STEPHEN ARNOLD, 190 acs. by Survey 23 Oct 1767 in Augusta Co. Adj. to his own Land on Elk cr. a br. of James Riv., Beginning in his old Survey, by the road; 1 Sep 1780, p.864. A.C. of £1 Sterl.

WILLIAM MOORE, 282 acs. by Survey 27 Apr 1780 in Rockbridge Co. on the waters of the Mary Cr., on the Great road, adj. John McClung & MacCrory; 1 Sep 1780, p.864. A.C. of 30 Shill. Sterl.

ALEXANDER McNUTT Ass'ee of JOHN McNUTT who was Ass'ee of JOSIAH EAST, 96 acs. by Survey 13 Jun 1771 in Bottetourt Co. Joining the Lines of John Reynolds/Rynolds on the North br. of James Riv. also the Lines of a Survey belonging to James Templeton containing 49 acs., to Locust Bushes in a Bushy Ground then to a bushy hill, on a hill above the riv.; 1 Sep 1780, p.865. A.C. of 10 Shill. Sterl.

Doctor JOHN NEELY, 157 acs. by Survey 20 Mar 1780 in Botetourt Co. on the South waters of Catawbo Cr. a br. of James Riv. by right of an Entry legally made with the Surveyor and Joining the Land of William McClenachan, John Hewit and Joseph Carroll; Beginning near the Tanyard; in the old Line; on the Side of a hill near an old Cabbin; in a Valley; near a Spring; 11 Dec 1780, p.866. A.C. of 20 Shill. Sterl.

WILLIAM NEELY, 264 acs. by Survey 29 Apr 1780 in Botetourt Co. on the Bent Mountain Joining a Survey of Said Neelys, in the low Ground of the cr.; 11 Dec 1780, p.867. A.C. of 30 Shill. Sterl.

WILLIAM NEELY Ass'ee of PATRICK MACKIN, 244 acs. by Survey 8 Apr 1772 in Botetourt Co. on the South bank of Masons Cr. a br. of Roanoke; adj. William Neely & Colo. Lewis, Carltons L.; 11 Dec 1780, p.867. A.C. of 25 Shill. Sterl. *125 acs. part thereof was Gtd. to Samuel Brown by Letters Pat. 12 May 1759 the right and title of which is since become vested in the sd William Neely and 119 acs. the residue never before Gtd.*

CHARLES MANN, 71 acs. by Survey 24 Feb 1773 in Augusta Co. on *Brocks Gap*, adj. his old C.; 1 Sep 1780, p.868. A.C. of 10 Shill. Sterl.

LODOVICK / LODEVICK / LODIVICK KELLOR ass'ee of LEONARD MILLER, 145 acs. by Survey 24 May 1774 in Rockingham Co. formerly Augusta on a br. of the North fork of Shenandore, adj. his old Line, near Gasper Fauts Line; 1 Sep 1780, p.869. A.C. of 15 Shill. Sterl. *bounded by the variation of the Magnetic from the true being 1° East.*

ANDREW HUDLOW, 12 acs. by Survey 12 Apr 1780 in Rockingham Co. Beginning on the point between and below the Mouth of Scotts Run and the North river Corner to his own Land and the Land formerly John Denestons, to Land formerly Robert Shanklens; 1 Sep 1780, p.870. A.C. of 5 Shill. Sterl.

JOSEPH REABURN, 53 acs. by Survey 14 Jan 1775 in Augusta Co. on the head Br. of Mill run a br. of the Calf pasture, near a Great road, crossing a draught, adj. Mathews; 1 Sep 1780, p.870. A.C. of 5 Shill. Sterl. *bounded by the Variation from the true Meridian it being 1°E.*

JOHN REAH, 54 acs. by Survey 20 Apr 1780 in Augusta Co. on a br. of Calf Pasture and Joining Alexander Crockets Entry; 1 Sep 1780, p.871. A.C. of 5 Shill. Sterl.

[Margin note: This Grant was altered in the name of Governour Harrison and dated 19th, August 1783 because the Grant was made out and recorded before Signed by Governour Jefferson who resign'd before it it could be signed or Seald]
ALEXANDER WALKER, 159 acs. by Survey 28 Mar 1770 in Augusta Co. on Some draughts of the Middle River of Shenandore, Beginning on the Side of a Pond, adj. Thomas Conolly; 19 Aug 1783 *in the 8th year of the Commonwealth In witness whereof the sd Benjamin Harrison Esquire hath hereunto Sett his hand and Caused the lesser Seal of the sd Commonwealth to be affixed at Richmond*, p.872. A.C. of 20 Shill. Sterl.

JOHN PEDAN, 180 acs. by Survey 14 Sep 1779 in Bottetourt Co. on Marshals Ridge and waters of Back cr.; 1 Sep 1780, p.872. A.C. of 20 Shill. Sterl. *including 114 acs. Surveyed for Robert Poage 22 Apr 1775 the property of which is Vested in the sd Pedan.*

JOHN RUNYAN, 98 acs. by Survey 20 Feb 1773 in Rockingham Co. in *Brocks Gap* on both Sides of Tunis's Cr.; 1 Sep 1780, p.873. A.C. of 10 Shill. Sterl.

JAMES GIVENS, 75 acs. by Survey 25 Jun 1769 in Augusta Co. Joining his patent Land, by the Great road, by the fraught, adj. George Crawford; 1 Sep 1780, p.874. A.C. of 10 Shill. Sterl.

MARTIN WETSALL, 33 acs. by Survey 26 Feb 1773 in Augusta Co. in *Wests Gap*, on a Ridge, adj. John Kepteners Land & one Rubles Line; 1 Sep 1780, p.875. A.C. of 5 Shill. Sterl.

JAMES REABURN, 130 acs. by Survey 18 Sep 1753 in Augusta Co. on a br. of Moffetts cr. Joining the Land of Joseph Reaburn and William Mathews, Beginning on a Ridge, near a draught; 1 Sep 1780, p.875. A.C. of 15 Shill. Sterl.

RICHARD KELLO, Gent., 300 acs. by Survey 13 Mar 1753 in Southampton Co. in Nottoway Par. and on the S side of Black water Sw., down the Trough Br., up the Horsebone br.; adj. John Bryants New Survey, Lewis Bryant, Thomas Beel, Richard Kello's old Lines, John Joyner & Joshua Joyner; 28 Dec 1780, p.876. A.C. of 30 Shill. Sterl.

SAMUEL VANCE, 47 acs. by Survey 9 Oct 1772 in Augusta Co. on the west fork of back cr. Joining his other Lands; 1 Sep 1780, p.877. A.C. of 5 Shill. Sterl.

DAVID PERKINS Ass'ee of GEORGE EASTERLY who was Ass'ee of SOLOMON GOOD PASTURE, 70 acs. by Survey 3 Mar 1773 in Rockingham Co. on Tunes's cr. in *Brocks Gap*; 1 Sep 1780, p.878. A.C. of 10 Shill. Sterl.

THOMAS HICKLIN, 85 acs. by Survey 29 Apr 1773 in Augusta Co. Joining the lines of James Bradshaws land on the waters of the Bull pasture, by a Buffalo run, to a fork'd Swamp, crossing Buffaloe run to a double Cherry tree; 1 Sep 1780, p.878. A.C. of 10 Shill. Sterl.

THOMAS BRADSHAW, 25 acs. by Survey 15 Apr 1767 in Augusta Co. on the S side of Moffetts Br., adj. his other L. & Alexander Gardner; 1 Sep 1780, p.879. A.C. of 5 Shill. Sterl.

JOHN HUNTER Ass'ee of PHILIP DAILEY, 150 acs. by Survey 5 Mar 1773 in Rockingham Co. onn the N side of the North fork of Shenandore, on a ridge; adj. his Old C. on the river bank, one Shoemakers Line, Fillinger, Chrisman, John Bear & Dalleys old Line; 1 Sep 1780, p.880. A.C. of 15 Shill. Sterl.

JOHN TANNER, 200 acs. by Survey 21 Feb 1775 in Augusta Co. on the brs. of Cortes run, on a ridge; adj. his own Old Line, Leonard Miller & Panthers Line; 1 Sep 1780, p.880. A.C. of 25 Shill. Sterl. *bounded by the variation of the Magnetic from the true Meridian being 1°E.*

WILLIAM BROWN, 210 acs. by Survey 16 Sep 1779 in Botetourt Co. on Mud Lick run a Br. of Roanoke, in the head of a Hollow, on a draft, on a ridge; 1 Sep 1780, p.881. A.C. of 30 Shill. Sterl. including 150 acs. formerly Surveyed.

JOHN WHITE, 209¾ acs. by Survey 25 May 1774 in Albemarle Co. on both Sides of Phills cr., adj. the L. of the late Philip Thurmond dec'd & Saxton; 1 Sep 1780, p.882. A.C. of 25 Shill. Sterl. [For Thurmond's l. see PB 19 p.677, for Saxton's l. see PB 26 p.570 to Abel Thaxton]

THOMAS GARAWAY, 98 acs. by Survey 13 Nov 1766 in Halifax Co. on the Mayo Riv., Crossing both forks of the sd riv., adj. Carter; 1 Sep 1780, p.883. A.C. of 10 Shill. Sterl.

BENJAMIN HUGHES (as assignee of ASHFORD NAPIERS), 313 acs. by Survey by Survey 26 Mar 1780 in Fluvanna Co. on both sides of Middle fork of Cunninghams cr., adj. William Fitzpatrick & Burnly; 1 Sep 1780,p.884. A.C. of 35 Shill. Sterl.

JOHN JARRETT Ass'ee of AUGUSTINE HACKWORTH who was ass'ee of JOHN NERVARD / NEWARD and JOHN HAYNES, 647 acs. by Survey 12 March 1773 in Bedford Co. on the head Branches of Bore Augurs cr. & Beaverdam Cr., on a large br. of Beaverdam cr., adj. Christian; 1 Sep 1780, p.884. A.C. of £3.S5 Sterl.

THOMAS NAPIER, 272 acs. by Survey 24 Mar 1767 in Albemarle Co. or the head brs. of Woodson's Great cr., on a Ridge, crossing a br. Just above its fork; 1 Sep 1780, p.885. A.C. of 30 Shill. Sterl.

JOHN NAPIER as ass'ee of ARTHUR COOPER, 82 acs. by Survey 26 Apr 1755 in Albemarle Co. on the S side of the Rivanna riv. on the Brs. of Cunninghams cr.; adj. George Hilton, William Creasy & Arthur Hopkins; 1 Sep 1780, p.886. A.C. of 10 Shill. Sterl.

JOHN CARTER LITTLEPAGE as Ass'ee of MARY BIRD & JOHN BYRD executors of the sd WILLIAM BYRD, 1,000 acs. by Survey 24 May 1774 in Jefferson Co. formerly Fincastle *called Mount Byrd* on the Ohio Riv. about 11 Miles below the Mouth of Kentucky in the lower end of the first Bottom and below the two Surveys made in sd Bottom, adj. the Second Survey in sd Bottom, on the top of a Steep Rock, by a draft; 28 Dec 1780, p.887. *in Consideration of Military Service perform'd by the Honourable William Byrd Esquire in the late war between Great Britain and France according to the terms of the King of Great Britains proclamation of 1763.*

JOHN CARTER LITTLEPAGE as ass'ee of MARY BYRD & JOHN BYRD executors of sd WILLIAM BYRD, 1,000 acs. by Survey 23 Jun 1774 in Jefferson Co. formerly Fincastle on the S side the Ohio riv., adj William Fleming & Thomas Bowyer, below Conelly's lower corner; 28 Dec 1780, p.888. *in Consideration of Military Service perform'd by the Honourable William Byrd Esquire in the late war between Great Britain and France according to the terms of the King of Great Britains proclamation of 1763.*

PATRICK NAPIER Ass'ee of JOHN BRUMET, 350 acs. by Survey 13 Mar 1761 in Albemarle Co. [on] the head of Smiths Camp br., crossing a fork of sd br.; 1 Sep 1780, p.888. A.C. of 35 Shill. Sterl.

PATRICK NAPIER, 160 acs. by Survey 14 Dec 1778 in Fluvanna Co. on the brs. of Cunninghams cr. and S Brs. of the Rivanna riv., on a ridge, adj. sd Napier & George Hardwick; 1 Sep 1780, p.889. A.C. of 20 Shill. Sterl.

SAMUEL ALEN, 107 acs. by Survey 18 Nov 1773 in Henry Co. on both sides of the North fork of Jacke's Cr.; 1 Sep 1780, p.890. A.C. of 15 Shill. Sterl.

JOHN MERRITT (As Ass'ee of WILLIAM KITCHEN), 78 acs. by Survey 3 Dec 1767 in Bedford Co. on the brs. of Joshuas cr., crossing Callehans br.; adj. Chenault, Callehan, one Kitchens line & Page; 1 Sep 1780, p.891. A.C. of 10 Shill. Sterl.

WILLIAM STEPHENS, 188 acs. [Pittsylvania Co.?] on the brs. of Home cr., adj. James Roberts & Walton; 1 Sep 1780, p.891. A.C. of £1 Sterl.

[Margin note: *NB this Grant was Altered and made out in the name of Governor Harrison Because Governor Jefferson resigned before the Grant could be signed or sealed tho made out & Recorded first in his Name*]
ROBERT PEREGOY, 291 acs. by Survey 22 Nov 1764 in Henry Co. formerly Halifax on Camp br. of Leathe[r]wood cr., adj. Lomax & Elkin; 1 January 1782 *in the 6th year of the Commonwealth, In witness whereof the sd Benjamin Harrison Governour of the Commonwealth of Virginia hath hereunto Sett his hand and caused the lesser Seal of the sd Commonwealth to be affixed at Richmond*, p.892. A.C. of 30 Shill. Sterl.

JOHN JOHNSON, 227 acs. by Survey 14 May 1779 in Goochland Co. on the waters of the broad br. of Tuckahoe cr.; adj. Paul Childress, Robert Wade, William Rowntree, William Roundtree, Charles Johnson, John Hutchins, John Ford, William Johnson & Drury Wood; 1 Jan 1781 in the 5th year of the Commonwealth, p.893. A.C. of 25 Shill. Sterl. *by the variation of the Magnetic from the true Meridian of 3½°W.* it being Surplus land found in a tract held by the sd John Johnson for 400 acs. [PB 14 p.481 to Charles Johnson dated 28 Sep 1732]

JOHN STARKEY SENR., 166 acs. by Survey 4 Nov 1771 in Bedford Co. on Ellots br. a N br. of Black water riv., adj. George Read; 1 Sep 1780, p.894. A.C. of 20 Shill. Sterl.

HENRY BARNS, 409 acs. by Survey 13 Dec 1771 in Halifax Co. on the draughts of Cherry tree Cr.; adj. Echolis, Tynes, Coleman & Cockerham; 1 Sep 1780, p.894. A.C. of 45 Shill. Sterl.

JOHN ACUFF, 450 acs. by Survey 18 Nov 1779 in Henry Co. on the brs. of Leatherwood; adj. Christopher Bowlings old line, his old Line and Lomax & Co.; 1 Sep 1780, p.895. A.C. of £2.S5 Sterl.

DAVID PARISH, 160 acs. by Survey 20 Apr 1780 in Pittsylvania Co. on the brs. of Sandy cr., in the low grounds; adj. Walker, Elijah King & Henry Terry; 1 Sep 1780, p.896. A.C. of 20 Shill. Sterl.

NATHANIEL COCK, 345 acs. by Survey 18 Feb 1775 in Pittsylvania Co. on the brs. of Stinking riv. and Sycamore; adj. Jones, Talbot & the Farriss line; 1 Sep 1780, p.897. A.C. of 35 Shill. Sterl.

JOHN VIA, 290 acs. by Survey 8 Nov 1768 in Amherst Co.; 1 Sep 1780, p.897. A.C. of 30 Shill. Sterl. This tract of Land lyes on the N brs. of fishing Cr.

WILLIAM WALTON, 400 acs. by Survey 27 Apr 1780 in Charlotte Co. on the said [side] of Cargills cr.; adj. Haskin, Finch & Blanks; 1 Sep 1780, p.898. A.C. of 40 Shill. Sterl.

JOHN GIBSON, 590 acs. by Survey 4 Mar 1774 in Bedford Co. on crooked run a N br. of the North fork of Black water riv., on a road, to a Mahogny tree on a Small br.; adj. Rentfro's Old Line, Isaack Rentfroes c., Mead & Leatherman; 1 Sep 1780, p.899. A.C. of £3 Sterl.

JOHN PEARSEY, 185 acs. by Survey 3 May 1770 in Bedford Co. on the S brs. of Goose cr., adj. Buford & Smith; 1 Sep 1780, p.900. A.C. of 20 Shill. Sterl.

JAMES LINSEY, 220 acs. by Survey 25 May 1777 in Bedford Co. on the E brs. of Senecca cr.; adj. Murray, Helms, Eldridge & Ornsbey; 1 Sep 1780, p.900. A.C. of 25 Shill. Sterl.

GEORGE RODGERS / ROGERS, 225 acs. by Survey 13 Oct 1769 in Henry Co. on the Brs. of Russells Cr., adj. David Rodgers & George Carter; 1 Feb 1781, p.901. A.C. of 25 Shill. Sterl.

JOHN FUSON, 235 acs. by Survey 4 May 1779 in Henry Co. on the North fork of Story Cr., adj. John Fuson & James Smith; 1 Feb 1781, p.902. A.C. of 25 Shill. Sterl.

GEORGE HARDY, 226 acs. by Survey 28 Mar 1774 in Pittsylvania Co. on the Brs. of Sandy Cr.; adj. Ben Terry, Joseph Terry, Lazarus Dodson, Thomas Terry & James Terry; 1 Feb 1781, p.903. A.C. of £1.S5 Sterl.

DANIEL COLLINS, 334 acs. by Survey 18 Feb 1777 in Pittsylvania Co. on the head brs. of Reedys Cr., Crossing Jonekin Cr., adj. David Ross & Ephraim Welcher; 1 Feb 1781, p.904. A.C. of 35 Shill. Sterl.

LUKE FOLEY, 176 acs. by Survey 18 Nov 1768 in Henry Co. Formerly Pittsylvania on the Waters of Great Sycamore Cr., Crossing a bold Br., on the Spur of a Mountain; 1 Feb 1781, p.906. A.C. of £1 Sterl.

LUKE FOLEY, 346 acs. by Survey 23 Nov 1768 in Henry Co. Formerly Pittsylvania on the Waters of Gobbling town Cr., adj. Adams's Order Line; 1 Feb 1781, p.907. A.C. of 35 Shill. Sterl.

JOHN HENDRICK, 231 acs. by Survey 13 Jan 1773 in Pittsylvania Co. on the draughts of Allens Cr. and Stinking riv., on Heickeys Road; adj. Jacob Faris, Joseph Fariss, Smith & Roberts; 1 Feb 1781, p.908. A.C. of 25 Shill. Sterl.

WILLIAM WITCHER / WETCHER, 144 acs. by Survey 1 Feb 1769 in Pittsylvania Co. on the N Brs. of Pigg riv.; adj. Simmon's L., David Polley, his old C. & William Adkins old Line; 1 Feb 1781, p.909. A.C. of 15 Shill. Sterl.

JACOB CHANCY, 234 acs. by Survey 3 Mar 1780 in Pittsylvania Co. on the Brs. of Birches Cr.; adj. sd Chancy, Terrys Order Line, Samuel Slate & Kerby; 1 Feb 1781, p.910. A.C. of 25 Shill. Sterl.

THOMAS WALTHERS, 181 acs. by Survey 29 Feb 1780 in Pittsylvania Co. on the brs. of the Double Creeks; adj. Daniel Slaton, William King, Weatherpoons order Line & Hughes Line; 1 Feb 1781, p.911. A.C. of £1 Sterl.

JOSEPH TERRY SENR., 420 acs. by Survey 10 Mar 1780 in Pittsylvania Co. on the Brs. of Sandy and Birches Creeks; adj. sd Terrys Order Line, Henrys Order

Line, Ingrams Line & Lazarus Dodson; 1 Feb 1781, p.912. A.C. of £2.S5 Sterl.

THOMAS ALSUP, 292 acs. by Surey 20 Nov 1768 in Pittsylvania Co. on the Brs. of Sandy Cr., on the Main road; adj. Thomas Callaway, James Cox & his old Line; 1 Feb 1781, p.914. A.C. of 30 Shill. Sterl.

JOHN BALLINGER, 414 acs. by Survey 2 Feb 1774 in Pittsylvania Co. on the Camp Cr. of Straight Stone Cr., adj. Collings & Dauthetey; 1 Feb 1781, p.915. A.C. of 45 Shill. Sterl.

JOSEPH CUNNINGHAM, 362 acs. by Survey 30 Mar 1770 in Pittsylvania Co. on the Waters of Sandy Riv., adj. sd Cunningham & Lumkins; 1 Feb 1781, p.916. A.C. of 40 Shill. Sterl.

JOSEPH MOTLEY, 346 acs. by Survey 5 Mar 1779 in Pittsylvania Co. on the S Brs. of Banister Riv. and on both sides of Shocko Cr., adj. John Markham & Claybrook; 1 Feb 1781, p.917. A.C. of 35 Shill. Sterl.

ENOCK JAMES, 356 acs. by Survey 2 Apr 1774 in Pittsylvania Co. on the brs. of Burches Cr., Crossing a Br. and a road; adj. William Walthers, Thomas Walthers & Robert Walthers; 1 Feb 1781, p.919. A.C. of 40 Shill. Sterl.

FRANCIS BENNITT, 410 acs. by Survey 21 Mar 1780 in Pittsylvania Co. on the Brs. of the old Womans Cr. and the head of the lower three Island Cr., Crossing the head of hemp Br., Crossing a bold Br., adj. Glasscock; 1 Feb 1781, p.920. A.C. of 45 Shill. Sterl.

WILLIAM BENNITT, 318 acs. by Survey 21 Mar 1780 in Pittsylvania Co. on the Brs. of Stanton Riv.; adj. sd Bennitts old Line, William Ward & Glasscock; 1 Feb 1781, p.921. A.C. of 35 Shill. Sterl.

EDWARD SPARKS, 569 acs. by Survey 6 Mar 1771 in Pittsylvania Co. on Rutledges Cr., adj. Bynum & Yeates Lines; 1 Feb 1781, p.923. A.C. of £3 Sterl.

CHARLES SMITH, 202 acs. by Survey 14 Mar 1774 in Pr. Edward Co. on the Brs. of Vaughans and Harris's Creek; adj. sd Smiths own lines, Joel Elam, Lockett, Alexander Guill, Fulton, & Jane Daniel; 1 Feb 1781, p.924. A.C. of £1 Sterl.

JOHN HARVIE & GEORGE NICKS, 489 acs. by Survey 28 Dec 1755 in Lunenburg Co. on both Sides of Cub Cr., adj. Thomas Christian & their own Line; 1 Feb 1781, p.925. A.C. of 50 Shill. Sterl.

THOMAS HOUSE, 400 acs. by Survey 13 Apr 1754 in Brunswick Co.; 1 Feb 1781, p.927. A.C. of 40 Shill. Sterl.

THOMAS HOUSE, 196 acs. by Survey 7 Mar 1773 in Brunswick Co., adj. Mason & sd House's old Line; 1 Feb 1781, pp.928-929 in the *5th year of the Commonwealth, Thomas Jefferson Esquire Governor.* A.C. of £1 Sterl.

End of Commonwealth Grant Book E

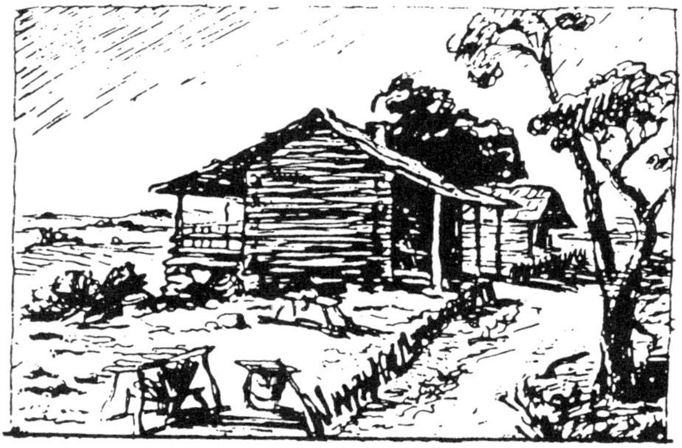

GRANT BOOK F

10 April 1781 to 1 June 1782

HENRY SMITH, 207 acs. by Survey 28 Apr 1780 in Henry Co. on the N brs. of Russels cr., Crossing a large br.; adj. Lyon, Shelton; 10 Apr 1781, *Thomas Jefferson Governor of the Commonwealth of Virginia, in the fifth year of the Commonwealth*; p.1. in Consideration of the Ancient Composition of 25 Shill. Sterl.

JOSHUA STONE, 300 acs. Pittsylvania Co. on both Sides of Milk cr., Crossing Mill cr., adj. William Tucker & William Payne; 10 Apr 1781, p.2. in Consideration of the sum of £1,600 Current Money paid by Joshua Stone unto Abraham Shelton Escheator for Pittsylvania Co.; being part of 595 acs. *late the property of John Smith Murdock and Comps. British Subjects and sold by the sd Abraham Shelton Escheator unto the sd Joshua Stone Agreeable to two Acts of Assembly passed in the year 1779 the one Intitled an Act Concerning Escheats and forefeitures from British Subjects the Other Intitled an Act Concerning Escheators.*

THOMAS STEWART/STUART Ass'ee of JAMES STEWART who was Ass'ee of CORNELIUS DOGHERTY who was Ass'ee of of ROBERT CAMPBELL, 100 acs. by Survey 3 Oct 1770 in Botetourt Co. on a br. of Carrs cr. the waters of James Riv., on the top of a ridge, on the bank of a run; 10 Apr 1781, p.3. A.C. of 10 Shill. Sterl.

SAMUEL SEEGAR of the State of North Carolina Ass'ee of CHARLES TALBOT, 850 acs. in three Entries by Survey 8 Apr 1779 in Bedford Co. including the head of Little Whipping cr. and heads of other E brs. of Whipping cr., Beginning in Watkins road, up Miry br.; adj. Dougherty, John Hall, George Jones & Talbot; 10 Apr 1781, p.5. A.C. of £4.S5 Sterl.

PHILLIP SILER Ass'ee of ALEXANDER WALKER, 70 acs. by

Survey 21 May 1769 in Augusta Co. upon Broad cr. in the forks of James Riv., adj. a tract of L. belonging to sd Walker & the Old Survey; 10 Apr 1781, p.6. A.C. of 10 Shill. Sterl.

ELIPHAZ SHELTON, 365 acs. by Survey 29 Apr 1780 in Henry Co. on the waters of Mayo Riv., on the Main Mountain; 10 Apr 1781, p.7. A.C. of £2 Sterl.

JOHN HANDCOCK, 136 acs. by Survey 23 Mar 1780 in Fluvanna Co. on the brs. of the South fork of Cunningham cr.; adj. Benjamin Fitzpatrick, Scott, Ross, Napier & Cockrin; 1 Mar 1781, p.8. A.C. of 15 Shill. Sterl.

STEPHEN SEAY, 334 acs. by Survey 15 Nov 1774 in Albemarle Co. on the Brs. of Great and little Bremore creeks, to the Secretarys old rolling road on the Mountain hill, Crossing the Secretary road; adj. William Williams, John Alloway, the sd Stephen Seays old Patent line & the sd Stephen Seays corner on a Cove; 1 Mar 1781, p.9. A.C. of 35 Shill. Sterl.

WILLIAM OLIVER, 400 acs. by Survey 20 Nov 1780 in Halifax Co. on the draughts of Childry cr., down little Childry, Crossing Bookers; adj. John Malicole formerly Charles Bosticks, Scater, Selcocke, Polley, Hill, Cruse, Handcock, Hunt, Yuille & Oliver; 10 Apr 1781, p.11. A.C. of £2. Sterl.

MICAJAH TERRELL, 366 acs. by Survey 17 May 1769 in Amherst Co. on the N side and Joining the Fluvanna riv. on both Sides of Bollings cr., Crossing the South fork of Bollings cr., on the bank of the North fork of Bollings Cr.; adj. Henry Harper, Bolling, Daniel Burford & his own lines; 10 Apr 1781, p.13. A.C. of £2 Sterl.

ROBERT STUART Ass'ee of JAMES STUART who was Ass'ee of PETER ANGLEY or OLNGLEY, 60 acs. by Survey 1 Apr 1773 in Augusta Co. on the south Mountain on the waters of Mary cr. a br. of James riv., Beginning in a draft, Crossing a Spurr; 10 Apr 1781, p.15. A.C. 10 Shill.

JAMES TOWNSLY/TOWNSLEY, 140 acs. by Survey bearing date 26 Aug 1779 in Botetourt Co. on the N and S brs. of Back Cr. a br. of James Riv., Crossing the south fork, on a Spurr, on a ridge; adj. Ward & Neelly; near Simpsons line; 10 Apr 1781, p.16. A.C. of 15 Shill. Sterl. *140a acs. being part of 182 acs. Surveyed for James Leatherdale Senr. the property of which is Vested in the sd Townsley.*

BARNETT LANCE, 98 acs. by Survey 13 Apr 1774 in Augusta Co. on the Middle fork of Crab Apple waters, Beginning on a ridge on the E side of the Br. above a Lick; 10 Apr 1781, p.17. A.C. of 10 Shill. Sterl.

ARMAGER LILLY, 400 acs. by Survey 24 Nov 1779 in Fluvanna Co. at the head of a drain, down the Bird cr.; 10 Apr 1781, p.19. £737 Currant Money paid unto Thomas Napier for Fluvanna Co. *lately the property of Lewis B. Martin Esq. a Subject of Great Britain and Sold by the sd Thomas Napier Escheater unto the sd Armager Lilly Agreable to two Acts of Assembly passed in the year 1779 the one Intitled an Act Concerning Escheats and forefeitures from British*

Subjects the other Intitled an Act Concerning Escheators.

JAMES LYON, 153 acs. by Survey 6 Mar 1780 in Henry Co. on the waters of Russells cr.; adj. Parr, Patitiah Shelton [his line], Walton, & Walton otherwise Lyons line; 20 Apr 1781, p.20. A.C. 15 Shill. Sterl.

JAMES LYON, 300 acs. by Survey 27 Apr 1780 in Henry Co. on both sides of Mathews cr.; adj. his [own] line, Shelton, Bartin & Fletcher; 20 Apr 1781, p.22. A.C. of 30 Shill. Sterl.

BERNARD FINCH, 350 acs. by Survey 21 Feb 1780 in Bedford Co. on both sides of the Lawyers road including heads of Brs. of Mollys cr. and Bear cr.; adj. Samuel Hubbard, John Farris, William Read, William Harris, James Campbell & Daniel; 10 Apr 1781, p.23. A.C. of 35 Shill. Sterl.

JOHN FARRISS/FARISS, 342 acs. by Survey 21 Feb 1779 in Bedford Co. on both sides of Moslys [Mollys] Cr., crossing flaggy br., up Molleys cr. aforesaid & through a Bent; adj. Richard Stith, the Patent lines & Smithers lines; 10 Apr 1781, p.25. A.C. of 35 Shill. Sterl. *270 acs. of which being part of a tract of 320 acs. first Gtd. by Pat. to Richard Stith and by Several Conveyances became the Property of sd John Farriss the Residue 72 acs. not Granted before.*

THOMAS KINKEAD Ass'ee of JOHN ANDERSON who was Ass'ee of WILLIAM GREENLEE, 160 acs. by Survey 9 Jun 1771 in Botetourt Co. Joining the lines of Hugh Berkleys l. in the fork of James riv., Crossing a run to near Cedar Bridge, on the top of a hill by a road, on the top of a high hill above Cedar cr., along a ridge, adj. sd Berklys l.; 10 Apr 1781, p.26. A.C. of £1 Sterl.

JOSEPH ANTHONY, 372 acs. Henry Co. formerly Pittsylvania on the Brs. of Marrow bone cr.; adj. Meredith, Taylor, Burns line, Randolph & Webb; 10 Apr 1781, p.28. in Consideration of the sum of £101 Current money paid unto Abraham Penn Escheator for Henry Co. *late the Property of James Smith a Subject of Great Britain and Sold by the sd Abraham Penn Escheator unto sd Joseph Anthony Agreable to two Acts of Assembly passed in 1779 the one Intitled an Act Concerning Escheats and forfertures from British Subjects the other Intitled an Act Concerning Escheators.*

AARON HIGGINBOTHAM, 54 acs. by Survey 13 Dec 1770 in Amherst Co. on both sides of Thrashers cr., adj. Henry Trent & his own line; 10 Apr 1781, p.30. A.C. of 5 Shill. Sterl.

SAMUEL BUCKLEY, 400 acs. in Henry Co. formerly Pittsylvania on the brs. of Marrow bone cr.; adj. Conway, Meredith & Webb; 10 Apr 1781, p.31. in Consideration of the sum of £1,080 Current Money paid unto Abraham Penn Escheator for Henry Co. *late the property of James Smith a Subject of Great Britain and sold by sd Abraham Penn Escheator Unto sd Samuel Buckley Agreable to two Acts of Assembly passed in 1779 the one Intitled an Act Concerning Escheats and forefeitures from British Subjects the other Intitled an Act Concerning Escheators.*

JOHN DICKERSON, 1,063 acs. Henry Co. on Leatherwood cr.; adj. Daniel

Hankins, Lomax and Com., Hawkins, Twinlly, his own line, Wills line, Samuel Johnston & Burches c.; 10 Apr 1781, p.33. A.C. £5.S10 Sterl.

DAVID DALTON, 57¼ acs. by Survey 9 Aug 1780 in Albemarle Co. on the N Side the North fork of the Rivanna Riv.; adj. John Dowell, William Herrin, Isaac Croswate & Croswaters line; 10 Apr 1781, p.35. A.C. 10 Shill. Sterl.

JAMES DICKERSON/DICKENSON, 361 acs. by Survey 11 Mar 1780 in Henry Co. on Spoon cr. Waters, on a Bald Nobb, Crossing the said Road; adj. his own lines, William Poor, William Wilson, Frazer, sd Dickensons line & Grisham; 10 Apr 1781, p.37. A.C. of £2 Sterl.

REUBEN DANIEL, 282 acs. in Pittsylvania Co. on Ralphs br. of Leatherwood cr., adj. Randolphs Order line; 10 Apr 1781, p.38. in Consideration of the sum of £236 Currant money paid unto Abraham Penn Escheator for Pittsylvania Co. *lately the property of James Smith a Subject of Great Britain and Sold by the sd Abraham Penn Escheator unto sd Reuben Daniel Agreable to two Acts of Assembly passed in 1779 the one Intitled an Act Concerning Escheats and Forfertures from British Subjects and the other Intitled an Act Concerning Escheators.*

AUGUSTINE BROUNE or BROWNE, 680 acs. by Survey 17 Apr 1780 in Henry Co. on the Waters of Peters cr.; adj. Smith, George Rogers & Carter; 10 Apr 1781, p.40. A.C. of £3.S10 Sterl.

PHILLIP BERRICK, BORRICK / BARRICK, 280 acs. by Survey 28 Feb 1780 in Augusta Co. on the W Side of the falling springs between the lands of John Poage and Lewis Mowra, on the side of a ridge; 10 Apr 1781, p.42. A.C. of 30 Shill. Sterl.

BANISTER HARPER, 102¼ acs. by Survey 24 Oct 1780 in Halifax Co. on the drafts of Tobys cr., Crossing a pair of Race paths; adj. his lines, Wall, Waddill & Lawson; 10 Apr 1781, p.43. A.C. of 10 Shill. Sterl.

JOHN HENDERSON JUNIOR, 200 acs. by Survey 12 Nov 1776 in Albemarle Co. on the S side the Rivanna Riv. and on the Brs. of Buck Island cr.; adj. John Henderson Senior, Thomas Priddy & William Rynolds line; 10 Apr 1781, p.44. A.C. of £1 Sterl.

STEPHEN HEARD, 106 acs. by Survey 13 Jan 1781 in Henry Co. on the brs. of Poplar Camp cr., adj. Heards own old line & Jesse Heard; 10 Apr 1781, p.46. A.C. of 15 Shill. Sterl.

JOHN HIND, 250 acs. by Survey 26 Sep 1780 in Augusta Co. adj. his, Michael Dickey, James Henderson and Casper Millers land; near Grattons line, near a great Road, on a ridge; 10 Apr 1781, p.47. A.C. of 25 Shill. Sterl.

DANIEL HANKINS, 316 acs. by Survey 28 Mar 1780 in Henry Co. on the waters of Turkey cock cr.; adj. William Hankins, Twitty & Twittys Order line; 10 Apr 1781, p.49. A.C. of 35 Shill. Sterl.

STEPHEN HEARD, 303 acs. by Survey 20 Jan 1781 in Henry Co. on the Brs. of Black Water Riv., adj. Blankinship & Lumsden; 10 Apr 1781, p.50. A.C. of 30 Shill. Sterl.

THOMAS HEARD, 100 acs. by Survey 16 Jan 1781 in Henry Co. on both Sides of Jacks cr., Crossing a large br., adj. his old Line; 10 Apr 1781, p.51. A.C. of 10 Shill. Sterl.

JAMES HARRIS, 40 acs. by Survey 26 Mar 1773 in Albemarle Co. on the foot of the Pastures fence Mountain on a br. of McWilliams cr., crossing a small br.; adj. Benjamin Brown, the sd James Harris & John Price; 10 Apr 1781, p.53. A.C. of 5 Shill. Sterl.

MOSES RUNNOLDS, 157 acs. by Survey 15 Apr 1780 in Henry Co. on the Nobusiness fork of Mayo Riv., adj. John Cameron & Cogars old line; 10 Apr 1781, p.54. A.C. of £1 Sterl.

JAMES HICKMAN Representative of THOMAS HICKMAN, 2,000 acs. by Survey 18 Jul 1775 in Fincastle Co. on the Brs. of Boons cr. which Runs into Kentucky About 4 Miles below Boons borough, Crossing a Small cr.; 10 Apr 1781, p.56. in Consideration of Military Service performed by Thomas Hicksman Granted unto James Hickman Representative of sd Thomas Hickman by Virtue of Lord Dunmores Warrant and Agreable to the King of Great Britains proclamation of 1763.

REUBEN HARRISON, 198 acs. by Survey 15 Apr 1780 in Rockingham Co. on the SW side of the big Spring a br. of Smiths cr. between Several tracts of his land, on his old Patent line, near a line of Bayes land; 1 Mar 1781, p.57. A.C. of £1 Sterl.

JOHN ACUFF, 176 acs. Pittsylvania Co. on the brs. of Leatherwood cr., in the Road, adj. Rowland; 10 Apr 1781, p.59. in Consideration of the sum of [£126] Current Money paid unto Abraham Penn Escheator for Pittsylvania Co. being *lately the property of James Smith a Subject of Great Britain and Sold by the sd Abraham Penn unto sd John Acuff Agreable to two Acts of General Assembly pass in 1779 the one Intitled an Act Concerning Escheats and forefeitures from British Subject and the other Intitled an Act Concerning Escheators.*

RICHARD BENNET / BENNETT, 225 acs. in Fluvanna Co. on the bank of a cr.; 10 Apr 1781, p.60. in Consideration of the sum of £356 Current Money paid unto Thomas Napier Escheator for Fluvanna Co. ... *late the property of Robert Payne a Subject of Great Britain and sold by the sd Thomas Napier Escheator unto the Aforesd Richard Bennett Agreable to two Acts of General Assembly passed in 1779 the one Intitled an Act Concerning Escheats and forefeitures from British Subjects and the other Intitled an Act Concerning Escheators.*

JOHN WILLS, 297 acs. by Survey 3 Apr 1780 in Henry Co. on the S brs. of Leatherwood cr., down a South fork of sd cr.; adj. Lomax and Co., Jacob Regin, William Brown & Heihres or Hichres line; 10 Apr 1781, p.62. A.C. of 30 Shill. Sterl.

JOHN POAGE, 107 acs. by Survey 26 Jun 1780 in Augusta Co. on black Thorn br. of the South br. of Powtomack Joining Swadleys Meadow Survey, on the bank of the Thorn, adj. sd Swadley; 10 Apr 1781, p.63. A.C. of 15 Shill. Sterl.

JOHN PARR JUNR., 241 acs. by Survey 20 Apr 1780 in Henry Co. on Russells cr., adj. his own & Azariah Shelton his line Otherwise Wilsons; 10 Apr 1781, p.65. A.C. of 25 Shill. Sterl.

JOHN PARR SENR., 374 acs. by Survey 6 Mar 1780 in Henry Co. on the N brs. of South Mayo Riv., adj. his old line & his New line; 10 Apr 1781, p.67.A.C. of £2 Sterl.

WILLIAM POOR, 391 acs. by Survey 11 Mar 1780 in Henry Co. on the Waters of Spoon cr., Cross a Road, adj. John Grisham & John Parr; 10 Apr 1781, p.68. A.C. of £2 Sterl.

JOSIAH WOOD Ass'ee of JOHN MARTIN, 127 acs. by Survey 20 Mar 1780 in Amherst Co. on the S brs. of Davisons cr.; adj. his own lines, Josiah Wood & Luke Rennion; 10 Apr 1781, p.69. A.C. of 15 Shill. Sterl.

PETER RANDOLPH Esq., a Certain lott or one Acre in Dinwiddie Co. in the new town of Peters burgh and Numbered in the plann of sd town Number 27 on the N side of the street adjoining Daniel Dodson and Others; 10 Apr 1781, p.71. in Consideration of the Sum of £12,500 paid unto Kennon Jones Escheator for Dinwiddie Co. *late the property of Joseph Elam a Subject of Great Britain and Sold by the sd Kennon Jones Escheator unto the sd Peter Randolph Agreable to two Acts of General Assembly passed in 1779 the one Intitled an Act Concerning Escheats and forefeitures from British Subjects the Other Intitled an Act Concerning Escheators.*

JOHN GRISHAM, 344 acs. by Survey 11 Mar 1780 in Henry Co. on the Brs. of Spoon cr., in a bottom; adj. his own line, John Parr & John Marr; 10 Apr 1781, p.72. A.C. of 35 Shill. Sterl.

JOHN & CHARLES CHRISTIAN, 300 acs. by Survey 3 May 1780 in Amherst Co. in the south hundred on the Brs. of Baree br. and the Brs. of fishing cr.; adj. George Hilton, William Horseley, John Jeslin, Elizabeth Evans [his line?], John Via & Reuben Tyra; 10 Apr 1781, p.74. A.C. of 30 Shill. Sterl. *Entered by Richard Fletcher Gregory 3 Sep 1768 now the property of the sd John & Charles Christian.*

HENRY PAWLING / PAWLINGS, 1,500 acs. by Survey 19 Mar 1779 in Botetourt Co. on the head waters of Glade cr. a br. of Roanoke, on the Great Road, on a ridge, by a dry Run, in a draft, Along the side of the Mountain, near the Spur of the Mountain; 10 Apr 1781, p.76. A.C. of £5 Sterl. *including three tracts of Patented land and a Survey of 700 acs. one of sd tracts Containing 179 acs. Another tract 141 acs. and the third of 213 acs. formerly Gtd. to Israel Christian and by him Conveyed to the sd Paulings the Residue 265 acs. Never Gtd. before.*

JOHN CHILES, 150 acs. by Survey 15 Mar 1750 in Albemarle Co. joining the N side of Appomatox Riv., cross a br. of Chiles road, adj. Henry Chiles; 10 Apr 1781, p.79. A.C. of 15 Shill. Sterl.

JAMES DUDLEY ROBERTS, 269 acs. by Survey 10 Feb 1769 in Pittsylvania Co. on the waters of Read cr. and Beaver cr.; adj. Col. Gordon, Walker, & Coplands Order line; 10 Apr 1781, p.80. A.C. of 30 Shill. Sterl.

JAMES ROBERTS, 335 acs. by Survey 9 Apr 1768 in Pittsylvania Co. on Sandy

Riv., adj. William Roberts & John Rizwell or Bizwell; 10 Apr 1781, p.81. A.C. of 35 Shill. Sterl.

JAMES ROBERTS, 162 acs. by Survey 19 Nov 1778 in Pittsylvania Co. on both Sides of Callaways Mill cr., Crossing Rocky fork; adj. Nash, & Samuel Moseley; 10 Apr 1781, p.83. A.C. of £1 Sterl.

DAVID ROSS, 3,160 acs. by an inclusive Survey bearing date 24 Mar 1780 in Pittsylvania Co. on the Brs. of Stanton and Pigg Rivers, crossing three bold Brs., on the side of Smiths Mountain, on the head of a br. of Ceder cr.; adj. his old lines, Austin, John Goad, John Smith, Bond, & William Lawson; 10 Apr 1781, p.84. A.C. of £17 Sterl. *257 acs. of which was Surveyed for John Smith, 216 acs. Surveyed for John Good, 240 acs. of Patent land Surveyed for John Good junr. and 2,447 acs. of the whole of which Surveys and new land is became the property of the sd Ross.*

JOHN BYRUM GOTHARD, 343½ acs. by Survey made 23 Mar 1780 in Buckingham Co. on the Brs. of Davids and Bent creeks, adj. Thomas Wright & William Young; 10 Apr 1781, p.87. A.C. of 35 Shill. Sterl. paid by John Byrum [Gothard].

BARNETT / BARNET LANCE, 395 acs. by Survey 12 Apr 1774 in Augusta Co. on the Middle fork of Crab Apple waters; adj. William Cunningham, Jacob Tross & sd Lances old line; 10 Apr 1781, p.88. A.C. of 40 Shill. Sterl.

ARCHIBALD HOPKINS, 128 acs. by Survey 21 Mar 1780 in Rockingham Co. on the E side of Muddy cr., Beginning near the cr. and near a line of Shanklins land in a line of his Patent land; 1 Feb 1781, p.90. A.C. of 15 Shill. Sterl.

JULIUS HATCHER, 668 acs. by Survey 10 Apr 1779 in Bedford Co. on Austin and Harricane creeks; adj. Jackson, the Patent lines, Campbell, Holt & Termon; 10 Apr 1781, p.91. A.C. of £3.S10 Sterl.

PETER HERMAN, 70 acs. by Survey 7 Feb 1781, in Bedford Co. on the North fork of Otter Riv., on the Road; adj. his lines, Banister & [Fuqua]; 10 Apr 1781, p.93. A.C. of 10 Shill. Sterl.

SAMUEL HIGGINBOTHAM, 140 acs. by Survey 3 May 1773 in Amherst Co. on the S brs. of the North fork of Buffaloe riv. and on the side of the bold Mountain; 10 Apr 1781, p.95. A.C. of 15 Shill. Sterl.

STEPHEN HEARD, 293 acs. by Survey 19 Jan 1781 in Henry Co. on Poplar camp cr. and foul Ground br., adj. his own old line; 10 Apr 1781, p.97. A.C. of 30 Shill. Sterl.

AARON HIGGINBOTHAM, 200 acs. by Survey 9 Mar 1780 in Amherst Co. on the S side and Joining the North fork of Buffaloe Riv., adj. Phillips Walker; 10 Apr 1781, p.98. A.C. of £1 Sterl.

SHADRACK HARRIMAN, 232 acs. by Survey 20 Aug 1773 in Botetourt Co. on both sides of Jacksons Riv., near a path, on a Steep hill, adj. Zophen Carpenters 90 Acre tract & 50 Acre tract; 10 Apr 1781, p.100. A.C. of 25 Shill. Sterl. *56 acs. of which being part of two Surveys made for Zophen Carpenter one Containing 90 acs. Surveyed 25 Oct 1770 the other of 50 acs. also 35 acs. Surveyed for Thomas Kelly 7 Nov 1766 also 53 acs. surveyed for Zophen Carpenter 4 Nov 1772 and a part of 60 acs. Surveyed for Michael Kelly 4 Sep 1772 the property of all which is now Vested in the sd Harremon.*

JEREMIAH MURDEN, 991 acs. by an **inclusive Survey** bearing date 16 Nov 1772 in Norfolk Co. Saint Brides parish, on the W side of the Old Main road; adj. sd Minden, Isaiah Nicholas, John Murden, William Butts, Joshua Hopkins, Samuel Wiles & William Etherege; 10 Apr 1781, p.103. A.C. of 30 Shill. Sterl. *498 acs. of which was Gtd. to John Minden or Murden by Pat. 30 Oct 1686 [PB 7 p.532 between the S & E branches of Elizabeth River which includes 250 acs. gtd. to Warren Godfrey & Isaac Barrington dated 23 Oct 1673] also 204 acs. Gtd. to Warren Godfrey and Isaac Barrenten by pat. 23 Oct 1673 [PB 6 p.471] the Residue 289½ acs. never before Gtd. the right of the whole being now Vested in the sd Murden.*

DANIEL HANKINS, 1,224 acs. by an Inclusive Survey bearing date 30 Sep 1772 in Pittsyl. Co. on the waters of the South fork of Sandy Riv.; adj. Joseph Austin, Martain, John Baker, Graham, John Hankins, Pidder, Fritter, Hankins old Line & Morton; 10 Apr 1781, p.106. A.C. of 30 Shill. Sterl. *436 acs. of which was Surveyed 21 Feb 1769 for William Graham also 526 acs. Surveyed 11 Apr 1770 for sd Hankins the Residue 262 acs. of new land never Gtd. before the whole being now Vested in sd Daniel Hankins.*

HENRY GAMBRELL, 738 acs. by an inclusive Survey bearing date 5 Feb 1777 in Louisa Co. in Trinity Parish, down the Road; adj. B. Smith, Ambler, Windston, the Glebe land, Barrett, Powers line now Thompsons, Davet, & Thomas Ballard Smith; 10 Apr 1781. p.109. A.C. of 55 Shill. Sterl. *207 acs. of which was Ptd. land the Residue 531 acs. of Surplus land never Gtd. before.*

JOHN HOGSHEAD JUNR., 257 acs. by Survey 5 Apr 1755 in Augusta Co. on both Sides of Bradshaws cr.; adj. his old Lines, William McEamey & David Hogshead; 10 Apr 1781, p.111. A.C. of 5 Shill. Sterl. *45 acs. of which being part of a tract of 400 acs. Gtd. to James Hogshead by Pat. 1 Jun 1746 and Also 172 acs. part of a tract of 285 acs. Gtd. to David Hogshead by pat. 16 Jun 1744 the Remainder 40 acs. Never Gtd. before the property of all which being now Vested in the sd John Hogshead Senr.*

SPENCER SHELTON, 235 acs. in Pittsylvania Co. on both Sides Mill cr., Along the old line; adj. Lightfoot, Thomas Payne & William Tucker; 10 Apr 1781 *in the 5th year of the Commonwealth, Thomas Jefferson Governor of the Commonwealth of Virginia hath hereunto Set his hand and Caused the Lesser Seal of the said Commonwealth to be Affixed at Richmond*, pp.113-115. in Consideration of the sum of £1,725 paid unto Abraham Shelton Escheater for Pittsylvania Co. *late the property of John Smith Murdock and Company Subjects of Great Britain and Sold by the sd Abraham Shelton Escheater unto the sd Spencer Shelton agreable to two Acts of General Assembly passed in 1779 the one Intitled an Act Concerning Escheats and forefeitures from British Subjects the Other Intitled an Act Concerning Escheators.*

REUBEN COUTTS, 45 acs. by Survey 5 May 1779 in Henrico Co., Beginning at a Stake on Shocoe cr. at High water Mark, crossing a Gutt of the River, to a Stake at the Corner of the stone dam, to an elm Stake on a Barr of Sand, to a Stake on the Sandy Barr, opposite Nappers Rock; 1 Jun 1782 *in the 6th year of the Commonwealth, Benjamin Harrison Governor of the Commonwealth of Virginia hath hereunto Set his hand and Caused the Lesser Seal of the said Commonwealth to be Affixed at Richmond*, p.116. A.C. of 5 Shill. Sterl.

ABRAHAM EKERT, 150 acs. by Survey 25 Jul 1780 in Augusta Co. on the SE Side of the south fork of the south br. of Powtomack joining George Possenberrys land, to fulls corner, also adj. Henry Pickle, by a path; 1 Jun 1782, p.118. A.C. of 15 Shill. Sterl.

WILLIAM McCLANACHAN, 85 acs. by Survey 8 Mar 1780 in Botetourt Co. on the waters of James Riv., on a ridge, in a hollow, Near a Spring, adj. William Preston & David McClanahan; 1 Jun 1782, p.119. A.C. of 10 Shill. Sterl.

PHILIP EKERT, 58 acs. by Survey 27 Jun 1780 in Augusta Co. on the South fork of the South br. of Powtomack on the NW side of his other land; 1 Jun 1782, p.121. A.C. of 10 Shill. Sterl.

JOSEPH ECHOLES, 406 acs. by Survey 2 Apr 1757 in Halifax Co. on the North fork of Bull cr., adj. Stephen Below; 1 Jun 1782, p.123. A.C. of 45 Shill. Sterl.

JOHN BOOKERHOY, 253 acs. by Survey 16 May 1780 in Henry Co. on the waters of Jennings cr.; 1 Jun 1782, p.124. A.C. 25 Shill. Sterl.

NICHOLAS SYBERT, 294 acs. by Survey 23 Feb 1781 in Augusta Co. on head of Straight cr. a br. of the south br. of Powtomack, adj. Samuel Black; 1 Jun 1782, p.125. A.C. of 30 Shill. Sterl.

GEORGE WALTON, 550 acs. by Survey 20 Apr 1752 in Lunenburg Co. on the S side of Otter Riv., on Orricks cr., down Mosse Run; adj. Womack, Perry & Stoner; 1 Jun 1782, p.127. A.C. of £4 Sterl.

JOHN STRANGE Ass'ee of WILLIAM HARRIS, 346 acs. by Survey 12 Apr 1765 in Bedford Co. on the S side of the South fork of Falling Riv.; adj. his own lines, Bell, & John Wood; 1 Jun 1782, p.129. A.C. of 35 Shill. Sterl. [For his own lines, see PB 33 p.488 to Jacob Earnest]

WILLIAM MEAD & ISHAM TALBOT, 225 acs. by Survey 11 Dec 1767 in Bedford Co. on both sides of Beaverdam cr., adj. Walton; 1 Jun 1782, p.130. A.C. of 25 Shill. Sterl.

JOSEPH ECKHOLS Ass'ee of the Coheirs of JOSEPH WILLIAM Decd., 377 acs. by Survey 1 Mar 1775 in Bedford Co. on the N side of Stantoun Riv., over a large br.; adj. Murray, & Moza Hart; 1 Jun 1782, p.132. A.C. of £2 Sterl.

JOHN DIGGS Ass'ee of DAVID DUNNOHO, 29 acs. by Survey 23 Mar 1771 in Amherst Co. on the S brs. of Rock fish Riv., adj. Thomas West & James Hurd; 1 Jun 1782, p.134. A.C. of 5 Shill. Sterl.

ALEXANDER BELL, 296 acs. by Survey 12 Oct 1781 in Norfolk Co. adj.

James Wilson decd.; 1 Jun 1782, p.135. A.C. of 30 Shill. Sterl.

LAUGHLIN McGRADY / McGRADDY, 150 acs. by Survey 15 Nov 1769 in Bedford Co. on both sides of Maggotty cr.; 1 Jun 1782, p.136. A.C. of 15 Shill. Sterl.

PLEASANT JOHNSON Ass'ee of ISAAC BROWN, 169½ acs. by survey 24 May 1780 in Mecklenburg Co. on the S side of Meherrin Riv.; adj. Mr Edward Collies c., Mr. Winfred Thompson, Jeffries, Burnett & Jackson; 1 Jun 1782, p.138. A.C. of £1 Sterl.

WILLIAM VINCENT, 175 acs. by Survey 30 Oct 1781 in Pittsylvania Co. on the draughts of Sandy and Strawberry Creeks; adj. Edward Atkins, Thomas Boaze, Josiah Cooke, Thomas Smith & Joshua Cantrill; 1 Jun 1782, p.139. A.C. of £1 Sterl.

JOHN WOOD Ass'ee of WILLIAM HARRIS, 265 acs. by Survey 1 May 1781 in Bedford Co. on the N brs. of the South fork of falling Riv.; adj. Thomas Jones, his own lines & Brookers or Brookess lines; 1 Jun 1782, p.141. A.C. of 30 Shill. Sterl. *being part of a tract of 590 acs. Surveyed 9 Feb 1781.*

PETER LEGRAND, 862 acs. by Survey 26 Oct 1774 in Pr. Edward Co. on the brs. of Appomatox Riv. and Vaughans cr.; adj. Harris, Childs now Woodsons lines, Phillips, Lee, Benjamin Harris, James Walker & Robert Harris; 1 Jun 1782, p.143. A.C. of £4.S10 Sterl.

WALTER WEST, 194 acs. by Survey 22 Nov 1780 in Bedford on the W Brs. of wreck Island cr., on the top of the Ridge between little Wreck Island and Stone well [Stonewall] creeks, adj. Rogers & Whitney; 1 Jun 1782, p.145. A.C. of £1 Sterl.

ANDREW FITZPATRICK Ass'ee of GEORGE SKILLER, 36 acs. by Survey 6 May 1773 in Augusta Co. on Jacksons riv. at a place called Kings bottom, Beginning by a path on the W side of the Riv., in a bent of the hill; 1 Jun 1782, p.147. A.C. of 5 Shill. Sterl.

ALEXANDER MAXWELL Ass'ee of ROBERT CRAVEN, 400 acs. by Survey 26 Oct 1780 in Augusta Co. on the E Side of Tygerts Valley Riv. Joining George Breadens and Isaac Shavers land; 1 Jun 1782, p.148. A.C. of £2 Sterl.

THOMAS MOOR, 5 acs. by Survey 7 Jun 1774 in Augusta Co. on both sides of South cr. between his own and John Phelps land; 1 Jun 1782, p.150. A.C. of 5 Shill. Sterl.

JOHN MARR Ass'ee of JOHN MILLER, 464 acs. Surveyed 13 Apr 1780 in Henry Co. on the N brs. of North Mayo Riv.; adj. Randolph & Co. order line, & his own line; 1 Jun 1782, p.151. A.C. of 50 Shill. Sterl.

WILLIAM HANKINS, 838 acs. by Survey 27 Mar 1780 in Henry Co. on the Waters of Turkey cock cr., adj. Twittys order line; 1 Jun 1782, p.153. A.C. of £4 Sterl.

EDWARD WOOD Ass'ee of WILLIAM JENNINGS, 282 acs. by Survey 20 Feb 1755 in Albemarle Co. on a south br. of fish pound cr., adj. Thomas Lee & John Jennings; 1 Jun 1782, p.155. A.C. of 30 Shill. Sterl.

JOHN WHITE, 195 acs. by Survey 24 Sep 1774 in Louisa Co. Fredericksville Parish on the head of the brs. of Hudsons cr.; Beginning at the Mountain Road; adj. David Jones, Smith & Kelleyham; 1 Jun 1782, p.156. A.C. of £1 Sterl.

GIDEON MARR, 334 acs. by Survey 26 Mar 1770 in Pittsylvania Co. on the S side of Sandy Riv., adj. John Gammon & Belling; 1 Jun 1782, p.158. A.C. of 35 Shill. Sterl.

JAMES EAST, 287 acs. by Survey 1 Feb 1781 in Henry Co. on the S Brs. of Horse pasture cr., adj. his line & Redman; 1 Jun 1782, p.160. A.C. of 20 Shill. Sterl.

JOHN OBRYAN, 178 acs. by Survey 11 May 1780 in Henry Co. on the Waters of Nicholas cr., adj. Dennis OBryan & Scockton [Stockton]; 1 Jun 1782, p.162. A.C. of £1 Sterl.

JOHN COOKE, 444 acs. by Survey 9 Apr 1772 in Pittyslvania Co. on the Grassey fork of Snow cr.; adj. Randolph, Richardson & Woodson; 1 Jun 1782, p.164. A.C. of 45 Shill. Sterl.

RALPH WILSON heir at law of SAMUEL WILLSON dec'd., 62 acs. by Survey 19 Feb 1768 in Augusta Co. between the head brs. of the Straight fork of Powtomack and the Crab Runs, Beginning near a Spring, on a ridge; 1 Jun 1782, p.165. A.C. of 10 Shill. Sterl.

WILLIAM TAYLOR, 85 acs. by Survey 11 Apr 1780 in Henry Co. on the brs. of Horse Pasture cr.; adj. his own, James East & Hooker; 1 Jun 1782, p.167. A.C. of 10 Shill. Sterl.

DARBY RION, 270 acs. by Survey 8 Nov 1753 in Halifax Co. now Henry on both sides Widgeon cr., adj. Harbour; 1 Jun 1782, p.168. A.C. of 30 Shill. Sterl.

DANIEL GOODE Ass'ee of JOHN STRATTON Ass'ee of MARY GILMORE heir of JOHN GILMORE, 133 acs. by Survey 2 Mar 1754 in Albemarle Co. on the N side and Joining the North br. of Piney Riv.; 1 Jun 1782, p.170. A.C. of 15 Shill. Sterl.

JOHN JORDEN or JERDEN, 177 acs. by Survey 20 Jan 1781 in Augusta Co. on a br. of the Bull pasture Joining the land he now lives on, Beginning near a path, to a Sugar tree in Purgatory, to a Lynn and Sugar tree in Purgatory; 1 Jun 1782, p.172. A.C. of £1 Sterl.

GEORGE NICHOLAS, 123 acs. by Survey 24 Jun 1780 in Augusta Co. on Sprucie pine Run a br. of South br. of Powtomack, near Bull Pasture Road; 1 Jun 1782, p.174. A.C. of 15 Shill. Sterl.

JOHN PHILLIPS, 164 acs. by Survey 7 Feb 1763 in Augusta Co. Between Smiths cr. and the Peeked Mountain and Joining his Other land, his patent land; 1 Jun 1782, p.175. A.C. of £1 Sterl.

JOHN CROUCH, 90 acs. by Survey 12 Nov 1772 in Bedford Co. on the brs. of Back cr., adj. his own line; 1 Jun 1782, p.177. A.C. of 10 Shill. Sterl.

THOMAS MATTHEWS, 1,626 acs. by Survey 27 Apr 1780 in Buckingham Co. on both sides of dry Beaver Pond cr. and a br. of Thornhill fork, crossing Mathews road, crossing his aforesaid Road, on a ridge; adj. Coll. John Harris, his own line cross his Spring br., Thomas Stevens, John Chambers, Wagsteffs now his own, John Patterson & Henry Moore; 1 Jun

1782, p.178. A.C. of 30 Shill. Sterl. 1,357 acs. of the same has been Surveyed in Severall differrent Surveys the whole being now included in one.

SAMUEL BEARD, 243 acs. by Survey 24 Oct 1751 in Bedford Co. on the S side of the south fork of Otter Riv., adj. Randolph; 1 June 1782, p.181. A.C. of 25 Shill. Sterl. [The survey is a duplicate of the 243 acs. Lunenburg Co. (Now Bedford) in GB K p.14 to Samuel Beard Devisee of Adam Beard Dec'd.]

JOHN BICKNALL Son and heir of JAMES BICKNALL, 52 acs. by Survey 16 Mar 1771 in Amherst Co. on both Sides the Dutch cr., on the S Bank of Rock fish Riv.; adj. Thomas Bicknall, Miles Raley & Josiah Woods line; 1 Jun 1782, p.183. A.C. of 5 Shill. Sterl.

JOHN WORMSLEY / WORMSLY / WORMLY, 384 acs. by Survey 2 Dec 1767 in Augusta Co. on the Mole hill draft a br. of Cooks cr., adj. Daniel Harrison; 1 Jun 1782, p.184. A.C. of £2 Sterl.

HUGH INNES, 358 acs. by Survey 16 Feb 1769 in Pittsylvania Co. on Bennetts cr. of Snow Cr.; adj. Tulley Choice, his old line, Remmington & Bennet; 1 Jun 1782, p.186. A.C. £2 Sterl.

DAVID KYLE, 190 acs. by Survey 27 Apr 1780 in Buckingham Co. on Davis cr.; adj. Robert Kyle, Robert Freeland & John Byrum Gothard; 1 Jun 1782, p.188. A.C. of £1 Sterl.

ROBERT GRIMMETT, 190 acs. by Survey 9 Oct 1773 in Henry Co. formerly Pittsylvania on the Brs. of Chesnut cr., Beginning on a fork of the Gap; 1 Jun 1782, p.190. A.C. of £1 Sterl.

MARK ANDREWS Ass'ee of SAMUEL SNEED, 450 acs. by Survey 13 Dec 1748 in Lunenburgh Co. on the Upper side of Tossekea cr.; adj. Stunck, Ellen [Ellis], Daniel Melone, Mechun [Michaux] & Irby; 1 Jun 1782, p.191. A.C. of 45 Shill. Sterl. [This survey is the same as in PB 31 p.576 to Penelope Parratt dated 10 Sep 1755 & the regrant in PB 35 p.406 to Samuel Snead dated 30 Aug 1763].

JOHN LEWIS, 26 acs. by Survey 11 Apr 1780 in Augusta Co. on the NW side of the Warm Spring tract; 1 Jun 1782, p.193. A.C. of 5 Shill. Sterl.

JOHN CALLAWAY Ass'ee of JESSEE RENTFROE, 338 acs. by Survey 11 Nov 1771 in Bedford Co. on the North fork of Black Water riv., in lick br.; adj. Mason, & Joseph Rentfroe; 1 Jun 1782, p.195. A.C. of 35 Shill. Sterl.

GEORGE WILKINS, 500 acs. Surveyed 3 May 1781 on a TW #420 issued 15 Oct 1779 in Lincoln Co. on the waters of Quirks Run, adj. Kirkham; 1 Jun 1782, p.197. £200.

JOHN SIZEMORE / SIZEMOND, 840 acs. by Survey 5 Nov 1771 in Halifax Co. on Cedar and Reedy branches; adj. Fields order Line, Trammel, Cox, & William McGill; 1 Jun 1782, p.198. A.C. of £4.S5 Sterl.

JOHN STUART, 30 acs. by Survey 23 Apr 1781 in Augusta Co. on the N side of the Middle Riv. of Shenandore, adj. John Dixon & Beverly; 1 Jun 1782, p.200. A.C. of 5 Shill. Sterl.

NICHOLAS SYBERT, 317 acs. by Survey 23 Feb 1781 in Augusta Co. on Straight cr. below and Joining a tract of land of sd Sybert; 1 Jun 1782, p.201. A.C. of 35 Shill. Sterl.

SARAH BOONE Ass'ee of SQUIRE BOONE who was Ass'ee of JOSEPH MORETON, 250 acs. by Survey 31 Mar 1781 on a TW #3,506 and issued 7 Mar 1780 in Jefferson Co. on fox Run fork of Brashears cr., crossing fox Run, at the head of a drain of sd Run; Beginning at John Porters NW corner of his preemtion, also adj. Pater; 1 Jun 1782, p.203. £100.

SQUIRE BOONE, 1,000 acs. Surveyed 8 Mar 1781 on a PTW #631 and issued 1 Apr 1780 in Jefferson Co. on both sides of Clear cr. a fork of Brashears cr. adjoining his Settlement Called the painted Stone tract; 1 Jun 1782, p.205. £400.

SQUIRE BOONE Ass'ee of GEORGE MEREWETHER, 200 acs. surveyed 8 Jul 1781 part of a TW #5,877 issued 15 Jul 1780 in Jefferson Co., cross Guess cr., at the head of drain of sd cr., adj. John Eastwood; 1 Jun 1782, p.206. £80.

SQUIRE BOONE Ass'ee of GEORGE MEREWETHER, 122 acs. surveyed 8 Jul 1781 on a TW #5,877 issued 15 Jul 1780 in Jefferson Co. on both sides of Clann or Clean cr. adjoining his settlement and preemption Called the Painted Stone tract; 1 Jun 1782, p.208. £44.S8.

SQUIRE BOONE Ass'ee of BENJAMIN VANCLERR, 400 acs. Surveyed 8 Mar 1781 by Virtue of a Certificate for Settlement Granted by the Commissioners of the district of Kentuckey in Jefferson Co. on Clare cr. a fork of Brashears cr. called the painted stone, Beginning on the W side of Clear cr.; 1 Jun 1782, p.210. A.C. of £2 Sterl.

JACOB MYERS Ass'ee of ANDREW HYNES who was Ass'ee of JAMES PIGOTT, 400 acs. Surveyed 15 Mar 1781 on a PTW #1,071 issued 16 Aug 1780 in Jefferson Co. on the upper Side of Salt River including David Alls Garrison, Beginning on the upper Bank of the River about 50 years above the ferry; 1 Jun 1782, p.211. £160.

ANN POAGE, 400 acs. Surveyed 4 Oct 1780 on a TW #4,532 issued 1 Apr 1780 in Kentucky Co. adjoining the lower side of her preemption land, on the side of a Ridge; 1 Jun 1782, p.213. £160.

GEORGE BUCHANNAN, 300 acs. surveyed 27 Jun 1780 part of a TW #4,523 issued 1 Apr 1780 in Kentucky Co. on both sides of a large br. of Salt Riv. and on the W side of sd Riv. opposite to William Adams preemption and Settlement about a mile from the Mouth of the Br., in a Hallow; 1 Jun 1782, p.214. £120.

GEORGE BUCHANNAN, 200 acs. Surveyed 30 Jan 1781 part of a TW #4,523 issued 1 Apr 1780 in Lincoln Co. on the E Side of Robert McAfees 200 Acs. survey, Beginning 23 poles S from his NE corner, adj. sd Robert McAfees land Standing on head of a draft; 1 Jun 1782, p.216. £80.

ARTHUR CAMPBELL, 280 acs. Surveyed 11 May 1781 in Washington Co. on both sides of big Mockison cr. in and above big Mockison Gap, Beginning at the foot of Clynch Mountain on the W side of the cr., adj. sd Campbells other

Survey, to a large hoop Ash at the foot of a high Barren hill, on a Spurr in sd Gap, on a Steep bank of the cr. at the foot of Coopers creek ridge, on the point of a Spurr of sd Ridge, along an inaccessible part of the Mountain; 1 Jun 1782, p.217. £31. 80 acs. part of which is in part of a TW #1,900 issued 25 Nov 1779 the Residue 200 Acs. by Virtue of a Military Warrant.

ARTHUR CAMPBELL, 1,140 acs. Surveyed 10 Nov 1780 on a TW #1,898 and part of Another TW #1,900 both issued 25 Nov 1779 in Washington Co. on both sides of the Middle fork of Holston riv. Known by the name of Goodwood including his patent land, on the top of a Ridge, crossing Mill cr., on the top of a high hill, by a Steep bank, at the head of Hollow; adj. David Campbell Senr., David Campbells land being the Second corner in the old Survey, & the sd David and Arthur Campbells patent land; 1 Jun 1782, p.220. £260.

ARTHUR CAMPBELL, 1,140 acs. Surveyed 10 Nov 1780 on a TW #1,898 and part of Another Treasury Warrant Number 1,900 both issued 25 Nov 1779 in Washington Co. on both sides of the Midle fork of Holston riv. Known by the name of **Goodwood** including his patent land, on the top of a Ridge, crossing Mill cr., on the top of a high hill, by a Steep bank, at the head of Hollow; adj. David Campbell Senr., David Campbells land being the Second corner in the old Survey, & the sd David and Arthur Campbells patent land; 1 Jun 1782, p.220. £260.

ARTHUR CAMPBELL, 120 acs. by Survey 11 May 1781 on a TW #1,900 issued 25 Nov 1779 in Washington Co. on both sides of big Mockison cr. a br. of the North fork of Holsten Riv. and a Little below Mockison Gap, Beginning on the E side of the cr. at the foot of a high Barren hill, at the foot of Clynch Mountain, at the foot of a Spurr; 1 Jun 1782, p.223. £60.

SQUIRE BOONE Ass'ee of THOMAS PIERCE, 200 acs. surveyed 8 Mar 1781 on a TW #683 issued 15 Oct 1779 in Jefferson Co. on a fork of Guess cr. adj. Thomas Daggerly or Duggerly; 1 Jun 1782, p.225. £80.

JULIUS LANE, 100 acs. by Survey 22 Mar 1781 in Hanover Co. on a br. of Black cr.; down a drain & the North fork of sd cr. & up the South fork to the Beg.; adj. William Bowes land, Blackwells land, & Alexander Bennetts field; 1 Jun 1782, p.227. A.C. of 10 shill. Sterl.

WILLIAM STEWART Ass'ee of RICHARD MORRISS & RICHARD TERRELL, 500 acs. surveyed 20 Jul 1781 on part of a TW #5,841 issued 5 Jul 1780 in Jefferson Co. on the waters of Rowling fork a br. of salt riv. about 4 Miles N of the Cedar licks, at the head of a small drain, on the top of a ridge; adj. Stewarts 1,000 Acre Preemption, his 1,000 Acre Survey; 1 Jun 1782, p.228. £200.

JACOB MYERS, 550 acs. Surveyed 6 Mar 1781 on a TW #7,062 issued 15 Oct 1779 in Lincoln Co. on the head of Scaggs cr. on the Trace leading from English Station to the Settlement; 1 Jun 1782, p.230. £220.

JACOB MYERS Ass'ee of JOHN DEREMIAH, 1,000 acs. surveyed 21 Jul 1780 on a preemption TW #1,070 issued

16 Aug 1780 in Jefferson Co. on the main br. of Buffaloe cr. about 2 Miles from Rogers Station, on the east fork of sd cr.; 1 Jun 1782, p.231. £400.

WILLIAM STEWART Ass'ee of RICHARD MORRISS & RICHARD TERRELL, 500 acs. Surveyed 7 Sep 1781 on part of a TW #5,841 issued 5 Jul 1780 in Jefferson Co. on the waters of the Rolling fork a br. of Salt Riv. about 2 Miles N of the Cedar lick, near a Small drain & near a Small Glade; adj. his 1,000 Acre Survey & his Preemption; 1 Jun 1782, p.233. £200.

WILLIAM STEWART, 300 acs. surveyed 1 Aug 1781 on a TW #796 in Lincoln Co. on Chaplins fork a Br. of salt Riv., Beginning at the SW corner of Thompsons land in Stewarts settlement line, also adj. Stewarts 560 Acre Survey; to a Cherry Walnut and Coffee tree the SE corner of Goodnights; 1 Jun 1782, p.234. £120.

WILLIAM & MARY KNIGHT of the one part & ANN PETERS of the Other part, heirs and Representatives of OTHO PETERS dec'd, 404 acs. by survey 28 Oct 1751 in Brunswick Co. Joining the lines of Vaughan, Love, Swanson, Conter & Lambert; 1 Jun 1782, p.236. A.C. of £2 Sterl. **paid by Otho Peters into the late Receiver Generals Office.**

WILLIAM STEWART Ass'ee of JOSEPH DIXON, 1,000 acs. Surveyed 20 Jul 1781 on a preemption TW #1,015 issued 29 Jun 1780 in Jefferson Co. on the waters of the Rowling fork a br. of Salt Riv. Lying about 3 or 4 Miles from the Cedar licks a North Course from the same; Beginning 60 poles from Perrickes N corner of his preemption a N Course from the same, crossing 2 small Runs, with Stewarts line Passing Penicks corner; 1 Jun 1782, p.238. £400.

CLOUGH OVERTON, 400 acs. on a PTW #12 issued 22 Jan 1780 in Kentucky Co. on the head of the east fork of Simpsons cr. a br. of Salt Riv., on the W side of a draft; 1 Jun 1782, p.239. £160.

CLOUGH OVERTON Ass'ee of THOMAS DENTON, 907 acs. by Survey 17 Oct 1780 on a PTW #11 issued 22 Jan 1780 in Kentucky Co. on the waters of Salt riv. corner at sd Dentons Settlement, on a Ridge, on the side of the dry br., on a draft; also adj. Thomas Denton, Thomas Gant & Silas Harlin; 1 Jun 1782, p.241. £362.S16 Sterl.

BENJAMIN LOGAN, 750 acs. Surveyed 15 Apr 1781 on a TW #4,524 issued 1 Apr 1780 in Lincoln Co. on a Br. of Dicks riv.; adj. John Montgomery, Benjamin Logan & John Logan; 1 Jun 1782, p.243. [£300]

CHARLES M. THRUSTON Ass'ee of JOHN HARVIE, JOHN LEWIS & CHRISTOPHER CLARK, 2,000 acs. Surveyed 13 Aug 1781 on two Treasury Warrants #107 & 108 issued 15 Oct 1779 in Jefferson Co., Beginning at the SE corner of the sd Thrustons Settlement, on the cr. bank, in the edge of the Bottom, crossing the cr. to a Stake in the Barrens; 1 Jun 1782, p.244. £800.

CHARLES M. THRUSTON, 400 acs. Surveyed 11 Aug 1781 by virtue of a certificate in right of Settlement in Jefferson Co. on the waters of Green riv. and Noleleonn cr., Beginning on the W side of the cr. about ½ Mile below the

Station, to a Stake in the Barrens; 1 Jun 1782, p.246. A.C. of £2 Sterl.

CHARLES W. THURSTON Ass'ee of JOHN LEWIS, CHRISTOPHER CLARK & JOHN HARVIE, 1,400 acs. surveyed 11 Aug 1781 on two treasury Warrants #113 and 1,170 issued 15 Oct 1779 in Jefferson Co. on NoleLinn cr. waters of Green Riv., Beginning at the SE corner of the sd Thrustons Settlement, to a Stake in the barrens; 1 Jun 1782, p.247. £560.

WILLIAM STEWART Ass'ee of WILLIAM WILSON, 300 acs. surveyed 28 Aug 1781 on a PTW #584 issued 1 Apr 1780 in Lincoln Co. on the waters of Black Run, Beginning at the SE corner of Robert Caldwell preemption on James Gilmores line; 1 Jun 1782, p.249. £120.

JACOB MEYERS Ass'ee of JOSEPH CARTWRIGHT, 400 acs. by Virtue of a Certificate in Right of Settlement Surveyed 20 Jul 1781 in Jefferson Co. on Pleasant Run a br. of the beech fork a br. of Salt riv., Beginning in a line of the 500 Acre Survey part of the Preemption 300 poles from the SE corner of sd Survey; 1 Jun 1782, p.250. A.C. of £2 Sterl.

JACOB MYERS Ass'ee of JOSEPH CARTWRIGHT, 500 acs. Surveyed 20 Jul 1781 on a PTW #1,166 issued 18 Sep 1780 in Jefferson Co. on Pleasant Run a br. of the beech fork a br. of salt riv., Beginning on the SE line of the settlement 90 poles from the SW corner of sd Settlement; 1 Jun 1782, p.251. £200.

JACOB MYERS, 100 acs. Surveyed 2 Apr 1781 on a TW #761 issued 15 Cct 1779 in Jefferson Co. on the waters of the Beech fork; 1 Jun 1782, p.253. £100.

JACOB MYERS Ass'ee of JOSEPH CARTWRIGHT, 500 acs. Surveyed 20 Jul 1780 on a PTW #1,166 issued 18 Sep 1780 in Jefferson Co. on Pleasant Run a br. of the beech Fork a Br. of salt Riv., adj. John Harden; 1 Jun 1782, p.254. £200.

THOMAS PRATHER, 1,000 acs. surveyed 4 Sep 1781 on part of a TW #2,590 issued 14 Feb 1780 in Jefferson Co. on Hardens cr., Beginning on the SW side of the cr. about 3 Miles SWwardly from Cartwrights Station, adj. Edward Bullock; 1 Jun 1782, p.255. £400.

JOSEPH EARLY Ass'ee of GEORGE MOSS, 1,400 acs. Surveyed 29 May 1780 in Kentucky Co. on the waters of Salt riv. near the head of Bentons fork, adj. the land of Elijah Craig, Elijah Craigs Settlement line; 1 Jun 1782, p.257. in Consideration of the Sum of £400 as paid by Joseph Early. 400 acs. of which is by virtue of a certificate in right of Settlement the residue being 1,000 acs. on a PTW #65 issued 26 Feb 1780.

JOHN FITCH, 300 acs. Surveyed 26 Mar 1781 on a TW #2,388 issued 2 Feb 1780 in Jefferson Co. on Coxes cr., on the top of a Ridge; 1 Jun 1782, p.259. £120.

BASIL PRATHER, 500 acs. Surveyed 30 Jun 1781 on part of a TW #2,595 issued 14 Feb 1780 in Jefferson Co. on the head of Pleasant run, on the SE side of a Small Sw., crossing a small br. of Pleasant run & the heads of the Waters of Rowling fork; adj. Evan Shelby, Joseph Hughes & Richard Swann/Swan; 1 Jun 1782, p.261. £200.

THOMAS MADISON Ass'ee of THOMAS QUIRK, 924 acs. Surveyed 29

Oct 1780 on part of a PTW #304 issued 23 Mar 1780 in Kentucky Co. on Harrods Run a Br. of Dicks riv.; adj. Henry Wilson about 25 poles from his and Davies's C., Azor Reise & George Smith; 1 Jun 1782, p.262. £376.S8.

GEORGE MAY Ass'ee of JOHN FLOYD Ass'ee of RICHARD PETERS, 400 acs. surveyed 13 Oct 1780 part of a TW #889 issued 15 Oct 1779 in Kentucky Co. on the Ohio Riv. about 49 Miles below the mouth of the Scioto riv., About 2 Miles below the Lower point of the 2 Islands, 11 or 12 Miles below the Island Opposite to Kennedys Cabbin, Beginning in the upper end of the 1st large Bottom below the 2 Islands on the River bank; 1 Jun 1782, p.264. £160.

HUBBARD TAYLOR, 400 acs. Surveyed 11 Apr 1781 by Virtue of a Certificate in right of Settlement in Lincoln Co.; adj. Joseph Bowmans Settlement line, Aser Rees c. & Hogans Settlement and preemption line; 1 Jun 1782, p.266. A.C. of £2 Sterl.

ANN POAGE, 400 acs. Surveyed 4 Oct 1780 on a PTW #563 issued 1 Apr 1780 in Kentucky Co. on both sides of a cr. running into Kentucky riv., Beginning on the SE side of the Falls trace and about 130 poles SW from Mr. Garrys Spring, crossing the Falls tract; 1 Jun 1782, p.267. £160.

CLIFF OVERTON Ass'ee of THOMAS DENTON, 93 acs. Surveyed 10 Aug 1781 in [part] of a preemption Warrant for 1,000 acs. in Lincoln Co. on a dry br. of Chaplains fork of salt Riv.; 1 Jun 1782, p.268. £38.S12.

STEPHEN TRIGG Ass'ee of JOHN GRAYSON, 400 acs. Surveyed 23 Jan 1781 by virtue of a Certificate in right of Settlement in Lincoln Co. on the waters of Cain run, adj. Jacob Fremees land, running through to a pond, passing John Gordens c. to the Beg.; 1 Jun 1782, p.270. A.C. of £2 Sterl.

STEPHEN TRIGG Ass'ee of JAMES ROBINSON, 344 acs. Surveyed 6 Apr 1781 on a TW #905 issued 15 Oct 1779 in Lincoln Co. on the waters of Shawnee run adj. John Gordons land on the N, John McMurtrie on the W and Henry Prather on the S; Beginning in John Gordens line, also sd Triggs settlement & Caves line; 1 Jun 1782, p.271. £137.S12.

HENRY GREER Ass'ee of ANDERSON BRYAN, 302½ acs. by survey 18 May 1774 in Albemarle Co. on the S side the Rivanna Riv. and on E side Smiths br.; adj. Henry Martin, Joseph Fitzpatrick Senior & Kenney/Kinney; 1 Jun 1782, p.273. A.C. of 30 Shill. Sterl.

HENRY LEE, 1,000 acs. surveyed 20 Jul 1781 on a TW #401 issued 15 Oct 1779 in Jefferson Co. on the waters of Mill cr. a br. of the Beech fork a br. of Salt riv.; adj. Stewarts 600 Acres Survey on a small Rise, Charles Stewarts line & William Stewarts line; 1 Jun 1782, p.274. £400.

BENJAMIN HARRISON Esq., 120 acs. in Surry Co. down the deep sw. and up the upper Chip Oaks cr., adj. Philip Best dec'd & Col. William Allen; 1 Jun 1782, p.275. £6,630 paid unto James Belshes Escheator for sd Co. *late the property of Richard Oswald a British Subject and Sold by sd James Belsches Escheator unto sd Benjamin Harrison agreable to two Acts of General Assembly passed in 1779 the one Intitled an Act concerning escheats and forefeitures from British Subjects the other Intitled an Act Concerning Escheaters.*

SIMEON MOORE, 1,000 acs. Surveyed 15 Jul 1780 on a preemption TW #487 issued 31 Mar 1780 in Kentucky Co. on the waters of Shawnee run about 2 Miles N of the Shawnee Spring, on the Top of a Ridge; adj. Deanna Donterns or Danlerns [Denton?] line, her line, & Henry Prather; 1 Jun 1782, p.276. £400.

SAMUEL MOORE, 400 acs. by Virtue of a Certificate in Right of Settlement Surveyed 9 Apr 1781 in Lincoln Co. on the N side of the Knob Lick; to the Corner white Oak, Coffee and Linn Wood [trees]; 1 Jun 1782, p.278. A.C. of £2 Sterl.

LEVEN POWELL, 1,200 acs. surveyed 5 Apr 1781 on a TW #4,144 and part of a TW #4,141 Both issued 20 Mar 1780 in Jefferson Co., Beginning at the Mouth of a small br. on the W side of Simpsons cr. about 100 poles below the Mouth of the main east fork of sd cr., up the small br. near where it is Supposed the line of Jacob Myers preemption will run, on a ridge in or near a line of a Survey made for Paul Froman on plumb Run and its waters, on the SW side of a rising on waters of Plumb Run west br. of Simpsons cr., on a W bank of Simpsons cr. about 20 poles above the Mouth of the sd Plumb Run and near a spring and Corner also to a tract of 2,000 Acres Surveyed for the sd Powel; 1 Jun 1782, p.279. £480.

ELIJAH CRAIG Ass'ee of JOHN MORTS who was Ass'ee of SWITHEN PALSON, 1,400 acs. surveyed 29 May 1780 in Kentucky Co., Beginning on the Run above Palsons Cabbin, adj. Joseph Early's Settlement line & John Briscoes Survey; 1 Jun 1782, p.281. £400. 400 acs. of which is by Virtue of a Certificate in right of Settlement the residue 1,000 acs. on a PTW #56 issued 26 Feb 1780.

SAMUEL McAFEE, 1,400 acs. Surveyed 11 Jun 1780 in Kentucky Co. on both sides of the Town fork of salt riv. adj. John McGees land on the S and James McGees land on the N, also adj. James McAfee; 1 Jun 1782, p.282. £400. 400 acs. of which is by Virtue of a certificate in right of Settlement.

NICHOLAS MEREWETHER Ass'ee of SQUIRE BOONE, 400 acs. by virtue of a Certificate in right of Settlement Surveyed 8 Mar 1781 in Lincoln Co. on Mulberry cr. a fork of Clear cr., adj. William Bryan; 1 Jun 1782, p.284. A.C. of £2 Sterl.

NICHOLAS MEREWETHER Ass'ee of SQUIRE BOONE, 1,000 acs. surveyed 8 Mar 1781 on a PTW #216 issued 20 Mar 1780 in Jefferson Co. on Mulberry cr. a fork of Clar cr., adj. his Settlement; 1 Jun 1782, p.285. £400.

DAVID COOKE Ass'ee of GEORGE DIXON, 115 acs. Surveyed 15 Feb 1781 on a TW #4,465 issued 31 Mar 1781 in Lincoln Co. on the waters of Dicks riv., Beginning on the point of a Bald hill; 1 Jun 1782, p.286. £46.

ISAAC HITE, ABRAHAM BOWMAN, JACOB BOWMAN heir at Law to JOSEPH BOWMAN dec'd and JOHN BOWMAN as tennants in Common, 837 acs. Surveyed 22 Jan 1781 on a PTW #559 issued 1 Apr 1780 in Lincoln Co. on the N side of Cain Run; adj. Richard

Hogans preemption lines, John Smiths Settlement line, a Settlement Surveyed for John Grissum, William Bryans land, Adam Smiths Settlement line now the property of John Bowman and Company, & the sd Joseph Bowmans Settlement; 1 Jun 1782, p.287. £327.S8. with its Appurtenances, to have and to hold the said tract or parcel of Land, with its Appurtenances, to the said JOHN BOWMAN and COMPANY and their heirs forever.

JOHN CURD, 454 acs. Surveyed 28 Mar 1781 on a PTW #982 issued 28 Jun 1780 in Lincoln Co. on Dicks riv. and Harrods Run adj. Adam Fishers Settlement on the SW; on the Clifts of sd riv.; up Wilsons Run; on the Clifts of sd run; also adj. Zachariah Smith & John Bowman; 1 Jun 1782, p.288. £181.S12.

JOHN CURD, 300 acs. Surveyed 29 Mar 1781 on part of a PTW #983 issued 28 Jun 1780 in Lincoln Co. adj. James Masons Settlement on the Bank of his Mill cr. & William Whitelys line; 1 Jun 1782, p.290. £120.

JOHN PITMAN, 750 acs. Surveyed 18 Jun 1781 on a TW #5,774 issued 24 June 1780 in Lincoln Co. on Quirks Run, Beginning on the SW corner of Gilmours land at the foot of a large row of Knobs, along the Knobs to 3 sugar trees on the hunters trace, along Gilmores line; 1 Jun 1782, p.291. £300.

JOHN HALL, 1,000 acs. surveyed 21 May 1781 on a PTW #756 issued 26 Apr 1780 in Lincoln Co. on Logans cr. the waters of Dicks riv.; 1 Jun 1782, p.292. £400.

THOMAS PRATHER, 759 acs. Surveyed 28 Apr 1781 on a PTW #912 issued 28 Jun 1780 in Lincoln Co. adj. James Harrods land on the W, Beginning at his NW corner; also adj. John Cowen, Joseph Early, Elijah Craig, John Briscoe, Henry Wilson & George Smith; 1 Jun 1782, p.293. £300.S16.

WILLIAM MAY Ass'ee of GEORGE MAY who was Ass'ee of THOMAS JOHNSON, 300 acs. Surveyed 28 Jul 1781 being part of a TW #4,201 issued 21 Mar 1780 in Jefferson Co. on waters or Green Riv. Known by the name of the head Mountain cr., Beginning on the W side of the sd cr. about 8 poles distant therefrom and about 130 poles Westward from Mays Spring, to a Stake in the Barrens; 1 Jun 1782, p.295. £120.

JOHN LEE Ass'ee of HANCOCK LEE, 1,000 acs. surveyed 2 Sep 1780 on a TW #390 issued 15 Oct 1779 in Kentucky Co. on panther cr. adj. William Bailey Smith & Ambrose Madison; 1 Jun 1782, p.296. £400.

WILLIAM LOGAN, 200 acs. Surveyed 11 Aug 1781 part of a PTW #583 issued 22 Jun 1780 in Lincoln Co. on Dicks Riv., Beginning at the NE Corner of his oldest preemption Survey, on his former line to the Beg.; 1 Jun 1782, p.297. £80. [Margin note: **This Grant is found to be Erroneous, therefore a New one Issued & Recorded in Book No. 20 Page 646**]

JOHN EDWARDS Ass'ee of ENOCH FURR, 150 acs. Surveyed 5 Apr 1781 on a TW #95 issued 15 Oct 1779 in Lincoln Co. on the Crab Orchard Run, down the Crab Run, on the point of a Mountain unfit for Cultivation, along the Spurs of the Mountain Beginning on the NW Corner of Williams land, also adj. Moor and Owsly or Orosly; 1 Jun 1782, p.298. £60.

MARK HARDEN, 500 acs. Surveyed 28 Jun 1781 on a TW #2,583 issued 14 Feb 1780 in Jefferson Co. on the waters of Hardens cr. adj. his preemption on the S and John Askings or Arkings on the N and S; on the side of a Ridge on the S side of a br. of Prathers cr. (crossed a br. at 60 poles and one at the Corner); 1 Jun 1782, p.299. £200.

ADAM WICKERHAM, 1,000 acs. Surveyed 14 Apr 1781 on a PTW #970 issued 28 Jun 1780 in Jefferson Co., Beginning at Allens S Corner of 2,000 Acre tract, cross the south fork of Clear cr. and cross a br. of sd fork to corner to his Settlement; 1 Jun 1782, p.301. £400.

JAMES COBURN, Surveyed 8 Mar 1781 by virtue of a Certificate from the Commissioners of the district of Kentucky, 400 acs. in Jefferson Co. on both sides of Mulberry cr. about 2 Miles E from **the painted Stone**; adj. William Bryan, & Nicholas Merewethers Settlement; 1 Jun 1782, p.302. £2 Sterl.

THOMAS PRATHER, 1,000 acs. Surveyed 4 Sep 1781 part of a TW #2,590 issued 14 Feb 1780 in Jefferson Co. adj. his other 1,000 Acre tract, Beginning on the NE line 180 poles from the SW Corner, also adj. Bullock; 1 Jun 1782, p.303. £400.

HUBBARD TAYLER / TAYLOR Ass'ee of JAMES PEYTON, 347 acs. Surveyed 4 Apr 1781 on a TW #4,353 issued 23 Mar 1780 in Lincoln Co. on the head waters of paint lick and Gilberts cr. adj. Lewis Craig's Survey of 200 Acres on the SW and Philip Buckner on the N; Beginning at a corner to Young and Buckner; 1 Jun 1782, p.304. £138.S16.

JAMES McAFEE, 200 acs. Surveyed 22 Jun 1780 in full of a PTW #34 issued 19 Feb 1780 in Kentucky Co. on the W side of the town fork of Salt Riv. adj. his Settlement lands on the E, crossing a small br. to a Hallow; 1 Jun 1782, p.305. £80.

NATHANIEL EVANS Ass'ee of THOMAS LOVEL, 336 acs. Surveyed 28 Apr 1781 on a PTW #511 issued 31 Mar 1780 in Lincoln Co. on the waters of the hanging fork of Dicks riv., on the side of a Ridge, in a Cain patch, adj. Bulger & sd Evans; 1 Jun 1782, p.306. £127.

NATHANIEL EVANS Ass'ee of ROBERT CRAIG who was Ass'ee of JAMES CRAIG, 228 acs. Surveyed 21 Apr 1781 part of a PTW #657 issued 4 Apr 1780 in Lincoln Co. on the hanging fork of Dicks riv., on the bank of a small cr., along the foot of large fall unfit for Cultivation; adj. Daniel McCormack, James McKenney & Nathaniel Evans; 1 Jun 1782, p.308. £85.S12.

JAMES McAFEE, 1,200 acs. Surveyed 12 Jun 1780 in Kentucky Co. [two surveys] 400 acs. of which is by virtue of a Certificate in right of Settlement, on both sides of the town fork of salt riv., crossing the riv. & a dry Run, adj. Samuel McAfee & James McCoun, passing the preemption Corner; the Residue 800 acs. being in part of a PTW #34 issued 19 Feb 1780 adj. the sd Settlement lands on the East, James McCoun & Samuel McAfee; 1 Jun 1782, p.309. A.C. of £2 Sterl. also the sum of £320.

CHARLES WILLS Ass'ee of GEORGE McCOLLOCK, 400 acs. Surveyed 2 Jun 1780 by Virtue of a Certificate in Right of Settlement in Ohio Co. on the waters of Buffaloe cr. adj. the land whereon he now lives; 1 Jun 1782, p.311. A.C. of £2 Sterl.

BENJAMIN WILLS, 400 acs. surveyed 2 Jun 1780 in Ohio Co. on the waters of Buffaloe cr.; adj. Edward Povien, & Charles Wells two tracts; 1 Jun 1782, p.312. A.C. of £2 sterl.

JAMES RAY Ass'ee of HUGH McGARY, 400 acs. Surveyed 19 Jul 1780 by Virtue of a Certificate in right of Settlement in Kentucky Co. on the waters of the Shawnee Run, near a pond, on the point of a low Ridge, on the edge of a Bald hill; 1 Jun 1782, p.313. £2 Sterl.

MARBELL STONE Ass'ee of THOMAS LAWHAUN, 200 acs. by Survey 4 Feb 1755 in Fluvanna Co. [formerly] Albemarle Co. on the S side of Hardware Riv. on the brs. of Darbys and Dicks creeks, cross Georges cr.; 1 Jun 1782, p.314. A.C. £1 Sterl.

JAMES GILMOUR / GILMORE, 1,000 acs. Surveyed 23 Mar 1781 on a PTW #1,053 issued 13 Jul 1780 in Lincoln Co. on the head of the town fork of salt riv., Beginning on the W side the South cr., on the point of a large row of Mountains unfit for Cultivation, adj. Caldwell; 1 Jun 1782, p.315. £400.

SHADRACK CARTER Ass'ee of GEORGE ROGERS CLARK, 560 acs. Surveyed 24 Oct 1780 on a State TW #2,169 issued 29 Jan 1780 in Kentucky Co. on the Beech fork, Beginning near the Mouth of Cedar cr., up Cedar cr. in a line agreed upon by sd Shadrack Carter and Evan Williams, in the edge of a small Glade, Crossing Cedar Run & Crossing Beach fork to the upper end of an Island; 1 Jun 1782, p.316. £224.

ROBERT BARNETT, 400 acs. surveyed 10 Apr 1781 on a PTW #514 issued 1 Mar 1780 in Lincoln Co. on the hanging fork of Dicks riv., Beginning on the bank of the cr. about a mile below Barnetts Station; 1 Jun 1782, p.317. £160.

JAMES WOODS, 200 acs. Surveyed 9 Mar 1781 on a TW #2,743 issued 19 Feb 1780 in Lincoln Co. on both sides of the town fork of salt Riv. Below William Adams Preemption, on the top of a Ridge; 1 Jun 1782, p.318. £80.

JOHN SMITH Ass'ee of JAMES WILLEY, 1,400 acs. Surveyed 23 Oct 1780 in Kentucky Co. [two surveys] 400 acs. of which is by Virtue of a Certificate in Right of Settlement; on the waters of Cain Run and joining Richard Hogan and Azor Rees on the N; Beginning in a Small draft in Hogans line; to the NW Corner to Hogans Settlement. the Residue 1,000 acs. on a PTW #33 issued 19 Feb 1780 adj. his Settlement, John Grisham, sd Grissum & Azor Rees; 1 Jun 1782, p.319. in Consideration of the A.C. of £2 Sterl. and the sum of £400.

CHARLES INGLISH Ass'ee of WILLIAM VAUGHAN, 116 acs. surveyed 23 Feb 1781 on a TW #2,808 issued 22 Feb 1780 in Lincoln Co. on Dicks riv. the N side thereof, Beginning on the NE Corner of the sd Inglishes preemption; 1 Jun 1782, p.321. £43.S4.

ISAAC WINSTON, 1,600 acs. Surveyed 4 Oct 1780 on a TW #3,992 issued 18 Mar 1780 in Kentucky Co. adj. the land of Ann Poage on the NW; 1 Jun 1782, p.322. £640.

JACOB MYERS Ass'ee of sd DAVID GRIFFITH, 43 acs. by Survey 6 Jun 1780 in Kentucky Co. near the falls of Ohio adj. John Conally / Connally, Beginning at a Rock on the small Stream at low Water Mark, from the Mouth of Bear Grass cr. running at low water Mark, to the lower end of the Island; 1 Jun 1782, p.323. in Consideration of Military Service Performed by David Griffith as a Surgeons Mate during the late war between Great Britain and France According to the King of Great Britains Proclamation of 1763.

PETER SHEPHERD, 900 acs. part of a TW #928 issued 15 Oct 1779 Surveyed 22 Mar 1781 in Jefferson Co., Beginning on the Bank of Salt Riv. at the lower part of the falls on the upper side of sd Riv., adj. McGee; 1 Jun 1782, p.324. £360.

THOMAS ROWLAND Ass'ee of GEORGE MAY, 400 acs. Surveyed 14 Jun 1780 on a PTW #639 issued 1 Apr 1780 in Kentucky Co. on the N side of Kentucky Riv. about 4 Miles above the Mouth of the Shawnee Run, Beginning a little Above a Spring, crossing the Spring Run thence up Riv.; 1 Jun 1782, p.325. £160.

DAVID GLENN Ass'ee of JOHN STROBE?, 500 acs. Surveyed 20 Jul 1781 being on half of a TW #2,551 issued 12 Feb 1780 in Jefferson Co. on the Waters of Coxes cr. and Stewarts cr. Waters of Salt Riv., adj. Charles Stewart & Henry Lee; 1 Jun 1782, p.326. £200

JOHN BRADFORD Ass'ee of SAMUEL BRYAN, 1,000 acs. Surveyed 24 Aug 1780 on a PTW #151 issued 15 Mar 1780 in Kentucky on David Jones fork of Elk horn, Beginning at a Corner to a former Survey made for William Philips and the Assignees of John Smith, with a line of the latter and adj. Samuel Bryan; 1 Jun 1782, p.327. £400.

NATHANIEL EVANS Ass'ee of JACOB MYERS, 400 acs. on a PTW #1,159 issued 6 Oct 1780 Surveyed 27 Apr 1781 in Lincoln Co. on both sides the Hanging fork of Dicks riv.; [two surveys] 200 acs. of which adj. McKenny, Craigs preemption, Evans, Barnets preemption & McKinney; the Residue 200 acs. on the side of a Ridge, adj. Ba[r]nett & McKenney; 1 Jun 1782, p.328. £160.

JOHN GORDON, 1,400 acs. Surveyed 19 Feb 1781, [two surveys] 400 acs. of which is by virtue of a Certificate in Right of Settlement in Lincoln Co. on the head Waters of the Shawnee and Cedar Run; adj. Trigg, Corn & his preemption land; the Residue 1,000 acs. on a PTW #570 issued 1 Apr 1780 adj. his Settlement land on the W and NE; also adj. the lands of Froman, Yoakum and Ingram; 1 Jun 1782, p.330. £400.

PETER SHEPHERD, 500 acs. part of a TW #928 issued 15 Oct 1779 Surveyed 22 Oct 1780 in Kentucky Co. Beginning on the hill of Beach fork Nearly Opposite the Mouth of Mill cr., at a Spring br., to three Cedars falling into the fork of a dry Run; 1 Jun 1782, p.332. £200. [Incorrectly given as Lincoln Co. in the Margin note]

JOHN LANE, 400 acs. by Virtue of a Certificate in Right of Settlement Surveyed 14 Dec 1770 in Ohio Co. on the waters of Buffaloe cr.; adj. Thomas Chaplain, John MacWilliams, Samuel Johnston & Thomas Chapman; 1 Jun 1782, p.333. A.C. of £2 Sterl.

JAMES HARROD Ass'ee of LEVEN POWELL, 1,000 acs. Surveyed 9 Apr 1781 on a TW #4,159 issued 20 Mar 1780 in Lincoln Co. on the Waters of Clarks Run, adj. Moores Settlement; 1 Jun 1782, p.334. £400.

MARGARET IRWIN, 150 acs. Surveyed 26 Mar 1781 on a TW #2,721 issued 19 Feb 1780 in Lincoln Co. on the head Brs. of the town fork of Salt Riv.; on the NW Corner of Myers preemption & on the NW Corner of Caldwells Survey; 1 Jun 1782, p.335 £60.

WILLIAM MONTGOMERY, JUNIOR, heir at law of ALEXANDER MONTGOMERY Dec'd, 1,400 acs. on a PTW #506 issued 31 Mar 1780 Surveyed 4 May 1781 in Lincoln Co. on a br. of Green riv. [two surveys] 400 acs. of which is by virtue of a Certificate in right of Settlement Beginning near his preemption about ½ a Mile South from Petills Station, at the foot of the Nobbs; the Residue 1,000 acs. adj. the Settlement 95 poles North from the Beginning Corner of sd Settlement, also at the foot of the Nobbs; 1 Jun 1782, p.336. £400.

JOSEPH RUSSELL Ass'ee of DAVID FINLEY, 250 acs. Surveyed 25 Apr 1781 on a TW #3,628 issued 10 Mar 1780 in Lincoln Co. on a Br. of Dicks Riv., adj. Benjamin Logans about 1½ North from Benjamin Logans house; 1 Jun 1782, p.338. £100.

ROBERT TYLER Ass'ee of SQUIRE BOONE Ass'ee of GEORGE MEREWETHER, 400 acs. surveyed 8 Jun 1781 on part of a TW #5,877 issued 15 Jul 1780 in Jefferson Co. on both Sides of Tick cr., cross lick cr.; adj. Meredith Helms 382 Acre tract, John Eastwood, & the sd Tylers former Survey; 1 Jun 1782, p.339. £160.

JOHN KENNEDY Ass'ee of THOMAS KENNEDY, 1,000 acs. Surveyed 24 Oct 178 on a PTW #455 issued 31 Mar 1780 in Kentucky Co. between Dicks riv. and the Hanging fork and adj. on the N of Richard Jackmans Settlement and preemption, on a remarkable Bend in the hanging fork, on the side of a path that leads from Richard Jackmans to Downeys Station; 1 Jun 1782, p.340. £400.

HUGH LOGAN, 1,000 acs. Surveyed 10 Apr 1781 on a PTW #600 issued 1 Apr 1780 in Lincoln Co. on the waters of the Hanging fork of Dicks Riv., Beginning on a hill Side about 4 Miles SW from Benjamin Logans Station, at the foot of the Nobbs near the little flatt lick; 1 Jun 1782, p.342. £400.

AARON LEWIS, 200 acs. Surveyed 29 Jun 1781 on a TW #4,002 issued 18 Mar 1780 in Jefferson Co. on the waters of Pleasant Run, on the N side of a Ridge; adj. John King on the West, Kings preemption land; 1 Jun 1782, p.343. £80.

JAMES ESTILL, 1,000 acs. surveyed 6 May 1781 on a PTW #53 issued 25 Feb 1780 in Lincoln Co. on the waters of Muddy and Otter cr., Beginning on a Ridge at the Corner of his fence, crossing the head br. of Otters cr., crossing little Muddy cr., crossing two Brs. of Muddy cr. and one of Silver cr.; 1 Jun 1782, p.344. £400.

THOMAS HELM Ass'ee of JAMES GARRANT, 500 acs. Surveyed 12 Jul 1781 on a TW #31 issued 15 Oct 1779 in Jefferson Co. on Freemans fork a br. of severns Valley of Green Riv., Beginning on the W side of the sd fork about 140 poles Nwardly from where the sd Helm now lives; 1 Jun 1782, p.345. £200.

ISHAM WATKINS, 400 acs. surveyed 19 Jul 1781 on a TW #3,315 issued 2 Mar 1780 in Jefferson Co. on the waters of Hardens cr. and the Waters of the Rowling fork brs. of Salt riv. about 3 Miles east from the head of Pottengers cr., adj. Edmond Eggleston; 1 Jun 1782, p.346. £160.

Col. WILLIAM McCLANACHAN, 50 acs. surveyed 21 Apr 1781 on a TW #5,782 issued 24 Jun 1780 in Botetourt Co. on the Waters of Roanoke and Joining the land of John Griffith and John Mesix; 1 Jun 1782, p.347. £20.

HENRY BOCKNER, 300 acs. Surveyed 4 Apr 1781 on a TW #949 issued 15 Oct 1779 in Lincoln Co. on the waters of Gilberts cr., at the head of a draft, on a ridge, adj. William Youngs preemption line; 1 Jun 1782, p.348. £120.

BENEDICK SWOAP Ass'ee of WILLIAM FLEMING who was Ass'ee of HENRY BAUGHMAN, 1,000 acs. Surveyed 28 Mar 1781 on a PTW #807 26 Apr 1780 in Lincoln Co. on Dicks Riv., binding with land unfit for Cultivation, adj. Henry Baughmans Settlement & George Smith; 1 Jun 1782, p.349. £400.

PETER SHEPHERD, 500 acs. surveyed 18 Aug 1781 on a TW #922 issued 15 Oct 1779 in Jefferson Co. on Soverns Valley cr., Beginning in the edge of the Barrens on the E side of the Cr. about half a Mile below Hooles Mill, on the bank of the west Br.; 1 Jun 1782, p.351. £200.

PETER SHEPHERD, 404 acs. surveyed 28 Mar 1781 on a TW #926 issued 15 Oct 1779 in Jefferson Co. on Mill cr. a br. of Salt riv. about 4 Miles from the Buffaloe crossing, Beginning about ¼ of a Mile from a Small Br. that empties into the sd cr. on the NW side; 1 Jun 1782, p.352. £161.S12.

HENRY BAUGHMAN, 1,000 acs. Surveyed 17 Feb 1781 on a preemption TW #414 issued 31 Mar 1780 in Lincoln Co. on Dicks riv., on the bank of Baughmans cr.; 1 Jun 1782, p.353. £400.

JAMES HARROD, 1,218 acs. surveyed 18 Oct 1780 on a PTW #544 issued 1 Apr 1780 in Kentucky Co. on the waters of Harrods Run [two surveys] 400 acs. of which is by Virtue of a Certificate in Right of Settlement adj. John Cowan & Smith; the Residue 818 acs. on a preemption Treasury Warrant Number 544 issued 1 Apr 1780 adj. his Settlement on the east, Smith, Bowman & Cowan; 1 Jun 1782, p.355. £323.S12.

LEVEN POWELL, 2,000 acs. Surveyed 5 Apr 1781 on two treasury Warrants #7 and #1,075 issued 15 Oct 1779 in Jefferson Co. Beginning on the west side of Simpsons cr. a br. of the town fork of Salt riv. about 20 poles above the Mouth of Plumb run and near a Spring, on the west Side of a Ridge about 18 poles south of a br. of the east fork of Simpsons cr., on a hill side on a drain Supposed to be the waters of Ashes cr.; 1 Jun 1782, p.356. £800. [Trees in the survey were marked "LP"]

WILLIAM OWSLEY / OWSLY Ass'ee of ENOCH FURR, 150 acs. Surveyed 4 Apr 1781 on part of a TW #95 issued 15 Oct 1779 in Lincoln Co. on Dicks riv.,

Beginning on the SW Corner of Thomas Owsley Assignee of Crockets Settlement, adj. the beginning of Manifields Settlement his line; 1 Jun 1782, p.358. £60.

THOMAS OWSLEY Ass'ee of WILLIAM MOORE, 1,000 acs. Surveyed 20 Feb 1781 on a PTW #632 issued 1 Apr 1780 in Lincoln Co. on Dicks Riv. [two surveys] 700 acs. Beginning on the NW Corner of Moores Settlement, on the west Bank of Owsleys Station Br., to an old survey of William Owsly, on the Point of a Mountain; the Other 300 acs. begins on Moors Settlement, adj. Moors line & the forementioned 700 acs. Survey; 1 Jun 1782, p.359. £400.

THOMAS HARGATE, 455 acs. by survey 5 Apr 1773 in Pittsylvania Co. on the North fork of Sandy Riv., crossing a fork of sd Riv. & two Bold Brs.; adj. the lines Surveyed for Abraham Baker, & John Martin; 1 Jun 1782, p.361. A.C. of £50 Shill. Sterl.

BENJAMIN CRAIG Ass'ee of JOHN CRAIG, 500 acs. Surveyed 27 May 1780 on a TW #548 issued 15 Oct 1779 in Kentucky Co. in the wates of Elk hork adj. an old Survey made for John Easter, & Elijah Craig in Carters old line; 1 Jun 1782, p.362. £200.

ELIJAH CRAIG Ass'ee of JOHN CRAIG Ass'ee of TOLIVER CRAIG, 500 acs. Surveyed 26 May 1780 on a TW #536 issued 15 Oct 1779 in Kentucky Co. Beginning at a corner to Carter and Philips about 3 or 4 Miles east from Bryans Station; 1 Jun 1782, p.363. £200.

PHILIP BUCKNER, 500 acs. Surveyed 4 Apr 1781 on a TW #2,080 issued 25 Jan 1780 in Lincoln Co. on a SE br. of Gilberts cr. adj. the lands of Lewis Craig on the NE, Wooleys on the N and Youngs preemption on the S; 1 Jun 1782, p.364. £200.

MARTIN HAWKINS Ass'ee of RICHARD CONNER, 1,000 acs. surveyed 20 Jun 1781 on a PTW #1,224 issued 23 Dec 1780 in Jefferson Co. on the head of the Middle fork of Simpsons cr. adj. the Lower side of sd Hawkins as Ass'ee of Charles Polke, beginning on the W side of a br. opposite the lower end of an Island, in a small draft, on the side of a Ridge ; 1 Jun 1782, p.365. £400. [Trees in the survey were Marked "RC"]

THOMAS BREND Ass'ee of JAMES BREND, 977 acs. Surveyed 14 Apr 1781 on a treasury Warrant Number 2,781 issued 19 Feb 1780 in Jefferson Co. on the lower side of Salt Riv., Beginning about 1½ Miles below the falls of sd Riv., adj. Honey & Shepherd; 1 Jun 1782, p.367. £395.S8.

STEPHEN TRIGG, 900 acs. surveyed 3 Feb 1781 on two treasury Warrants #912 and #913 issued 15 Oct 1779 in Lincoln Co. on the two Main brs. of Hammons cr. a br. of Salt Riv. adj. Todds Tract of 400 Acres, Beginning on a large level, on the head of a draft; 1 Jun 1782, p.368. £360.

JOHN ASKINGS, 1,000 acs. Surveyed 28 Jun 1781 on a PTW #1,006 issued 29 Jun 1780 in Jefferson Co. on Hardens cr. adj. Lewis Thomas and Mark Harden, on an Island in an east fork of Hardins cr., by a drain on a hill side, in Hardins line; 1 Jun 1782, p.369. £400.

ASEL DAVIS, 1,400 acs. surveyed 21 Oct 1780 [two surveys] 400 acs. by virtue of a Certificate for Settlement from the Commissioners in the district of Kentucky in Kentucky Co. on Clare cr. a br. of Dicks Riv., passing through a Bend of sd riv.; also 1,000 acs. adj. the E and N side of his Settlement; 1 Jun 1782, p.371. £400.

PAUL FROMAN Ass'ee of NICHOLAS CRISTE, 1,000 acs. Surveyed 9 Oct 1780 on a PTW #170 issued 16 Mar 1780 in Kentucky Co. on the E brs. of Polkes Run the waters of Coxes Cr., in the edge of a Glade, crossing a Small Run Making into the Beech fork, crossing Polkes Run and a dry Run; 1 Jun 1782, p.372. £400.

JOHN BRISCOE Ass'ee of JOHN HAWKINS who was Ass'ee of THOMAS BARTON, 1,400 acs. on a PTW #10 issued 27 Jan 1780 surveyed 30 Apr 1781 in Lincoln Co. on both sides of the Dry Run of Salt Riv. near the Mouth thereof at Henry Willsons Station [two surveys] 400 acs. of which is by Virtue of a Certificate in right of Settlement, in the Bent of a Small drain; the Residue 1,000 acs. adj. the settlement on the N and W side, Beginning on the bank of the dry run of Salt riv. 50 poles from the Mouth at Henry Willsons station; 1 Jun 1782, p.374. £400.

JAMES SMITH, 400 acs. Surveyed 17 Oct 1780 on a PTW #409 issued 31 Mar 1780 in Kentucky Co. on the waters of Dicks riv., Beginning at the NW Corner of Samuel Scotts Settlement, to Andrew Gemblins Settlement line, on the bank of Smiths br.; 1 Jun 1782, p.376. £160.

JOHN BAKER, 400 acs. Surveyed 11 May 1781 on a PTW #981 issued 28 June 1780 in Jefferson Co. on the Waters of the Beech fork; adj. James Rogers [at a large poplar marked with a J or cross in a Capitol D, 40 poles from Rogers beginning], near a Small drain Crossing Cedar cr.; 1 Jun 1782, p.377. £160.

WILLIAM WHITLEY / WHITELEY Ass'ee of VALENTINE HARMON, 400 acs. Surveyed 17 May 1780 by Virtue of a Certificate in right of Settlement in Kentucky Co. on Whitley cr. a br. of Dicks Riv. Including sd Whitleys Station; 1 Jun 1782, p.378. A.C. of £2 Sterl.

THOMAS OWSLY Ass'ee of ANDREW CROCKET, 400 acs. surveyed 19 Feb 1781 on a PTW #598 issued 1 Apr 1780 in Lincoln Co. on the waters of Dicks Riv., Beginning on the second Corner of the sd Owlys Settlement, on the dividing Ridge between Drake Camp and the fall lick Waters, along a Ridge of Mountain unfit for Cultivation to a point of Rocks on the North a br., along a large Ridge of Bald Hills unfit for Cultivation till the line Intersects the sd Owsleys Settlement line on a bald Hill; 1 Jun 1782, p.379. £160.

THOMAS MONTGOMERY Ass'ee of WILLIAM MONTGOMERY, 400 acs. Surveyed 15 Jun 1781 on a PTW #535 issued 1 Apr 1780 in Lincoln Co. on Carpenters cr. a br. of Green Riv., at the foot of the Nobs, adj. John Carpenters preemption; 1 Jun 1782, p.380. £160.

SAMUEL ESTILL Ass'ee of JOHN WEBBER, 400 acs. surveyed 7 May 1781 on a PTW #381 issued 29 Mar 1780 in Lincoln Co. on the waters of Muddy and silver cr., crossing a br. of Silver cr. & a br. of little Muddy cr., adj. James Estill; 1 Jun 1782, p.382. £160.

THOMAS OWSLEY Ass'ee of ANDREW CROCKET, 600 acs.

Surveyed 19 Feb 1781 part of a PTW #598 issued 1 Apr 1780 in Lincoln Co. on Drakes Camp cr., Beginning on the first Corner of his Settlement, on a large Ridge of Bald hills unfit for Cultivation, on a point Opposite the Mouth of three forks of Drakes Camp cr. thence west Agreable to an Agreement between the sd Owsly and Kennedy; 1 Jun 1782, p.383. £240.

MICHAEL TROUTMAN, 500 acs. Surveyed 22 Oct 1780 on two treasury Warrants #2,430 and #2,438 issued 7 Feb 1780 in Kentucky Co. on the Beech fork waters, Beginning on the N side of the cr. on the side of a hill in the hunters path side near the Mouth of a br. of sd cr., on the top of a Ridge; 1 Jun 1782, p.384. £200.

WILLIAM MOORE, 400 acs. surveyed 27 Oct 1780 by Virtue of a Certificate in right of Settlement in Kentucky Co. on the W side of Dicks Riv. Known by the Name of **the Crab Orchard**, Beginning near the Crab Orchard Run bank Supposed to be About half a mile from Dicks riv., About 20 poles from a very Remarkable Round hill about 50 poles from Housleys Station on the S side of sd Station; 1 Jun 1782, p.385. A.C. of £2 Sterl.

DANIEL TRIGG Ass'ee of JAMES INGRAM, 400 acs. Surveyed 9 Apr 1781 by Virtue of a Certificate in Right of Settlement in Lincoln Co. on the waters of the Shawnee run adj. Methias Yocum on the N, John Gorden on the W, Abraham Chaplin on the E, George Thompson and Slaughter on the S; near a Small Sinking Spring, crossing Slaughters Spring br.; 1 Jun 1782, p.386. A.C. of £2 Sterl.

THOMAS HYNES Ass'ee of JAMES EWING, 122 acs. by survey 2 Mar 1775 in Augusta Co. on the head brs. of the Midle riv. of Shenandore, adj. John McCleary, Robert Patterson, Mathew Wilson & Samuel McClearey; 1 Jun 1782, p.388. A.C. of 15 Shill. Sterl.

JOHN COOPER Ass'ee of WILLIAM CALLAWAY, 354 acs. by Survey 14 Dec 1762 in Bedford Co. on both sides of Prathers run; 1 Jun 1782, p.389. A.C. of 35 Shill. Sterl.

THOMAS SKIDMORE, 288 acs. by survey 14 Nov 1780 in Augusta Co. in Tygerts Valley Joining the land of Robert Cunningham and Andrew Skidmore, Beginning near a Great lick; 1 Jun 1782, p.390. A.C. of 30 Shill. Sterl.

DAVID HOGSHEAD, 30 acs. by survey 2 Nov 1780 in Augusta Co. in the Camp Run, on a bank near the Mountain, adj. his old line & John Hogshead; 1 Jun 1782, p.391. A.C. of 5 Shill. Sterl.

WILLIAM EWING, 283 acs. by survey 6 Apr 1775 in Bedford Co. on the brs. of the south fork of Otter riv. including a Small survey made for Michael Tanner and Transferred to sd William Ewing; adj. Randolphs old line, sd Tanners old line & Ewings line; 1 Jun 1782, p.392. A.C. of 30 Shill. Sterl.

JOHN OLIVER Ass'ee of ROBERT HALL who was Ass'ee of JOHN HAMILTON, 125 acs. by Survey 30 Oct 1766 in Augusta Co. on Jacksons riv., adj. Jackson; 1 Jun 1782, p.394. A.C. of 15 Shill. Sterl.

BENNETT GOODE, 275 acs. by Survey 26 Mar 1768 in Mecklenburgh Co. on the brs. of mine cr. and Mitchells cr., in the lick br.; adj. Eastland, Kitt, & Thomas Lanier; 1 Jun 1782, p.395. A.C. of 30 Shill. Sterl.

CHARLES, SAMUEL & GEORGE EWING Legatees of CHARLES EWING dec'd, 390 acs. by Survey 19 Dec 1771 in Bedford Co. on the brs. of the south fork of Otter Riv., adj. Charles Ewing & Randolph; 1 Jun 1782, p.396. A.C. of £2 Sterl.

MATTHEW TALBOT, 304 acs. by Survey 12 Apr 1770 in Bedford co. on both sides of Gills cr.; adj. Hawkins, Green, Patial & sd Hakins line; 1 Jun 1782, p.397. A.C. of 30 Shill. Sterl.

JOHN DAVIS, 43 acs. by Survey 10 Oct 1772 in Augusta Co. on back cr. a br. of Jacksons riv., Beginning near his old corner, adj. William Hutcheson; 1 Jun 1782, p.399. A.C. of 5 Shill. Sterl.

ALEXANDER WYLIE, 91 acs. by Survey 9 Feb 1782 in Augusta Co. on Jacksons Riv. on the E, S and W of **Kings bottom** now belonging to Andrew Kilpatrick/Killpatrick; Beginning on the side of a Steep Bank on the W side the riv., near a Gully, crossing a deep hollow; 1 Jun 1782, p.399. A.C. of 10 Shill. Sterl.

JOHN CALDWELL Ass'ee of JOHN TRABUE who was Ass'ee of JOHN RICHARDSON, 400 acs. Surveyed 31 Mar 1781 on a TW #1,927 issued 4 Dec 1779 in Lincoln Co. on the waters of Dicks Riv. Joining Boofmans land, at the head of a draft near a Bald hill; 1 Jun 1782, p.401. £160.

JOHN & JAMES BELL Orphans of DAVID BELL dec'd, 92 acs. by Survy 17 Jan 1781 in Augusta Co. on a br. of Black Thorn Joining the Land of Hugh Bodkin; 1 Jun 1782, p.402. A.C. of 10 Shill Sterl.

JOHN OLIVER Ass'ee of SAMUEL McCLEAN, 106 acs. by survey 12 Nov 1775 in Augusta Co. on a Small br. of Jacksons Riv.; 1 Jun 1782, p.403. A.C. of 15 Shill. Sterl.

WILLIAM NEELLY, 74 acs. by Survey 19 Dec 1771 in Botetourt Co. on the W Side of Masons cr. a br. of Roanoke, Beginning on a hill near the Great Road, adj. Col. Lewis & James Neely; 1 Jun 1782, p.404. A.C. of 10 Shill. Sterl.

JOHN & JAMES BELL Orphans of DAVID BELL Dec'd, 150 acs. by Survey 19 Feb 1781 in Augusta Co. on a br. of Black Thorn Joining a tract of Hugh Bodkins; 1 Jun 1782, p.405. A.C. of 15 Shill. Sterl.

HENRY MARTIN Ass'ee of DANIEL CONNER Ass'ee of JOHN TUGLE JUNIOR, 98 acs. by Survey 13 Apr 1773 in Amherst Co. on the S brs. of the North fork of the dutch cr. on the Spurrs of the Rockey Mountain, adj. William Tiller & Daniel Conner; 1 Jun 1782, p.406. A.C. of 10 Shill. Sterl.

JOHN CALLAWAY Ass'ee of JESSEE RENTFROE Ass'ee of NICHOLAS LEATHERMAN, 99 acs. by Survey 1 Mar 1774 in Bedford Co. on the south br. of the North fork of Black Water Riv., Beginning at W on Balls run Earnests Corner, on Lazy Run in Rentfroes old line; 1 Jun 1782, p.407. A.C. of 10 shill. Sterl.

JOHN DIGGS Ass'ee of OWEN HERNDEN, 50 acs. by Survey 21 Apr

1774 in Amherst Co. on the brs. of hatt cr., Beginning on the top of a Mountain; 1 Jun 1782, p.408. A.C. of 5 Shill. Sterl.

PAUL SUMMERS, 50 acs. by Survey 20 Feb 1781 in Augusta Co. on a br. of Bull Pasture Joining the land whereon he lives, Hughes line & George Sheetzs line; 1 Jun 1782, p.409. A.C. of 5 Shill. Sterl.

JOHN HOPKINS Ass'ee of THOMAS MONTGOMERY Ass'ee of LUKE BENNION, 164 acs. by Survey 9 Nov 1769 in Amherst Co. on the brs. of Davisons cr., adj. Thomas Montgomery; 1 Jun 1782, p.410. A.C. of £1 Sterl.

WILLIAM STEWART Ass'ee of WALTER BEAL & JAMES DOWDALL, 600 acs. surveyed 30 Apr 1781 on two Treasury Warrants #3,117 and #5,812 issued the one 29 Feb 1780 and the Other 29 Jun 1780 in Lincoln Co. on doctors fork; 1 Jun 1782, p.412. £240.

CHARLES CALLAWAY, 295 acs. by Survey 3 Mar 1770 in Pittsylvania Co. on Stantoun Riv., crossing Hancocks cr. 4 times, adj. sd Callaways old line; 1 Jun 1782, p.413. A.C. of 30 Shill. Sterl.

JOHN NEELLY, 500 acs. by Survey 20 Nov 1772 in Botetourt Co. on Peters cr. a br. of Roanoke, Beginning near a Spring a Corner of John Griffiths Survey; 1 Jun 1782, p.414. A.C. of 50 Shill. Sterl. including a Survey of 187 acs. made for Nathaniel Evans 29 May 1767 the title of which is now in the sd Neelly.

HENRY MILLER, 160 acs. by Survey 9 Feb 1781 in Augusta Co. on the NW side of Mossey cr. a br. of the North Riv. of Shenandore, in a hallow; adj. Hugh Divers corner, sd Millers line & Abel Griffith; 1 Jun 1782, p.416. A.C. of £1 Sterl.

RICHARD CAMPFIELD, 145 acs. by Survey 22 Nov 1780 in Rockingham Co. on the N side of the North riv. of Shenandore on the head drafts of fort Run, on a Ridge near a line of Raders Survey; adj. John Kennestick/Kenestrick, Hite, Greens Survey & Wedins land his open line; 1 Jun 1782, p.417. A.C. of 15 Shill. Sterl.

WILLIAM POAGE, 400 acs. by survey 6 Nov 1780 in Greenbrier Co. in the little levells, in a Glead, in the edge of the Savannah; adj. the land of William and George Clandenen, Nathan Gillelan and Edward Kennison which he's Intitled to by Settlement; 1 Jun 1782, p.418. A.C. of £2 Sterl.

JOHN EASTWOOD Ass'ee of JAMES McCOY, 900 acs. Surveyed 8 Mar 1781 on a TW #3,132 issued 29 Feb 1780 in Jefferson Co., Beginning about 50 poles from Guess cr. on the E side thereof; 1 Jun 1782, p.420. £360.

JOHN CAFFRY, 403 acs. Surveyed 24 Apr 1781 on a TW #6,241 issued 29 Mar 1781 in Bedford Co. on W head Brs. of Beaver cr. on both sides of Hairstones Road to New London, upon the Ridge Between the waters of Beaver cr. and flat cr., adj. Thompson; 1 Jun 1782, p.421. £640.

JOHN HOPKINS, 23 acs. by Survey 11 Jan 1763 in Augusta Co. on the head br. of Muddy cr. a br. of the North Riv. of Shenandore between his patented land and the North Mountain, also adj. Love; 1 Jun 1782, p.422. A.C. of 5 Shill. Sterl.

HUGH INNES Ass'ee of WILLIAM INGLES Ass'ee of PATRICK COUTTS who was Ass'ee of sd THOMAS BOOTH, 2,000 acs. by Survey 17 Jul 1774 in Fincastle Co. on the waters of Elk horn cr. a North br. of Kentucky Riv. about 20 Miles from the same about 90 Miles from the Ohio and on the S side thereof, crossing a Small cr. 5 times; adj. his own land, John Draper & William Russell; 1 Jun 1782, p.423. in Consideration of Military Service performed by Thomas Booth as a Lieutenant in the late war Between Great Britain and France Agreable to the terms of the King of Great Britains proclamation of 1763 and the Governors Warrant Obtained under the former Goverment.

REUBEN PAIN Ass'ee of HENRY McDANIELL, 720 acs. by Survey 10 Jun 1772 in Pittsylvania Co. on the brs. of sandy cr. and Shockoe cr., crossing a br. of Johns Run; adj. Walton, Dudgeon, Hicks line, Henry Empry, Givens line & Benjamin Terrys new line; 1 Jun 1782, p.424. A.C. of £3.S15 Sterl.

JOHN JOHNSTON / JOHNSON, 294 acs. by Survey 29 Oct 1773 in Botetourt Co. on back cr. a br. of Looneys Mill cr., on a Small cr. & a Small br.; adj. Samuel Johnston/Johnson, John Mills corner & Evans corner; 1 Jun 1782, p.426. A.C. of 30 Shill. Sterl.

ANDREW SKIDMORE, 336 acs. by Survey 13 Nov 1780 in Augusta Co. on the W side of Tygerts Valley riv. Joining the land of Thomas Skidmore and Thomas Warms, by a Sw.; 1 Jun 1782, p.428. A.C. of 35 Shill. Sterl.

GEORGE WALTON, 200 acs. by Survey 28 Apr 1752 in Lunenburgh Co. on the brs. of Juniper cr.; adj. Walker, Hawkins line & Pachans line; 1 Jun 1782, p.430. A.C. of £1 Sterl. [For Pachan's land, see PB 36, p.645 to Thomas Nance; for Hawkins land, see PB 32, p.32 to Benjamin Hawkins; for Walker's land see GB D, p.602 to Daniel Crenshaw ass'ee of Silvanus Walker heir to Tandy Walker]

WILLIAM JEANS, 131 acs. by Survey 21 Feb 1781 in Augusta Co. on the waters of Straight cr. and the waters of Crab Runs, on the top of a Ridge, adj. Nicholas Sibert; 1 Jun 1782, p.431. A.C. of 15 Shill. Sterl.

JOHN KING, 178 acs. by Survey 1 May 1781 in Augusta Co. on the south fork of the North Riv. of Shenandore below the big lick, at the foot of the Mountain adj. George Learight/Leawright; 1 Jun 1782, p.432. A.C. of £1 Sterl.

JOHN LEAWRIGHT, 210 acs. by Survey 27 Sep 1780 in Augusta Co. on the North fork of the North riv. of Shenandore above the Great white Oak lick near Harrisons Survey, by the foot of the Mountain, at the foot of a Ridge; 1 Jun 1782, p.433. A.C. of 25 Shill. Sterl.

WILLIAM BROWNLEE, 83 acs. by Survey 3 Jun 1780 in Augusta Co. joining his other tract Between William Mulcher and John Brownlee, by a road; 1 Jun 1782, p.434. A.C. of 10 Shill. Sterl.

SAMUEL BELL, 150 acs. by survey 15 Mar 1781 in Augusta Co. Between him and James Givens on Harless's draft, crossing the Spring br. to a Stake by the bank, adj. Harless & sd Bell; 1 Jun 1782, p.435. A.C. of 15 Shill. Sterl.

JAMES McCOUN SENR., 1,400 acs. Surveyed 12 Jun 1780 on a PTW #27 issued 12 Feb 1780, [two surveys] 400 acs. of which is by Virtue of a Certificate in right of Settlement in Kentucky Co. on both sides of the town fork of Salt Riv. adj. James McAfee; the Residue 1,000 acs. Crossing Salt Riv.; Adj. the Settlement land, George McAfee & James McAfee; 1 Jun 1782, p.436. £400.

WILLIAM ADAMS, 1,400 acs. surveyed 9 Mar 1781 [three surveyes] 400 acs. of which is by virtue of a Certificate in right of Settlement in Lincoln Co. on both sides of the town fork of Salt Riv. adj. George McAfees preemption on the NE side, Beginning on the W side of the Riv., on the side of a Ridge; also 600 acs. on part of a PTW #23 issued 12 Jan 1780 adj. the sd Settlement on the NE side, crossing the river 3 times; the Residue being 400 acs. in full of the sd preemption Warrant adj. the 600 Acre Survey on the NE side, cross a large br., cross the river to an Island, on a Ridge, adj. Hill; 1 Jun 1782, p.438. £400 also £2 Sterl.

GEORGE CALDWELL Ass'ee of JOHN DOWNIE, 200 acs. Surveyed 27 Mar 1781 on a TW #3,324 issued 3 Mar 1780 in Lincoln Co. on the town fork of Salt Riv.; adj. Harlins line & Steells Settlement; 1 Jun 1782, p.440. £80.

GEORGE CALDWELL, 1,400 acs. surveyed 20 Apr 1781 on a PTW #27 issued 12 Feb 1780 in Lincoln Co. on the town fork of Salt Riv. [three surveys] 400 acs. of which is by Virtue of a Certificate in right of Settlement; also 540 acs. adj. the Settlement on the SW side; the Residue 460 acs. adj. the Settlement on the NE side; 1 Jun 1782, p.441. £400.

ANTHONY BLEDSOE Ass'ee of WILLIAM COCKE, 1,400 acs. Surveyed 6 Oct 1780; [two surveys] 400 acs. of which is by Virtue of a Certificate in right of Settlement in Kentucky Co. on a fork of Tates cr. About 3 or 4 Miles N of Binneys Mill seat on silver cr., on a Ridge that is Remarkable for white Ash timber; the Residue 1,000 acs. on a PTW #552 adj. sd Settlement on the E side; 1 Jun 1782, p.443. £400.

CHARLES INGLISH, 400 acs. Surveyed 23 Feb 1781 on a PTW #609 issued 1 Apr 1780 in Lincoln Co. on Dicks riv. adj. the Settlement Trace & Rogers line; 1 Jun 1782, p.444. £160.

DAVID COX, 1,000 acs. Surveyed 28 Mar 1781 on a PTW #984 issued 29 Jun 1780 in Jefferson Co. on a Small Hallow crossing Coxes cr.; adj. Isaac Cox, Osborn Sprigg & Col. Cox; 1 Jun 1782, p.445. £400. [Trees in the survey were marked "D.C."]

ISAAC COX, 1,000 acs. by Survey 28 Mar 1781 on a PTW #955 issued 29 Jun 1780 in Jefferson Co. Crossing Fitches br. a fork of Coxes cr., crossing also Cane fork of Coxes cr., below Murrays Run, near the head of a drain; 1 Jun 1782, p.446. £400. [Trees in the survey were marked "I.C." or "J.C."]

JAMES BROWN, 400 acs. surveyed 10 Apr 1781 by Virtue of a Certificate in right of Settlement in Lincoln Co. on Clarkes Run, adj. Crow; 1 Jun 1782, p.447. A.C. of £2 Sterl.

DAVID ADAMS, 736 acs. Surveyed 14 Apr 1781 on a PTW #22 issued 12 Feb 1780 in Lincoln Co. on both sides of the town fork of Salt Riv.; [two surveyes]

400 acs. of which is by Virtue of a Certificate in Right of Settlement, Beginning on the W side of the Riv. at the head of a deep hollow, down a dry Run with Wilsons line to the Mouth thereof at Wilsons Station thence up the town fork of Salt riv., adj. Briscoe; the Residue 336 acs. adj. his Settlement, at the deep Hollow, near Natts br., adj. Wilson; 1 Jun 1782, p.448. £127.S4.

DAVID ADAMS, 469 acs. Surveyed 14 Apr 1781 part of a PTW #22 issued 12 Feb 1780 in Lincoln Co. on the W side of the town fork of Salt Riv.; adj. his Settlement, Briscoe, Gant, Overton & Thompson; 1 Jun 1782, p.450. £183.S16.

GEORGE SMITH, 1,000 acs. Surveyed 7 Oct 1780; [two surveys] 400 acs. of which is by Virtue of a Certificate in Right of Settlement in Kentucky Co. on the waters of Harrods Run; adj. James Harrod, Bowman & Quirk; the Residue 600 acs. on a PTW #943 issued 23 Jun 1780 adj. the Settlement on the West; 1 Jun 1782, p.451. £240.

HENRY WILSON, 1,000 acs. Surveyed 2 Jun 1780 on a PTW #54 issued 26 Feb 1780 in Kentucky Co. on the dry br. of the town fork of Salt Riv. and both sides the sd Riv., on a Small ridge, near a Gully; adj. John Briscoe, David Adams, Robert McAfee and Azariah Davis; 1 Jun 1782, p.453. £400. [Trees in the survey were marked "D.A." & "J.B."]

WILLIAM MONTGOMERY Ass'ee of JOHN MONTGOMERY, 400 acs. surveyed 23 Jun 1781 on a TW #6,178 issued 10 Feb 1781 in Lincoln Co. on the dividing Ridge between Green Riv. and the hanging fork; adj. William Montgomery Senrs. preemption, Abram James, Conrod Carpenter, & John Carpenters preemption; 1 Jun 1782, p.454. £640.

THOMAS GANT ass'ee of JAMES McAFEE who was Ass'ee of sd GANT, 500 acs. Surveyed 2 Feb 1781 on a PTW #491 issued 31 Mar 1780 in Lincoln Co. on both sides of the town fork of Salt Riv.; adj. John Briscoes preemption & Overtons preemption; passing Denters corner; 1 Jun 1782, p.456. £200.

PATRICK SHOAN, 400 acs. Surveyed 3 Apr 1781 by virtue of a Certificate in Right of Settlement in Lincoln Co. on Daughertys Run a br. of Dicks Riv., Beginning about a Mile from James Logans in a line of John Patersons, crossing a br. to James Logans line; 1 Jun 1782, p.457. A.C. of £2 Sterl.

JOHN LEWIS & RICHARD MAY, 1,000 acs. surveyed 21 Jul 1781 on a preemption Treasury Warrant in Jefferson Co. on waters of Hardens cr. and the waters of the Rowling fork Waters of the Salt Riv. about 4 Miles E and NE from the head of Pottengers cr., adj. Eggleston; 1 Jun 1782, p.458. £400.

PATRICK SHONE, 730 acs. surveyed 7 Apr 1781 on a PTW #601 issued 1 Apr 1780 in Lincoln Co. on the waters of Doughertys Run; adj. Dodd, Read, Shones Settlement & Logan; 1 Jun 1782, p.459. £286.

THOMAS HILL, 200 acs. Surveyed 28 Jun 1780 on a PTW #1,365 issued 18 Oct 1779 in Kentucky Co. on both sides of a fork of George Buckannans Br. about ¼ Mile North of his 300 Acre Survey, down a Small Run; 1 Jun 1782, p.460. £80.

SAMUEL HOPKINS, 613 acs. in Lunenburgh Co. [three surveys] 146 acs. of which *late the Property of John Patterson a British Subject* in Lunenburgh Co. adj. DeGraffenridt & Staples line; also 100 acs. late the property of John Graham a British Subject in Lunenburg Co. on the Brs. of flat Rock; adj. Thomas Tabbs corner over Whites Br., Robert Chappel & Henry Buford; the Residue 357 acs. on the N side of the south fork of Meherrin Riv. late the Property of Messr. Cunningham and Company British Subjects, adj. Elliot; 1 Jul 1782, p.461. £180 paid unto David Stokes Escheater for Lunenburg Co. the sd 613 acs. was sold by the Aforesd David Stokes Escheater unto sd Samuel Hopkins *agreable to two Acts of General Assembly passed in 1779 the one Intitled an Act Concerning Escheats and forfeitures from British Subjects the other Intitled an Act Concerning Escheators.*

DAVID STOKES JUNR Ass'ee of SAMUEL HOPKINS, 145½ acs. in Lunenburgh Co. on the brs. of Fucking cr., along the road; adj. Allen Stokes, Ludwill Evans, Elisha Betts, William Betts & John Winn; 1 Jul 1782, p.463. £600 paid unto David Stokes Escheator for sd Co. *late the Property of Andrew Johnston a British Subject which sd Land was Sold by the Aforesd David Stokes escheater for sd Co. unto David Stokes Junior Assignee of Samuel Hopkins Agreable to two Acts of General Assembly Passed in 1779 the one Intitled an Act Concerning Escheats and forfeitures from British Subjects the Other Intitled an Act Concerning Escheators.*

PATRICK WRIGHT Ass'ee of ALEXANDER BELL, 157 acs. surveyed 12 Oct 1781 in Norfolk Co. adj. Soloman Butt Talbutt; 1 Jun 1782, p.465. A.C. of £1 Sterl.

PATRICK HENRY Esq., the heirs of JOHN WILSON Decd, WILLIS WILSON and GEORGE KELLY, 2,800 acs. in Norfolk Co. adj. Richard Jones, Henry Halstead, William Hall & Benjamin Armstrong; 1 Jun 1782, p.466. A.C. of £14 Sterl. Surveyed by Virtue of Entrys made with the sd County Surveyor 19 Feb 1779.

GEORGE THOMPSON Ass'ee of PATRICK DOLAN, 890 acs. in Lincoln Co. on the waters of Shawnee Run adj. Henry Prather on the SW, Daniel Trigg on the N and E, and Stephen Trigg on the W; [three surveys] 400 acs. of which is by Virtue of a Certificate for Settlement from the Commissioners of the district of Kentucky adj. Henry Prather, Prathers Settlement and Preemption; also 380 acs. by virtue of a PTW #864 issued 22 Jun 1780, on a path; adj. sd Settlement, Hugh McGary & Henry Prather; and 110 acs. surveyed 9 Apr 1781 on the aforesd Preemption Warrant adj. John Gordon, Stephen Trigg, Daniel Trigg, sd Thompson, & Henry Prather; 1 Jun 1782, p.467. £196 Current Money.

PATRICK HENRY Esq., the heirs of JOHN WILSON dec'd, WILLIS WILSON & GEORGE KELLY, 4,000 acs. in Norfolk Co. adj. Alexander Bells land by the Green Lea Road [Green Sea Road], along the Road and adj. James Webbs land; 1 Jan 1782, p.470. A.C. of £20 Sterl. surveyed by virtue of Entrys made with the Surveyor of sd Co. 19 Feb 1779.

SAMUEL KIRKHAM, 400 acs. Surveyed 3 Mar 1781 on a PTW #307

issued 23 Mar 1780 in Lincoln Co. on Quirks cr.; 1 Jun 1782, p.471. £160.

ANDREW DODDS, 400 acs. surveyed 9 Mar 1781 on a PTW #432 issued 31 Mar 1780 in Lincoln Co. on both sides of Gevens cr. a br. of Dicks riv. adj. John Reads Preemption on the SE, crossing a large br. of Gevens cr., on the side of a Ridge; 1 Jun 1782, p.472. £160.

WILLIAM McCLANAHAN, 150 acs. by survey 20 Apr 1781 in Botetourt Co. on the waters of Tinker cr. a br. of Roanoke, near a Glade; adj. William Cavin/Carvin, Joseph Robinson, Cormack McCakery and his own land; 1 Jun 1782, p.473. A.C. of 15 Shill. Sterl.

JOSEPH WILSON as Ass'ee of WILLIAM DANDRIDGE, 768 acs. in Fluvanna Co. [two surveys] 320 acs. on Bird cr. the Residue 448 acs. up the Bird cr. adj. John Ashley; 1 Jun 1782, p.475. £3,652 paid by William Dandridge unto Thomas Napier Escheator for Fluvanna Co. which two tracts was *late the Property of Samuel Martin Esq. a Subject of Great Britain and was Sold by the sd Thomas Napier Escheater as aforesd unto William Dandridge and by him Assigned to sd Joseph Wilson Agreable to two Acts of General Assembly passed in 1779 the one Intitied an Act Concerning Escheats and forfeitures from British Subjects the other Intitled an Act Concerning Escheators.*

HUGH INNES, 420 acs. by survey 18 Jan 1760 in Halifax Co. on both sides the long br. of Panther cr., Crossing a Meadow, crossing the south and North fork of sd br.; 1 Jun 1782, p.476. A.C. of 45 Shill. Sterl.

NATHANIEL GARNET Ass'ee of THOMAS GOODSEY, 67 acs. by survey 28 Nov 1769 in Buckingham Co. on both sides of Sams or Jams cr. a br. of Slate Riv.; adj. his own line, Allen Tryes line & Charles Mosely; 1 Jun 1782, p.477. A.C. of 10 Shill. Sterl.

WILLIAM McCLANAHAM Ass'ee of ANDREW ARMSTRONG, 112 acs. by survey 31 Aug 1772 in Botetourt Co. Beginning on the N Side of the Riv. below the land of John Kinkead, Near Thomas Meadows, adj. Kinkead, on a path at the foot of a ridge; 1 Jun 1782, p.478. A.C. of 15 Shill. Sterl.

JAMES McNEEL / McNEAL, 917 acs. by survey 28 Sep 1781 in Buckingham Co. on the S brs. of Frisbys cr., in the low Grounds of sd cr.; adj. Charles Maxey, Col. Joseph Cabell, Archelaus Austin, James Bolling, Nicholas Corner, William Spencer & Robert Smith; 1 Jun 1782, p.479. £4.S15 Sterl.

CHARLES CALLAWAY, 240 acs. by Survey 16 Feb 1775 in Pittsylvania Co. on both sides of Sycamore cr., adj. Major Early & Talbot; 1 Jun 1782, p.480. A.C. of £1 sterl.

DAVID HOGSHEAD, 53 acs. by survey 6 Apr 1775 in Augusta Co. on the S side of Bradshaws cr., adj. his Fathers land; 1 Jun 1782, p.481. A.C. of 5 Shill. sterl.

BENJAMIN HARRISON, 260 acs. by survey 12 May 1780 in Rockingham Co. on the head drafts of the west fork of Cooks cr.; adj. Alexander Miller, Love, Harrison, another tract of sd Harrisons, & a line of the Meeting house land; 1 Jun 1782, p.482. A.C. of 30 shill. Sterl.

MICAJAH CLARK JUNR. Ass'ee of CHRISTOPHER CLARK who was Ass'ee of PETER JOHNSON, 250 acs. by survey 4 Apr 1739 in Goochland Co. crossing Cavets cr.; 1 Jun 1782, p.484. A.C. of 25 shill. Sterl.

HUGH DONOHO, 98 acs. by survey 15 Dec 1769 in Augusta Co. on the NE side of the North riv. of Shenandore, adj. Donoho; 1 Jun 1782, p.485. A.C. of 10 shill. Sterl.

DAVID BLY Ass'ee of JOHN GREGORY Ass'ee of WILLIAM BRUMMET, 50 acs. by Survey 26 Jan 1769 in Amherst Co. on the S side and Joining Buffaloe riv.; adj. Fry, & William Gatewood; 1 Jun 1782, p.486. A.C. of 10 shill. Sterl.

LEONARD BELL, 262 acs. by Survey 10 Feb 1781 in Augusta Co. on Stuarts cr. a br. of Cow pasture riv., adj. his patent land; 1 Jun 1782, p.487. A.C. of 15 shill. sterl. including 150 acs. gtd. to James Hall by pat. 3 Nov 1750 and thence to his son Robert Hall heir at law of sd James who Conveyed the sd land to Andrew Donolly by deed and was by sd Donolly Conveyed to sd Leonard Bell.

CHARLES WHITLOCK Ass'ee of GEORGE WALTON, 270 acs. by Survey 19 Apr 1752 in Lunenburgh Co. on the Brs. of Meherren riv. and Spring cr.; adj. Boulden, Dabbs line, Jones & Mitchel; 1 Jun 1782, p.488. A.C. of 30 Shill. Sterl.

WILLIAM BURNIT, 230 acs. by survey 22 Nov 1780 in Bedford Co. on W Brs. of little wreck Island cr. including the head br. of Stonewall cr., on the top of a Ridge Between little [wreck] Island and stonewall creeks; adj. Rogers, & Robert Wright; 1 Jun 1782, p.489. A.C. of 25 Shill. Sterl.

JOHN WALKER, 186 acs. by survey 1 Sep 1779 in Botetourt Co. in the fork of James Riv., by a path, adj. W. Carrell/Carroll; 1 Jun 1782, p.490. A.C. of £1 sterl.

THOMAS FUQUA, 120 acs. by survey 5 Feb 1781 in Bedford Co. on the North fork of Otter Riv., on Austins or Auslin Cr., adj. Hermen; 1 Jun 1782, p.491. A.C. of 15 Shill. Sterl.

THOMAS LOFTIS, 105 acs. by survey 6 May 1773 in Halifax Co. on the Drafts of Aarons cr., Beginning at the Mouth of Staffords br., adj. sd Loftis, Cox, Sizemore, Thomas Poole; 1 Jun 1782, p.492. A.C. of 15 Shill. Sterl.

DAVID FRAME, 77 acs. by survey 20 Mar 1761 in Augusta Co. on a draft of Naked cr., to a high rock, on a ridge, adj. sd Frame & Robert McCutchan; 1 Jun 1782, p.493. A.C. of 10 shill. Sterl.

THOMAS BOYD, 80 acs. by Survey 3 Mar 1775 in Augusta Co. on the waters of Marys cr. the Waters of James Riv., adj. Samuel Steel & sd Boyd, near Robert Campbells line; 1 Jun 1782, p.494. A.C. of 10 shill. Sterl.

JOHN ARCHER, 2,400 acs. by an inclusive Survey made 3 Nov 1780, 1,153 acs. thereof new land the remainder in Different Parcells and Gtd. to the sd John Archer by Patents the whole in Augusta Co. on Moffetts br. a br. of the Midle riv. of Shenandore, on a Ridge, crossing a draft to a Rock, by a Spring, on a hill near Moffett's line, near his Meadow; adj. William Matthews, John

King, John Beard, sd Archers old Corner & John Gardner; 1 Jun 1782, p.495. A.C. of £12 Sterl.

ALEXANDER FORBES, 110 acs. by survey 6 Apr 1775 in Bedford Co. on the North br. of Goose cr.; adj. Zac Bunch, Harris, Christian & Churches lines; 1 Jun 1782, p.498. A.C. of 15 Shill. Sterl.

JOSHUA TAYLOR, 351 acs. by survey 22 Dec 1779 in Buckingham Co. on both sides of slate riv.; 1 Jun 1782, p.499. A.C. of 35 Shill. Sterl.

HUMPHREY POSEY, 185 acs. by Survey 14 Dec 1773 in Pittsylvania Co. on the S side of Smiths Riv., on a high clift of Rocks on the aforesd Riv.; 1 Jun 1782, p.500. A.C. of £1 Sterl.

SAMUEL ANDERSON, 34 acs. by Survey 6 Oct 1779 in Augusta Co. near the long Glade joining his other land, near John Francis's line; 1 Jun 1782, p.501. A.C. of 5 Shill. Sterl.

WILLIAM & GEORGE CLENDINEN Ass'ee of DANIEL TAYLOR & SAMUEL DELANY, 352 acs. by Survey 4 Nov 1780 in Greenbrier Co. in the little Levells adj. the lands of Alexander Waddle and John Poage, Beginning at the foot of the Buckeye Mountain; 1 Jun 1782, p.502. A.C. of 35 Shill. Sterl.

WILLIAM WEBB, 186 acs. by survey 18 Mar 1780 in Botetourt Co. on Bordens run a Br. of James Riv. and Joining the lands of Robert Caldwell, James Gaunt dec'd and Benjamin Hawkins dec'd; by a Gully; 1 Jun 1782, p.503. A.C. of £1 Sterl. including 148 acs. of Patent land.

JOHN WRIGHT, 322 acs. by Survey 21 Apr 1780 in Buckingham Co. on Bent cr.; adj. his own line, Pendleton, Christians order Council line & Nalley Gordens line [on him]; 1 Jun 1782, p.505. A.C. of 35 Shill. Sterl.

NATHANIEL DAVIS Ass'ee of ROBERT JOHNSTON, 324 acs. by Survey 11 Dec 1781 in Amherst Co. on the N brs. of Pedlar riv.; adj. Roderick McCullock, his own lines & Charles Ellis's Orphans; 1 Jun 1782, pp.506-507. A.C. of 35 shill. sterl. [There is no margin note to explain why this grant was crossed out]

ROBERT WEAKLEY / WEAKLY, 253 acs. by survey 29 May 1780 in Halifax Co. on the brs. of Runaway and Brush creeks; adj. Swenny, sd Weaklys old line, James Ridgeway & Robert Williams; 1 Jun 1782, p.508. A.C. of 25 shill. Sterl.

ABSOLOM LOONEY Ass'ee of BENJAMIN DAVIS, 114 acs. by survey 1 Nov 1754 in Botetourt Co. on the waters of Craigs cr. a Br. of James Riv., Beginning at the foot of a Mountain, by a Spring, adj. Lee; 1 Jun 1782, p.509. A.C. of 15 Shill. Sterl.

JOSEPH ECHOLLS, 304 acs. by Survey 22 Apr 1755 in Halifax Co. on both Sides of Buffaloe cr., crossing the Cherry tree fork; adj. Joshua Echolls, Cornelius Short & Joseph Echolls; 1 Jun 1782, p.510. A.C. of 30 Shill. Sterl. [Margin note: This Grant was altered in the name of Governour Harrison and date]

THOMAS HILL, 200 acs. surveyed 24 Jan 1780 being one half of a TW #1,365 issued 18 Oct 1779 in Lincoln Co. on a large br. running into the town fork of salt riv. and N of his former Survey, on the side of a Hallow; 1 Jun 1782, p.511. £80.

MATTHEW WILSON, 92 acs. by Survey 30 Mar 1779 in Botetourt Co. on Looneys mill cr. a br. of James Riv. joining his Patented land, the land of Jeremiah Jenkins, John Drake, James Leatherdale and Solomon Simpson; 1 Jun 1782, p.512. A.C. of 10 Shill. Sterl.

CHARLES CALLAWAY, 98 acs. by survey 7 Mar 1770 in Pittsylvania Co. on bothsides of Tinkers cr.; 1 Jun 1782, p.513. A.C. of 10 shill. sterl.

EDWARD SMOOT Ass'ee of FRANCIS SMITH, 335 acs. by Survey 14 Apr 1780 in Botetourt Co. in Carvins Cove on Masons cr. a br. of [Roanoke] joining the land of Samuel Crawford; 1 Jun 1782, p.514. A.C. of 35 Shill. Sterl.

SOLOMOM TROWER, 273 acs. by survey 24 Sep 1774 in Louisa Co. and Fredericksville parish on the Waters of Cuffeys cr. and about the head thereof, Beginning on the N side of the Mountain road near the head of Cuffeys Cr.; adj. Murray, David Saunders & David Jones; 1 Jun 1782, p.515. A.C. of 30 Shill. Sterl.

JOHN BIGGS, 36 acs. by survey 19 Apr 1774 in Amherst Co. on the N brs. of Rodes cr., Beginning on the side of a Mountain; 1 Jun 1782, p.516. A.C. of 5 Shill. Sterl.

DANIEL McDONALD & DANIEL MONROW, 70 acs. by Survey 15 Feb 1780 in Augusta Co. on Stuarts cr. above and near the land of Van Swearingham; 1 Jun 1782, p.517. A.C. of 10 Shill. Sterl.

ROBERT GROGG Ass'ee of THOMAS GROGG, 400 acs. by Survey 2 Apr 1781 in Augusta Co. on the SE side of the North riv. of Shenandore, in pine hill draft, Beginning at Robert Groggs Corner on the side of Castle hill; also adj. John Stevenson / Stephenson, John McDougal, John Lowry & John Hare; *Benjamin Harrison Governor of the Commonwealth of Virginia hath hereunto set his hand and Caused the lesser seal of the sd Commonwealth to be Affixed at Richmond on the 1st day of June 1782 and of the Commonwealth the sixth*, pp.518-519. in Consideration of the Ancient Composition of £2 Sterling paid into the treasury of this Commonwealth.

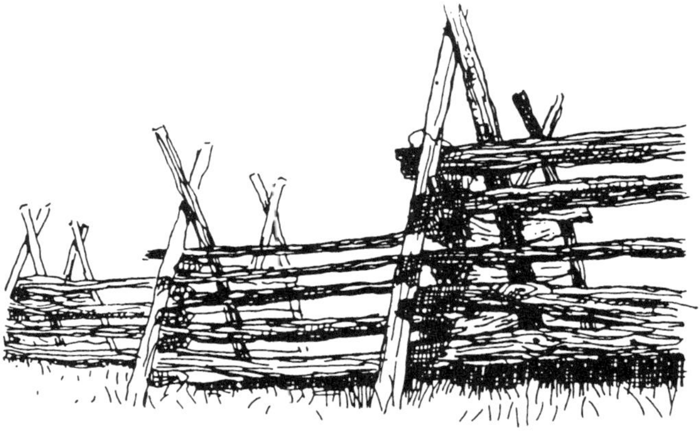

A Note To The User

Personal Names: The user of this index should be as imaginative in his pursuit of a surname as a colonial clerk might have been in his spelling. Virtually all variant spellings of personal names in the abstracts are unchanged in the index. The indexer has not presumed to decide, for example, whether *Thomas Bailey* is the same person as *Thomas Bayley*. Nor have "see also's" been included since it would be impossible to suggest all of the possibilities. When the sub-entry Capt. or other title is listed without a given name, no given name appears in the abstract (or in the patent book). The underline (_____) is used in place of given names or surnames if information was missing or illegible in the patent.

Place-Names: Variant spellings of place-names and variant abbreviations of geographical terms have been retained in the index. The user should remember that colonial clerks were recording many names for which there were no standard English spellings. No attempt is made to indicate the best or most frequent spellings of place names used during the colonial period.

Patentees: The given names of all patentees appear in capital letters in the index.

Subject Headings: Researchers will find entries under the following subject headings in the index:

bends (bents)	forks	orchards
Bermuda	forts	ordinaries
Beverly Manor	gaps	Parishes
Boonsborough	General Court	paths
bottoms	glades	pilot pine
boundary line (Fairfax)	glebe	plantations
branches	Golgotha	pocosons
bridges	governors	points
cabins	Grassy Hill Company	ponds
cane break	Great Britain	race grounds
caves	Green Sea	regiments
cliffs	gullies	ridges
churches	guts	rivers
cities	hills	roads
clerks	hollows	rocks
corners	houses	runs
counties	hunting ground	settlements
Country Line	islands	slashes
county lines	Kentucky	springs
courthouses	knobs	spurs
creeks	landings	stables
districts	levels	streets
drafts	licks	surveyors
fences	marshes	swamps
escheators	meadows	towns
falls	mills	tracts
ferries	Mingo	valleys
fields	mountains	Waughoo tree
fords	North Carolina	

INDEX

Aaron
  DANIEL, 232
  WILLIAM, 232
Abanathey, 182
Abner
  John, 182
Abney, 222, 223, 225
  Abraham, 224
  Dennit, 224
Abrams
  Robert, 128
Absten, 206
  JOSHUA, 206
Abston
  John, 214
Achold, 36
Acres
  ABRAHAM, 123
Acris, 77
Acuff
  JOHN, 277, 285
Adam
  Robert, 268
Adams, 1, 34, 45, 56, 108, 169, 184, 203, 224, 234, 256, 278
  David, 312
  DAVID, 311, 312
  GEORGE, 243
  HOWELL, 273
  Isaac, 2
  ISAAC, 37
  James, 104, 128
  JAMES, 238
  John, 139, 170, 211
  JOHN, 169

Adams, *cont'd*
  NATHAN, 243
  Richard, 204
  RICHARD, 119, 203
  Robert, 53, 97, 191, 238, 258
  ROBERT, 77, 253
  ROBERT JUNIOR, 234
  Silvester, 186
  SYLVESTER, 242, 243
  Thomas, 273
  THOMAS, 20, 204, 273
  William, 293, 301
  WILLIAM, 311
Addams
  James, 76
Aderson, Senior
  JAMES, 154
Adey
  WALTER, 145, 146
Adkerson, 38, 46
  Owen, 30
Adkins
  Edward, 252
  JOEL, 40
  John, 52
  Owen, 73
  RICHARD, 73
  William, 114, 278
Adkinson, 70, 110, 221, 240
  Richard, 170
  Roger, 78, 82
  William, 166
Adkison
  Elias, 156

Ady
  WALTER, 145
Agee
  JOSHUA, 266
Ager, 267
  John, 250
Agus
  Matthew, 50
Ainge
  William, 43, 107, 108
  Wm, 97
Airs, 142
  Aaron, 203
Aker, 123
Akers
  WILLIAM, 23
Akin
  Joseph, 95
  JOSEPH, 67, 237, 238
  PEEDMT, 117
  THOMAS, 31
  WILLIAM, 117
Akins, 64, 235
Alcorn, 199
  JAMES, 199
Alderson, 173
Aldridge
  John, 104
Alen
  SAMUEL, 276
Alexander, 108
  Andrew, 200
  Joseph, 206, 221
  JOSEPH, 112
  William, 112, 246
  WILLIAM, 206

Alford, 184, 196
　William, 158
Allegre
　DANIEL, 107
　Giles, 108
Allegree, 62, 128, 186
　Giles, 185
　GILES, 83
Allen, 128, 129, 144, 165,
　　210, 259
　ARCHER, 165
　BENJAMIN, 119
　George, 176
　GEORGE, 144
　Hugh, 33
　HUGH, 94, 117
　James, 176
　JAMES, 93
　JOHN, 93, 94, 179
　ROBERT, 259
　Samuel, 165, 192, 193,
　　198
　Valentine, 49
　William, 173
　WILLIAM, 256
　William, Captain, 99
　William, Col, 297
Allen, Colo.
　William, 135
Allen, Senior
　James, 195
Alley, 2, 18
　HENRY, 191
Allin, 199
Allison, 141
　JAMES, 146
　John, 152, 195
　JOHN, 79
Alloway
　John, 282
Almond
　Christopher, 165
Alsup
　ROBERT, 172
　THOMAS, 279
Alverson
　Becknal, 202
Ambler, 288
Ambrose
　Thomas, 194

Amos, 163
　Francis, 111
　FRANCIS, 48
　WILLIAM, 255
Amose, 156
　WILLIAM, 119
Anderson, 26, 40, 54, 85,
　　122, 154, 190, 206, 238
　Alexander, 8
　Bartlett, 35, 36
　Francis, 221
　GEORGE, 137
　James, 64, 82, 159
　JAMES, 147
　John, 179, 194, 253, 267
　John, 283
　JORDAN, 179
　MATTHEW, 8
　NATHANIEL, 137
　Richard, 11, 12, 85
　Richard, Colo, 85
　SAMUEL, 316
　THOMAS, 61, 179
　William, 115, 136, 173
　WILLIAM, 26-29, 194
　William and Samuel, 147
Andrews
　MARK, 292
　Richard, 121
　RICHARD, 141
Angela, 119
Angles
　James, 100
Angley
　PETER, 282
Anglin
　John, 97, 203
　JOHN, 38
Angling
　Philip, 120
Angus
　JOHN, 242
Anthony, 60, 102, 214, 248
　JOHN, 140
　Joseph, 164
　JOSEPH, 216, 283
Apperson
　LITTLEBURY, 238
Appleberry, 11
Applebury, 129

Apshear, 268
Arbuckle
　James, 92
　MATTHEW, 92
Archer, 62
　John, 115, 116, 177
　JOHN, 115, 315
Archers, 316
Aris, 77
Arking
　John, 300
Armantrout
　GEORGE, 254
Armantrouts, 194
Armentrout
　John, 182
Armontrout
　JOHN, 130
Armouist, 22
Armstrong, 141, 164
　Andrew, 133
　ANDREW, 133, 314
　Benjamin, 313
　James, 116
　John, 141
　JOHN, 212, 213
　Robert, 216
　ROBERT, 173
　Thomas, 133
　THOMAS, 142
　WILLIAM, 140, 216
Arnold, 144, 197, 264
　JAMES, 167
　John, 119, 132
　JOHN, 193
　STEPHEN, 249, 273
Arther, 156, 161, 253
　THOMAS, 140, 247
　William, 159
Arthur, 238, 240
　BENJAMIN, 221
　John Junr, 240
　THOMAS, 215, 240, 247
Asberry, 120
　THOMAS, 222
Asbury
　THOMAS, 222
Ashberry, 120
Ashby
　John, 1

Ashby, *cont'd*
  JOHN, 68, 69
Ashley
  John, 209, 314
Ashton, 177
Ashworth, 53
  JOHN, 44
Askew, 129
  ANTHONY, 184
Askey
  SAMUEL, 97
Asking
  John, 300
Askings
  JOHN, 305
Askins
  John, 164
Asten
  William, 266
Astin, 141
Aswoerth, 8
Asworth
  John, 8
Atcheson
  Thomas, 32
Atkeison
  Jesse, 190
Atkerson, 270
  JESSE, 123
  Jesser, 194
Atkins
  Edward, 38, 290
  EDWARD, 38
  HENRY, 40
  JACOB, 149
  Owen, 14
  WILLIAM, 1
Atkinson, 41, 121, 160, 269
  Elias, 156
  PARKER, 246
  Roger, 141, 142
  ROGER, 141, 142, 215
  Samuel, 206
  THOMAS, 128
Atkisson
  Roger, 15
Austen
  Richard, 262
Austin, 25, 56, 255, 264, 287
  Archelaus, 314

Austin, *cont'd*
  Joseph, 288
  JOSEPH, 53
  William, 214, 249
  WILLIAM, 60
Avent, 272
  THOMAS, 272
Ayler
  ANTHONY, 155
Aylor
  Anthony, 116, 249
  ANTHONY, 258
Ayres
  MOSES, 36, 170
Baber
  ROBERT, 215
  Thomas jr, 100
  Thomas Junr, 3, 10
  THOMAS SENR, 3
  William, 65
  WILLIAM, 55
Bachellor
  DAVID, 53
Bacon
  Lidal, 262
Bagbey
  William, 138
Bagg
  Alexander, 232
Baggs
  ALEXANDER, 171, 173
  THOMAS, 173
Bags
  ALEXANDER, 149, 251
  JAMES, 149
Bailey, 50, 263
  Gamiliel, 181
  John, 161
  JOHN, 42
  JOSEPH, 61
  RICHARD, 215
  WILLIAM, 33
Baily
  JOHN, 238
Baine, 55
  ALEXANDER, 39
Bains
  Patrick, 64
Baird, 81
  John, 191

Baison
  PATRICK, 176
Baker, 14, 150
  Abraham, 305
  James, Col, 18
  John, 96, 288
  JOHN, 177, 224, 306
  ROBERT, 10, 177
Baldwin, 51, 119
  William, 111
Baldwins, 258
Ball
  James, 216
  John, 60, 253, 257
  JOHN, 200, 253
  WILLIAM, 124
Ballamy, 129
Ballard
  Richard, 54
  RICHARD SENR, 48
Ballenger, 6
  Isaac, 252
  John, 3, 30, 149, 176
  JOHN, 21, 30
Ballentine
  JOSEPH, 183
Ballew
  Joseph, 150
Ballinger
  JOHN, 279
Ballow
  John, 204
  LEONARD, 238
  Robert, 84
  STEWARD, 229
  Thomas, 63
Bandfield, 76
Bane
  JAMES, 112
Banfield, 76
Banister, 141, 264, 287
Bank
  Laurel, 203
Banks
  Henry, 22
  South, 7
  TUNSTALL, 76
  WILLIAM, 76
Barber
  John, 160

Barbey
  HUGH, 131
Barby
  HUGH, 131
Bardel, 37
Barenett, 142
Barkdale
  HICKERSON, 25
Barker, 47, 140
  Benjamin, 138
  EDMUNDS, 47
  Henry, 138
  Jesse, 38
  John, 77
Barket, 11
Barksdale
  HENRY, 120
  HICKERSON, 23, 119
Barlour, 239
Barlow, 235
Barnard, 119, 179
  ABNER, 121
Barner
  Barners Mill, 244
  Francis, 244
  Jacob, 235
Barnes, 37
Barnet, 13, 55, 142
  Thompson, 55
Barnets, 302
Barnett, 179, 249, 301
  JAMES, 13, 105
  JOHN, 149
  Robert, 132
  ROBERT, 301
Barns, 245, 266
  HENRY, 149, 277
Barrenten
  Isaac, 288
Barret, 3
Barrett, 200, 238, 288
  John, 190
  Robert, 200
  William, 15
Barrick
  PHILLIP, 284
Barrington
  Isaac, 288
  Samuel, 208
Barrott, 15

Barrow
  John, 206
Bartin, 283
Bartman
  HENRY, 18
Barton
  JOSHUA, 264
  THOMAS, 306
  William, 108
  WILLIAM, 107
Basham, 262
Baskam, 262
Baskerville, 239
Basket
  WILLIAM, 11
Batersby, 103
Bates, 74, 81, 121, 220
  DANIEL, 26
  FLEMING, 225
  James, 121
  JAMES, 39, 222, 224, 225
  John, 221, 224
  JOHN, 221
  SAMUEL, 224
  STEPHEN, 224
  THOMAS, 252
  WILLIAM, 224
BATTALLIONS
  Third, 261
Battersby
  William, 227
Batterson
  William, 144
  WILLIAM, 176
Baugh, 80
  Isham, 191
  James, 191, 219
  John, 191
  MARTHA, 247
  Thomas, 247
Baughan, 223
Baughman
  HENRY, 304
  HENRY, 304
Baughmans
  Henry, 304
Bausher
  Thomas, 33
Baxter
  GEORGE, 198

Bayes, 119, 285
Bayley
  William, 162
Baylor
  John, 164
Baynes
  Joseph, 18
Bays
  JOHN, 11
  PETER, 114
  WILLIAM, 113
Bayses, 167
Ba[r]nett, 302
Beal, 94
  James, 81
  WALTER, 309
Bear
  John, 161, 275
Beard, 13, 19, 73, 177, 227
  Adam, 292
  John, 47, 116, 217, 316
  JOHN, 176
  Samuel, 292
  SAMUEL, 292
  Thomas, 177
Beasley
  PHILIP, 48
Beaver, 57
  JAMES, 54
Beazley
  John, 228
  JOHN, 97
Beck
  PAUL, 130
Beckham
  James, 192
  JAMES, 22
Beckley, 79
Bedford, 140
  THOMAS, 135, 181
Beel
  Thomas, 275
Been, 52
Beggs
  THOMAS, 155
Belcher, 177
  Isham, 213
Bell, 193, 253, 289
  ALEXANDER, 60, 61,
    289, 313

Bell, *cont'd*
  DAVID, 22, 65, 308
  Henry, 71, 149
  HENRY, 246
  James, 110, 144
  JAMES, 203, 247, 308
  JOHN, 308
  John Miller, 181
  JOHN MILLER, 181
  LAURENCE, 130
  Lawrence, 254
  LEONARD, 315
  SAMUEL, 310
  THOMAS, 180
  WILLIAM, 99, 111
Bellamy, 75
  JOHN, 75
Bellew
  Joseph, 150
Belling, 291
Bellomy, 184
Bells
  Alexander, 313
  Laurence, 194
Below
  Charles, 208
  Stephen, 289
Belsches
  James, 135
Belsher
  Edmund, 182
Belshes
  James, 297
BENDS, (see bents)
Benet
  JOSEPH, 199
Benge
  THOMAS, 119
Bennet, 168, 292
  John, 148
  Joseph, 42
  Peter, 113
  RICHARD, 285
  THOMAS, 30
  William, 268
Bennett
  John, 153
  JOHN, 257
  Richard, 285
  RICHARD, 285

Bennetts
  Alexander, 294
Benning, 265
  Anthony, 265
Bennion
  LUKE, 309
Bennit
  Peter, 77
Bennitt
  FRANCIS, 279
  WILLIAM, 279
Bentley, 87
BENTS, 32
  Adrian's Cr., 33
  Bells River, 24
  First Sharp, 61
  Great, 63
  Peters Creek, 24
Berkley
  Hugh, 283
Berkly, 283
  Edmund, 75
BERMUDA, 47
Bernard
  Abner, 85
  John, 85
  William, 168
Berrick
  PHILLIP, 284
Berry
  DAVID, 154
  JOHN, 201
Best
  Philip, 297
Bethel, 129, 184
Bethell, 11
Betterson
  WILLIAM, 176
Betts
  Elisha, 313
  William, 313
Beverly, 115, 116, 195, 292
BEVERLY MANOR, 17, 132
Bibb
  ROBERT, 17
  William, 134, 158, 266
Bibe
  JOHN, 254

Bibee
  David, 83
  JOHN, 127
Bible
  ADAM, 155
Biby
  Peter, 193
Bicknall
  JAMES, 292
  JOHN, 292
  Thomas, 292
BICKNALL
  James, 292
Bife
  JOHN, 19
Biggs
  JOHN, 317
Bilberry
  James, 273
Billings, 8, 9, 38, 80, 205
  Jasper, 7
  Mill Survey, 7
Billup, 207
Billups
  JOSEPH, 207
Bings
  John, 201
Birch
  GARROT, 54
Birches
  Garrot, 124
Bird, 12, 145, 170, 177, 218
  Colo, 85
  Francis, 254
  FRANCIS, 218
  Joseph, 76, 130
  JOSEPH, 218
  MARY, 276
Birk
  ROWLAND HORSELY, 194
Birt
  Philip, 135
Bishop
  Francis, 198
  Mason, 254
  MASON, 25
Bizwell
  John, 287

Black, 205
  Henry, 181
  James, 64
  Samuel, 48, 289
  THOMAS, 71
  William, 62
  WILLIAM, 149
Blackley
  JAMES, 128
Blackmore
  NATHANIEL, 94
Blackwelder, 206
Blackwells, 294
Blagg
  JOHN, 33, 74
  John, Capt, 34
Blaickley, 161
Blain
  George, 158
  John, 138
  JOHN, 253
Blaine
  ALEXANDER, 209
  JOSEPH, 16
Blair, 58, 253
  Alexander, 250
  ARCHIBALD, 172
  James, 172, 250, 253
  John, 147
  JOHN, 172, 250
  William, 161
  WILLIAM, 147, 148, 258
Blairs, 147
Blan
  Charles, 231
  John, 226
Bland
  Merritt, 163
  Thomas, 75
  William, 75
Blane
  ALEXANDER, 209
  John, 228
Blankenship
  HUDSON, 222
  JOSEPH, 223
  NOVELL, 15
  Nowel, 222
Blankes, 129

Blankinship, 284
  HUDSON, 222
  JOEL, 138
Blanks, 277
  Henry, 31
  John, 15
Blanton
  JAMES, 269
  THOMAS, 222, 223
Blayr
  James, 115
  William, 73
Bleake, 59
Bledsoe
  ANTHONY, 311
  Joseph, 155
Blevens, 99
Blevir, 186
Bliver
  James, 186
Bluford, 166
Bly
  DAVID, 315
Boad
  JAMES, 234
Board
  James, 237
  JAMES, 234
  JOHN, 77
  William, 213, 262
  WILLIAM, 56
Boaz
  James, 37, 241, 243
  JAMES, 21, 22
  Thomas, 22, 37, 38, 40, 190, 195
  THOMAS, 37, 38, 190, 195
Boaze
  Thomas, 290
Bobbet
  James, 250
Bobbit
  James, 170
Bockner
  HENRY, 304
Bodkins
  Hugh, 308
Boggs
  THOMAS, 259

Bohannan
  John, 165, 196
  WILLIAM, 247, 254
Boles
  JOHN, 16
Boling
  JOSEPH, 70
Bolling, 123, 152, 156, 186, 214, 234, 239, 241, 251, 267, 282
  Christopher, 186, 256
  Edward, 233
  James, 314
Bolton, 182
  Robert, 188
  ROBERT, 188
Boman, 71
Bome, 238
Bond, 83, 287
  Charles, 266
Bondurant
  John, 265
  JOHN PETER, 65
  PETER, 65
Booker, 22, 50, 78, 141, 157, 239, 263, 264
  Parham, 263
  Thomas, 9
  WILLIAM, 46, 54
Bookerhoy
  JOHN, 289
Boone
  SARAH, 293
  SQUIRE, 293, 294, 298, 303
BOONSBOROUGH, 63, 210, 212, 285
Booth
  John, 179
  JOHN, 77, 214
  Thomas, 310
  THOMAS, 310
Borden, 94, 132, 191, 221
  Benjamin, 46
Bordin, 176
Borne, 238
Borrick
  PHILLIP, 284
Boss
  NICHOLAS, 155

INDEX

Bostick, 12, 68, 108, 119, 240
  Charles, 78, 108, 167
  John, 243
  Nathan, 243
Bosticks
  Charles, 282
Boswell
  George, 154
  GEORGE, 147, 251
  John, 104
BOTTOMS, 206
  Crages, 76
  Larg Rich Bottom, 35
  Large, 7
  Mingo, 35
  White Walnut, 17
Bough
  MARTHA, 247
Boughman, 259
Boughton
  John, 244
  JOHN, 235, 244
Boulden, 46, 315
  Thomas, 262
  THOMAS JUNR, 262
Boulding, 198
Boulton, 207
  Robert, 182
BOUNDARY LINE
  Lord Fairfax, 12
Bounds, 214
Bousher
  Thomas, 37
Bover, 146
Bowcock
  John, 47
Bowden
  Burwell, 253
  BURWELL, 78
Bowder
  Burwell, 37
Bowen
  Rice, 222
Bowes
  William, 294
Bowin
  REICE, 223
Bowling
  Christopher, 277

Bowling, cont'd
  James, 189
  JOSEPH, 70
Bowman, 304, 312
  ABRAHAM, 69, 298
  ESUM, 71
  JACOB, 298
  John, 171, 299
  JOHN, 69, 71, 126, 163, 298
  JOSEPH, 69, 298
  Peter, 108
  THOMAS, 80
Bowmans
  Joseph, 297, 299
Bowyer
  John, 113, 172, 249
  JOHN, 82
  Thomas, 83, 92, 276
  THOMAS, 92, 209
  WILLIAM, 92
Bowyers
  John, 191
Boxley
  BENJAMIN, 122
Boyd, 45, 160, 183, 221, 223, 269, 315
  ALEXANDER, 39
  Andrew, 182
  James, 191, 200, 244
  JAMES, 170, 222
  John, 132
  JOHN, 99
  Robert, 196
  Thomas, 120, 132
  THOMAS, 315
  WILLIAM, 200
Boyer, 194
  INGLE, 182, 193, 194
Boyle
  JAMES, 248
Boyles
  ROBERT, 221
Brackey
  Thomas, 115
Brackfield
  CHRISTOPHER, 148
  JACOB, 148

Bracy
  John, 93
Bradfield, 163
Bradford
  JOHN, 302
  Samuel, 188
Bradley, 33
  WILLIAM, 33, 181
Bradly
  William, Capt, 34
Bradshaw, 56, 58, 64, 101, 115, 214, 246
  James, 275
  JAMES, 260
  PETER, 140
  THOMAS, 275
  WILLIAM, 140
Bramble, 18, 221
Bramblett, 222, 247
  William, 162
Bramblitt, 238
Brammer
  JAMES, 152
  John, 204
  JOHN, 272
Branch
  John, 56
  Samuel, 236
BRANCHES, 92
  Adams's Spring, 224
  Agers, 244
  Austins, 244
  Austons, 223
  Back, 57, 253
  Bare, 60
  Bates's, 224
  Bays, 15
  Beaver Creek, 127
  Beaver Dam, 127
  Beaver Pond, 262
  Beaverpond, 252
  Big, 260
  big run, 114
  Birch, 6
  Black Thorn, 183, 285, 308
  Bold, 2, 4, 8, 14, 39, 40, 53, 97, 100, 216, 250, 278, 279

BRANCHES, *cont'd*
Bold Branch of
  Leatherwood Creek-, 134
Bradshaws, 115
Briahry, 80
Briary, 247
Brieary, 127
broad, 264
Bryary, 80
Buck, 14, 53, 103, 235, 244, 266
Buck Horn, 45, 60, 67
Buck run, 131
Buck Shoal, 80
Buck-horn, 62
Buckhorn, 261
Buffaloe Creek, 129
Bull, 238
Burges, 108
Burks's, 11
Burnt Bride, 265
Butterys, 118
Cabben, 56
Cabbin, 56
Callehans, 277
Camp, 8, 12, 15, 30, 68, 70, 79, 213, 277
Cattail, 23, 243
Cattail Spring, 214
Cattamount Falls, 246
Cedar, 292
Chappel, 219
Coles, 245
Cool, 48
Corn, 114
Corn feild, 247
Corn Field, 80
Corner, 54
Cornfield, 226
Cory, 60
Cow, 68, 223
Crab apple tree, 235
Cribbons, 227
Cron, 102
Crooms Quarter, 49
Crossing Bens, 129
Cut Shin, 129
Deans, 71
Deep, 236, 240

BRANCHES, *cont'd*
Dividing, 3
Dolaps Creek, 114
Double, 219
Dry, 92, 267, 312
Dry Branch Gap, 173
Dung, 54
Dutchmans, 129, 237, 263
Elk, 28, 29
Elk horn, 209
Ellots, 277
Falls, 222, 224
Firns, 44
Fitches, 311
Flaggy, 283
Flat, 81, 248
Folfits, 19
Foul Ground, 287
Fowl Ground, 97
Fox, 217
Gap, 56
Glady, 15, 236
Golloways, 239
Grassy, 84
Grave, 234
Great, 18, 33, 37, 38, 55, 77, 230
Grindstone, 4
Gundstone, 4
Half way, 245
Harbour, 54
Haw, 57, 68, 210
Hay stack, 122
Head, 238
Hemp, 279
Hicks, 273
Hill Powder, 220
Hog, 217
Hogpen, 100
Horse Pen, 6
Horse Shoe, 12, 21, 77, 207
Horsebone, 275
Hungry Camp, 54
Indian, 5
Indian Field, 77
Ivi, 7
Ivry, 4
Jacks, 271
Jacobs, 79

BRANCHES, *cont'd*
Jannings, 19
Jennings, 217
Jennings's, 115, 216
Johns, 14, 61
Johns Creek, 117
Johnson, 38
Johnsons, 33, 123
Kents, 243
Keytons, 2
Kirks, 247
Knuckold, 12
Large, 245, 267, 271
Leynors, 97
Lick, 10, 64, 105, 222
Lillys, 29
Lils, 221
Long, 10, 23, 39, 40, 54, 59, 75, 100, 103, 217, 239, 243, 314
long Meadow, 135
Low Ground, 97
Lower Long, 83
Lynous's, 97
Manallys, 227
Manalys, 64
Maple, 8, 236
Mary creek, 115, 120
McBride, 223
McBrides, 223
McDaniels, 264
McDowels, 68
Meadow, 67, 68, 220, 236, 263
Meherrin, 37
Merrewethers, 104
Middle, 22, 92
Middle fork of
  Cunningham Creek, 121
Miery, 95
Millstone, 265
Mire, 265
Miry, 15, 59, 281
Mobberly's, 263
Moffets, 116, 269
Moffetts, 270, 275, 315
Morsons, 36
Mudlick, 71
Muster, 62, 119

BRANCHES, *cont'd*
Narrow Passage, 62
Natts, 312
Nob lick, 116, 117
North, 5, 7, 19, 31, 55, 69, 74, 93, 99, 115, 273, 316
North branch of fishing Creek, 122
North of Naked Creek,, 110
North West Branch of Linvils Creek/, 137
Nothing, 131
Nusery, 265
NW, 89
of Mossey Creek, 115
of Ruffets Creek, 113
Old Field, 103
Pates, 215
Pattons, 231
Peters, 4
Pinsons Shoal, 80
Plowmans, 273
Plum, 267
Pole Bridge, 10
Pole Cat, 266
Pond, 24, 52
Poplar, 111
Pounding Mill, 2, 13
Prathars run, 130
Raccoon, 223
Ralphs, 243, 284
Rattle Snake, 238
Rays, 61
Reads, 222
Reedy, 56, 92, 292
Rius, 36
Robbins, 9
Robersons, 8
Robertsons, 73
Robins, 6
Robinsons, 8
Rock castle, 96
Rockey, 47, 243, 253, 265
Rocky, 25, 52
Rogers, 215
Rounding Mill, 2
Ruis, 36
Russels, 122

BRANCHES, *cont'd*
Sandy, 265
Sarahs, 83
Saw Scaffold, 52
Sawpets, 248
Seths, 51, 122
Shears, 122
Shoars, 241
Sholes, 244
Simmons, 123
Sinking, 92
Sinking Spring, 87
Siths, 80
Slavary, 78, 79
Small, 238
Small Branch of the S Side of the Middle river;, 115
Small branch of the South river, 123
Small Spring, 117
Smiths, 132
Smiths Camp, 276
Snake horn, 108
Snake run, 120
Sorrel, 85
South, 6, 23, 39, 55, 70, 76, 83, 94, 102, 123, 285
south branch of Potomack River, 126
south Branch of Potowmac River, 126
south branch of Potowmack River, 126
Speeds, 33
Spring, 67, 95, 102, 243, 310
Staffords, 315
Standefers, 6
Steep, 15, 135
Stith's, 87
Stone Spring, 243
Stones Spring, 243
Stoney, 239
Suck, 95, 158, 245
Sucks, 97
Sullens, 77
Tabacco House, 209
Tantraugh, 262

BRANCHES, *cont'd*
Todds run, 113
Tollesons, 227
Tomkins Meadow, 138
Toms, 240
Trough, 275
Turkey pen, 118
Ugleys creek, 114
Wain Writes Grave, 234
Wainwrights grave, 234
Wallace, 98
Watry, 15, 124, 214
Weary, 82
West, 103, 123, 214
Western, 19
Western branch of Linwell Creek, 124
Whealers, 243, 244
Whill's, 100
White Marsh, 251
White Oak, 6, 11, 119
White Walnut Bottom, 17
Whites, 313
Wicks, 59
Wolf, 84
Wolfpen, 111
Worsham's, 220
Branham
Benjamin, 108
Branscomb, 2
THOMAS, 2
Brawner
BENJAMIN, 147
Braxton, 246
Carter, 81, 134, 227
Braze
William, 31
Breadens
George, 290
Breadon
JOHN, 138
Brechen, 85
Breden
Edward, 115
Brend
JAMES, 305
THOMAS, 305
Brett
BENJAMIN, 205

Brewer, 207, 272
  JAMES, 100
  Nicholas, 272
  SACKVILL, 212
  William, 207
Brewis
  Robert, 190
BRIDGES, 207
  Baree, 286
  Cedar, 283
Bridgwater
  Charles, 104
Bries, 179
Briggs
  JOHN, 259
Bright
  GEORGE ADAM, 120
Brillemon
  Jacob, 67
Brinson
  ZEBULON, 14
Brintle
  William, 25
Briscoe, 312
  John, 299, 312
  JOHN, 306
Briscoes
  John, 298, 312
Bristo
  BENJAMIN, 130
British (see Great Britian)
Broadnan
  Stephen Edmards, 168
Broadnax
  Stephen Edward, 168
Brodnor [Broadnax]
  Edward, 151
Broles, 72
Brook, 72
Brooker, 290
Brookes, 290
  Anne, 206
Brooks, 149, 267
  WILLIAM, 186
Brothers
  Francis, 96
Broune
  AUGUSTINE, 284
Browder, 37

Brown, 17, 19, 54, 130, 138, 156, 158, 160, 188, 212, 213, 224, 225, 263
  ABSALOM, 124
  AUGUSTINE, 62, 201
  Benjamin, 285
  BENJAMIN, 245
  Goram, 221
  Gorom, 225
  Henry, 56
  HENRY, 150
  ISAAC, 151, 212, 213, 290
  Israel, 212
  ISRAEL, 151, 212, 213
  JAMES, 54, 311
  John, 47, 104, 140, 228
  JOHN, 47, 196, 199, 201, 226
  JOHN JUNIOR, 226
  John Junr, 206
  John Senr, 206
  MARGARET, 54
  Richard, 31, 83
  RICHARD, 21, 56, 130
  Samuel, 140, 274
  Sheldrake, 153
  Shildrakes, 153
  Thomas, 142, 245
  THOMAS, 40, 116
  Valentine, 207
  William, 51, 85, 104, 105, 156, 217, 235, 249, 285
  WILLIAM, 82, 147, 222, 227, 261, 263, 275
Browne
  AUGUSTINE, 284
Brownlee
  John, 310
  WILLIAM, 310
Broyles
  Coatney, 72
Bruas
  ROBERT, 257
Bruce
  JOHN, 129
  WILLIAM, 210
Brumet
  John, 131
  JOHN, 276

Brumfield
  Lacosta, 174
  Lacoste, 174
BRUMFIELD & COMPANY
  LACOSTA, 174
Brummet
  WILLIAM, 315
Bryan, 305
  ANDERSON, 196, 297
  David, 126
  J, 26
  John, 226
  JOHN, 238
  Peter, 132, 221
  Samuel, 302
  SAMUEL, 302
  William, 142, 298, 300
  WILLIAM, 160
  William Junr, 71
Bryan, Senior
  William, 113
Bryans, 113
  William, 299
  WILLIAM, 113
Bryans, Senior
  William, 113
Bryant, 100, 129, 130, 162, 163
  Benjamin, 131, 132
  Cornelius, 155
  JAMES, 18, 160
  John, 275
  Lewis, 275
  Sylvanus, 48
  Thomas, 135, 155
  THOMAS, 155
  WILLIAM, 18
Buchanan
  JOHN, 88
Buchannan
  GEORGE, 293
  JAMES, 191
  JOHN, 90, 91
Buche
  John, 57
Buchellor
  DAVID, 53
Buckannan
  JOHN, 88

Buckannans
  George, 312
Buckley
  James, 173
  John, 176
  JOHN, 6
  Samuel, 283
  SAMUEL, 283
Buckly
  James, 114
Bucknall
  FRANCIS, 62
Bucknel, 184
Buckner
  Philip, 300
  PHILIP, 305
Buford, 158, 264, 278
  David Junior, 226
  Henry, 313
  HENRY, 225
  James, 34
  JAMES, 81, 221, 255
  JOHN, 156
  Miles, 164
  THOMAS, 19, 148, 221
  William, 223, 262
  WILLIAM, 18, 55
Buggs, 99
Bulger, 300
Bullen
  Joseph, 161
Bullerton, 6
Bullet
  CUTHBERT, 13
  THOMAS, 13, 75
  THOS, 13
Bullett
  CUTHBERT, 75
Bullock, 105, 240, 300
  Edward, 296
  John, 20
Bumgardner
  GODFREY, 199
Bumk
  John, 19
Bumpass
  Robert, 216
Bumsider
  John, 23

Bunch, 73, 236
  HENRY, 148
  Samuel, 100
  Zac, 316
Burch, 284
  Garrot, 121
Burches
  Garrot, 124
Burchet, 168
Burchett
  Ben, 207
Burcks
  Samuel, 225
Burden, 250
  ARCHIBALD, 225
Burdett
  WILLIAM, 110
Burford
  BURFORD, 215
  Daniel, 81, 226, 282
  DANIEL, 228
  John, 228
  Miles, 164
Burge
  WOODY, 60
Burger
  Menes, 227
Burges
  Main, 64
  William, 103
  Woody, 201
Burgess
  EDWARD, 15
  Thomas, 7
  THOMAS, 43, 45
  WILLIAM, 144
Burk
  Charles, 96
  David, 143
  John, 81, 210
  JOHN PARTREE, 242
Burke
  WILLIAM, 136
Burkett
  FREDERICK, 115
Burkly
  Edmund, 75
Burks
  ROWLAND HORSELY, 150

Burks, *cont'd*
  Samuel, 229
Burnet, 24, 33, 241
  James, 136, 194
  JAMES, 241
Burnett, 24, 266, 290
  CHARLES, 109
  JAMES, 48, 241
  Joseph, 136, 137
Burnit
  WILLIAM, 315
Burnley, 165, 252
  AUSTIN, 189
  Harden, 197, 266
  Hardin, 104, 266
  ISREAL, 262
Burnly, 198, 276
Burns, 283
  JOHN, 200
  PATRICK, 193
Burnside
  James, 195
  John, 115
Burnsides
  JAMES, 195, 210
Burrass
  John, 185
Burrus
  John, 104
  William, 104
Burruss
  John, 185
Burton, 188
  Benjamin, 118
  Charles, 241
  CHARLES, 8
  Isaiah, 24
  Jesse, 133
  JESSE, 133, 196
  JESSEE, 270
  William, 196
Burwell, 247
Butler, 25, 156, 236
  WILLIAM, 214, 247
Butterworth, 140
  ISAAC, 110
  ISAACK, 110
Butts
  William, 288

Buzzard
  Philip, 119
  PHILIP, 203
Bybee, 186
  JOHN, 128, 180
  JOSEPH, 180
Byble
  Adam, 155, 259
Byer
  William, 211
Bynam, 15
Bynom, 178
Bynum, 64, 77, 279
  Samuel, 257
Byrd, 122, 241
  Colo, 80
  Honble Col, 45
  JOHN, 276
  Joseph, 68
  MARY, 276
  William, 74, 129
  WILLIAM, 276
Cabbel, 249
Cabell, 107, 204
  JOHN, 202, 204
  Joseph, 96, 157, 233
  JOSEPH, 96, 157
  Joseph Col, 314
  Nicholas, 229
  NICHOLAS, 85
  William, 122, 158, 225, 229
  WILLIAM, 157, 158
  William, Docter, 228
Cabell, Esquire
  William, 134
CABINS, 31
  Kennedys, 297
  Old, 164, 273
  Palsons, 298
  Willsons, 164
Caffrey
  Charles, 265
Caffry, 239
  Charles, 237
  CHARLES JUNR, 237
  JOHN, 309
Cafre
  JOHN, 118

Cagar
  Jacob, 200, 204
Caghey
  JAMES, 114
Calaway, 219, 220
  James, 220
  JAMES, 143, 218-220
Calbreth
  William, 64
  WILLIAM, 227
Caldwell, 2, 239, 265, 301
  David, 71
  GEORGE, 311
  JOHN, 308
  JOSEPH, 16
  Robert, 296, 316
  William, 117
Caldwells, 303
Calferry
  JOHN, 189
Call
  William, 191
  WILLIAM, 104, 217
Callaham
  Nicholas, 210
Callaway, 67, 68, 70, 71, 73, 102, 109, 130, 151, 159, 166, 216, 222, 233, 249, 263, 264 & Co., 76
  CHARLES, 309, 314, 317
  Francis, 236
  GEORGE, 238
  James, 77
  JAMES, 110, 170, 263
  John, 214
  JOHN, 159, 237, 292, 308
  Randolph, 172
  Thomas, 187, 279
  William, 161, 172, 237
  WILLIAM, 236, 237, 307
  Wm, 156
Callehan, 277
Calloway, 4, 18, 23, 31, 56, 62
  James, 2, 64
  JOHN, 218
Callwell, 235
  John, 227
Caloway, 5

Cambril
  HUGH, 118
Camden
  WILLIAM, 232, 233
Cameron, 126
  John, 160, 285
  JOHN, 120, 269
  JOHN, Revd, 80
  John, Reverend, 269
Cammeron
  JOHN, 120
Camp, 149
Campbel, 199
  ARTHER, 76
Campbell, 3, 144, 157, 191, 239, 287
  ALEXANDER, 191
  Archibald, 135
  ARCHIBALD, 239
  Arthur, 209, 294
  ARTHUR, 293, 294
  CHARLES, 18
  Daniel, 218
  David Senr., 294
  GEORGE, 113
  Hugh, 110
  Jacob, 259
  James, 19, 145, 176, 283
  JAMES, 124, 161, 181
  John, 23, 117, 118, 159, 219
  JOHN, 17, 96, 116
  Josiah, 266
  Neil, 233
  Neill, 230, 233
  ROBERT, 154, 281
  THOMAS, 42, 154, 223
  William, 20
  WILLIAM, 88, 90, 91, 154
Campbells
  David Senr., 294
  John, 183
  Robert, 315
Campble
  ROBERT, 260
Campell
  ABRAHAM, 70
Campfield
  RICHARD, 309
CAMPS, 54, 150

Camron
  Joseph, 212
CANADY
  DAVID, 76
Candler
  DANIEL, 15
  WILLIAM, 222
Candles
  Stephen, 137
CANE BREAK, 34, 79, 94
Canefax, 184
  JOHN, 140
Canifax, 184
Cannaday
  WILLIAM, 68
Cannady
  DAVID, 76
Cannefaxe, 196
Cannon, 39
Canterberry, Junior
  JOSEPH ,, 121
Cantley
  John, 211
Cantrell, 38, 252
  Joshua, 152
Cantril
  JOSHUA, 195
  SARAH, 42
Cantrill
  Joshua, 38, 290
  JOSHUA, 11
Cantwell
  JOHN, 251
Caplenger
  JOHN, 259
Cargel, 8
Cargell
  John, 241
Cargett, 31, 40
Cargetts
  JOHN, 40
Cargil, 215
Cargill, 31, 142, 195, 252, 257
  John, 142
Carlton, 274
Carnall
  THOMAS, 52
Carney
  Thomas, 163

Carolile
  JOHN, 249
  ROBERT, 258
Carpenter, 52
  Conrod, 312
  George, 201
  ZOPHAN, 177
  ZOPHAR, 178
  ZOPHER, 120
Carpenters
  John, 306, 312
  Zophen, 287
Carr
  James, 102, 114
  JAMES, 48
  Samuel, 191
  Thomas, 136, 181, 191
  William, 43
  WILLIAM, 43
Carrel
  JOHN, 122
Carrell
  Roger, 134
  W, 315
Carrington
  George, 228
  PAUL, 262
Carroll
  Joseph, 273
  Roger, 137
  W, 315
Carson, 239, 258, 267
  Ezekiel, 23
  James, 158
  John, 23, 25
  JOHN, 237
  Thomas, 158
Carter, 62, 67, 177, 245, 268, 276, 284, 305
  Col, 9
  E, Colo, 9
  Edward, 174
  EDWARD, 17, 33
  Edward, Colo., 104
  ELIJAH, 8
  George, 149, 278
  GEORGE, 114, 171, 251, 268
  Isaac, 7
  JOHN, 8

Carter, *cont'd*
  JOSEPH, 3
  JOSIAH, 10
  Peter, 225, 228
  PETER, 229
  Richard, 3
  S, 7
  Shadrack, 301
  SHADRACK, 301
  Solomon, 225
  THEODORICK, 3
  THOMAS, 8, 109
Cartwright, 296
  JOSEPH, 296
Carver, 111
  Joseph, 20
Carvin
  William, 314
Cary, 73, 108, 236
  Archibald, Honble. Esq., 219
  Miles, 137
Casey
  Roger, 231
Cash
  Howard, 227
Casson, 125
Cato
  SARLING, 240
  STARLING, 240
  STERLING, 38
Cauchey
  JOHN, 23
Caudle
  Stephen, 137
Caudler
  CAUDLER, 15
CAUSEWAY
  at the Bridge, 207
Cave
  RICHARD, 8
Cavenaugh
  Wm, 156
CAVES
  Cave Run, 7
  Cave Spring, 82
  Cave Spring Tract, 1
  caving land, 63
Cavin
  William, 314

Cerby
 John, 4
Certain, 3
 Isaac, 112
Chadwell, 24, 52, 135, 252
 DAVID, 187
 Georg, 52
 George, 52
Chaffin, 165
Chafin
 Joshua, 36
Chaldwell, 7
Challiss, 260
Chamberlain, 11, 33, 41, 128, 152, 153
Chamberlaine, 150
Chambers
 John, 291
 JOHN, 244
 THOMAS, 37
 William, 24, 273
Chamourlain, 179
Champion, 162
Chancy
 JACOB, 278
Chandler, 43, 222, 237
 ISAAC, 192
 WILLIAM, 64
Chaney, 208
 JACOB, 67, 148
Channey, 6
Chaplain
 Thomas, 302
Chaplin
 Abraham, 307
 Joshua, 36
Chapman, 2
 Chares, 59
 JOHN, 50
 JOSEPH, 58
Chappel
 Robert, 313
Charleton, 74
 Richard, 261
Charlton, 94
 RICHARD, 75
Charter, 145
Cheak
 William, 102

Cheatham, 140, 195
 ABIA, 44
Cheldress, 50
Chenault, 277
 STEPHEN, 125
Cherry
 Thomas, 76
 THOMAS THEOPHILUS, 183
Cheswell, 17
Chetwood
 John, 103
Chew[n]ing, 163
Chezenhall
 ALEXANDER, 50
Chick
 William, 137, 183
Chigley, 181
Childers
 Benjamin, 270
 HENRY, 81, 232
 John, 233
 WILLIAM, 236
Childres, 79, 96
 JOHN, 226, 241, 242
Childress
 John, 51
 JOHN, 226
 MAJOR, 185
 Paul, 277
Childrie, 121, 122
 John, 122
Childris
 HENRY, 81
Childs, 255, 290
 John, 54
 JOHN, 251
 PAUL's Heirs, 218
Chiles, 218, 239
 Henry, 286
 John, 111, 268
 JOHN, 149, 286
Chirtwood, 4
Chistian
 ISRAEL, 99
Chiswell, 147, 208
 Colo., 227
Chitwood
 JAMES, 215

Chitzenhall
 ALEXANDER, 50
Choat, 5, 109, 216
 Christopher, 4, 248
 EDWARD, 218, 219
 EDWARD JUNR, 218
 SABERET, 119
Choice
 Tulley, 292
 TULLEY, 143
 Tully, 64, 257
 TULLY, 53, 64
Choise, 2
Chowning, 163
 THOMAS, 186, 189
Chrisam
 John, 15
Chrishan
 James, 227
Chrisman, 275
Christian, 49, 103, 148, 276, 316
 Charles, 131, 185, 196
 CHARLES, 286
 Christian, 104
 CHRISTIAN, 76
 Col, 8
 David, 128
 Drury, 230, 233
 Israel, 32, 133, 286
 ISRAEL, 32, 94, 99
 ISREAL, 266
 James, 17, 25, 71, 129, 149, 190, 227, 229, 267
 JAMES, 146, 149, 248
 John, 229, 246
 JOHN, 230, 286
 Nathaniel, 198
 Robert, 230
 ROBERT, 229
 ROSANNA, 32
 Thomas, 279
 William, 32, 73, 79, 94
 WILLIAM, 14, 33, 34, 37, 247
Christian, Junior
 CHARLES, 131, 196
Christians, 316
 Roberts Orphans, 230

INDEX

Church, 223
  ROBERT, 223
CHURCHES, 316
Cinsey, 72
Circle
  LEWIS, 189
CITIES
  Alexandria, 257, 258, 268
  Petersburg, 25-6, 29-30
  Richmond, 32, 95
Clack, 38
Claiban
  William, 125
  WILLIAM, 125
Claiborne
  William, 125
Clak
  James, Lt, 51
Clancy, 130
Clandenen
  George, 309
  William, 309
Clardy
  MICHAEL, 252
Clark, 17, 18, 56, 186, 208, 243
  Archibald, 57
  Benjamin, 156
  CHRISTOPHER, 295, 296, 315
  Edward, 15
  Francis, 78
  GEORGE, 201
  GEORGE ROGERS, 301
  James, 18
  JAMES, 51
  James, Lt, 51
  Micajah, 15, 156
  MICAJAH JUNR, 315
  Rances, 163
  Robert, 242
  ROBERT, 160, 234, 238
  Thomas, 34, 190, 221
  THOMAS, 145
  William, 103
  WILLIAM, 230
Clarke, 78
  F, 17
  Francis, 153
  WILLIAM, 232

Clarkson
  DAVID, 54
  WILLIAM, 150
Clasby, 128
Claunch
  Jeremiah, 114
Claunche's, 152
Clausel
  Clausel, 270, 272
Clay, 44, 58, 81, 151, 160, 205, 255
  Abia, 195
  Charles, 44, 85, 103, 249
  CHARLES, 36, 80, 188, 205
  CHARLES Rev'd, 101
  ELEAZER, 206
  JESSE, 245, 254
  Jessey, 168
Claybrook, 3, 21, 22, 25, 31, 37, 79, 130, 149, 279
Claywell
  PETER, 253
Cleaver
  JOHN, 160
Cleavland, 111
Cleek
  MATHIAS, 79
Clement, 264
  ADAM, 248
  Stephen, 190
Clements, 216
  BENJAMIN, 243
  ISAAC, 8, 243
  Isacc, 77
Clemment
  ISAAC, 8
Clemon
  John, 24
Clendening, 221
  CHRISTOPHER IRVINE, 264
  Christopher Irvine, 221
Clendinen
  WILLIAM, 316
Clerk, 2
  William, 48, 136, 194
CLERKS
  Thomas, Edmund, C.L.Off., 41

Cleveland
  Jacob, 17
Clever, 145
Cliborn
  JOHN, 77
CLIFFS
  Ivy Clift, 238
Clift, 53, 241
Clinch
  William, 261
Clonche, 218
Clopton
  George, 153
  GEORGE, 153
  Robert, 17
  ROBERT, 51
  William, 25
Cloud, 7
  ISAAC, 168
Cloyds, 141
Clyert, 140
Coak, 10
Cobb, 167, 177, 188
  Charles, 159, 245
  James, 225
  Robert, 225
  Samuel, 5
Cobbin
  Richard, Colo, 75
Cobbs
  Ambrose, 225
  CHARLES, 245
Coburn
  JAMES, 300
Cock, 171, 265
  George, 245, 247
  James, 104
  NATHANIEL, 165, 277
  Richard, Col, 206
Cocke, 27-29
  Abraham, 207
  NATHANIEL, 61
  Peter, 207
  Richard, 171
  Richard, Colo, 61
  William, 135
  WILLIAM, 311
Cockerham, 150, 277
Cockran, 184
  Andrew, 181, 270

Cockran, cont'd
  THOMAS, 19
Cockran and Company, 174
Cockrin, 282
Codgar
  JACOB, 55
Coffer
  JOSIAS, 189
Coffey, 170
  James, 227
Coffman, 198
Cogar
  Jacob, 122, 199, 200, 203
Cogars, 285
Cogbill
  CHARLES, 192
  Jesse, 48, 219
  Jessee, 219
Coger, 120
  JOHN, 256
Coghey
  James, 176
Cohorn, 118
Coil
  GABRIEL, 126
Colborth
  William, 64
Cole, 83, 103, 163, 211, 220, 224
  Isaac, 78
  James, 57
  John, 101
  MARK, 55, 57, 77
  Walter, 225
Coleman, 153, 155, 159, 165, 235, 277
  CLUVERIUS, 270
  James, 180
  JAMES, 100
  John, 22
  Vincent, 193
Coles
  ISAAC, 223
  JOHN, 103, 104
  Mark, 109
  Mary, 167
  WALTER, 34
Colin, 43
Colin, Dunlop, Son, and Co:y Merchants, 43

Collaice
  WILLIAM, 36
Collen
  William, 30
Collens
  James, 79
  WILLIAM, 79
Collar
  JOHN, 61
Collice
  JAMES, 36
  WILLIAM, 36
Collie
  Edward, 290
Collier, 176, 221
  Aaron, 129
  AARON, 129
  HENRY, 176, 255
Colliers
  Aaron, 129
Collin
  Thomas, 161
  William, 30
Colling
  William, 30
Collings, 279
  JOSEPH, 25
  William, 149
Collins, 51, 183
  Aaron, 129
  DANIEL, 278
  James, 112
  John, 131
  Joseph, 167
  Moses, 16
Collises
  Henry, 2
Colly
  JOHN, 33
Colyer
  JOHN, 15, 78, 186
Comer, 108, 122, 205, 211
  THOMAS, 108
Commack
  WILLIAM, 127
Compton, 83, 224
  JOHN, 150, 259
Conally
  John, 302

Conary
  JOHN, 21
Confrey, 64
Connally
  John, 302
Connelly, 92, 118, 276
  John, 103, 209
Conner, 95
  ALLEN, 56
  DANIEL, 308
  Nicholas, 48, 245
  NICHOLAS, 187
  RICHARD, 305
  Samuel, 41
Conners, 244
  Darby, 141
  Nicholas, 48
Connoley, 117
  ARTHUR, 118
  THOMAS, 117
Connolly
  John, 76
Conolly
  ARTHUR, 118
  Thomas, 274
Conrad
  John, 192
Conrod
  GEORGE, 272
  PETER, 113
Conter, 295
Conway, 144, 146, 283
  Henry, 31, 224
  HENRY, 246, 248
  JOHN, 186
  Richard, 268
Coock
  William, 5, 11
Cook, 5, 109, 220
  Andrew, 235
  Harmon, 30
  John, 211
  JOSHUA, 33, 37
  JOSIAH, 40
  William, 6, 150, 256
  WILLIAM, 151
Cooke
  DAVID, 298
  JOHN, 291
  Josiah, 290

Cooley
  JAMES, 11
Cooper, 124, 136
  Arthur, 255
  ARTHUR, 276
  JOHN, 307
  THOMAS, 9
Copeland, 153, 188, 191
  PETER, 184
Copland, 73, 103, 180
  Peter, 62
  PETER, 192
Coplands, 286
Coplin, 109, 181, 182
Corben
  THOMAS, 153
Corbet
  James, 188
  JAMES, 188
Corbin
  John Tayloe, 82
  JOHN TAYLOR, 206
  Richard, Colo, 75
Cormer
  Samuel, 163
Corn, 302
  JESSE, 104
  JOHN PETER, 223
Cornelius
  ANN, 266
Corner
  Daniel, 230
  Huginges, 109
  Nicholas, 314
  Thomas, 61
CORNERS
  Choat's, 109
  Dreadens old, 137
  Erwins old, 116
  Grays and Waltons, 120
  Mullings, 110
  Nicholas, 48
  old, 114
  Thomas Hornsbys, 132
Cornet
  WILLIAM, 190, 195
Cornwell
  Edmund, 7
Cottrell
  Edward, 190

Cottril
  Edward, 267
Cottrill
  WILLIAM, 4
Couch
  JOHN, 47
Couger, 201
Coughland
  Benjamin, 193
COUNTIES, 21, 30, 261
  Albemarle, 9, 17, 18, 24,
    25, 33, 43, 47, 49, 65,
    75, 93, 99-101, 103,
    104, 108, 119, 121,
    122, 124-126, 129, 131,
    132, 134, 136-139, 157,
    161, 166-167, 170, 177,
    180-182, 184, 185,
    189-192, 194, 196-198,
    201, 202, 205, 207,
    209, 210, 216, 223,
    226, 227, 232, 241,
    243, 246, 250, 255,
    265-6, 275, 276, 282,
    284-6, 290-1, 297, 301
  Amherst, 11, 15, 17, 33,
    40, 43, 57, 61, 64, 65,
    71, 81, 82, 84, 85, 97,
    104, 121, 123, 125,
    128, 129, 131, 132,
    134, 143, 146, 149,
    156-158, 164, 167, 180,
    190, 193, 196, 197,
    204-5, 210, 219, 221,
    225-234, 242, 247, 248,
    266, 270, 277, 282,
    283, 286, 287, 289,
    292, 308, 309, 315-317
  Appomattox, 47
  Augusta, 6, 11-13, 17, 19,
    20, 22, 23, 32, 39,
    41-43, 46, 48-50, 62,
    65, 70, 71, 73, 79,
    86-92, 94, 95, 97, 98,
    102, 104, 110-118,
    120-128, 130-132,
    135-142, 144-148, 150,
    152, 154, 155, 159,
    161, 163, 171, 173-180,
    183, 188-190, 192-204,

COUNTIES, cont'd
  Augusta, cont'd
    206, 211-213, 216,
    217, 221, 223, 245-247,
    249-256, 258-260,
    264-270, 272-275, 282,
    284, 285, 287-293,
    307-310, 314-317
  Bedford, 9, 10, 12, 15,
    17-19, 23, 25, 31, 39,
    40, 42, 54-58, 60-62,
    72, 73, 77, 82-85, 95,
    96, 101-103, 105, 108,
    111, 118, 120, 122-124,
    128-130, 135, 138,
    140-150, 152, 155-162,
    165-167, 177, 179, 181,
    184-186, 188, 189, 196,
    199, 200, 204, 205,
    213-216, 221-225, 227,
    234-253, 255, 257,
    260-268, 276-278, 281,
    283, 287, 289-292,
    307-309, 315, 316
  Berkeley, 15, 16, 86
  Botetourt, 9, 10, 12, 13,
    16, 31, 32, 34, 36,
    39-41, 45, 49, 50, 63,
    64, 71, 73, 75, 78, 93,
    94, 97, 98, 103-105,
    112-114, 116-120, 126,
    127, 129, 131-134,
    139-141, 143, 147-149,
    161, 163-165, 170-173,
    176-178, 181, 183, 185,
    188, 190, 191, 196,
    199-202, 204, 210-213,
    222, 223, 232, 248-252,
    268, 270, 272-275,
    281-283, 286, 287, 289,
    304, 308-310, 314-317
  Brunswick, 1-3, 33, 37,
    38, 47, 52, 70, 137,
    168, 171, 178, 188,
    205-208, 216, 255, 272,
    273, 279, 295
  Buckingham, 22-25, 44,
    47-50, 61, 63, 65, 96,
    99, 107, 111, 119, 125,
    131, 132, 134, 136,

COUNTIES, *cont'd*
Buckingham, *cont'd*
138, 167, 170, 182,
187, 189, 190, 192,
194, 195, 202, 204,
250, 265, 287, 291,
292, 314, 316
Campbell, 95, 156, 235,
244
Caroline, 163, 164, 271
Charles City, 104
Charlotte, 4, 10, 36, 70,
87, 96, 98, 129, 140,
165, 186, 213, 223,
236, 245, 262, 268, 277
Chesterfield, 48, 192, 206,
219-221, 272
Culpeper, 127, 181, 183
Cumberland, 49, 63
Dinwiddie, 32, 61, 80, 82,
104, 125, 179, 247, 286
Essex, 82, 107, 139, 164,
193
Fairfax, 162, 257, 258,
268
Fincastle, 74, 75, 96, 155,
185, 194, 212, 261,
276, 285, 310
Fluvanna, 3, 6, 10, 11,
26-29, 43, 48, 55, 61,
62, 69, 75, 83-85, 97,
100, 101, 104, 107,
108, 127-130, 132, 133,
136, 137, 162, 163,
166, 180, 184, 186,
194, 196, 198, 199,
223, 259, 269, 270,
276, 282, 285, 301, 314
Gloucester, 102
Goochland, 17, 26-30, 63,
102, 277, 315
Greenbrier, 33, 34, 75, 95,
209, 211, 262, 309, 316
Greensville, 37, 206
Halifax, 2-4, 6, 7, 9, 10,
12-3, 21-22, 25, 30-32,
34, 37, 39-42, 45-6,
50-54, 57-8, 61, 62, 67,
68, 71, 78-81, 83-4, 96,
98, 103, 108-110, 112,

COUNTIES, *cont'd*
Halifax, *cont'd*
113, 118, 121-22, 124,
127-28, 130, 132, 134,
135, 137, 141-143, 145,
149-50, 152, 153, 155,
165-168, 170, 171, 176,
177, 179, 182, 184,
187, 192, 193, 205-7,
211, 215-219, 221-225,
238, 241-243, 246, 248,
252, 254-257, 260, 275,
277, 282, 284, 289,
291, 292, 314-316
Hampshire, 182
Hanover, 35, 139, 153,
177, 294
Henrico, 25, 26, 48, 100,
137, 220, 289
Henry, 2-6, 8-12, 14, 23,
24, 34, 41, 42, 45, 46,
48-50, 53-55, 57, 58,
61, 62, 64, 67-76, 80,
84, 95, 98-101, 103,
109, 110, 112, 114,
115, 118-124, 126, 128,
130-136, 138, 140, 142,
143, 145-153, 157, 160,
164-166, 168, 169, 171,
177-182, 184-196,
198-204, 213, 215-220,
222, 232, 240, 243,
245-249, 251-256, 266,
268, 270-272, 276-278,
281-287, 289-292
Isle of Wight, 47, 56,
58-60
Jefferson, 83, 271, 276,
293-300, 302-306, 309,
311, 312
Kentucky, 1, 4-9, 14, 16,
19, 32-34, 37, 43-45,
47-49, 51, 63, 68, 69,
71-76, 79-85, 87, 92-7,
99, 101, 103, 116, 117,
155, 175, 185, 208,
210, 212, 261, 293,
295-307, 310-313
King & Queen, 75, 102,
206

COUNTIES, *cont'd*
Lincoln, 116, 117, 175,
292-309, 311-314, 316
Louisa, 6, 11, 12, 17, 19,
20, 22, 23, 60, 78, 82,
83, 85, 100, 111, 136,
138, 139, 202, 288,
291, 317
Lunenburg, 2, 15, 18, 19,
24, 25, 34, 36, 39, 64,
70, 71, 87, 96, 110,
123, 134, 137, 140,
144-5, 151, 165, 168,
171-2, 182, 183, 187,
195, 197, 198, 207,
210, 212-213, 215, 218,
223, 239, 246, 247,
254, 262, 272, 279,
289, 292, 310, 313, 315
Mecklenburg, 10, 41,
50-52, 57, 69, 80, 92-3,
99, 147, 160, 163, 198,
206-207, 210, 215, 220-
221, 269-272, 290, 307
Montgomery, 36, 139,
211, 212
Nansemond, 207-8
Nelson, 43
New Kent, 153
Norfolk, 60, 61, 127, 183,
206, 207, 288, 289, 313
Ohio, 15, 34, 35, 76, 86,
301, 302
Orange, 46, 217
Pittsylvania, 2-15, 20-22,
24-26, 30, 31, 33-34,
36-50, 52-7, 60-62, 64,
67-73, 76-80, 85, 96-8,
100-103, 109-115, 119,
122, 124-128, 130-131,
133-137, 140-153, 155,
159-60, 164-6, 168-73,
176-180, 183-195, 197,
199, 200, 203, 205,
208, 212, 215-219,
221-225, 239-258, 260,
264, 266, 268, 270-272,
277-279, 281, 283-288,
290-292, 305, 309-310,
314, 316, 317

COUNTIES, cont'd
  Prince Edward, 14, 47, 51,
    54, 62, 64, 84, 100-102,
    111, 119, 128, 132,
    149, 165, 170, 179,
    180, 188, 193-4, 197,
    205, 223, 261, 279, 290
  Prince George, 51, 95,
    104, 123, 185, 191,
    194, 217
  Prince William, 43, 44,
    163
  Princess Anne, 35, 185
  Rockbridge, 16, 45, 71,
    79, 81, 85, 92-94, 112,
    113, 129, 131, 133,
    135, 137, 147, 149,
    161, 171-173, 175, 180,
    188, 191, 195, 199,
    218-220, 246, 249, 251,
    268, 273
  Rockingham, 41, 42, 48,
    96, 97, 102, 119, 121,
    123-4, 126, 127, 133,
    136-138, 141, 147, 152,
    154, 155, 161, 176,
    178, 180-183, 186, 188,
    190-194, 196-199, 201,
    251, 253, 255, 256,
    258-260, 270, 272, 274,
    275, 285, 287, 309, 314
  Southampton, 56, 205,
    273, 275
  Spotsylvania, 174, 189
  Surry, 14, 70, 83, 104,
    135, 137, 138, 170,
    186, 206, 297
  Sussex, 14, 70, 137, 138,
    206, 272, 273
  Washington, 293, 294
  Yohogania, 16, 35, 86,
    210
COUNTRY LINE, 24, 41,
  42, 50, 51, 53, 57, 80,
  93, 210, 215, 255, 271
COUNTY LINE, 24, 41, 50,
  51, 57, 100, 266, 273
  Goochland, 17
COURTHOUSES
  Courthouse Road, 11

Coutts
  PATRICK, 310
  REUBEN, 289
COVES, 17, 20, 34, 282
  Carvins, 317
  Ragged Mountain, 250
Covinton, 96
Cowan, 48, 266
  John, 304
  ROBERT, 224
Cowden
  JAMES, 81
Cowen
  John, 299
Cox, 81, 207, 225, 292, 315
  Charles, 215
  CHARLES, 192
  DAVID, 311
  Francis, 119
  FRANCIS, 153
  HENRY, 110
  Isaac, 311
  ISAAC, 311
  JACOB, 251
  James, 279
  JAMES, 166
  John, 21, 24, 49
  JOHN, 12, 33, 34, 39, 41,
    42, 53, 96, 97, 205
  MATHEW, 125
  SAMUEL, 61
  William, 170, 256
Coxey, 273
Craddle, 245
Craddock
  JOHN, 114
Crafford
  William, 189
Crag
  ROGERT, 201
Craggit
  Peter, 109
Craig
  BENJAMIN, 305
  Elijah, 8, 296, 299, 305
  ELIJAH, 8, 298, 305
  James, 116
  JAMES, 300

Craig, cont'd
  JOHN, 305
  Lewis, 300, 305
  LEWIS, 33
  ROBERT, 300
  TALIAFERRO, 163
  TOLIVER, 305
Craigs, 302
Craine
  JAMES, 248
Crank
  Henry, 29
  Thomas, 29
Craven
  FRANCIS, 181
  John, 270
  Joseph, 270
  ROBERT, 290
Cravens
  Robert, 270
Crawford, 172, 193
  David, 65, 226
  DAVID, 81
  George, 118, 275
  JOHN, 193
  Patrick, 6, 118
  Samuel, 200, 317
  SAMUEL, 2, 114
  VALENTINE, 76
  William, 173
  WILLIAM, 76, 173, 267
Crawley
  ROBERT, 93
Creasy, 207
  William, 276
  WILLIAM, 227
Creddel, 143
CREEKS
  Aarons, 10, 51, 80, 96,
    124, 160, 163, 215,
    269, 315
  Adran's, 75
  Adreans, 11, 104
  Adrians, 33, 75
  Alens, 15
  Allens, 3, 6, 13-15, 18, 22,
    77, 144, 150, 173, 176,
    206, 269, 270, 278
  Allins, 256
  Archers, 84, 239

CREEKS, *cont'd*
 Arons, 10, 50, 52, 269
 Arthers, 24
 Ash Camp, 96
 Auslins, 122, 315
 Austin, 120, 287
 Austins, 315
 Avents, 99, 206
 back, 2, 10, 19, 34, 88,
   114, 128, 138, 147,
   171-173, 196, 199, 201,
   214, 249, 253, 260,
   264, 274, 275, 282,
   291, 310
 Back Draft, 253
 Ballenger's, 184
 Ballengers, 3, 10, 83, 100,
   101, 103, 167, 184
 Ballingers, 108, 127, 128,
   132
 Balls, 109
 Barbers, 252
 Bareskin, 73
 Bargrass, 1, 33
 Batterrem town, 145
 Baughmans, 304
 Bea's, 152
 Beans, 24
 Bear, 185, 283
 Bear Grass, 6, 68, 71, 75,
   83-85, 94, 99, 302
 Bear Skin, 14, 72
 Beard, 5
 Beards, 109, 114, 204
 Beargrass, 33, 74, 103
 Bears Element, 171
 Bearskin, 2, 6, 9, 30, 34,
   64, 70, 152, 169, 187
 Beaver, 9, 12, 24, 48, 98,
   110, 124, 126-128, 157,
   160, 181, 189, 216,
   228, 237, 239-241, 245,
   248, 257, 263, 264,
   267, 286, 309
 Beaver dam, 17, 77, 144,
   166, 205, 223, 234, 246
 Beaver Pond, 272, 291
 Beaverdam, 19, 138, 146,
   162, 202, 247, 253,
   266, 276, 289

CREEKS, *cont'd*
 Beaverpond, 151
 Beavers, 179
 Bedingsfields, 207
 Been, 243
 Beens, 52, 135, 172, 240
 Beffelo, 252
 Bennetts, 292
 Bent, 134, 287, 316
 Berches, 4, 108
 Bever, 57, 191
 Bever Pond, 57
 Big, 51
 big Mockison, 294
 Bigg Bone, 76
 Bigg pasture, 203
 Birches, 4, 9-11, 52, 130,
   216, 218, 278
 Birc, 21, 26-29, 31, 166,
   177, 282, 314
 Black, 153, 294
 Black Thorn, 22, 23, 62,
   65
 Black Water, 12, 156
 Blackberry, 188
 Blackwater, 147, 166
 Blue Wing, 53
 Bluestone, 129, 207
 Bluewing, 121, 122, 215
 Bobbs, 157
 Boings, 24
 Bollings, 81, 82, 125, 233,
   282
 Bomans, 265
 Boons, 101, 285
 Bore Auger, 221, 223,
   225, 237, 238, 255, 266
 Bore Augurs, 276
 Botetourt, 12
 Bowmans, 235, 244
 Bradley, 221
 Bradleys, 132, 221
 Bradshaws, 288, 314
 Brashears, 293
 Bremore, 69
 Brier, 131
 Briery, 197, 216, 234
 Broad, 282
 Brock, 41
 Brock's, 163

CREEKS, *cont'd*
 Brown Mountain, 228, 233
 Browns, 227
 Brush, 51, 142, 165, 316
 Bryery, 101, 142
 Buck, 231
 Buck Island, 104, 198,
   202, 284
 Buck Mountain, 136
 Buckskin, 34, 224
 Buffala, 69
 Buffalo, 79-81, 149, 171,
   264, 269
 Buffaloe, 16, 32, 50, 60,
   79, 92-94, 109, 113,
   129, 133, 173, 176,
   177, 191, 198, 211,
   216, 218-220, 269, 295,
   301, 302, 316
 Buffalow, 255
 Buffelo, 113, 114, 147,
   152, 199
 Buffelow, 131
 Buffesons, 168
 Buffellow, 246
 Buffles, 249
 Buffloe, 112
 Buflow, 264
 Bull, 55, 119, 167, 289
 Bull Mountain, 171
 Bulls, 110
 Bulskin, 34
 Bunches, 138
 Burches, 10, 42, 43, 67,
   98, 111, 114, 153, 171,
   225, 279
 Burets, 143
 Burkes, 83
 Burks, 75, 127
 Bush, 71
 Butram Town, 110, 255
 Butrams town, 147
 Butramtown, 128, 150,
   247
 Butterwood, 32, 82
 Buttramtown, 254
 By, 80, 224
 Byrd, 6, 77
 Cabells Mill, 232
 Cain, 142

INDEX

CREEKS, *cont'd*
Callaway's Camp, 155
Callaways Mill, 287
Camp, 17, 20, 82, 100, 111, 204, 279
Cane, 215
Careys, 184
Cargill's, 129
Cargills, 277
Carrs, 43, 281
Carvans, 268
Carvins, 268
Cary, 134, 137, 269
Carys, 129
Cascade, 24, 81, 85, 205
Cashade, 166
Cashaw, 81
Cataber, 12
Catabo, 173
Catawba, 46, 179, 252
Catawbo, 121, 213, 222, 225, 273
Cates, 263
Cattail, 272
Cattawba, 121
Cavets, 315
Cawtaba, 250
Cedar, 12, 13, 16, 137, 283, 301
Ceder, 287
Chain, 46
Cheese, 140, 237
Cherry Stone, 39, 40, 52, 72, 77, 78, 100, 134, 189, 250, 257
Cherry tree, 149, 150, 155, 277
Chery tree, 108
Chesnut, 2, 3, 10, 11, 31, 62, 64, 69-71, 100, 110, 128, 133, 136, 142, 164, 168, 178, 216, 219, 222, 232, 253, 292
Childree, 167
Childrees, 108
Childres, 125
Childres's, 144
Childress, 108
Childreys, 31, 50
Childrie, 179

CREEKS, *cont'd*
Childry, 78, 79, 282
Childry's, 25
Childrys, 22, 167, 238
Chiles's, 168
Chip Oaks, 135, 297
Christian, 115
Christians Mill, 146, 248
Clar, 298
Clare, 293, 306
Clarks, 242
Clean, 293
Clear, 94, 262, 293, 298, 300
Clerks, 24
Cliffts, 149
Clift, 111
Clout, 166
Clove, 222
Coartks, 22
Cody's, 149
Cogers, 256
Coles, 69
Colliers, 251
Collins, 16
Cook's, 150
Cooks, 42, 43, 46, 95, 102, 152, 176, 253, 270, 292
Coopers, 294
Cove, 209
Cow, 71, 184
Cox's, 227
Coxes, 227, 296, 302, 306, 311
Crab Apple, 22, 282, 287
Crab Orchard, 214, 247
Craddocks, 56
Craigs, 49, 93, 94, 97, 112, 113, 131, 143, 148, 149, 172, 200, 251, 252, 316
Crooked, 15, 41, 146, 186
Crooks, 25
Cross, 34, 35, 86, 147
Cub, 101, 111, 143, 165, 195, 227, 279
Cubb, 98, 166, 198
Cuffeys, 317
Cunningham, 121, 126, 127, 131, 196-198, 282

CREEKS, *cont'd*
Cunningham's, 163
Cunninghams, 83, 104, 121, 184, 255, 276
Cuthe, 67
Cuttawbo, 224
Damson, 196
Dancing, 233
Daniels Mill, 184, 254
Darbys, 301
Davids, 47, 48, 138, 189, 190, 194, 202, 287
Davis, 136, 250, 292
Davis's, 81, 229
Davisis, 270
Davisons, 286
Delaps, 232
Dicks, 301
Difficult, 17, 61, 83, 168, 182, 206, 207, 224, 225, 236
Dinner, 160
Dittoes, 208
Dockayes, 269
Doe, 216-219
Dog, 48, 239, 264
Dolaps, 114
Double, 32, 53, 96, 110, 150, 153, 170, 177, 251, 257, 278
Doubles, 251
dowble, 141
Drag, 130, 186
Dreaming, 84
Driver, 270
Dry, 31, 53, 207, 241
Dry Beaver Pond, 23
Dunlaps, 120, 248, 270, 272
Dunlop, 104
Dunlops, 171, 177, 178
Dutch, 121, 180, 228, 230-232, 292
Ekhorn, 32, 33
Elk, 24, 31, 110, 168, 172, 188, 189, 253, 273
Elk horn, 45, 69, 74, 79, 80, 82, 84, 92, 94-96, 99, 147, 155, 208, 310
Elk Island, 167, 233, 234

CREEKS, *cont'd*
Elk-horn, 5
Elkhorn, 1, 7-9, 32-34, 37, 45, 47, 49, 51, 81, 257
Ellis's, 223
Ellises, 37
Enochs, 18
Enocks, 15
Entry, 82, 265
Enuck's, 237
Ewin, 34
Ewins, 34
Fall, 4, 7, 8, 40, 44-46, 50, 97, 98, 101, 189, 195, 248, 249
Falling, 18, 25, 165, 179, 252
Falls, 233
Fawl, 225
First, 97
Fish Pond, 49, 190
fish pound, 290
Fishing, 15, 122, 156, 241, 242, 277, 286
Flat, 15, 24, 57, 110, 118, 140, 214, 217, 221, 241, 253, 263, 264, 269, 309
Flat Rock, 34, 151
Flatrock, 168
Flatt, 57
Flintstone, 214, 237
Floods, 225
Floyds, 82
Fly blow, 22, 26, 76, 206, 221, 256
Fointerack, 218
Fork, 17
Fountains, 208
Franklins, 75
Frisbeys, 96
Frisbys, 314
Frying Pan, 113, 170, 250, 266
Fucking, 313
Gammons, 38
George's, 165
Georges, 21, 61, 78, 301
Gevens, 314
Gilberts, 226, 300, 304

CREEKS, *cont'd*
Gills, 42, 56, 57, 82, 83, 144, 145, 155, 166, 215, 245, 256, 268, 308
Gist's, 93
Glade, 164, 190, 222, 223, 286
Glover, 49
Gobbling Town, 278
Gobblingtown, 251
Gobling town, 113, 114, 130, 151, 152, 194
Gocs, 236
Goose, 15, 17, 39, 73, 96, 111, 128, 138, 144, 147, 148, 156, 175, 222-224, 236-238, 240, 242, 247, 262, 264, 278, 316
Gralde, 39
Grass, 76
Grassey, 185, 210
Grassy, 84
Great, 137, 139, 183, 269, 272, 282
Great Baraskin, 178
great bear, 195
Great Bone, 76
Great Byrd, 103
Great Cherry Stone, 5, 40, 78, 97
Great Cherrystone, 241
Great Georges, 63
great Mychunk, 186
Great Nut Bush, 271
Great Sycamore, 21, 278
Great Wreck Island, 99
Green, 119, 121, 177
Green Rock, 38, 78, 222
Green Spring, 246
Greenrock, 223
Greys, 178
Griffith, 161
Griffiths, 40, 56, 214, 215, 238, 245, 247
Guess, 293, 294, 309
Gum, 27-29
Gum Spring, 246
Hammons, 305
Hances, 41

CREEKS, *cont'd*
Hancocks, 309
Hanus, 41
Hard Bargain, 20
Hardens, 296, 300, 304, 305, 312
Harpen, 170
Harpin, 30, 52
Harping, 30, 253
Harricane, 287
Harris's, 226, 229, 230, 279
Harrises, 228
Harrods, 1, 33, 72
Harwoods, 261
Hat, 225, 266
Hatt, 132, 229, 239, 309
Hawksbill, 259
head Mountain, 299
Heatt, 144
Hendricks, 142
Henry, 2, 263
Hickeys Mill, 255
Hickmans, 4
Hickory, 161, 221, 228, 232, 233, 238
Hills, 105, 237, 249
Home, 277
Honey, 96
Horn Pasture, 4
Horsalys, 82
Horse Pasture, 123, 126, 133, 202, 212, 291
Horse Pen, 49, 140
Horse Shoe, 12
Horseleys, 226
Horsely, 259
Horsepen, 36, 87
Horsley, 128
Horsleys, 64, 84, 85, 210, 225, 227, 229
Hounds, 34
Hubboards, 50
Hudsons, 291
Huffs, 233
Hunting, 34, 37, 83
Hurricane, 9, 12, 18
Inchanted, 226
Indian, 95, 211
Ingle Mill, 36

CREEKS, *cont'd*
Ingles Mill, 39, 210, 212, 213
Irish, 112, 150, 206, 226, 273
Irvines, 155, 234, 262
Irvins, 262
Island, 25, 56, 93, 102, 222, 238
Ivey, 60, 143
Ivy, 77, 85, 102, 136, 137, 243
Jacke's, 276
Jacks, 14, 64, 70, 143, 157, 285
James Daniels Mill, 62
Jams, 314
Jaspers, 56
Jennings, 116, 185, 271, 289
Jennings's, 170
Jessamine, 97
Jessemine, 44
Joes, 198
John, 31
John's, 97
Johnakin, 31
Johnaykin, 248
Johneykin, 246
Johns, 31, 113, 117, 127
Johnson's, 155
Johnsons, 250
Join crack, 128
Joinerack, 152, 250
Jonakin, 144, 224
Jonekin, 278
Jones's, 24, 160
Joninausk, 143
Jordans, 218
Joshua, 99
Joshuas, 277
Jourdans, 118
Juniper, 11, 64, 187, 310
Keatons, 143
Keiths, 146
Kents, 252
Kettlestick, 254
Kings, 231
Large, 51
Laws, 175

CREEKS, *cont'd*
Lawsons, 111
Laytons, 220, 221
Leatherwood, 2, 54, 55, 61, 62, 64, 100, 112, 119, 121, 124, 134, 135, 153, 168, 178-180, 186, 198, 243, 263, 266, 277, 283-285
Ledbetter's, 182
Leewatts, 21
Lenvells, 156
Lenvills, 155, 157, 182, 186, 190
Lenvils, 138, 181, 192
Lick, 23, 261, 265
Licking, 16, 45, 48, 93, 212
Lime Kill, 247
Lime Kiln, 229
Limekiln, 149
Linvell, 56
Linvells, 19, 123, 255
Linvells Mill, 201
Linvels, 54, 137, 198, 199
Linwells, 123, 124
Little, 4, 10, 26, 55, 57, 77, 96, 145, 147, 150, 182, 187, 198, 215, 238
Little Back, 57, 173
Little Baraskin, 178
Little beaver, 184
Little Blewing, 242
Little Blue Wing, 51
Little Bluewing, 121, 122, 242
little Bremore, 282
Little Childreys, 223
little Childry, 282
Little Georges, 63
Little Leewatts, 21
Little Linvel, 56
Little Linvells, 146
Little Marrowbone, 169
Little Mary, 71
Little Mechunk, 62
Little Mill, 95
Little Mine, 163
little My chunk, 128
little MyChunk, 128

CREEKS, *cont'd*
Little Otter, 4, 248
Little Peters, 268
Little Reedy, 221
Little Rough, 101, 111
Little Sinking, 33
Little Stewarts, 37
Little strait, 144
Little Stuarts, 241
Little Turkey Cock, 153, 254
Little Whipping, 105, 144, 238, 261, 281
Little Wolf Island, 197, 243
little wreck Island, 159, 290, 315
Locust, 261
Logans, 299
Long Entry, 170
Long Island, 11
Looks, 175
Loone's Mill, 73
Loones Mill, 70, 71
Looneys mill, 127, 200, 204, 310, 317
Loonies, 98
Loony's, 182
Lower Double, 12, 42, 46, 58, 62, 96
Lower Three Island, 279
Lyme Kiln, 71, 149
Lynch's, 234
Lynches, 216
MacDonalds, 111
Machunk, 11, 139
Maggotty, 161, 190, 246, 248, 260, 268, 290
Magot, 144
Magotty, 39, 55, 56, 140, 146
Mahoggony, 146
Main Bird, 166
Main Sandy, 8
Maple, 210
Marrow, 283
Marrow bone, 178, 186, 187, 283
Marrowbone, 191, 253

CREEKS, cont'd
- Mary, 11, 85, 115, 120, 174, 273, 282
- Marys, 268, 315
- Masons, 250, 274, 308, 317
- Mathews, 283
- Mathis's, 148
- Matrimony, 255
- Matthews, 112
- Mayes, 226
- Mayos, 226, 228
- Mays, 37
- Mayss, 228
- McWilliams, 285
- Meadow, 181, 191
- Meadowry, 54
- Meadows, 182
- Mechunk, 83
- Merry, 6
- Middle, 78, 130
- Milbery, 37
- Milk, 281
- Mill, 12, 15, 16, 21, 33, 39, 93, 96-98, 111, 128, 191, 203, 204, 236, 258, 281, 288, 294, 297, 302, 304
- Mills, 201
- Mirery, 3
- Miry, 245
- Mobberleys, 53
- Moberlys, 24
- Mobleys, 125
- Mockison, 293
- Moffetts, 275
- Molleys, 129, 142, 238, 261, 263, 264, 283
- Mollys, 142, 267, 283
- Moore's, 161, 181
- Moores, 119, 205
- Mores, 250
- Moriss's, 80
- Morocosick, 164
- Morriss's, 182
- Moslys, 283
- Mossey, 30, 115, 126, 136, 148, 190, 246, 309
- Mountain, 24, 50, 52, 53, 72, 84, 224, 241

CREEKS, cont'd
- Muddy, 46, 124, 136, 194, 262, 287, 303, 306, 309
- Mulberry, 62, 109, 234, 298, 300
- Mychunk, 180
- Naked, 73, 110, 115, 120, 135, 137, 147, 193, 199, 236, 237, 239, 249, 315
- Nicholas, 291
- Nicholas's, 2, 5, 6, 149, 151, 249, 254
- Nicholasses, 184
- Nichols's, 204
- Noleleonn, 295
- NoleLinn, 296
- North, 237, 256
- North East, 22
- Old Womans, 3, 15, 78, 153, 279
- Orricks, 289
- Orter, 98
- Orucks, 249
- Otter, 57, 68, 98, 143, 151, 225, 226, 231, 247, 256, 303
- Owens, 188, 234, 240, 244
- Owl, 64
- Palls, 210
- Panther, 21, 33, 53, 314
- Pattersons, 172
- Peahill, 33, 37
- Peek, 91
- Peeping, 219
- Peggs, 65
- Peters, 24, 60, 62, 108, 112, 122, 150, 169, 201, 205, 211, 252, 271, 284, 309
- Phelp's, 265
- Phelps, 186
- Philips, 96
- Phills, 11, 275
- Piggs, 81
- Plumb, 89
- Polecat, 152, 207
- Poplar, 178
- Poplar Camp, 68, 151, 213, 284, 287

CREEKS, cont'd
- Porrage, 129, 246, 267
- Porrige, 128, 190
- Possum, 15, 224, 237, 249
- Pottengers, 304, 312
- Potters, 25, 30, 64, 112, 142, 149, 170, 249
- Potts, 63, 103, 143, 210
- Potts's, 104
- Prathers, 300
- Preed, 192
- Pudding, 8, 10
- Puppies, 227, 232
- Pye, 200
- Quirks, 314
- Raccoon, 184
- Rackoon, 76, 166
- Racoon, 86, 132
- Ramseys, 187
- Read, 78, 169, 286
- Read Island, 20
- Ready, 34
- red, 182
- Reed, 11, 73, 91
- Reed Island, 20
- Reedy, 23, 109, 120, 123, 134, 182, 222, 224, 240, 251, 260
- Reedy's, 109
- Reedys, 278
- Riconnet Bag, 68
- Roberts's, 226
- Robertsons, 20
- Rock cassel, 236
- Rock Castle, 20, 84, 120, 187, 222, 242, 256
- Rock Island, 18, 201
- Rockbridge, 6
- Rockcastle, 122, 242
- Rockey, 60, 189
- Rocks, 97
- Rocky, 24
- Rodes, 317
- Rodes's, 227
- Roscastle, 166
- Rossells, 60, 135
- Rossels, 54
- Rough, 47, 62, 64, 101, 149, 193, 194, 205, 223
- Roundabout, 17

CREEKS, *cont'd*
Rowling fork, 296
Rudys, 257
Ruffets, 113
Ruine, 96
Runaway, 79-81, 108, 206, 238, 316
Runetbag, 218
Runnetbag, 218
Runnett Bagg, 57, 143
Runnettbagg, 217
Rusks, 127
Russells, 53, 60, 62, 118, 122, 149, 195, 200, 202, 251, 278, 283, 285
Russels, 54, 185, 204, 281
Rutledges, 57, 81, 257, 279
Salt Spring, 19
Sams, 314
Sandy, 3, 4, 7, 8, 13-15, 36-42, 44, 45, 47, 49, 52, 53, 61, 69, 78, 80, 97, 101, 110, 141, 142, 169, 177, 203, 205, 207, 219, 240, 242, 243, 266, 277-279, 290, 310
Sapony, 80
Savana, 262
Savil, 151
Sawners, 188
Sawneys, 14, 64, 128
Scaggs, 294
Second, 272
Seneca, 62, 85, 120, 154, 156-158, 160, 184, 214-216, 234-236, 246, 249, 261, 265, 267
Senecca, 278
Shallow, 88, 90
Sharps, 65
Shepherds, 246, 266
Shirtee, 20, 86
Shirtees, 76, 94, 210
Shocco, 37, 55
Shoccos, 238
Shock, 21, 153
Shocko, 130, 242, 279
Shockoe, 310

CREEKS, *cont'd*
Shocks, 21
Shoco, 3, 21, 22, 62, 247
Shocoe, 289
Short, 86
Shoulder Camp, 159, 244
silver, 303, 306
Simmons, 68
Simpsons, 295, 298, 304, 305
Sinking, 88, 90, 209
Sinrells, 146
Sleaves, 150
Small, 51, 194, 310
small S, 186
Smith's, 154
Smiths, 41, 50, 119, 126, 130, 178, 182, 189, 192, 194, 198, 201, 218, 254, 255, 272, 285, 291
Snow, 2, 5, 12, 54, 58, 63, 64, 70-72, 101, 103, 132, 133, 137, 188, 291
Sotry, 168
South, 101, 290, 301
South Mill, 17, 70
Soverns Valley, 304
Spider, 132
Spoon, 119, 200, 203, 284, 286
Spring, 51, 85, 111, 315
Stag, 68
Standifers, 73
Stephens, 97
Stephens's, 167
Steuarts, 243
Stewards, 256
Stewarts, 22, 37, 38, 69, 167, 249
Stone House, 227
Stone Wall, 25, 103, 150
Stone well, 290
Stones, 4, 122, 199, 200, 203, 204
Stonewall, 103, 160, 243, 290, 315
Stoney, 81, 96, 151, 165, 212, 214, 247
Stony, 2, 3, 5, 25, 46, 220

CREEKS, *cont'd*
Storey, 146, 254
Story, 46, 72, 109, 149, 151, 169, 244, 245, 252, 278
Stovalls, 15, 84, 242
Stovals, 84, 128, 228
Stovauls, 84
Straight, 203, 289, 293, 310
Straight Stone, 21, 30, 70, 131, 137, 190-192, 197, 279
Strait Stone, 22
Straite Stone, 79
Straitstone, 6
Straught stone, 137
Strawber, 252
Strawberry, 11, 38, 41, 128, 152, 195, 290
Strawbery, 241
Streight Stone, 149, 150, 183, 185, 188, 189, 257
Strouds, 138, 169
Stuarts, 179, 315, 317
Sugar Tree, 24, 38, 81
Swan, 226, 246
Swaping Camp, 230
Swepstone Mill, 41
Sycamore, 18, 21, 34, 77, 119-121, 133, 142, 159, 200, 206, 219, 243, 244, 277, 314
Sycamore Island, 182
Talbots, 266
Tates, 311
Taylors, 231-233
Terrible, 7, 39, 81, 132
Tewahominie, 80
Thomas's, 47
Thomas's Mill, 65, 143, 230
Thrashers, 75, 283
Three, 1, 3, 37, 272
Tick, 251, 303
timber, 171
Tinker, 10, 164, 314
Tinkers, 217, 317
Tinkey, 64
Toby's, 85

CREEKS, cont'd
- Tobys, 148, 225, 284
- Togeir, 101
- Tomahauk, 73
- Tomahawk, 147, 153, 253, 257
- Tomahock, 60
- Tommahawk, 253
- Toms, 139, 211, 212
- Tossekea, 292
- Totear, 101, 103, 104, 192, 227
- Toteir, 103
- Totier, 101, 103
- Touslout, 266
- Town, 5, 70, 130, 168, 254
- Trawbury, 38
- Troublesome, 101, 159, 214, 240, 244, 253, 263
- Troubleson, 240
- Tuckahoe, 277
- Tunes's, 275
- Tunis's, 259, 274
- Turkey, 43, 69, 103, 219
- Turkey Cock, 21, 186-189, 217, 284, 290
- Turkey cok, 215
- Turners, 75, 164, 184, 188, 249, 255, 271
- Turnip, 110, 145, 195, 197, 223, 244, 268
- Turnup, 186
- Turpins, 99
- Twitteys, 140
- Twitty's, 87
- Twittys, 87, 96, 213
- Ugleys, 114, 134
- Upper Double, 42, 98, 110, 218
- Vaughans, 111, 279, 290
- Wagion, 217
- Wajion, 143
- Walkers, 87, 89-91, 94
- Wallaces, 98
- Waqua, 137, 188
- Warf Mountain, 120, 169
- Wash Arse, 216
- Wenfords, 50
- Wetsleave, 41, 128

CREEKS, cont'd
- Whipping, 105, 234, 235, 239, 257, 261, 265, 281
- White Oak, 7, 11, 36, 43, 45, 61, 77, 97, 98, 101, 112, 173, 272, 273
- White Oak, 42
- White thorn, 15, 21, 171, 257
- White Walnut, 7, 72
- wide mouth, 109
- Widgeon, 291
- Wiggon, 167
- Willies, 252
- Willis's, 23, 47, 122
- Wilson's Mill, 206
- Wins, 192
- Witch Island, 22
- Wogion, 218
- Wolf, 23, 24, 190
- Woodson's Great, 276
- Wreck Island, 22, 24, 25, 47, 49, 101, 108, 111, 131, 134, 145, 157, 158, 187, 192, 204, 234, 235, 237, 239, 267, 290
- Wymes, 81
- Wynnes, 81

Crenk
- Henry, 29
- Thomas, 29

Crenshaw
- Daniel, 310
- DANIEL, 187
- David, 63
- DAVID, 63

Cresp
- William, 158
- WILLIAM, 158

Crew, 18

Crews, 227
- Joseph, 228

Cribbin
- WILLIAM, 227, 231

Criddle, 265
- HUMPHREY, 265

Criste
- NICHOLAS, 306
- Nicholas, 306

Critze
- HAMAN, 200
- Hayman, 203
- HAYMAN, 200, 203

Critze, Junior
- HAYMAN, 203

Crocker
- Sarah, 206

Crocket
- Alexander, 274
- ANDREW, 306
- WALTER, 13

Crockets, 305

Crockett, 13

Cromwell
- NATHAN, 34, 35
- WILLIAM, 20, 94

Cron
- Walter, 255

Crook, 122
- Solomon, 104

Cross
- Henry, 79, 108, 206

CROSSING
- Buffaloe, 304
- Very Large Buffaloe Road, 51

Croswate
- Isaac, 284

Croswater, 284

Crouch
- JNO, 10
- JOHN, 291

Crouches, 164

Crow, 311
- Captain William, 182
- John, 192
- Walter, 192
- WALTER, 190
- William, 252
- WILLIAM, 204

Crowder, 221, 269

Crowly
- Elizabeth, 187

Cruse, 282

Crutcher
- LEONARD, 119

Cub
- Marcus, 196

INDEX

Cubb
  MARCUS, 118
Cummings
  CHARLES, 81
Cummins
  John, 112
Cuningham, 269
  William and co., 219
Cunningham, 22, 24, 69, 199, 313
  JAMES, 178
  John, 144
  Joseph, 69, 72
  JOSEPH, 169, 279
  Mapes, 43
  Matthew, 5
  MOSES, 129
  Robert, 307
  THOMAS, 16
  William, 19, 125, 260, 270, 287
  William & Co., 44, 48
Cunningham and Company, 164
Cunninghams
  James, 147
Curd
  JOHN, 299
  William, 25
Cureton
  WILLIAM, 194
Curl
  John, 38
Currey
  Samuel, 154
  SAMUEL, 159
Currie, 6
Curry
  Alexander, 120
  ALEXANDER, 146
  James, 175
  JAMES, 175
  NICHOLAS, 99
  ROBERT, 246
Curvey
  WILLIAM, 148
Custard
  CONROD, 259
Dabbs, 315

Dabney, 17
  John, 98, 244
Dades, 258
  Baldwins, 258
Daggerly
  Thomas, 294
Dailey
  PHILIP, 275
Dale
  John, 144
Dallas
  John, 127
Dalley, 275
Dalton
  DAVID, 284
  ROBERT, 21
  Timothy, 140
Dalyell
  David, 162
Dalzell
  JAMES, 173
DAMS
  Beaver, 127
Damson
  George, 47
Dandridge, 82
  Alexander S, 79
  ALEXANDER SPOTSWOOD, 5
  Alexander Spotswood, 185
  BARTHOLOMEW, 7
  William, 314
  WILLIAM, 314
Dandy
  Thomas, 51, 127
Daniel, 164, 185, 283
  James, 62
  JAMES, 110
  Jane, 279
  JOHN, 177
  Peter, 149, 159, 260, 266
  REUBEN, 284
  WALKER, 37
Daniel, Junior
  William, 164
Danlern
  Deanna, 298
Darnel
  John, 84

Darnell
  NICHOLAS, 135
Dashper
  John, 85
Daughaty, 238
Daugherty, 144, 173, 176, 238, 240, 256, 263-265
  George, 248
  THOMAS, 241
Daughtey
  Thomas, 178
Daughton, 9
  JOHN, 14
Daughty
  Thomas, 108
Daulton
  Robert, 166
Daun
  JOHN, 129
Dauthetey, 279
Davanport
  WILLIAM, 143
Davenport
  David, 65
  Edward, 123
  RICHARD, 129
David
  Davids, 167
  ISAAC, 50
  PETER, 48
Davidson, 130, 148
  ALEXANDER, 157
  DAVID MOSBY, 62
  David Mosley, 215
  John, 52
Davies, 60
  John, 183
  Nicholas, 242
  ROBERT, 117
Davis, 158, 188, 214, 221, 222, 238
  Arther, 59
  ASEL, 305
  Azariah, 312
  Benjamin, 6
  BENJAMIN, 222, 316
  CHARLES, 230
  David, 63
  GEORGE, 81
  Henry, 159

Davis, cont'd
  HENRY, 237, 244
  Isaac, 123
  ISAAC, 239
  James, 151, 196
  John, 92, 133, 137, 272
  JOHN, 19, 30, 81, 199,
    215, 240, 244, 308
  JONATHAN, 216, 232
  Joseph, 176
  JOSEPH, 176
  Nathaniel, 231
  NATHANIEL, 230, 316
  Nicholas, 60, 229, 230,
    242
  Robert, 87, 206
  ROBERT, 143, 226, 233
  Samuel, 10
  SOLOMON, 115, 131
  Stephen, 63
  Thomas, 176
  THOMAS, 78
  William, 3, 59, 111, 165
  WILLIAM, 146, 196, 244,
    245, 250
  Zacheriah, 36
Davitt
  TOLLY, 247
Daws
  James, 15
Dawson
  & Company, 24
  John, 24
  JOHN, Capt, 233
Day, 124
  Edmund, 206
  James, 59
  PETER, 134
  Samuel, 244
De Francey
  LAZARUS, 35
Dealey
  Philip, 161
Dean, 197
  EDWARD, 7
  Jacob, 72
  THOMAS, 7
Debnam
  MONTEAU, 94

Debrael
  ANTHONY, 264
Deer Pens
  Mitchels, 92
Degarnet
  James, 13
DeGraffenridt, 313
Degraffenriedt, 210
Deiver
  Lewis, 12
Dejarnett
  CHRISTOPHER, 261
Delany
  SAMUEL, 316
Delosair, 124
Delosure
  LEONARD, 60
Demul
  MALACHI, 143
Dendy
  Thomas, 165
Deneston
  John, 274
Dennis
  JOSEPH, 171
Denny
  Benjamin, 225
  BENJAMIN, 266
Denton, 62, 128, 240
  Deanna, 298
  JOHN, 62
  JOSEPH, 152
  Thomas, 295
  THOMAS, 295, 297
Depriest
  John, 167
  JOHN, 167
Deremiah
  JOHN, 294
Derret
  William, 177
Deupree
  LEWIS, 245
Devan
  WILLIAM, 150
Dewer
  Lewis, 12
Dibrael
  ANTHONY, 264

Dichey
  John, 93
Dick
  ABRAHAM, 114
  DAVID, 134
  Robert, 162
  ROBERT, 162
Dick
  DAVID, 179
Dickenson, 178, 284
  JACOB, 192
  James, 203
  JAMES, 284
  John, 134
  JOHN, 71, 72, 109, 119,
    120, 136, 161, 177,
    178, 224
  NORTON, 70
Dickerson, 142, 198
  JAMES, 284
  JOHN, 283
Dickey
  James, 110
  JAMES, 119, 177, 178
  Michael, 284
  MICHAEL, 178
  Robert, 194
Dickinson
  John, 104
  JOHN, 48, 100, 161
  Joseph, 13
Dickison
  John, 104
Dickons
  RICHARD, 178
Dickson
  Thomas, 80
  THOMAS, 207
Diek
  DAVID, 179
Digge
  Anthony, 104
Digges
  Dudley, 25
  John, 231
  JOHN, 229, 231
Diggs, 17
  JOHN, 289, 308
Dilingham, 147
Dillan, 45

Dillar
  Thomas, 192
Dillard, 21
  James, 137
  JAMES, 128, 129, 190, 266
  John, 102
  JOHN, 6
  JOSEPH, 231
  Major, 137, 197
  Moses, 22
  Thomas, 6, 137, 189, 197
  THOMAS, 243
  THOMAS JUNIOR, 71
Dillian
  HENRY, 138, 169
Dillon, 68
Dinwiddie, 62
  JAMES, 131, 234
  JOHN, 131, 177
  Robert, 202
  ROBERT, 121
  William, 156
  WILLIAM, 125
Dirkam
  Isaac, 11
Dismang
  WILLIAM, 210
DISTRICTS
  Kentuckey, 175
Dive
  Hugh, 30
Diven, 11
  JAMES, 10, 11
  William, 10, 11
Diver
  HUGH, 48, 61, 136
  JAMES, 196
  John, 137
  JOHN, 117
  WILLIAM, 266
Divers
  Hugh, 309
  James, 191, 193
DIVIDING LINE, 14
Dix
  JOHN, 41
  WILLIAM, 40
Dixan, 70

Dixen
  James, 70
Dixon, 144, 147, 236, 252
  GEORGE, 298
  Henry, 80
  JAMES, 157, 239
  John, 80, 102, 146, 292
  JOHN, 144, 152
  JOSEPH, 295
  Thomas, 80
  THOMAS, 116
Dixons, 152
Dixson, 236, 239
  James, 240
  JAMES, 245
  JOHN, 135
Dizmang
  WILLIAM, 210
Doak
  David, 219
Doaks
  Samuel, 17
Dobbins
  ALEXANDER, 158
Doby
  John, 272
Dobyns, 267
Dodd, 312
Dodds
  ANDREW, 314
Dodgett
  Capt, 69
Dodson, 8, 40, 43, 98, 114, 130, 141
  Daniel, 286
  George, 148
  JESSE, 171
  Joseph, 92
  JOSEPH, 52, 62
  LAMBOTH, 80
  Lazarus, 110, 278, 279
  LAZARUS, 38
  THOMAS, 4, 62
Doggatt
  Richard, 100
Doggel, 215, 247
Dogget, 245
  Miller, 165
Doggett, 244

Dogherty
  CORNELIUS, 281
Dolan
  PATRICK, 313
Dolson, 38
Dolton, 167
  ROBERT, 21
  Timothy, 139
Donald, 269
  Matthew, 191
Donalds, 35
Donalds, Scott & Company, 35
Donalson, 4, 7
  John, 4, 15, 70
Donavant, 165
Donelson, 37, 39, 79, 149, 193, 253
  John, 70, 77, 248, 257
  John Jr, 47
Donelson\, 220
Donilly, 213
  John, 213
Donnelson, 38, 257
Donnely
  CHARLES, 249
Donnilly
  John, 213
Donoghe
  Hugh, 117
Donogho, 12
  Hugh, 13
  HUGH, 12, 13, 73
Donoho, 199
  Hugh, 147, 249, 251
  HUGH, 199, 315
Donohoe
  EDWARD, 17
Donohoo, 236
Donolly
  Andrew, 315
Dontern
  Deanna, 298
Dooley, 223
  Abraham, 185
  HENRY, 39
  THOMAS, 19
Dooly
  ABRAHAM, 185

Doran
  HARTMAN, 82
Dorough
  JAMES, 257
Doss, 25
  James, 168
  JAMES, 144, 184
  Thomas, 134, 192
  THOMAS, 153, 187
  William, 150
Doswell
  THOMAS, 205, 206
Dotson, 38
  Labmert, 120
  Lambeth, 190
Dougherty, 82, 144, 186, 240, 281
  THOMAS, 266
Doughton
  JOHN, 2, 14
Douglas, 238, 267
Douglass, 2
  George, 232
  Hugh, 96, 141
  HUGH, 96
  James, 4
  JOSEPH, 96, 141, 183
Dowdall
  JAMES, 309
Dowell
  John, 284
Downey, 114, 303
Downie
  JOHN, 311
Downnen
  JAMES, 170
Dozer, 182
DRAINS, 16, 26, 35, 76, 86
Drake
  FRANCIS, 51
  Francis, Corporal, 52
  John, 317
Draper, 213
  John, 99, 310
  JOHN, 84
Drapier
  John, 49
Drapur
  John, 49

DRAUGHTS/DRAFTS, 7, 10, 11, 16, 17, 37, 43, 51, 63, 64, 69-72, 79, 80, 84, 86-90, 94, 98, 99, 111, 113-119, 123, 126, 129, 136, 137, 148, 150, 152, 155, 161, 171-176, 178, 179, 190, 191, 198, 209, 210, 223, 246, 248, 249, 258-260, 273-276, 282, 286, 293, 295, 304, 305, 308, 315
Aarons Creek, 51, 182, 215, 315
Allens Creek, 278
Berches Creek, 108
Black Water Run, 8
Blackwater River, 168
Bluewing, 121, 122, 141, 179, 215
Bluewing Creek, 122
Brieary Branch, 127
Buck horn, 45
Buffaloe Creek, 109, 153
Bush Creek, 71
By Creek, 224
Catawbo Creek, 222, 225
Cherry stone Creek, 134
Cherry tree Creek, 108, 155, 277
Childrie Creek, 179
Childry Creek, 282
Colliers Creek, 251
Cooks Creek, 42, 46, 102, 150, 152, 176, 253, 314
Cow Creek, 184
Daniels Mill Creek, 184
Deep, 71
Double Creek, 153
Dry Creek, 53
Dry fork of White Oak Creek(, 112
Ellises Creek, 37
Falling Spring, 174
Fiers Spring, 183
Fork Run, 309
Gobling Town Creek, 114
Harless's, 310
James River, 41

DRAUGHTS, *cont'd*
Johnaykin Creek, 248
Leatherwood Creek, 55, 135
Lenvills Creek, 190, 192
Little Reedy Creek, 221
Livells Creek, 255
Long Meadow, 182
Looks Creek, 175
Middle River, 116
Middle River Shenandore$, 274
Mile Hill, 292
Mirery Creek, 3
Mossey Creek, 148
Mountain Creek, 53
Naked Creek, 315
Nicholas's Creek, 5, 254
North river Shanandore, 180
Peters Creek, 122, 211, 252
Pigg River, 4
Pine Hill, 317
Richmans, 220
Rock castle Creek, 142
Roscastle Creek, 166
Runaway Creek, 81
Saney Creek, 290
Shoco Creek, 22
Small, 32, 84, 301, 305
Smiths Creek, 192
Smiths River, 165, 256
Snow Creek, 54
Southern of Peter Creek$, 108
Stanton River, 165
Stewarts Creek, 167
Stinking River, 222, 225
Stones Spring Branch,, 243
Straight stone Creek,, 191
Strait Stone Creek, 21
Streight Stone Creek,, 149
Sugar tree, 273
Sweetnings fork, 3
Tobys Creek, 284
Touslout Creek, 266
Wajion Creek, 143
Willises River, 170

Dreaden, 137
Drewit
  Richard, 104
Drinkwater
  John, 234, 236
  JOHN, 240, 257
Driskill, 264
  DANIEL, 155
Drummon
  Aron, 34
Dubrel
  ANTHONY, 265
Dudgeon, 110, 149, 310
Dudley
  George, 207
  GEORGE JR, 104
Dudly, 246
Duen, 6
Duggan, 165
Dugger, 263
Duggerly
  Thomas, 294
Duggin
  ALEXANDER, 232
Duggins
  Thomas, 198
Duglas
  Hugh, 265
Duiguid
  William, 187
  WILLIAM, 134
Duke, 57
  JOHN TAYLOR, 57
Dumoss
  THOMAS, 56
Dunbore
  JOHN, 43
Duncan, 24
  BENJAMIN, 60
  Charles, 24, 52, 243
  James, 109
  JOHN, 49, 143, 226
Duncanson
  JAMES, 261
Duncas
  WILLIAM, 50
Duning
  William, 190
Dunkin, 53, 109, 172, 197
  Charles, 241

Dunkin, *cont'd*
  CHARLES, 109, 172, 252
  James, 172
Dunkley, 211
Dunlairy
  John, 75
Dunlap
  ADAM, 179
  Moses, 40
  MOSES, 40, 41, 173
  WILLIAM, 146
Dunlavy
  John, 75
Dunlop, 43
  Colin and Son, 258
Dunmore, 185
Dunmores
  Lord, 285
Dunn
  ANDREW, 128
  MICHAEL, 62
  WATERS, 2
  WILLIAM, 119
Dunning
  WILLIAM, 3
Dunnoho
  DAVID, 289
Duprie, 247
Dupriest
  John, 167
Durham
  DAVID, 188
Durrell?
  William, 219
Durrett
  WILLIAM, 150
Duval
  WILLIAM, 71
Duverse, 73
Dyer
  ISAAC, 108
  John, 78, 108, 238
Dyerly
  Peter, 173
  PETER, 13, 78
Dyers, 142
Ead, 184
Eades
  Abraham Senr, 101
  Joseph, 244

Eagar
  THOMAS, 176
Eager
  John, 114
  JOHN, 176
Eaken
  William, 31
Eakins
  ISABELLA, 41
Eakon
  WILLIAM, 143
Ealidge
  Francis, 18
Earby, 3
Earley, 67, 222
  JACOB, 31
  JEREMIAH, 143, 147, 159, 218-220
  Joshua, 189
Early, 5, 70, 71, 109, 220, 314
  JEREMIAH, 220
  JEREMIAH and COMPANY, 220
  Jocob, 189
  Joseph, 296, 298, 299
  JOSEPH, 296
Earnest
  GEORGE, 166
  Jacob, 289
Easley, 67
  WILLIAM, 152
Easly
  John, 111
East
  James, 123, 138, 291
  JAMES, 202, 203, 212, 291
  JOHN, 225
  JOSIAH, 273
  Thomas, 78, 157
  THOMAS, 265
Easter
  John, 305
Easterly
  GEORGE, 275
Eastheart
  JOHN, 129
Eastland, 308
  Thomas, 272

Eastwood
  John, 293, 303
  JOHN, 309
Echolds, 152
  ABNER, 151
Echoles, 206
  JOSEPH, 289
Echolis, 277
Echolls, 76
  Joseph, 316
  JOSEPH, 316
  Joshua, 316
Echols, 152
  BENJAMIN, 240
  Joseph, 135
Eckholds
  MARY, 223
Eckhols
  ISAAC, 79
  JOSEPH, 289
Eckol, 225
Eckolds, 81
Eckole, 263
Eckols
  ISAAC, 78
  Joseph, 78
  RICHARD, 78
Ecoles
  John, 4
Edey
  Walter, 224, 266
Edge
  Robert, 250
Edger, 251
  THOMAS, 250
Edloe, 151
  John, 15
Edlow, 210
Edmerson, 243
Edmeston, 241, 263, 264, 267
Edmiston, 19, 263
  Guin, 145
  Matthew, 176
  MATTHEW, 145
Edmiston's, 142
Edmonds
  JOHN, 215
Edmonson, 8
  RICHARD, 8

Edmunds, 108
Edmundsen, 67
Edmundson, 6
Edmuston
  ROBERT, 150
Edson
  Henry, 237, 244
  HENRY, 214
Edwards, 4, 138
  ARTHUR, 103
  EDMOND, 256
  Edmund, 118
  ISHAM, 166
  JAMES, 255
  JOHN, 224, 299
  Joseph, 229, 233
  JOSEPH, 225, 226, 228, 231
  THOMAS, 266
  William, 170, 266
Eeal Root Level, 95
Eggleston
  Edmond, 304
Egleston, 41
Eidson
  BOYCE, 228
  Edward, 246
  HENRY, 253
Ekert
  ABRAHAM, 289
  FRANCIS, 116
  PHILIP, 289
Elam
  Jarvis, 63
  Joel, 279
  Joseph, 286
Elan
  Jarvis, 102
Elder
  Andrew, 129
  ANDREW, 129
  Matthew, 172
Elcridge, 278
Eliot
  Robert, 11
Elkin, 277
  James, 186
Elkins
  JAMES, 256
  RALPH, 100

Elledge
  Francis, 18
Ellen, 292
Ellingon
  John, 181
Ellington
  DAVID, 151
Elliot, 257, 313
  James, 173
  Richard, 225
  Robert, 11
Elliott
  GEORGE, 87
  John, 173
  ROBERT, 210
Ellis, 187, 292
  Charles' Orphans, 210, 316
  JOHN, 64
  Joseph, 256
  JOSEPH, 256
  Josiah, 229
  JOSIAH, 225, 229
Ellison, 42
  Henry, 163
Embrough, 244
Embry, 62
Emmerson, 11, 72
  Exrs, 72
  SAMUEL, 2, 6, 9
Empry
  Henry, 310
Emry, 188
English, 294
  STEPHEN, 19
EnRoughty, 84
Epperson, 170
  JAMES, 136
  Littlebury, 31
Eppeson
  DAVID, 136
Ergabright
  ADAM, 253
Ergebright, 180
Erskin, 247
Ervin, 136, 186, 203
  Edward, 110
  Francis, 183
  FRANCIS, 133
  Samuel, 133

Erving
  CALEB, 73
  ROBERT, 73
Erwin
  Charles, 116
  Jane, 116
  JARED, 126
  SAMUEL, 116, 176
Erwing
  Samuel, 115
ESCHEATORS
  Anderson, Bartlett, 35, 36
  Clausel, Clausel, 270, 272
  Cogbill, Jesse, 49, 219
  Gregory, John, 208
  Hardy, Samuel, 47, 58-60
  Harrison, William, 26-30, 63
  Napier, Thomas, 25-29, 43, 48, 282
  Pendleton, Edmund Junr, 271
  Penn, Abraham, 283, 284
  Peyton, Henry, 44
  Ross, Hector, 258, 268
  Shelton, Abraham, 281
  Shepherd, David, 40, 57
  Thomas Napier, 97, 100
  Walker, Thomas P, 35
  William Harrison, 102
Eslin
  James, 35
Estill
  James, 306
  JAMES, 303
  SAMUEL, 306
Etherage
  William, 288
Euing
  Henry, 95
  HENRY, 42
  JOHN, 46
  William, 42
Eustace
  Hancock, 261
  Hancok, 71
Evans, 126, 141, 150, 245, 302, 310
  ALEXANDER, 263
  Charles, 232

Evans, *cont'd*
  Elizabeth, 286
  HARDEN, 237
  Ludwill, 313
  Nathaniel, 300, 309
  NATHANIEL, 300, 302
  STANHOPE, 61
  Thomas, 61, 210
  THOMAS, 93
  WILLIAM, 164, 243, 253
Eves
  John, 2
Evins
  NATHANIEL, 152
Ewell, 163
Ewin, 138, 198
Ewing, 19, 236
  Capt, 60
  Charles, 159
  CHARLES, 308
  CHARLES, 308
  GEORGE, 308
  Henry, 102, 176
  HENRY, 42
  JAMES, 307
  John, 234
  JOHN, 55
  Robert, 159
  ROBERT, 161
  SAMUEL, 308
  William, 307
  WILLIAM, 159, 307
Ewins
  JOHN, 138
Exum
  Joseph, 56
  Robert, 56
  William, 56
Eye
  Christopher, 128
  CHRISTOPHER, 183
Eyvers
  Charles, 247
Failing
  THOMAS, 265
Faire
  Edward, 81
Fairfax
  Lord, 12
Fallen, 13

Falling, 80, 205
FALLS, 8, 31, 72, 74, 83-85, 92, 103, 221
  Cattamount Falls Br., 246
  Great, 6, 14, 229
  of the Ohio, 6
  Ohio, 261
Famborah
  ANDERSON, 108
Famborough
  ANDERSON, 108
Fan
  Charles, 17
Farguson, 165, 220
  Andrew, 164
  JOHN, 152, 165
  WILLIAM, 109
Faris, 6
  Jacob, 278
  James, 160
  Thomas, 76
Fariss
  BENJAMIN, 138
  James, 78
  John, 129
  JOHN, 129
  Joseph, 145, 225, 278
  William, 143
Farlor, 215
Farlow
  THOMAS, 58
Farmer, 47, 108
  FREDERICK, 4
  JOHN, 215
  THOMAS, 250
Farr
  Thomas, 3
Farrar
  JOHN, 197, 206
  JOSEPH, 197
Farrer
  Thomas, 18
Farres
  JAMES, 165
  Thomas, 172
Farris, 26
  Charles, 165
  Jacob, 78, 79
  John, 283
  Thomas, 3, 78, 79, 172

Farris, *cont'd*
  William, 143
  WILLIAM, 82
Farriss, 277
  Benjamin, 111
  CHARLES, 82
  Jacob, 22
  James, 21
  JOHN, 283
  Joseph, 173
  Michael, 50
  Thomas, 21
  WILLIAM, 82
Farrow
  Thomas, 18
Faut
  Gasper, 274
Fear, 205
  Soloman, 170
Fears
  ABSALOM, 14
  Absolom, 64
Fee
  Henry, 194
  HENRY, 133
Feild, 122
  Theophilus, 217
Felt
  ANDREW, 122
FENCES, 104
  Baughs, 80
  Bowcocks, 47
  Mortons, 14
Fendley
  JOHN ARMOUR, 205
Fenn
  Frances Massenburg, 104
  Francis Massenburg, 217
Fenny, 3, 7
Fergrea
  Moses, 105
Ferguson
  THOMAS, 113
Fernando
  Benjamin, 191
Ferrell, 240
  David, 156
FERRIES
  Boyds Ferry Road, 45, 211
  Mayes's Ferry Road, 224

FERRIES, *cont'd*
  Mays Ferry Road, 78
  Wards Ferry Road, 240
Ferrill
  John, 130
  JOHN, 166
Field, 122, 269
  PETER, 17
Fielder
  JOHN, 180
FIELDS, 179, 255, 265, 292
  Corn, 247
  Galbrath's, 94
  JOHN, 192
  John Buches, 57
  NATHANIEL, 100
  Old, 25
  Old Field, 80
  Potts, 251
  Small, 82
Fields, 122
Filler
  WILLIAM, 180
Fillinger, 275
Finch, 277
  BERNARD, 283
  CHARLES, 253, 254
Finley, 19, 263
  DAVID, 303
  GEORGE, 115
  JAMES, 84
  John, 136, 162
  JOHN, 123
Finney, 42, 71, 152, 253
Finnie, 74
  WILLIAM, 75
Finny, 25, 37, 250
  TIMOTHY, 228
  WILLIAM, 75
Fips, 109
Fish
  Peter, 260
Fisher, 110
  John, 188
  JOHN, 205
Fishers
  Adam, 299
Fitch
  JOHN, 296

Fitzgarrell
  EDMUND, 14
Fitzgarrett, 47
Fitzgerral
  JARREL, 145
Fitzpatrick, 136
  ANDREW, 290
  Benjamin, 184, 282
  BENJAMIN, 61, 136
  John, 236
  JOHN, 142, 240
  JOSEPH, 129
  Joseph Senior, 297
  THOMAS, 13
  William, 197, 198, 231, 232, 276
  WILLIAM, 131
Fitzpatrick, Junior
  Joseph, 132
FitzWater
  John, 259
  JOHN, 259
Flake, 207
Flannakin, 252
Flannikin
  JAMES, 252
Fleming, 12, 101
  THOMAS, 32
  Thomas, Capt, 32
  William, 83, 164, 276
  WILLIAM, 92, 164, 304
Fletcher, 92, 283
Floid, 206
Florney
  WILLIAM, 181
Floures
  Andrew, 111
Flours
  Ralph, 111
Flower
  THOMAS, 140
Flowers
  Andrew, 111
  Ralph, 111
  RALPH, 131, 187
  WILLIAM, 202
Floy'd
  John, 74
  JOHN, 81, 84
  William, 82

INDEX

Floyd, 94
  John, 33
  JOHN, 64, 84, 103, 210, 297
  William, 65
Folbot
  Charles, 105
Foley, 152
  BARTLEY, 34, 250
  LUKE, 114, 251, 278
Folier
  BARTHOLOMEY, 256
Follie
  Luke, 133
Follin, 13
Folue
  Bartley, 218
  Luke, 218
Fonk
  Peter, 101
Fontain, 251
Fontaine, 122
  JOHN, 198
Forbes
  ALEXANDER, 148, 316
  JOHN, 237
Forbis
  JOHN, 12
Forbus
  ANGUS, 270
  William, 270
  WILLIAM, 227
Ford
  Anthony, 48
  JAMES, 99
  John, 277
  JOHN, 33
  Micael, 163
  MICHAEL, 41
  PETER, 50
  William, 17
  WILLIAM, 51, 75, 128
FORDS
  Anthony, 48
  Buffaloe, 45, 84
  Great Buffaloe, 61
  Great Crossing, 99
  Island, 92
  Kings, 215
  Large Buffaloe, 7

FORDS, *cont'd*
  Old Rod, 245
  Phelps old Road, 235
  Remarkable Buffaloe Fording Place, 45
  Sandy, 64
Forgason, 108
  JOHN WESTBROOK, 159
Ferguson, 152, 188
  JOHN, 151, 152
  PETER, 18
  WILLIAM, 151
FORKS, 1, 2, 54, 102, 246, 250, 257, 259, 266
  Bantrees, 10
  Buffaloe, 10
  Bull Mountain, 57
  Burks, 20
  Callael, 240
  Cat Tail, 77, 78
  Crab Tree, 54
  Cross Creek, 34
  Dry, 7, 198
  East, 24, 78, 84, 85, 177, 205, 270
  Ellingtons, 261
  Fary's, 202
  First, 54
  Fishing, 61, 64, 121
  Fluvanna & Rivanna Rivers, 25
  fork, 263
  Fusys, 202
  Glady, 15, 21, 53, 205
  Grassey, 72, 101, 145, 222
  Grassy, 22, 37, 38, 58, 64, 121, 256
  Greasy, 3
  Guttery, 64
  Head, 216
  Horse, 77
  Ivy, 238
  James River, 12, 16, 17, 69, 79, 81, 117, 124, 126, 131, 134, 137, 146, 171, 180, 251, 283, 315
  Jeremiah, 52
  Jeremys, 130, 148

FORKS, *cont'd*
  Lawless's, 40
  Lick, 36, 237
  Little, 15
  Main, 10, 76, 78, 256
  Middle, 8, 11, 48, 81, 88, 101, 103, 104, 143, 207, 229, 231, 232, 276
  Middle fork of Crab Apple Waters, 282
  Mitchel's, 207
  Mortons, 10
  Muddy, 10, 253
  Mullins's, 84
  Nals, 11
  Nats, 11
  Nobusiness, 179
  North, 2, 9, 11, 14, 15, 18, 19, 25, 31, 32, 35, 43, 50, 54, 64, 74, 77, 80, 81, 98, 100, 102, 104, 117, 139, 143, 205, 211, 213, 217, 218, 221-223, 226, 228, 230, 233, 234, 236, 238, 245, 246, 248, 251, 256, 260, 262, 263, 266, 267, 271, 274-276, 278
  Open Ground, 24, 243
  Piney, 244
  Roaring, 257
  Robt. Walters, 96
  Rocky, 30
  Rough, 184
  Second, 90
  Seneca Creek, 265
  Shanendore, 260
  Snows, 247
  South, 1, 2, 6-9, 12, 13, 18-21, 23, 24, 32, 47, 64, 67, 68, 72-74, 80-82, 84, 86, 87, 98, 99, 103, 140, 143, 144, 206, 210, 217, 218, 222, 226, 228, 230-232, 236, 240, 243, 245, 247, 252, 253, 255, 257, 260, 262, 264, 266, 267, 269, 271, 272

FORKS, *cont'd*
  Southern, 104
  Stoney, 262
  Sweating's, 260
  Sweatings, 3
  Sweatons, 3
  Sweetens, 3
  Sweetnings, 3
  Sycamore, 20
  Timber, 53
  Vals, 252
  Waltons, 24, 265
  Watkins's, 46
  West, 20, 22, 23, 65, 101, 275
Formby
  NICHOLAS, 4
Forrest
  RICHARD, 50
FORTS, 272
  Fort Road, 2
  Fourt Road, 2
Fosh
  Tasker, 175
  THOMAS, 175
Foster
  FRANCIS, 96
Foulis
  James, Reverend, 224
Fountain
  ABRAHAM, 41
  ARON, 41
  PETER, 41
Foushee, 165
Fowler, 206
  Joshua, 228
Fowles, 45
Fowless, 4
Fox
  JOHN, 61, 101, 116, 117, 175
  SAMUEL, 248
Fraim, 258
  Thomas, 260
Frame, 315
  DAVID, 117, 315
  Margaret, 266
  William, 250
  WILLIAM, 120

Frames
  David, 132
  William, 137
France, 32-35, 44, 47
Francis
  JACOB, 131
  John, 316
  Reubin, 103
  REUBIN, 243
  Thomas, 23
Franciscor [Francisco], 180
Frank, 87
Frankhum
  William, 115
Franklin, 210, 227
  Edmund, 236
  EDMUND, 227
Franks
  Nehemiah, 87
Fraser, 163
  Daniel, 125
Frazer, 154, 284
  Abraham, 203
  ABRAHAM, 203
  DAVID, 255
  Robert, 10
Frazier, 165, 190
  GEORGE, 33
  George, Lieut, 33
  James, 230, 232
  JAMES, 231
  JOHN, 154
  MARY, 33
Freeding, 43
Freedly
  GEORGE, 130
Freeland
  James, 61, 125, 134, 233, 234
  Robert, 125, 292
Freeman, 4, 23, 112, 208
Fremees
  Jacob, 297
French
  DANIEL, 161
Friel
  DANIEL, 144
  Jeremiah, 144
  John, 245
Frigus, 141

Frisl
  John, 245
Fritter, 288
Froman, 302
  Paul, 298
  PAUL, 306
Frowmans
  Frowman's Mill, 94
Fry, 140, 315
  and Company, 77, 102, 240
  Colo, 50
  Henry, 15, 84
  John, 61, 170, 196
Fry, Colo.
  John, 125
Fulkerson
  FREDRECK, 202
Fulton, 10, 279
  James, 10, 39, 69
  JAMES, 8
  John, 37, 242
  JOHN, 9, 36, 241, 243
Fuqua, 287
  THOMAS, 315
Furbish
  Robert, 137
Furgason
  Andrew, 75
  EDWARD, 23
  John, 76, 220
  JOHN, 24
Furguson
  JOHN, 24
  William, 23
  WILLIAM, 2
Furr
  ENOCH, 299, 304
Fuson
  John, 109, 168, 169, 278
  JOHN, 68, 278
Gabert
  MATTHIAS, 152
Gaddy, 214, 227
  GEORGE, 60, 102
Gaines
  Daniel, 246
  DANIEL, 125
Gains
  Daniel, 246

Gains, *cont'd*
  HENRY, 34, 35
  ROBERT, 34, 35
Galbrath
  MARTHA, 93
Galbraths, 94
Gallaway, 240
Galloway
  CHARLES, 24
  WILLIAM, 202
Gamble
  James, 116, 120
  JAMES, 137
Gambrell
  HENRY, 288
Gammon, 38, 52, 53, 241, 252
  John, 241, 291
  JOHN, 114
Gant, 312
  Thomas, 295
  THOMAS, 312
GAPS, 9, 19, 94, 170, 171, 199, 249, 272, 292
  Bells Mountain, 24
  Brock's, 150
  Brocks, 118, 155, 188, 259, 260, 274, 275
  Dry Branch, 173
  Gap Br., 56
  Gap Run, 143
  Jennings, 200, 217
  Madisons, 147
  Mockison, 293, 294
  Peters Mountain, 270
  Rocks, 155
  Sugar Lick, 178
  Vander Pools, 121
  Vanderpooles, 132
  West, 259
  West's, 154
  Wests, 154, 155, 163, 259, 275
  Woodes, 123
Garaway
  THOMAS, 275
Gardener
  THOMAS, 257
Gardner
  Alexander, 275

Gardner, *cont'd*
  ALEXANDER, 115
  FRANCIS, 145
  John, 316
Garland, 231
  David, 25, 212
  JOHN, 15
  PETER, 34, 151
  William, 125
Garner, 266
Garnet
  NATHANIEL, 314
Garrant
  JAMES, 303
Garrel
  ROBERT, 235
Garrell
  GARRELL, 235
Garret, 23
Garrett, 161, 234, 238, 244
  JACOB, 252
  LEWIS, 176
  Robert, 235, 265
  ROBERT, 235, 238, 239
Garrison
  David Alls, 293
Garry, 297
Gartin
  URIAH, 138
Garvin, 204
  HUGH, 204
Gates
  James, 159
  JAMES, 159
  SAMUEL, 255
Gatewood
  JAMES, 140
  Larkin, 71, 229
  William, 315
  William, Junior, 134
Gathbrath, 94
Gatlive
  MARTHA, 112
Gaulding, 234
  Samuel, 144, 265
  SAMUEL, 238
Gaunt
  James, 316
Gausnel
  CHARLES, 245

Gay
  Robert, 20
Gearheart
  LEONARD, 253
  PETER, 147
Gee
  Charles, 171
  Henry, 25
  James, 3
Geen
  Henry, 25
Gelchrist
  ROBERT, 271
Gell
  Joseph, 10
Gemblins
  Andrew, 306
GENERAL COURT, 39, 46
George
  Ansil, 102
  James, 173
  JAMES, 77
  John, 77
  JOHN, 150
Gibbs
  SARAH, 20, 35
  THOMAS, 20
Gibson, 92
  GEORGE, 92, 132
  Gilbert, 132
  GILBERT, 132
  JOHN, 110, 160, 260, 278
  Miles, 265
  Robert, 116
  WILLIAM, 133
Gilbert, 128, 186, 235, 249, 261, 265
  Acquila, 237
  Aquela, 184
  Aquila, 235
  Benjamin, 85, 261
  BENJAMIN, 156, 234, 237
  Henry, 131
  JOHN WEBSTER, 214
  MICHAEL, 31, 224
  PRESTON, 157
  Samuel, 85, 215
  Thomas, 261

Gilchrist
  ROBERT, 271
Giles
  JOHN, 18
Gill, 10, 130, 242
  FRANCIS, 53
  James, 220
  John, 141
  JOHN, 55
  Joseph, 122, 124
  JOSEPH, 215
  JOSEPH SENIOR, 53, 241
  Joseph Senr, 241
  Richard, 168
  William, 168, 215
  WILLIAM, 51, 121
  WILLIAM SENIOR, 50-52
Gill, Junior
  Joseph, 124
  WILLIAM, 122
Gill, Senior
  JOSEPH, 122
  William, 121
Gillam
  ZACHERIAH, 17
Gillelan
  Nathan, 309
Gilley, 186
  FRANCIS, 188
Gilliam, 263
  ARCHELAUS, 15
  Dyche, 47
  John, 180
  JOHN, 63, 210
  William, 119, 187
  WILLIAM, 23
Gillington
  John, 167
Gillium
  John, 181
Gills, 179
Gillum
  DEBERIX, 203
  John, 180, 181
  PETER, 4
Gilmer
  George, 181, 182
Gilmore, 299
  James, 79, 131, 296

Gilmore, *cont'd*
  JAMES, 301
  John, 55
  JOHN, 291
  MARY, 291
Gilmour, 299
  JAMES, 301
Gist
  CHRISTOPHER, 93
  NATHANIEL, 93
  THOMAS, 93
Givan, 242
Givans
  EDWARD, 52
Given, 39, 145
  JOHN, 253
  RICHARD, 53
Givens, 8, 11, 13, 241, 310
  James, 310
  JAMES, 274
  JOHN, 6, 239
  RICHARD, 53
Givens Junr.
  JOHN, 145
Givin, 98
Givins, 53, 145
  David, 242
  EDWARD, 52
  JOHN, 239
GLADES, 20, 33, 64, 78, 91, 249
  Long, 246, 250, 253, 316
Glasbey
  James, 31
Glasby, 177
  JAMES, 38
Glascock, 6
Glasford, 162
Glass
  DANIEL, 179
  DUDLEY, 71, 221
  Thomas, 179
  THOMAS, 179
  VINCENT, 235
Glasscock, 113, 279
Glaves, 154
GLEBE land, 288
Gledewell, 122, 179
Glen, 85
  Tyree, 87

Glenn
  DAVID, 302
  JOSEPH, 122
Glidewell, 122, 179
  WILLIAM, 122
Glynn
  NATHAN, 222
Goad, 168
  Charles, 113
  CHARLES, 113
  John, 113, 144, 287
Goade
  John, 112
Goard
  John, 171
Godfrey
  Warren, 288
Godfry
  Thomas, 170
Goen
  WILLIAM, 222
Goff
  John, 109
Goggin, 241, 263
  STEPHEN, 118
Goggin, Junior
  STEPHEN, 118
Going, 137
  Philip, 4
GOLGOTHA, 27
GOLGOTHA ROCKS, 26, 30
Golightly
  John, 104
Gollaher
  THOMAS, 245
Gollaway, 240
Golloway, 239
Gooche
  William, 161
Good, 69, 80
  John, 287
  John Junr., 287
  ROBERT, 14
  SAMUEL, 14
Good Pasture
  SOLOMON, 275
Goodall
  Richard, 163
Goode, 62, 101, 165, 262
  BENNETT, 307

Goode, *cont'd*
  DANIEL, 291
  PHILIP, 165
  Samuel, 236
  SAMUEL, 165, 252
  Thomas, 272
  THOMAS, 272
  WILLIAM, 122, 198
Goodman, 18, 23
Goodrich
  John, 59, 258
Goodricks
  Edward, 59
Goodsby
  Daniel, 190
Goodsey
  THOMAS, 314
Goodwin, 80
  Boswell, 104
  DANIEL, 249
  John, 14, 138
  JOSEPH, 46
Goodwood, 294
Goodwyn, 80
  ROBERT, 19
Gooff
  John, 109
Gooldsby
  Thomas, 233
Goosby
  DANIEL, 110
Gordan, 73, 237
  Ephraim, 266
  ROBERT, 252
Gorden
  John, 307
Gordens
  John, 297
  Nalley, 316
Gordin, 257
Gordon, 169, 214
  Alexander, 217
  Col, 286
  John, 199, 313
  JOHN, 302
  MARY, 4
  ROBERT, 165
  Samuel, 217
Gordons
  John, 297

Gorman, 72
Gothard
  John Byrum, 287, 292
  JOHN BYRUM, 287
Gouer, 37
Gouern, 39
Gough
  John, 163
Gover
  JOHN, 241
Govern
  Archibald, 35
GOVERNORS
  Harrison, Benjamin , Esq.,
    36, 62
  Jefferson, Thomas, 36
Gowen
  Moses, 226
Gower, 37
  William, 3
Gowin, 272
Gowing
  Philip, 4
Gradge
  Benjamin, 50
Grag
  ROBERT, 201
Gragg
  William, 154
  WILLIAM, 120
Graham, 216, 268, 288
  Archibald, 32
  ARCHIBALD, 219
  Duncam, 229
  FRANCIS, 268
  John, 313
  WILLIAM, 48
Grahams Old Place, 32
Grammar
  John, 125
  JOHN, 125
Grammer
  William, 95
Grant
  BURWELL, 61
  DAVID, 61
GRASSY HILL COMPANY,
  67
Gratton
  JOHN, 118

Grattons, 284
Grauby
  JOSEPH, 64
Grauly
  JOSEPH, 64
Graves
  Elijah, 202
  Indian, 117
  John, 219
  WILLIAM, 42
Gravley, 61
Gray, 15, 21, 24, 43, 49, 77,
  96, 130, 136, 205, 258
  Edmond, 12
  Edmund, 39
  Edward, 12
  JAMES, 251
  John and Company, 271
  Joseph, 101
  ROBERT, 138
Grayham, 216, 248
  ARCHIBALD, 219
Grays, 70
Grayson, 174
  JOHN, 297
Grear
  AGUILLA, 55
  AQUELLA, 19
  James, 19
GREAT BRITAIN, 25-30,
  32-35, 37, 43-4, 47, 49
Green, 26, 69, 127, 142, 156,
  183, 308, 309
  GARDINER, 69
  George, 212
  GEORGE, 143
  Hugh, 114
  HUGH, 204
  JAMES, 140, 214
  JOSEPH, 140
  Messrs, 270
  MOSES, 244
  Peter, 137
  Thomas, 25
GREEN SEA, 206
Greenhorn
  Andrew, 202
Greenlee
  WILLIAM, 283
Greenstreet, 77, 98

Greenway
  JAMES, 80, 82
Greer, 108, 245, 268
  Acquilla, 140
  Benjamin, 166
  HENRY, 297
  James, 251
  JAMES, 214
  John, 251
  Joseph, 19
  ROBERT, 101
  William, 148, 214
Gregory
  John, 231
  JOHN, 315
  John, Escheator, 208
  MARY, 147
  Richard Fletcher, 286
  RICHARD FLETCHER, 122
  WILLIAM, 253, 260
Gresham
  THOMAS, 38
Grey, 178
Greyham
  Archelaus, 132
Grier
  Acquilla, 19
Griffeth
  CHRISTOPHER, 179
Griffin, 69, 130, 269
  Anthony, 39
  ELY, 207
  James, 269
  John, 80, 198
  JUDITH, 72
  LERAY, 72
  Leroy, 209
  Samuel, 194
  Thomas, 40
  William, 194
Griffith, 40, 112, 145, 161, 238
  Abel, 309
  ABEL, 126, 190
  BENJAMIN, 245, 267
  CHRISTOPHER, 179
  David, 302
  DAVID, 302

Griffith, *cont'd*
  George, 56
  John, 250, 262, 304
  THOMAS, 178
Griffiths
  John, 309
Griggs
  JOHN, 172
Griggsby
  JAMES, 188
Grigsby
  JAMES, 133, 188
  JOHN, 126
Grimes, 140, 268
  Francis, 195
  FRANCIS, 151
  JOSEPH, 194
  Mosser, 183
  MOSSER, 183
  STEPHEN, 192
Grimitt, 109
Grimmet
  JOHN, 249
Grimmett, 222
  ROBERT, 292
Grimmitt
  Robert, 133
Grisham, 284
  John, 203, 240, 286, 301
  JOHN, 286
Grisham, Junior
  JOHN, 203
Grissom
  THOMAS, 226
Grissum
  John, 299
Grobbs [Grubbs]
  ANDREW, 167
Groce
  GARROT, 218
Grogg
  ROBERT, 317
  THOMAS, 317
Groggs
  Robert, 317
Groom
  Robert, 75
Gross
  Jarrott, 141

Grubb
  JOHN, 126
Gruheart
  PETER, 2
Grundy, 166
Grunmet, 131
Gudgens
  Benjamin, 50
Gudger, 145
  Benjamin, 190
Guilintine
  John, 50
Guill
  Alexander, 279
Guin, 50, 51, 68
  BARTLET, 132
  Richard, 12
Guinn, 50
GULLIES, 10, 49, 64, 72, 73, 79, 88, 94, 103, 110, 119, 142, 154, 178, 191, 196, 210, 259, 270, 308, 312, 316
  Small, 7
Gum
  Jacob, 155
Gums
  Isaac, 201
Guthrey
  Henry, 102
GUTS, 26, 27, 69, 78
  Canoe, 92
  Island, 26, 30
  Small, 14, 208
Gwin, 53, 244, 268
  JOHN, 223
Gwinn
  RICHARD, 52
Gwyn
  RICHARD, 52, 101
Gwynn
  RICHARD, 61
Hacket, 163
  Jones, 10
Hackett, 163
Hackworth, 144
  AUGUSTINE, 276
  GEORGE, 264
Haden, 162
  John, 126, 197

Haden, *cont'd*
  JOHN MOSLEY, 127
  Joseph, 127
  William, 127
  WILLIAM, 83
  Younger, 197
Haggard
  JAMES, 186
  Nathaniel, 181, 196
Hagood
  JOHN, 150
Hagues, 182
Haiden
  John, 75
  WILLIAM, 83
Hail, 220, 238, 239
  Joseph, 271
  Stephen, 56
  THOMAS, 5, 68, 71, 256
Haile, 18, 236, 238
  John, 214
Hailey, 11, 12, 152
Hains
  Henry, 50
Hainser
  WILLIAM, 248
Hainston
  Andrew, 12
Hairston, 241, 263
  Andrew, 12
  GEORGE, 135
  ROBERT, 57
  Samuel, 237
  SAMUEL, 57, 160, 263
  SAMUEL, 246
Hairston and Company, 187
Hairstone
  Andrew, 159
  ANDREW, 144, 264, 265
  GEORGE, 128
  SAMUEL, 264, 267
Hakins, 308
Hal
  Joseph, 271
Halbert
  WILLIAM, 200
Halcon
  GRIMES, 128
Hale, 15
Halecomb, 54

Haley
  David, 33, 71, 168, 258
  William, 78
Hall, 10, 36, 171
  HENRY, 152, 189
  James, 315
  JAMES, 171, 252
  John, 53, 140, 141, 281
  JOHN, 32, 251
  JOHN, 299
  Robert, 224, 315
  ROBERT, 145, 307
  Thomas, 102, 216
  THOMAS, 4
  William, 80, 313
  WILLIAM SENIOR, 224
Hallaway, 151
Halliard
  William, 75
Halloway, 109
Halls
  James, 147
Halstead
  Henry, 313
Ham
  William, 201
Hamack
  John, 147
Hamblett, 3
  Hambletts Mills, 3
  WILLIAM, 3
Hames
  William, 21
Hamilton
  ANDREW, 115
  GAWIN, 46
  JOHN, 307
  THOMAS, 203
  WILLIAM, 47, 124
Hamlin, 14, 262
Hammelton
  SAMUEL, 248
Hammer
  Nicholas, 129
Hammett
  John, 163
Hammock, 236
Hammon, 118, 129, 163
  JOHN, 129
  JOSEPH, 190

Hammond, 163
  JOHN SENR, 21
  PETER, 194
Hamner
  William, 9
  WILLIAM, 138
Hamond
  JOHN, 259
Hampton, 15
  Micajah, 108, 221
Hamrick
  Patrick, 108
Hanbey, 251
  JONATHAN, 169
Hanby, 251
Hancock, 49, 130, 136
  JOHN, 163
  RICHARD, 25
  Simon, 138
  THOMAS, 5
Handcock, 31, 282
  BENJAMIN, 121
  JOHN, 282
Handeford
  John, 246
Handley
  John, 211
  William, 212
Handy
  WILLIAM, 249
Hanken, 219
Hanking, 3
Hankins
  Daniel, 283
  DANIEL, 197, 284, 288
  John, 288
  William, 284
  WILLIAM, 290
Hanly
  Jonathan, 150
Hann, 213
Hanna
  John, 141
Hannah
  ALEXANDER, 81
  John, 81, 148
  JOHN, 79
  Joseph, 154
Hannan
  ESUM, 71

Hansby
  Jonathan, 62
Hansford
  JOHN, 82
  LEWIS, 58
Harber
  NOA, 108
Harbord, 167
Harbour, 34, 119, 218
  Tilmon, 151
Harchey, 41
Harchy
  HARCHY, 41
Hard, 64
Hardaway
  DRURY, 236
Hardeman, 53
Harden
  Gabriel, 269
  GEORGE, 11
  Henry, 7
  HENRY, 3, 4
  John, 296
  John M, 83
  Mack, 4, 7
  Mark, 4, 305
  MARK, 3, 300
Hardeway
  Joseph, 219
Hardiman
  John, 187
  JOHN, 111
Hardin, 113, 305
  Henry, 3
Hardman
  John, 187
Hardway
  Joseph, 51
Hardwick
  George, 104, 276
  John, 228
Hardy, 3, 153, 207
  George, 38
  GEORGE, 278
  John, 34
  JOSHUA, 32
  Samuel, 47, 58-60
  Thomas, 3, 34, 36, 42,
    110, 189, 250, 251, 253
  THOMAS, 32, 37, 38, 77

Hardyman, 53
Hare
  John, 317
Harey/Harvey
  John, 189
Hargar
  JOHN, 64
Hargate, 241
  THOMAS, 305
Harger
  JOHN, 64
Hargrove
  JOHN, 229
Harkey
  CONRAD, 97
Harkin, 129
  EDWARD, 117
  Ned, 137
Harler, 111
Harless, 117, 310
Harley, 11
Harlin
  Silas, 295
Harlins, 311
Harlor, 111
Harlow, 20, 100
  Thomas, 82
Harman, 33, 37, 203
  Great House, 20
Harmer
  John, 57, 157, 158, 193,
    197, 231
  JOHN, 218
Harmon, 33, 37, 141
  DAVID, 203
  Jacob, 211
  VALENTINE, 306
Harmour, 178
Harnes
  GEORGE, 209
Harness, 6, 14
Harold
  GILBERT, 143, 250
Harper
  BANISTER, 284
  Henry, 82, 233, 282
  HENRY, 225
  JOHN, 2, 259
  NICHOLAS, 126
  William, 137

Harress
  JOHN jr., 9
Harriman
  SHADRACK, 287
Harris, 11, 17, 44, 52, 53,
    119, 207, 223, 227,
    238, 240, 260, 267,
    290, 316
  & Company, 24
  Benjamin, 290
  Fuller, 257
  Gideon, 207
  James, 285
  JAMES, 181, 201, 285
  John, 43, 291
  JOHN, 227
  Leonard, 181
  Robert, 290
  Samuel, 39, 98, 113, 241
  SAMUEL, 195
  Thomas, 236
  William, 62, 261, 283
  WILLIAM, 128, 149, 266,
    289, 290
Harrison, 42, 53, 76, 95, 122,
    124, 151, 153, 156,
    180, 184, 192, 198,
    272, 310, 314, 316
  Battle, 233
  Ben, 160
  Benjamin, 112, 138, 181,
    195, 266-269, 271, 274,
    277, 289, 297, 317
  BENJAMIN, 265, 297,
    314
  Benjamin, Governor, 62,
    124, 137, 248, 266-269,
    270, 277,
  CARY, 186
  Daniel, 198, 292
  HARMON, 2
  HENRY, 83
  Jeremiah, 102
  John, 152, 194
  JOSIAH, 102
  NEHEMIAH, 102
  PRESBY, 51
  Reuben, 135, 192, 194,
    198
  REUBEN, 50, 192, 285

Harrison, *cont'd*
  Reubn, 119
  RICHARD, 230
  Thomas, 178
  William, 26-30, 63, 102
  WILLIAM, 30, 53
Harriss, 122, 129, 195
  George F., 151
  James, 220
  John, 111
  JOHN EVANS, 99
  Samuel, 114, 142
  SAMUEL, 98
  THOMAS, 185
Harrisson
  Daniel, 175
  Jeremiah, 176
  John, 176
  Reuben, 182
  William, 150
Harrod
  James, 312, 299
  JAMES, 303, 304
Harston, 191, 218
  GEORGE, 181, 186, 191
  Robert, 217
Harstone, 272
Hart, 136
  Moza, 289
  Silas, 48, 136
  William, 104
  WILLIAM, 104
Harter
  GEORGE, 154, 259
Hartless
  HENRY, 150
Hartsough, 94, 251
Hartwell
  JOHN, 73, 245
  PAUL, 272
  RICHARD, 2
Harvey, 195
  James, 131
  John, 101, 255
  JOHN, 166
  William, 264
Harvie
  JOHN, 279, 295, 296
  Richard, 181, 191
  RICHARD, 181, 230

Harwell, 178
Harwood
  Harwoods Landing, 94, 209
Haskin, 277
Hatcher, 108, 120, 266
  EDWARD, 108, 251
  JULIUS, 287
  RICHARD, 56
Hatchet
  John Junior, 220
Hatchett, 10
  John, 220
Hauston, 12
Hawkin
  Herbert, 215
  Martin, 182
Hawkins, 12, 64, 206, 284, 305, 308, 310
  Benjamin, 46, 310, 316
  BENJAMIN, 200
  Harbert, 51
  John, 193, 306
  JOHN, 193, 197, 306
  JOSEPH, 189
  MARTHA, 45
  Martin, 136, 181, 191
  MARTIN, 305
  William, 51
  WILLIAM, Junior, 172
  Wm, Junior, 172
Hay, 165
  Nicholas, 23
Hayes, 225
  Andrew, 176
  William, 190
  WILLIAM, 120
Hayley
  David, 258
Haymes
  William, 21
  WILLIAM, 21
Haynes, 48, 50, 166, 199
  Henry, 48, 109, 110
  HENRY, 56
  JOHN, 19, 276
  JOHN, 250
  William, 54, 108, 169, 226
  WILLIAM, 160, 256

Hays, 166, 224, 227, 266
  NICHOLAS, 227, 236
Haythes, 162
Hazlewood, 134
Head
  JOHN, 8
  Thomas, 170
Heal, 201
  PETER, 201
Heard, 64, 72, 284
  GEORGE, 68
  Jesse, 284
  JESSE, 196
  John, 45, 220
  JOHN, 8
  Stephen, 255
  STEPHEN, 45, 55, 151, 199, 213, 284, 287
  THOMAS, 14, 285
  William, 70, 103, 151
Hearold
  GILBERT, 143
Heart, 15
Heath, 142, 144, 159, 261
  THOMAS, 263
  WILLIAM, 42
Heihres or Hichres, 285
Helm, 156
  JACOB, 196
  MOSES, 235
  THOMAS, 156, 303
Helms, 278
  Meredith, 303
Helton, 73
Hemphil, 253
Hemphill
  JOHN, 23
Hemphit
  SAMUEL, 150
Henbey
  JONATHAN, 169
Hencock, 124, 236
  WILLIAM, 188
Henderson, 83, 127, 136, 162, 176, 196, 236, 253
  Alexander, 232
  ALEXANDER, 162
  BENNET, 191, 196
  DAVID, 119, 177, 178
  James, 178, 284

Henderson, *cont'd*
  John, 42
  JOHN JUNIOR, 123, 196, 284
  John Senior, 284
  Samuel, 6, 118
  SAMUEL, 236, 237
  Thomas, 256
Hendrick, 153, 155
  Hance, 41
  JOHN, 242, 278
  Nathaniel, 114
  NATHANIEL, 112
Hendricks
  JOHN, 242
  Nat, 131, 191
Hendrickson, 128
Henry, 39, 110, 171, 278
  Col, 33
  Hugh, 22, 96, 242
  HUGH, 37
  John, 223
  JOHN, 196
  Patrick, 74, 95
  PATRICK, 32, 51, 263, 313
  WILLIAM, 34, 74
Hensley
  William, 202
Hensly
  William, 47
Herbert
  William, 268
  WILLIAM, 268
Herbinson, 200
Herd
  James, 219
Herdman
  JOHN, 42, 95
Herman
  PETER, 287
Hermen, 315
Hermon, 196
Hernden
  OWEN, 308
Herndon
  OWEN, 219, 229
Hernsberg
  HENRY, 260

Heron
  William, 265
Herons
  SAMUEL, 198
Herrin
  Leonard, 182
  LEONARD, 192
  William, 198, 284
Herrins
  Leonard, 190
Herryford
  HENRY, 152
Heth
  HENRY, 102
Hetton, 254
Hevit
  James, 262
Hewit
  John, 46, 273
Heyndman
  John and Company, 58
Hickerson
  THOMAS, 72
Hickey, 4, 67, 110, 266
  John, 103
  Mill Cr., 255
Hickey
  JOHN, 145
Hickinbottom
  WILLIAM, 61
Hicklin
  JOHN, 195
  THOMAS, 275
Hickman
  JAMES, 101, 285
  JOHN, 74
  Joseph, 183
  RICHARD, 101
  THOMAS, 285
Hicks, 149, 257, 310
  JAMES, 98
  JAMES J, 75
  William, 268
Higginbotham
  AARON, 283, 287
  JOSEPH, 231, 232
  Moses, 134, 228
  SAMUEL, 287
  William, 229
  WILLIAM, 233

Highs
  NATHANIEL, 96
Hight
  NATHANIEL, 96
  RICHARD, 212, 213
Hightower
  Joshua, 188
Higingbotham
  Benjamin, 81
Hill, 3, 4, 10, 11, 14, 64, 67, 70, 74, 109, 146, 147, 165, 170, 179, 196, 220, 272, 282
  Ephraim, 83
  Hills Powder Mill, 220
  Hills Powder Mill Br., 220
  JAMES, 189
  Jonathan, 141
  JONATHAN, 42
  ROB, 5
  Robert, 216, 219, 249
  ROBERT, 13, 68, 76, 97, 206, 248, 254
  ROBT, 67
  SWENFIELD, 68
  Swenkfeild, 220
  SWENKFIELD, 67
  Swinfield, 14
  SWINFIELD, 168
  SWINGFIELD, 168
  Swinkfield, 143
  SWINKFIELD, 5, 74, 76, 254
  THOMAS, 5, 9, 67, 68, 76, 254, 312, 316
HILLS
  Bald, 298, 308
  Barran, 211
  Buffelo, 152
  Creek, 143
  Flintstone, 244
  High, 7, 98
  High Rocky, 89
  Ivy, 235
  Mole, 175, 292
  River, 30
  Seneca, 249
  Short, 94, 219, 220
  Steep, 232, 237
  Toads or Touds, 155

HILLS, *cont'd*
  Turkey, 177
  Whilting, 14
  Whiskey, 133, 199
  Whistling, 3, 5, 165
Hilton, 11, 12, 240
  George, 101, 107, 125,
    233, 234, 255, 276, 286
  GEORGE, 122, 192
  George Junr, 255
Hilyard
  CORNELIUS, 188
  JONATHAN, 126
Himbeecher, 69
Hind
  JOHN, 284
Hinds
  John, 178
  Samuel, 117
  THOMAS, 95
Hines, 273
Hinge
  Ambrose, 197
Hinton
  James, 2
  William, 182
Hitchcock
  William, 129
Hite, 309
  ABRAHAM, 4, 19, 82
  ISAAC, 69, 298
Hix, 77, 129, 241
  JOHN, 225, 226, 231
  Joshua, 140
  WILLIAM, 58, 226, 233
Hoal
  GEORGE, 200
  Peter, 39
Hoard
  Mordecai, 181
Hobson
  WILLIAM, 122
Hodge
  FRANCIS, 181
Hodges, 10
  Edmund, 221
  Edward, 2, 221
  Isham, 136
  ISHAM, 133, 178
  JOSIAH, 194

Hodges, *cont'd*
  MOSES, 179
  Robert, 232
  ROBERT, 222
  SAMUEL, 127
  Thomas, 72
  THOMAS, 72
  WILLIAM, 82, 124
Hogan, 41
  James, 40, 142
  Richard, 301
Hogans, 297
  Richard, 298
Hoges
  Edmund, 72
  EDMUND, 72
  THOMAS, 72
  WILLIAM, 82
Hogg
  James, 62
  JAMES, 23
  John, 143, 226
  JOHN, 210
  Milburn, 203
  PETER, 19, 70
Hogshead
  David, 288
  DAVID, 307, 314
  James, 288
  John, 19, 145, 307
  JOHN JUNR, 288
  John Senr., 288
  Michael, 19, 115
Hogus, 182
Hole
  Peter, 39
Holland, 15, 18, 56, 140, 160,
    206, 244
  BENJAMIN, 77, 219
  EZEKIAH, 177
  Hezekiah, 177
  J, 6
  John, 6
  JOHN, 177
  Peter, 262
  PETER, 55, 214, 239
  RICHARD, 32
Holley
  FRANCIS, 122, 177
  John, 123

Holligan, 156
Hollingsworth
  THOMAS, 188
Holloway
  James, 272
  John, 219
  JOHN, 102
HOLLOWS, 70, 78, 275
  Panther, 223
Holly
  FRANCIS, 177
Holsingers
  Michael, 121
  Michl, 119
Holston
  HENRY, 97
Holt, 18, 287
  AMBROSE, 101
Holton, 136
Honeman
  Andrew, 148
Honey, 305
Hooe
  Bastion, 23
  John, 163
  JOHN, 163
Hook, 154, 238, 244
  James, 255
  JOHN, 95
  Robert Junr, 255
  Wiliam, 154
  WILLIAM, 154
  WILLIAM JUNR, 255
Hooker, 291
  ROBERT, 200
Hooks, 235
Hoone, 57
Hooper
  GEORGE, 170
  Joseph, 170
Hoopery, 269
Hope
  THOMAS, 168, 206
Hopkins, 138
  ARCHIBALD, 124, 194,
    287
  Arthur, 276
  Dolton, 11
  FRANCES, 168
  JAMES, 81

Hopkins, *cont'd*
JANE, 168
John, 75
JOHN, 11, 182, 309
Joshua, 288
Samuel, 313
SAMUEL, 11, 313
Hornsby
John, 233
Thomas, 132
Horseley
William, 192, 286
Horsely
William, 192
Horsley
Robert, 233
WILLIAM, 233, 234
Horsleys, 225
Houchins
John, 229
Hough
Thomas, 168
Hour
CHRISTOPHER, 119
House
GASPER, 222
Lawrence, 206
THOMAS, 279
HOUSES, 35
Dwellings, 59
Harman Great House, 20
John Nunnaly's, 82
Large Store, 257
Raffertys, 264
School House Spring, 32, 61
Store Houses, 43, 44
Ware House Road, 104
Wooden, 258
Housley, 307
Houtchin
JOHN, 230
Howard, 47, 85, 186
JOHN, 92
Howel, 161
Howell
ELIZABETH, 250
JAMES, 250
Howett, 11

Hoy
JOHN BOOKER, 44
JOHN ROOKER, 44
Hubbard, 183, 189
Benjamin, 79, 108
BENJAMIN, 255
Samuel, 283
SAMUEL, 185
THOMAS, 82
Hubboard, 22
Hubbord, 253
Huchenson
ROBERT, 31
Huddlestone
BENJAMIN, 125
Hudlow, 255
ANDREW, 154, 274
Hudson
Charles, 190
Joshua, 97
JOSHUA, 53
OBADIAH, 193
Huff, 68, 164, 223
JOHN, 67, 164
Leanard, 116
Richard, 152
Thomas, 60, 168
Hufman
FREDERICK, 231
Hugar
JOHN, 64
Hugart, 45
THOMAS, 48, 206
WILLIAM, 48
William, Lieutenant decd,, 48
Huges
SAMUEL, 14
Huggings
LUKE, 50
Hughes, 3, 70, 126, 185, 199, 203, 241, 264, 269, 278, 309
Archelaus, 203
ARCHELAUS, 121
Archeleus, 177
ARCHELIUS, 182
Archelous, 119
ARCHELUS, 49
BENJAMIN, 198, 276

Hughes, *cont'd*
Joseph, 296
Mrs, 269
NATHANIEL, 42
ROBERT, 240
SAMUEL, 14
Hughin, 3
Hughs, 241, 269
NATHANIEL, 10
ROBERT, 240
Huland
Andrew, 189
Humphit
SAMUEL, 150
Humphrey
DAVID, 6
E, 6
Humphries, 270
JOHN, 220
Humphris
Daniel, 167
Hundley
CALEB, 22
CALEP, 22
Hunnicut
Robert, 185
Hunt, 6, 140, 141, 165, 179, 206, 225, 245, 262, 282
David, 21
DAVID, 70, 188
ELIJAH, 223, 224
Gilbert, 21, 149
GILBERT, 50
James, 70, 224
Joseph, 224
Nathaniel, 7
Robert Robertson, 222
ROBERT ROBERTSON, 222, 224
THOMAS, 214
Hunter, 19, 58, 108, 157, 159, 267
Alexander, 23
Andrew, 23
David, 108
James, 265
JAMES, 160
JOHN, 275
JOSEPH, 232
NATHANIEL, 151

Hunter, *cont'd*
  William, 258
  WILLIAM, 110
  William Junior, 258
  WILLIAM JUNIOR, 258
HUNTING GROUNDS, 102
Hunton
  THOMAS, 124
Huntsman
  Benjamin, 124
Hurd
  James, 289
  WILLIAM, 5
Hurt, 119
  JOEL, 191
  MOZO, 31
Huskey
  William, 33, 37
Hust
  THOMAS, 51
Huston
  JAMES, 148
  JOHN, 251
  PETER, 242
  WILLIAM, 165
Hutcheson
  David, 239
  William, 236
  William, 252
Hutcheson
  William, 308
Hutching, 22
  Christian, 38
  Christopher, 42
Hutchings, 10, 64, 122
  Christopher, 10, 152
  CHRISTOPHER, 152
  Robert, 51
  Thomas, 67, 73, 149, 216
  THOMAS, 67, 197
Hutchings and Company, 187
Hutchins, 122
  John, 277
Hutchison
  JAMES, 252
  PHILLIP, 103
Hutson, 96
Hutt, 223
  JACOB, 138
Hylton, 235, 248, 264, 265

Hyndman
  & Co., 59
  John, 59
Hynes
  ANDREW, 293
  THOMAS, 307
Hynton
  James, 52
Ingland, 127
Ingles, 213
  WILLIAM, 49, 310
  William, Lt, 49
Inglis
  William, 139
Inglish
  CHARLES, 301, 311
  STEPHEN, 19
  William, 139
Ingram, 279, 302
  ABRAHAM, 131, 202
  JAMES, 152, 307
  John, 56
Innes, 73
  Hugh, 153
  HUGH, 292, 310, 314
Inness, 13
Innis
  HUGH, 62
Innise, 153
Irby, 50, 236, 292
  Charles, 18
  DAVID, 135
  FRANCIS, 206
Ironmunger
  Joseph, 42
Irvin, 240, 241, 245
  John, 159
Irvine, 118, 140, 177, 234, 263
  Abraham, 245
  CHRISTOPHER, 214
  David, 214, 244
  DAVID, 148, 262, 263
  John, 262
  William, 57, 102
Irwin, 177
  MARGARET, 303
Isbell, 64
  Henry, 97

ISLANDS, 7, 18, 20
  Island Ford, 92
  Large, 271
  Little Wolf Island Cr.", 243
  Small, 102, 210
  Third, 8, 72
Ison
  CHARLES, 232
Jack
  SAMUEL, 157
Jackmans
  Richard, 303
Jackson, 37, 38, 287, 290, 307
  Henry, 38
  JACOB, 251
  JOHN JUNR, 39
  JOSEPH, 42
  Thomas, 38, 111
  THOMAS, 101
  WILLIAM, 101
Jamerson
  THOMAS, 131
James, 170, 224, 266
  Abram, 312
  ENOCK, 279
  JEMMY, 187
  JEREMIAH, 170
  John, 170
  JOHN, 187
  Richard, 48
  THOMAS, 131, 184
  William, 166
  WILLIAM, 237
JAMES
  Edmiston, 152
  Patton, 139
  Roberts, 141
  Speed, 140
Jameson, 111
  ARTHUR, 111
  John, 201, 208
  SAMUEL, 124
  WILLIAM, 143
Jarrard, 138
Jarrett
  JOHN, 276
Jarvis
  JOHN, 231

Jeans
  WILLIAM, 310
Jefferson, 154, 156, 180, 184, 192, 257
  George, 15, 84, 229, 242
  JOHN, 49
  Peter, Colo, 61
  Thomas, 107, 112, 124, 139, 160, 204, 264, 288
  Thomas, Gov., 1, 3, 20, 36, 62, 65, 67, 95, 107, 112, 124, 137-139, 154, 156, 160, 180, 184, 192, 204, 248, 264, 266-271, 274, 277, 279, 281, 288
Jefferus or Jefferees
  Nathaniel,, 170
Jeffreis, 269
Jeffries, 290
Jenkings, 70
Jenkins
  Jeremiah, 200, 317
Jenning, 131, 156, 160, 188
Jennings, 144, 175, 176, 236, 238, 239, 245
  John, 100, 290
  Jonathan, 216
  MILES, 110, 133, 190, 271
  WILLIAM, 290
Jerden
  JOHN, 291
Jeron
  Jacob, 126
Jeslin
  John, 286
Jeter, Junr.
  WILLIAM, 182
Jinkings
  DANIEL, 22
  LEWIS, 69
Joe, 189
Joes, 156
John, 112
  John, 236
  Robert, 128
JOHN HALL
  Glover, 143
Johns, 4

Johnson, 11, 93, 109, 123, 145, 153, 155, 191, 207, 248, 271
  Andrew, 198
  ASHLEY, 241
  Ben, 137
  Benjamin, 139
  Charles, 277
  CHARLES, 241
  CHRISTOPHER, 240
  George, 55, 161
  James, 216, 236
  JAMES, 134
  John, 199, 271
  JOHN, 15, 260, 273, 277, 310
  Jonathan, 163
  JONATHAN, 233
  Joseph, 21, 78
  MOSES, 38
  Mosses, 152
  Patrick, 260
  Peter, 315
  PETER, 62, 315
  PLEASANT, 290
  RICHARD, 17
  Robert, 143
  ROBERT, 51, 64, 65, 104
  SAMUEL, 124, 179
  THOMAS, 138, 177, 299
  Thomas, Major, 17
  William, 118, 156, 205, 277
  WILLIAM, 10, 191, 242
Johnston, 118
  Andrew, 313
  Andrew Jr, 272
  Andrew Junr, 272
  Benjamin, 11
  GEORGE, 260
  Hugh, 115
  James, 173
  JOHN, 245, 310
  JOHNSTON, 233
  JONATHAN, 233
  Michael, 272
  PETER, 64
  Robert, 143, 229
  ROBERT, 64, 81, 210, 225, 229, 316

Johnston, *cont'd*
  Samuel, 284, 302, 310
  SAMUEL, 121, 124, 178
Jones, 1, 5, 14, 33, 47, 50, 64, 68, 87, 95, 108, 137, 149, 160, 164, 179, 199, 206, 225, 271, 277, 315
  Abraham, 4, 130
  AMBROSE, 180
  Andrew, 160
  Benjamin, 269
  CHARLES, 33, 37
  David, 109, 195, 291, 302, 317
  DAVID, 138
  Eanos, 118, 194, 196
  Gabriel, 13
  George, 266, 281
  GEORGE, 145, 234
  Henry, 2, 10, 109, 130, 136, 165
  HENRY, 3, 4, 67, 68
  Isaac, 2, 4, 67
  Jacob, 2
  James, 40, 188, 196
  JAMES &, 10
  James Boisseau, 138
  John, 4, 10, 46, 149, 179, 188, 257
  JOHN, 137, 160, 163, 184, 253
  JOHN ARMSTED, 254
  Jonathan, 21
  JONES, 254
  Joseph, 125
  JOSEPH, 125
  JOSIAS, 96
  Kennon, 125, 286
  Mary Ann, 132
  MARY ANN, 132
  MICHAEL, 239
  Peter, 262
  Richard, 37, 313
  RICHARD, 53, 127
  Robert, 4, 9, 109, 130, 165, 271
  ROBERT, 5, 9
  Robt, 76
  Stephen, 269

INDEX

Jones, *cont'd*
  Thomas, 68, 75, 76, 96,
    123, 149, 165, 184,
    187, 199, 256, 290
  THOMAS, 5, 9, 21, 67,
    240, 255
  THOMAS CAPT, 249
  Thomas, Junior, 123
  William, 37, 131
  WILLIAM, 33, 37, 123
  Wm, 33
  Wood, 82, 143, 239, 266
Jopling
  Thomas, 231
Jordan, 169, 180
  Edward, 208
  Sarah, 208
Jorden
  JOHN, 291
Joslin
  John, 122
Jouet, 78
Jouett, 78
Jourdan, 134, 169, 180
Joyner
  John, 275
  Joshua, 275
Judd, 188
  JOHN, 188
Jude
  George, 137
Judkins
  Charles, 104
Junior
  William Junior, 70
Justice, 144, 146
  JAS, 30
  SIMON, 30
  WILLIAM, 144
Kay, 141
Kea
  Charles, 104
Keeny, 248
Keerbey, 260
Keerby, 243
Keerly, 248
Keese, 225
Keesee, 190
  George, 188
  JEREMIAH, 172

Keesey
  JESSEY, 153
Keesus
  Arthur, 78
Keetin, 200
Keiton, 220, 221
Keley, 273
Kellam
  Henry, 185
  HENRY, 185
Kelleyham, 291
Kello
  Richard, 275
  RICHARD, 56, 275
Kellor
  LODEVICK, 274
  LODIVICK, 274
  LODOVICK, 274
Kelly
  Alexander, 257
  ALEXANDER, 234
  Anthony, 94
  GEORGE, 313
  ISAAC, 200
  JOHN, 130, 131
  MICHAEL, 151, 254
  Thomas, 288
  THOMAS, 120, 178
  WILLIAM, 83
Kelso
  Hugh, 94
Kemp, 8
  John, 98
  JOHN, 8, 68
Kendrick, 166
  EZEKIEL, 119
  John, 218
  JOHN, 60, 168
Kennady
  JOHN, 18
Kennedy, 307
  JOHN, 303
  THOMAS, 303
Kennerley
  James, 179
Kennerly, 124
Kennestick/Kenestrick
  John, 309
Kenney
  BRYANT, 115

Kenney, *cont'd*
  William, 126
Kenney/Kinney, 297
Kennison
  Edward, 309
Kennon, 52, 61, 78, 101, 266
  Richard, 70
  William, 17, 107
  WILLIAM, 17
  Williams, 42
Kennons, 98
Kensly
  William, 47
KENTUCKY, 285
  Lincoln County, 83
  Lincoln District, 83
Keplener
  John, 259
Kepliner, 259
  GEORGE, 155
  JOHN, 259
Keplinger
  JOHN SENR, 259
Keptener
  John, 275
Ker
  James, 146
Kerbey, 98
  Francis, 246
  John, 97
Kerby, 3, 39, 52, 98, 146, 278
  FRANCIS, 188
  HENRY, 7
  Jessey, 240
  JOHN, 39
  Josiah, 240
  JOSIAH, 188
  Kerby, 61
  Richard, 7
  RICHARD, 120, 265
Kerby, Senior
  JOHN, 202
Kerlly, 260
Kern, 154
Kerr, 48, 115, 152
  JAMES, 115
Kersee
  ARTHER, 21
Kersey, 11

Kesee
 Arthur, 50
Kester
 CONRAD, 150
Key, 221, 239, 247
 JACOB, 143
 Martin, 167, 270
 MARTIN, 40
 MARTIN JUNR, 39
 Roger, 45
Keys
 John, 174
Kickey
 JOHN, 145
Kile
 George, 182
Kilpatrick/Killpatrick
 Andrew,, 308
Kincade, 188
Kincaid
 ROBERT, 16
Kinder
 Conrad, 211
 Michael, 139, 211
Kindrick
 JOHN, 168
King, 3, 41, 49, 104, 166,
  169, 195, 203, 215, 240
 Daniel, 84, 184
 DANIEL, 83
 Danl, 85
 Edmond, 137
 Edward, 189
 Elijah, 37, 47, 277
 ELIJAH, 260
 George, 173
 John, 73, 101, 174, 193,
  303, 316
 JOHN, 42, 83, 84, 116,
  310
 Joseph, 232
 JOSEPH, 109, 231
 Martin, 104, 128, 184, 198
 Thomas, 193
 THOMAS, 58, 60
 Walter, 25, 40, 121, 134,
  157, 167, 193, 197
 Walter Esq., 132, 134,
  158, 167
 WALTER Esq., 218

King, *cont'd*
 William, 42, 98, 278
 WILLIAM, 130
Kingcaid
 ROBERT, 16
Kinge
 AMBROSE, 194
Kinkead
 Burrow, 227
 John, 314
 THOMAS, 283
Kinkel
 ISAAC, 178
Kinkell
 ISAAC, 178
Kinkle
 ISAAC, 178
Kinley
 Ben, 154
 BENJAMIN, 136, 137,
  186
Kinney, 126
 William, 197
Kinton
 William, 194
Kirby
 John, 4, 112
Kirk
 John, 216
Kirkham, 292
 SAMUEL, 313
Kirkland
 Betty, 207
 BETTY, 207
 William, 207
Kirlland
 Snowden, 241
Kirtley, 260
Kirtly, 260
Kirtty, 260
Kitchen, 243, 277
 James, 143
 JAMES, 226
 JOHN, 243
 WILLIAM, 277
Kitt, 308
Knight
 MARY, 295
 Thomas, 140
 WILLIAM, 295

KNOBS
 Bald Nobb, 284
 Caravans Nob, 63
 High, 33, 90
 Oars Nob, 39
Koff
 James, 133
Kurbey, 97
Kurkland, 50
Kyle
 DAVID, 292
 Robert, 292
Kyler
 Robert, 167
Kyseers, 148
Lace
 BARNETT, 287
 Matthias, 19
Lacey, 266
Lackey
 Adam, 41
 ADAM, 120, 178
 ALEXANDER, 257
Lacky
 Adam, 128
Lacy, 266
 THEOPHELUS, 265
Lainhart, 18
 JOHN CHRISTOPHER,
  18
Laird
 JAMES, 120, 177, 178
Lamax
 Lunsford, 65
Lamb
 WALTER, 64
 William, 145, 176, 255
Lambert, 269, 295
Lamkin
 RICHARD, 207
Lamme
 WILLIAM, 157, 270
Lamont
 JOHN, 39
Lancaster, 180
Lance
 BARNET, 287
 BARNETT, 282
Lancer
 Barnet, 22

Lancier [Lanier], 163
Land, 48
  JOHN, 25
LANDINGS
  Harwoods, 94, 209
Landsdown
  GEORGE, 257
Lane, 207, 234, 265
  JOHN, 72, 234, 302
  JOSEPH, 81, 231
  JULIUS, 294
  Thomas, 234
  THOMAS, 143
  William, 170
Lane, Junior
  JOHN, 159
Langdon
  SAMUEL, 214
Langford, 6, 15
  Ben, 256
  BENJAMIN, 15, 78
Langley
  ROBERT, 183
Lanier, 37
  Thomas, 308
  THOMAS, 92
Lankford, 52, 176
  Benjn, 77
  John, 50, 53
  JOSEPH, 165
Lanniam
  JOSEPH, 180
Lapsley
  ISABEL, 199
Lark
  Robert, 269
Larke, 57
Larky
  Adam, 241
Lastly
  Menoah, 85
Latany, 193
Latimer
  Jack, 188
  John, 188
Lauderdale
  WILLIAM, 9
Law
  James, 80
  William, 51

Lawhaun
  THOMAS, 301
Lawhon
  HENRY, 81
Lawless, 4, 40, 225
  Ben, 45
  Benj, 7
  Benjamin, 142
  BENJAMIN, 42
  James, 44
  JAMES, 249
Lawrence, 58
  SAMUEL, 147
Lawrey
  JAMES, 155
Laws
  John, 257
Lawson, 45, 284
  ANTHONY, 35
  John, 268
  JOHN, 69, 77
  Jonas, 101
  JONAS, 43, 97
  Jones, 203
  William, 287
Lawsons, 149
Lax, 83, 245
Layman
  JOSEPH, 199
Layne, 133
  DULTON, 123
  THOMAS, 233
Lea
  JAMES GREEN, 148
Leak, 150, 153, 179
Lear
  WILLIAM, 18
Leard
  David, 201
Learight/Leawright
  George, 310
Leatherdale
  James, 317
  JAMES, 200
  James Senr, 282
Leatherman, 278
  NICHOLAS, 308
Leatherwood, 198
Leawright
  JOHN, 310

Leche
  Matthias, 155
Ledbeter, 206
Ledbetter, 33, 37
  John, 33, 37
Leddesdale, 5
Lee, 290, 316
  EVAN, 49
  HANCOCK, 299
  Henry, 44, 302
  HENRY, 44, 297
  JOHN, 299
  RICHARD, 132
  Samuel, 191
  Thomas, 49, 290
  Timothy, 177
  William, 227, 235
Leeake, 112
Leeneve
  JOHN, 54
Leeper
  Gawan, 73
  James, 73
Leftwich
  William, 236
Leftwick, 10
Leftwitch
  WILLIAM, 10
Legrand
  John, 83
  PETER, 111, 290
Lei
  Stephen, 99
Leich, 42
Leikh
  John, 240
Lelba
  LELBA, 64
Lemon
  JOHN, 163
Leneaue
  JOHN, 54
Lenous, 119
Lenox, 267
  THOMAS, 267
Lentecom, 11
Lenvills, 162
Lenvils, 162
Lesley
  THOMAS, 132

Lester
  THOMAS, 235
Letbetter
  Charles, 38
Levells, 316
LEVELS
  Eeal root, 95
Levinston
  AARON, 246
Leviston
  AARON, 246
Lewellin
  THOMAS, 206
Lewis, 2, 19, 38, 83, 93, 141, 145, 177, 251
  AARON, 303
  Andrew, 13
  ANDREW, 33, 34, 95, 209
  Charles, 26, 155, 194
  CHARLES, 209
  Col, 308
  Col. A, 45
  Coles, 37
  Colo, 274
  James, 271
  JAMES, 55, 271
  John, 119, 192, 209
  JOHN, 208, 292, 295, 296, 312
  Nicholas, 181
  NICHOLAS, 102
  Orphans, 93
  Robert, 175
  SARAH, 161
  THOMAS, 189
  William, 173, 202
  WILLIAM, 141, 171, 174, 270
  William Terrel, 250
  William Terrell, 181
  William Terril, 119
Lewis, Junior
  THOMAS, 116
LICKS, 18, 282
  Buffaloe, 14, 76
  Lick Hole, 39
  Mud, 76
Lidderdale, 262
Liftwick
  Thomas, 147

Ligget
  Alexander, 219
Liggin
  JOHN, 201
  JOSEPH, 201
Liggins, 122
Lightfoot, 33, 83, 127, 222, 288
  Col., 38
Ligon, 84, 179
  JOHN, 179
Lilly
  ARMAGER, 282
Linch, 82, 98
  William, 98
Lindon
  Joseph, 259
Lindsey
  ROBERT, 267
Lingell
  Jacob, 211
Lingole
  Jacob, 139
Linsey
  James, 161
  JAMES, 278
  ROBERT, 267
Lipscomb, 83
  WILLIAM, 60
Lipscomb]
  Thomas, 97
Little, 80, 205
  CHARLES, 80
  Jesse, 104
Littlepage, 245, 265
  JOHN CARTER, 276
  RICHARD, 245
Lively
  JOSEPH, 20
Loae
  James, 44
Loard
  David, 13
Lockett, 279
Lockhart
  PATRICK, 12, 49
  THOMAS, 133
Locust Thickett Land, 235
Loftis, 315
  THOMAS, 315

Loftus
  RALPH, 126
Logan, 312
  Benjamin, 295, 303
  BENJAMIN, 99, 295
  DAVID, 16
  HUGH, 303
  James, 155
  JAMES, 94
  John, 257, 265, 295
  JOHN, 80
  WILLIAM, 299
Logans
  Benjamin, 303
  James, 312
Loggon
  DAVID, 129
Logherd
  William, 20
Logwood, 18
  THOMAS, 160, 263
  THOMAS, 246
Lomax, 52, 112, 124, 135, 153, 186, 190, 197, 277, 285
  & Co, 54, 61, 64, 124, 135, 153, 169, 263, 266, 277, 284
  Colo, 230
  Lunsford, 65, 157, 158, 206
  Lunsford, Colo, 266
  THOMAS, 139
London
  William, 114
  WILLIAM, 153, 206
Long, 83, 220
  John, 252
  JOSEPH, 249
  Lewis, 104
Looney
  ABSOLOM, 316
  Joseph, 181
Lord Dunmore, 33, 185, 285
Lord Fairfax, 12
Lorton, 211
Love, 198, 295, 309, 314
  Alexander, 13
  EPHRAIM, 198
  JOHN, 71

Love, *cont'd*
  Joseph, 39
  Phillip, 74
  PHILLIP, 69
Lovel, 165, 197
  GEORGE, 195
  THOMAS, 300
  William, 203
Lovell, 77
  CHARLES, 205
  DANIEL, 40, 97, 152
  W, 6
Lovesay
  John, 123
  William, 123
Loving, 243
  JOHN, 228
  John Junr, 206
  William, 228
  WILLIAM, 228
Low
  Thomas, 177
Lowrey
  James, 259
Lowry
  James, 259
  John, 171
  JOHN, 118
Lowry
  John, 317
Loy
  Martin, 212
Lucas, 150
  Barton, 210
  BURTON, 210
  WILLIAM, 269
Luck, 70
  Francis, 185
Lucks
  Francis, 131
Lumkin, 279
Lumpkin, 39
Lumpkins, 38
Lumsden, 199, 284
  John, 103, 220
Lundy, 206
Luney
  Robert, 182
Lunsfords
  Thomas, 139

Lyell
  Joseph, 212
  JOSEPH, 72
Lyle
  James, 191
  SAMUEL, 172
Lynch, 81, 82, 84, 160, 237, 239
  Charles, 164, 234, 262
  CHARLES, 216
  Christopher, 143, 156
  John, 222, 242, 272
  JOHN, 39, 156, 164, 242
  William, 39
  WILLIAM, 7
Lyne
  GEORGE, Colo, 75
  JOHN, 75
Lyon, 281, 283
  JAMES, 60, 204, 283
Lyons
  Shelton, 283
Lysle, 45
Mabary
  Frances, 241
  Francis, 40
Mabery, 161
Mabray
  Francis, 10
Mabry, 161, 269
  BRAXTON, 242
  Joshua, 269
  NATHANIEL, 273
MacAdow
  JOHN, 190
Macbee, 98
MacCord
  William, 131
MacCormack
  William, 119
MacCrory, 273
MacCulloch
  John, 124
MacDaniel
  ROTHERICK, 114
MacDearmanroe, 197
  BRYAN, 197
MacDowel
  EPHRAIM, 123
  Samuel, 191

MacDuff
  Laurence, 107
MacDugall
  John, 121
MacGill
  JOHN, 198
MacHany
  Cornelius, 185
Machen, 264
  John, 221
Mackee
  Samuel, 115
MacKenny
  MORRIS, 188
Mackettrick
  Robert, 115
Mackey, 123
Mackie
  Alexr, 137
  ANDREW, 59
Mackin
  PATRICK, 274
Macklin
  John, Col, 33
Maclin
  Frederick, 3
  John, 37
MacNair
  ROBERT, 124
MacNutt
  JOHN, 118
Macollough
  Barnet, 69
Macoy
  RICHARD, 272
Madding
  John, 42, 257
Maddison
  WILLIAM STROTHER, 103
Maddox
  Benjamin, 55
Madion
  WILLIAM STROTHER, 103
Madison, 99
  Ambrose, 299
  John, 270
  JOHN, 85
  JOHN JUNIOR, 270

Madison, *cont'd*
  THOMAS, 32, 296
  WILLIAM, 82, 165
  WILLIAM STROTHER,
    63, 64, 103
Madly, 212
Magabey, 213
Magann
  Joseph, 246
Magee
  JOHN, 213
Maggot, 258
  Hans, 259
Major
  Philip, 25
Malcom, 193
Malicole
  John, 282
Mallet, 206
Mallott, 41
Mallow
  GEORGE, 196
Malther
  John, 110
Mamon
  NATHANIEL, 166
Mamurdy
  JAMES, 61
Manaley
  David, 64
Manally
  David, 227
  John, 227
Mandley, 270
Mankin
  James, 122
  JAMES, 202
Manking
  JAMES, 134
Manley
  William, 142
Manly, 238
Mann, 157, 204
  ANDREW, 145
  CHARLES, 274
  Francis, 219
  JOHN, 75
Mannen
  Beverley, 178

Mannus
  James, 81
Manry, 122
Manuel
  Philemon, 262
Manyfee, 220
  William, 220
Maples
  JOSEPH, 257
  WILLIAM, 77
Marberry
  HENRY, 60
Marbry, 60
  HENRY, 60
Marham
  Pat, 73
Markam, 22
Markham, 21, 160
  ABNER, 215
  John, 279
Marks
  Edwards, 95
Marley, 268
Marr
  GIDEON, 291
  John, 286
  JOHN, 24, 135, 181, 199,
    290
Marrable, 220, 221
  MATTHEW, 270
  WILLIAM, 69
Marray, 240
Marshal
  Francis, 125
  John, 198
Marshall, 31, 105, 234, 238,
    257, 265
  William, 235
  WILLIAM, 239
MARSHES
  Marsh Land, 35
  White, 239
Martain, 288
  SAMUEL, 252
Martian
  James, 222
Martin, 78, 128, 157
  Charles, 95, 209
  David, 63, 145, 160

Martin, *cont'd*
  Henry, 33, 75, 76, 132,
    297
  HENRY, 33, 75, 230, 308
  James, 2, 3, 71, 128, 196,
    222
  JAMES, 2, 71, 225, 226
  James Junr, 104
  John, 127, 305
  JOHN, 10, 36, 286
  John, Capt, 26, 48, 100
  JOSEPH, 134
  Lewis B, 282
  Lewis Burwell, 26-30
  Robert, 165, 169
  Samuel, 26-30, 48, 100,
    314
  SAMUEL, 252
  Thomas, 160, 191
  William, 195
  WILLIAM, 166, 167, 230
  WILLIAM, 245
Maryfee
  William, 220
Mashall
  THOMAS, 7
Mason, 62, 64, 147, 160,
    166, 171, 186, 207,
    238, 279, 292
  David, 25
  David, Colo, 272
  James, 299
  John, 114, 268
  JOHN, 244
  JOSEPH, 114, 171
  MARTIN, 101
  Robert, 164
  ROBERT, 10, 100
Massenburg Fenn
  Frances, 104
  Francis, 217
Massey, 123
Massie
  THOMAS, 161
Mathewes
  Townsend, 137
Mathews, 128, 274
  GEORGE, 12, 49
  James, 101
  JAMES, 230, 231

Mathews, *cont'd*
  Joshua, 31
  Phillip, 25
  Richard, 195
  SAMPSON, 12, 49
  Samuel, 26
  SAMUEL, 12
  Thomas, 138
  Townsend, 119
  William, 258, 275
  WILLIAM, 233
Matlock
  ISON, 228
Mattenly
  Mack, 43
  MARK, 241
Matthew
  ROBERT, 182
Matthews, 171
  GEORGE, 12
  James, 100
  JAMES, 189
  John, 171
  Phillip, 25
  Sampson, 173
  SAMPSON, 12
  Samuel, 21, 31
  THOMAS, 23, 291
  Townsend, 186
  William, 238, 315
  WILLIAM, 143, 154, 226, 238
Mattox
  Wilson, 207
Maulding
  John, 31
Mauray, 240
Maurey, 122
Maurice, 265
Maurius, 265
Maury, 122
Mausey, 122
MaVaes
  John, 127
Mavily, 271
  ROBERT, 4
  William, 271
Mavity, 165, 256
  WILLIAM, 14, 67, 168

Mawkin
  Thomas, 239
Max, 39
Maxey, 146, 165, 266, 268
  Charles, 314
  JOSIAH, 268
  Radford, 225
  Walter, 188
  WALTER, 168
Maxwel
  John, 81
Maxwell, 22, 37
  ALEXANDER, 290
  THOMAS, 63, 210
  William, 232
Maxy, 50
May
  GEORGE, 297, 299, 302
  JOHN, 92
  RICHARD, 312
  William, 222
  WILLIAM, 299
Maye, 82
Mayes, 39, 136
  Joseph, 167
Mayfee, 109
Mayfield
  John, 134, 196
  JOHN, 131
Maynard, 93
  Nicholas, 138, 194
Mayo
  JAMES, 255
  Joseph, 129, 190
  Philip, 25, 190
  ROBERT, 270
  Valentine, 187
  William, Colonel, 226
Mays, 37, 78
  John, 118
  Joseph, 31
  JOSEPH, 22
  MATOX, 37
  MATTOX, 31
McAdow, 190
  JOHN, 190
McAfee
  George, 311
  James, 311
  JAMES, 300, 312

McAfee, *cont'd*
  Robert, 312
  Samuel, 300
  SAMUEL, 298
McAfees
  George, 311
  Robert, 293
McAlnary
  JAMES, 96
McBride, 97, 165, 204, 243
  Daniel, 169
  DANIEL, 135
McCaines
  DAVID, 30
McCakery
  Cormack, 314
McCalpin
  Robert, 251
McCamish
  WILLIAM, 159
McCanner
  Beverly, 17
McCarneys
  John, 180
McCarry
  RICHARD, 180
McCary
  RICHARD, 121
McCaul
  Alexander, 228, 242
McCetrick
  Robert, 20
McClain
  JOHN, 257
McClan, 17
McClanacha
  WILLIAM, Col, 304
McClanachan
  WILLIAM, 289
  WILLIAM, Col, 304
McClanaham
  WILLIAM, 314
McClanahan, 60
  ABSALOM, 55
  David, 289
  WILLIAM, 314
McClara
  John, 202
  JOHN, 202

McClean
  SAMUEL, 308
McClearey
  Samuel, 307
McCleary
  John, 307
McClellon
  John, 70
  WILLIAM, 70, 73
McClenachan
  DAVID, 211
  JOHN, 211
  William, 273
  WILLIAM, 112, 211
McCloure
  DAVID, 188
McCluney
  WILLIAM, 158
McClung
  James, 6, 11
  JAMES, 11, 71
  John, 273
McCluny
  JOHN, 263, 264
McClure, 161
  ALEXANDER, 135
  Andrew, 152
  David, 135
  DAVID, 188
  JNO, 265
McClures
  Arthur, 199
  Samuel, 126
McClurle, 161
McColan
  PATRICK, 16
McCollin
  KENNETH, 183
McCollock
  GEORGE, 300
McColloug
  Barnet, 37
  Bernet, 37
McCollough, 243
McColough
  BARNET, 37, 39
  Barnett, 21
McComb
  Andrew, 147
  ANDREW, 146

McConnel
  PATRICK, 92
McCord, 245
  David, 124
  William, 184
McCorkel
  John, 172
  Samuel, 250
McCorkle, 17, 85
  JAMES, 74
  SAMUEL, 146
McCormack
  Daniel, 300
  DAVID, 119
  JOSHUA, 148
McCormick
  Daniel, 173
McCoun
  James, 300
  JAMES SENR, 311
McCowen, 198
McCown, 186
  Hugh, 265
McCoy
  Hugh, 208
  JAMES, 190, 309
McCoyes, 182
McCrae
  Christopher, 85
McCraw
  Saml, 65
McCrery
  William, 207
McCrocle
  SAMUEL, 146
McCullock
  Rederick, 65
  Roderick, 316
  RODERICK, 226
McCullough
  Barnetts, 243
McCurdy
  HENRY, 16
McCutchan
  Robert, 73, 315
McCutchen
  Robert, 148, 258
McCutchens
  Robert, 193

McDaniel, 6, 62, 77
  Angus, 232, 233
  ANGUS, 226, 230
  George, 229, 233
  GEORGE, 229
  GEORGE JUNR, 226
  Henry, 149, 229
  JOHN, 57, 233
  ROTHERICK, 114
McDaniell
  HENRY, 310
McDavid
  James, 70
McDearmanroe
  BRYAN, 197
McDonal
  GEORGE, 148
McDonald, 213
  Bryan, 141
  BRYAN, 141
  Bryan Senior, 213
  DANIEL, 317
  GEORGE, 173
  John, 260
McDonel
  GEORGE, 148
McDonold
  Henry, 47
McDougal
  John, 317
McDowel
  SAMUEL, 74
McDowell, 45
  EPHRAIM, 123
  JAMES, 45
  Samuel, 45
  SAMUEL, 45
  WILLIAM, 41
McDugal
  JOHN, 148
McEamey
  William, 288
McElhenny
  SAMUEL, 173
McElheny
  Robert, 173
  ROBERT, 114
McElhony
  Samuel, 114
McElroy, 234

McEndry, 50
McFeeters
  WILLIAM, 17
McGaffey
  Henry, 225
McGary
  Hugh, 313
  HUGH, 301
McGee
  John, 78
McGeehe
  JAMES, 36
McGeehee
  JAMES, 36
McGees
  John, 298
McGehee, 224, 241
  JAMES, 36
McGehee, Senior
  WILLIAM, 185
McGill
  JAMES, 183
  John, 265
  JOHN, 198
  William, 175, 292
  WILLIAM, 175
McGlammery
  MATTHIAS, 272
McGlaughlin, 264
McGleasters
  Nul, 148
McGraddy
  LAUGHLIN, 290
McGrady
  LAUGHLIN, 290
McGriff, 98
McGuff, 24, 172
McGuffey
  Henry, 225
McHaney
  Cornelius, 183
Mchany
  Cornelius, 130
McHauley
  Peter, 138
Mckahey, 161
McKeachey
  JAMES, 250
McKeachy
  JAMES, 176

McKee
  JOHN, 16
  Samuel, 23
McKenney, 302
  James, 300
McKenny, 302
  John, 22
McKenzie
  Robert, Capt, 74
McKetterick
  ROBERT, 146
Mckettrick
  Robert, 216
  ROBERT, 146
McKinsey
  Daniel, 30
McKittrick
  Robert, 20, 217
  ROBERT, 146
McKutchen
  Robert, 148
McLaughlin, 157
  CHARLES, 141
McLoughlin, 166
McLoyes
  John, 183
McMahan
  John, 23, 73
  JOHN, 266
McMahon, 225
  John, 117
  Thomas, 259
McMillan
  JAMES, 213
McMillion, 57
McMurtrie
  John, 297
McMurtry, 238
McNare
  Daniel, 175
  DANIEL, 175
McNaris
  Daniel, 217
McNeal
  GEORGE, 259
  JAMES, 314
McNeel
  JAMES, 314
McNeely
  Robert, 93

McNeese
  John, 195
McNeill
  Daniel, 164
McNelley
  John, 227
McNelly
  JOHN, 35
McNutt
  ALEXANDER, 273
  JOHN, 118, 273
McPike
  WILLIAM, 214
McQue, 270
McRae
  DANIEL, 75, 93
McRandle, 123, 234
  JAMES, 239
McRaw, 199
McRoberts
  John, 41
  Samuel, 252
McVae
  JOHN, 130
McVeaty
  WILLIAM, 76
McVety
  WILLIAM, 76
McVia
  JOHN, 181
McViaty
  WILLIAM, 67
McWilliams
  John, 302
Mead, 15, 18, 42, 55, 56, 58,
    122, 138, 161, 214,
    215, 221, 236, 238,
    247, 252, 253, 268, 278
  Order of Council, 238
  Robert, 140
  W, 156
  William, 18, 54, 57, 237
  WILLIAM, 23, 60, 102,
    146, 161, 236, 246, 289
  William Junr, 244
Meader, 239
Meador, 56, 58
  JAMES, 213
  JOEL, 56, 250

Meadow, 246
  JOEL, 57
MEADOWS, 7, 19, 30, 52,
  53, 68, 72, 83, 85, 91,
  92, 246, 263, 270, 272
  Dyes, 270
  Great, 48, 224
  Ground, 159, 240, 264
  Hanns, 213
  Harts, 136
  Iveys, 273
  Long, 19, 255
  Small, 12, 238
  Swadleys, 285
  Tash's, 163
  Thomas, 314
Meads, 159, 161
Meanes
  HUGH, 252
Means
  HUGH, 148
  Robert, 129, 142
Meaveaty
  ROBERT, 247
Mecheaux, 271
Mechum
  Paul, 63
Mechun [Michaux], 292
Medirff
  John, 21
Medkiff, 208
  NATHANIEL, 112
  THOMAS, 270
Megginson
  BENJAMIN, 49
  William, 125, 234
  WILLIAM, 125
Melone
  Daniel, 292
Melther, 110
Melton, 11, 73
  JAME, 135
  Richard, 255
Menifee
  WILLIAM, 68
Mercer
  Hugh, 209, 271
  HUGH, 155, 261
Meredith, 283
  James, 96

Meredith, cont'd
  Samuel, 32
  SAMUEL, 79
Mereman
  MICAJAH, 82
Merewether
  DAVID, 231, 233
  FRANCIS, 232
  GEORGE, 293, 303
  NICHOLAS, 12, 17, 23,
    298
Merewethers
  Nicholas, 300
Merick
  Edward, 164
Merimon
  JOHN, 49
Merrick
  Edward, 164
Merrit
  JOHN, 228
Merritt, 157
  JOHN, 108, 160, 228, 277
Merriwether
  Thomas, 161
Merser
  Hugh, 7
Mesix
  John, 304
Messersmith
  CUNROD, 269
Meyers
  JACOB, 296
Mice
  James, 96
  Jeremiah, 96
Michael
  John, 215, 261
Michal
  John, 85
Michel, 82
Michell, 25
Middleton
  John, 98
  THOMAS, 267
Midriff
  Jacob, 4
Milam, 12, 18, 141

Military Service, 1, 4-9, 13,
  14, 16, 19, 20, 32-35,
  37, 43-45, 47-49, 51,
  52, 63
Millar
  JOHN, 195
Miller, 23, 42, 136, 146, 207
  ABRAHAM, 131
  Alexander, 46, 96, 102,
    314
  Daniel, 268
  David, 142
  Henry, 136, 196, 203
  HENRY, 79, 121, 180,
    309
  JOHN, 15, 290
  JOHN FREDERICK, 4,
    199
  Leonard, 274, 275
  Peter, 180
  SAMUEL, 16, 248
  SIMON, 18, 23
  Thomas, 23
Millers, 309
  Casper, 284
  Henry, 127
Million, 57
Milloner, 18
MILLS, 23, 128, 158
  Barners, 244
  Billings Mill Survey, 7
  Boughton's, 244
  Cabells Mill Cr., 232
  Christians Mill Cr., 248
  Daniels Mill Cr., 254
  Dunkins Mill Run, 224,
    266
  Frowman's, 94
  Hambletts, 3
  Hickeys Mill Cr., 255
  Hills Powder, 220
  Hills Powder Mill Br., 220
  Hooles, 304
  James Daniels Mill Cr., 62
  John, 221, 310
  JOHN, 127, 181, 263
  Little Mill Cr., 95
  Mill Path, 80
  Old, 23, 27
  Old Mill Place, 267

MILLS, *cont'd*
  Spencer Mill Road, 75
  Thomas's Mill Cr., 65, 230
  Wades Mill Tract, 206
  Whitney's, 111
  Wilson's Mill Creek, 206
Milum
  Thomas, 12
Minden
  John, 288
MINGO
  Bottom, 35
  Old, 35
  Path, 76
  Town
Minor
  GEORGE, 92, 179
  John, 163
  JOHN, 163
Minter, 190
Mitchel, 82, 83, 118, 315
  DANIEL, 108
  James, 82, 131
  Mitchels Deer Pen, 92
  Robert, 82, 93, 245
Mitchell, 141, 153, 215, 239
  ALEXANDER, 125
  Daniel, 143, 144, 239, 265
  DANIEL, 167
  David, 21
  DAVID, 172
  Isaac, 215
  James, 140, 192
  JAMES, 30, 262
  JOHN, 187
  Robert, 143, 262, 265
  STEPHEN, 224
  WILLIAM, 112
Mitchells, 308
Mize
  James, 140
Moar
  GARRAT, 134
  GARRATT, 134
Moberley
  Clement, 102
Moberry
  HENRY, 60
Modding
  John, 46

Modsfield
  JOHN, 52
Moffet, 116, 194
  George, 175
  GEORGE, 122, 217
Moffett, 85, 154
  George, 175, 177
  GEORGE, 43, 96
Moffett's, 315
Moira
  William, 13
Monrow
  DANIEL, 317
  Thomas, 120
Montgomery
  ALEXANDER, 303
  DAVID, 228
  DAVID JUNIOR, 230
  David Junr, 229
  JAMES, 50
  John, 295
  JOHN, 312
  Samuel, 171
  Thomas, 309
  THOMAS, 306, 309
  WILLIAM, 306, 312
  WILLIAM JUNIOR, 303
  William Senr., 312
Moody
  Jno, 2
  THOMAS, 2
Moor, 101, 111, 299
  David, 230
  John, 111
  THOMAS, 290
Moore, 9, 10, 184
  Alexander, 112
  ALEXANDER, 30
  David, 233
  George, 121, 257
  GEORGE, 170
  Henry, 291
  James, 79, 98
  JAMES, 15
  JAMES JUNR, 71
  JNO SENR, 20
  John, 38, 55, 141, 266, 272
  JOHN, 87, 98, 149
  SAMMY LAMKIN, 266

Moore, *cont'd*
  Samuel, 198
  SAMUEL, 298
  SIMEON, 298
  Thomas, 2
  William, 191
  WILLIAM, 147, 268, 273, 305, 307
Mooreman, 242
Moores, 303, 305
  David, 147
Moorman, 222
  CHARLES, 15
  ZACHERIAH, 15
Moors, 305
Morain
  JOHN, 111
Morefield, 206
Morehead, 37, 224
Moreland
  John, 248
Moreley
  John, 248
Moreman
  Micajah, 233
  Robert, 227
  ZACHARIAH, 83
Moreton
  JOSEPH, 293
Morgan, 6, 119, 236, 273
  Daniel, 150
  DANIEL, 14
  HAYNES, 25
  Jeremiah, 254
  JOHN, 166
Morgin, 159
Morra
  Samuel, 216
Morran
  Nicholas, 227
Morris, 238, 273
  HENRY, 23
  Hugh, 65, 81, 143, 230
  John, 101
  JOSEPH, 228
  Richard, 82, 111
  Richd, 100
  Samuel, 237, 263
Morrison, 249
  MICHAEL, 221

Morrison, *cont'd*
  Thomas, 119, 133
  THOMAS, 200
  William, 233
  WILLIAM JUNR, 231
Morriss, 127, 138
  John, 194
  RICHARD, 294, 295
Morrisson, 185
Morrow, 5
  Jeremiah, 2
  John, 170
Morten
  Thomas, 102
Morton, 14, 25, 98
  John, 9, 153, 242
  JOHN, 153
  Patrick, 108
Morts
  JOHN, 298
Mosbey, 36
Mosby, 36
Moseby, 103
  Edward, 231
Moseley, 129
  Charles, 202
  Edward, 232
  John, 187
  JOHN, 202
  Samuel, 187, 287
  SAMUEL, 257
Mosely
  Charles, 314
  EDWARD, 233
  JNO, 47
  SAMUEL, 256, 257
Mosey
  Elihu, 123
Moss
  David, 96
  GEORGE, 296
  WILLIAM, 186
Motley
  Joseph, 47
  JOSEPH, 55, 62, 279
Mouldin, 167
MOUNT BYRD, 276
MOUNTAIN
  Brown, 226

MOUNTAINS, 13, 18, 19, 22, 23, 31, 34, 40, 41, 43, 46, 54, 61, 63, 68, 87, 89-91, 95, 102, 213, 250-252, 254, 259, 267, 272, 278
Banister, 248
Banisters, 3
Beards, 227
Bells, 24
Bent, 116, 196, 273
Berrys, 233
Blue Ridge, 95, 227, 229, 230, 232
Blue Ridge of, 46
Brown, 97, 228, 226
Brown Mountain Cr., 233
Brushey, 71
Brushy, 240
Buck, 192, 227
Buckeye, 316
Bucks elbow, 184
Bull, 57, 114
Bushy, 113
Byrd, 276
Camp, 170
Candlers, 84, 242
Chesnut, 10, 81, 143, 169, 253
Clynch, 293, 294
Coopers, 160, 224
Flat top, 236
Flemings, 60
Fork, 205
Glenvar, 89
Grassey Hill, 168
Great, 131, 136, 271
Griffith's, 145
Harpeth, 237
Holland's Mountain Line, 244
High, 210
House, 16
Hurricane, 12
Jameson's, 189
Johnsons, 140
Johnstons, 250
Linvell, 56
Little, 166, 190, 191, 209, 221

MOUNTAINS, *cont'd*
Long, 237, 265, 267
Main, 50, 217, 282
Main Blue Ledge, 246
Marrow bone, 180
Mcfalls, 55, 223, 234
Mountain, 236
Naked, 47
Nochollow, 89
Nobusiness, 177
North, 144, 198, 217, 267
Painter, 273
Paris, 31
Pastures Fence, 285
Peeked, 259, 291
Peters, 270
Pilot, 156, 232, 235
Pyburns, 244, 262
Ragged, 250
Rocky, 230
Rorks, 239
Shalum, 237
Slate river, 170
Smiths, 224
South, 123, 127, 138, 154, 161, 176, 180, 183, 249
Tobacco Row, 228, 229, 232
Turkey Cock, 178
Warf, 254
whereby Extreem Cold the trees None Exceed ten feet highF, 246
White Oak, 8, 44, 97, 249
Widdows, 223
Wilsons, 237
Wrights, 183
Montgomery
  DAVID, 229
  John, 206, 231
  MONTGOMERY, 228
  William, 231
Mountgumery
  ALEXANDER, 147
  ROBERT, 147
Mowra
  Lewis, 284
Mowras
  Lewis, 196

Mucklehonney
   Thomas, 171
Muir, 258
Mulcher
   William, 310
Muldwick
   JANE, 201
Mullin
   John, 201
Mullines, 146
Mulling
   William, 31
Mullins, 112
Munger
   Henry, 38
Munkous
   WILLIAM, 242
Murchie
   John, 219
   JOHN, 219
Murden
   JEREMIAH, 288
Murdock, 281
Murphey, 39, 111, 145, 156, 238
   James, 262
   JAMES, 184
   John, 161
   JOHN, 156, 271
Murphie
   HUGH, 70
Murras, 68
Murray, 31, 160, 184, 246, 249, 278, 289, 317
   ANTHONY, 61, 63
   Atholbrose family, 105
   James, 105
   JOHN, 61, 63
   RICHARD, 61, 63
   WILLIAM, 105
Murrel, 153
   Samuel, 232
Murrey
   Nathaniel, 251
   NATHANIEL, 110
Murril
   William, 83
Murrill, 62
Murry, 246
   James, 198

Musick, 110
   Election, 42
   George, 78, 240
Musteen?, 96
Musterd
   WILLIAM, 225
Muston, 33, 77
Mustun, 77
Mutter, 122, 179
Myers
   Jacob, 298
   JACOB, 293, 294, 296, 302
Myias
   William, 121
Naked Ruff, 205
Nalle
   WILLIAM, 258
Naly
   DAVID, 246
Nance
   GILES, 81
   REUBEN, 54
   Thomas, 187, 206, 310
   William, 183
Napier, 121, 126, 129, 163, 282
   Ashford, 197, 198
   ASHFORD, 121, 126, 162, 197, 198, 276
   Bouth, 207
   CHAMPION, 197
   JOHN, 276
   P, 61
   Patrick, 184, 207
   PATRICK, 43, 97, 101, 130, 162, 163, 198, 276
   RICHARD, 132, 207
   Thomas, 25-29, 48, 97, 100, 107, 108, 282, 285, 314
   THOMAS, 132, 266, 276
Napper, 43
Narber, 108
Nash, 58, 62, 177, 287
   Arthur, 103
   Enoch, 230
   Henry, 243
   HENRY, 177
   JOHN, 103

NASH, *cont'd*
   Norvell, 103
   Thomas, 208
   Thomas Senior, 208
   William, 5
Neadham
   JOHN, 50
Neal
   ANN, 230
   Pater, 23
   Roger, 31
   ZACHARIAH, 120
   ZEPHENIAH, 199
Nealey
   WILLIAM, 165
Neavells
   HENRY, 249
Needham, 272
Neelly, 282
   JOHN, 309
   WILLIAM, 308
Neely
   James, 252
   JOHN, 16
   JOHN, Doctor, 273
   WILLIAM, 172, 273, 274
Neilly
   ROBERT, 32
Neilson, 85, 156, 158, 261, 267
Neison, 267
Nelson, 246
   AMBROSE, 4
   THOMAS, 164
Nerrell
   James, 121
Nervard
   JOHN, 276
Nevel
   John, 256
Nevil
   JAMES, 228
Nevills
   JNO, 76
   JOHN, 133
Neward
   JOHN, 276
Newell, 41
Newkam
   JOHN, 182

Newman, 236
  Daniel, 200
  DANIEL, 199, 204
  JOHN, 200
  NIMROD, 15
Newsum
  William, 2
Newton, 57
Niax
  WILLIAM, 2
Nichol
  JOHN, 148
Nicholas, 111, 118, 259, 288
  GEORGE, 291
  JAMES, 200
  John, 170
  JOHN, 270
  Julias, 183
  JULIAS, 183
  ROBERT CARTER, 18
  Samuel, 43
  William, 127
Nicholes
  John, 260
  WILLIAM, 260
Nicholl, 127
Nicholls
  ANDREW, 269
  John, 258
Nichols
  John, 221
Nickles
  ANDREW, 258
Nicks, 195
  GEORGE, 279
Niman, 156
Nobb
  John, 4
  Jones's, 149
Noble
  John, 67
Noline
  James, 119
Norflet
  Thomas, 208
Norman, 108, 109, 150
Norris, 245
North
  Abraham, 82, 233

NORTH CAROLINA, 281
  Gilford Co., 41
Northington
  JABEZ, 206
Norton, 129
  Nehemiah, 240
  NEHEMIAH, 242
Nowill, 41
Nowland
  William, 24
Nowlin, 112, 149, 150, 165, 170, 206
  JAMES, 231
Nowling
  Bryant Ward, 30
  BRYANT WARD, 25
Nuckles
  CHARLES, 64
Nuckolds, 152
Nuckols
  James, 78
Nugan
  Richard, 156
Nunally
  William, 221
Nunnally
  John, 82
Nuqan, 156
Nuquan, 156
Nutt, 184
  Richard, 184, 199
  RICHARD, 184, 199, 269
Oak, 33
Oaks
  JAMES, 50
  John, 241
Oar
  ROBERT, 153, 257
Obryan
  Dennis, 291
  JOHN, 291
Ogleby
  THOMAS, 235
Oglesby, 159
  Richard, 104
  Thomas, 22
  THOMAS, 49
Oglisby, 111
  THOMAS, 111

Old
  JOHN, 138
Oldham
  William, 176
Oldhouser
  HENDRY, 249
Oldum
  JOHN, 112
Oliver, 127, 207, 282
  Dionysias, 104
  DRURY, 26
  Isaac, 206
  JAMES, 249
  JAMES, Sr., 155
  JOHN, 115, 307, 308
  Nicholas, 139
  WILLIAM, 50, 282, 317
Olliver
  Dionysias, 104
  John, 269
  JOHN, 269
Olngley
  PETER, 282
Omohundro
  RICHARD, 51
  Richard, Corporal, 51
Oneal, 206
  Neal, 212
  NEAL, 4
  WALTER, 18
Oneil
  DANIEL, 222
ORCHARDS
  Crab Orchard, 307
  Haw, 102
ORDER LINES, 38, 41, 42, 52, 78, 101, 150, 184, 189, 192
  Adams, 34
  Adams's, 278
  Adkinsons, 110, 240
  Bells, 253
  Birds, 177
  Christians, 316
  Clay's, 151
  Copelands, 188
  Coplands, 103, 286
  Donelsons, 39, 77
  Feilds, 122
  Fennys, 3

INDEX

ORDER LINES, *cont'd*
  Fields, 179, 292
  Finneys, 253
  Finnys, 25, 250
  Grays, 77
  Greys, 178
  Henry, 171
  Henry's, 110
  Henrys, 278
  James Terrys, 169
  Leatherwood, 198
  Lomax and Company's, 112, 153
  Randolph & Co., 290
  Randolphs, 191, 246, 253, 271, 284
  Samuel Harris's, 113
  Terry's, 21, 166
  Terrys, 11, 22, 37, 62, 130, 278
  Twittys, 284, 290
  Walkers, 245
  Waltons, 121, 145
  Weatherpoons, 278
  Wittens, 68
  Wittons, 213
  Woodson and Companys$, 141
ORDINARIES
  Dragon, 102
Ornsbey, 278
Ornsby, 160, 236, 238, 246, 261, 264, 267
  John, 142
Orrick, 15
Oswald
  Richard, 135
Oswaldd
  Richard, 297
Overby
  OBADIAH, 124
  Peter, 80
Overby, Senr.
  Peter, 124
Overstreet, 17, 236
Overton, 312
  CLIFF, 297
  CLOUGH, 295
  SAMUEL, 34
  Samuel, Capt, 34

Overtons, 312
Owen, 38, 53, 67
  Henry, 221, 224
  John, 15, 31, 37, 38, 221, 224, 260
  JOHN, 221
  Richard, 221
  Thomas, 52, 124, 260
  THOMAS, 241, 243
  William, 36, 221
  WILLIAM, 77, 184
Owens, 197
  JOHN, 41
  WILLIAM, 131
Owin, 103
Owings
  SAMUEL, 20
Owlys, 306
Ownby, Junior
  John, 196
  JOHN, 131
Ownby, Junr.
  John, 131
Owsley, 305
  Thomas, 305
  THOMAS, 305, 306
  WILLIAM, 304
Owsly, 307
  THOMAS, 306
  William, 305
  WILLIAM, 304
Owsly or Orosly, 299
Ozwald
  & Co., 60
Pace
  William, 257
Pachans, 310
Page, 277
  William, 108
  WILLIAM, 103
Pain
  REUBEN, 310
Paine
  JOSEPH, 190, 195
Palsel
  PETER, 12
Palson
  SWITHEN, 298
Pamplin
  James, 192

Pankey
  STEPHEN, 215
Pannel
  John, 64
  LUKE, 227
  Thomas, 227
Panther, 275
Panther Hollow, 223
Parbary
  JAMES, 21, 169
Parham, 1, 151
  Lewis, 104, 217
Parish, 41, 67, 130
  David, 63
  DAVID, 63, 277
  JAMES, 137
  John, 269
PARISHES
  Bath, 32
  Bristol, 247
  Broomfield, 127
  Drysdale, 164
  Fredericksville, 202, 291, 317
  Lynhaven, 185
  Nottoway, 56, 273, 275
  Saint Brides, 288
  Saint Patrick, 255
  Saint Paul, 153
  Trinity, 11, 12, 288
Parker, 237
  JAMES, 115
  John, 140
Parkins, 243
Parks
  JOHN, 174, 273
Parr, 203, 283
  HENRY, 204
  John, 148, 200, 286
  JOHN, 54
  JOHN JUNR, 285
  JOHN SENR, 204, 286
Parrish, 78
Parrither, 42
Parrow, 12
Parsley
  RICHARD, 245
  Robert, 83
Parsly
  RICHARD, 245

Parsons
  JOHN, 73
Partns, 112
Partridge
  John, 111
Passons
  THOMAS, 254
Pasture
  SOLOMON GOOD, 275
Pate, 156
  ANTHONY, 145
  Thomas, 156, 223, 246
Pater, 293
Paterson, 115, 125, 232
  James, 110
  JAMES, 116
  Samuel, 110, 136
Patersons
  John, 312
Patey, 78
  JESSE, 78
PATHS, 16, 39, 55, 75, 85, 103, 209, 211, 227, 236, 245, 264, 265
  Browns, 224
  Cart, 59
  Deans, 108
  from William Robinsons, 31
  Mill, 80
  Mingo, 76
  Old, 265
  Pates, 250
  Path, 234
  Race Ground, 85
  Ridge, 55
  Thompsons, 235
Patial, 308
Paton
  James, 86
Patrick
  John, 130
Patten
  Alexander, 232
Patterson, 235, 236, 238, 239
  CHARLES, 23, 131, 132
  DAVID, 20, 95, 182
  James, 110
  John, 44, 118, 132, 211, 291, 313

Patterson, *cont'd*
  JOSEPH, 244
  Nathaniel, 156
  Robert, 199, 201, 307
  ROBERT, 201
  Samuel, 133, 222
  SAMUEL, 142, 216, 217
  Thomas, 24
  William, 47, 116
Patteson
  Charles, 202
  CHARLES, 131, 132, 202
  JOHN, 136, 138
  WILLIAM, 194
Pattey, 38
Pattillo
  George, 197
Patton
  James, 139
  JAMES, 49, 86-92, 211, 212
  MATHEW, 131
  MATTHEW, 122
  Roger, 202
  THOMAS, 56
Pattons
  Jacob, 195
Paul
  John, 45
Pawling
  HENRY, 286
Pawlings
  HENRY, 286
Paxton
  John, 172
  Samuel, 117, 221
  SAMUEL, 117, 221
  THOMAS, 180
  William, 118
  WILLIAM, 117, 137
Payne, 43, 52, 130, 141, 170, 262
  Edmund, 21
  EDMUND, 77
  John, 33, 36, 177
  JOHN, 102, 219
  John, Colo, 103
  Jonas, 62
  Philemon, 12, 39
  Reuben, 258

Payne, *cont'd*
  REUBEN, 78, 130
  Robert, 285
  Thomas, 15, 156, 288
  THOMAS, 258
  William, 15, 42, 45, 58, 85, 281
  WILLIAM, 257
  William Senior, 218
Paynor
  JOHN, 243
Payson
  Thomas, 145
Payton
  Robert, 233
Peachey
  William, 72
  WILLIAM P, 71
Peachy, 34
  William, 69
  WILLIAM, 73, 74
Peak, 180
  George, 52
  WILLIAM, 153
Pearsey
  JOHN, 278
Peart
  Griffin, 194, 209
  GRIFFIN, 194
Peburn, 141
Peck
  Jacob, 115
  JACOB, 136
Pedan
  JOHN, 274
Pedigon
  ROBERT, 73
Pedigow
  ROBERT, 266
Pedigrow
  ROBERT, 168, 179
Peebles
  JOHN, 135
  JOSEPH, 33
Peek
  Robert, 119
Pelfry
  JOHN, 131
Pemberton, 6, 15, 77
  JOHN, 130

Pendleton, 235, 244, 265, 316
  BENJAMIN, 231
  Edmund, 163, 164
  Edmund Junior, 271
  William, 229
Pendletons, 235
Penicks, 295
Penington
  Sack, 99
  William, 99
Penix, 102
Penn
  Abraham, 193, 283-285
  ABRAHAM, 128
  GABRIEL, 11, 228
  JOHN, 72
Pennell, 265
Pennix, 14
Perdue
  Richard, 219
Peregen
  WILLIAM, 176
Peregoy
  ROBERT, 277
Perham
  Matthew, 269
Perigen
  WILLIAM, 176
Perkey, 255
Perkin, 172
Perkins, 50, 53, 241, 252
  Constant, 135, 243
  CONSTANT, 24
  DAVID, 275
  Nicholas, 241
  NICHOLAS, 24
  PETE, 53
  PETER, 13, 24, 50, 52
  WILLIAM, 204
Perrickes, 295
Perriman
  Richard, 21
Perron
  Charles, 233
Perry, 81, 289
  Agness, 247
  JAMES, 171
Persinger
  Jacob, 180

Persinger, *cont'd*
  JACOB, 155
Peter
  Richard, 128, 267
Peters, 57
  ANN, 295
  Otho, 295
  OTHO, 295
  RICHARD, 297
Petill, 303
Pettet
  William, 17
Pettit
  William, 82
Petty, 38, 64
  FRANCIS MOORE, 222, 223
Pettycrew, 239
  MATTHEW, 234
Peyton
  Henry, 43, 44, 163
  JAMES, 300
  William, 44
Pharis
  Edward, 62
Phelp
  John, 186
Phelps, 44, 111, 157, 192, 214, 215, 225
  James, 145
  John, 159, 244, 290
  Phelps, 267
  SAMUEL, 18, 64
  Thomas, 44
  WILLIAM, 49
Philips, 305
  CHARLES, 175
  John, 116, 189
  Jonathan, 249
  RICHARD, 136
  SAMUEL, 124
  William, 302
Phillips, 78, 80, 290
  Hartwell, 56
  JACOB, 231
  James, 247
  John, 104
  JOHN, 291
  JONATHAN, 142
  Moses, 56

Phillips, *cont'd*
  Richard, 12
  RICHARD, 11, 78, 136
  Richard Senr, 11
  Stephen, 137
  THOMAS, 228
  William, 8, 79
  WILLIAM, 69, 78
Philp
  John, 163
Philpott
  JOHN, 169
Phip
  John, 41
Piburn
  Jacob, 159
Pickett, 99
  John, 164
  JOHN, 164
  Mace, 164
  MACE, 164
  MARTIN, 69
  Thomas, 164
Pickins
  Israel, 70
Pickle
  Henry, 289
Pidder, 288
Pierce, 222
  THOMAS, 294
Pigg, 2, 6, 14, 38, 178
  HEZEKIAH, 10
  John, 9, 10
  JOHN, 178
  William, 64
Pigott
  JAMES, 293
Pilis, 246
PILOT PINE, 24, 252
Pine
  JAMES, 94
Pineaes, 14
Pinkard, 153
Pinners of Pigg River, 6
Pistol
  Thomas, 142
Pistole
  THOMAS, 113
Pitman
  JOHN, 299

Pittillo
  James, 194
Pittillow
  James, 217
PLANTATIONS
  John Hewits, 46
  Richard Taylors, 104
  Summer's Manor, 208
Pleasant, 60, 62
Pleasants
  THOMAS, 26
  THOMAS JUNIOR, 27-29
  THOMAS JUNR, 26, 27, 29, 30
Pledger, 64
Plunkett, 57
Poag
  John, 126
  JOHN, 123, 126
  ROBERT, 126
Poage
  Ann, 301
  ANN, 293, 297
  George, 195
  John, 200, 204, 284, 316
  JOHN, 17, 19, 23, 123, 173, 180, 195, 217, 285
  Robert, 196, 274
  ROBERT, 249
  WILLIAM, 309
POCOSONS, 82, 104
Podigrow
  ROBERT, 168
Poindexter, 83
POINTS, 274
  East, 89
  High Point of Rocks, 91
  Island, 214
  Point of Rocks, 8, 87, 91, 104, 160, 191, 305
  Rocky, 213
  Sandy, 265
  Stoney, 263, 264
Polke
  Charles, 305
Pollard
  William, 144, 191
Polley, 140, 282
  David, 114, 278
  DAVID, 109

Polley, cont'd
  JOHN, 130
Polly, 21
  David, 257
  JOHN, 130
PONDS, 42, 53, 102, 237, 263
  Ceder, 113
  Great, 188
  High Land, 214
  Horsepound, 104
  Little, 188
  Maple, 216
  Mill, 107
  Round, 104
  Small, 20
Pool
  BENJAMIN PETTY, 182
  Seth Petty, 179
Poole, 57
  BENJAMIN PETTY, 182
  Petty, 182
  Thomas, 315
  WALTER, 57
Pooles
  Walter, 57
Poor
  GEORGE, 202
  William, 284
  WILLIAM, 286
Porter, 36, 188, 237
  Benj, 7
  JOHN, 131
  Nathaniel, 111
Porters
  John, 293
Posey, 173
  HUMPHREY, 316
Possenberrys
  George, 289
Poteeat
  JAMES, 173
Poteet, 82
  James, 255
Poteete
  James, 218
  JAMES, 68
Pothress
  Polly, 32

Potter
  THOMAS, 198
Potty
  David, 102
Potty or Polly, 161
Poul
  John, 98
Pound
  JANE, 211
Powel, 7
  Edmund, 227
  Lucas, 167
  Richard, 227
  THOMAS, 227
  William, 80
Powell
  John, 129
  LEVEN, 298, 303, 304
  Robert, 273
  William, 31, 224
Power
  Walter, 230-232
Powers, 288
Powers and Company, 181
Poythress
  Peter, 92
  PETER, 32, 95
Prather, 159
  BASIL, 296
  Henry, 297, 298, 313
  THOMAS, 296, 299, 300
Pratt, 156
  Jacob, 86
Prayther
  NEHEMIAH, 201
Preedle
  JOHN, 237
Prenty
  JAMES, 58
  Thomas, 10
  THOMAS, 2
Prentys
  Thomas, 103
Preston, 63, 64, 97, 103, 104, 113, 173, 213
  Col, 6, 127
  FRANCIS, 87
  JOHN, 91
  William, 69, 80, 117, 139, 143, 289

Preston, *cont'd*
  WILLIAM, 49, 63, 64, 79,
    82, 84-91, 103, 139,
    210-212
  WM, 87
Prestone
  William, 1, 41
  WILLIAM, 19
Prewet
  Daniel, 199
Prewit, 22, 142
  Daniel, 203
  DAVID, 12
  JAMES, 184
  MICHAEL, 264, 265
Prewitt
  DAVID, 70
  Hugh, 167
Price, 101, 207, 211, 259
  ABRAM, 266
  AUGUSTINE, 180
  John, 285
  JOHN, 60
  JOSHUA SHORE, 168
  RICHARD, 165
  Thomas, 264
  William, 210
  WILLIAM, 17
Priddy, 186
  Thomas, 284
Pride, 168
Prince
  JOSEPH, 2
Procise
  WILLIAM, 169
Proclamation of 1763, 1, 4-9,
  13, 14, 16, 19, 20
Prossett
  William, 63
Pruit, 186, 244, 263
  MICHAEL, 264, 265
Pruits
  Michael, 155
Pruntey
  ROBERT, 151
Prunty
  JAMES, 208
Pryor, 182
  William, 226
  WILLIAM JUNIOR, 226

Pryor, *cont'd*
  WILLIAM SENIOR, 226,
    229
Pucket
  ROBERT, 235
Puckett
  DRURY, 112
  ROBERT, 235
Pullam
  JAMES, 183
Pulliam, 182
  JOSEPH, 182
Purdie
  George, 59
  GEORGE, 59
Purdue
  William, 220
Purkens
  Harden, 18
Purkins
  Constant, 252
  CONSTANT, 24
  PETER, 13
Purnell
  Mrs, 12
Pursley, 159
  William, 185
Purvis
  George, 228
Pyne
  Isaac, 71
Quarles, 11, 128, 140, 163,
  166, 237
  JOHN, 155
Quirk, 312
  THOMAS, 296
Raby
  James, 207
  Kedah, 207
RACE GROUND
  Bibees, 85
Rackoon Tract, 262
Radar
  ADAM, 256
Radcliff, 234
  JAMES, 239
Raders, 309
Rafferty, 264, 265
  JOHN, 244, 264
  Thomas, 56, 239

Rafferty, *cont'd*
  THOMAS, 141
Ragen
  JEREMIAH, 255
  RICHARD, 152
Raggin
  Jerry, 190
Ragland, 4, 60
  JOEL, 271
  John, 23
  SAMUEL, 85
  William, 167
Ragsale
  Edward, 254
Ragsdale
  DANL, 42
  Edward, 25
  JOHN, 171
  JOSEPH, 2
Rain
  George, 163
Raines, 163
Raley
  Miles, 292
Ralph, 112
Ralston
  David, 182
  Robert, 195
Ralstons
  William, 148
Ramey, 173
  ABSALOM, 149
  Absolom, 173
  DANIEL, 246
  JOHN, 173, 177
Ramey, Senior
  ABSALOM, 176
Ramsey, 164
  ANDREW, 127
  JOHN, 11, 69, 123, 183
  Thomas, 128, 257
  THOMAS, 250
  William, 137, 258
  WILLIAM, 231
Randel
  John, 52
Randle, 205
  Bernard, 52
  BERNARD, 52
  William, 52

Randolph, 4, 5, 13, 38, 43,
    56, 58, 72, 84, 100,
    101, 103, 105, 108,
    111, 118-120, 123, 126,
    133, 134, 141, 145,
    157, 158, 161, 166,
    168, 169, 181, 191,
    203, 213, 214, 222,
    224, 225, 236, 246,
    248, 249, 252-254,
    262-264, 271, 283, 284,
    290-292, 307, 308
  Beverly, 78
  Henry, 104
  M, 10
  PETER, 286
  Richard, 98, 159
  RICHARD, 63
  Thomas Mann, 167, 229
  THOMAS MANN, 218
Randolph and Company, 133,
    181, 187, 199, 203
Rankin, 199
  JAMES, 258, 269
  Thomas, 259
Ranking, 76
Rankins, 210
Rawlings
  HENRY, 195
Ray, 39, 56, 129, 145
  JAMES, 169, 301
  JOHN, 198
  Joseph, 25
  Moses, 246
  Samuel, 137
  William, 228
Rayley
  PHILIP, 109
Raysois, 170
Rea
  Andrew, 186
  ANDREW, 133
  John, 76
  JOHN, 75
Reabourn
  Adam, 154
Reaburn
  JAMES, 275
  JANE, 259
  Joseph, 275

Reaburn, *cont'd*
  JOSEPH, 274
Read, 62, 73, 80, 101, 129,
    160, 199, 222, 240,
    245, 265, 312
  AJONADAB, 236
  Ajonadal, 142
  Casper, 18
  CLEMENT, 195, 198
  Elizabeth, 242
  Francis, 224
  FRANCIS, 224
  George, 277
  JONES, 264
  Mary, 216
  MARY, 145, 195, 198,
    236, 264
  THOMAS, 4, 70, 98
  William, 95, 142, 247, 283
  WILLIAM, 133, 245
Reading
  Francis, 14
Reads
  John, 314
  Thomas, 126
Reah
  JOHN, 274
Real
  MICHAEL, 149
Reas
  John, 263
Reaves, 142, 211
  George, 254
  GEORGE, 255
  JOHN, 9, 12
Reavis
  ISHAM, 206
Redar
  ADAM, 256
Reddy
  Samuel, 174
  SAMUEL, 174
Rediford
  WILLIAM, 131
Redman, 98, 291
Reed, 96
  AJONADAB, 236
  Robert, 116, 176
  SAMUEL, 172
  Thomas, 137

Rees
  Aser, 297
  Azor, 301
Reeve
  John, 163
Reeves
  Brewer, 119
  BREWER, 121
  JOHN, 135
  Thomas, 119
  THOMAS, 119
Regan
  Jeremiah, 176
Reger [Rogers]
  Reger, 169
REGIMENTS
  Pennsylvania, 261
  Second Virginia, 47, 99,
    155, 261
  Virginia, 93
Regin
  Jacob, 285
Regney, 257
Reid
  Adam, 231
  John, 95
  Robert, 114
Reise
  Azor, 297
Reives
  GEORGE, 256
Reivs
  John, 168
Rely
  Barnabas, 172
Remmington, 292
Renalds
  BARTLET, 200
Renffrow
  James, 152
Renick, 171
Rennion
  Luke, 286
Rentfro, 260, 278
  Isaac, 236
  John, 147
  JOHN, 159, 166
  WILLIAM, 260
Rentfroe, 68, 76, 166
  Isaack, 278

Rentfroe, *cont'd*
  James, 67, 68
  JESSEE, 292, 308
  Joseph, 160, 292
  JOSHUA, 256
  Stephen, 127
Rentfroes
  Jessey, 159
Rentfrow, 9, 23, 109, 136
  James, 2, 164
Rentsfrd, 247
Reubil, 164
Reynolds
  JAMES, 267
  John, 273
  SUSANNA, 55
Rheaburn
  JOSEPH, 114, 115
Rhodes, 9
  John, 151
Rice
  John, 23, 166, 191
Rich
  Nimrod, 24
Rich Hill, 86
Richards, 11, 12, 64, 110
  EDWARD, 62
  THOMAS, 110
Richardson, 54, 143-145, 240, 241, 246, 248, 291
  AMOSE, 72
  Henry, 43
  John, 240
  JOHN, 133, 187, 234, 308
  JONATHAN, 144, 215
  Joseph, 236
  JOSEPH, 96
  LANDIE, 100
  TURNER, 184
  William, 141
Richel
  Thomas, 84
Richey, 223
  JAMES, 148
Richmans Draft, 220
Richmond
  John, 12
Rickets
  WILLIAM, 112

Riddell
  CORNELIUS, 19
Riddle, 19, 269
  CORNELIUS, 19
  William, 183
RIDGES, 4, 7, 10, 13, 14, 16, 17, 19, 22, 29, 31, 34, 39, 41-43, 68, 82, 83, 87, 89, 92-96, 98, 100, 102, 211-213, 216, 234, 238, 241, 245, 247, 250, 252-255, 259-261, 264-266, 270, 273, 275, 276
  Barren, 89
  Blue, 64, 95, 230
  Buffaloe, 17
  Bushey, 92
  Dividing, 31, 86, 266, 272
  Flat, 7, 63, 74, 93, 94, 99
  High, 86
  Hucklebury Hill, 94
  Lime Stone, 12, 41, 102
  Limestone, 95
  Main, 40, 237, 239
  Marshals, 274
  McCalisters, 94
  Naked, 4, 90
  Painters Mountain, 273
  Ridge, 223, 234, 271
  Rocky, 88
  Steep, 70, 105
  Timber, 68, 88
Ridgeway
  James, 316
Ridgway
  JAMES, 127
Rigby
  Hugh, 129
Rigers, 135
Right, 72
  William, 40, 100
Rigney, 72
  Charles, 150
Rion, 58
  AARVIEL, 57
  D, 14
  Daniel, 68, 218, 255
  DANIEL, 68
  Darby, 196

Rion, *cont'd*
  DARBY, 57, 68, 167, 291
  DERBEY, 6
Ripley
  RICHARD, 24
  Richd, 24
Riser
  HENRY, 254
Risk
  JOHN, 176
Ritchey, 223
Ritchie
  MATTHEW, 210
Ritchie & Company, 174
River Hill, 30
RIVERS, 6, 42, 71, 285
  Appamatox, 44, 47, 101
  Appamattox, 64, 100
  Appomatox, 63, 111, 119, 132, 180, 286, 290
  Arrarat, 24
  Banister, 10, 11, 25, 26, 31, 36, 37, 42, 70, 77, 78, 96, 130, 145, 150, 152, 153, 169, 179, 207, 250, 253, 257, 279
  Bannister, 11, 50
  Bells, 24
  Big Mearne, 261
  Big Miami, 7
  Bigg, 54
  Bill Pasture, 309
  Black, 254
  Black water, 4, 6, 8, 10, 13, 23, 25, 45, 48, 55, 58, 68, 69, 73, 97-100, 103, 109, 111, 146, 151, 159, 160, 168, 214, 215, 220, 224, 236, 244, 245, 254-256, 260, 267, 272, 277, 278, 284, 292, 308
  Blackwater, 159, 165, 168, 170, 213, 237
  Bluewing, 122, 179
  Bryery, 54
  Buffaloe, 61, 131, 134, 196, 227, 230, 287, 315
  Buffalow, 54

RIVERS, *cont'd*
  Bull Pasture, 195, 249, 258, 260, 275, 291, 309
  Calf Pasture, 20, 111, 115, 274
  Camp, 202
  Catawber, 140
  Catawbo, 173
  Catheyes, 17
  Catheys, 216
  Contrary, 83
  Cow Pasture, 135, 202, 249, 315
  Dan, 7, 12, 20, 24, 31, 38, 40, 41, 52, 53, 77, 109, 124, 177, 178, 186, 192, 193, 197, 205, 221, 241, 243
  Dicks, 98, 116, 117, 175, 176, 295, 297-308, 311, 312, 314
  Dry, 46, 138, 198, 206, 265
  Elizabeth, 288
  Elk, 13, 75
  Ervin, 140
  Falling, 10, 56, 61, 62, 72, 95, 123, 129, 141, 144, 149, 152, 155, 159, 161, 179, 186, 214, 227, 234-240, 245, 247, 260, 263-267, 289, 290
  Fluvanna, 18, 25, 47, 49, 99, 101, 107, 111, 133, 156, 164, 186, 189, 190, 196, 227, 231, 233, 234, 241, 270, 282
  Great Byrd, 177
  Great Kanawa, 209
  Great Kanhawa, 209
  Great Kanhaway, 75
  Great Kenhawa, 13
  Green, 295, 296, 299, 304, 306, 312
  Green brier, 33, 34, 95
  Green Brire, 262
  Hallidays, 195
  Hardware, 9, 101, 129, 138, 163, 191, 194, 223, 301

RIVERS, *cont'd*
  Hico, 51, 80, 241
  Holadays, 119
  Holladay, 132
  Holliday, 190
  Holsten, 294
  Holston, 96
  Horse Pasture, 199
  Indian, 87, 88, 92
  Irven, 21
  Irvens, 95
  Irvine, 217
  Irwin, 216
  Jackson, 131, 232
  Jackson's, 98
  Jacksons, 13, 17, 121, 122, 125, 126, 132, 147, 173, 177, 178, 197, 202, 206, 260, 287, 290, 307, 308
  James, 2, 11, 12, 16, 17, 26, 27, 30, 31, 34, 41, 46, 63, 64, 69, 71, 73, 79, 81, 85, 92-94, 97, 98, 103, 104, 113-117, 120, 124, 126, 127, 129, 131, 134, 137, 141, 143, 146-150, 161, 170-174, 176-182, 188, 191, 199-202, 204, 210, 213, 218-220, 237, 248, 250-252, 264, 270, 273, 281-283, 289, 315-317
  Kentuck, 209
  Kentuckey, 69, 98, 99, 185, 209, 212
  Kentucky, 1, 4, 5, 7-9, 19, 32, 34, 37, 43-45, 47, 51, 63, 69, 73, 74, 79, 80, 82, 84, 85, 87, 92-95, 97, 209, 210, 276, 297, 302
  Little, 20, 89
  Little Falling, 95, 159, 165, 234-236, 238, 239, 244, 245, 262, 265
  Little Kentucky, 87
  Little Otter, 157, 166
  Little Piney, 231
  Mattapony, 164

RIVERS, *cont'd*
  Mayo, 41, 53, 55, 57, 80, 110, 112, 114, 118, 120, 122, 130, 134, 147, 166, 171, 180, 182, 184, 185, 190, 191, 194, 199, 201, 204, 218, 251, 276, 282, 285
  Mayo's, 49
  Mayos, 41
  Mechams, 93
  Mechums, 180, 181
  Meherin, 38
  Meherren, 315
  Meherrin, 2, 145, 151, 178, 206, 247, 254, 290, 313
  Middle, 6, 23, 114-117, 136, 144-6, 152, 174-6, 179, 204, 245, 247, 258, 266, 267, 274, 292
  Middle Slate, 111, 187
  Midle, 118, 315
  Missisippie, 86, 88
  Moremans, 124, 201
  New, 20, 87, 88, 90, 91, 211, 212
  nob Lock, 175
  North, 12, 13, 30, 73, 118, 121, 127, 130, 131, 133, 136-138, 154, 155, 159, 178, 180, 183, 198, 201, 250, 259, 266, 274, 309, 310, 317
  North Mayo, 120, 123, 131, 133, 185, 199, 203, 290
  North Shanando, 96
  North Shanandore, 141
  North Shennendore, 265
  Nottoway, 137, 206
  Occaquan, 162
  Occoquan, 163
  Ohio, 1, 5-9, 14-16, 20, 32-5, 37, 44-5, 48, 51, 52, 69, 71-6, 79, 83-87, 92-95, 97, 99, 103, 155, 185, 194, 209, 261, 271, 276, 297, 310

INDEX

RIVERS, *cont'd*
Otter, 18, 19, 55, 57, 60, 102, 140, 141, 148, 150, 159, 160, 162, 199, 200, 214-216, 221-223, 237, 244, 246, 248, 262-264, 287, 289, 292, 307, 308, 315
Pamonkey, 12, 17
Pamonky, 11
Patomack, 39
Patowmack, 19, 126, 154
Pedlar, 97, 225-233, 316
Pedler, 143
Pigg, 2-6, 9, 14, 20, 53, 54, 67-69, 71-74, 76, 97, 102, 109, 112, 114, 115, 120, 125, 130-132, 136, 142, 144, 146, 149, 151-153, 160, 164-166, 168, 170, 188, 195, 196, 213, 218-220, 240, 244-246, 248, 249, 253, 255, 256, 264, 271, 278, 287
Piney, 123, 291
Potawmack, 178
Potomack, 22, 23, 70
Potowmac, 268
Potowmack, 102, 126
Powtomack, 123, 182, 183, 192, 197, 199, 202-204, 289, 291
Rappahannock, 139, 164
Rappahanock, 127
Revanna, 166
Riv, 9, 61
Rivanna, 3, 6, 10, 11, 25, 27, 28, 33, 48, 55, 75, 76, 83-85, 100, 104, 107, 108, 121, 126-129, 136, 137, 177, 180-182, 184, 186, 191, 196-199, 207, 243, 259, 269, 276, 284, 297
Roan, 31
Roan Oak, 10, 12, 13, 36, 39, 40, 50, 71, 78, 93, 147, 148, 163, 165, 250, 268

RIVERS, *cont'd*
Roan Oke, 41, 210, 222, 223
Roan-oak, 32
Roanoak, 31, 32, 39, 71, 73, 114, 139, 249, 271
Roanoake, 105, 119, 250
Roanoke, 112-114, 117, 126, 141, 172, 173, 175, 176, 183, 190, 202, 210-213, 274, 275, 304, 317
Rock fish, 85, 228, 232, 233, 289, 292
Rockfish, 17, 104, 219, 231
Ronoak, 172
Rowanoak, 215
salt, 14, 93, 293-298, 300-306, 311, 312, 316
Sandy, 7-10, 14, 21, 24, 33, 36, 38, 39, 43, 52, 68, 69, 72, 102, 103, 114, 135, 153, 169, 171, 187, 203, 205, 217, 239-243, 252, 256, 268, 279, 286, 288, 291, 305
Scioto, 297
Sciotto, 51
Shanadore, 23, 258
Shanadow, 6, 19
Shanando, 73, 96, 114, 259, 260
Shanandoah, 154
Shanandoe, 19
Shanandore, 115-118, 136, 145, 146, 152, 159, 161, 174, 176, 178-180, 183, 245, 247, 255, 256, 259
Shandore, 12
Shandow, 13
Shanendo, 161
Shanendore, 247, 260
Shanido, 133
Shannandore, 155, 267
Shanondore, 250
Shenando, 116, 201

RIVERS, *cont'd*
Shenandore, 115-118, 121, 124, 127, 130, 135, 136, 138, 198, 201, 204, 274, 275, 292, 307, 309, 310, 315, 317
Shendandore, 155
Sioto, 52
Slate, 24, 48, 50, 65, 96, 99, 131, 170, 187, 202, 265, 314, 316
Smith, 68, 140
Smith's, 168, 185, 186
Smiths, 20, 43, 46, 52, 54, 109, 128, 130, 131, 133, 135, 165, 168, 169, 173, 178, 181, 186-191, 198, 204, 218, 246, 254-256, 263, 272, 316
South, 115, 123, 127, 154, 161, 164, 178, 180, 183, 201
South Hardware, 17
South Mayo, 120, 122, 133, 186, 202, 204, 251, 268, 286
Southanna, 6
Stan, 196
Stanton, 3, 18, 19, 31, 50, 55, 56, 58, 105, 108, 111, 124, 130, 156, 162, 165, 167, 169, 170, 214, 217, 246, 250, 263, 266, 268, 279, 287
Stantoun, 289, 309
Staunton, 70, 71, 77, 78, 98, 105, 129, 140, 144, 146, 184, 214, 216, 224, 235, 238, 244, 246, 248, 251
Stinking, 3, 21, 50, 78, 79, 135, 136, 145, 160, 172, 222, 225, 277, 278
Tye, 33, 205, 206, 227-229, 233
Tygerts Valley, 290, 310
Walkers, 262
Willises, 170

RIVERS, *cont'd*
  Woods, 86, 88-91, 139,
    211, 212
Rizwell
  John, 287
Roach, 145
Road, 10
ROADS, 3, 5, 9, 11-13, 19,
    27, 34, 42, 46, 51, 52,
    54, 56, 61, 71-73, 83,
    92, 93, 99, 102, 103,
    214, 215, 219-221, 223,
    236, 237, 239, 241,
    242, 247, 249, 252,
    255, 256, 258, 260,
    262, 265, 267, 268,
    270, 272, 273, 278,
    279, 284
  Arbor, 10
  Arbors, 100
  Arbox, 10
  Bairds, 24, 190
  Beards, 227, 235
  Bibees, 85
  Black water, 214
  Bookers, 81, 132, 179, 221
  Boyd's, 205
  Boyds, 167
  Boyds Ferry, 45, 211
  Bradleys, 107
  Bremore, 197
  Bryants, 27, 100
  Buffaloe, 44, 209
  Bull Pasture, 291
  Burch Island, 170
  Callaways, 172
  Chiles, 286
  Church, 55, 57, 194
  Clarks, 138
  Colemans, 22, 49
  Coles, 70, 71, 222
  Coles Church, 103
  Country, 119
  County, 62, 107, 195
  Court hourse, 150
  Court House, 138, 158,
    197, 219
  Courthouse, 11
  DAVID, 189
  Dennys, 140, 195, 246

ROADS, *cont'd*
  Doughertrys, 240
  Ferry, 156
  Fort, 2
  Fourt, 2
  frm Dragon Ordinary to
    King and Queen/, 102
  from Barners Mill, 244
  from Drapers to Hanns
    Meadow&, 213
  from Reid's store to
    Boughton's Mill /, 244
  Fuquas, 224
  Glovers, 50
  Great, 31, 45, 51, 78, 79,
    118, 180, 196, 223,
    273, 274
  Green Lea, 313
  Hairstones, 309
  Hardens, 55
  Hatt Creek, 132
  Heickeys, 278
  Heikey's, 167
  Heikeys, 167
  Hickeys, 76, 110, 152,
    167, 184
  Hicky's, 9
  Hogans, 207
  Holloways, 219
  Howards, 65
  Hunts, 225
  Irby's, 205
  Irish, 75
  Irvins, 240, 241
  Jefferson, 22
  Jeffersons, 52
  Jeremiah Whitneys, 107
  John Coles Church Road,
    101
  John Piggs, 2, 6, 38
  Keiheys, 64
  Large Buffaloe, 43
  Large Buffaloe, 19
  Lawyers, 283
  leading to Charlotts ville$,
    203
  Leftwich's, 156
  Linches Old, 101
  Locust Thicket, 85, 235
  Locust thicket Oald, 235

ROADS, *cont'd*
  Lynch's, 242
  Main, 27, 82, 95, 234,
    236-238, 261, 265, 267,
    279
  Main fish day, 263
  Main River, 28
  Martin Kings, 104, 128,
    184, 198
  Mathews, 291
  Mayes's, 224
  Mayes's Ferry, 224
  Mays Ferry, 78
  Mickeys, 76
  Migginsons, 204
  Mill, 252
  Millstone, 132
  Moseleys, 202
  Mountain, 291
  Napier's, 166
  New, 56, 75, 202, 206
  New London, 157, 235,
    263, 265, 309
  Old, 110, 266
  old Court house, 196
  Old Irish, 101
  Old Main, 288
  Old Mountain, 23
  Otter River, 216
  Parks, 131
  Pates, 262
  Paynes, 63, 102
  Penny Lain, 59
  Penny Lane, 59
  Phelp's, 261
  Phelps, 235
  Phelps old, 215, 235
  Phelps old Road Ford, 235
  Phelps's old, 85, 156, 236
  Pick Skin, 187
  Pigg River, 12, 21, 30, 33,
    39, 52, 142
  Piggs, 2, 6, 38, 152
  Piggs river, 132
  Pocket, 234, 238
  Pounceys tract, 137
  Randolph's Long Island,
    95
  Rices, 245
  River, 28

ROADS, *cont'd*
  Rockfish, 123
  Rosser, 239
  Russells, 242
  Sappony, 220
  Secretaries, 184
  Secretary's, 184
  Secretarys old rolling, 282
  South, 184
  South Thickett, 235
  Spencers, 193
  Spencers Mill, 75
  Store, 244
  Stovals, 187, 204, 228
  Taylors, 95, 235
  Three Notch'd, 83, 100
  Three Notched, 17
  to Anthony Ford, 48
  to Charlotte, 268
  Tribles, 238
  Turners, 168
  Valentine Woods
    Rollings", 108
  Verdeman's Mountain, 155
  Very Large Buffaloe Road
    Crossing Place1, 51
  Waggon, 18, 42, 102, 150
  Wards, 234
  Wards Ferry, 240
  Ware House, 104
  Watkins, 281
  Winstons, 242
  Woodsons, 129
Roane, 193
  WILLIAM, 107, 193
Roberson, 8, 25, 57
  David, 19
  DAVID, 31
  John, 243
  Nicholas, 92
  THOMAS, 38
Robert
  James, 10
Roberts, 36, 77, 122, 187,
  202, 221, 245, 257, 278
  George, 251
  James, 40, 185, 277
  JAMES, 199, 203, 286,
    287
  JAMES DUDLEY, 286

Roberts, *cont'd*
  John, 159
  JOHN, 228, 238, 260
  MATTHEW, 209
  Morris, 11
  THOMAS, 130
  William, 209, 238, 287
Robertson, 38, 73, 92, 93,
  153, 159, 180, 184,
  206, 220, 238, 244, 263
  ALEXANDER, 112, 195
  Archabald, 47
  ARCHIBALD, 215
  DAVID, 13, 31, 75, 161
  Edward, 165
  EDWARD, 145
  GEORGE, 90
  JAMES, 12, 73
  JOHN, 110, 139, 248, 264
  Mathew, 195
  Matthew, 161
  Orphans, 93
  Thomas, 240, 268
  THOMAS, 223, 232
  William, 115
  WILLIAM, 161, 195
Robinson, 113, 184, 255
  Arthur, 233
  David, 71
  DAVID, 161, 185, 212
  Field, 113
  FIELD, 113
  GEORGE, 89-91
  Isaac, 161
  James, 10, 185
  JAMES, 32, 95, 134, 297
  John, 36, 208, 268
  JOHN, 3, 104, 114, 139,
    210, 212, 213, 232, 272
  Joseph, 314
  LITTLEBURY, 208
  William, 31, 101
  WILLIAM, 202
  WILLIAM JUNIOR, 272
  William Senr, 272
  Zachariah, 119
Rockett, 137
ROCKS
  Great Rock, 63
  Gray Rock, 4

ROCKS, *cont'd*
  Grey Rock Mark'd JD
    1779, 68
  Nappers, 289
  Point of Rocks, 8, 87, 91,
    104, 160, 191, 306
Rodes
  DAVID, 189
  John, 124
Rodger
  George, 160
Rodgers, 186
  David, 278
  GEORGE, 278
  JOHN, 244
  JOHN, 262
  Thomas, 61, 186
  THOMAS, 186
Rogers, 108, 149, 164, 234,
  244, 265, 268, 290,
  295, 311, 315
  David, 47, 195
  DAVID, 54, 149
  George, 284
  GEORGE, 278
  James, 306
  John, 244
  JOHN, 262
  JOHN JUNR, 242
  Joseph, 77
  JOSEPH, 7, 79, 80
  Thomas, 238, 239, 245
  THOMAS, 197
  William, 195, 238
Roles, 16
Rolin, 102
Rollins, 94
Rolston, 41
Rork
  CHARLES, 239
Rose
  HUGH, 125
  John, 132
  John, Colo., 225
Roser/Rosser
  Peter, 191
Ross, 163, 184, 235, 238,
  244, 257, 282
  Daniel, 228
  DANIEL, 204, 228

Ross, *cont'd*
  David, 26, 109, 202, 242, 278
  DAVID, 25-30, 92, 95, 287
  Hector, 162, 258, 268
  James, 47
  JAMES, 194
  John, 23, 60
  JOHN, 203
  Peter, 177, 243
Rosser, 149, 266
  David, 10
  JONATHAN, 10
Roundtree, 166
  William, 277
Rousey
  James, 134
  JAMES, 134
  JOHN, 196
Routon
  WILLIAM, 165
Row
  William, 137
Rowland, 188, 285
  John, 120, 185
  THOMAS, 302
Rowlett
  WILLIAM, 220
Rowntree
  William, 277
Roy, 223
Ruble, 275
  OWEN, 6, 75
Rubsaman
  JACOB, 111, 268
  JACOB Esq., 48
Rubsamon
  Jacob, 48
  JACOB, 170
Rucker
  AMBROSE, 229
  JOHN, 227
Rudd, 160, 163
  James, 220
  THOMAS, 220
Rudder
  ALEXANDER, 168
  CHARLES, 208

Ruddle
  CORNELIUS, 48
Ruffin, 18
  Edmund, 261
  John, Col, 18
Runkle
  SAMUEL, 217, 247
Runnold, 120
  George, 168
Runnolds, 119, 187
  George, 153
  GEORGE, 62
  MOSES, 285
  RICHARD, 128, 187
RUNS
  Back, 57, 63, 77, 113
  Balls, 308
  Beverly's, 164
  Big, 102, 114
  Bisket, 196
  Black, 63, 296
  Black Water, 8
  Bordens, 316
  Buck, 131
  Buffalo, 275
  Buffaloe, 275
  Bull, 4, 48, 50, 54, 64, 72, 84, 109, 169, 256, 272
  Burdens, 12
  Burdins, 250
  Burtons, 16
  Cabin, 111
  Cain, 297, 298
  Camp, 307
  Camping, 54
  Cauthans, 85
  Cave, 7
  Cedar, 213, 301, 302
  Ceder, 212
  Christopher, 83
  Clarkes, 311
  Clarks, 303
  Colepit, 86
  Cortes, 275
  Corteses, 255
  Cortesses, 176
  Cove, 259
  Crab, 291, 310
  Crab Orchard, 299, 307
  Crooked, 212, 213, 278

RUNS, *cont'd*
  Daniel's, 151
  Daughertys, 312
  Den, 210
  Doe, 218
  Doughertys, 312
  Dunkins Mill, 224
  Dunkins Mill, 266
  fort, 309
  fox, 293
  Gap, 143
  George's, 155
  Gullery, 2
  Guttery, 2, 63, 64
  Gutterys, 54
  Hacket, 2
  Hardens, 15
  Harrods, 297, 299, 304, 312
  Hatchet, 70, 136
  Hatchett, 3, 10, 11, 73
  Hatchetts, 5
  Hayses, 247
  Hazle, 208
  Hungry, 155, 259
  Inak, 67
  Indian, 57
  John, 3
  John's, 110
  Johns, 47, 141, 198, 310
  Jumping, 213, 215, 234, 237
  Kettlestick, 3
  Lazy, 23, 308
  Lick, 39, 50, 56, 58
  Lickinhole, 131
  Little Bull, 110, 148
  Little Indian, 239
  Lusks, 113
  Mackeys, 123
  Main, 185, 193
  Main Dragon, 82
  Marimon, 140
  McNutts, 137
  Meadow, 115, 262
  Meriman, 214
  Merimons, 141
  Merrymans, 77, 245
  Miligans, 9
  Mill, 274

RUNS, *cont'd*
  Mountain, 239
  Mud Lick, 275
  Murrays, 311
  Nicklestons, 230
  North Ruckers, 57
  Paid, 63
  Painters, 76
  Pine, 216
  Pleasant, 296, 303
  Plumb, 298, 304
  Point Bank, 103
  Polkes, 306
  Prathars, 130
  Prathers, 18, 56, 307
  Prize, 10
  Quirks, 292, 299
  Rich, 140, 217
  Roaring, 18, 23
  Rock, 120, 187
  Rock Castle, 209
  Rockey, 196, 205
  Rocky, 2, 53
  Ruckers, 40, 134, 157, 158, 167, 193, 197, 206, 228, 266
  Scotts, 274
  Shawnee, 297, 298, 301, 302, 307, 313
  Skidmore, 201
  Snake, 120, 177, 178
  Sorry, 16
  Spring, 220, 302
  Sprucie pine, 291
  Stoney, 222
  Stony, 17
  Terrys, 262
  Todds, 113
  Walkers, 23
  white Walnut, 183
  Wilsons, 299
Runyan
  JOHN, 188, 274
Rush, 18
  JOHN, 138
Rusher, 18
  GEORGE, 18, 77
Russel
  William, 9, 62, 101

Russell, 118, 166, 205, 214
  Henry, 185
  HENRY, 185
  JOSEPH, 303
  William, 42, 46, 49, 58, 310
  WILLIAM, 98, 185
Rust
  JEREMIAH, 264
Rutherford, 130, 181, 252
  James, 262
  JOHN, 85
  ROBERT, 16, 86
  THOMAS, 15, 86
  William, 239
Rutledge
  THOMAS, 31
Rutlidge
  THOMAS, 31
Ruttledge
  Edward, 115
Ruvsemen
  JACOB, 144
Ryan
  DERBEY, 6
  PHILIP, 183
Rynolds
  John, 116, 273
  William, 284
Ryon, 58, 165
  DARBY, 165
  WILLIAM, 64, 101
Sadler, 163
  JOHN, 61
Saffold
  William, 15
Salley
  Peter, 50
  William, 99
Salmon
  JACOB, 104, 134
  JOHN, 118, 120, 178
Samford
  WILLIAM, 137
Sample
  Robert, 201
Samples, 138
Sampson, 238
Sams, Junior
  WILLIAM, 130

Sandage, 126, 197
Sandefur
  James, 6
Sanders
  JESSE, 247
  John, 23, 25, 108
  Julius, 33
  Peter, 151
  Thomas, 49
  William, 138
Sandridge
  Thomas, 170
Sanford
  JOHN, 109, 114
Sanhen
  HENRY, 81
Sansom
  John, 140
Sarjeant
  John, 183
Saulsburey
  JEREMIAH, 224
Saulsbury
  JEREMIAH, 224
Saunders
  David, 317
  John, 35, 78, 185
  Julius, 33
  PETER, 98
  William, 138
Savage
  JOHN, 82
Savarywood
  John, 220
Savige
  HENRY, 170
Savorie, 257
Saxton, 275
Scam, 41
Scarborough
  JAMES, 150
Scater, 282
Scham, 41
Scockton, 291
Scoggin, 167
Scot, 84, 227
Scott, 35, 130, 184, 282
  JAMES, 104
  John, 132, 136
  JOHN, 132

Scott, *cont'd*
  JOHN Junior, 184
  Nim, 141, 170
  Nimrod, 150
  Nimrodd, 251
  Robert, 154
  Samuel, 306
  Thomas Junr, 13
  THOMAS JUNR, 13, 205
  Thos, 207
  WILLIAM, 204
Scruggs
  GROSS, 242
Scrugs, 103
Seaberry
  JOHN, 79, 80
Seal
  JAMES, 58
Seale
  JAMES, 58
Seares
  Paul, 81
Searight
  John, 249
Sears
  John, 80
Seat, 121
Seawright
  John, 73
Seay
  Abraham Junr, 206
  STEPHEN, 282
Seegar
  Samuel, 265
  SAMUEL, 281
Seely, 161
Sehorn
  JOHN, 12
  NICHOLAS, 12
Seidmore
  Samuel, 197
Selcocke, 282
Seldon, 122
  MILES JUNR, 32
Sellars
  MICHAEL, 178
Seneca waters, 102
Senter
  Stephen, 188
  STEPHEN, 103

Serjeant, 127
  John, 127
  WILLIAM, 183
Server
  Casper, 127
Seth, 122
SETTLEMENTS, 117, 175,
  176, 293, 294, 296,
  298, 300-304, 306, 307,
  311-313
  Adam Fishers, 299
  Adam Smiths, 299
  Andrew Gemblins, 306
  Bowmans, 299
  Crockets, 305
  Dentons, 295
  Elijah Craigs, 296
  Henry Baughmans, 304
  Hogans, 297, 301
  James Masons, 299
  John Grissum, 299
  John Smiths, 299
  Joseph Bowmans, 297
  Joseph Early's, 298
  Manifields, 305
  Moores, 303, 305
  Moors, 305
  Nicholas Merewethers,
    300
  Owlys, 306
  Owsleys, 306
  Painted Stone tract, 293
  Prathers, 313
  Richard Jackmans, 303
  Samuel Scotts, 306
  Shones, 312
  Steells, 311
  Stewarts, 295
  Thrustons, 295, 296
  Triggs, 297
Sevadley
  March, 23
Sever
  Valentine, 121
Seveyor
  VALNTINE, 255
Sevill, 127
Sewer
  John, 143

Shackelford
  Roger, 153
Shanklen
  Robert, 274
Shanklin, 194
  Robert, 255
Shanklins, 287
Shanks
  JAMES, 43
Shannon
  WILLIAM, 118
  William Jr, 46
Shanond
  James, 138
Shard
  JAMES, 185
Sharp, 221
  George, 211, 212
  Hardness, 211
  JOHN, 103, 223
Sharps
  WILLIAM, 191
Shaver
  GEORGE, 155
Shavers
  Isaac, 290
Shaw, 6, 71
  JOHN, 83
  Joseph, 83, 224
  ROBERT, 6, 71
Shawdon
  MATTHEW, 140
Shearee, 264
Shearing
  John, 2
Shearse, 264
Sheetz
  JACOB, 161, 193
Sheetzs
  George, 309
Sheilds
  Jane, 229
  SAMUEL, 242
  WILLIAM, 268
Shelby
  Evan, 296
  EVAN, 1
  ISAAC, 116, 117, 175
Sheltman, 152
  JOHN, 253

INDEX 397

Shelton, 9, 11, 21, 111, 126, 130, 182, 202, 281, 283
   Abraham, 21, 281, 288
   ABRAHAM, 15, 21
   ABRAM, 21
   Armistead, 78
   ARMSTEAD, 21, 171
   ARMSTED, 21
   ARMSTRONG, 21
   Azariah, 286
   AZARIAH, 148
   BENJAMIN, 21
   ELIPHAZ, 57, 282
   HESEKIAH, 112
   JEREMIAH, 166
   Mach or Mack, 9
   PALIKAH, 185
   Palitiah, 204
   PALITIAH, 195
   Patitiah, 283
   Ralph, 182
   RALPH, 53
   Spencer, 288
   SPENCER, 78, 288
   Thomas, 112
   William, 7, 181, 243
   WILLIAM, 180, 181
Shelton
   HESEKIAH, 147
Shelton, Junr.
   RALPH, 192
Shelton, Senior
   RALPH, 112
Shepherd, 3, 4, 305
   David, 40, 57, 132, 134, 157, 158, 167, 193, 197
   JOHN, 11
   PETER, 302, 304
Sheridan
   PHILIP, 169
   Phillip, 168
Shever
   NICHOLAS, 19
Shield, 39, 240
   William, 240
Shields
   John, 229
   JOHN, 240
   Samuel, 153
   SAMUEL, 242

Shiflet
   John, 137
Shilby, 175
   ISAAC, 175
Shipman
   Josiah, 191
Shipmans
   Iseah, 196
Shitze
   Jacob, 258
Shoan
   PATRICK, 312
Shockley, 30, 153
   James, 153
   JAMES, 153, 254
Shoemaker, 275
   PETER, 97
   ZEDEKIAH, 226
Shone
   PATRICK, 312
Shones, 312
SHOPS
   Black Smiths, 27
   Smiths, 27
   Weavers, 27
Short, 121
   Cornelius, 316
   John, 22, 169
   JOHN, 25
   Peyton, 83
   William, 190
Shotwell, 50, 52
   John, 269
Shouls
   CHARLES, 198
Shrewsberry, 166
Shrewsbury
   NATHANIEL, 166
Shrosberry
   SAMUEL, 162
Shrousbury
   JEREMIAH, 6
Shud, 24
Sibert
   Nicholas, 310
   NICHOLAS, 203, 204
Sibley, 153
Sikes
   Jones, 207
   WILLIAM, 206

Siler
   PHILLIP, 281
Silver, 306
Silvester, 205
Sim
   Robert, 165
Simmon, 123, 278
Simmons, 130, 236, 239, 247, 248
   Charles, 193
   CHARLES, 214
   GEORGE, 55
   John, 95, 142
   JOHN, 123, 126, 185
   JOSEPH, 56
   SHOCKLEY, 109
   Stephen, 56
   William, 238
Simpson, 200, 282
   James, 171
   JEREMIAH, 177
   Solomon, 317
   WILLIAM, 144
Sims
   JOHN, 186
   William, 2
Sinate
   PATRICK, 123
Sinclair
   ROBERT, 255
Singleton, 15
   WILLIAM, 239
SINK HOLES, 9, 16, 41, 42, 250, 256
   Little, 95
Sinks
   Daniel, 260
Siveir
   Valentine, 119
Sivel
   Daniel, 127
Sizemond
   JOHN, 292
Sizemore, 53, 121, 124, 242, 315
   JOHN, 292
Skeen
   ROBERT, 113
Skidmore, 192
   Andrew, 307

Skidmore, *cont'd*
  ANDREW, 310
  JOHN, 23, 39, 180, 192
  JOSEPH, 201
  Thomas, 310
  THOMAS, 307
Skidwell
  CHARLES, 221
Skiller
  GEORGE, 290
Skillern, 164
  George, 164
  GEORGE, 80
Skilliem
  GEORGE, 85
Sladon
  JOSEPH, 251
SLASHES, 23, 82, 136, 151, 272
  Middle, 217
Slate
  Samuel, 278
Slater
  Joseph, 15
Slaton
  Daniel, 278
Slaughter
  John, 127, 183
  JOHN, 127
Slaughter, Colo.
  John, 127
Slaugter, 1
Slavan
  JOHN, 202
Slone
  James, 170
  JAMES, 144, 268
Slover
  Daniel, 181
Slow
  Joel, 38
Slunbergen
  Peter, 4
Small
  JOHN, 57, 256
  Matthew, 187
Smeley, 172
Smelser
  POLSER, 222
Smely, 172

Smileys
  John, 118
Smily
  Alexander, 172
Smith, 2, 3, 7, 39, 51, 58, 64, 72, 98, 100, 107, 109, 110, 114, 120, 126, 131, 142, 147, 150, 153, 163, 169, 173, 179, 182, 189, 191, 194, 198, 203, 219, 238, 243, 266, 268, 278, 284, 291, 304
  Abraham, 127, 141, 225
  ABRAHAM, 39, 46
  Alexander, 96
  ALEXANDER, 23
  ANTHONY, 199
  AUSTIN, 250
  B., 288
  Barbara, 176
  BENJAMIN, 154
  Bradley, 123, 131, 190
  BRADLEY, 194
  CHARLES, 19, 279
  CONROD, 126
  Daniel, 178
  DANIEL, 128, 154, 254-256, 259
  Edward, 7
  Elex, 134
  Francis, 117
  FRANCIS, 41, 87, 173, 317
  George, 60, 127, 253, 297, 299, 304
  GEORGE, 147, 253, 312
  Gray, 11
  GRAY, 33
  Grey, 11
  GUY, 162
  Henry, 63, 103
  HENRY, 55, 63, 64, 103, 127, 210, 224, 281
  HEZEKIAH, 8
  JACOB, 227
  James, 60, 62, 75, 193, 219, 230, 278, 283-285
  JAMES, 80, 253, 306

Smith, *cont'd*
  John, 37-39, 64, 69, 160, 169, 196, 197, 239, 243, 244, 281, 287, 302
  JOHN, 7, 9, 10, 43, 54, 69, 72, 80, 85, 87, 144, 160, 169, 191, 200, 242, 301
  John Smith, 288
  John Smith Murdock & Comps, 281
  JOSEPH, 198, 208
  Josiah, 199
  JOSIAH, 122, 126, 180
  Luke, 13
  Orlander, 46
  ORLANDER, 101
  PEYTON, 146
  Robert, 145, 314
  Solomon, 25
  Thomas, 241, 242, 290
  THOMAS, 7, 9, 10, 35, 40, 114, 225, 243
  Thomas Ballard, 288
  Timothy, 207
  Tobias, 211
  WILLIAM, 122, 225, 244, 249, 255, 268
  William Bailey, 299
  Willis, 170
  Zachariah, 299
  ZACHARIAH, 120
Smither, 142
Smithers, 263, 283
Smiths, 297, 306
  Adam, 299
  John, 299
Smithson, 129, 259
  John, 207
  William, 207
Smitther
  Gabriel, 263
Smoot
  EDWARD, 317
Sneed
  SAMUEL, 292
Snelson, 40
  Thomas, 134
Snider, 196
Snoddin, 198

INDEX

Snodgras, 211
Snodgrass, 213
  ALEXANDER, 213
  JAMES, 173
  William, 173
Snow
  JAMES, 235
  JOHN, 240
Sollomon
  JOHN, 77
Soloman
  ISHAM, 253
Sommer
  John, 251
Sommon
  George, 258
Sommor
  John, 251
Sorrel
  John, 233
Sorrell
  William Hodges, 120
Sorsby
  Thomas, 135
South, 165, 268
Southall, 94
  James, 99, 261
  JAMES, 74, 75
  Turner, 7
  TURNER, 7
Southeland, 52
Southerland
  GEORGE, 52, 109
  WILLIAM, 242
Southerlin, 12
  JOHN, 8
Southern
  JAMES, 47
Sowel
  WILLIAM, 190
Sowell
  MANN, 33
  THOMAS, 55, 100, 101, 228
  WILLIAM, 190
Sowell/Sowel
  WILLIAM, 190
Sowsbury
  Jeremiah, 109

Spangleg
  DANIEL, 6
Spangler, 12
  DANIEL, 67, 68
Spark, 169
Sparkes
  MATTHEW, 240
Sparks, 43
  EDWARD, 279
  MATTHEW, 240
  Samuel, 268
  THOMAS, 241
Sparrow, 81
  James, 163
Spead
  John, 215
Speed, 215
  JAMES, 213
  John, 92
Spence
  Widow, 251
Spencer, 247, 251
  ROBERT, 3
  Samuel, 182, 226, 233
  THOMAS, 127
  William, 157, 314
  WILLIAM, 40
  WILLIAM, 238
Spenser
  WILLIAM, 238
Spicer
  WILLIAM, 252
Spiers
  WILLIAM, 205
Spiller, 83
Spilson, 38
Spotswood
  Alexander, 6
  ALEXANDER, 5
Spradlin, 124
Spraggin, 121, 222
Spraggins
  THOMAS, 121, 179
  WILLIAM, 121
Spratley
  Benjamin, 170
Spratly
  Benjamin, 170
Springlan, 2

SPRINGS, 12, 16, 22, 31, 34, 40, 41, 63, 65, 71, 87, 94, 95, 98, 206, 213, 235, 237, 244, 249, 258, 260, 264, 267, 270, 273
Anthonys, 137
Black Water, 95
Buring, 209
Cave, 82
Cave Spring Tract, 1
Colt, 23
Falling, 284
Fiers, 183
Head, 95, 99, 272
Garrys, 297
Hot, 13
Hot Spring Survey, 13
Large, 88, 97
Mays, 299
Pudding, 115
Pulpits, 42
Salt, 14
Salt Spring Creek, 19
School House, 32, 61
Shawnee, 298
Spring, 31
Stones Spring Br., 243
Sulpher, 91
Sweet, 34, 270, 272
Sprouce
  VINSON, 167
Sprout
  John, 248
SPURS, 11, 12, 16, 71, 85, 91, 210, 237, 250, 252, 259, 265, 267, 272
High, 89
Piney, 89
Srum
  DAVID, 176, 255
STABLES, 258
Stafford, 52
Stallings
  JACOB, 109
Stamp, 153
  Timothy, 49, 58
Stamps, 142
  TIMOTHY, 42, 62

Stampts
  TIMOTHY, 42
Stanback
  John, 269
Standefer, 6, 11
  ISRAEL, 6
  James, 160
  JAMES, 252
  James Junior, 72
  JAMES SENR, 3
  Luke, 72, 252
  LUKE, 98
Standefor, 219
Standeford
  JAMES, 146, 151, 249, 254
  LUKE, 46
Standerfer, Junior
  James, 169
Standerfer, Senior
  JAMES, 169
Standifer, 140
  ISRAEL, 73
Standley
  JOSEPH, 30
Standuff
  JOHN, 16
Stanfiel
  William, 197
Stap
  John, 62
Staple
  William, 250
Staples, 72, 149, 313
  David, 17
  Isaac, 111
  ISAAC, 25
  John, 17
  JOHN, 231, 232
  Samuel, 25
  SAMUEL, 231, 232
Stapleton, 183
Stapp, 62
Starkey, 145
  JOHN SENR, 277
Starnel
  WILLIAM, 175
Starnet
  WILLIAM, 175

Starret
  ROBERT, 200
Starrett
  ROBERT, 200
STATIONS, 296
  Barnetts, 301
  Benjamin Logans, 303
  Bryans, 305
  Cartwrights, 296
  Downeys, 303
  English, 294
  Henry Willsons, 306
  Housleys, 307
  Owsleys Station Br., 305
  Petills, 303
  Rogers, 295
  Whitleys, 306
  Wilsons, 312
Staunton, 224
Steardman, 75
Stearman
  VALENTINE, 144
Steegal, 142
Steegale
  AARON, 96
Steegall
  GEORGE, 96
  WILLIAM, 137
Steel, 239
  ALEXANDER, 152, 159
  AUGUSTINE, 81, 82
  David, 132
  DAVID, 246
  Samuel, 315
Steell
  FREDERICK, 201
Steells, 311
Steen
  John, 25, 142
Steep Rockey Bank, 210
Steerman, 263
  WILLIAM, 263
Stegal, 58, 70
Stegall
  WILLIAM, 219
Steinbergen
  PETER, 4
Stell, 72
  ALEXANDER, 152
Stellwell, 57

Stemmon, 15
Stepen
  ADAM, 45
Stephen
  ADAM, 45
  Adam, Col, 45
Stephends
  ADAM, 97
Stephens, 119
  ADAM, 44
  Adam. Col., 44
  Adam, Col., 44
  PETER, 36
  SAMPSON, 168
  Samuel, 96
  Thomas, 167
  WILLIAM, 277
Stephenson, 258
  James, 86
  John, 161, 254, 317
  JOHN, 161
  Robert, 114
  Thomas, 195
  William, 210
Stephey
  PETER, 36, 39
Stephinson
  Marcus, 210
Stepney
  PETER, 39
Stevens
  ADAM, 97
  Thomas, 291
Stevenson
  John, 193, 317
  JOHN, 193
  Robert, 116, 204
  Thomas, 204
Steward
  JAMES, 216
Stewart, 2, 71, 94, 147, 222, 232
  ALEXANDER, 94
  ALEXANDER, 93
  Charles, 302
  David, 175
  David, Colo., 71
  JAMES, 234, 281
  Richard, 217
  ROBERT, 51

Stewart, *cont'd*
  Thomas, 48, 211
  THOMAS, 281
  WALTER, 16
  William, 297
  WILLIAM, 294-296
  WILLIAM, 309
Stewarts, 294, 295, 297
  Charles, 297
Stile
  JOHN, 39
Stiles, 122
Still, 64
  Patrick, 39
  Thomas, 136
  THOMAS, 190
  William, 189
  WILLIAM, 190
Stinnet
  Benjamin Junr, 231
Stinson
  Alexander, 23, 25
Stith, 15, 129, 144, 158, 198, 207
  Richard, 62, 146, 156, 215, 234, 235, 237, 265, 283
  RICHARD, 62, 144, 236, 237, 262
  Richard, Surveyor, 235
  THOMAS, 195, 198
Stocks
  SILVANUS, 45, 98
  SYLVANIUS, 97
Stockton, 291
  ROBERT, 54, 149
  Thomas, 201
Stoke
  SYLVANUS, 101
Stokes, 242
  Allen, 313
  CHARLES, 179
  David, 313
  David Junior, 313
  DAVID JUNR, 313
  Evan, 7
  Henry, 182
  Jonathan, 208
  SILVANUS, 45, 98, 248
  SYLVANIUS, 97

Stokes, *cont'd*
  William, 208
  WILLIAM, 182
  Young, 182
Stomp, 148
Stone, 24, 30, 96, 109, 179, 184, 243
  GEORGE, 15
  Henry, 52
  JEREMIAH, 166
  John, 186, 243
  JOHN, 243
  JOHN JUNR, 240
  John Senr, 240
  JOSHUA, 13, 79, 281
  MARBELL, 301
  Thomas, 163
Stoner, 289
Stony Ground, 90
STORES
  Reid's, 244
  Ross and Hooks, 244
Stort, 23
Stoval
  GEORGE, 84
Stovall, 145, 204, 243, 267
  GEORGE, 15, 84, 101, 103
  George Junior, 101
  GEORGE JUNR, 84
  THOMAS, 221
Stow
  Joel, 252
  JOEL, 252
Strange, 128, 184, 199
  JAMES, 84
  Jno, 100
  John, 3, 55, 83, 127, 128, 184
  JOHN, 83, 84, 128, 171, 184, 289
  John Allaway, 107
  John Alloway, 108
  JOHN ALLOWAY, 107, 108
Stratton
  JOHN, 291
  SERAIAH, 197
  Thomas, 192

Street, 179, 215
  Anthony, 172
  ANTHONY, 172, 207
  BUTLER STONE, 243
  HENRY, 82
  JOSEPH, 108
  Quitrents, 172
STREETS
  Carolina, 174
  Caroline, 174, 189
  Cross, 32
  Essex, 162
  Fairfax, 162
  Green, 135
  Hanover, 174
  King, 257
  Main, 32
  Oronooko, 268
  Paussia [Prussia], 189
  PM, 257
  Princess Anne, 174
  Prusia, 174
  River, 32
  Sophia, 174
Strobe
  JOHN, 302
Strol, 23
Stuart, 195
  Charles, 220
  James, 238
  JAMES, 282
  JOHN, 168, 292
  Robert, 201
  ROBERT, 282
  THOMAS, 281
Stugall
  WILLIAM, 137
Stunck, 292
Stunkard
  John, 201
Sturdivant, 123
  Daniel, 191
  JOHN, 123
Sturman, 239, 264
  WILLIAM, 263
Styles
  JOHN, 241
Sudderth
  Lawrence, 266
Sullavan, 159

Sullavants, 159
Sulleven
  JOHN OWEN, 252
Sullin, 108
Sulling
  John, 223
Sullivan, 142
  JOHN OWEN, 148
Sullivant
  John, 87
Sulliven
  JOHN OWEN, 148, 252
Sulpher Spring, 91
SUMER
  John, 79
Summer, 208
Summers
  PAUL, 309
  WILLIAM, 4
Sumner
  JOHN, 92
  Sumners Forest, 92
Sumners Forest, 92
Sumpter
  HENRY, 187
Sumter
  HENRY, 254
SURVEYORS
  Prestone, William, 41
Sutherlin
  JOHN, 8, 68
Sutton
  WILLIAM, 74, 241
Swadley
  Mark, 62
Swaldley
  Mark, 62
SWAMPS, 98
  Black, 14, 70, 138, 185
  Black water, 14, 51, 70,
    95, 104, 138, 217, 275
  Chickahomy, 177
  Cross, 78
  Dragon, 82, 102, 206
  Fork'd, 275
  Gautley, 59
  Gualtney, 59
  Guatney, 59
  Large, 115
  Little, 206

SWAMPS, cont'd
  Long Grass, 93, 271
  Maple, 206, 220
  Piscataway, 193
  Quarrel, 205
  Round Hill, 56
  Second, 104, 191
  Warwick, 191
  Whortleberry, 191
Swan
  Richard, 296
Swann
  Richard, 296
Swanson, 169, 295
  NATHAN, 169
  WILLIAM, 169
Swearingham
  Van, 317
Sweet Springs, 34
Sweeting, 4, 241
  Robert, 207, 242
Swenney
  JOHN, 257
  MOSES, 150
Swenny, 316
  JOHN, 257
  MOSES, 150
Swilivent
  JOHN, 109
Swinny
  John, 100
  MOSES, 5
Swoap
  BENEDICK, 304
Sybert
  NICHOLAS, 289, 293
Sydnor
  EPAPHRODITUS, 50
Syke
  Barnaby, 185
Sylen
  CASPER, 196
Sylin
  Casper, 118
Sylvester, 80
Symm
  Andrew, 58
Synamon Tree, 20
Tabbs
  Thomas, 313

Tabler
  WILLIAM, 190
Tadlock
  Thomas, 191, 194
Tait
  James, 135
  JAMES, 135
Talbot, 56, 99, 111, 157, 159,
  162, 166, 169, 213,
  214, 221, 223, 236-238,
  244-247, 253, 262, 277,
  281, 314
  Charles, 265
  CHARLES, 240, 265, 281
  Charles M, 156
  Isham, 54
  ISHAM, 60, 144, 146,
    148, 161, 185, 215,
    246-248, 263, 289
  James, 140, 146, 196
  John, 215, 262, 268
  JOHN, 15, 77, 156, 236
  M, 236
  Matthew, 156
  MATTHEW, 146, 156,
    162, 166, 247, 264, 308
  WILLIAM, 249
Talbots
  John, 155
Talbott, 56
  MATTHEW, 157
Talbutt
  Soloman Butt, 313
Taliaferro
  BENJAMIN, 75
  John, 75
  JOHN, 42, 243
  Samuel, 76
  SAMUEL, 104
  Walker, 139
  ZECHARIAH, 75
Taliaferroe
  Charles, 227
Talley, 49
  Henry, 96
Talliaferro, 42
Tally, 49, 80
  Henry, 251
  John, 122

Taloe
    JOHN, 86
Tandy, 107
    John, 121
Tanner, 47, 235
    BENJAMIN, 238
    FLOYD, 110
    Floyed, 262
    JOHN, 275
    Michael, 307
Tanyard, 273
Taply, 57
Tarrance
    Benjamin, 144
Tarrence
    Leonard, 170
Tarry
    William, 114
Tary
    William, 114
Tate, 143, 156
    Charles, 221, 237, 255
    DAVID, 272
    HENRY, 181
Tatum, 37
    EDWARD, 150
    Henry, 38
    Richard, 194
Tayler
    HUBBARD, 300
    JOHN, 82
Taylon
    William, 230
Taylor, 40, 50, 69, 75, 99, 100, 123, 129, 184, 271, 283
    Charles, 36, 237
    CHARLES, 263
    DANIEL, 316
    David, 129
    EDMUND, 1, 207
    George, 185, 194
    GEORGE, 1, 131, 219, 220
    GEORGE JUNIOR, 231
    H, 6
    Hancock, 6
    HANCOCK, 47, 99
    Hancocke, 69
    Henry, 251

Taylor, *cont'd*
    HUBBARD, 297, 300
    Isaac, 40, 41, 173
    James, 164, 174
    JAMES, 1, 78, 113, 174, 179, 218
    Jessee, 258
    JESSEE, 257
    JOHN, 58, 90, 117, 186
    JOHN JUNIOR, 93
    JOSHUA, 316
    Richard, 23, 47, 104
    RICHARD, 92, 111, 271
    ROBERT, 58
    William, 57, 200, 230, 232
    WILLIAM, 4, 148, 151, 291
    ZACHARY, 99
    ZACHERY, 47
Tedford
    JOHN, 16
Teese
    Charles, 180
Telford
    JAMES, 85
Temple
    BENJN, 76
Templeton, 109
    James, 118, 273
    JAMES, 116
    John, 157
Tenants, 185
Teneson
    Henry, 246
Tenison
    JOHN, 230
Tennant
    JOHN, 271
Terancis, 144
Terence
    JOSEPH, 236
Termon, 287
Terrel
    Harry, 10
    MACAJER, 122
    MICAJAH, 241
    MICAJER, 122
Terrell, 236, 237, 240
    David, 235
    GABRIEL, 156

Terrell, *cont'd*
    Harry, 236, 265
    John, 11
    JOHN, 21
    MICAJAH, 282
    RICHARD, 294, 295
Terril
    John, 31
    Micajah, 82, 241
    MICAJAH, 81
Terrill
    MICAJAH, 164
Terry, 11, 21, 22, 31, 37, 40, 55, 62, 110, 130, 166, 171, 208, 278
    Ben, 278
    Benjamin, 42
    BENJAMIN, 47, 110
    Champness, 4
    David, 169
    HARRY, 41
    Henry, 277
    HENRY, 169
    James, 20, 42, 141, 169, 278
    Joseph, 10, 11, 42, 43, 111, 218, 278
    JOSEPH, 111
    JOSEPH SENR, 278
    Moses, 42
    Mosses, 98
    Nathaniel, 141, 142
    Peter, 41
    Stephen, 22
    Thomas, 42, 278
Terry, Senior
    JOSEPH, 130
Terry, Senr.
    JOSEPH, 110
Terry's Order, 166
Terrys
    Benjamin, 310
Terrys Order, 37, 130
Tery
    James, 169
Terys Order, 169
Thacker
    BENJAMIN, 129
Thackston
    WILLIAM, 80

Tharp
  Joseph, 272, 273
Thaxton
  Abel, 275
  William, 179
the late War, 47
Theeds
  ELIZABETH, 137
Thiff, 168
Thimade, 30
Thomas, 31, 39, 268
  Charles, 204
  Cornelius, 228-230
  Edmund, 41
  HENRY, 201
  Job, 49
  John, 49, 163, 228
  JOHN, 189
  Jonathan, 241
  Lewis, 305
  LODOWICK, 113
  LUDOWVICK, 127
  PHILIP, 177, 272
  William, 38
  WILLIAM, 31
Thomason
  ELIAS, 22
  Gentry, 17
Thomerson
  Elias, 23
Thompson, 56, 83, 84, 214,
    239, 240, 265, 309. 312
  ANTHONY, 51
  Barnet Line, 55
  GEO, 55
  George, 85, 197, 307
  GEORGE, 55, 85, 196,
    313
  John, 55, 84, 263
  JOHN, 167, 246
  Leonard, 55
  LEONARD, 75
  Matthew, 154
  Waddy, 23
  Wady, 23
  William, 139, 159, 174,
    244, 245
  WILLIAM, 86-91, 139,
    170, 211, 212, 235
  Winfred, 290

Thompsons, 288, 295
Thomson, 245
  GEORGE, 133
  JAMES, 134
  THOMSON, 49
Thornhill, 107
  THOMAS, 107, 167
Thornill
  THOMAS, 250
Thornton
  John, 26, 100, 183
  William, 183
  WILLIAM, 183
Thorp, 158, 272
  FRANCIS, 158, 264
Thorpe
  FRANCIS, 255
Thruston
  CHARLES M, 295
  John, 63, 102
Thurman, 78
  NATHAN, 3
  RICHARD, 78, 85
  WILLIAM, 100
Thurmand
  Thomas, 11
Thurmon
  John, 209
  WILLIAM, 47
Thurmond
  Philip, 275
  PHILIP, 229
Thurston, 75, 239
  CHARLES W, 296
  William, 75
Thweat, 191
  James Jr, 82
Tiller, 206
  William, 121, 228, 230,
    308
Tillevier, 148
Tilman
  Thomas, 192
Tilues, 151
Timberlake
  JOHN, 83
  RICHARD, 243
Tinley, 236
Tinsley, 179

Tirdle
  JOHN, 23
Tittle, 151
Todd, 156, 238, 239, 264
  Low, 235, 239
  LOW, 263
  MALLORY, 47
  WILLIAM, 76
Todds, 305
Tolbert, 19
Tolbot, 73
  Charles, 105
Tolbut, 73
Tolifaro, 97
Tolleson
  DANIEL, 227
Tollifarro, 98
Tolman
  Benjamin, 116
Tomason
  ELIAS, 22
  Samuel, 23
Tomkies
  Charles, 116, 175
  CHARLES, 116, 117, 175
Tomkins
  John, 138
Tomlinson
  AMBROSE, 230
  Richard, 14
Tommerson
  ARNOLD, 84
  JOHN, 270
  Richard, 84
Tompson
  WILLIAM, 216
Toney
  WILLIAM, 25
Tool
  John, 196
Tooley
  John, 192
Tooll
  John, 196
Tosh, 117
  Jonathan, 117
  THOMAS, 117, 250
Toulis
  James, Revd, 80

Toup
  HENRY, 259
Towns
  THOMAS, 45
  WILLIAM, 165
TOWNS,
  Charlottsville, 191
  Colchester, 162
  Dumfries, 43, 44
  Fairfax, 181
  Fredericksburg, 174, 189
  Hanover, 35
  Manchester, 48, 219
  New London, 265, 309
  Old Mingo, 35
  Petersburg, 125, 286
  Port Royal, 271
  Richmond, 32
  Smith field, 47, 58-60
Townsley
  JAMES, 282
Townsly
  JAMES, 282
Trabue
  JOHN, 308
TRACTS
  Cave Spring, 1
  Painted Stone, 293
  Pounceys, 137
  Rackoon, 262
  Wades Mill, 206
Tracy, 18
Traime, 148
Trammel, 292
Travis
  Edward, 178
Treadaway
  Thomas, 221
Treadway, 167
  Richard, 70
  Thomas, 260
  WILLIAM, 100
Treadwell, 179
Treble
  John, 108
  Paler, 78
  Peter, 108
  Shadrach, 78
Tredley
  George, 49

Tredway
  JAMES, 51
Tredwell
  William, 36
Tremble
  James, 146, 247
  JOHN, 273
Trent, 134
  Alexander, 49
  Henry, 223, 283
  John, 223
  OBADIAH HENRY, 141
  PETER F, 17, 33
  PETER FIELD, 34
Tribble, 22, 149
  Shadrach, 21, 79
Tribel
  Peter, 167
Trible
  George, 167
  Peter, 71
Trigg, 302
  Daniel, 313
  DANIEL, 74, 307
  Stephen, 313
  STEPHEN, 297, 305
  William, 141
  WILLIAM, 160
Trimble, 22, 65
  David, 115, 136
  DAVID, 115, 116
  James, 146
  JAMES, 146, 148, 170, 250
  John, 144, 167, 172, 180
  JOHN, 111, 113, 116, 146, 250, 273
  MOSES, 117
  THOMAS, 249
  Walter, 144
  Walton, 121
Trip, 109
Tross
  Jacob, 287
Trotter
  Joseph, 132
  JOSEPH, 132
Trout
  Jacob, 131

Troutman
  MICHAEL, 307
Trower
  SOLOMOM, 317
Tryes
  Allen, 314
Tuck
  EDWARD, 109
Tucker, 51
  Abraham, 217
  FRANCIS, 121
  James, 18
  John, 153, 183
  William, 281, 288
  Wood, 80
Tuggle
  JOHN, 206
  LODOWICK, 20
  LODWICK, 246
Tugle
  JOHN JUNIOR, 308
Tullos, 140
Tullus, 140
Tully
  JOHN, 170, 225, 226
Tune
  Travis, 80
Tunley
  JOHN, 54
Tunly
  JOHN, 54
Tunsall
  THOMAS, 222
Tunstall
  THOMAS, 222, 224, 225
Turdale
  JOHN, 23
Tureman, 75
Turk, 124
  THOMAS, 123, 180
Turmon, 223
Turner, 25, 26, 40, 77, 87, 203, 222, 223, 236
  ANDREW, 267
  JOSIAH, 150
  MESHACK, 77
  SHADRACH, 5, 78
  Shadrack, 150
  SHADRACK, 147
  Terisha, 128

Turner, *cont'd*
  William, 151
Turpin, 11, 68, 136
  HENRY, 220
  James, 2, 10
  JAMES, 73
  SOLOMAN, 255
  Thomas, 99
  THOMAS JUNIOR, 48, 100
Turpine
  JAMES, 136
Twedwell, 6
Tweedwell, 9
Tweedy, 267
Twilley, 20
Twinlly, 284
Twitty, 20, 284
Twittys, 290
Tyins, 184
Tyler
  Charles, 85
  CHARLES, 226
  ROBERT, 303
Tylers, 303
Tynes, 277
Tyra
  Reuben, 286
Tyrce
  David, 44
  DAVID, 44
Tyre
  William, 233
  WILLIAM, 229
Tys
  Allen, 202
Ubank
  George, 129
Uest
  Thomas, 17
Underwood
  JOHN, 145
  JOSEPH, 77
Upshar, 15
Upshaw, 15
Usery, 214
Ussery, 212
  John, 212

VALLEYS, 32, 51, 79, 87, 88, 94, 161, 163, 202, 237, 267, 273
  Deep, 94, 96
  Dry, 116
  Falling Spring, 161
  Gravelly Walk, 139
  Narrow, 259
  Paint Bank, 63
  Rich, 96
  Severns, 304
  Soverns, 304
  Steep, 163
  Tygerts, 307, 310
  Tygerts Valley River, 290
Vamon
  Richard, 63
Vance, 150
  SAMUEL, 173, 275
Vanclerr
  BENJAMIN, 293
Vander Pool, 121
Vanderpoole, 132
Vaner
  Mathew, 15
Vardeman, 68
Vardiman, 220
Varnon
  Richard, 63
Vason
  WILLIAM, 3
Vaugh
  ALEXANDER, 47
Vaughan, 15, 26, 37, 79, 80, 87, 92, 295
  Abraham, 87
  John, 21, 22
  JOHN, 22
  SARAH, 26
  SHADRACH, 9
  Thomas, 22
  WHITE, 81
  William, 198
  WILLIAM, 38, 156, 301
Venable, 78, 165, 180, 262
  Abraham, 195
  Nathaniel, 195
Verdaman
  William Jur, 263

Verdeman, 68
  PETER, 67
Verdiman, 5
Vermon
  Johnathan, 70
Vest
  James, 157
  JAMES, 196
  Thomas, 196
  THOMAS, 246
  William, 157, 236, 244
  WILLIAM, 235
Vestler
  HENRY, 43
Via
  John, 286
  JOHN, 277
Vincent, 241, 243
  Charles, 146
  Moses, 10
  MOSES, 169
  WILLIAM, 290
Vineyard
  CHRISTIAN, 190
Vollintine
  JOHN ARMSTED, 254
Waddell
  JAMES, 178
  Thomas, 175
Wadden
  John, 32
Waddill, 284
Waddle
  Alexander, 316
  Joseph, 175
  Thomas, 175
  THOMAS, 175
Wade, 21, 168, 206, 217, 221, 252
  DANIEL, 137
  Edward, 112, 122, 252
  Jeremiah, 227
  JOHN, 111
  Pearce, 75
  PEARCE, 227
  PEYTON, 166
  Robert, 208, 225, 277
  STEPHEN, 165
Wadey, 8

Wadlow
 William, 24, 53
 WILLIAM, 52
Wagener
 Peter, 162
Waggoner
 ANDREW, 1
 CHRISTIAN, 22
 CHRISTOPHER, 135
 EDMUND, 1
 Edmund, Subaltern
  Officer&, 1
 THOMAS, 1
Wagner
 Thomas, Capt., 1
Wagsteffs, 291
Waid
 BALLENGER, 242
 Nathaniel, 11
Wainright
 John, 264
Wainwright, 234
Wakeling
 William, 164
Walden, 156
 MOSES, 31
 Richard, 50, 75
 RICHARD, 56
Waldon, 179
Waldrope
 John, 168
 LUKE, 121
Waldrops
 John, 168
Waldrum
 GEORGE, 123
Walker, 23, 54, 99, 114, 134,
 169, 185, 245, 266,
 277, 286, 310
 Alexander, 116-118
 ALEXANDER, 94, 274,
  281
 BUCKLEY, 214
 DANIEL, 37
 David, 242
 Doctor, 11
 GEORGE, 103
 James, 4, 290
 JESSE, 119
 JOEL, 167

Walker, *cont'd*
 JOHN, 94, 153, 315
 Joseph, 188
 PHILIP, 230
 Phillips, 287
 SAMUEL, 12
 Silvanus, 310
 SILVANUS, 187
 Sylvanus, 207
 TANDY, 187
 THOMAS, 139, 262
 Thomas P, 35
 Thomas R., 185
 WILLIAM, 113, 172, 252
Walker's, 310
Walker]
 Tandy, 310
Wall, 45, 108, 167, 178, 284
 Daniel, 61, 182, 211
 David, 211
 JAMES, 2
 John, 61
 JOHN, 225
 Richard, 179, 182
Wallace, 165, 234, 245
 CALEB, 32
 Josiah, 181
 SAMUEL, 119
 William, 171
 WILLIAM, 127
Waller, 3, 7, 225
 John, 47
 JOHN, 47, 49, 99
 Robert, 49
Walling
 ELISHA, 191
Wallox, 213
 JOHN, 215
Walls
 Miles, 60
Walson
 William, 241
Walter
 William, 10
Walters, 96, 251
 John, 167, 225
 JOHN, 42
 Robert, 11, 46
 ROBERT, 43, 46
 Robt. Walters Fork, 96

Walters, *cont'd*
 Thomas, 46
 THOMAS, 46, 98, 167
 William, 98
Walthal
 Henry, 192
Walthel
 John, 192
Walther, 70, 170
 Robert, 42, 110, 114
 William, 114
Walthers
 Robert, 98, 279
 Thomas, 279
 THOMAS, 278
 William, 279
Walton, 19, 24, 30, 41, 52,
 57, 68, 84, 118, 121,
 122, 133, 140, 145,
 146, 161, 162, 177,
 185, 186, 195, 202,
 204, 205, 213, 214,
 221, 222, 224, 236,
 240, 248, 251, 256,
 262, 264, 265, 277,
 283, 289, 310
 George, 14, 18, 96, 108,
  159, 169, 187, 236
 GEORGE, 118, 289, 310,
  315
 JEREMIAH, 221
 John, 189
 JOHN, 56
 Joseph, 172
 JOSEPH, 69
 Robert, 110, 195, 250
 Robert, 215
 SHERWOOD, 31
 WILLIAM, 277
Wamack
 James, 95
Ward, 20, 55, 56, 68, 109,
 133, 140, 166, 238,
 256, 282
 Daniel, 168
 Edward, 45
 JAMES, 176, 250
 Jeremiah, 109
 JEREMIAH, 109, 168,
  250

Ward, *cont'd*
  John, 27, 98, 216
  JOHN, 20, 95, 142, 143,
    155, 157, 166, 168,
    215-218, 244
  Nathaniel, 11
  William, 268, 279
  WILLIAM, 128, 183
Ware, 137
  Capt, 6
  Edward, 228
  EDWARD, 225, 232
  John, 34, 83, 92, 124
  JOHN, 8, 32, 124, 223
  John, Capt, 32
Warin, 182
  MICHAEL, 182
Waring, 107
Warms
  Thomas, 310
Warmsley
  JOHN, 175
Warrain, 62
WARRANTS
  Dunmores, 6
Warrantstaff
  Charles, 209
Warren, 11
  JAMES, 227
  John, 227
  Robert, 228
Warsham
  JEREMIAH, 78
Warsley
  JOHN, 175
Warter
  Thomas, 42
Warwick
  Abraham, 230
  ABRAHAM, 57, 230
Washam, 223
  Jeremiah, 38
Washington
  Charles, 174, 189
  General, 257
  GEORGE, 209
  LUND, 76
Wathal
  John, 192
  William, 192

Wathall
  JOHN, 221
Wathan, 156
Wathen, 144, 186, 235, 236,
  238, 239, 245, 260
Watkins, 32, 41, 46, 61, 101,
  121, 128, 152, 156,
  167, 186, 197, 224, 240
  BENJAMIN, 239
  GEORGE, 208
  ISHAM, 304
  Joel, 167, 229
  John, 110
  JOHN, 21, 42, 148
  JOSIAH, 151
  MOSES, 267
  Nathaniel, 101, 103
  Thomas, 96
  WILLIAM, 9
Watson, 5, 24, 43, 52, 77,
  100, 202, 240, 242
  James, 241
  JAMES, 153
  John, 203, 257
  JOHN, 77, 223
  Matthew, 78
  R, 6
  WILLIAM, 51, 166
Watts, 18
  EDWARD, 55
  RICHARD, 130
Wattson, 100
Waugh, 6
  Alexander, 74
  ALEXANDER, 47, 84, 99,
    103
WAUGHOO TREE, 20
Wayles, 143, 240, 243
Weak
  William, 168
Weakley, 208
  Robert, 79, 262
  ROBERT, 80, 316
Weakly
  ROBERT, 79, 81, 316
Weaklys, 316
Weaks
  WILLIAM, 109
Weathan, 159
Weathen, 264, 267

Weatherford, 10, 42, 225
  Charles, 12, 96
  William, 98
Weatherpoon, 278
Weaver, 18, 124, 248, 263
  David, 101
Weavers Shop, 27
Web, 190
  Merray, 109
Webb, 21, 52, 189, 263, 283
  JACOB, 47
  JEDIAS, 33
  Martin, 165
  MARY, 191
  Merrah, 109
  Merry, 243
  SMITH, 219
  Theoderick, 231
  THEODORICK, 47
  WILLIAM, 316
Webber
  JOHN, 306
Webbs
  James, 313
Webster
  JOHN, 166
  JOSEPH, 246
Wedin, 309
Weedon
  Genl. GEORGE, 174
  GEORGE, 261
Weekes
  Thomas, 14
Weekly, 81
  ROBERT, 81
Weir
  THOMAS, 8
Welch, 85, 238, 247
  JOHN, 215
Welcher
  Ephraim, 278
Welden, 193
Weldon
  JONATH, 96
Wells
  Abraham, 198
  Alexander, 86
  ALEXANDER, 34, 35
  Charles, 301
  Edward, 301

Wells, *cont'd*
  ELEXANDER, 20
  JAMES, 134
  JOHN, 193
  MILES, 60
Welsh
  John, 189
  JOHN, 189
Weron
  Michael, 126
  MICHAEL, 123, 126
Wesson
  William, 273
West, 3, 250, 303
  FRANCIS, 226, 228
  John, 131, 192, 197
  JOHN, 197
  JOHN JUNIOR, 85
  JOSEPH, 137, 190
  OWEN, 136, 189, 192
  Thomas, 17, 154, 163, 259, 289
  THOMAS, 259, 260
  WALTER, 290
Westmorland
  John, 69
Wetcher
  EPHRAIM, 257
  William, 114
  WILLIAM, 278
Wetherford, 42
Wetsall
  Martin, 259
  MARTIN, 163, 275
Wetsell
  MARTIN, 154, 163
Wetzell
  MARTIN, 154
Whain
  John, 157
Whaley
  James, 163
Whealer, 15
  John, 3
Wheeler, 52
  Micajah, 161
  MICAJAH SENIOR, 161
Wheler, 15
Wherry
  James, 124

Whetley
  JOHNATHAN, 93
White, 10, 21, 41, 57, 128, 149, 150, 198
  Arthur, 103, 104
  BENJAMIN, 38
  ELIZABETH, 227
  EPHRODITUS, 36
  JAMES, 96, 219
  Jeremiah, 190
  JEREMIAH, 36, 149
  JNO, 23
  JOHN, 275, 291
  Joseph, 264
  MATTHEW, 227
  Moses, 17
  Reuben, 47
  Richard, 82
  SAMUEL, 75, 96
  Stephen, 255
  William, 17
Whitebread
  Zachevrel, 125
Whitehead, 270
  BENJAMIN, 270
  WILLIAM, 206
Whiteley
  WILLIAM, 306
Whitelys
  William, 299
Whitley, 99, 306
  JOHN, 227
  WILLIAM, 306
Whitlock, 23
  CHARLES, 315
  SARAH, 208
  WILLIAM, 208
Whitlow
  FRANCIS, 84
Whitney, 49, 108, 159, 290
  Jeremiah, 22, 111
  JEREMIAH, 47, 99
Whittle
  JOSEPH, 17
  Matt, 17
Whitton
  Richard, 195
  Robert, 228
Whorley
  SILAS, 187

Whorly
  SILAS, 187
Wickerham
  ADAM, 300
Wicomb
  Andrew, 120
Wier
  JOHN, 17
Wilbourn
  John, 207
Wilches
  Joseph, 131
Wilcox
  Edmond, 158
  Edmund, 167
  EDMUND, 229
  EDWARD, 229
Wiles
  Samuel, 288
Wiley, 197
  Allen, 174
  ROBERT, 126, 197
Wilkerson, 243
Wilkins
  GEORGE, 292
  JOHN, 41
  Robert, 12
Will
  ANN, 56
Willcox, 150
Willey
  JAMES, 301
William
  JAMES, 30
  JOSEPH, 289
WILLIAM
  Forguson, 151
  Lain, 153
Williams, 30, 134, 145, 149, 212, 299
  Aaron, 182
  David, 25, 130
  Evan, 301
  HENRY, 166, 211
  John, 25, 47, 254
  JOHN, 145, 212, 213
  Joseph, 187
  JOSEPH, 191
  Lazs, 34
  LEWIS, 70, 243

Williams, *cont'd*
  LUKE, 6
  Richard, 170
  Robert, 177, 316
  ROBERT, 85, 142, 217, 260
  Thomas, 198, 223
  William, 21, 37, 130, 282
  WILLIAM, 22
  WYATT, 212, 213
Williamson, 71, 82
  JOHN, 57
  Thomas, 187
Willingham
  Jesse, 133
  JESSE, 186
Willis, 10, 20, 242
  HENRY, 12
  John, 12
  JOHN, 10, 11, 70, 254
  Richard, 269
  Thomas, 198
Willis or Wills, 178
Willoughby
  Hugh, 230
Wills, 284
  BENJAMIN, 301
  CHARLES, 300
  EUCLID, 143
  JOHN, 193, 285
Willson, 42, 164, 268
  Henry, 306
  Henry Willsons station", 306
  John, 244
  JOHN, 17, 268
  Mathew, 200
  SAMUEL, 291
Wilson, 48, 54, 62, 71, 135, 146, 186, 239, 240, 242, 243, 312
  David, 143
  EDMUND, 43
  Henry, 297, 299
  HENRY, 312
  James, 61, 290
  JAMES, 12, 52
  John, 52, 72, 124, 171, 244

Wilson, *cont'd*
  JOHN, 7, 17, 37, 68, 186, 190, 241, 313
  Joseph, 314
  JOSEPH, 314
  Mathew, 200, 307
  MATTHEW, 317
  Peter, 7
  PETER, 53, 72
  RALPH, 291
  SAMUEL, 115
  Thomas, 4, 263
  THOMAS, 115
  Thos, 4
  William, 72, 203, 240, 284
  WILLIAM, 7, 98, 119, 178, 296
  WILLIS, 313
Wilsons, 147, 286
Wimbish
  JOHN, 187
Wimbush, 126
  John, 26
Wimbushe, 199
Wimbut
  John, 30
Wimpee
  David, 129
Wims
  William, 189
Winder, 147
Windham
  CHARLES, 14, 70
Windston, 288
Winfield, 80
  John, 80
Winford, 235, 264, 265
Wingfield
  CHARLES, 17
Wingo
  JOHN, 194
Winn
  John, 313
Winston, 3, 100, 156, 171
  EDMUND, 189
  ISAAC, 301
  Nathaniel, 214, 263
Winter
  James, 157

Wintham
  GEORGE, 231
Wise
  William, 272
Wisson
  Edward, 273
Witcher, 109
  Ephraim, 54
  JOHN, 114
  WILLIAM, 278
Wither, 22
Withers
  JOHN, 213
Witoker
  Daniel, 22
Witt
  ANN, 56
  Benjamin, 131
  BENJAMIN, 25
  Charles, 3, 187
Witten, 68
  Wittens Order, 68
Witton, 213, 235
  and Company, 55
  Richard, 72
Wittshire
  JOSEPH JUNIOR, 227
Wolf, 182
Womack, 289
  Alexander, 235
  CHARLES, 53
  Richard, 37
Wood, 17, 70, 188, 253
  Andrew, 71
  Archebald, 93
  Drury, 277
  EDWARD, 290
  Henry, 161
  James, Lt.Gov., 41
  John, 10, 72, 145, 289
  JOHN, 290
  Joseph, 127, 181, 183
  Josiah, 286
  JOSIAH, 286
  Josias, 81
  THOMAS, 160
  Valentine, 203
  Zechariah, 70
Woodard
  Thomas, 127

Woodford
  WILLIAM, 271
Wooding, 81
  Robert, 224, 241
  ROBERT, 49, 80, 81, 225
Woodnett
  John, 23
Woodroof, 227
Woods, 200
  ARCHIBALD, 12
  BENJAMIN, 113
  ELIZABETH, 113
  Hugh, 3
  HUGH, 222
  JAMES, 301
  JOHN, 3
  Josiah, 292
  Michael, 12
  MICHAEL, 12
  RICHARD, 113
  SAMUEL, 113, 219
Woodson, 62, 103, 141, 149, 156, 159, 166, 254, 291
  Ben, 137
  Benjamin, 129
  BENJAMIN, 166
  BOOTH, 134
  Joseph, 181, 183
  SHADRACH, 99, 100
Woodson and Company, 157, 166
Woodson and Companys Order, 141
Woodson's and Company's Order ", 166
Woodsons, 290
Woodward, 122
Wooldridge, 227
  GEORGE, 40, 41
  THOMAS, 23
Wooldrige
  GEORGE, 40
Woollom
  John, 236
Woolloms
  JOHN, 157
Woolster, 52
Wormly
  JOHN, 292

Wormsley
  JOHN, 292
Wormsly
  JOHN, 292
Worsham
  Joshua, 207
Wray
  James, 96
Wreek, 72
Wright, 39, 56
  DAVID, 157, 159, 166
  FRANCIS, 11
  Isaac, 226
  James, 132, 154
  John, 19, 140
  JOHN, 253, 316
  JOSEPH, 251
  PATRICK, 313
  Peter, 188
  PETER, 132, 188
  Robert, 315
  ROBERT, 134, 150
  Solomon, 140
  Thomas, 287
  THOMAS, 48
  William, 37
  WILLIAM, 145, 146, 246, 248
Write
  John, 19
Wyatt
  EDWARD, 232
  Francis, 82
Wych
  Henry, 208
  WILLIAM, 38
Wyche, 208
  William, 38
Wylie
  ALEXANDER, 308
Wyn
  Thomas, 221
Wynn, 36, 57, 219
  CHARLES, 57
  Samuel, 34
Wynne
  JONES, 265
  JOSHUA JUNR, 246
  Peter, 32

Xlian
  James, 17
Yancey
  CHARLES, 210, 232
Yancy
  ROBERT, 269
  YANCY, 232
Yarbroug, 214
Yarrington, 9, 205
Yates, 15
Yearley
  Benjamin, 145
Yearly
  Ben, 201
Yeates, 279
Yoakum, 302
Yocum
  Methias, 307
Yongue
  SAMUEL, 163
York, 53
  William, 241
Young, 132, 257, 300, 305
  EDWARD, 253
  HENRY, 165
  James, 79
  JAMES, 110
  John, 159, 176
  JOHN, 176
  ROBERT, 81
  SAMUEL, 147, 163, 269
  William, 71, 103, 107, 114, 147, 164, 188, 287
  WILLIAM, 5, 54, 68, 69, 102, 132, 133, 137
Young,
  John, Senior, 110
Younger
  George Younger & Co., 125
Youngs
  William, 304
Yuille, 253, 282
  Thomas, 244
  THOMAS, 159
Zachary
  James, 239
Zachery
  Bartholemy, 23

Richmond Falls, New River.